International Trade

T0338236

International Trade

Charles van Marrewijk

By nature all men are alike, but by education widely different.

Chinese proverb (*The Economist* app, 20 May 2015)

OXFORD
UNIVERSITY PRESS

OXFORD
UNIVERSITY PRESS

Great Clarendon Street, Oxford, OX2 6DP,
United Kingdom

Oxford University Press is a department of the University of Oxford.
It furthers the University's objective of excellence in research, scholarship,
and education by publishing worldwide. Oxford is a registered trade mark of
Oxford University Press in the UK and in certain other countries

First edition 2017

Impression: 1

Published in the United States of America by Oxford University Press
198 Madison Avenue, New York, NY 10016, United States of America

British Library Cataloguing in Publication Data

Data available

Library of Congress Control Number: 2017932601

ISBN 978–0–19–875375–9

Printed in Great Britain by
Bell & Bain Ltd., Glasgow

Contents

Detailed Contents

List of Figures

List of Tables

List of Boxes

List of Technical Notes

Preface

The objective of this book is to give a succinct yet fairly complete, up-to-date, and thorough intro-duction to the study of international trade. It is the result of about three decades of experience in analysing and teaching international economics at the undergraduate and postgraduate level in four different countries (Australia, China, the Netherlands, and the USA). The target audience includes first- and second-year university and college students in economics, management, and business with a working knowledge of microeconomics and macroeconomics. Elementary comprehension of math-ematics for economists (simple functions and differentiation) is recommended. Additional support and learning material is available on the **online resources** (www.oup.com/uk/vanmarrewijk_it/), which provides review questions, data-based empirical questions, user-friendly simulations, all figures and tables, and additional resources for instructors (indicative answers to questions and pres-entations of chapters).

I briefly discuss the main features of the book below.

Structure of the book

The book is organized in six parts.

- *Part I Introduction*. This part consists of three chapters. In Chapter 1 we provide a brief overview of the international world economy as it is today. In Chapter 2 we discuss some historical information on international economic developments over time from a broader 'globalization' perspective. Chapter 3 concludes with some information necessary for the rest of this book on the principles of national income accounting and the balance of payments.

- *Part II Comparative advantage*. The three chapters in this part of the book analyse comparative advantage in perfectly competitive economies. Such advantages may explain international trade flows and are based either on the classical theory of technology differences, analysed in Chapter 4, or on the neoclassical theory of differences in factor abundance, analysed in Chapters 5 and 6.

- *Part III Competitive advantage*. This part of the book, which consists of three chapters, moves away from the classical and neoclassical world of perfect competition into the world of competitive advantages. We start in Chapter 7 with an overview of imperfect competition (monopoly, oligopoly, and monopolistic competition) and its main consequences for international trade flows. Chapter 8 provides empirical information on intra-industry trade and how to measure this, as well as theoretical explanations for such trade flows. Chapter 9 analyses international capital and labour mobility, with a focus on empirical information. The theoretical foundations for these flows, leading to foreign direct investments and multinational firms, are analysed in Part V of the book, which is on international firms.

- *Part IV Trade policy*. This part of the book, on international trade policy, consists of three chapters. We start in Chapter 10 by providing a brief overview of the international economic order (the World Trade Organization—WTO—and so on) before analysing the main possibilities and implications of trade restrictions (tariffs, quotas, and so on) under perfect competition. Chapter 11 analyses different types of WTO trade disputes and the possibilities and limitations of strategic trade policy under imperfect competition. Chapter 12 concludes with an overview of different types of regional trade agreements (which are becoming more popular) and the economic consequences and limitations of such agreements, with special attention for the European Union.

- *Part V International firms.* This part focuses on the role of international firms in international trade flows and consists of three chapters. We start in Chapter 13 by providing an overview of the enormous differences between firms (in size, productivity, and so on) before analysing the economic trade consequences of this heterogeneity. Chapter 14 analyses the rising importance of (heterogeneous) multinational firms in international trade flows, with a focus on horizontal foreign direct investment. Chapter 15 concludes with an overview of global supply chains and offshoring, examining the role of multinationals in vertical foreign direct investment.

- *Part VI International interactions.* This part concludes our analysis of international trade with a discussion of international interactions, consisting of two chapters. We start in Chapter 16 with two empirical regularities (Zipf's Law and the gravity equation) and explain how a proper mix of the insights we have learned about throughout the book helps us to understand these regularities in terms of three variations on geographical economics models. Chapter 17 analyses the dynamic aspects of international economics through the accumulation of physical and human capital, endogenous growth, and knowledge spillovers. Through this analysis, we provide insights into the changing role of global competitiveness as countries mature from factor-driven economies in their early stages, to efficiency-driven economies in their intermediate stages, to innovation-driven economies in their most advanced stages of economic development.

Foundations and recent developments

The progress of (economic) science never stops. The objective of this book is to provide both a solid foundation of international trade flows and theories for students to build on, as well as up-to-date information on empirical developments and new theoretical insights. The 'foundations' part is concentrated in Chapter 3 on national income accounting and the balance of payments, in Part II on classical and neoclassical comparative advantage, in Part III on 'new trade' competitive advantage, and in part IV on trade policy. From an empirical perspective, 'recent developments' can be found throughout the book, as all chapters use the most recent available information for illustration purposes. From a theoretical perspective, 'recent developments' are concentrated in part V on international firms and in part VI on international interactions. The fundamental changes in our view of the role of the firm in international trade flows and organization, in terms of firm heterogeneity, multinational activity, horizontal and vertical foreign direct investments, and global supply chain activities, are particularly worth mentioning in this respect.

Two-tier analysis

The body of the text represents the first tier of analysis, by providing extensive verbal, graphical, and intuitive explanations of the structure of international trade. The reader's understanding of the first tier is supported by structural analysis, empirical information, boxes discussing areas of special interest, and applications. The second tier of analysis is provided by the Technical Notes at the end of a chapter, which explicitly derive most results used and discussed in the body of the text. As such, the second tier represents background information for a better understanding of the body of the text. A proper understanding of the first tier, however, does not require knowledge and comprehension of the Technical Notes, as long as the reader is willing to take the results derived in those notes for granted.

Empirics: applications, boxes, and examples

The ultimate objective of economic model building is to provide a better understanding of the (forces of the) world economy. The empirical information provided throughout the book therefore serves a dual purpose. First, it is there to give a better insight in the structure of the world economy, for example on the size of trade and capital flows or the rising importance of multinational firms, such that the reader has a better idea of what we are trying to explain. Second, the empirical information is used to test the main conclusions of the economic models by applying them to real world problems. By directly using the models we also make the exposition livelier, through case studies and by pointing out vivid examples in special interest boxes.

Thorough, but simple

As already mentioned, I want to provide a thorough analysis, which means that (virtually) all the analysis is based on explicit economic models. Nonetheless, I want to keep the analysis as simple and tractable as possible. For that reason all analysis in the text and the derivations in the Technical Notes at the end of each chapter are based on the most simple functional forms. This is also to our advantage for the simulation exercises in the online Study Guide, which are based on the figures in the book and help the student understand what happens, for example, if the capital stock rises or the preference structure changes.

Charles van Marrewijk
Suzhou, China

Acknowledgements

Over the past decades I have accumulated a substantial intellectual debt to colleagues, friends, co-authors, students, and reviewers: for comments and suggestions, for joint work providing the basis for certain sections or boxes, for pointing out errors and omissions, and for general encouragement. In many cases the feedback I received was anonymous. In particular, I would like to thank the seven anonymous reviewers who provided detailed and useful comments and suggestions for further improvement for the first version of this book.

At the non-anonymous personal level, I would like to thank:

Name	Affiliation	Country
Ralph Bayer	University of Adelaide	Australia
Brian Bentick	University of Adelaide	Australia
Koen Berden	Ecorys Consultancy	Netherlands
Marcel van den Berg	Statistics Netherlands (CBS)	Netherlands
Peter van Bergeijk	Institute of Social Studies (ISS)	Netherlands
Sjoerd Beugelsdijk	University of Groningen	Netherlands
Rob Bolder	Utrecht University	Netherlands
Steven Brakman	University of Groningen	Netherlands
Han-Hsin Chang	Private consultant	USA
Yang Chen	Xi'an Jiaotong—Liverpool University	China
Wilfrid Csaplar	Bethany College	USA
Gerrit Faber	Utrecht University	Netherlands
Joe Francois	World Trade Institute	Switzerland
Harry Garretsen	University of Groningen	Netherlands
Jeroen Hinloopen	Utrecht University	Netherlands
Franz Xaver Hof	Technical University Vienna	Austria
Shiwei Hu	Beijing Foreign Studies University	China
Robert Inklaar	University of Groningen	Netherlands
Tristan Kohl	University of Groningen	Netherlands
Ger Lanjouw	University of Groningen	Netherlands
Julian Emami Namini	Erasmus University	Netherlands
Peter Neary	Oxford University	UK
Doug Nelson	Tulane University	USA
Daniël Ottens	IMC Trading	Netherlands
Mark Partridge	Ohio State University	USA
Victor Pontines	Asian Development Bank Institute	Japan
Hein Roelfsema	Utrecht University	Netherlands
Ward Rougoor	SEO research	Netherlands
Nimesh Salike	Xi'an Jiaotong—Liverpool University	China
Mark Sanders	Utrecht University	Netherlands
Teun Schmidt	Erasmus University Rotterdam	Netherlands
Marc Schramm	Utrecht University	Netherlands
Stephan Schueller	APG	Netherlands
Joachim Stibora	Kingston University London	UK

Julia Swart	Utrecht University	Netherlands
Saara Tamminen	VATT	Finland
Mark Taylor	University of Warwick	UK
Albert de Vaal	Radboud University Nijmegen	Netherlands
Jean-Marie Viaene	Erasmus University Rotterdam	Netherlands
Rien Wagenvoort	European Investment Bank	Luxembourg
Arjen van Witteloostuijn	University of Tilburg	Netherlands
Maurizio Zanardi	Lancaster University	UK

My special thanks go out to my wife Mira Flor van Marrewijk-Flores and my son Marco for support, encouragement, love, and simply making my life beautiful.

Charles van Marrewijk
Suzhou,China

Part I

Introduction

The Introduction to this book consists of three chapters. In Chapter 1 we provide a brief overview of the international world economy as it is today. In Chapter 2 we discuss some historical information on international economic developments over time from a broader 'globalization' perspective. Chapter 3 concludes with some information necessary for the rest of this book on the principles of national income accounting and the balance of payments.

The world economy

◉ Objectives

- To get an overview of the current state of the world economy.
- To understand the distinction between real and monetary analysis, as well as between partial equilibrium and general equilibrium analysis.
- To become familiar with the World Bank's global regions.
- To identify powerful nations in terms of land area, population, and income levels.
- To know the difference between gross domestic product and gross national income.
- To understand the importance of correcting for price differences (purchasing power parity) when comparing income levels between different countries.
- To distinguish between developing and economically advanced countries, partially based on income per capita levels.
- To identify strong trading nations and distinguish between import and export flows.

1.1 Introduction

We present basic information on the structure of the world economy in terms of land area, population, income, and trade flows. This serves as background information for observations to be explained by international economics models discussed in the remainder of this book. More detailed empirical information on specific topics, raising new questions to be answered, will be presented in individual chapters as we go along. This chapter provides an introduction to the world economy as it is today. Chapter 2 on 'globalization' analyses the growing importance of international economics over time; it shows how international connections are becoming ever more important in our everyday life.

What is international economics? To paraphrase a well-known definition of economics, it is 'what international economists do'. Although this does not seem very helpful at first sight, the underlying message is clear: you will know what international economics is about only once you have studied it yourself. In fact, this probably holds for many fields of study outside economics. This does not mean that you have to devote four years of your life to studying international economics before you get an idea of why we like this field so much, although I can highly recommend it. Instead, you can get a good overview by studying this book. The field of international economics is divided into two parts, namely international *real* analysis and international *monetary* analysis. This book covers international real analysis, investigating trade and investment flows, imperfect competition, trade policy, multinationals, economic integration, and so on. International monetary analysis investigates the demand for and supply of (international) money and the interactions between nations through the exchange rate, capital flows, and other means.

A final remark before we get started. I was asked by students what sets international economics apart from other fields of study. After contemplating the question for a while, I think an important distinguishing characteristic is the *general equilibrium* approach in our field. It is true that many discussions in the chapters to follow are analysed in a *partial equilibrium* setting, for example determining the optimal production level for a producer *given* the demand for its good, or determining the optimal consumption level for a labourer *given* the wage rate she earns and the prices charged for the goods on the market. However, international economists are not truly satisfied with an explanation of empirical observations until the partial equilibrium explanations are put together like a jigsaw puzzle in a consistent general equilibrium framework, providing a miniature world in which the demand for a producer's goods is explained by the consumer's optimization problem and in which the wage rate and the prices are also determined within the model. The main advantage of insisting on a general equilibrium framework is, of course, that it forces us to be precise and complete in our explanations. Essentially, it prevents us from cheating. It is important to keep this in mind as we continue.

1.2 World Bank regions

The World Bank provides a lot of information at the country level in its World Development Indicators online (www.worldbank.org). We will use this information as a basis for discussion throughout this book. For presentation and discussion purposes it is sometimes useful to group countries together in bigger regions. Based on historical, cultural, and geographic information, the World Bank identifies seven main regions, as listed in Table 1.1. The East Asia and Pacific (EAP) region consists of 32 countries and includes such diverse countries as China, Indonesia, and Australia. Occasionally, we will subdivide this group into smaller parts (East Asia, Southeast Asia, and Oceania). The Europe and Central Asia

Table 1.1 Overview of the World Bank regions

Code	Region	Example countries	No. of countries
EAP	East Asia and Pacific	China, Japan, Indonesia, Australia	32
ECA	Europe and Central Asia	UK, Germany, France, Russia	49
LAC	Latin America and Caribbean	Brazil, Mexico, Argentina	35
MNA	Middle East and North Africa	Egypt, Saudi Arabia, Algeria	21
NAM	North America	USA, Canada	3
SAS	South Asia	India, Pakistan, Bangladesh	8
SSA	Sub-Saharan Africa	Nigeria, South Africa, Ethiopia	48

Source: World Development Indicators online.

(ECA) region consists of 49 countries, including the core European countries, such as France, Germany, and the UK, and Central Asian countries, such as Kazakhstan and Russia. This group too is occasionally split into smaller parts (Europe and Central Asia). The Latin America and Caribbean (LAC) region consists of 35 countries. It includes virtually all American countries south of the USA, such as Mexico, Brazil, and Argentina. From a geographical point of view, a cut at Panama would have been understandable. The World Bank decided to include Mexico and the Central American countries in the LAC region in view of their historical and cultural links. As a consequence, the North American (NAM) region consists of only three countries: USA, Canada, and Bermuda. As the connection between Europe and Africa, the Middle East and North Africa (MNA) region consists of 21 countries, including Egypt, Saudi Arabia, and Algeria, and thus stretches over parts of both the African and the Asian continents. The remainder of Africa (48 countries) is grouped together in the Sub-Saharan Africa (SSA) region. It includes Nigeria, South Africa, and Ethiopia. The final region is South Asia (SAS), which consists of eight countries, including India, Pakistan, and Bangladesh.

1.3 Land area and population

There are many countries in the world. In the World Development Indicators the World Bank distinguishes between 214 different countries. Some of them are so small in terms of land area, population, and economic clout that you may never have heard of them. The small Polynesian island state of Tuvalu, for example, has a land area of 26 km^2 and a population smaller than 10,000 people. Even the tiny land area of Washington DC is more than six times as large, while its population is more than 60 times as large. As usual when you gather information, some data are missing. Taiwan, for example, is considered by China to be one of its provinces. Taiwan was thus expelled from the United Nations in 1971 when China took its place there. As a result there are no official data available for Taiwan at the World Bank. Similarly, for some countries specific types of data are not available or only somewhat older data is available. For the purposes of this chapter we proceeded as follows. First, we took the most recently available information from the World Development Indicators, covering the period 2010 2014. Second, for all countries with missing information that have a larger population than 300,000 people we looked up this information in the CIA's World Factbook.[1] In this way we created a complete dataset for the 'world' as a whole consisting of 196 countries. Fewer than 1.3 per cent of the observations are from the World Factbook.

We focus attention in this chapter on the most important countries. Important in what sense? Clearly, if you are one of the few inhabitants of Tuvalu, this is an important country to you and your family. However, for the world as a whole we will assume that 'large' countries are important. Again, the question arises: large in what sense? There are, of course, several options available, their suitability depending on the object of study. In general terms, we can look at land area or population. Since this is a book on economics, we can look at various income measures. More specifically, since this is a book on *international* economics, we can look at exports or international capital flows. In the rest of this chapter we will look briefly at all these aspects, indicating some of the relationships between them if appropriate.

Table 1.2 Top ten countries in land area and agricultural land area, 2014

Rank	Country	Land area	%	Country	Agricultural	%
1	Russia	16,380	12.6	China	5,146	10.5
2	China	9,388	7.2	USA	4,087	8.3
3	USA	9,147	7.0	Australia	4,055	8.2
4	Canada	9,094	7.0	Brazil	2,756	5.6
5	Brazil	8,358	6.4	Russia	2,144	4.4
6	Australia	7,682	5.9	Kazakhstan	2,080	4.2
7	India	2,973	2.3	India	1,793	3.6
8	Argentina	2,737	2.1	Saudi Arabia	1,734	3.5
9	Kazakhstan	2,700	2.1	Argentina	1,488	3.0
10	Algeria	2,382	1.8	Mongolia	1,134	2.3
	World	129,936	100	World	49,152	100

Notes: land area and agricultural land area in 1,000 km^2; % is relative to world total; 196 countries included.
Source: based on the most recently available information in the World Development Indicators online for the period 2010–2014 and CIA World Factbook for supplementary data.

1.3.1 Land area and agricultural land area

As the central piece left over after the break-up of the Soviet Union, the Russian Federation, henceforth Russia for short, is still by far the largest country in the world in terms of land area. With 16.4 million km^2, as indicated in Table 1.2, or 12.6 per cent of the world total, Russia is about 75 per cent larger than China, the world's second-largest country. Other non-surprising large countries are Canada, the USA, and Brazil. Perhaps more remarkable in the top ten list are the ninth place for Kazakhstan, formerly a part of the Soviet Union, and Algeria (tenth) in Africa. Other African countries follow: Sudan (eleventh) and Congo DR (Zaire[2], twelfth). As a result of the most frequently used methods for projecting the world globe on a flat piece of paper, most people tend to underestimate the size of the African land area. To avoid this problem and get a better indication of the land area at different locations, panel a. of Figure 1.1 provides a simple equilateral projection of bubbles proportional to a country's total land area, where the centre of the bubble is located at the country's geographic centre. We will provide similar diagrams for other variables for the same reason in the remainder of this chapter. For discussion purposes, the figure displays individual country data and at the same time groups the countries together in the seven regions of the World Bank (see Table 1.1).

The top six countries in Table 1.1 clearly stand out in panel a. of Figure 1.1. Together these six countries already account for 46 per cent of the world's total land area. This graph also clearly illustrates the size of the African continent. Only one African country makes it to the top ten, but there are many African countries and they tend to be large in size. Taken together, the African countries account for more than 23 per cent of the world's total area. If we realize that Russia (for its land area at least) and Kazakhstan are located in Asia, we also note that Europe is rather small in total land area (the sum of the other bubbles is not so large).

Since some large land areas consist of deserts, are almost permanently frozen, or receive hardly any rain at all, one may wonder how useful the land area is for humans. A first indication is to look at agricultural land area rather than total land area. This is done in

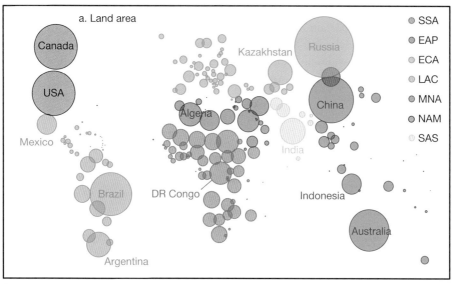

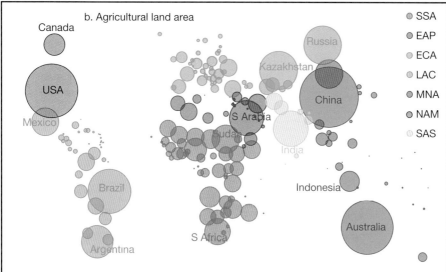

Figure 1.1 Land area and agricultural land area, 2014.

Notes: bubbles are proportional to a country's land area (panel a.) and agricultural land area (panel b.), located at the geographic centre—except for the USA, which is at the geographic centre of the 48 contiguous states—(CIA world fact book), equilateral projection; for the world as a whole agricultural land area is about 38 per cent of total land area; 196 countries; see Table 1.1 for the World Bank region abbreviations.

Source: see Table 1.2.

panel b. of Figure 1.1, where the bubbles are proportional to agricultural land area rather than total land area. For the world as a whole, agricultural land area is about 38 per cent of total land area. We should therefore note that when we compare the bubbles in panel b. with the bubbles in panel a. this gives us an indication of a country's relative importance (as a share of the world's total) only in one case compared to the other. We observe that Russia and Canada are not nearly as important in terms of agricultural land area. The reverse holds for China, Kazakhstan, Australia, Argentina, and South Africa, which all are significantly more important in terms of agricultural land area. As a group, the East Asia and Pacific region and the Sub-Saharan Africa region gain in importance. We must realize, of course, that this provides no information regarding the intensity of agricultural production, which is low in Kazakhstan, Australia, and Mongolia.

1.3.2 Population

As an indicator of economic importance, a country's land area is of limited use. Many of the countries listed in Table 1.2 incorporate vast stretches of desert, rocks, swamps, or areas frozen solid year round. Such uninhabitable land cannot be used to sustain and feed a population engaged in commerce, production, and trade. In this respect, the total population of a country is a better indicator of its fertility and potential economic viability. Table 1.3 lists the top 15 countries in terms of total population.

Two Asian countries, China and India, clearly stand out in terms of total population. Together they have 2.61 billion inhabitants, or almost 36 per cent of the world total of 7.12 billion people. The USA, ranked third with 316 million inhabitants, has only about 25 per cent of the Indian population, which is ranked second. Asian countries dominate the population list. Apart from China and India, this includes Indonesia (fourth), Pakistan (sixth), Bangladesh (eighth), Japan (tenth), the Philippines (twelfth), and Vietnam (fourteenth). Note that we do not include Russia (ninth) in this list of Asian countries, despite the fact that its largest land mass is in the Asian continent, because the largest share of its population is on the European continent. This makes it the only European country on the

Table 1.3 Top 15 countries by population, 2014

Rank	Country	Population	%
1	China	1,357	19.1
2	India	1,252	17.6
3	USA	316	4.4
4	Indonesia	250	3.5
5	Brazil	200	2.8
6	Pakistan	182	2.6
7	Nigeria	174	2.4
8	Bangladesh	157	2.2
9	Russia	143	2.0
10	Japan	127	1.8
11	Mexico	122	1.7
12	Philippines	98	1.4
13	Ethiopia	94	1.3
14	Vietnam	90	1.3
15	Egypt	82	1.2
	World	7,124	100

Note: population in millions.

Source: as Table 1.2.

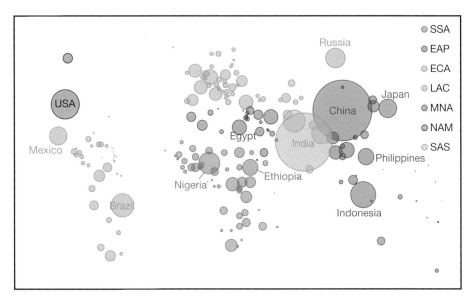

Figure 1.2 Total population, 2014.

Notes: bubbles are proportional to a country's total population located at the geographic centre; 196 countries; see Table 1.1 for the World Bank region abbreviations.

Source: see Table 1.2 and Figure 1.1.

list (Germany is sixteenth). The Americas (USA, Brazil, and Mexico) and Africa (Nigeria, Ethiopia, and Egypt) both have three countries on the list.

Figure 1.2 provides an indication of the distribution of the world's population across the globe. When we compare it with Figure 1.1 on the distribution of land area we notice that the Americas shrink substantially (from 29.5 per cent of land area to 13.6 per cent in terms of population). Asia, in contrast, becomes much more important. This holds in particular for South Asia (from 3.7 per cent in terms of land area to 23.5 per cent in terms of population) and the countries in East Asia and Southeast Asia. Together the EAP and SAS countries account for 55 per cent of the world population.

1.4 Income

The best indicator of the economic power of a nation is, of course, obtained by estimating the total value of the goods and services produced in a certain time period. Actually doing this and comparing the results across nations is a formidable task, which conceptually requires taking three steps. First, a well-functioning statistics office in each nation must gather accurate information on the value of millions of goods and services produced and provided by the firms in the economy. This will be done, of course, in the country's local currency: that is, dollars in the USA, pounds in the UK, yen in Japan, etc. Second, we have to decide what to compare between nations: gross domestic product or gross national income? Third, we have to decide *how* to compare the outcome for the different nations. We will elaborate on the second and third steps below.

1.4.1 Domestic or national product?

As mentioned above, we can compare either gross domestic product (GDP) or gross national income (GNI, formerly known as gross national product, GNP) between nations. GDP is defined as the market value of the goods and services produced by labour and property *located* in a country. GNI is defined as the market value of the goods and services produced by labour and property of *nationals* of a country. If, for example, a Mexican worker is providing labour services in the USA, these services are part of American GDP and Mexican GNI. The term 'located in' sometimes has to be interpreted broadly: for example if a Filipino sailor is providing labour services for a Norwegian shipping company, this is part of Norwegian GDP despite the fact that the ship is not actually located in Norway most of the time. The difference between GNI and GDP holds not only for labour services, but also for other factors of production, such as capital, that is:

GDP + net receipts of factor income = GNI   1.1

So does it really matter whether we compare countries on the basis of GDP or GNI? Essentially: no. This is illustrated in Figure 1.3 using a logarithmic scale with the size of the bubbles proportional to the size of GNI. Almost all observations are close to a straight 45° line through the origin, at least for the large countries. This implies that the values of GDP and GNI are usually close to one another. If we restrict attention to the 30 largest countries, which together account for 93 per cent of total GNI and GDP, the (unweighted) average deviation between GNI and GDP is only 2.1 per cent, while the GNI or GDP weighted average deviation is only 1.3 per cent. The maximum deviation for this group of countries is in Russia, where GDP is 4.7 per cent higher than GNI.

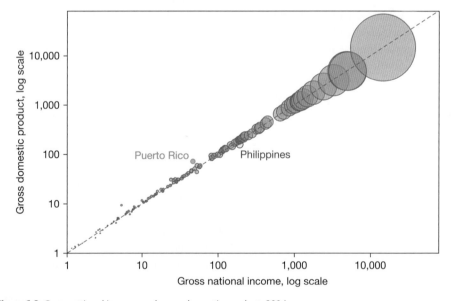

Figure 1.3 Gross national income and gross domestic product, 2014.

Notes: GNI and GDP in billion constant 2005 USD (most recent in the period 2010–2014); the dotted line is a 45° line; logarithmic scales; bubbles are proportional to the size of GNI; 126 countries included.
Source: World Development Indicators.

Table 1.4 Top ten countries by GDP and GDP PPP, 2014

Rank	Country	GDP xrate	%	Country	GDP PPP	%
1	USA	16,768	22.2	USA	16,768	16.3
2	China	9,240	12.2	China	16,162	15.7
3	Japan	4,920	6.5	India	6,784	6.6
4	Germany	3,730	4.9	Japan	4,613	4.5
5	France	2,806	3.7	Germany	3,539	3.4
6	UK	2,679	3.5	Russia	3,623	3.5
7	Brazil	2,246	3.0	Brazil	3,013	2.9
8	Italy	2,150	2.8	France	2,475	2.4
9	Russia	2,097	2.8	UK	2,453	2.4
10	India	1,875	2.5	Indonesia	2,389	2.3
	World	75,628	100	World	102,762	100

Note: GDP and GDP PPP in billion current USD; xrate = exchange rate; 196 countries included.
Source: as Table 1.2.

Figure 1.3 also illustrates that for some smaller countries the deviation between GDP and GNI can be more substantial. This is shown in the graph for the Philippines (ranked 31 in terms of GNI), where GNI is 20 per cent larger than GDP because of the many Filipino people working abroad as sailors, in construction, in hotels, and as domestic helpers. It is also shown for Puerto Rico (ranked 54), where GDP is 35 per cent larger than GNI because of investments by American multinationals.

1.4.2 Comparison

The left side of Table 1.4 reports the top ten countries in terms of GDP level when the outcome for each nation in local currency is simply converted to the same international standard currency on the basis of the average exchange rate in the period of observation (referred to as GDP xrate). The total value of all goods and services produced in the world in 2014 was estimated to be $75,628 billion. Taken together, the top ten countries account for about 64 per cent of the world production value.

Based on exchange rates, the USA is by far the largest economy in the world, producing more than 22 per cent of all goods and services. This is almost twice as much as China, which is ranked second (at 12.2 per cent of world production), followed by Japan. There are five European countries in the top ten, namely Germany (fourth), France (fifth), UK (sixth), Italy (eighth), and Russia (ninth). With the exception of Russia, none of the European countries makes it to the land area top ten of Table 1.2 or the population top 15 of Table 1.3.

1.4.3 Purchasing power parity

The ranking of production value on the left side of Table 1.4 is deceptive because it tends to overestimate production in the high-income countries relative to the low-income countries. To understand this we have to distinguish between *tradable* and *non-tradable* goods and services. As the name suggests, tradable goods and services can be transported to or provided in another country, perhaps with some difficulty and at some costs. In principle, therefore, the providers of tradable goods in different countries compete with one another fairly directly, which implies that the prices of such goods are related and can be compared effectively on the basis of observed (average) exchange rates. In contrast, non-tradable goods and services have to be provided locally and do not compete with international providers. Think, for example, of housing services, getting a haircut, or going to the cinema.

Since (i) different sectors in the same country compete for the same labourers, such that (ii) the wage rate in an economy reflects the average productivity of a nation (see also Chapter 4), and (iii) productivity differences between nations in the non-tradable sectors tend to be smaller than in the tradable sectors, converting the value of output in the non-tradable sectors on the basis of observed exchange rates tends to underestimate the value of production in these sectors for the low-income countries. For example, on the basis of observed exchange rates, getting a haircut in the Netherlands may cost you $18 rather than the $4 you pay in China or the $2 you pay in the Philippines, while going to the cinema in Sweden may cost you $12 rather than the $2 you pay in Jakarta, Indonesia. In these examples the value of production in the high-income countries relative to the low-income countries is overestimated by a substantial amount.

To correct for these price differences, the United Nations International Comparison Project (ICP) collects data on the prices of goods and services for virtually all countries in the world and calculates 'purchasing power parity' (PPP) exchange rates, which better reflect the true value of goods and services that can be purchased in a country for a given number of dollars. Reporting PPP income levels therefore gives a better estimate of the actual value of total production in a country.

Suppose, for example, that people in the USA and China spend about 70 per cent of their income on non-traded goods and 30 per cent on traded goods. Also assume that if we use exchange rates to compare income levels, the average Chinese person earns $7,000 and the average American $49,000, or *seven* times as much. When we calculate PPP income levels the average American still earns $49,000 since it is the benchmark country. The average Chinese person spends $4,900 on non-traded goods (70 per cent of 7,000) before correcting for PPP and $2,100 on traded goods (30 per cent of 7,000). After correcting for PPP, spending on traded goods is still $2,100, but spending on non-traded goods will rise because the price for non-traded goods is lower in China than in the USA. Suppose that non-traded goods are on average about twice as expensive in the USA, such that spending on non-traded goods by the average Chinese person is $9,800(= 4,900 × 2) after PPP correction. Average income in China after PPP correction is then $11,900 (= 9,800 + 2,100). As a consequence, income in the USA is no longer 7 times higher but only 4.12 times higher (49,000/11,900). The PPP correction raises income in China by 11,900/7,000 = 1.70 since prices are the same for traded goods and twice as high for non-traded goods (0.3 × 1 + 0.7 × 2 = 1.70).

The right side of Table 1.4 lists the top ten countries in terms of income corrected for PPP. By construction, the value for the USA remains the same. Since the world income level is about 36 per cent higher for GDP PPP than for GDP exchange rates, the share of the US economy in the world's total declines from 22.2 per cent to 16.3 per cent. Note that the ordering on the right side of Table 1.4 has changed compared to that on the left side, but that Indonesia is the only new country in the table (tenth) at the expense of Italy (which moved to eleventh). Total production in China is about the same as in the USA (in fact,

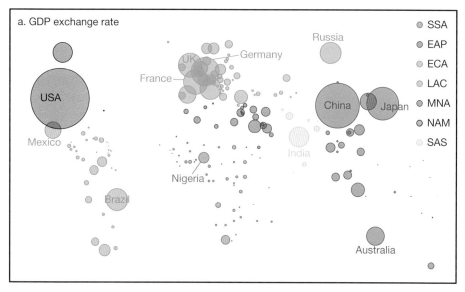

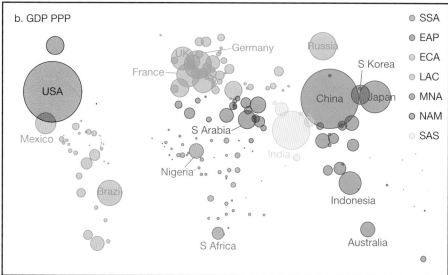

Figure 1.4 GDP exchange rate and GDP PPP, 2014.

Notes: bubbles are proportional to a country's GDP exchange rate (panel a.) and GDP PPP (panel b.); 196 countries; see Table 1.1 for the World Bank region abbreviations.
Source: see Table 1.2.

China's income level is larger than that of the USA from 2015 onwards). India moved up from ten to three, while Russia moved up from nine to six.

Figure 1.4 illustrates the distribution of world income across the globe using bubbles located at a country's geographic centre, as used in Figures 1.1 and 1.2. Panel a. is based on GDP exchange rates and panel b. on GDP PPP. When we compare the income bubbles in panel a. with the land area bubbles of Figure 1.1 or the population bubbles of Figure 1.2, we note immediately that Africa virtually disappears: it is important in terms of land area, somewhat less important in terms of population, and almost unimportant in terms of income level. A similar observation holds for South Asia (particularly relative to population) and for Latin America (particularly relative to land area). The opposite holds for North America and Europe: these regions are more important in terms of income levels than in terms of population and land area (the latter particularly for Europe).

When we compare panel b. of Figure 1.4 with panel a., we note that the above observations are mitigated. Sub-Saharan Africa is somewhat more important when we correct for PPP and South Asia is substantially more important. In contrast, Europe and North America become somewhat less important. This is, of course, an indication of the generally high price levels in these regions. All these observations are, naturally, related to differences in income per capita for the various countries. This is the next issue we discuss.

1.5 Income per capita

For an individual inhabitant of a country the total production value of the country is hardly relevant. More important is the production value per person, which is per capita. It should be noted that income per capita gives an idea of the well-being for the 'average' person in the country, but gives no information on the distribution of the income level within the country. If Juan and Pedro together earn $100, the average income level is $50, which holds if they both earn $50 *and* if Juan earns $1 while Pedro earns $99. The average income level is therefore a poor indicator of the 'representative' situation in a country if the distribution of income is more uneven. In general, the income level is more evenly distributed in Europe and Japan than in the USA, where it is in turn more evenly distributed than in many developing nations.

Table 1.5 gives an overview of the ten richest (left side) and poorest (right side) countries in terms of income per capita, corrected for purchasing power. The average income level in the world was $14,426 per person. The highest income level ($138,025, almost ten times

Table 1.5 Top ten rich and poor countries by income per capita, 2014

Rank	Rich country	GDP PPP	%	Poor country	GDP PPP	%
1	Macao	138,025	957	Somalia	544	3.8
2	Qatar	127,562	884	C African Rep	584	4.1
3	Luxembourg	88,850	616	Burundi	747	5.2
4	Kuwait	79,471	551	Malawi	755	5.2
5	Singapore	76,237	528	DR Congo	783	5.4
6	Brunei	69,474	482	Liberia	850	5.9
7	Norway	62,411	433	Niger	887	6.1
8	Un Arab Em	56,187	389	Mozambique	1,070	7.4
9	Switzerland	54,993	381	Eritrea	1,157	8.0
10	Saudi Arabia	52,068	361	Guinea	1,213	8.4
	World average	14,426	100	World average	14,426	100

Notes: GDP PPP in current USD; 196 countries included.
Source: as Table 1.2.

the world average) was generated in the tiny, casino-rich state of Macao. The top ten is dominated by small countries (the population average is only 6.4 million and the median 4.2). Six of the top ten nations are rich in oil and natural gas: Qatar, Kuwait, Brunei, Norway, United Arab Emirates, and Saudi Arabia. The lowest income level ($544 per capita), less than 4 per cent of the global average, was measured in Somalia (see the right side of Table 1.5). To put this in perspective: the average income level in Macao is more than 250 times higher. All poor countries in the top ten are located in Sub-Saharan Africa. In fact, the poorest 17 countries are located there. Estimated income levels are even lower than in eighteenth-ranked North Korea.

1.6 International trade

As the title of this book suggests, the interactions between nations, the underlying forces they reflect, and the implications of economic policy are our primary focus of attention. We also analyse the welfare consequences of policy decisions and reasons for imposing trade restrictions (see, for example, Box 1.1). Before we continue it should be noted that the comparison problems between countries discussed in Sections 1.4 and 1.5, arising from the distinction between tradable and non-tradable goods, do not occur when investigating and discussing trade flows, which can readily be compared using the exchange rates. So what are the large trading nations? Table 1.6 shows the largest exporting nations in terms of goods (left side) and in terms of services (right side). The total value of goods exports is $18,552 billion. The total value of services exports is $4,754 billion. This implies that about 80 per cent of all exports are in terms of goods and the remainder are in terms of services.

China was the world's largest goods exporter (11.6 per cent of total exports), followed by the USA (8.6) and Germany (7.8). Taking into consideration that the USA's share of world production is about 16–22 per cent (see Section 1.4), the American share of world exports (8.6 per cent) is rather modest. Most countries in Table 1.6 have a larger share in world exports than in world production. To some extent this can be explained by the artificiality of drawing borders between nations on the globe. For example, if an American firm in Boston sells goods 5,000 km away in Los Angeles, this is not counted as export because both cities are located in the USA. Compare this to a Dutch firm in Rotterdam, Europe's largest harbour, selling goods to a Belgian consumer in Antwerp less than 100 km away, which of course is counted as part of Dutch exports.[3] Consequently, some countries in the left side of Table 1.6 are relatively small, high-income open economies such as the Netherlands, Hong Kong, Singapore, and Switzerland.

The right side of Table 1.6 lists the top 15 commercial services exporters. Relative to the left side there are four new countries on the export list, namely India, Spain, Ireland, and Belgium, which replace Russia, Canada, Switzerland, and Mexico. Although we can therefore conclude that large goods exporters are generally also large services exporters, the order on the list differs quite remarkably. The USA, for example, moves up to first place (from third) and the UK moves up to second place (from eleventh). China, on the other hand, drops from first to fifth place, while Japan drops from fourth to eighth. Evidently, the USA and the UK specialize to some extent in exporting services while China and Japan specialize in exporting merchandise trade.

BOX 1.1 Tariffs as a source of government revenue

In this book (Parts II–VI) we analyse the economic forces underlying international trade flows, their welfare impact for different agents in the economy, and the consequences of policy measures restricting trade flows. In general we will argue not only that international trade flows lead to efficiency gains and welfare improvements for a country as a whole, but also that policy measures restricting trade flows lead to a deterioration of welfare and reduce efficiency, sometimes in unexpected and covert ways. In view of these conclusions, which are supported by almost all international economists (see, however, Section 2.9 on globalization and income inequality), the question arises *why* countries impose (welfare-deteriorating) trade restrictions.

We analyse the more complicated distribution effects of trade restrictions, which may help to explain why trade restrictions are imposed, in Part IV of this book. In this box, however, we want to point to the problems facing the governments of many developing nations which do not have an efficient tax-collecting system available. After all, tax collection requires detailed information on the inhabitants of the country, their income level, specific circumstances that may be relevant for an individual, and many public servants to gather and process the information. The governments of all nations, however, require funds to perform basic duties, such as protecting the country, providing law, order, and education, and so on.

In the absence of an efficient tax-collecting apparatus it is thus tempting to collect government revenue by imposing tariffs on (relatively easily controlled) international trade flows (imports duties, export duties, exchange profits, and the like). This is illustrated in Figure 1.5, which ranks countries in terms of taxes on international trade as a percentage of government revenue. It shows not only that the countries imposing high tariffs are generally developing nations, but also that some countries are highly dependent on taxing international trade flows for their tax revenue. This holds in particular for the Bahamas (56 per cent), Saint Lucia (48), and Madagascar (41). It is more than one-third for Ivory Coast, Antigua and Barbados, Botswana, and Liberia. For all countries in the figure it is above 22 per cent. Even for a large country such as Russia, the government's revenue dependence on international trade taxes can be as high as 26 per cent.

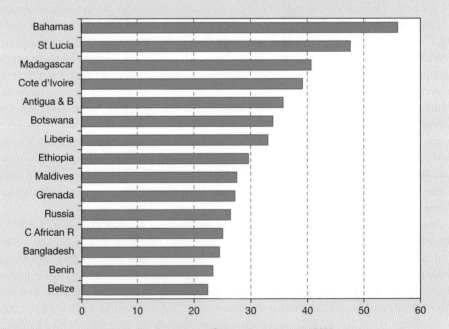

Figure 1.5 Taxes on international trade: per cent of government revenue, 2013.

Source: World Development Indicators; most recent 2010–2013; top 15 countries.

Table 1.6 Top 15 exporting countries: goods and services, 2013

Rank	Country	Export goods	%	Country	Export services	%
1	China	2,148	11.6	USA	687	14.5
2	USA	1,593	8.6	UK	298	6.3
3	Germany	1,440	7.8	Germany	261	5.5
4	Japan	695	3.7	France	255	5.4
5	S Korea	617	3.3	China	215	4.5
6	France	581	3.1	India	149	3.1
7	Netherlands	551	3.0	Spain	145	3.1
8	Russia	523	2.8	Japan	135	2.8
9	Hong Kong	509	2.7	Singapore	130	2.7
10	Italy	502	2.7	Ireland	118	2.5
11	UK	477	2.6	Netherlands	117	2.5
12	Canada	465	2.5	Belgium	114	2.4
13	Singapore	438	2.4	Italy	113	2.4
14	Mexico	381	2.1	Hong Kong	105	2.2
15	Switzerland	379	2.0	S Korea	102	2.1
	World	18,552	100	World	4,754	100

Notes: values in billion current USD; based on balance of payments items for goods and services.
Source: as Table 1.2.

1.6.1 Exports relative to imports

Figure 1.6 illustrates the international exports and imports of goods in 2014 for 227 countries using a logarithmic scale.[4] It also depicts a 45° line where exports are equal to imports and the trade balance is zero (see also Chapter 3). The bubbles are proportional to a country's share in total trade flows (average of exports and imports). The five largest trading nations (together accounting for 37 per cent of total trade) are listed in the figure: China (11.5), the USA (10.8), Germany (7.3), Japan (4.0), and the Netherlands (3.7). Although a country's export value is generally roughly in line with its import value, the deviations between the two are clearly more substantial than the deviations between GDP and GNI illustrated in Figure 1.3. For China, Germany, and the Netherlands exports are substantially larger than imports. The reverse holds for the USA and Japan.

The figure also identifies 'remarkable' cases. First, as an oil-exporting nation, Qatar is somewhat of an outlier with much larger exports than imports ($132 versus $31 billion, respectively). Similar observations hold for other oil-exporting nations such as Kuwait and Brunei. Second, on the left side of the diagram there is an outlier for 'ship stores and bunkers', indicating that there may be fluctuations between reported export and import values based on goods being carried on their way in ships or goods stored in bunkers. Finally, note that for many small trading nations (circled in the lower part of the diagram) the import value exceeds the export value (the observations are above the 45° line). Most of these observations are of developing nations which can finance their

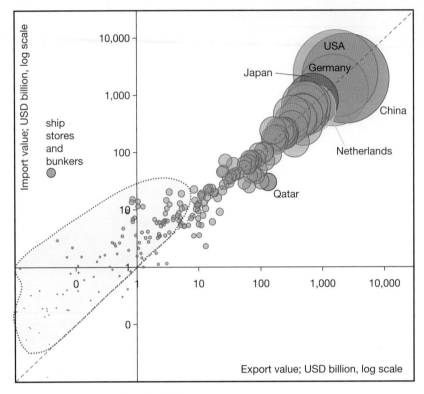

Figure 1.6 Exports and imports of goods, 2014.

Notes: bubbles are proportional to the country's percentage of total trade (average of exports and imports); top five countries are listed (together accounting for 37 per cent of total trade), as are two special cases; the diagonal line is a 45° line; data for 227 countries included; for discussion of circled area see main text.

Source: based on data from the International Trade Centre (www.trademap.org; downloaded on 18 June 2015).

high imports through foreign aid flows and remittances from workers abroad; again, see Chapter 3.

1.6.2 Exports relative to production

The reader may wonder how it is possible that small countries such as Hong Kong (7 million inhabitants) and Singapore (5 million inhabitants) are able to reach the world's top 15 in trade flows. The reason is that countries may re-export goods and services they import from other countries, with only modest value added in the country itself. This is illustrated in Figure 1.7, which shows the top 15 value of exports of goods and services relative to GDP. Hong Kong and Luxembourg both export more than twice as much as the total value of production (230 and 203, respectively). Singapore has almost reached that level (191). Three other countries (Maldives, Macao, and Ireland) are also above the 100 per cent mark. The other countries are 83 or higher. All countries are small in terms of population and GDP. Most of them are rich countries; only Vietnam and the Maldives are below the world average (at 36 and 78 per cent, respectively).

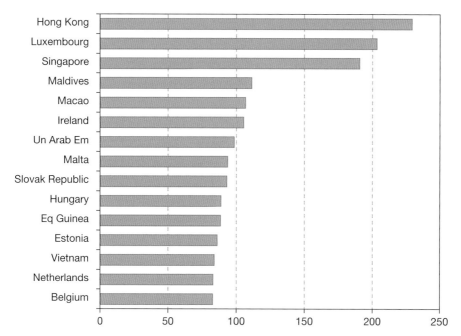

Figure 1.7 Exports of goods and services: per cent of GDP, 2013.

Source: World Development Indicators; most recent 2010–2013; top 15 countries.

1.7 Conclusions

This chapter presents basic, but essential, information on the structure of the world economy. We give an impression of the importance of various countries using different measures. In terms of land area, Russia is the largest country, while some relatively unknown African nations are also important. In terms of population, China and India stand out, as do Asian nations in general. In terms of income, using either GDP or GNI, North America, Japan, and many European nations are important. This holds even when current dollars, which tend to overestimate the importance of high-income countries, are corrected for purchasing power. Nations from North America and Europe also hold top positions with respect to income per capita. The differences in this respect are enormous. International trade flows are dominated by China, the USA, and (relatively small) European and Southeast Asian countries. In general, the different rankings change the composition of important countries considerably. Only *four* countries, namely China, the USA, India, and Russia, make it to the top lists in terms of land area, population, total income, and trade flows (Tables 1.2, 1.3, 1.4, and 1.6).

With this information in the back of our minds we are ready to embark on our journey into international economics, which values the consistency of a general equilibrium approach. Clearly, we will not be able to 'explain' all the empirical observations above, although international economists do work on all these issues. We will discuss how the insights we derive can be helpful for tackling important policy problems. Many other topics touched upon above will also be explored. Along the way we will present more detailed empirical information on specific topics to raise new questions and guide us in our search. Before we can analyse these issues, however, we want to provide an historical understanding of the process of globalization in Chapter 2 and get a firm grip of international accounting principles and practices in Chapter 3 in order to better understand the interconnections between goods and services flows on the one hand and international capital flows on the other.

 ## Notes

1   https://www.cia.gov/library/publications/resources/the-world-factbook/

2   There are two 'Congo' countries in Africa, the largest of which in terms of both population and size, a former Belgian colony, is also sometimes known by its old name, Zaire.

3   Some argue that the focus should be only on extra–European Union (EU) trade flows to make data between the USA and the EU more comparable. This ignores the fact, of course, that the states of the USA are not comparable to EU countries in terms of autonomy. In any case, doing so would make the EU the world's largest exporter (16.2 per cent of the world total), ahead of China (12.8 per cent) and the USA (11.2 per cent); see WTO (2010, p. 31).

4   The differences relative to Table 1.6 arise because Figure 1.6 is based on both a different source and a different year.

 ## Questions

Question 1

The difference between GDP converted by the current and the PPP exchange rate can be illustrated with a simple example. Assume that Germany and Poland both produce 1,000 machines (to remove oil remains) and 500 pedicure treatments every year. Machines can be traded between both countries while pedicure treatments cannot be traded. Further assume that the current exchange rate is one euro for four Polish zloty, the hourly wage in Germany is 10 euro and the number of hours it takes to produce one machine or to give one pedicure treatment in both countries is given in Table 1.7:

Table 1.7 Number of hours to produce one unit

	Germany	Poland
Machine	10	20
Pedicure treatment	2	2

a. If machine producers do not make any profit, what is the price of a machine in Germany (in euro) and in Poland (in zloty)?

b. What is the hourly wage rate in Poland?

c. If pedicures also do not make any profit, what is the price of a pedicure treatment in Germany (in euro) and in Poland (in zloty)?

d. What is the GDP figure in Germany (in euro) and in Poland (in zloty)?

e. What is the PPP exchange rate between the euro and the zloty?

f. Convert the Polish GDP figure to euro with the current exchange rate and the PPP exchange rate. Explain the difference between these two figures.

Question 2

Trade statistics are not always reliable. It is a well-known fact that there is a discrepancy between figures on the value and number of products leaving a country and figures on the value and number of products entering another country as reported by the national statistical agencies. Table 1.8 gives a striking example.

Table 1.8 Indonesian sawnwood exports to major trading partners in thousand m^3 according to Indonesian statistics (export) and statistics of importers (import)

	1998			1999			2000		
	export	import	% diff	export	import	% diff	export	import	% diff
Japan	148	336	127	109	261	139	35	271	674
China	52	317	510	77	580	653	20	931	4,555
Malaysia	4	335	8,275	7	289	4,029	7	450	6,329

Source: Johnson (2002), 'Documenting the undocumented', *Tropical Forest Update*, vol. 12, no. 1.

a. Why do statistics on exports and imports differ between different national statistical agencies?

b. What do you think is the main source of discrepancy in the case of Indonesian sawnwood?

Question 3

According to World Bank data China's GDP at market prices (in current US dollars) was $10,355 billion in 2014. In that same year the GDP at market prices (in current US dollars) in the USA was $17,419 billion.

a. Your neighbour argues that China is the biggest economy in the world since 2014. Could she be right, or not? Explain why, or why not.

According to World Bank data the export of goods and services was 22.6 per cent of GDP in China in 2014 and 23.1 per cent of GDP in Guatemala in that same year.

b. The same neighbour argues that China is actually a more open economy than Guatemala in 2014. Could she be right this time, or not? Explain why, or why not.

 See the **online resources** *for a Study Guide and questions:*
www.oup.com/uk/vanmarrewijk_it/

2 Globalization

Objectives

- To understand that there are different types of globalization that may be interpreted differently.
- To know that world income per capita growth has been fluctuating around 1.3 per cent per year since 1980 and world trade per capita growth around 3.8 per cent per year.
- To know that global income per capita has been rising rapidly only for the last 200 years.
- To have an idea of leading and lagging nations in terms of income per capita and the widening disparity between leaders and laggards over the past 1,000 years.
- To have an idea of the waves of globalization in an historical perspective.
- To understand the narrowing role of the price wedge in the globalization debate for trade, capital, and migration flows.
- To know that global income inequality has been mostly rising over time and to understand why the decline since the 1970s is likely to be reversed in the near future.
- To understand that within-country income inequality may rise or fall and to know that there has been no clear trend in within-country inequality at the global level over the past 30 years.

2.1 Introduction

Chapter 1 provided a brief overview of the current state of international economic affairs. Before we start to analyse how we can better understand current economic interactions, it will be useful to provide a brief, non-technical overview of the long-run developments of the world economy, which we do using the term 'globalization'.[1] We explain in Section 2.2 that there are different types of globalization and that the term is interpreted in different ways by different people. This book will focus on economic globalization. We then provide an overview of 'recent' history by analysing the development of global trade and income flows since 1960, both in total (Section 2.3) and per capita (Section 2.4). Most of the remainder of this chapter focuses on 'long-run' history. First, we provide an overview of the developments of income per capita over a two-thousand-year period (Section 2.5). Second, we discuss globalization in history and the two waves of globalization for trade flows (Section 2.6). Third, we analyse the role of the price wedge in globalization for trade flows (Section 2.7) and for flows of capital and migration, both with their own waves of globalization (Section 2.8). We conclude by analysing developments of income inequality, both for the world as a whole (Section 2.9) and within countries (Section 2.10). These analyses rely heavily on data collected and evaluated by Angus Maddison (see Box 2.1).

BOX 2.1 Angus Maddison

Figure 2.1
Angus Maddison
(1926–2010).

Born in Newcastle upon Tyne (England) and educated at Cambridge, McGill, and Johns Hopkins, Angus Maddison (Figure 2.1) spent most of his professional career in various functions at the Organization for Economic Cooperation and Development (OECD; see Chapter 10) in France and as a professor of economics at the University of Groningen in the Netherlands. As one of the most important economic historians and a self-confessed chiffrephile, he published a wide range of articles and books on historical statistical data. He estimated, for example, the levels of population, income, trade, and urbanization throughout the world for the past 2,000 years. Of his many publications, which are also used as a source of data throughout this book, we should at least mention *Monitoring the World Economy, 1820–1992* and *The World Economy: A Millennial Perspective*, published in 1995 and 2001 respectively.

The portrait was painted by Carla Rodenburg in 2001.
I am grateful to Angus Maddison for his permission to reproduce this painting.

2.2 What is globalization?

The short and uninformative—but correct—answer to the question 'What is globalization?' is: 'Everything you want it to be.' Many of the heated disputes on the streets and in the media about the advantages and disadvantages of the globalization process arise from the fact that this phrase means different things to different people. At the infamous 1999 meeting of the World Trade Organization (WTO) in Seattle, the environmentalists dressed in sea-turtle outfits cared about different issues than the French farm leaders protesting against 'McDonaldization' driving out the consumption of Roquefort cheese. So in turn did the trade unionists and the human right activists. We identify five key globalization debates.[2]

- *Cultural globalization*: this debate asks whether there is a global culture or a set of universal cultural variables and the extent to which these displace embedded national cultures and traditions. To an unprecedented extent we have similar cultural experiences in virtually all countries of the world: we see similar (American) movies, listen to similar (American and British) music, eat at McDonald's, drink Coca Cola, drive Toyotas, and so on. The carriers of culture globalization are argued to be large multinational corporations, hence the term 'McDonaldization'. Some people are afraid that this will lead to a boring, homogeneous global culture at the expense of local cultures and traditions. Others are not so gloomy, and see enough room for local traditions and new developments against a globally oriented background. After all, there is great regional cultural variety in China even after thousands of years of common experiences, and the same holds for Europe. Cultural globalization is not the focus of this book.

- *Economic globalization*: this debate centres on the decline of national markets and the rise of global markets, be it for the production and sale of final and intermediate goods and services or for the procurement of inputs (labour and capital). Driven by fundamental changes in technology which permit new, complicated, and more efficient ways of internationally organizing production processes, the rules of competition are being redefined along the way and firms and governments will have to learn how to adapt. We *do* analyse the consequences of economic globalization: the increased interdependence of national economies, and the trend towards greater integration of goods, labour, and capital markets (Neary, 2003).

- *Geographical globalization*: this debate refers to the sensation of compressed time and space as a result of reduced travel times between locations and the rapid (electronic) exchange of information. Knowledge and production previously confined to certain geographical areas may now cross borders and can be made available anywhere because of the rapid transfer of information and transport innovations. Some argue that this leads to the 'end of geography', a time in which the 'world is flat' such that location no longer matters and 'footloose' global capital can quickly cross borders. We will argue instead in Chapter 16 that the declining costs of trade and interaction make location and geography more important and lead to the agglomeration of economic activity. Think, for example, of the clustering of international finance in three global centres (London, New York, and Tokyo).

- *Institutional globalization*: this debate relates to the spread of 'universal' institutional arrangements across the globe. In the aftermath of the neoliberal policies pursued by President Ronald Reagan (USA) and Prime Minister Margaret Thatcher (UK) in the 1980s, in combination with the collapse of communist Soviet-type economic systems, more and more countries adopted similar reforms (Albert, 1993) with an emphasis on making markets more flexible, privatizing former state-owned organizations, reducing the size of welfare arrangements, and so on. In an international context, these policies were promoted by institutions such as the International Monetary Fund (IMF) and the World Bank, which, it may be argued, aimed to force the 'Washington Consensus' upon the developing world (Stiglitz, 2002). In a similar vein, micro-level business institutions are influenced by global trends. Multinationals adopt similar policies under the pressure of competition and regulation. For instance, benchmarking practices are promoted by global consultancy businesses such as the Boston Consulting Group and McKinsey, and the regulations of the New York Stock Exchange (NYSE) are imposed upon many non-American enterprises (Sorge and van Witteloostuijn, 2004).

- *Political globalization*: this debate refers to the relationship between the power of markets and (multinational) firms versus that of the nation-state, a relationship that is undergoing continuous change and updating in reaction to economic and political forces—from counter-cyclical national demand policies and international cooperation after World War II to the renaissance of the belief in the power of the price mechanism and market forces for efficient allocation of resources in the 1970s. The globalization process is conditioned by (financial) institutions and dominant market players, such as multinational corporations and large investment firms. Some argue that the competitive pressure of international markets will 'hollow out' the functions of the nation-state and lead to an erosion of sovereignty and a race to the bottom (be it in corporate tax rates or environmental policies; see also Section 3.5).

2.3 World income and trade since 1960

The world income level, measured as GDP in constant 2005 PPP dollars for all countries of the world combined, rose from \$9,306 billion in 1960 to \$58,148 billion in 2014: see Figure 2.2. This is a substantial 6.2-fold increase over a 54-year period at a compounded growth rate of about 3.4 per cent per year.

One important aspect of globalization is the international trade of goods and servic-es, which we will measure as the sum of exports and imports.[3] The world trade volume, measured in constant 2005 PPP dollars for all countries of the world combined, rose from \$2,162 billion in 1960 to \$37,208 billion in 2014, as shown in Figure 2.2. This represents an even more substantial 17.2-fold increase over this 54 year period at a compounded growth rate of about 5.3 per cent per year. Trade flows thus rise more quickly than income flows. In percentage terms the difference between income growth and trade growth seems modest

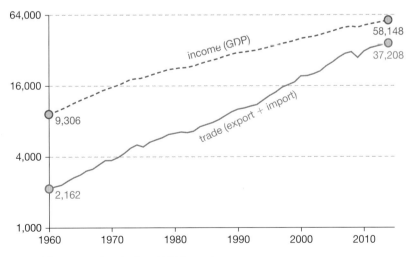

Figure 2.2 World income and trade since 1960, log scale.

Source: calculations based on World Development Indicators; values in constant 2005 billion USD.

BOX 2.2 Logarithmic graphs and a rule of thumb

To graphically analyse the growth rate of income and trade we used a logarithmic scale in Figure 2.2. The important advantage is that the *slope* of the income line reflects the growth rate of income (and similarly for trade), since:

$$y \equiv ln(Y) \Rightarrow dy = d\,ln(Y) = \frac{dY}{Y} \qquad\qquad 2.1$$

If the slope of a logarithmic graph is thus relatively stable over time then the long-run growth rate is also relatively steady. A careful look at the graphs for trade and income in Figure 2.2 suggests that the slope is declining for income, indicating that income growth slows down, but not for trade. This is further analysed in the main text.

A disadvantage of logarithmic graphs is the large step-wise increase in values along the vertical axis. The vertical distance from 1,000 to 4,000 in Figure 2.2 is the same as from 4,000 to 16,000. One such step therefore represents a 4-fold increase, two steps represent a $4 \times 4 = 16$-fold increase, three steps represent a $4 \times 4 \times 4 = 64$-fold increase, and so on. The increase in the level values is extremely rapid as you go up a graph, which may not be fully appreciated by a careless reader.

Rule of thumb: a growth rate of x per cent per year implies a doubling in $70/x$ years.

In evaluating the impact of seemingly small differences in growth rates it is useful to apply the rule of thumb above. According to the rule, which is surprisingly accurate, output doubles in 70 years if the growth rate is 1 per cent, whereas output doubles in 35 years if the growth rate is 2 per cent, and so on.

(namely 3.4 versus 5.3 per cent per year). Over a 54-year period this modest difference nonetheless adds up to substantial differences as a result of compounded growth, namely a 6.2-fold versus a 17.2-fold increase (see Box 2.2 on a rule of thumb and the use of log scales).

As a consequence of the rapid increase in trade flows, trade relative to income rises from 23 per cent in 1960 to 64 per cent in 2014. Relative to either exports or imports only, this thus represents an increase from 11.5 per cent in 1960 to 32 per cent in 2014. Figure 2.2 also suggests that the development of trade flows is more volatile than the development of income: there are larger fluctuations in the trade graph than in the income graph. This is confirmed and illustrated in Figure 2.3, where panel a. depicts annual growth rates and panel b. depicts five-year moving average growth rates.

The average growth rate for income is 3.5 per cent per year, ranging from a minimum of −2.1 per cent in 2009 to a maximum of 6.6 per cent in 1964, with a standard deviation of 1.6 per cent. In contrast, the average growth rate for trade is 5.5 per cent per year, ranging from a minimum of −10.6 per cent in 2009 to a maximum of 13.2 per cent in 2010, with a standard deviation of 4.0 per cent. Trade flows are thus substantially more volatile than income levels, but on average grow much faster.

There is only one year in which the world income level declines, namely in 2009 by 2.1 per cent as a result of the Great Recession. There are three years in which the world trade level declines, namely in 1975 by 4.0 per cent as a result of the first oil crisis, in 1982 by 0.9 per cent as a result of the second oil crisis, and in 2009 by 10.6 per cent as a result of the Great Recession.

To get a better view of the longer-term growth rates of world trade and income, panel b. of Figure 2.3 depicts five-year moving averages. This illustrates three main points. First, none of the five-year moving average growth rates is negative. Second, in all cases the moving average for trade growth is higher than that for income growth. So over five-year periods for the past half century trade has always grown more rapidly than income. Third, the growth rate of income seems to decline over time, certainly before 1980 and perhaps more slowly after that. A similar conclusion cannot be drawn for world trade flows.[4] The next section analyses this aspect in more detail.

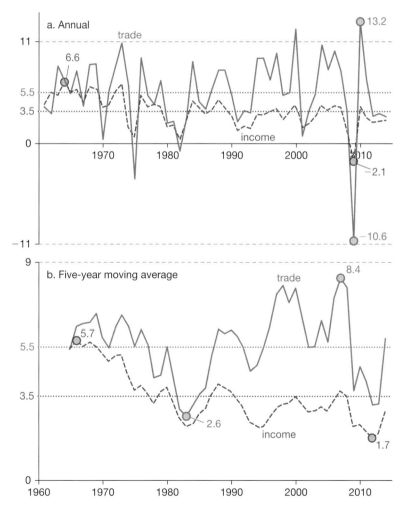

Figure 2.3 World income and trade growth rates since 1960, per cent.

Source: see Figure 2.2; panel b. five-year moving averages located at most recent year; average growth rate for income is 3.5 per cent per year, for trade 5.5 per cent per year; st. dev. is 1.6 and 4.0, respectively.

2.4 World trade and income per capita since 1960

Over the period 1960 to 2014 world population increased from 3.03 billion people to 7.26 billion people, a 2.4-fold increase over 54 years at an annual compounded growth rate of about 1.6 per cent per year. Disasters aside, population growth does not vary much from one year to the next, but it does change significantly over longer time periods. Global population growth peaked at 2.1 per cent per year in 1969; it was above 2 per cent per year for each year of the ten-year period 1963–1972. In 2014 population growth was about 1.2 per cent per year; it was below 1.25 per cent per year for each year of the ten-year period 2005–2014. Population growth is thus declining over time, which may be one of the reasons we observe a declining growth of income over time, as illustrated in panel b. of Figure 2.3.

Why does declining population growth lead to declining GDP growth? This is simple arithmetic. Let y be income per capita and let p be the population. Total income is then given by $Y = p \times y$. If we let a tilde indicate a relative change, so $\tilde{p} = dp/p$ and so on, then this implies that $\tilde{Y} = \tilde{p} + \tilde{y}$, so the growth rate of GDP is the sum of the population growth rate and per capita GDP growth.[5] Since the population growth rate is declining over time, total income growth will decline over time even if per capita income growth is steady. To analyse if this is true we thus have to investigate the development of world trade and income in per capita terms.

A logarithmic graph of the developments over time of income and trade per capita looks, of course, very similar to Figure 2.2 since we are dividing both graphs by total population. Trade per capita thus rises from 23 per cent of income per capita in 1960 to 64 per cent of income per capita in 2014. The slopes of the graphs are, of course, less steep, since we are dividing by a total population that rises over time. In particular, income per capita rises from $3,066 in 1960 to $8,009 in 2014, a 2.6-fold increase in 54 years at a compounded growth rate of about 1.8 per cent per year (= 3.4 − 1.6: income growth minus population growth). Trade per capita rises from $712 in 1960 to $5,125 in 2014, a 7.2-fold increase at a compounded growth rate of 3.7 per cent per year (= 5.3 − 1.6: trade growth minus population growth).

When we calculate growth rates of income and trade per capita (see Figure 2.4), the annual data per capita look similar to a shifted-down version of the total data (see Figure 2.3a, so we do not provide it separately). Our main interest lies in the five-year moving averages depicted in Figure 2.4. These show that income per capita growth slowed down considerably before 1980 and fluctuated around a stable rate since then. The high growth rates in the 1960s and 1970s are generally attributed to a recovery catch-up process after World War II, in particular for Europe and Japan. In fact, the peak in income per capita growth was 3.7 per cent per year over the period 1961–1966. The average income per capita growth rate before 1980 (the period 1960–1980) is 2.7 per cent per year, which declines to 1.3 per cent per year since 1980 (the period 1980–2014). In contrast, there seems to be no noticeable slowdown in the growth rate of trade per capita. Indeed, the average growth rate of trade per capita is *the same* before 1980 (3.8 per cent per year for the period 1960–1980) and after 1980 (3.8 per cent per year for the period 1980–2014).

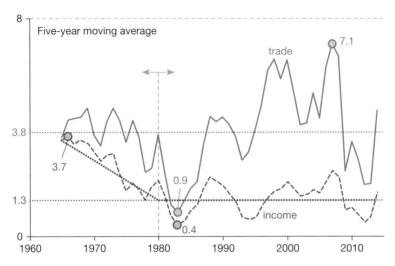

Figure 2.4 World income and trade per capita growth rates since 1960, per cent.

Notes: five-year moving averages located at most recent year; average growth rate for income per capita is 1.8 per cent per year, for trade 3.8 per cent per year.

Source: see Figure 2.2.

Table 2.1 Trend analysis of world income per capita and trade per capita since 1960

	1960 to 1980		1980 to 2014	
	coefficient	p-value	coefficient	p-value
Income per capita	−0.1354**	0.0175	0.0128	0.5642
Trade per capita	−0.0575	0.6740	0.0482	0.5148
Observations	20		35	

Notes: dependent variable is annual growth rate in per cent for world income per capita and trade per capita; ** *significant at the 5 per cent level.*

Source: as Figure 2.2.

Table 2.1 confirms the impression provided by Figure 2.4 using a trend analysis. The growth rate of world income per capita declined significantly over the period 1960–1980, namely by about 0.1354 percentage points per year.[6] Since 1980 the growth rate of world income per capita stabilized at about 1.3 per cent per year (the estimated coefficient is low at 0.0128 percentage points per year and not significant, with a high p-value of 0.5642). If we repeat the same exercise for the growth rate of trade per capita we note that the estimated coefficient is small both before and after 1980 and is not significant in either period (high p-values of 0.6740 and 0.5148, respectively), which indicates there is no time trend for trade per capita.

Conclusion. The worldwide growth rate of income per capita declined over the period 1960–1980 and has fluctuated around 1.3 per cent per year since 1980. The worldwide growth rate of trade per capita has fluctuated around 3.8 per cent per year since 1960. This implies that since 1980 trade per capita has grown about 2.5 per cent per year faster than income per capita.

In Chapter 15 we will analyse supply chains, another aspect of international trade flows, which is based on international fragmentation: see Box 2.3.

BOX 2.3 Fragmentation

Another globalization phenomenon that deserves our attention is 'fragmentation'. Part I of Figure 2.5 depicts a traditional production process in which firm 1 located in country A uses inputs to produce a final good. International economics can help to clarify under what circumstances the firms of a country have a comparative advantage in the production of a certain type of good, which will then be exported. However, technological and communication advances have enabled many production processes to be subdivided into different phases which are physically separable, a process known as fragmentation. This enables a finer and more complex division of labour, as the different phases of the production process may now be spatially separated and undertaken at locations where costs are lowest.

Part II of Figure 2.5 shows an example of fragmentation in which the production process consists of four phases, performed in three countries by two firms. Service links—such as transportation, telecommunications, insurance, quality control, and management control—facilitate the fragmentation process. International economics can help to clarify in this more complex setting why the firms in a country will have a comparative advantage in a phase of the production process where the coordination (service links) will take place, why some phases of the production process will be internally organized (blocks 1, 2, and 4 in part II of Figure 2.5) and why outsourcing is better for some other phase of the production process (block 3 in part II of Figure 2.5). It is clear that these more complex production processes lead to increased *interdependence* of national economies and more intricate international connections, as well as to large exports (and re-imports) of parts of products (as holds, for example, for country A in part II of Figure 2.5).

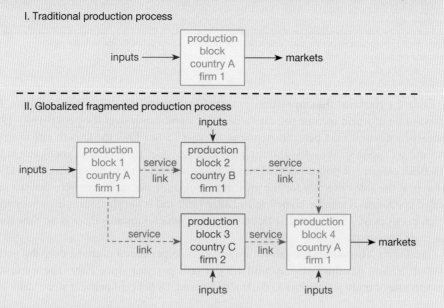

Figure 2.5 Traditional and fragmented production processes.

2.5 A longer-term perspective: the past 2,000 years

In his impressive work full of historical detail, *The World Economy: A Millennial Perspective* (2001), Angus Maddison collects detailed statistics on a wide range of economic variables— such as income, population, and international trade and capital flows—for all the major regions and countries in the world over the past 2,000 years. To describe the evolution of income over time Maddison uses '1990 international Geary-Khamis dollars' (which correct for PPP) and takes great care to ensure transitivity, base-country invariance, and additivity. He collects data for virtually all countries in the world.

The development of world *per capita* income is illustrated in Figure 2.6 using a logarithmic scale. As explained in Box 2.2, the advantage of using a logarithmic scale is the simultaneous depiction of the *level* of a variable (measured by its vertical height) and the *growth rate* of that variable (measured by the slope of the graph) in one figure. Average world per capita income in year zero is estimated to have been $467. The subsistence income level is $400. Where the governing elite could maintain some degree of luxury and sustain a relatively elaborate system of governance, Maddison estimates the income level in the year zero to be higher, as was the case for Italy ($809), North Africa ($550–600), the Fertile Crescent ($500–550), and China and India ($450).

As shown in Figure 2.6, there was no advance in per capita income on a global scale in the first millennium. From the year 1000 to 1820, global per capita income started to increase in what we now consider a slow crawl—the world average rose by about 50 per cent in 820 years, to $666. A clear increase in the global economic growth rate started in 1820 with the industrial revolution. Since then, per capita income rose more than 11-fold in a period of 188 years. The nineteenth and twentieth centuries have been unprecedented in terms of economic growth rates. Moreover, as Maddison argues (2001, p. 17): 'Per capita income growth is not the only indicator of welfare. Over the long run, there has been a dramatic increase in

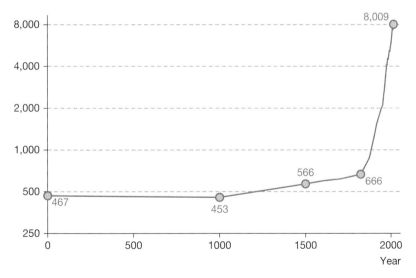

Figure 2.6 Development of world income per capita, 0–2014, log scale.

Note: 1990 international Geary–Khamis dollars.
Data Source: Maddison Historical Statistics 1–2008 AD and World Development Indicators.

life expectation. In the year 1000, the average infant could expect to live about 24 years. A third would die in the first year of life, hunger and epidemic disease would ravage the survivors . . . Now the average infant can expect to survive 66 years.' According to World Bank data, average life expectancy increased from 52.5 years in 1960 to 71.2 years in 2014 (with a steady four-year-longer life expectancy for females than males throughout this period).

We now focus attention on the leading and lagging nations and regions in *relative* terms over the last 2,000 years, by calculating a deviation index of income per capita above the world average (with the world average as base) and below the world average (with the country as base).[7] The calculations over this long period are available for 28 individual countries (15 in Europe, 6 in Asia, 3 in the Americas, 2 in Africa, and 2 in Australia) and 6 country groups, together comprising the global economy. Figure 2.7 summarizes our conclusions for leading and lagging nations.

At the beginning of our calendar (the year zero), the leading country by far was Italy (+73 per cent) while there were many countries and regions lagging behind (in Europe, the Americas, and Australia: namely −17 per cent). During the first millennium there was a convergence of income per capita: in the year 1000 Iran and Iraq became the world leaders (+43 per cent) while many countries still qualify as laggard (−13 per cent). The second millennium witnesses increasing divergence. The leading nations in terms of per capita income were, in turn, Italy (+94 per cent), the Netherlands (+246 per cent), the UK

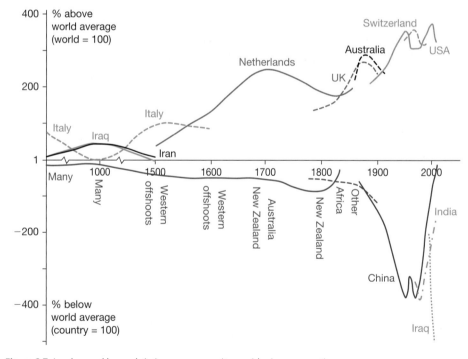

Figure 2.7 Leaders and laggards in income per capita: a widening perspective.

Note: 'Other Africa' here refers to all of Africa except Egypt and Morocco; deviation relative to world average; world index = 100 for positive deviations; country index = 100 for negative deviations.

Data source: Maddison Historical Statistics 1–2008 AD.

(+260 per cent), Australia (+276 per cent), the USA (+353 per cent), Switzerland (+353 per cent), and the USA again (+371 per cent). The lagging nations were, in turn, the 'western offshoots' (Australia, Canada, New Zealand, and USA: −49 per cent), Australia and New Zealand (−54 per cent), New Zealand (−66 per cent), Africa (−74 per cent), China (−371 per cent), India (−381 per cent), and Iraq (−626 per cent). A clear common feature for both positive and negative deviations is that the gap has widened considerably over the past thousand years (see also Sections 2.9 and 2.10 on income inequality).

2.6 Globalization in history

The relative rise of international trade flows is not something new. Trade flows have always been central in economic interactions: for the ancient cultures of Egypt and Greece as well as for China, India, and Mesopotamia. According to Maddison, trade has been most important for the economic rise of western Europe in the past millennium. Based on improved techniques of shipbuilding and navigation (the compass), Venice played a key role from 1000 to 1500 in opening up trade routes within Europe, on the Mediterranean, and to China (via the caravan routes), bringing in silk and valued spices as well as technology (glassblowing, also used for making spectacles; the cultivation of rice; and sugar-cane cutting). Venice's role in the development of banking, accounting, and foreign exchange and credit markets was equally important, thus establishing a system of public finance which made it the lead economy of the period. The fall of Byzantium and the rise of the Ottoman Empire eventually blocked Venetian contacts with Asia.

Portugal began more ambitious interactions between Europe and the rest of the world in the second half of the fifteenth century by opening up trade and settlement in the Atlantic islands and developing trade routes around Africa to China, Japan, and India. It took over the role of Venice as the major shipper of spices. Portugal's location on the south Atlantic coast of Europe enabled its fishermen to gather knowledge of Atlantic winds, weather, and tides. Combined with maritime experience, the development of compass bearings and cartography, and adjustments in ship design to meet Atlantic sailing conditions, this allowed the Portuguese (such as Vasco da Gama) to embark on their explorations and play a dominant role in intercontinental trade. As Maddison (2001, p. 19) puts it: 'Although Spain had a bigger empire, its only significant base outside the Americas was the Philippines. Its two most famous navigators were Columbus who was a Genoese with Portuguese training, and Magellan who was Portuguese.' Portugal was able to absorb Jewish merchants and scholars, who were required to undergo a *pro forma* conversion and who played an important role in science, as intermediaries in trade with the Muslim world, and in attracting foreign capital (Genoese and Catalan) for business ventures.[8]

From 1400 to the middle of the seventeenth century the Netherlands had the most dynamic European economy, using power from windmills and peat, creating large canal networks and transforming agriculture into horticulture, but most of all developing shipping, shipbuilding, and commercial services. As illustrated in Figure 2.8, by 1570 the carrying capacity of Dutch merchant shipping was about the same as that of the combined fleets of Britain, France, and Germany. The Dutch were then able to maintain this lead for a century by more than doubling this capacity. Holland created a modern state which provided

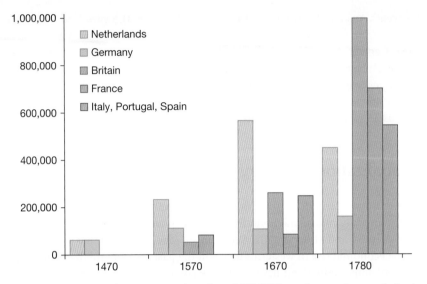

Figure 2.8 Carrying capacity of European merchant fleets, 1470–1780, metric tons; absence of a bar in a year for a particular country /group indicates that no data are available.

Data source: Maddison (2001, p. 77).

property rights, education, and religious tolerance and had only 40 per cent of the labour force in agriculture. This attracted a financial and entrepreneurial elite from Flanders and Brabant, who emigrated to Holland on a large scale and made it the centre for banking, finance, and international commerce.

Britain became the leading economy in the eighteenth century, initially by improving its financial, banking, fiscal, and agricultural institutions along the lines pioneered by the Dutch, and subsequently through a surge in industrial productivity. The latter was based not only on the acceleration of technical progress and investments in physical capital, education, and skills, but also on commercial trade policy, which in 1846 reduced protective duties on agricultural imports and by 1860 had unilaterally removed all trade and tariff restrictions. The British willingness to specialize in industrial production and import a large part of its food had positive effects on the world economy and diffused the impact of technical progress, but most of all it allowed Britain to achieve unprecedented rates of economic growth and establish itself as a global economic and political power by taking over the lands that the French and Dutch had lost in Asia and Africa. The soundness of its monetary system (the gold standard) and public credit gave Britain an important role in international finance. At the end of the nineteenth century and the beginning of the twentieth, there was a massive outflow of European capital (French, Dutch, and German, but most of all British—up to half of British savings) for overseas investment, mostly in the Americas and Russia. The British economist John Maynard Keynes (1919, Chapter 2) summarized the high degree of global economic progress and development in this epoch as follows:

> What an extraordinary episode in the economic progress of man that age was which came to an end in August 1914! . . . The inhabitant of London could order by telephone, sipping his morning tea in bed, the various products of the whole earth, in such quantity as he

might see fit, and reasonably expect their early delivery upon his doorstep . . . But, most important of all, he regarded this state of affairs as normal, certain, and permanent, except in the direction of further improvement, and any deviation from it as aberrant, scandalous, and avoidable.

The old liberal order came to end, as indicated by Keynes' quote, as a result of two world wars (1914–18 and 1939–45) and the Great Depression in the 1930s, with its beggar-thy-neighbour policies, which drastically raised trade impediments and led to a collapse of flows of trade, capital, and migration. As a consequence, the world economy grew much more slowly from 1913 to 1950 than it had from 1870 to 1913.[9] The institutional arrangements with codes of behaviour and cooperation set up after World War II, such as the General Agreement on Tariffs and Trade (GATT), the International Monetary Fund (IMF), the Organization for Economic Cooperation and Development (OECD), and the World Bank, created a new liberal international order which abolished beggar-thy-neighbour policies in favour of liberal trading. In the post–World War II period, this contributed to remarkable growth rates of income per capita (3 per cent per year), total world income (5 per cent per year) and world trade flows (8 per cent per year). At the same time, the world economy became more closely connected than ever before, as illustrated in Figure 2.9.

This type of globalization is not a monotone process, as clearly illustrated in Figure 2.9, which depicts the development of merchandise exports relative to income for the world as a whole, the USA, and Japan from 1870 to 2014. It is now customary to identify two 'waves' of globalization: the first wave at the end of the nineteenth century and the beginning of the twentieth, and the second wave after World War II. Evidently, international trade rose much more rapidly than output for the period as a whole, but there was a long and substantial interruption as a result of two major international conflicts and economic policy changes.

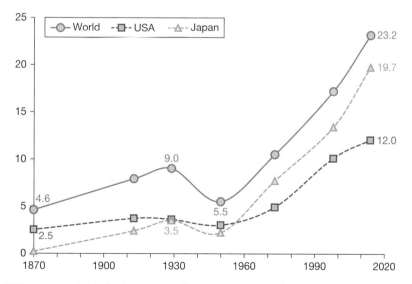

Figure 2.9 Two waves of globalization: merchandise exports, per cent of GDP.

Data sources: Maddison (2001, table F–5) in constant 1990 prices, extended to 2014 using World Development Indicators Online.

2.7 The price wedge and trade flows

The most basic economic picture consists of a downward-sloping demand curve (on the assumption that people buy less of a good if its price is higher) and an upward-sloping supply curve (on the assumption that firms produce more of a good if its price rises). International trade flows can also be depicted in this most basic framework, with two twists. We assume there are two countries, the USA A and the UK B, and we focus attention on the UK's import market. The first twist is that the UK's downward-sloping demand curve for *imports* actually consists of the UK's demand for the good *not* provided by its domestic suppliers (it is therefore also called the UK's *net* demand curve). The same applies, necessary changes being made, for the USA's export supply curve (or net supply curve). The second twist is that there may be a number of reasons for a deviation between the price received by American producers and the price paid by British consumers, which is called a *price wedge*—for example, because American firms have to overcome transport costs, tariffs, trade impediments, cultural differences, and all sorts of other extra costs before they can export the good to the British market.

Figure 2.10 illustrates international trade equilibrium, which results from the intersection of the downward-sloping British import demand curve and the upward-sloping American export supply curve, taking the price wedge into consideration. Suppose the initial equilibrium is situation D, where trade volume is q_d, the price received by American exporters is p_d, and the price paid by British consumers is $p_d + g_0$. The difference between the price paid in the UK and the price received in the USA is thus the price gap g_0.

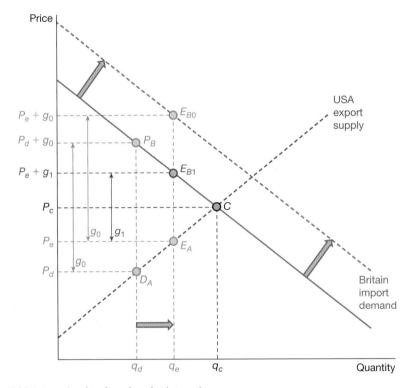

Figure 2.10 International trade and market integration.

International trade flows can now increase for two main reasons.

- First, a shift to the right in either the USA's export supply curve or the UK's import demand curve at a constant price wedge g_0 will result in increasing trade flows. As an example, Figure 2.10 shows that a shift in the UK's import demand curve to the right as a result of a demand shock (as indicated by the arrows) for a given price wedge g_0 raises the price received by American producers to p_e, the price paid by British consumers to $p_e + g_0$, and the volume of trade to q_e. The demand shift might, for example, be caused by changing preferences, population growth, or per capita income growth.

- Second, a decrease in the price wedge between what consumers pay and what producers receive will also lead to rising trade flows. Figure 2.10 shows that the same increase in trade volume from q_d to q_e can be obtained if the price wedge decreases from g_0 to g_1; in that case the price received by American producers is again p_e but the price paid by British consumers falls to $p_e + g_1 < p_e + g_0$. The decrease in the price wedge may be caused, for example, by lower transportation costs, lower tariffs, a reduction in other types of trade restrictions, lower communication costs, and so on.[10]

Globalization, as measured for example by the rising volume of trade or increased capital flows, may thus be caused by volume effects or a decrease in the international price wedge. O'Rourke and Williamson (2002) argue that early growth of international trade was mostly of the first kind: rising trade in non-competing goods, such as spices, special dyes (indigo), coffee, tea, and sugar, which could not be produced in substantial amounts in the importing countries themselves. Usually, these were expensive luxury items and their buyers could afford to pay for the price wedge. The discovery of the New World and its commodities created a market for these goods, shifting the British import demand curve to the right without necessarily reducing the price wedge. O'Rourke and Williamson then provide evidence that the post-1492 trade boom was most likely caused by the demand for luxury items and by population growth and hardly reduced the price wedge on traded goods, as measured by changes in the mark-up. Moreover, there is some evidence that the retreat of China and Japan from world markets from the mid-fifteenth century to the mid-nineteenth further stimulated European–Asian trade.

The two waves of globalization illustrated in Figure 2.9 provide examples of the second kind of growth in international trade. During the first wave in the nineteenth century there was an increase of trade in basic and homogeneous commodities. During the second wave after World War II there was an increase of trade in basic and differentiated manufactured products. Decreases in transports costs, technology improvements, falling trade restrictions, international cooperation, and improved communication possibilities have all been important underlying forces in these two waves of globalization. The spectacular decline in transport costs in the nineteenth century is considered to have been the most important cause for increased trade flows. The railway and the steamship revolutionized the means of transportation, while the opening of the Suez Canal and the Panama Canal dramatically cut travel times and meant that traders could avoid the dangerous routes around the Cape of Good Hope and Cape Horn.[11] Technological inventions, such as effective means of refrigeration which enabled the transportation of perishable goods (meat and fruit) across the equator, further stimulated trade, as did reductions in protectionist measures. Table 2.2 shows empirical estimates from O'Rourke and Williamson (2000) for both the declining transport costs and the reduction in the price wedge for commodities produced in different markets, indicating closer market integration.

The rise in trade during the first wave of globalization was also caused by reductions in protectionist measures. Under the influence of Adam Smith's doctrine of free trade, many restrictions to trade were removed during the nineteenth century. By 1860 the UK and the Netherlands had unilaterally virtually removed all trade restrictions. Special bilateral arrangements were made between the UK and France (the Cobden–Chevalier Treaty of 1860).[12] Other bilateral arrangements involving other countries soon followed. Table 2.3 shows that tariffs were very high at the beginning of the nineteenth century and declined considerably until 1875. Around the 1880s, the tariff reductions more or less came to a stop. Cheap Russian grain increased competition in agricultural markets. The real earnings of British farmers, for example, declined by more than 50 per cent between 1870 and 1913 (Findlay and O'Rourke, 2001). Soon Britain, France, Germany, Sweden and other countries returned to protectionist practices and tariffs were raised again. Perhaps the integration of product markets, due to better transport systems, was so successful that it undermined its own success. In general, it seems that the transport revolution could flourish in an environment that already tended towards free trade, but that the income consequences led to adverse reactions. The continued efforts of the GATT/WTO after World War II to reduce trade barriers has now driven tariff measures to unprecedented low levels (see Chapter 10).

Table 2.2 Price convergence and declining transport costs, 1870–1913

Transport cost reductions (index)		
American export routes, deflated freight cost	1869/71–1908/10	100 to 55
American east coast routes, deflated freight cost	1869/71–1911/13	100 to 55
British tramp, deflated freight cost	1869/71–1911/13	100 to 78
Commodity price convergence at selected markets (per cent deviation)		
Liverpool–Chicago, wheat price gap	1870–1912	58 to 16
London–Cincinnati, bacon price gap	1870–1913	93 to 18
Philadelphia–London, pig iron price gap	1870–1913	85 to 19
London–Boston, wool price gap	1870–1913	59 to 28
London–Buenos Aires, hides price gap	1870–1913	28 to 9

Source: O'Rourke and Williamson (2000, Table 1).

Table 2.3 Tariffs on manufactures imposed by selected countries: 1820–2010, per cent

	1820[a]	1875[a,b]	1913[a,b]	1931[c]	1950[c]	2010[c]
Denmark	30	15–20	14	–	3	1.9 (EU)
France	Prohibition	12–15	20	30	18	1.9 (EU)
Germany	–	4–6	13	21	26	1.9 (EU)
Italy	–	8–10	18	46	25	1.9 (EU)
Russia	Prohibition	15	84	Prohibition	Prohibition	6.0
Spain	Prohibition	15–20	41	63	–	1.9 (EU)
Sweden	Prohibition	3–5	20	21	9	1.9 (EU)
Netherlands	7	3–5	4	–	11	1.9 (EU)
UK	50	0	0	–	23	1.9 (EU)
USA	45	40	44	48	14	3.0

Note: – = data unavailable.
Sources: [a] Baldwin and Martin (1999, Table 8); [b] O'Rourke and Williamson (1999, Table 6.1); [c] Beugelsdijk et al. (2013, Table 1.6).

The reduction in trade cost and the narrowing of the price gap are driving forces of the globalization process, to a large extent based on international fragmentation (see Box 2.3). It should be noted at this point that the country where the final product is manufactured is not necessarily the most important country in terms of added value. This is analysed in Box 2.4, which shows that an iPad assembled in China may have 'made in China' written on the product, although China receives only a small fraction of the total retail price.

BOX 2.4 Who earns what when an iPad is sold?

In 2011 the retail price of an iPad was about $500 in the United States. But who earns what when you buy an iPad? In a thought-provoking analysis of the entire value chain of the iPad, Linden, Kraemer and Debrick (2009, 2011) show that most of the value added goes to American shareholders and workers: see Figure 2.11.

The costs of material inputs are about 31 per cent of the retail price, while Apple's profits of the iPad are about 30 per cent of the retail price. Apple's design, software development, and marketing are located in the United States. Moreover, distribution and retail costs are about 15 per cent, meaning that for each iPad sold in the United States another 15 per cent goes to American workers. The remaining 24 per cent of the retail price is divided over a number of other contributors. About 7 per cent goes to South Korean firms such as Samsung and LG, which provide key components. The production of an iPad takes place at the Taiwanese Foxconn firm located in China, which explains the Taiwanese profits of about 2 per cent. The most striking observation is the fact that although production takes place in China, only 2 per cent of the retail price goes to Chinese labour (for assembling). This analysis triggered a response by many economists, business scholars, and policy makers, in particular because of the finding that production may take place in China, but the added value generated there is pretty small.

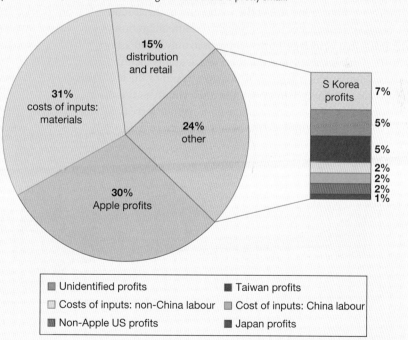

Figure 2.11 Value-added distribution for an Apple iPad, 2011.

Source: Brakman et al. (2013); the figure is based on data provided by Linden et al. (2009, 2011). See also *The Economist,* 21 January 2012.

2.8 More waves: capital and migration flows

The reduction in the price wedge for international trade flows during the first wave of globalization and the increase in the inter-war years analysed in Section 2.7 is also visible on the capital market. This is illustrated in Figure 2.12, which depicts the mean bond spread for 14 core and empire countries surrounded by a measure of dispersion (a band equal to ± 2 standard deviations).[13]

Obstfeld and Taylor (2003) studied government bonds traded in London, focusing exclusively on bonds denominated in gold or in sterling so as to isolate the effects of default risk. The interest rate spread for these countries was small, usually within 1 or 2 percentage points of Britain's. Moreover, there was a convergence in bond spreads up to 1914, and a widening in spreads and increased volatility in the inter-war years. As with international trade flows, it is customary to identify two 'waves' of globalization for capital flows as well. This is illustrated in Figure 2.13, where foreign capital stocks relative to world GDP are relatively high towards the end of the nineteenth century and the beginning of the twentieth, then drop dramatically in the inter-war years, only to reach unprecedented heights after the capital market liberalizations beginning in the 1960s.

We can also apply the idea of the price wedge to international migration flows. In principle, real wage differences between countries explain the direction of migration flows to a large extent. Large wage differences between countries exist: see Section 1.5. These differences are caused, for example, by migration quotas, the perceived probability of actually finding a job in the destination country, or the lack of knowledge of foreign countries. Such factors contribute to the size of the wedge and to the absence of labour market integration.

UN evidence indicates that although absolute migration numbers have increased, world migrants—that is, foreign-born—comprised only about 3.1 per cent of the world population in 2010.[14] This relatively low number, which seems inconsistent with popular opinion that the level of migrants is large, is primarily a result of the low number of migrants in developing countries. Indeed, in some individual countries these numbers are much larger. The share of foreign-born as a percentage of the labour force is relevant, as this number gives an impression of competition on the labour markets. In Australia, for example, 26.5 per cent of

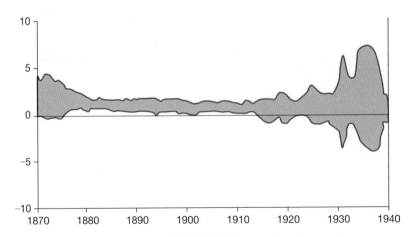

Figure 2.12 London external bond spread, 1870–1940, 14 core and empire countries.

Note: units are percentage points.

Source: Beugelsdijk et al. (2013), based on Obstfeld and Taylor (2003).

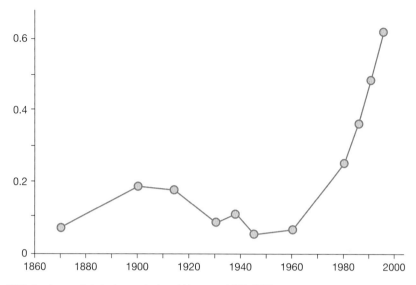

Figure 2.13 Foreign capital stocks: assets / world income, 1860–2000.

Source: Beugelsdijk et al. (2013), based on Obstfeld and Taylor (2003).

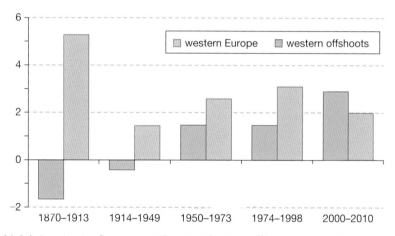

Figure 2.14 Relative migration flows: western Europe and western offshoots, 1870–2010.

Note: data for 1999 not included. Western Europe consists of Belgium, France, Germany, Italy, Netherlands, Norway, Sweden, Switzerland, and UK.

Sources: net migration in the period (Maddison, 2001, table 3.4) is divided by the (simple) average population and length of the period, normalized per 1,000 inhabitants; updated for the period 2000–2010 with data from UN Population Division, Migration Section.

the labour force in 2008 was foreign-born; in the USA this number was 16.5 per cent; in the UK 12.6 per cent; in the Netherlands 11.4 per cent; and in Denmark 6.8 per cent.[15] In addition, the United Nations High Commissioner for Refugees (UNHCR) estimated that there were some 15.4 million refugees in the world in 2010; see also Chapter 9.

Historians have also identified two modern 'waves' of migration (see Figure 2.14). The first took place between 1820 and 1913. More than 50 million migrants departed (mostly) from Europe to Australia, Canada, South America, and the USA. Almost 60 per cent of the migrants went to the USA. Most were young and relatively low-skilled. After 1850, most migrants came from Ireland.

The second 'wave' started after World War II and has not yet ended. Between 1913 and 1950 migration was only a fraction of what it had been during the nineteenth century. The USA remained the main destination country. Immigration grew from a low of 252,000 per year in the 1950s to 916,000 in the 1990s, but the source countries changed dramatically. Before the 1950s most immigrants came from Europe; in the 1990s most came from Asia and (from 1990 onwards) also from the former eastern European countries. During this second wave, immigration restrictions became more binding than before. Many countries use a quota and allow in migrants only for reasons such as a family reunion or specific labour needs. In Europe most migration flows are in the form of intra-European Union migration. From 1990 to 2010 the number of migrants in Europe increased from 49 million to 70 million, compared to an increase from 28 to 50 million in North America. In contrast to globalization with respect to trade and capital, labour markets are thus less globally integrated.

2.9 Globalization and income inequality

Section 2.5 on the long-term perspective of globalization suggests that income inequality is rising over time; see in particular Figure 2.7 on the widening perspective of leader versus laggard income per capita over the past thousand years. An important part of the globalization debate is focused on the question of whether globalization fosters income inequality. We address this question in two steps. This section focuses on changes in global income inequality, while the next section analyses changes in within-country income inequality. Our discussion is based on Rougoor and van Marrewijk (2015; see their paper for references), who also make a projection of expected changes in global income inequality for the next 40 years. The discussion in this section groups countries together in larger regions. One should be cautious in doing so, however, as discussed in Box 2.5.

BOX 2.5 The BRIC(S): emerging market economies

The term 'BRIC countries', which later became 'BRICS countries', is based on the initials of the names of four (later five) countries and was introduced in 2001 by consultancy firm Goldman Sachs to refer to major emerging market economies. The included countries are Brazil, Russia, India, China, and South Africa.

The term 'BRICS countries' quickly became popular in the media as a catch-all term for major emerging market economies, which are then grouped together in subsequent discussions. Figure 2.15 provides information on the income developments in these countries using GDP PPP in constant 2011 international dollars with a log scale, both per capita (panel a.) and in total (panel b.). Based on this information, we just want to point out how remarkable the grouping of these countries together, and the popularity of the term BRICS, is.

First, as panel a. of Figure 2.15 shows, there have been enormous differences between the countries in terms of the development of income per capita. The compounded growth rate of income per capita over the period 1990–2014 ranges from a meagre 0.8 per cent per year for Russia and South Africa to a remarkable 8.8 per cent for China. The growth rate for Brazil is rather standard (1.6 per cent) and for India is substantial (4.7 per cent). Also note the high variability of growth for Russia. On the basis of this information alone it seems unwise to group China and India together with the other three countries.

Second, as panel b. of Figure 2.15 shows, there is an enormous difference between the countries in terms of total economic power and the speed at which this power is rising. In 2014, for example, total income in

(continued...)

South Africa is less than 4 per cent of total income in China, which makes it hard to understand the inclusion of South Africa. The total economic power of Brazil and Russia is also modest compared to that of China (about 18 and 20 per cent of China's GDP in 2014, respectively). In this respect only India comes close (about 41 per cent of China's GDP in 2014, or twice as important as Brazil and Russia). The average compounded growth rate of total income over the period 1990–2014 ranges from a meagre 0.7 per cent per year for Russia to a remarkable 9.6 per cent for China. It is 2.5 per cent for South Africa, 2.9 per cent for Brazil, and 6.3 per cent for India. The difference relative to panel a. is based on differences in population growth, which is fast in India and South Africa in this period (1.7 and 1.8 per cent per year), negative in Russia (–0.1 per cent), and in between in China and Brazil (0.8 and 1.3 per cent). Future demographic differences are also substantial.

In short, when listing 'major emerging market economies' it seems wise to include only the IC countries, India and China. That term is, of course, not catchy enough to become popular.

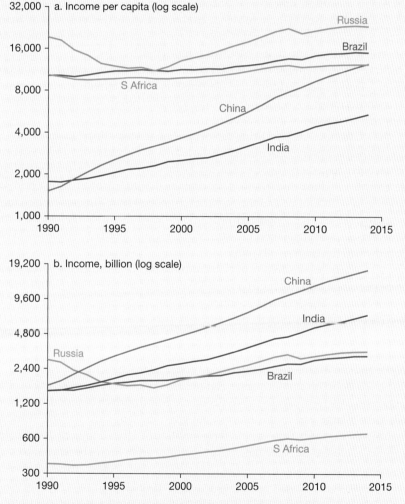

Figure 2.15 BRIC(S) countries: income and income per capita, 1990–2014.

Note: GDP PPP constant 2011 int. dollar.

Source: based on data from World Development Indicators.

Global income inequality measures, in principle, treat all people in the world equally and try to provide indicators regarding the degree of income inequality for poor and rich people in Tanzania versus poor and rich people in Russia, USA, China, and so on. Various income inequality measures exist, each with specific benefits and drawbacks. In this section we focus our discussion on the Gini coefficient, a widely used measure of income inequality. It ranges from zero (when all people in the world have the same income level in a certain period) to one (when one person earns all income and everyone else earns nothing).

Around 200,000 years ago, when *Homo sapiens* first walked on the earth, global income inequality (by which at this point in history we mean inequality in material well-being, as money did not exist) must have been very small as most people were simply trying to stay alive. In Angus Maddison's measure of income per capita used in Section 2.5, this means that most people just lived at the subsistence level equivalent to that provided by an income of $400 per year. The Gini coefficient is close to zero. Since then global income inequality has been rising, particularly in the past two centuries, driven by the strong and continuous growth of a small number of (OECD) countries after the industrial revolution. This resulted in a twin-peaks world income distribution, characterized by a large number of people (countries) with a low income level and a smaller group of people (countries) with a high income level, and not much in between.

From the 1970s onwards 'equalizing' factors proved stronger than 'disequalizing' factors and a trend towards lower global inequality started, largely because of a decline in between-country income inequality. Major equalizing factors were the faster-than-world-average income growth in China and South Asia combined with a slower-than-world-average population growth in Europe and the western offshoots. Major disequalizing factors were slower-than-world-average income growth in Sub-Saharan Africa (combined with faster-than-world-average population growth in that region) and faster-than-world-average income growth in the western offshoots.

Figure 2.16 illustrates the decline in global income inequality since the 1970s using data on income per capita for 176 countries as well as information on the distribution of income within each country. The decline is slow at first and not monotonic; the Gini coefficient falls by about 2.4 per cent from 1970 to 1983 and then rises again by 1.5 per cent from 1983 to 1991. In the new millennium the decline in global income inequality is more rapid; the Gini coefficient falls by about 7.9 per cent from 2000 to 2009.

Rougoor and van Marrewijk (2015) develop several global growth scenarios up to 2050 in order to project global income inequality. Figure 2.16 also shows a projection of global income inequality up to 2050 for a 'base scenario'. Economic growth, driven by productivity increases, naturally plays a large part in this process, but given the long time horizon, demographic developments do so as well. For example, the population of Africa is projected to double in the coming four decades. At the same time, Asian countries profit from a beneficial age structure, as many economically advanced countries have over the past decades. These advanced countries are now starting to struggle with aging populations and fertility rates below replacement levels. All these developments directly (through economic growth) or indirectly (through the proportion of working-age people in the population) affect global income inequality.

Up to 2050 Asia's income share is expected to rise by about 15 percentage points and that of Africa and Oceania by less than 1 percentage point. The income shares of Latin

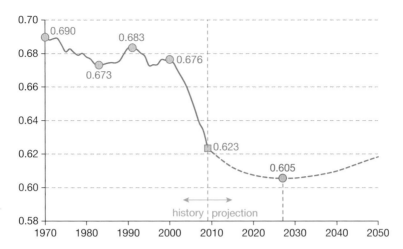

Figure 2.16 Global Gini coefficient, 1970–2050, base scenario.

Source: Rougoor and van Marrewijk (2015).

America and North America decline by about 4 percentage points, and that of Europe by about 9 percentage points. These changes are, of course, the result of changes in the total population, the working population, and production per worker. Total population more than doubles in Africa, compared to an increase of about 30 per cent for most of the rest of the world, except for Europe, which has a stagnant population. Africa is the only continent where the share of the working population increases by 6.6 percentage points. In the other continents it declines, ranging from 1.5 percentage points for Latin America to 11.2 percentage points for Europe.

This base scenario projects a reversal of the current trend towards lower global income inequality.[16] The turning point is expected to be reached around 2027. Rising income levels in many Asian economies and continuing high population growth rates in Sub-Saharan Africa are the most important drivers behind this trend reversal. By 2050 global income inequality is expected to have returned to levels similar to that of today. To analyse the dynamics behind this development, a closer look at the data is required. This is done by constructing a 'world distribution of income', which is the result of a so-called kernel density function in which all income groups are population-weighted and effectively integrated into one global income distribution. Figure 2.17 has the income level (log scale) on the horizontal axis and millions of people on the vertical axis. The areas under the graphs are equal to the total world population in the respective years.

Each consecutive world distribution of income is larger (larger area under the graph) and shifted to the right relative to the one before. This corresponds to a growing world population and rising income levels. Because of these two large-scale developments most other shifts are small in comparison and therefore hardly visible. Figure 2.18 takes this approach one step further and looks at different regions (based on the World Bank classification) in relation to one another. Sub-Saharan Africa (SSA), South Asia (SA), East Asia (EA), and the OECD countries are each shown as individual distributions for 2010 and 2050.

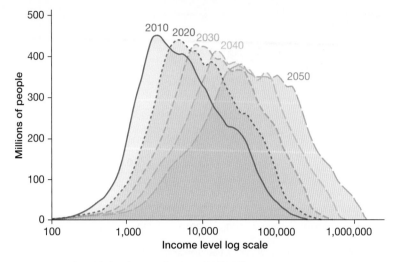

Figure 2.17 Projection of world distribution of income, 2010–2050.

Note: units for real income are in constant 2005 international dollars.
Source: based on Rougoor and van Marrewijk (2015).

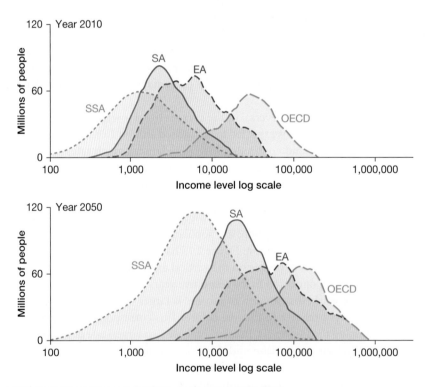

Figure 2.18 Projection of regional distributions of income, 2010–2050.

Note: units for real income are in constant 2005 international dollars; EA=East Asia; SA=South Asia; SSA=Sub Sahara Africa.
Source: Rougoor and van Marrewijk (2015).

First, note that considerable shifts are visible, both in individual distributions as well as in distributions in relation to each other. All distributions shift to the right, but South Asia and East Asia move relatively faster. A consequence of this is that East Asia has more overlap with the income distribution of the OECD countries in 2050 than it had in 2010. The same holds for South Asia.

Second, note that the continent distributions shift relative to each other. Some of these shifts result in an overall decrease of inequality and some result in an overall increase of inequality. With respect to South Asia and East Asia the situation is more complex. While these countries *catch up* to OECD countries, they simultaneously *pull away* from most other African and Asian countries (the latter are not shown in the graph). For example, China has over the past few decades grown faster than the OECD average. At the same time it over took most African countries, which resulted in a diverging trend relative to Africa and a converging trend relative to the OECD. The net result for global income inequality depends on the relative size of such trends.

Finally, note that the OECD countries and East Asia (mainly China) show a modest population growth. South Asia (India) and Sub-Saharan Africa are projected to significantly increase in population.[17] This impacts global inequality in at least two ways. First, a rapid increase in population is often associated with a higher youth dependency ratio and subsequent lower economic growth. Countries with an extremely high population growth are thus at risk of (economically) lagging behind countries with a lower population growth. A similar observation can be made for very low population growth, which results in a larger old age dependency ratio.[18] Second, population size also directly influences inequality measures such as the Gini coefficient. The bulk of low-income countries are situated in Sub-Saharan Africa. As the population in Sub-Saharan Africa grows more rapidly than in the rest of the world the relative weight of the continent increases. Therefore, inequality would increase *even if* GDP per capita is assumed to stay the same in all countries over the entire period.

Conclusion. In a long-term perspective, global income inequality has been mostly rising. Since the 1970s global income inequality has been falling (thanks in large part to the economic rise of China and India). This recent trend is likely to reverse again in the 2020s, mainly as a result of the rising population in Africa, which is still lagging behind.

2.10 Within-country income inequality

Our discussion in Section 2.9 has ignored changes in within-country income inequality. To analyse these changes we use the latest version of the UNU-WIDER database on World Income Inequality (WIID3.b1, version September 2014), where we focus on the quintile distribution of the included studies if this is provided. Since our objective is to determine long-run trends in within-country income inequality, we want to compare the first information for the country as a whole that is available for any country with the latest (most recent) information.[19] We also want to incorporate the quality of the observations, as indicated by the database in the four classes 'not known', 'low', 'average', and 'high'. We therefore compare the first observation of average or high quality with the last observation of average or high quality. Only if observations of average or high quality were *not* available did we select low or not known quality (in that order).[20] On the basis of these observations we calculated implied Gini coefficients to determine if within-country income inequality is rising or falling for the country under consideration.

Table 2.4 summarizes our findings for the 148 countries with more than one observation.[21] Panel a. provides summary statistics on the year and Gini index of the first and last observation, as well as the change in the Gini index. The median first observation is in the year 1988 (average is 1985). The median last observation is in the year 2009 (average is 2007). The median difference between the first and last observation is thus 21 years (average is 22). The median Gini index for the first observation is 0.361 (average is 0.373) and for the last observation is 0.339 (average is 0.353). For the average country, therefore, the median Gini index has *fallen* by 0.019 or a modest 5 per cent (the average by 0.020,

Table 2.4 First and last quintile information and associated Gini coefficients

a. First and last observation year and Gini coefficient					
Statistic	First observation		Last observation		Change
	Year	Gini	Year	Gini	Gini*
Average	1985	0.373	2007	0.353	−0.020
Median	1988	0.361	2009	0.339	−0.019
Minimum	1951	0.175	1978	0.186	−0.283
Maximum	2007	0.651	2012	0.647	0.202
Standard deviation	13.8	0.100	5.9	0.083	0.074
Observations	148	148	148	148	148
Population weighted average Gini index[#]		0.3598		0.3597	−0.000

b. Change in Gini coefficients per continent						
Statistic	Asia	Africa	Europe	Latin America	Oceania	North America
Average	−0.016	−0.027	−0.007	−0.039	−0.045	0.060
Median	−0.009	−0.035	−0.018	−0.036	−0.023	0.060
Minimum	−0.283	−0.205	−0.110	−0.265	−0.177	0.056
Maximum	0.094	0.202	0.122	0.098	0.042	0.063
Standard deviation	0.075	0.086	0.062	0.069	0.093	0.005
Observations	41	35	40	26	4	2
Falling inequality	23	25	25	20	3	0
Falling per cent	56	71	63	77	75	0

Notes: * The Gini index falls for 96 out of 148 countries (65 per cent) and rises for the other 52 countries.
[#] *The population-weighted average Gini index uses the total population in 2000 as weights (data from World Development Indicators; plus Maddison (2011) for Taiwan).*
Observations for countries that no longer exist (Czechoslovakia, the USSR, and Yugoslavia) are excluded from the calculation of the weighted average.
Source: Rougoor and van Marrewijk (2015), calculations based on UNU-WIDER World Income Inequality Database (WIID3.0b, September 2014).

also 5 per cent) over a period of 21 years. Indeed, the Gini index fell for most countries (96 out of 148, or 65 per cent). The largest decline was in Armenia from 1996 to 2011 (by 0.283, or 50 per cent). The largest increase was in Rwanda from 1985 to 2006 (by 0.202, or 76 per cent).

The information above does not necessarily imply that the declining within-country income inequality as summarized in Table 2.4a. translates into a decline in global income inequality if these trends continue in the future. This depends, among other things, on (i) regional differences and (ii) the trend for the most populous nations. Regarding (i), Table 2.4b. provides further information by detailing the changes in the Gini index for the six continents. We do not observe big differences between the continents regarding the change in the Gini index: the decline is small and holds for about two-thirds of the countries. The only exception is North America, where the two countries involved (Canada and USA) both experienced an increase in within-country income inequality. Regarding (ii), Table 2.4a. also provides a 'population-weighted average Gini index', which thus takes the size of the population in a country into consideration. It shows that although there is a majority of countries where income inequality declined, this is almost perfectly compensated for by the fact that income inequality increased for some populous nations, such as (in order of population size) in China (by 19 per cent), the USA (by 15 per cent), Indonesia (by 17 per cent), Bangladesh (by 21 per cent), and Nigeria (by 9 per cent).[22] As a consequence, the population-weighted average Gini index is *constant* at 0.360.

Conclusion. Over the period 1988–2009 there is no clear trend in changes in within-country income inequality; the population-weighted average Gini index is constant.

2.11 Conclusions

We explain that there are different types of globalization and that the term is interpreted in different ways by different people. We then show that at the global level trade flows have risen considerably faster than income flows since 1960. We also note that there is a slow-down in total income growth that is related to the declining population growth rate. On a per capita basis, income growth slowed down from 1960 to 1980, but has fluctuated around 1.3 per cent growth per year since then. Trade flows per capita have fluctuated around 3.8 per cent per year since 1960, implying that trade per capita has been growing more rapidly than income per capita by about 2.5 per cent per year since 1980. From a long-run perspective we note that income per capita growth has been particularly fast for the last two centuries and that the gap between the leading and lagging nations seems to have been rising for the past thousand years. We discuss the role of the price wedge in globalization and the waves of globalization in trade flows, capital flows, and migration flows. Finally, we argue that global income inequality has been mostly rising throughout history. The recent (modest) decline since the 1970s as a result of the economic rise of China and India looks to be temporary and is likely to be reversed in the 2020s because of the rising population in Africa, which is still lagging behind. We return to the issues raised above throughout the remainder of the book. First, however, we need to provide a solid accounting basis for our analysis, which we do in the next chapter.

Notes

1 This chapter is partially based on Beugelsdijk et al. (2013); I am grateful to my co-authors Sjoerd Beugelsdijk, Steven Brakman, and Harry Garretsen for permission to use our joint work.

2 See also McDonald and Burton (2002).

3 Even at the world level the balance of trade is not zero, for example as a result of statistical errors or because goods are en route to their destination during a particular time period. Over the period 1960–2013 the average world external balance was –0.11 per cent of GDP, indicating that the value of measured imports was slightly higher than the value of measured exports.

4 The variance of five-year moving averages for world trade is still quite high; looking at moving averages over longer periods does not reveal clear changes for world trade growth over time either.

5 Differentiating gives $dY = ydp + pdy$; divide both sides by Y to get: $\tilde{Y} \equiv \dfrac{dY}{Y} = \dfrac{dp}{p} + \dfrac{dy}{y} \equiv \tilde{p} + \tilde{y}$.

6 The 'p-value' in the table refers to probability values. It estimates on the basis of standard errors the probability that the coefficient does *not* differ significantly from zero. For income per capita in the period 1960–1980 this value is 0.0175, or 1.75 per cent. This is such a low probability that we conclude instead that the coefficient *does* differ significantly from zero. It is customary to have certain cut-off levels of significance; in this case the coefficient is significant at the 5 per cent level as indicated by ** since 1.75 per cent is lower than 5 per cent. See Box 3.3 on basic econometrics for further details.

7 The asymmetric construction of the index for leading and lagging nations is for comparability of the degree of deviation; if both indices used the world average as base there is no upper bound for leading nations while there is a lower bound (of 100 per cent) for lagging nations.

8 Unfortunately, Portugal also initiated the slave trade to the New World and carried about half of the slaves from Africa to the Americas between 1500 and 1870.

9 That is, 0.91 per cent per annum rather than 1.30 per cent. Although this difference might seem to be small, world income would have been 15 per cent higher in 1950 if the slowdown had not occurred and the economy had maintained its 1.30 per cent growth rate.

10 If the price wedge completely disappears, trade flows increase to q_c in Figure 2.10 and the price consumers pay in the UK becomes equal to the price producers receive in the USA (equal to p_c).

11 The size and speed of Atlantic liners, for example, increased spectacularly: it took the *Britannic* (using a combination of steam power and sails) 8 days and 20 hours to cross the Atlantic with 5,000 tons of payload in 1874, whereas it took the *Mauritania* (using steam power only) 4 days and 10 hours to cross the Atlantic with 31,000 tons of payload in 1907. During the same period railway mileage also increased dramatically: from 1850 to 1910 railway mileage in the UK increased from 6,621 to 23,387 miles, in the USA from 9,021 to 249,902 miles, and in Germany from 3,637 to 36,152 miles (O'Rourke and Williamson, 1999).

12 The treaty was also important because it introduced the 'most favoured nation' (MFN) principle as the cornerstone of European trade policies (Findlay and O'Rourke, 2001).

13 The core and empire countries are Australia, Belgium, Canada, Denmark, France, Germany, India, the Netherlands, New Zealand, Norway, South Africa, Sweden, Switzerland, and the USA.

14 Based on UN Population Division, Migrant Section, data.

15 Based on OECD labour force statistics.

16 Several alternative scenarios and measures of income inequality lead to similar conclusions.

17 Population growth between 2010 and 2050 according to United Nations Population Department (2011): OECD from 1.23 to 1.40 billion, East Asia from 1.89 to 2.01 billion, South Asia from 1.63 to 2.31 billion, and Sub-Saharan Africa from 0.85 to 1.95 billion people.

18 This is most relevant for OECD countries such as Germany and Japan.

19 We thus exclude studies covering only part of a country or only rural or urban areas. The only exception is for Germany, where we use the distribution of West Germany in 1968 and of Germany as a whole in 2011. This choice does not affect our findings.

20 If our rules resulted in two or more estimates for the same year, the highest-quality estimate was chosen. In case of a tie we chose the most recently modified or updated one. In case of a further tie, the first entry in the database was chosen.

21 There are 23 countries with just one observation, which are thus not included in the table. For these countries, the median observation is in 2003 (average in 1999) and the median Gini index is 0.408 (average is 0.420). The within-country income inequality is thus substantially higher for these countries than for the countries included in the table.

22 Income inequality on average *declined* by less in other populous countries, such as (in order of population size) in India (by 5 per cent), Brazil (by 10 per cent), Russia (by 7 per cent), Pakistan (by 12 per cent), and Mexico (by 22 per cent).

 ## Questions

Question 2.1

Please answer the brief review questions below.

a. Which five main types of globalization debates can we distinguish?

b. What grows faster since 1960: world income or world trade?

c. Is it appropriate to compare the growth rates in question b? Explain why, or why not.

d. On a per capita basis: is there a noticeable trend in the growth rates for income and trade?

Question 2.2

Briefly discuss the development of global income per capita over the past 2,000 years and indicate if (using national average income per capita levels for comparison) global income inequality has been steady, rising, or falling over this period. Explain.

Question 2.3

What are two main ways to measure increased economic globalization? Briefly explain.

 See the **online resources** *for a Study Guide and questions:*
www.oup.com/uk/vanmarrewijk_it/

3 The balance of payments

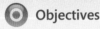

Objectives

- To know the main principles of national income accounting.
- To understand why savings are equal to investments in a closed economy and how their difference is reflected in the current account balance for an open economy.
- To know that a surplus in the current account is a net capital and financial outflow.
- To understand that private savings can be used for either domestic investment, acquiring foreign wealth, or purchasing new government debt.
- To understand the difficulties of comparing the economic power of firms with the economic power of countries.
- To know the Feldstein–Horioka puzzle and its relation to capital market integration.
- To know the difference between endogenous and exogenous variables and to understand the basic econometrics problems with running a regression to test a model.

3.1 Introduction

The balance of payments records a country's transactions with the rest of the world. As such, it provides essential information on a nation's trade and capital flows in a consistent accounting framework. James Meade was one of the key contributors in this area: see Box 3.1. We start in Section 3.2 with the basics of national income accounting in a closed and open economy.[1] Accounting may not be viewed as the most exciting field of economics, but the products provided by accountants, such as a country's balance of payments or a firm's annual report, are indispensable as building blocks for other research. As we will see, accounting helps us, for example, to establish the link between international trade and capital flows in Sections 3.3 and 3.4. We continue in Section 3.5 by discussing the difficulties associated with comparing the economic power of firms with that of nations. We conclude in Section 3.6 with a discussion of the Feldstein–Horioka puzzle and how it may be used to measure the degree of capital market integration. For readers not familiar with basic econometric methods, we provide a brief overview of the main issues involved with estimating economic relationships and testing economic parameters in Box 3.3.

BOX 3.1 James Meade

Figure 3.1
James Meade
(1907–1995).

James Meade (Figure 3.1) studied and worked at the University of Cambridge and the University of Oxford. He also worked at the London School of Economics and was active outside academia, for the League of Nations and for the British Cabinet Office, where he collaborated with Richard Stone on national income accounts for Britain. He incorporated the Keynesian framework in the textbook *An Introduction to Economic Analysis and Policy*, which appeared in 1936, only a few months after Keynes's *General Theory*. He systematically analysed internal and external balance in a general equilibrium framework. His work on trade policy and welfare analysis led to the 'theory of second best'. In 1977 he shared the Nobel Prize in economics with Bertil Ohlin.

3.2 National income accounting

In Chapter 1 we briefly discussed the total value of production of all goods and services as measured by a nation's income level in a given period, as well as the difference between gross domestic product and gross national product. In this section we review the main components of a nation's income level, for both a closed economy and an open economy.

3.2.1 Closed economy

In a closed economy we can focus attention on the three main players in the economy: households, firms, and the government. We let C denote the consumption of goods and services by households (food, housing, entertainment, and so on), G denote the purchases of the government (military expenditures, education, infrastructure, and so on), and I the investment level of firms (machines, buildings, inventory, and so on). Total output, denoted by Y, is equal to the sum of these three components in a closed economy: see equation 3.1. We define *national savings* to be the share of output not spent on household consumption or government purchases: see equation 3.2. Consequently, *in a closed economy national savings is always equal to investment*: see equation 3.3. The total wealth in a closed economy can therefore only increase by accumulating more capital.

$$Y = C + I + G \qquad\qquad 3.1$$

$$S = Y - C - G \qquad\qquad 3.2$$

$$S = I \qquad\qquad 3.3$$

3.2.2 **Open economy**

When we look at an open economy we realize, of course, that part of household consumption, government purchases, or a firm's investment may not be produced in the home economy but may be imported from abroad. Denoting the import of goods and services by M, we should thus subtract these from the determination of output given in equation 3.1. Similarly, part of home production may be exported to foreign consumers, firms, or governments. Denoting the export of goods and services by X we should thus add these to the determination of output given in equation 3.1. The resulting adjustments are given in equation 3.4.

$$Y = C + I + G + (X - M) \qquad\qquad 3.4$$

$$S - I = X - M \qquad\qquad 3.5$$

Since our definition of national saving does not change, this implies that the difference between national saving and investment is equal to the difference between the export and import of goods and services: see equation 3.5. A closed economy can thus only save by building up the capital stock (investing), whereas an open economy can either do this or acquire foreign wealth. The difference between exports and imports is known as the *current account* balance.[2] If imports exceed exports there is a current account *deficit*, while if exports exceed imports there is a current account *surplus*. If there is a current account deficit we are spending more on goods and services than we produce domestically. We must finance this deficit somehow, either by borrowing from foreigners or by selling some of our wealth to foreigners. *The current account balance is thus equal to the change in net foreign wealth.*

Figure 3.2 depicts the various components of output for the 28 countries of the European Union in 2015 (in € trillion). Total output, Y, is €14.6 trillion. Its largest component (57 per cent) is household consumption C. The second-largest component (43 per cent) is the export of goods and services X, which is slightly larger than the import

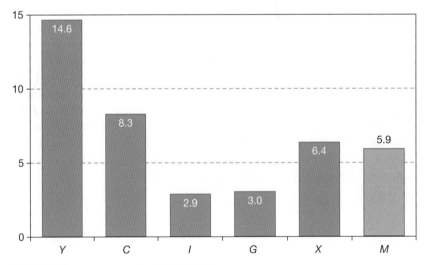

Figure 3.2 EU-28 income components, 2015, in € trillion.

Source: based on Eurostat data.

of goods and services M (40 per cent). Government expenditure G is slightly bigger than investment I (both are close to 20 per cent). Finally, it is useful to distinguish between private saving S_p and government saving S_g: see equation 3.6. If we let T denote the government's net tax revenue, then government saving is the difference between government income T and government spending G, see equation 3.7. Combining this with equation 3.5 we thus get equation 3.8, which indicates that private saving S_p can be used for either (i) domestic investment I, (ii) acquiring foreign wealth $(X - M)$, or (iii) purchasing new government debt $(G - T)$.

$$S = S_p + S_g \qquad\qquad 3.6$$

$$S_g = T - G \qquad\qquad 3.7$$

$$S_p = I + (X - M) + (G - T) \qquad\qquad 3.8$$

3.3 The balance of payments

This section is divided into two parts. First, we briefly review some accounting principles. Second, we discuss some accounting identities at the macroeconomic level.

3.3.1 Accounting principles

The balance of payments records a country's transactions with other countries on the basis of a set of agreed-upon accounting definitions and principles. The balance of payments thus involves macro-level accounting for nation-states and is based on the rules of double-entry bookkeeping, with matching credit and debit entries. By definition, the balance of payments is therefore equal to zero. We distinguish between two main parts of the balance of payments, namely the current account on the one hand and the capital and financial account on the other hand, each with subdivisions as summarized in Figure 3.3.

The transactions on the current account are income related, pertaining to produced goods, provided services (also known as invisibles), income (from investment), and unilateral

Current account
　Goods　⎫
　Services ⎬ Trade balance
　Income
　Current transfers

Capital and financial account
　Capital account
　Financial account
　　Direct investment
　　Portfolio investment
　　Other investment
　　Reserve assets

Figure 3.3 The balance of payments.
Source: IMF (1996).

transfers. Exports are recorded as credit items (+) and imports as debit items (−). After all, with exports money is earned, and with imports it is spent. The sum of the merchandise and services balance is called the trade balance, indicating the net money earned with trade (exports minus imports), which may of course be negative if more is imported than exported, in terms of money value.

More important than the trade balance is the current account balance, which also includes unilateral transfers and income generated abroad, such as dividend payments which reflect the remuneration for the use of capital, a factor of production, by another country. It is therefore essentially the payment for trade in (capital) services. Unilateral transfers, such as foreign aid to a developing nation, remittances or military aid, are included as they represent income transfers to another country and not claims on another country. As a result, the current account balance measures the net change in claims on the outside world, which is recorded on the capital and financial account. This includes, in the capital account, capital transfers and transactions (purchases/sales) in an economy's non-produced, non-financial assets (such as patents and copyrights) and, in the financial account, transactions in an economy's external financial assets and liabilities.

3.3.2 Accounting identities

The transactions on the capital and financial account are asset related. An increase in claims on foreigners is a *capital outflow* and appears as a debit. An increase in claims by foreigners on our country is a *capital inflow* and appears as a credit. If the claim is longer than one year, it is called long-term capital—for example, foreign direct investment and long-term portfolio investment such as securities and loans. Otherwise, it is called short-term capital. Sometimes, the classification is difficult. Purchasing foreign stocks is a short-term capital flow, unless you buy so much of the company that it becomes a foreign direct investment. Changes in reserve assets may refer to changes by the central banking system in gold stocks, IMF credits, Special Drawing Rights (SDRs), or foreign exchange reserves. As mentioned above, the balance of payments is zero by definition such that

$$current\ account\ balance + capital\ account\ balance = 0 \qquad\qquad 3.9$$

Suppose there is a surplus on the current account. This implies, roughly speaking, that the value of our exports (credit) is higher than the value of our imports (debit)—that is, the current account represents a net credit item. By the rules of double-entry accounting this must be matched by a net debit item on the capital account, and thus a net capital outflow, that is:

$$surplus\ current\ account \Leftrightarrow net\ capital\ \&\ financial\ outflow \qquad\qquad 3.10$$

To see how the current account and capital account are related and how the 'books are balanced', consider the following example. Suppose a country exports goods for one billion euro (net proceeds) and imports no goods at all. The country has a current account *surplus*. If the exporting firms decide to spend their proceedings on buying financial assets abroad, such as foreign shares or bonds, this constitutes a capital outflow and hence a debit because by buying these assets the country has *imported claims (on future production) on foreigners*. This means that the capital account displays a *deficit* because of the capital outflow of one billion euro.

Of course, the net export proceeds do not have to be spent on foreign financial assets. The exporting firms may simply put their money on deposits with their banks. In that case the reserve asset position of this country will increase by one billion and the result will be the same as with the acquisition of foreign shares or bonds. To see this, note that our exporting firms will have to be paid in local currency, which means that the foreigners who have bought the goods will first have to go to the bank to exchange their currency for that of the exporting firms, leading to an increase in the foreign exchange reserves of the exporting country (the item 'Reserve assets' in Figure 3.3). A similar line of reasoning helps to explain why a net capital inflow is booked as a credit.

The principle underlying the balance of payments is exactly the same as the one related to an individual's budget constraint.[3] If the income you earn this month (export of labour services, your only factor of production) is higher than the money you spend on consumption (import of goods and services), this will increase your claims on the outside world (for example, by an increase of the balance on your checking account). If your income is less than your consumption spending this month, this will decrease your claims on the outside world.

3.4 Capital flows

As is clear from equation 3.10, analysing a country's current account balance over a somewhat longer period of time gives a good idea of the net change in claims on the rest of the world. This is illustrated in Figure 3.4 for a selection of countries, where the current account balance is measured relative to income (GDP). The USA has accumulated such large current account deficits that it is now the world's largest debtor. Considering the size of the US economy, the current account deficit of 5.8 per cent of GDP in 2006 was enormous. The extent of the deficit then fell to 2.2 per cent in 2014. An historical example of large

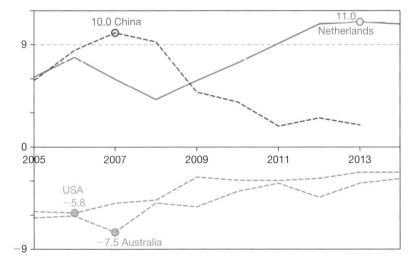

Figure 3.4 Current account balance (per cent of GDP); selected countries, 2005–2014.

Source: based on data from World Development Indicators online.

American financial flows is provided by the Louisiana Purchase: see Box 3.2. Australia is another country with substantial current account deficits, reaching 7.5 per cent of GDP in 2007 but declining to 2.8 per cent in 2014. These observations indicate that funds are flowing into the USA and Australia, financed by other countries. Their willingness to finance can be viewed as a strength of the recipient's economy, provided of course that the funds are used to increase productive capacity which makes it possible to generate the funds needed to repay in the future.

BOX 3.2 International financing of the Louisiana Purchase

A little more than 200 years ago, on 20 December 1803, and only 27 years after the Declaration of Independence, the United States of America was involved in the best real estate deal in history: the Louisiana Purchase.[4] The French general Napoleon Bonaparte had acquired the huge territory west of the Mississippi river, an area of 828,000 square miles (more than two million square kilometres), from Spain only three years earlier. The United States were primarily interested in the harbour city of New Orleans, providing access from the mighty Mississippi to the Gulf of Mexico for its trade flows. France, however, urgently needed funds to finance its war efforts in Europe and was willing to sell the entire Louisiana Territory, raising the price from the initially offered 10 million dollars to 15 million dollars. The deal between American president Thomas Jefferson and Napoleon Bonaparte doubled the size of the United States, provided the desired harbour access, and enabled westward expansion: see Figure 3.5. In 1804, the famous Lewis and Clark expedition embarked on charting the newly acquired territory.

The Louisiana Purchase was financed by the banks Hope & Co in Amsterdam and Baring & Co in London; they issued bonds on behalf of the US Treasury with an interest rate of 6 per cent. Business bankers, such as the Scotsman Henry Hope who lived in Amsterdam, were indispensable links in the global network of international financing. It was a lucrative deal for the bank, which made a return on investment of 6.5 per cent in the decades before the Louisiana Purchase and of 10 per cent for a substantial period afterward. Hope was particularly well connected with Russia, which bought most of the bonds. Ironically, therefore, Napoleon financed his European expansion with a transaction of American land via Amsterdam and hostile London with funds provided in substantial part by Russia, his later target. Hope & Co later evolved to the present Dutch bank MeesPierson, a subsidiary of the Dutch Fortis group. The London-based Baring & Co went bankrupt in 1995 after massive speculation by one of its employees in Singapore. It was bought by another Dutch financial conglomerate: ING. *Source: NRC Handelsblad (2003).*

Figure 3.5 The Louisiana territory relative to the present continental USA.

China and the Netherlands present the mirror image of the USA and Australia. Both countries have had a current account surplus since 2005 and have been accumulating claims on the rest of the world. China's surplus peaked at 10.0 per cent of GDP in 2007 and has created a lot of tension, particularly with the USA, regarding the management of its exchange rate. China's surplus had declined to 1.9 per cent of GDP by 2013. The Netherlands has a long history of current account surpluses. In part this reflects the large forced savings for pension funds, which is generating revenue for the future income of its ageing population. This is an example of consumption smoothing over time. The lowest Dutch surplus was 4.2 per cent of GDP in 2008; the highest surplus was 11.0 per cent in 2013. Since the Dutch economy is much smaller than the Chinese economy, its surplus, unlike China's, does not generate animosity. The recent large surplus is also partially caused by the Dutch membership of the European Economic and Monetary Union.

3.5 Nations and firms: a classic mistake

The usefulness of accounting is also illustrated by the rhetoric in the anti-globalization debate claiming that powerful multinationals are larger than many—if not most—nation-states. Noreena Hertz (2001) and Naomi Klein (2001), for instance, passionately oppose the increased power of large multinationals, referring to lists that rank the size of countries versus multinationals, with many multinationals much larger than many countries. In such rankings, the size measure used for countries is GDP and for firms is sales.

Table 3.1 shows sales and profits for the smallest and the largest firms from the Fortune Global 500 largest companies in 2010. The firm-level data on sales and profits come from the Fortune Global 500; country income (GDP) is taken from the World Development Indicators provided by the World Bank. Indeed, in sales terms some firms are larger than some countries. For example, Sweden's GDP is almost equal to the total sales of Walmart, which is the largest firm in the world (both in sales and profits). The total profits of Walmart are approximately as large as the total GDP of Honduras. Whereas Honduras has almost 8 million inhabitants, Walmart has slightly more than 2 million employees. The Japanese Dai Nippon Printing firm takes the five-hundredth position of the Fortune Global 500 with a profit level of 253 million dollars, which is almost equal to the total GDP of Tonga, one of the Polynesian islands.

Such comparisons are problematic for three main reasons.

- First, comparing firm sales to GDP country scores is like comparing apples and oranges. Sales are the result of numbers of products sold and the price paid for these products. Value added (and the sum of it reflecting a country's GDP) is a part of the

Table 3.1 Country GDP compared to firm sales and profits (USD billion)

Country GDP	Firm sales	Firm profits
Sweden: 406	Walmart (1): 408	Walmart (1): 14.3
Honduras: 14.3	Dai Nippon Printing (500): 17	Dai Nippon Printing (500): 0.3

Source: Brakman et al. (2013); based on Fortune Global 500 and World Development Indicators.

total sales. Using sales as a size measure inflates firm size by cumulating double counts. After all, many expenses of a multinational relate to intermediate transactions. For instance, Daimler must pay billions of dollars or euros to suppliers of raw materials (such as steel) and intermediate products (such as tyres). Therefore, a multinational's sales cannot be compared with a country's GDP, which is a value-added measure. For a true comparison, only value added matters: the value that is really produced by the multinational itself, and not by its large set of suppliers.

- Second, even the comparison with value added is not perfect. The profit levels of firms may fluctuate over time, and firms that were on the Global 500 list years ago (such as Enron) disappear later on. A country's GDP is the sum of the value added by *all* firms, which obviously fluctuates less than the value added by a single firm. Nevertheless, it is clear that some multinationals are large compared to some countries, making these multinationals powerful economic actors. Large multinationals can influence policy making in countries, enticing governments to provide interesting packages when a multinational locates in their country.
- Third, Sweden and Honduras are sovereign states with the ability to pass laws and regulations imposing restrictions and conditions on individuals and firms, to impose taxes, organize police, justice, and defence systems, and so on. Walmart, or any other company in the world, does not even remotely have the same powers.

3.6 The Feldstein–Horioka puzzle

From the analysis in Section 3.2 we know that the current account balance (CA, say) is equal to the difference between national savings S and investments, that is $CA \equiv S - I$. The term 'national' indicates that both the private and government sector are included. From this accounting identity it becomes clear that a national savings surplus ($S - I > 0$) has to be invested abroad (as reflected in a corresponding capital outflow), and vice versa for a deficit.

A major implication of international capital mobility and integrated financial markets (illustrated in Figure 3.4) is that national savings are not necessarily equal to national investment: that is, $S - I \neq 0$ is possible. National savings and investment no longer move in unison and there is no longer a perfect correlation between these two. Particularly for a small country, national investment will not be constrained by a lack of national savings: it is world savings that matter.

Based on these observations, the seminal study by Feldstein and Horioka (1980) found, surprisingly, that the correlation between national savings and investment ratios was typically very high. For their sample of OECD countries they found this correlation to be almost equal to 1. They concluded that the degree of international capital market integration, and hence of international capital mobility, was still rather limited. This finding is puzzling because it is in contrast to the popular conviction that the world is highly globalized and that capital markets are highly integrated. Their result became known as the Feldstein–Horioka puzzle.

$$\frac{I}{Y} = \alpha_0 + \alpha_1 \frac{S}{Y} \qquad\qquad 3.11$$

Table 3.2 The Feldstein–Horioka test

Period	α_0		α_1		explained variance (R^2)
1960–64	7.02	(1.50)	0.70	(3.75)	0.50
1965–69	8.78	(2.07)	0.65	(3.90)	0.50
1970–74	5.93	(1.96)	0.74	(6.62)	0.74
1975–79	6.47	(1.45)	0.78	(4.17)	0.54
1980–84	12.17	(4.36)	0.48	(3.81)	0.49
1985–89	10.41	(3.91)	0.54	(4.57)	0.58
1990–94	10.26	(5.88)	0.53	(6.46)	0.74
1995–97	7.83	(2.93)	0.56	(4.74)	0.58

Notes: t-statistics in brackets; for the test, see equation 3.11.
Source: Ostrup (2002) based on OECD National Accounts.

In response to the Feldstein–Horioka puzzle, Table 3.2 presents some evidence of increasing capital market integration based on a pooled estimate of equation 3.11 for a large set of countries for various sub-periods of 1960–1997 (see Box 3.3 on basic econometrics). The core information is captured by the estimated coefficient α_1. The lower this coefficient, the lower the correlation between domestic savings and investment, and thus the higher the degree of international capital mobility. The year 1980 is often considered an important watershed year: on average, international capital mobility gradually increased after that point compared to the period 1945–1979. Table 3.2 illustrates this. The α_1-coefficient in the period after 1980 is lower than in the period 1960–1980, which suggests that international capital mobility and international capital market integration increased after that time.

BOX 3.3 Basic econometrics

When we are developing different theories to try to better understand various economic phenomena, we often assume that the relationships between the economic variables we are analysing are exact. In principle, our theories should lead to results, that is propositions or predictions that should hold empirically if the theory is true. If we gather economic data to test if the theoretical implications do indeed hold in reality, we need a method to determine if a theory is refuted or not. This is the work of econometricians. In practice, things are—as usual—not quite that simple, for four main reasons.

- First, we must recast the theory in a manner suitable for empirical evaluation and testing. This means we have to acknowledge the fact that the relationships between the economic variables of our theories are not exact due to simplifications and disturbances. There may, therefore, be deviations from the exact relationships which we can attribute to other phenomena, such as measurement errors or the weather, which do not immediately refute the theory. The point is, of course, that these deviations should not be 'too large'.
- Second, it can be complicated, even after overcoming the first problem, to actually test the implications of a theory for technical or econometric reasons. Numerous examples can be given of the many hurdles econometricians sometimes have to go over, and traps they have to avoid, before they can devise an adequate test of what may at first look like a simple implication of a theory.

(continued...)

- Third, it can be virtually impossible, even after overcoming the first and second problems, to pinpoint the nature of an observed friction between theory and empirics. Remember that our theories are usually based on a range of assumptions. In many cases, economic theorists may be convinced by the arguments of econometricians that an implication of a theory does not hold in practice, but disagree strongly on the particular assumption on which the theory was based which caused this friction. It can take several decades of scientific research, involving the development of new theories, new tests, and so on, before some, if any, consensus on the nature of the problem is reached.
- Fourth, even if an empirical test confirms our theory, this does not necessarily prove it. Maybe some other theory can also explain the observations; we are never really sure.

The remainder of this box focuses on the simplest version of the first problem. Suppose we have an economic theory which predicts a linear relationship between the economic variables y and x, such that $y = a + bx$. Since all theories are simplifications of reality (which is what makes them theories), there is always a range of other phenomena which might influence the actual relationship between the variables y and x. There can be other, more complicated, economic forces not modelled in the theory which could affect the relationship; there can be forces outside of economics (such as the weather, volcanic eruptions, or political changes) which could affect the relationship; there can be errors in measurement; and so on. This leads us to posit that the observed relationship is as follows:

$$y_t = a + bx_t + u_t \hspace{4cm} 3.12$$

The sub-index t denotes different observations (for example different time periods or different countries) and the variable u_t denotes the deviation between the structural linear part of an observation and the actual value of the observation. This deviation should not be 'too large', so when we average it over many observations its value should be zero (it is, for example, normally distributed with mean 0 and variance σ^2).

An econometrician is, of course, not given the 'true' parameters a and b of the structural linear equation (although there may be 'implied' theoretical values). Instead, she is given a number of observations, that is joint pairs (x_t, y_t) of the economic variables x and y. These are depicted as the dots (or balls) in Figure 3.6. Her task is then to find the best line to fit these empirical observations, that is estimate an intercept (say $\hat{a}$) and a slope (say $\hat{b}$) to minimize the (quadratic) distance from the observations to the

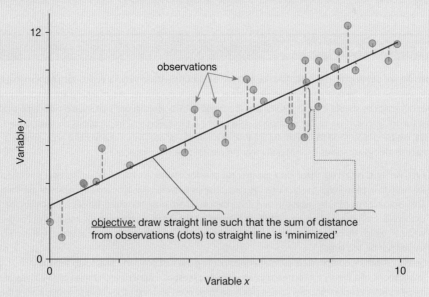

Figure 3.6 Basic econometrics: observations and regression line.

(continued...)

line. We are not concerned with how this is done here. Instead, we briefly discuss how hypotheses can be tested using this procedure.

Figure 3.6 was artificially constructed using a 'true' model with intercept 2 and slope 1 ($a = 2, b = 1$) by adding (normally distributed) disturbances u_t using a random number generator. Since the econometrician is only given the observations and not the true parameters, she tries to estimate their values ($\hat{a}$ and $\hat{b}$) based on the observations. The terminology is to 'run a *regression*', where y is the *endogenous* variable (the variable to be explained) and x is the *exogenous* variable (the explanatory variable). She finds:

$$y = \underset{(0.4730)}{2.776} + \underset{(0.0744)}{0.872}\, x \qquad\qquad\qquad 3.13$$

The numbers in parentheses in equation 3.13 are estimated standard errors of the estimated coefficients (see below). Instead of the true parameter 2 the econometrician therefore estimates the intercept to be 2.776 and instead of the true parameter 1 she estimates the slope to be 0.872. Well, we do not expect her to find the exact parameters, but how far off is she? Is this within acceptable limits? And how good is the 'fit' of the estimated line?

It is clear that the fit of the line is better the closer the observations are to the estimated line. A popular measure for this fit is the share of the variance of the variable y explained by the estimated line, the so-called R^2. In this case, 83.1 per cent of the variance is explained by the regression ($R^2 = 0.831$). In general, the higher the R^2 the better the fit. It should be noted, however, that the share of the variance that can be explained differs widely per application, with some areas of economics where researchers are happy if they can explain 20 per cent of the variance and others where less than 90 per cent is considered bad.

In this respect, the standard errors reported in equation 3.13 are more useful as they indicate the reliability of the estimated coefficients. They can be used for hypothesis testing. Based on the so-called t-distribution, we can calculate the probability that the true parameter has a particular value, given the observations on the pairs (x_t, y_t) available to us and the associated regression line. As a rule of thumb: hypotheses within two standard deviations away from the estimated coefficient are accepted; in this case this means a slope in between 0.7232 and 1.0208 and an intercept in between 1.830 and 3.722. Note that the true values of a and b (equal to 1 and 2) are within these limits. Alternatively, the rule of thumb implies that an absolute t-value larger than 2 denotes a 'significant' parameter as the estimated coefficient differs from the hypothesis 'equal to zero' by more than two standard deviations.

3.7 Conclusions

We provide some elementary information on national income accounting and the balance of payments, which records a country's transactions with the rest of the world. We distinguish between the current account (which records flows from trade in goods and services, income from investment, and unilateral transfers) and the capital and financial account (which records changes in claims on the rest of the world). Since the balance of payments is based on the rules of double-entry bookkeeping, the current account balance is always offset by an equal and opposite balance on the financial and capital account. As such, the current account balance measures the change in claims on the outside world. We use this identity to illustrate the size of international capital flows for a selection of countries. After a brief discussion on comparing the economic power of nations and firms, we provide some evidence of increased international capital market integration based on the Feldstein–Horioka approach.

Notes

1   I am grateful to my co-authors Sjoerd Beugelsdijk, Steven Brakman, and Harry Garretsen for allowing me to use some of our joint work (see Beugelsdijk et al., 2013) for parts of this chapter.

2   The discussion in the text ignores investment income and unilateral transfers for simplicity; see Section 3.3 for further details.

3   In fact, budget constraints are additive, so we can do this for all individuals in a country.

4   Arguably, the second-best deal is president Andrew Johnson's 1867 purchase of Alaska on behalf of the USA from Russia for $7.2 million.

 ## Questions

Question 3.1

Imagine you work at the Statistical Bureau of Singapore and have to record the value changes in GDP, GNI, exports, and imports. What value changes do you record and when?

a.   A shipload of 1,000 trousers arrives from India that has cost the Singapore importer 5 Singapore dollars per piece. This shipload is immediately re-exported to the USA for 6 Singapore dollars per piece.

b.   A bundle of 1,000 trousers has been purchased from a Singapore producer for 5 Singapore dollars per piece. This bundle is exported to the USA for 6 Singapore dollars per piece.

c.   The same transaction is executed as in Question 3.1a, but this time the Indian producer of trousers has to pay 1 Singapore dollar per trouser to a Singapore investor who has helped to establish the Indian trouser factory.

d.   An Indonesian nanny returns home after babysitting in Singapore for four months. She takes her total wage of 1,000 Singapore dollars with her.

e.   An Indonesian woman, married to a Singapore man, returns home and gives her parents 1,000 Singapore dollars.

Question 3.2

If there is more money flowing into a country than there is flowing out, that country has a positive balance of payments; if, on the other hand, more money flows out than in, the balance of payments is negative.

Source: Wikipedia encyclopaedia (http://en.wikipedia.org/wiki/Balance_of_payments).

a.   Is the definition above correct? Explain.

In this book, we follow the accounting principle that this balance is equal to zero. In practice, different definitions for the balance of payments exist. They sometimes exclude reserve assets or short-term capital account transactions from the balance, such that imbalances are possible. Consider the following quote: 'The US is able to attract funds from the rest of the world to finance its balance of payments deficit.'

b.   Explain the quote with the help of equation 3.9. What happens when the US is unable to attract funds from the rest of the world?

Suppose that the Chinese central bank publishes a report that blames expected balance of payments surplus reductions on lower trade tariffs (taxes on imports) and higher oil prices.

c. Which balance of payments definition does the Chinese central bank probably use? Explain how tariff reductions and higher oil prices can contribute to a lower surplus.

When a country has a deficit in its balance of payments, politicians and the press often portray this as a cause of major concern. This concern is groundless for two reasons: (1) there never is a deficit, and (2) it is not necessarily bad if there is a deficit.

d. Explain for both reasons whether you agree or disagree.

e. Can you explain why politicians and the press are often concerned?

Question 3.3

The developments of the Chinese and US current account balances since 1990 are shown in Figure 3.7. The current account is a flow variable. It represents the build-up of net foreign claims by an economy. Many US politicians blame China for their country's growing current account deficit and negative international investment position.

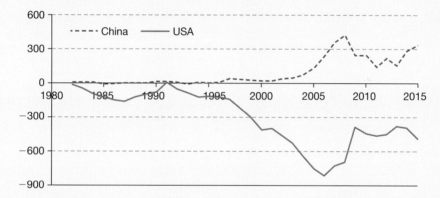

Figure 3.7 Current account balance, USD billion.

Source: Based on data from World Development Indicators online.

a. Why do US politicians blame China for their deficit, while the Chinese current account surplus is initially fairly small compared to the US deficit?

b. The current account balance is not exactly equal to changes in the international investment position. Can you explain why this is so?

c. The Chinese and US economies both attract a lot of foreign direct investment (FDI). Does this represent a capital inflow or outflow?

d. If the current account remains unchanged, which offsetting capital account transactions can occur to maintain a balance of payments (use Figure 3.3)?

e. Suppose the US government wants to improve relations with China and does so by giving emergency assistance after a flooding of the Yangtze River. How does this affect the Chinese balance of payments?

 *See the **online resources** for a Study Guide and questions:* **www.oup.com/uk/vanmarrewijk_it/**

Part II

Comparative advantage

The three chapters in this part of the book analyse comparative advantage in perfectly competitive economies. Such advantages may explain international trade flows and are either based on the classical theory of technology differences, analysed in Chapter 4, or on the neoclassical theory of differences in factor abundance, analysed in Chapters 5 and 6.

4 Technology: the classical approach

Objectives

- To be able to distinguish between absolute advantages and comparative advantages.
- To understand how differences in technology can be the driving force for trade flows based on comparative advantages.
- To know what a production possibility frontier is and how it relates to technology.
- To be able to distinguish between an autarky equilibrium and a free trade equilibrium.
- To know the principles of constant returns to scale and perfect competition.
- To understand the terms of trade and the gains from trade.
- To be able to empirically measure comparative advantage using the Balassa index.
- To know the difference between goods and services, and to understand the changing role of agricultural production and services production in the development process.

4.1 Historical introduction

From the classical point of view, the driving forces behind international trade flows are technological differences between nations. If another country can produce a good (relatively) more cheaply than we can make it, it is better to import this good from abroad as it will increase our welfare. The per capita welfare level, however, depends on absolute cost differences, which also explain the large international differences in wage levels.

Adam Smith (1723–1790; see Chapter 9) will provide us with the starting point of our analysis. On the peculiar notions of the costs and benefits of international trade before Adam Smith, for example considering the role of merchants, the reader is encouraged to consult Douglas Irwin's (1996) *Against the Tide: An Intellectual History of Free Trade*. It suffices for our present purposes to note that various authors had already advocated a policy of free trade before the publication of Smith's (1776) influential masterpiece, *An Inquiry into the Nature and Causes of the Wealth of Nations*. The emergence of a doctrine of free trade at the time was largely a reaction to the mercantilist literature of the seventeenth century, which advocated state regulation of trade to promote wealth and growth, maximize employment, achieve a favourable balance of trade, and protect the home industry.

If a free trade doctrine was already advocated by others before the *Wealth of Nations*, why do we pay so much attention to Adam Smith's analysis? First, because it is an economic *analysis* of trade flows. Second, because many people still needed to be convinced of the benefits of international trade, as illustrated by James Steuart's (1767) *An Inquiry into the Principles of Political Economy*. Third, because Smith was able to put many different arguments and elements together in a coherent and systematic framework, organized using a few general principles, and thus providing a new way of thinking about political economy. After a few years, this had a large impact on the profession. As Irwin (1996, p. 75) put it:

> While drawing upon the work of others, Smith created such a compelling and complete case for free trade that commercial policy could no longer be seriously discussed without contending with his views, and herein lies one of Smith's foremost contributions to economics.

An issue associated with the theory of absolute cost advantages as set forth by Smith continues to puzzle thinkers up to this day, as illustrated by the well-known historian Paul Kennedy (1995), criticizing the case for free trade more than 200 years after Adam Smith argued his case (italics mine): 'What if there is *nothing* you can produce more cheaply or efficiently than anywhere else, except by constantly cutting labour costs?' The suggestion is that less developed nations cannot compete on the international scene, and that they do not benefit from the international exchange of commodities. How can you participate on the global market and gain from trading different goods and services if there is nothing you can produce more efficiently than anyone else? These problems were analysed in the first half of the nineteenth century in England by Robert Torrens, James Mill, and, most importantly, David Ricardo (see Box 4.1). All were in favour of free trade, and in the popular debate were particularly hostile towards the (in)famous Corn Laws, restricting grain imports into Britain. The most important contribution of this era was the *classical model*, or the *Ricardian model*. American Nobel laureate Paul Samuelson once even remarked that the theory of comparative advantage is 'one of the few ideas in economics that is true without being obvious'.

BOX 4.1 David Ricardo

Born in London, the third son of a Jewish family that had emigrated from Holland, David Ricardo (Figure 4.1) married the daughter of a Quaker and was disinherited by his parents. Ricardo nonetheless accumulated a fortune as a stock-jobber and loan contractor. As Blaug (1985: 201) puts it: 'Ricardo may or may not be the greatest economist that ever lived, but he was certainly the richest.' His fame today rests mainly, of course, on his contributions to the theory of comparative advantage.

Figure 4.1
David Ricardo
(1772–1823).

Sections 4.2 and 4.3 summarize Adam Smith's and David Ricardo's contributions. These sections can be skipped without affecting the main line of argument. Section 4.4 introduces technology differences as the basis for comparative advantage. Section 4.5 discusses the production possibility frontier, an important concept used in many subsequent chapters, and the determination of the autarky equilibrium. Section 4.6 analyses the terms of trade and the gains of trade. The remaining sections provide more insight and background information, on the classical view of agricultural production as an example of technology (Section 4.7), on expanding our model to include more countries and on the world production possibility frontier (Section 4.8), on measuring trade advantages (Section 4.9), and on the structure of production (Section 4.10).

4.2 Smith's argument for free trade

Smith's argument for free trade runs roughly as follows. First, he emphasizes the *opportunity costs* of regulations in general (IV. ii. 3):[1]

> No regulation of commerce can increase the quantity of industry in any society beyond what its capital can maintain. It can only divert a part of it into a direction into which it might not otherwise have gone; and it is by no means certain that this artificial direction is likely to be more advantageous to the society than that into which it would have gone of its own accord.

This aspect of the analysis—that regulations, for example promoting the interests of shoemakers, imply that resources, such as capital and labour, are drawn away from other sectors of the economy—is probably Smith's most important contribution in this respect. Until then, the 'successfulness' of such regulations was measured, for example, by the increasing production of shoes, or by the increase in profits for the shoemakers. Smith pointed out that there were costs to this increase, now known as opportunity costs, because the extra capital and labour used for shoe production might have been more advantageously employed in some other sector.

Second, Smith applies the opportunity cost principle to individuals in a society (IV. ii. 11):

> It is the maxim of every prudent master of a family, never to attempt to make at home what it will cost him more to make than to buy. The taylor does not attempt to make his own shoes, but buys them of the shoemaker. The shoemaker does not attempt to make his own cloaths, but employs a taylor. The farmer attempts to make neither the one nor the other, but employs those different artificers. All of them find it for their interest to employ their whole industry in a way in which they have some advantage over their neighbours, and to purchase with a part of its produce, or what is the same thing, with the price of a part of it, whatever else they have occasion for.

His general conclusion is therefore that each individual is specializing in the production of those goods and services in which s/he has some advantage.

Third, he applies the same opportunity cost principle to international commercial policy (IV. ii. 12):

> What is prudence in the conduct of every private family, can scarce be folly in that of a great kingdom. If a foreign country can supply us with a commodity cheaper than we ourselves can make it, better buy it of them with some part of the produce of our own industry, employed in

a way in which we have some advantage. The general industry of the country, being always in proportion to the capital which employs it, will not thereby be diminished, no more than that of the above-mentioned artificers; but only left to find out the way in which it can be employed with the greatest advantage.

This leads to the conclusion that international trade flows reflect the fact that goods and services can sometimes be imported at lower cost from abroad than they can be produced at home. This increases the consumption opportunities for a nation, and is therefore beneficial for the nation as a whole, just as the specialization of the artificers, the shoemaker and the tailor, is advantageous at the individual level.[2]

4.3 Ricardo's contribution

As indicated in Section 4.1, at the beginning of the nineteenth century various people were working on the same problem at the same time, namely how a country that is less efficient than another country in all sectors of production can still trade with other countries. They were all close to reaching the same conclusion. As Irwin (1996, p. 89) put it, 'Mill and Torrens were on the verge of an even more important insight', by which he means the theory of comparative advantage. After a quote from Torrens involving Poland, Irwin (1996, p. 90) concludes: 'this formulation lacks only the comparison of the cost ratios in both countries . . . whereby the theory is stated in its entirety. David Ricardo . . . provided this finishing touch in his *On the Principles of Political Economy and Taxation* in 1817.' In that work Ricardo discusses a famous example of England and Portugal exchanging wine and cloth to complete the theory of comparative advantage, for which he therefore receives almost full credit (Ricardo, 1817, Chapter VII):[3]

> England may be so circumstanced that to produce the cloth may require the labour of 100 men for one year; and if she attempted to make the wine, it might require the labour of 120 men for the same time. England would therefore find it her interest to import wine, and to purchase it by the exportation of cloth.

> To produce the wine in Portugal might require only the labour of 80 men for one year, and to produce the cloth in the same country might require the labour of 90 men for the same time. It would therefore be advantageous for her to export wine in exchange for cloth. This exchange might even take place notwithstanding that the commodity imported by Portugal could be produced there with less labour than in England. Though she could make the cloth with the labour of 90 men, she would import it from a country where it required the labour of 100 men to produce it, because it would be advantageous to her rather to employ her capital in the production of wine, for which she would obtain more cloth from England, than she could produce by diverting a portion of her capital from the cultivation of vines to the manufacture of cloth.

> Thus England would give the produce of the labour of 100 men for the produce of the labour of 80. Such an exchange could not take place between the individuals of the same country. The labour of 100 Englishmen cannot be given for that of 80 Englishmen, but the produce of the labour of 100 Englishmen may be given for the produce of the labour of 80 Portuguese, 60 Russians, or 120 East Indians.

Ricardo therefore argues that it is beneficial for Portugal to specialize in the production of wine and exchange the wine for cloth from England, even though it would require less

Portuguese labour to produce this cloth than English labour. The details of this reasoning will be further explained in the next section. The essence of the argument was summarized by James Mill in 1821 as follows:[4]

> When a country can either import a commodity or produce it at home, it compares the cost of producing at home with the cost of procuring from abroad; if the latter cost is less than the first, it imports. The cost at which a country can import from abroad depends, not upon the cost at which the foreign country produces the commodity, but upon what the commodity costs which it sends in exchange, compared with the cost which it must be at to produce the commodity in question, if it did not import it.

4.4 Technology as a basis for comparative advantage

In general, to convince modern economists of the validity of an argument, one must be precise. This implies that one must specify the exact circumstances in a small economic model under which the conclusion is valid. Although some economists, and presumably many non-economists, bemoan the modern approach, for example because it results in much of the richness of Smith's analysis (the eloquence of his writing, the examples he uses) being lost in the process, the advantages are substantial. First, and most importantly, cheating is not allowed. You are forced to think your analysis through in detail and get your story right. The importance of this aspect cannot be stressed too much, because it is easy (and tempting) to sweep some of the loose ends and the details of the analysis (intentionally or unintentionally) under the mat in a purely verbal approach. Second, knowing the exact circumstances under which a conclusion is valid frequently points the way to a more general approach under which the conclusion is still valid, or to circumstances under which we may arrive at different conclusions.

To show a specific set of circumstances such that under free trade all goods will be produced where their relative or comparative costs in terms of labour are lowest, assume that there are two countries, Germany (G) and China (Ch), producing two goods, toys (T) and cars (C), using one factor of production, labour (international economists refer to this setting as a $2 \times 2 \times 1$ model). The production function in both countries and for both goods exhibits constant returns to scale, indicating that if we double the amount of inputs in an industry (that is, labour), the output level (that is, production) will also double. We assume that there are many firms in both countries, each behaving perfectly competitively; that is, each firm wants to maximize profits, taking the price levels in the output and input markets as given. Taken together, the assumptions of constant returns to scale and perfect competition imply that if a good is produced in equilibrium, the price level in the output market must be equal to the unit cost of production; see Box 4.2.

Since the production functions use only one input (labour) and exhibit constant returns to scale, they can be summarized using a table specifying how much labour is required to produce one unit of either good in either country: see Table 4.1. The left-hand side of the table gives the labour requirements in general terms, where a_T^G is the number of units of labour required in Germany to produce one unit of toys, a_C^{Ch} is the number of units of labour required in China to produce one car, and so on. The right-hand side of the table gives an example using specific numbers for the unit labour requirements.

BOX 4.2 Constant returns to scale and perfect competition

In classical and neoclassical economics we frequently combine the technological assumption of constant returns to scale with the behavioural assumption of perfect competition. This implies a simple, but important, relationship between the costs of production and the equilibrium price of a good on the market.

Under constant returns to scale, knowing the (minimum) costs of producing one unit of a good, say c, gives us enough information to determine the (minimum) costs of producing an arbitrary number of goods, even if there are many different inputs into the production process. More specifically, if the firm wants to produce x units of a good, its costs are cx.

Under perfect competition, the firm takes the unit costs of production c as a parameter; that is, it assumes that it has no control over the unit cost level, which will depend in particular on the level of technology (the production function) and the cost of the inputs (for example the wage rate). Similarly, the firm will treat the price it can fetch for a unit of output, say p, as a parameter beyond its control determined on the marketplace. If a firm sells x units of a product, its total revenue will be px. The firm's profits π, total revenue minus total costs, can therefore be written as:

$$\pi = px - cx = (p - c)x \qquad\qquad 4.1$$

Since the firm's objective function is to maximize profits and, as argued above, it treats the price p and the unit cost of production c as parameters, we can logically distinguish between three different possibilities:

- $p < c$. If the price p of the good on the marketplace is smaller than the unit cost of production c, profits are obviously maximized by not producing any units of the good: $x = 0$.

- $p = c$. If the price p of the good on the marketplace is equal to the unit cost of production c, profits are zero independently of the level of production; the production level x is undetermined at the firm level since the firm always maximizes profits independently of the scale of production (which in equilibrium can then be determined by other economic forces, such as the equality of total supply and demand for the good).

- $p > c$. If the price p of the good on the marketplace is larger than the unit cost of production c, profits are maximized at the firm level by producing an infinite number of goods ($x = \infty$), which also leads to infinite profits. Although this possibility may appeal to the entrepreneurs among the readers, an infinite production level cannot be reached in any economy with a finite number of inputs, implying that this logical possibility cannot be an economic equilibrium and therefore has to be discarded.

Summarizing the above arguments, we can conclude that under perfect competition and constant returns to scale: $p \leq c$, where $x > 0 \Rightarrow p = c$ and $p < c \Rightarrow x = 0$.

Table 4.1 Productivity table: labour required to produce one unit of output

	General specification		Example	
	Toys	Cars	Toys	Cars
Germany	a_T^G	a_C^G	2	8
China	a_T^{Ch}	a_C^{Ch}	4	24

As is clear from the table, Germany is more efficient in the production of both goods; it requires two rather than four units of labour to produce one unit of toys and eight rather than 24 units of labour to produce one car. Based on a theory of absolute cost advantages, China would not be able to trade with Germany. However, the theory of comparative cost advantages argues that only relative, or comparative, costs are important for determining a nation's production advantages. In the example we see that China is twice as inefficient as Germany in producing toys (requiring four units of labour, rather than two) but three times as inefficient as Germany in producing cars (requiring 24 units of labour, rather than eight). It should therefore specialize in the production of toys, and export this to Germany in exchange for cars.

Let's see how this works exactly. Suppose China produces one unit of cars less. This frees up 24 (that is a_C^{Ch}) units of labour. These 24 units of labour can be used in China to produce $24/4 = 6$ (that is a_C^{Ch}/a_T^{Ch}) units of toys. The opportunity costs of producing a car in China is thus six units of toys. China has now produced one unit of cars less and six units of toys more. Suppose, however, that it wants to consume the same quantity of cars as before. It must then import one car from Germany. To produce one extra car, Germany needs eight (that is a_C^{G}) units of labour. These labourers must come from the toys sector, where production therefore drops by $8/2 = 4$ (that is a_C^{G}/a_T^{G}) units of toys, reflecting the opportunity costs of producing cars in Germany. Now note that this hypothetical reallocation of labour between sectors in both countries results in China producing one car less, but six units of toys more, while Germany produces four units of toys less, but one car more. The total world production of cars therefore remains unchanged, while toy production rises by two units. These two extra units of toys reflect the potential gains from specialization if both countries concentrate in the production of the good for which they have a comparative advantage, that is the good they produce *relatively* most efficiently, namely cars for Germany and toys for China. In principle, therefore, there is room for both countries to gain from trading with each other. We now analyse what determines the terms of trade and the division of gains from trade in the classical setting.

4.5 The production possibility frontier and autarky

If we want to determine the terms of trade if two Ricardian-type countries are trading goods with each other, we have to determine the equilibrium relationships in the economy. Although this is not too complicated in the Ricardian model, it is instructive to start the analysis from a situation of *autarky*, that is if the two countries are *not* trading any goods. This is done most easily using the production possibility frontier (see Box 4.3).

To determine the production possibility frontiers for Germany and China for the example of Table 4.1, we have to specify the available factors of production in each country. Given that labour is the only factor of production, it suffices to specify the number of workers available: say 200 labourers for Germany and 480 labourers for China. This implies that Germany can produce a maximum of $200/2 = 100$ units of toys if it produces no cars at all, or $200/8 = 25$ cars if it produces no toys at all. Similarly, China can produce a maximum of $480/4 = 120$ units of toys, or a maximum of $480/24 = 20$ cars. This is summarized in Table 4.2.

This is actually all the information we need to calculate in full the production possibility frontiers for China and Germany in a Ricardian model, since there are constant returns to scale and there is only one factor of production. If Germany currently produces 100 toys and 0 cars (which is a point on the production possibility frontier) and wants to produce one unit of cars, it has to transfer eight labourers from the toys sector to the cars sector.

BOX 4.3 The production possibility frontier

Another tool introduced in this chapter is that of the production possibility frontier (or curve). It is defined as *all possible combinations of efficient production points given the available factors of production and the state of technology*. The production possibility frontier therefore gives all production combinations for which it is not possible to produce more of some good without reducing the production of some other good. In our two-good setting of toys and cars it depicts the maximum amount of toys the economy can produce for a given number of cars or, equivalently, the maximum number of cars the economy can produce for a given level of toy production. An example for the Ricardian model is depicted in Figure 4.2, where point D is a production point beyond the scope of the production possibility frontier (PPF) for the German economy (for lack of labourers or technology). Point A, on the other hand, is below the German PPF since Germany can produce more toys without producing fewer cars at point B or more cars without producing fewer toys at point C. More examples will follow in the next chapters. Note that:

- the production possibility frontier is a technical specification: it does not depend on any type of market competition;
- the production possibility frontier depends on the available factors of production: if more labourers are available, more goods can be produced;
- the production possibility frontier depends on the state of technology; if new production techniques become available, more goods may be produced using the same amount of factors of production.

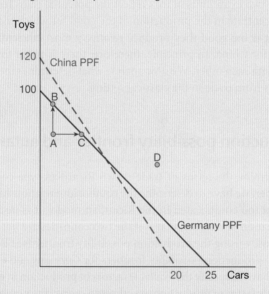

Figure 4.2 Ricardian production possibility frontiers for Germany and China.

Table 4.2 Total labour available and maximum production levels

	Total labour available	Maximum production	
		Toys	Cars
Germany	200	100	25
China	480	120	20

These eight labourers could have produced $8/2 = 4$ units of toys, so toys production drops to $100 - 4 = 96$, which gives us another point on the production possibility frontier. Similarly, if Germany wants to produce another unit of cars (two rather than one), toys production drops again by four units (to 92). These changes are therefore *equiproportional*, such that the Ricardian production possibility frontiers are *straight lines*. All we really have to do, therefore, is calculate the maximum production points and connect these with a straight line. This is illustrated using the information of Table 4.2 in Figure 4.2.

We can now determine the equilibrium price of cars in terms of toys (which we take as our measurement unit, known as the numéraire) for both countries, provided we are willing to make one simple and rather weak assumption: *both countries want to consume at least some units of both goods*. Why does this assumption suffice to determine the price of cars in terms of toys? Well, recall Box 4.2 and take Germany as an example:

- If the price of a car is higher than the price of four toys, the entrepreneurs want to produce only cars and no toys. Since the economy wants to consume at least some toys this cannot be an equilibrium price.

- If the price of a car is less than the price of four toys, the entrepreneurs want to produce only toys and no cars. Since the economy wants to consume at least some cars this also cannot be an equilibrium price.

- The price of a car is therefore four units of toys in autarky in Germany.

Similar reasoning for China leads to the conclusion that the price of a car is six units of toys in autarky. This implies that the production possibility frontier coincides with the economy's budget line generated by the production levels in autarky for both countries. The consumers in both countries therefore choose the optimal consumption point along the production possibility frontier in autarky, while the entrepreneurs adjust their production levels along the PPF to accommodate the wishes of the consumers.

Thus the autarky price ratio in a Ricardian model is exclusively determined by the technical coefficients of the productivity table; the price of a car in terms of toys equals $a_C^G/a_T^G = 8/2 = 4$ in Germany and $a_C^{Ch}/a_T^{Ch} = 24/4 = 6$ in China. Opportunities for trade between nations arise whenever the relative, or comparative, productivity ratios differ. They do not depend on absolute productivity levels.

4.6 Terms of trade and gains from trade

Determining the price of cars in terms of toys in autarky in both countries does not allow us to determine exactly the terms of trade if the two countries decide to open up opportunities to trade with each other, as this requires more detailed information on the demand structure of the economies than the simple assumption made in Section 4.4. We can, however, determine the range within which the terms of trade can vary, and we can demonstrate that both countries may gain from trade. To start with the former, the autarky price of a car in terms of toys is 4 in Germany and 6 in China. The relative price can only vary within this range, endpoints included. If the price falls below 4, both countries want to produce only toys, which cannot be an equilibrium, and if the price rises above 6, both countries want to produce only cars, which also cannot be an equilibrium.

As for the gains from trade, we can distinguish three separate cases: (i) if the relative price of a car is strictly in between 4 and 6, both countries will gain; (ii) if the relative price of a car is 4, only China will gain while welfare in Germany will not change; and (iii) if the relative price of a car is 6, only Germany will gain while welfare in China will not change. Possibility (i) is illustrated in Figure 4.3, where we assume that the relative price is 5 units of toys per car in the trading equilibrium. At that price China will produce only toys (120 units at point C) and will purchase abroad the required amount of cars at a price of 5 (to a maximum of 120/5 = 24 cars, not shown in the figure). Similarly, at that price Germany will produce only cars (25 units at point G) and will purchase the amount of toys it wants abroad (to a maximum of 25 × 5 = 125 units, not shown in the figure).

How can we decide that if the relative price is 5 units of toys per car, both countries will gain from trade? Quite simply because at this relative price the production decisions of the entrepreneurs allow the consumers to choose a consumption point *beyond* the old autarky optimum because the budget line has pivoted outwards (around point C for China and around point G for Germany). By revealed preference the consumption point chosen on the new budget line must be preferred to the old consumption point at autarky. So *if* a price of 5 is a trading equilibrium, both countries will gain from trade (and similar reasoning holds for any other price that is strictly in between 4 and 6). The *if* above reflects the fact that a price of 5 can only be an equilibrium price if the consumers of Germany and China combined want to consume the total world production of both goods at that price (120 units of toys and 25 units of cars) given their income levels. This is illustrated in Figure 4.4 for specific consumption points (C_2 for China and G_2 for Germany). In this case, China exports toys and imports cars to go from production point C to consumption point C_2, thereby generating the 'China trade triangle'. Similarly, Germany exports cars and imports toys to go from production point G to consumption point G_2, thereby generating

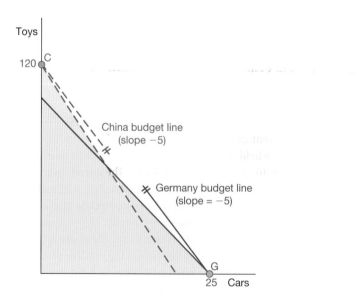

Figure 4.3 The terms of trade is five units of toys per car.

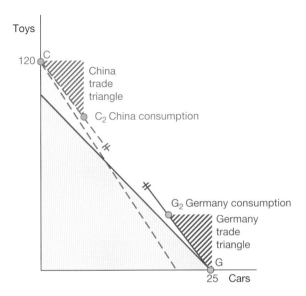

Figure 4.4 Trade triangles coincide in international equilibrium.

the 'German trade triangle'. If China and Germany are the only two countries in the world, total demand is equal to total supply for both products if the two trade triangles coincide (are equally large with flows in the opposite direction).

4.7 Ricardo and agriculture

A nice empirical test of Ricardo's theory of comparative advantage was recently provided by Costinot and Donaldson (2012).[5] One of the main difficulties in testing the Ricardian theory is the observability of relative productivity differences in the trade equilibrium. Note that if Germany and China specialize completely according to comparative advantage in our example in Section 4.6, Germany produces only cars and no toys, which makes it impossible to determine the relative productivity difference from the data. Costinot and Donaldson circumvent this difficulty by focusing on agricultural production, a sector for which agronomists have scientific knowledge on how inputs (water, soil, land) translate into outputs (different crops) for a certain field of land. In principle, therefore, we know the productivity of a field of land for all possible agricultural crops grown on the field, such that we can determine relative productivities. The authors analyse 17 major agricultural crops for 55 major agricultural countries. They base their information on the Global Agro-Ecological Zones (GAEZ) project run by IIASA/FAO (2012). The 'resolution' of the data produces 'fields' across the globe of 5 arc-minutes (land area of these fields vary by latitude, but is 9.2 × 8.5 km at the tropics, so these are sizeable fields). The GAEZ project then estimates the potential output for each field for each of the 17 agricultural crops.

Figure 4.5 provides an example of the relative productivity differences for wheat compared to sugar cane. Evidently, there is great variation across the world with some areas that are much more suitable to grow wheat (high wheat productivity) and other areas

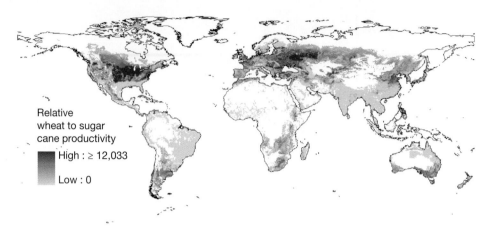

Figure 4.5 Ratio of productivity in wheat to productivity in sugar cane.

that are better suited to grow sugar cane (low wheat productivity). Similar graphs can, of course, be made for the relative productivity of any other combination of agricultural products. The authors then test Ricardo's theory using the calculated relative productivities by regressing data of actual output on measures of predicted output. They find reasonably strong support for the Ricardo model, with a positive and rather precisely estimated slope coefficient. Nonetheless, the model does not fit the data perfectly because (i) the authors focus on land productivity and abstract from all other determinants of comparative costs, (ii) the GAEZ project imperfectly predicts field productivity for the various crops, and (iii) the 'fields' are rather large (with in-field heterogeneity) and may be used for other economic activities.

4.8 More countries and the world production possibility frontier

The exposition in Sections 4.4–4.6 uses two final goods and two countries. Both restrictions can be relaxed quite easily, as long as we continue to restrict ourselves to the analysis of only one production factor. Dornbusch, Fischer, and Samuelson (1977), for example, analyse a setting with many goods ranked from high to low in terms of comparative advantage for some country, say Germany. If we use the index i to identify a good and there are N goods, $i = 1, \ldots, N$, then Germany will have the highest comparative advantage for good 1, the second highest for good 2, and so on. Dornbusch et al. show that there is a critical good, say n, such that Germany will produce the goods $1, \ldots, n$ and the other country produces the goods $n + 1, \ldots, N$.[6] Each country therefore produces the range of goods for which its comparative advantage is highest.

Figure 4.6 illustrates the other case, in which there are two goods and three countries. This also allows us to discuss another concept, that of the world production possibility frontier. Suppose that the USA is also able to produce cars and toys. Its production possibility frontier has a flatter slope than that of either Germany or China, see Figure 4.6. The

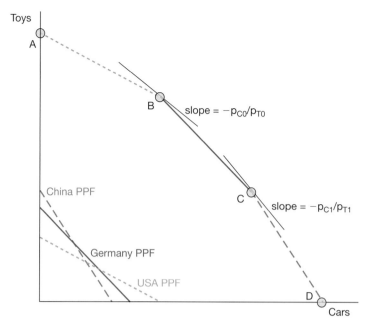

Figure 4.6 Three countries and the world production possibility frontier.

figure also shows the world production possibility frontier; that is, all combinations of efficient production points for the world as a whole (but without factor mobility). The maximum world production level of toys is obtained at point A if all countries only produce toys. Since the USA has the flattest slope for its production possibility frontier, indicating that its opportunity costs for producing toys are highest, it will be the first country to stop producing toys; that is, close to point A the slope of the world PPF is equal to the slope of the USA's production possibility frontier. Once point B is reached, the USA will have completely specialized in the production of cars. Since Germany has the second-flattest slope for its production possibility frontier it will be the second country to start producing cars. This process continues until all countries specialize in the production of cars at point D. The various line segments connecting points A, B, C, and D depict the world production possibility frontier.

Once we have derived the world production possibility frontier it is easy to determine the world production point in a free trading equilibrium. Suppose, for example, that the relative price of cars is equal to p_{C0}/p_{T0}. Then the maximum value of world production is obtained at point B; that is, the USA will produce cars and Germany and China will produce toys. The USA will therefore export cars in exchange for toys with the other countries. Next, suppose that the relative price of cars is equal to p_{C1}/p_{T1}. Then the maximum value of world production is obtained at point C; that is, China will produce toys and the USA and Germany will produce cars. China will therefore export toys in exchange for cars with the other countries, and similarly for other relative prices. Finally, note that all these comparative advantage principles have been analysed for nations, but they can also be applied for other types of organizations: see Box 4.4.

> **BOX 4.4 Comparative advantage and the organization of firms**
>
> It should be noted that the principles underlying an efficient production process in the international economy also hold at the firm level. A company employing 2,000 people should steer its workers to those labour activities they perform relatively most efficiently. The wage rate paid to an individual worker depends on absolute costs; see Box 4.2. The vivid example sometimes used here is that of a hospital employing a brain surgeon who also happens to be the world's fastest typist. This brain surgeon should nonetheless leave the typing work to her secretary, as she has a comparative advantage performing surgery (assuming that the typist cannot perform this activity). To assist her in making this choice, the wage she can earn as a brain surgeon is higher than the wage she can earn as a typist.

4.9 Measuring trade advantages: the Balassa index[7]

We have seen that it is beneficial for a country to specialize in the production of those goods that it can produce relatively more efficiently than another country, and to export these goods in exchange for imports of goods it can produce less efficiently. This provides a concise and simple explanation for international trade flows. Section 4.7 discussed some empirical support for the Ricardian model for agricultural products. We can, however, also turn the question around by first empirically investigating which countries are exporting which goods and then wondering which theory, or theories, may explain this export pattern. Since the idea is that investigating a country's actual exports 'reveals' the country's strong sectors, the first step in this procedure is known as establishing a country's 'revealed comparative advantage'.[8] The index most frequently used in this respect was pioneered by Liesner (1958), but refined and popularized by Bela Balassa (1965, 1989), and it is therefore known as the *Balassa index*.

Many countries are, for example, producing and exporting cars. To establish whether a country, say Japan, holds a particularly strong position in the car industry, Balassa argued that one should compare the share of car exports in Japan's total exports with the share of car exports in a group of reference countries' total exports. The Balassa index is therefore essentially a normalized export share. More specifically, if BI_j^A is country A's Balassa index for sector j, this is equal to:

$$BI_j^A = \frac{\text{share of sector } j \text{ in country } A \text{ exports}}{\text{share of sector } j \text{ in reference countries' exports}} \qquad 4.2$$

If $BI_j^A > 1$, country A is said to have a revealed comparative advantage in industry j, since this industry is more important for country A's exports than for the exports of the reference countries.

Before actually calculating the Balassa index, we have to decide which exports to which countries to include and which countries to use as 'reference' countries. In this section we use world trade flows as a reference and focus on 96 manufacturing sectors (which is the two-digit level of the Harmonized System).[9] Table 4.3 lists the sectors with the highest Balassa index in 2013 for the 40 largest exporting countries.[10] A number of observations stand out.

First, some of the strongest export sectors are the 'usual suspects', as the combination of product and country is based on a well-known, long-running tradition of production and specialization. This holds, for example, for the exports of clocks from Switzerland (and

Table 4.3 Sectors with highest Balassa index in 2013: two-digit Harmonized System level, selected countries

Sector		Country (BI value)
1	Live animals	Hungary (3.4)
3	Fish and crustaceans, etc.	Norway (11.7)
6	Live trees and other plants, bulbs, flowers, etc.	Netherlands (15.9)
7	Edible vegetables and certain roots and tubers	Mexico (4.1)
9	Coffee, tea, maté, and spices	Vietnam (12.5)
13	Lac (gums, resins, and other vegetable saps, etc.)	India (18.5)
15	Animal or vegetable fats and oils, etc.	Malaysia (13.2)
16	Preparations of meat, fish, or crustaceans, etc.	Thailand (11.4)
17	Sugars and sugar confectionery	Brazil (18.0)
24	Tobacco and manufactured tobacco substitutes	Poland (4.5)
26	Ores, slag, and ash	Australia (25.1); S Africa (11.3)
27	Mineral fuels, mineral oils, etc.	Kuwait (6.3); Qatar (5.8); Saudi Arabia (5.7)
31	Fertilisers	Russia (5.0)
33	Essential oils and resinoids, etc.	Ireland (11.5)
36	Explosives, pyrotechnic products, matches, etc.	Czech Rep (5.1)
37	Photographic or cinematographic goods	Japan (6.5)
43	Fur skins and artificial fur; manufactures thereof	Denmark (24.7)
45	Cork and articles of cork	Spain (9.2)
48	Paper and paperboard; articles of paper pulp etc.	Sweden (6.5)
51	Wool, fine or coarse animal hair, etc.	Italy (5.6)
57	Carpets and other textile floor coverings	Belgium (4.6); Turkey (17.0)
66	Umbrellas, sun umbrellas, walking-sticks, etc.	China (6.4)
74	Copper and articles thereof	Chile (34.6)
75	Nickel and articles thereof	Canada (6.7)
79	Zinc and articles thereof	Kazakhstan (7.5)
80	Tin and articles thereof	Indonesia (28.2)
86	Railway or tramway locomotives, etc.	Austria (5.8)
87	Vehicles other than railway or tramway, etc.	Germany (2.2); Slovakia (3.2)
88	Aircraft, spacecraft, and parts thereof	France (5.6); USA (4.1)
89	Ships, boats, and floating structures	S Korea (8.2)
91	Clocks and watches and parts thereof	Hong Kong (6.0); Switzerland (33.1)
97	Works of art, collectors' pieces, and antiques	UK (9.0)

Notes: two-digit Harmonized System codes; 40 largest export countries are reported.

Source: calculations based on data from UN Comtrade data, extracted 23 April 2015.

Hong Kong), of cars from Germany (and Slovakia), of flowers from the Netherlands, and of carpets from Turkey and Belgium.

Second, some of the strongest export sectors are based on a factor of production or input that is abundantly available in the country or in its direct vicinity. This holds, for example, for the exports of ores, slag, and ash from Australia and South Africa, of paper and wood from Sweden, of oil from Kuwait, Qatar, and Saudi Arabia, of zinc from Kazakhstan, of tin from Indonesia, of nickel from Canada, of copper from Chile, of cork from Spain, and of fish from Norway.

Third, the highest value of the Balassa index varies substantially between countries. In Table 4.3 it is only 2.2 for Germany compared to 34.6 for Chile. In general, it is harder for a sector to score a high value in an economically large country that exports a wide range of products, such as Germany, the USA, and France. In contrast, the value can be quite high for smaller trading nations specializing to a large extent on a particular products, such as Denmark and Chile. This holds even more so for even smaller countries not listed in Table 4.3. The highest Balassa index for Zimbabwe, for example, is 116 for the export of tobacco, while the highest Balassa index for Portugal is 179 for the export of cork. The bottom line is to remember that it is not useful to compare the value of the Balassa index for a sector in one country with the value of that same sector in another country as the underlying distributions are different (Hinloopen and van Marrewijk, 2001), but we *can* meaningfully compare values within the same country. The most important cut-off value is one for all countries, as only sectors with a value above one are revealed as strong in any country.

This leaves us to explain some of the other strong sectors as listed in Table 4.3. Why do we have photographic goods in Japan, umbrellas in China, railways and locomotives in Austria, aircraft and spacecraft in France and the USA, or ships and boats in South Korea? We will argue below that this is also to some extent based on abundantly available, yet more hidden, factors of production (think of human capital and knowledge intensity), as will be discussed in Chapter 5 and Chapter 6. To some extent, however, it is also based on the interaction between the comparative advantages at different locations, the ability to cut up the production process into smaller pieces (fragmentation), and the opportunity to make full use of increasing returns to scale in parts of the production process. These issues are addressed in Chapter 7 and Chapter 8. Some examples of revealed comparative advantage are discussed later for oil (Box 5.3), textiles (Box 5.8), precious stones (Box 6.2), electronics (Box 6.3), and cars (Box 8.5).

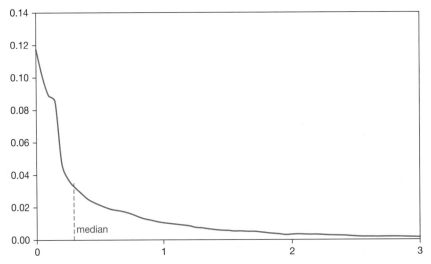

Figure 4.7 Global Balassa index distribution; two-digit Harmonized System sectors, 2013.

Notes: median value is 0.29; 75.2 per cent of the observations are below 1; the distribution is at the two-digit HS level, based on 108 available countries.

Source: see Table 4.3.

Figure 4.7 illustrates the global distribution of the Balassa index at the two-digit level. We already noted above that the values for sectors in one country cannot be compared to those of another country. The figure nonetheless gives some indication regarding the distribution of the Balassa index. The distribution is almost monotonically declining, with many values close to zero. The median value is thus only 0.29. Recall that 1 is the most important value as it indicates whether or not a country has a revealed comparative advantage (above 1) or not (below 1). It turns out that (at the two-digit level) about one-fourth of all observations are above 1. So, on average, only about a quarter of the sectors are identified as 'strong' using the Balassa index. In general, sectors with a high comparative advantage tend to sustain this advantage for a fairly long time, as the example for Swiss clocks and Belgian carpets illustrates. Changes over time are, however, also possible, as discussed in the Chinese case study in Section 8.10.

4.10 Production structure: services and agriculture

We want to make some final observations regarding technology, services, and the production structures of various economies before continuing with the rest of the book. In the remainder we will use the term 'goods' to also refer to the production and trade of services, because our theories apply both to goods and services. This does not mean that the distinction between goods and services is unimportant, or that there are no special issues associated with dealing with services instead of goods. In fact, as illustrated in Figure 4.8, the services sectors tend to become increasingly important as economies become wealthier and more sophisticated. The diagram uses bubbles proportional to population size to identify the most important countries. The graph also shows the World Bank regions discussed in Chapter 1. Although we can clearly identify the relatively poor Sub-Saharan Africa (SSA) countries in the left part of the figure, the remaining colours are hard to distinguish; this indicates that the transition to a more service-oriented economy as countries develop is a general phenomenon, not dependent on specific regions. The dotted line in the figure is a regression line, with a positive and highly significant slope, indicating that a 10 per cent higher income per capita level increases the services sectors by about 0.46 per cent.

The unweighted average added value generated in the services sectors in 2014 was 58.7 per cent of GDP, the median value was 60, and the population-weighted average was 54.4. The observations ranged from a minimum of 6.4 per cent for oil-rich Equatorial Guinea to a high of 93.8 per cent for Macao. Typical examples of the rising importance of the services sector for development are provided by the Democratic Republic of the Congo, with an income per capita of $809 and 41 per cent added value generated in the services sector, and the USA, with an income per capita of $53,042 and 78 per cent added value generated in the services sector. A popular method for distinguishing between goods and services is to argue that services, such as getting a haircut, are produced and consumed simultaneously, although not necessarily at the same place. A less sophisticated, but effective, method is to argue that if you can drop it on your foot it must be a good.

If the share of services in value added increases, it must be at the expense of the share of some other type of economic activity.[11] As illustrated in Figure 4.9, the agricultural sectors

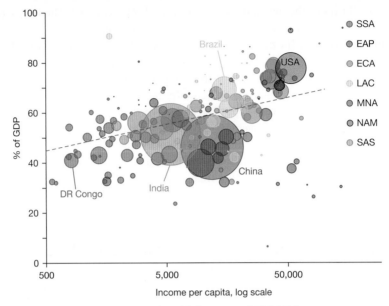

Figure 4.8 Income per capita and services value added: per cent of GDP, 2014.

Note: figure represents the most recently available information on the period 2010–2014; income in current GDP PPP; see Table 1.1 for the World Bank region abbreviations; bubbles proportional to population size; dashed line is a regression line; 195 countries included.

Source: as Table 1.2.

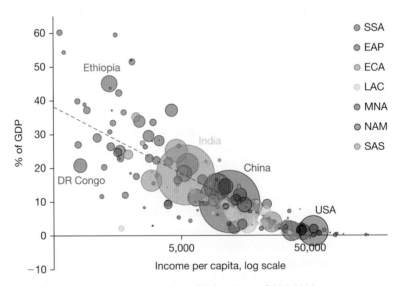

Figure 4.9 Income per capita and agriculture value added: per cent of GDP, 2014.

Note: figure represents the most recently available information on the period 2010–2014; income in current GDP PPP; see Table 1.1 for the World Bank region abbreviations; bubbles proportional to population size; dashed line is a regression line; 195 countries included.

Source: as Table 1.2.

tend to become *less* important as economies develop. The graph shows quite effectively that the share of agriculture in total output can vary substantially for low- and middle-income countries, but it is always low for high-income countries. The dotted line is a regression line, with a negative and highly significant slope, indicating that a 10 per cent higher income per capita level reduces the agricultural sectors by about 0.86 per cent. The intercept of the regression line with the horizontal axis is at $47,000. Beyond that level the agricultural sectors tend to be very small. In fact, there are only 13 countries with a higher income level, and their average share of value added in agriculture is only 0.65 per cent.

The unweighted average value added in the agricultural sectors in 2014 was 12.8 per cent of income, the median was 8.6 per cent, and the population-weighted average was 13.1 per cent. The minimum value was 0.0 per cent for Macao and Singapore (0.1 for Hong Kong). The maximum value was 60.2 for Somalia. Typical examples illustrated in the figure are Ethiopia (per capita income $1,380 and 45 per cent of income generated in agriculture), India ($5,418 and 18 per cent), China ($11,907 and 10 per cent), and the USA ($53,042 and 1.3 per cent).

4.11 Conclusions

To determine a country's strong (export) sectors on the classical basis of technology differences, as well as its terms of trade, only comparative costs are important. International trade leads to welfare gains irrespective of absolute costs. This was illustrated using empirical data for agriculture. Note, however, that the per capita welfare level largely depends on absolute cost differences, rather than comparative cost differences (see Box 4.5). This may explain the large international differences in wage rates, namely as the result of productivity differences. The analysis can be generalized quite easily to incorporate more goods and more countries. The incorporation of more than one factor of production, however, is more complicated. This issue is addressed in Chapters 5 and 6.

BOX 4.5 Comparative costs, absolute costs, and international wages

This chapter argues that differences in comparative costs are crucial for determining international trade flows and gains from trade. Absolute cost advantages, however, are crucial for determining a country's per capita welfare level, and thus help explain differences in international wages. To be concrete, take the example in Table 4.1 as the point of departure. Take the Chinese wage rate as numéraire and assume that Germany specializes in the production of cars, China specializes in the production of toys, and the exchange rate is 1. In a perfectly competitive economy with constant returns to scale the price of a product is equal to the cost of production, see Box 4.2. Given that toys are produced in China, that the Chinese wage is 1, and that it takes four units of Chinese labour to produce one unit of toys, the price of a toy must be 4 ($= 4 \times 1$). Let w_G be the German wage. Since Germany produces cars and it requires eight units of German labour to produce one unit of cars, the price of cars must be $8w_G$.

Now note that Germany can, in principle, also produce toys. If it were to do this, and in view of the fact that it requires two units of German labour to produce one unit of toys, the price would be $2w_G$. Since we have assumed that only China produces toys, this price must be higher than the actual price of a toy ($= 4$). We conclude therefore that $2w_G > 4$, or equivalently that $w_G > 2$.

Similarly, China can, in principle, also produce cars. If it did, the price would be 24 ($= 24 \times 1$), since it requires 24 units of Chinese labour to produce one unit of cars and the Chinese wage is 1. Since China

(continued...)

does not actually produce cars, this price must be higher than the price currently prevailing (= $8w_G$). We conclude therefore that $8w_G < 24$, or equivalently that $w_G < 3$.

Combining this information, we can conclude that the German wage rate is at least twice as high as the Chinese wage rate, and at most three times as high. (As with the terms of trade, to calculate the wage rate exactly requires information on the demand structure to determine the trading equilibrium.) Evidently, this difference in the international wage rates depends on the difference in absolute costs in the two countries, that is on the difference in productivity levels. German per capita welfare, based on this wage difference, therefore also depends on the difference in absolute cost levels, and is primarily based on its own productivity.

With the Ricardo model in mind, the information given in Figure 4.10 for 47 different countries can help us to understand the world economy. The bubbles are proportional to population size in order to quickly identify the main observations. Countries with a low labour productivity, such as Brazil ($11.48 per hour) or Mexico ($17.26 per hour), have a low income level per capita ($15,037 and $16,370, respectively). Countries with a high labour productivity, such as the USA ($58.98 per hour) and Norway ($76.76 per hour), have a high income level per capita ($53,042 and $64,406, respectively). The (regression) line in Figure 4.10 (which explains about 77 per cent of the variance in income per capita and is highly significant) summarizes this relationship. On average, a 10 per cent higher income level leads to a $3.2 higher wage rate per hour.

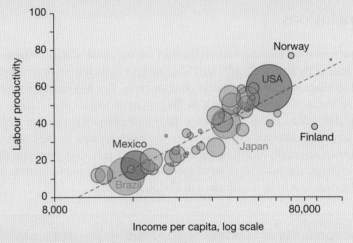

Figure 4.10 Labour productivity and income per capita.

Notes: income per capita GDP PPP, log scale (see Table 1.2); labour productivity per hour worked in USD (2009), based on Conference Board Total Economy Database; bubbles proportional to population; dotted line is a regression line; 47 countries included.

Source: adapted from Beugelsdijk et al. (2013, Figure 3.1).

 Notes

1   The reference numbers for Adam Smith follow the Glasgow convention of book, section, paragraph.

2   An important forerunner of Adam Smith in terms of opportunity costs was Henry Martyn, who in 1701 argued (Irwin 1996, p. 57): 'Things may be imported from India by fewer hands than as good would be made in England, so that to permit the consumption of Indian manufactures is to permit the loss of few

men's labour . . . a law to restrain us to use only English manufactures, is to oblige us to make them first, is to oblige us to provide for our consumption by the labour of many when that of few might be sufficient.'

3 See Allen (1965, pp. 63–4). Some economists question the contribution of David Ricardo—see e.g. Chipman (1965, p. 480)—or even suggest that James Mill rather than Ricardo came up with the example (Thweatt, 1976). Since his contemporary, Mill, gives full credit to Ricardo on at least two occasions (Irwin, 1996, p. 91), I think it is fair to conclude that Ricardo does deserve most credit.

4 Irwin (1996, p. 91).

5 The discussion in this section is based on Section 3.2 in Brakman, Garretsen, and van Marrewijk (2013).

6 In some cases, the other country may also produce good n.

7 This section is based on Hinloopen and van Marrewijk (2001).

8 The 'comparative' part of this term also reflects the developments discussed in Chapter 5 and Chapter 6.

9 The Harmonized System is an international nomenclature developed by the World Customs Organization, which is arranged in six-digit codes allowing all participating countries to classify traded goods on a common basis. Beyond the six-digit level, countries are free to introduce national distinctions for tariffs and many other purposes.

10 We ignore category 99, commodities not specified; this excludes Singapore from Table 4.3.

11 The share of manufacturing employment and value added tends to first increase and then decrease with income per capita: see Chapter 17.

 ## Questions

Question 4.1

Table 4.4 gives the units of labour needed to produce one ship, one bicycle, and one aeroplane in Russia and the European Union.

Table 4.4 Units of labour needed for the production of one unit

	Ship	Bicycle	Aeroplane
Russia	200	50	500
EU	100	30	200

a. Which country has an absolute advantage in the production of ships, bicycles, and aeroplanes?

b. What is the EU's comparative advantage if we look only at ships and bicycles?

c. What is the EU's comparative advantage if we look only at bicycles and aeroplanes?

d. Can you infer from your calculations in Question 4.1b and 4.1c which product the EU will export for sure and which product it will surely not export?

Question 4.2

Some politicians and trade activists argue that developing countries should not participate in the global economy as their industries cannot compete with their Western counterparts. According to these observers, trade does not benefit the developing countries and will only result in the exploitation of the labour force. Let's analyse this argument in a simple Ricardian framework. Suppose there are only two countries, Indonesia and the USA, producing only two goods, clothes and machines. Labour is the only factor of production. Table 4.5 shows how many man-hours are needed in Indonesia and the USA to make one unit of cloth or one machine. Assume that 2,000 man-hours are available in the USA and 36,000 in Indonesia.

Table 4.5 Number of man-hours needed to produce one unit

	Indonesia	USA
Cloth	50	3
Machine	100	5

a. Explain which country has a comparative advantage in which product.

b. What is the autarky price of machines in Indonesia and the USA?

c. Indicate exactly what range of prices for machines should be offered on international markets for both countries to profit from international trade. What will Indonesia and the USA import and export?

d. Explain in a consistent graph with production possibility frontiers why both countries gain from trade when prices on the international markets are within the range you indicated for Question 4.2c.

Some trade activists who think that developing countries are exploited on the international market may not be convinced by your arguments above. They claim that even in the Ricardian framework trade is based on unequal wages between developed and developing countries.

e. Explain whether wages are unequal in the example of Indonesia and the USA. If both countries trade with each other, what is the maximum and minimum difference between the wage rate in Indonesia and the USA?

f. Discuss whether abolishing trade is an effective instrument to raise Indonesian wages. Use the observations you made in your analysis above.

Question 4.3

Three countries, Hungary, Bulgaria, and Czech Republic, have Ricardian technologies as listed in Table 4.6 and can produce two types of goods, namely butter and beer.

Table 4.6 Number of labour units required to produce one unit of output

Country	Butter	Beer
Hungary	2	4
Bulgaria	3	7
Czech Republic	4	5

a. Which country has an absolute advantage in the production of beer and which country in butter? Explain.

b. The three countries start to trade with each other without any impediments whatsoever. Which country will export butter and which country will export beer (comparative advantage)? Explain.

c. What happens to the country not mentioned in your answer to Question 4.3b? Which good will it export? Your friend argues that it will lose from engaging in international trade for sure. Is she right? Explain.

 *See the **online resources** for a Study Guide and questions:*
www.oup.com/uk/vanmarrewijk_it/

5 Technology: the neoclassical approach

Objectives

- To become familiar with the size of intra- and inter-regional global trade flows.
- To understand the basic neoclassical production structure.
- To know what isoquants are and how to minimize costs.
- To understand the connections between constant returns to scale and perfect competition.
- To distinguish between products based on capital intensity (capital–labour ratios).
- To know and understand the four main neoclassical results (factor price equalization, Stolper–Samuelson, Rybczynski, and Heckscher–Ohlin).
- To be able to derive factor price equalization and Stolper–Samuelson with the Lerner diagram, making use of unit value isoquants and the unit value isocost line.

5.1 Introduction

In the neoclassical view, the driving forces behind international trade flows are differences in factor endowments between nations. The conclusions depend to a large extent on the production structure of the economy, based on identical technology, constant returns to scale, and perfect competition. The classical theory discussed in Chapter 4 focuses attention on technological differences between nations to explain international trade flows. At this point we may note at least three problems associated with this theory.

First, the largest technological differences between nations presumably arise when these nations are very different in their state of economic development. Even if we acknowledge that only the relative differences are influential in determining comparative advantage, we would still expect substantial trade flows between nations with large differences in technology. However, as we discuss in Section 5.2, there are only small trade flows between, for example, African countries and the United States.

Second, the empirical discussion in Section 4.7 on the explanatory power of the Ricardian model was only moderately supportive of this theory. Some of the difficulties were discussed at the end of Chapter 4. Evidently, however, other economic forces may be useful for explaining some of the remaining trade flows.

Third, the focus on only one factor of production seems too restrictive and precludes the analysis of many interesting issues. In effect we attribute *all* value added in a sector to only one factor of production: labour. Clearly, some sectors, such as oil refineries, are much more capital-intensive than other sectors, such as hairdressers. A larger part of the value added in the oil refinery is used to remunerate the capital investments involved than for the hairdresser. Similarly, some sectors, such as electronics firms, use more highly educated labourers than other sectors, such as domestic services. Differences in remuneration therefore may reflect differences in years of education and skills. To analyse these and other distributional economic aspects of production and trade flows requires the distinction of at least two different factors of production.

These observations bring us to the core of international trade theory: factor abundance theory, or the neoclassical theory of international trade, as developed by Paul Samuelson (see Box 5.1). Before we start our discussion, however, we provide some empirical information on the international trade flows between and within large global regions. This information is useful as a frame of reference. Once we summarize and better understand the direction and size of international trade flows between groups of countries we also have a better picture of what our trade theories should help us to explain.

BOX 5.1 Paul Samuelson

Born in Gary, Indiana, Samuelson (Figure 5.1) contributed from his MIT offices to virtually all parts of economic analysis, applying and developing the neoclassical apparatus of optimization to the problems of consumers and producers. His influence on the mind-set of today's economist cannot be overestimated. For international economics in particular he is important for the development of factor abundance theory.

Figure 5.1
Paul Samuelson
(1915–2009).

5.2 Inter- and intra-regional trade flows

We want to characterize the size and direction of international trade flows. To do that and simplify our picture we will aggregate countries into global regions based on the World Bank classification discussed in Section 1.2. We make two adjustments. First, we subdivide the large East Asia and Pacific region (31.3 per cent of the world population) into three parts: East Asia (including China, Korea, and Japan), Southeast Asia (including Indonesia and the Philippines), and Pacific (including Australia and New Zealand). Second, we subdivide the Europe and Central Asia region into Europe and Central Asia (including Russia) separately. We thus have ten different global regions, as shown in Table 5.1. We contemplated including Mexico into North America for geographic and trade agreement reasons (see Chapter 12), but decided not to do so to keep the World Bank region classification intact as much as possible.

Total trade within a global region is the sum of all trade flows for the countries that are part of that global region. These flows can be subdivided into *intra*-regional flows (within the same region; so from a country in the region to another country in the same region) and *inter*-regional flows (between regions; so from a country in the region to a country in some other region). The results of our calculations are visualized in Figure 5.2, while more details on the size of the flows are provided in Table 5.2.

The visualization in Figure 5.2 uses a map for reference, circles located more or less at the geographic centre of a region on that map which are proportional to the size of the region's total trade flows (average of exports and imports), and arrows between those circles to show trade flows from one region to another. In order not to clutter the diagram, only inter-regional flows of 1 per cent or more are shown in the figure. To get an indication of the importance of these flows, the thickness of the line is proportional to the size of the flow. To get an indication of the size of the intra-regional versus the inter-regional trade flows, each circle is subdivided into a light-shaded part and a dark-shaded part. The intra-regional flows are represented by the dark-shaded part.

A number of important observations can be made by looking at Figure 5.2 and the details provided in Table 5.2 regarding the trade flows as a whole (average of exports, the column totals in Table 5.2, and imports, the row totals).

- Europe is by far the most important region for international trade flows; it represents more than 37 per cent of global trade. Other important regions are East Asia (China and Japan) with 20 per cent of global trade and North America with 13.5 per cent. Together these three regions account for 71 per cent of all trade flows.

Table 5.1 Global regions: World Bank regions, further subdivided

Region	Code	Population				No. of countries
		million	%	million	%	
East Asia and Pacific	EAP	2,225	31.3			36
Pacific	PAC			31	0.4	17
East Asia	EAS			1,570	22.1	7
Southeast Asia	SEA			624	8.8	12
Europe and Central Asia	ECA	899	12.7			57
Europe	EUR			542	7.6	45
Central Asia	CAS			357	5.0	12
Latin America and Caribbean	LAC	615	8.7			41
Middle East and North Africa	MNA	403	5.7			21
North America	NAM	351	4.9			3
South Asia	SAS	1,671	23.5			8
Sub-Saharan Africa	SSA	937	13.2			48
Total		7,101	100			214

Source: based on World Bank Development Indicators classification, 2015.

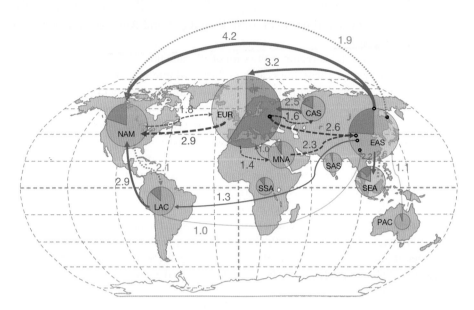

Figure 5.2 Global intra- and inter-regional trade flows, per cent of world total (value shown near each arrow).

Notes: bubbles proportional to size of trade flows in 2011; light-shaded area is extra-regional trade; dark-shaded area is intra-regional trade; weight of inter-regional trade flow is proportional to size (in per cent); only flows of 1 per cent or more are shown. *Source:* see Table 5.2.

- There is a limited number of sizeable inter-regional trade flows. Out of the 90 possible flows only 18 exceed the 1 per cent threshold.

- There are large flows between the three main centres: from East Asia to North America (4.2 per cent), from East Asia to Europe (3.2), from Europe to North America (2.9), etc.

- There are large flows from regions in the vicinity of the main centres to the main centre: from Latin America to North America (2.9 per cent), from Southeast Asia to East Asia (2.6), from Central Asia to Europe (2.5), and so on. We return to this geographical component in Chapter 16.

- Two or three global regions are rather isolated with relatively little interaction with the rest of the world. This certainly holds for Sub-Saharan Africa and South Asia (without any connecting arrow to any other region in Figure 5.2). To a somewhat smaller extent it also holds for Pacific (with one connecting arrow), which is geographically isolated, but in view of its relatively small population has a reasonable interaction with the world economy, particularly with East Asia (the destination of 59 per cent of its export flows).

To provide some more perspective on the relative interaction of some regions: the share of Pacific in world trade flows is 1.7 per cent, of Sub-Saharan Africa is 2.2 per cent, and of South Asia is 2.7 per cent. The share of the Netherlands, a small European country with a population of 16.8 million people, in world trade flows is 3.6 per cent. This is 30 per cent larger than South Asia (with a population that is 99 times larger), 60 per cent larger than Sub-Saharan Africa (with a population that is 54 times larger), and 110 per cent larger than Pacific (with a population that is twice as large). An alternative visualization at the country level (without connecting arrows) is provided in Figure 5.3. The reader may want to compare the size of a country's trade flows with the country's area (see Figure 1.1) or population (see Figure 1.2).

Table 5.2 Intra- and inter-regional trade flows, 2011

a. Including intra-regional trade: per cent of total trade

Importing region	Exporting region										
	CAS	EAS	EUR	LAC	MNA	NAM	PAC	SAS	SEA	SSA	Sum
CAS	1.0	0.8	1.6	0.1	0.1	0.2	0.0	0.1	0.1	0.0	3.9
EAS	0.6	6.3	2.6	1.0	2.3	1.9	1.1	0.3	2.6	0.7	19.3
EUR	2.5	3.2	**25.9**	0.8	1.0	1.8	0.1	0.5	0.8	0.6	37.2
LAC	0.1	1.3	0.8	0.9	0.1	2.1	0.0	0.1	0.2	0.1	5.8
MNA	0.3	0.8	1.4	0.1	0.5	0.4	0.1	0.4	0.2	0.0	4.3
NAM	0.3	4.2	2.9	2.9	0.7	3.4	0.1	0.3	0.8	0.5	16.1
PAC	0.0	0.5	0.3	0.0	0.1	0.2	0.1	0.0	0.3	0.0	1.7
SAS	0.1	0.7	0.6	0.1	0.9	0.2	0.1	0.1	0.3	0.2	3.3
SEA	0.1	2.2	0.7	0.1	0.6	0.6	0.2	0.2	1.6	0.1	6.4
SSA	0.0	0.5	0.6	0.1	0.1	0.1	0.0	0.1	0.1	0.3	2.0
Sum	5.0	20.6	37.4	6.1	6.3	11.0	1.8	2.2	7.0	2.5	100

b. Excluding intra-regional trade: per cent of total trade

Importing region	Exporting region										
	CAS	EAS	EUR	LAC	MNA	NAM	PAC	SAS	SEA	SSA	Sum
CAS		1.3	2.6	0.2	0.2	0.4	0.0	0.1	0.2	0.1	4.9
EAS	1.0		4.4	1.7	3.8	3.1	1.8	0.6	4.3	1.1	21.8
EUR	4.2	5.4		1.3	1.7	3.0	0.2	0.8	1.3	1.0	18.9
LAC	0.1	2.2	1.4		0.2	3.5	0.1	0.2	0.3	0.2	8.1
MNA	0.4	1.4	2.3	0.2		0.8	0.1	0.7	0.3	0.1	6.3
NAM	0.5	7.0	4.8	4.8	1.1		0.2	0.5	1.4	0.8	21.1
PAC	0.0	0.9	0.6	0.1	0.1	0.4		0.0	0.6	0.1	2.7
SAS	0.1	1.2	1.0	0.1	1.5	0.3	0.2		0.6	0.3	5.3
SEA	0.2	3.7	1.3	0.2	1.0	1.0	0.3	0.3		0.1	8.1
SSA	0.1	0.9	0.9	0.1	0.2	0.2	0.0	0.2	0.2		2.9
Sum	6.7	23.9	19.2	8.6	9.8	12.7	2.9	3.4	9.1	3.7	100

Notes: lightest shade are flows between 1 and 2 per cent; next shade between 2 and 4 per cent; next shade between 4 and 8 per cent; darkest shade and in bold are flows above 8 per cent; 166 countries included; for region abbreviations see Table 5.1.
Source: calculations based on UN Comtrade data for 2011.

When evaluating the performance of our trade theories we have to keep in mind to what extent they are able to explain the main trade flows discussed above. There is, however, one important aspect that we have not yet discussed, namely the extent of intra-regional trade relative to inter-regional trade flows. For the world as a whole the intra-regional trade flows are substantial: if we exclude all intra-regional trade flows from the analysis (as is done in panel b. of Table 5.2) total trade falls by 40 per cent. What remains is a slightly different picture of the importance of some regions. We draw some more conclusions.

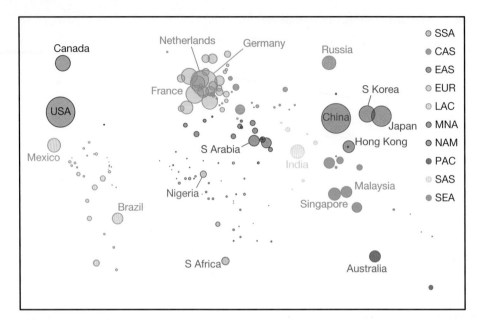

Figure 5.3 International trade flows.

Notes: bubbles are proportional to a country's trade flows in 2011 located at the geographic centre; 166 countries included; for region abbreviations, see Table 5.1.
Source: see Table 5.2.

- Europe has by far the largest intra-regional trade flows: more than 25 per cent of world trade flows from one European country to another European country, while 69 per cent of Europe's exports flow to another European country. This is by far the highest for all regions. Only 31 per cent of North American exports are destined for North America and 30 per cent of East Asian exports are destined for East Asia. The simple average for the other regions is only 12 per cent.

- If we exclude intra-regional trade flows from the analysis, the importance of Europe in global trade drops substantially, from 37.3 to 19.0 per cent. All other regions become more important; in relative terms this holds particularly for South Asia, Pacific, Middle East and North Africa, and Sub-Saharan Africa.

- All major observations discussed above still hold if we exclude intra-regional trade flows: (i) there are three main trade regions (Europe, East Asia, and North America), (ii) there are large flows between these main regions, (iii) there are large flows between the main regions and the regions in the vicinity, and (iv) there are three rather isolated regions (Pacific, South Asia, and North Africa).

5.3 Neoclassical economics

A proper understanding of the forces behind international trade and capital flows cannot be obtained without thoroughly studying the foundations of neoclassical economics. For many practical applications and problems, an understanding of the small general equilibrium model known as the neoclassical model provides valuable economic intuition for the most important forces playing a role in production and consumption decisions. The foundations for the neoclassical model were laid by Eli Heckscher and his pupil Bertil Ohlin, two Swedish economists. Undoubtedly the most influential publication in this respect is Bertil Ohlin's *Interregional and International Trade* (1933). After a brief discussion of some simplifications and the definition of a region, Ohlin (1933, Chapter I) remarks:[1]

> We have evidently pushed the analysis one step further, to an inquiry under what circumstances relative commodity prices will actually be different in two isolated regions. The starting point for such an investigation is the fact that all prices, of goods as well as of industrial agents, are ultimately, in each region, at any given moment, determined by the demand for goods and the possibilities of producing them. Behind the former lie two circumstances to be considered as known data in the problem of pricing: (1) the wants and desires of consumers, and (2) the conditions of ownership of the factors of production, which affect individual incomes and thus demand. The supply of goods, on the other hand, depends ultimately on (3) the supply of productive factors, and (4) the physical conditions of production.

Ohlin is thus well aware that the circumstances under which relative commodity prices in two isolated regions differ depend on interplay between demand and supply conditions, each in turn depending on various other factors. Before we can derive any definite conclusions, therefore, we have to specify these demand and supply conditions. We will elaborate on various details in this chapter and the next. First, however, we give an overview of the most important results of the neoclassical model.

Each serious student of international economics must be familiar with the four main results of neoclassical trade theory, namely:

- The *factor price equalization* proposition (Samuelson, 1948, 1949). This result argues that international free trade of final goods between two nations leads to an equalization of the rewards of the factors of production in the two nations.

- The *Stolper–Samuelson* proposition (Stolper and Samuelson, 1941). This result argues that an increase in the price of a final good increases the reward to the factor of production used intensively in the production of that good.

- The *Rybczynski* proposition (Rybczynski, 1955); see Section 6.2. This result argues that an increase in the supply of a factor of production results in an increase in the output of the final good that uses this factor of production relatively intensively.

- The *Heckscher–Ohlin* proposition (Ohlin, 1933); see Section 6.4. This result argues that a country will export the good which intensively uses the relatively abundant factor of production.

The precise formulation of these results and the conditions under which they can be derived will be analysed next. It is important to keep the final conclusion (the Heckscher–Ohlin proposition) clearly in mind: the neoclassical view that the driving forces behind international trade flows are based on differences in factor endowments between nations; that is, a country will export those goods and services that intensively use its abundant factors of production. In a sense the other results only pave the way for the Heckscher–Ohlin proposition. Before we continue, we must point out that most technical details and the precise conditions under which the four main results of neoclassical trade theory can be derived were analysed and specified by Paul Samuelson. Instead of the term 'neoclassical trade theory' or 'factor abundance theory' the term 'HOS theory' (short for Heckscher–Ohlin–Samuelson) is also often used.

The first two main results of neoclassical economics, namely (i) factor price equalization and (ii) Stolper–Samuelson, are related to an economy's factor prices. The results will be more precisely stated below, and discussed and derived in more detail in this chapter. The other two main results will be discussed in Chapter 6. We start the discussion with result (i), as result (ii) derives almost immediately from it. The term 'factor price equalization' refers to the idea that trade in final goods between two nations leads to an equalization of the rewards for the factors used to produce these goods. As Bertil Ohlin (1933, Chapter II) put it:[2]

> The most immediate effect of trade between a number of regions under the conditions which have been assumed to exist is that commodity prices are made to tally. . . . Trade has, however, a far-reaching influence also on the prices and the combination and use of the productive factors, in brief, on the whole price system. . . . In both regions . . . the factor which is relatively abundant becomes more in demand and fetches a higher price, whereas the factor that is scantily supplied becomes less in demand and gets a relatively lower reward than before.

Carefully reading the above quote makes it clear that Ohlin did not actually think that the rewards for the factors of production would be equalized between the two regions, just that there is a tendency for the rewards of the factors of production to become more equal between the regions (to understand this the reader must realize that the factor of production relatively abundant in one country is relatively scarce in the other country). The term 'factor price equalization' derives from Paul Samuelson's (1948, 1949) work on the formalization of Ohlin's ideas on the tendency of factor prices between nations to converge as a result of international trade in final goods, which shows that these factor prices will in fact become equal. It is this version of the idea, discussed below, that became one of the cornerstones of the neoclassical economics framework. To be fair to Ohlin, however, in a more general setting, allowing for more final goods, more factors of production, and other complications, factor prices will not become equal as a result of trade in final goods, but there is a tendency for factor rewards to move closer together, just as Ohlin argued. This prompted Paul Samuelson (1971) to write an essay with the title 'Ohlin was right'.

5.4 General structure of the neoclassical model

The general structure of the neoclassical model can be summarized as follows.

- There are two countries, the USA (index A) and the UK (index B); two final goods, manufactures (index M) and food (index F, representing agriculture); and two factors of production, capital (index K) and labour (index L). This is, therefore, a $2 \times 2 \times 2$ model. When appropriate, we will point out if the results to be derived below can be generalized to a setting with more goods, more countries, and more production factors.

- Production in both sectors is characterized by constant returns to scale. The two final goods sectors have different production functions.

- The state of technology is the same in the two countries, such that the production functions for each sector are identical in the two countries. Any trade flows arising in the model therefore do not result from Ricardian-type differences in technology.

- The input factors capital and labour are mobile between the different sectors within a country, but are not mobile between countries.

- All markets are characterized by perfect competition. There are no transport costs for the trade of final goods between nations, nor any other impediments to trade.

- The demand structure in the two countries is the same (identical homothetic preferences).

- Finally, the available amounts of factors of production, capital K and labour L, may differ between the two nations. These differences in factor abundance will give rise to international trade flows.

Because it imposes strong restrictions on the production structure (constant returns to scale) and the market structure (perfect competition) of the economy, the neoclassical model in general does not require strong restrictions on the functional form of the production functions to derive its four basic propositions. This is in contrast with the theories of absolute and comparative advantage discussed in Chapter 4, and with the new trade theories and geographical economic theories to be discussed in later chapters, all of which use simple specific functional forms to get the main points across as clearly as possible. As explained in the Preface, for expository balance and clarity we will use only the simplest (Cobb–Douglas) production function to derive the main results of neoclassical economics. The remainder of this chapter will briefly review the main implications of the production structure of the neoclassical model. Box 5.2 shows that the inclusion of capital in the production function is empirically relevant. Box 5.3 presents the first of several examples in this book of the classification of international merchandise trade flows into categories based on the intensity of their use of different factors of production. Box 5.4 briefly discusses the results obtained in a more general framework.

BOX 5.2 The importance of capital per worker

The neoclassical model discussed in this part of the book argues that countries will export the final goods making intensive use of the relatively abundant factor of production. Since we distinguish between two main types of factors of production, capital and labour, the empirical question arises of the extent to which countries differ in their capital and labour endowments. This question is not so easy to answer because it requires us to aggregate many different varieties of capital and labour into one measure. The construction of a consistent data set that can be compared for a large number of countries is therefore complicated and involves a lot of work. The data used in this box is taken from Feenstra, Inklaar, and Timmer (2015).

Table 5.3 provides information on the capital stock per worker for a selection of countries. It also provides information on the income level per capita and the population size of the country. We already discussed the variation in income per capita levels in Chapter 1; for the countries in the table it ranges from $2,296 for Tanzania to $51,340 for the USA, or 22 times as large. The variation in capital stock per worker is even larger, ranging from $6,098 for Tanzania to $288,607 for the USA, or 47 times as large. In general, countries with low capital per worker, such as Tanzania, India, and the Philippines, have low income per capita, while countries with high capital per worker, such as Australia, Japan, and the USA, have high income per capita.

(continued...)

Table 5.3 Capital per worker: selected countries, 2011

Country	Income per capita	Capital per worker	Population
Tanzania	2,296	6,098	44.9
India	5,244	20,776	1,241.5
Philippines	6,326	34,181	94.9
China	11,525	56,920	1,324.4
Brazil	14,555	63,367	196.7
Russia	23,564	108,830	142.8
UK	36,931	170,365	62.4
Australia	42,834	269,899	22.6
Japan	35,614	280,226	126.5
USA	51,340	288,607	313.1

Notes: income per capita GNI PPP 2011 USD; capital per worker in 2005 USD; population in millions.
Source: Penn World Table 8.1 and World Development Indicators.

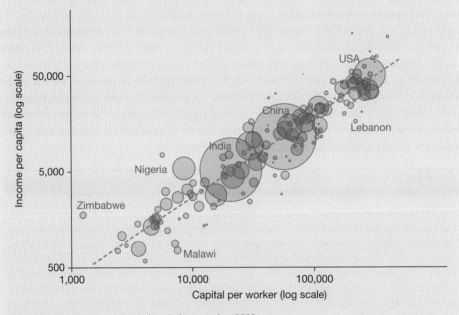

Figure 5.4 Income per capita and capital per worker, 2011.

Notes: 164 countries included; bubbles proportional to population size; dashed line is a regression line.
Source: calculations based on sources mentioned in Table 5.3.

It is not always true, however, that higher capital per worker leads to higher income per capita: Japan, for example, has a lower income per capita than Australia despite higher capital per worker.

Figure 5.4 illustrates the relationship between capital per worker and income per capita for 164 countries using logarithmic scales. It clearly shows the strong (but imperfect) positive association between

(*continued...*)

these two variables. The estimated regression line shown in the figure explains 85.5 per cent of the variance in income per capita and has an estimated slope coefficient of 0.847. This implies that, on average, when the capital stock per worker rises by 10 per cent the income per capita level rises by about 8.5 per cent. Most big countries, such as India, China, and the USA, have observations close to the regression line. Some resource-rich countries, such as Zimbabwe and Nigeria, have higher income per capita levels than expected on the basis of capital stock per worker only. Other countries, such as Malawi and Lebanon, have lower than expected income per capita. In any case, it is safe to conclude that capital per worker is an important determinant of income per capita.

BOX 5.3 Exporters in relative and absolute terms: oil exports

In this chapter we analyse the main properties of the neoclassical production functions by distinguishing between just two factor inputs and two final goods. In reality one can, of course, identify several thousand different factors of production and final goods: for example, many types of capital goods, such as printing presses, desks, and computers, or many types of labour, such as unskilled labour, engineers, and accountants. Empirical research usually tries to find some middle ground in between the two factors of production and two final goods used in the exposition of this book and the thousands one can identify in reality by distinguishing a limited number of each.

On the basis of data from the International Trade Centre (the joint UNCTAD/WTO organization: see http://www.intracen.org) we can classify the international merchandise trade flows into five categories, based on the intensity of the use of factors of production in the production process, namely (i) primary products, (ii) natural-resource-intensive products, (iii) unskilled-labour-intensive products, (iv) technology-intensive products, and (v) human-capital-intensive products.[3]

In this chapter and later ones, we briefly discuss the world's main exporters in relative and absolute terms for some examples at the two-digit level within these five categories (here and in Boxes 5.8, 6.4, 6.7, and 8.5). We start with sector 27, 'mineral fuels, oils, distillation products, etc.', which is an example of natural-resource-intensive exports. Total world exports in this sector, which we will refer to as 'oil' for short, is $3,052 billion, or 16.3 per cent of world total exports. Oil exports are thus a substantial part of total world exports.

The left-hand side of Table 5.4 lists the largest oil exporters in absolute terms. On top of the list is Saudi Arabia with exports of $299 billion, representing 9.8 per cent of all world oil exports. The list is completed

Table 5.4 Sector 27 exports: mineral fuels, oils, distillation products, etc., 2014

Top five in absolute terms			Top five in relative terms		
Country	% of world*	USD bn	Country	% of country	USD bn
S Arabia	9.8	299	Iraq	99.6	85
Russia	9.4	288	Angola	98.4	63
USA	5.2	157	Chad	97.3	3
Un Arab Em	4.5	138	Algeria	97.3	61
Canada	4.2	129	Nigeria	96.7	90
World	16.3	3,052			

Notes: *world flows are per cent of total world exports represented by sector 27; country flows are each country's per cent of sector 27 total world exports.
Source: calculations based on ITC data: www.intracen.org, downloaded 18 June 2015.

(continued...)

by Russia, USA, United Arab Emirates, and Canada, in that order. The right-hand side of Table 5.4 lists the top five oil exporters in relative terms, starting with Iraq ($85 billion, or 99.6 per cent of Iraq's exports), followed by four African countries: Angola, Chad, Algeria, and Nigeria. In relative terms oil exports are important for these countries: their export revenue depends almost completely on oil exports. In fact, this is a characteristic for many countries: no less than 35 countries depend on oil exports for more than half of their total export revenue. Together these 35 countries represent 57 per cent of all oil exports.

Figure 5.5 illustrates the top ten oil exporting nations in absolute terms (panel a.) and relative terms (panel b.). Added to the list in absolute terms are the Netherlands, Qatar, Kuwait, Norway, and Nigeria. An outlier in this setting is the Netherlands, which does not have large oil reserves in its soils. It is, however, a large trader of oil and distillation products, importing raw material from oil-producing countries and re-exporting these and distillation products to final markets. The list in relative terms (panel b.) shows the Balassa index: the indicator of revealed comparative advantage (if the value is above 1) which was discussed in Section 4.9. The Balassa index for Iraq is 6.1 (since oil represents 99.6 per cent of Iraq's exports compared to 16.3 per cent for the world as a whole; 99.6/16.3 = 6.1). In fact, the Balassa index is close to 6 for all ten countries in panel b., which now includes Libya, Yemen, Venezuela, Equatorial Guinea, and Kuwait.

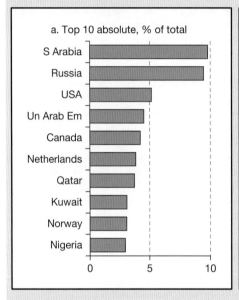
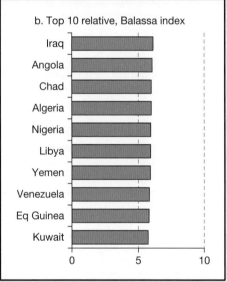

Figure 5.5 Sector 27 exports: mineral fuels, oils, distillation products, etc., 2014.

Notes: Balassa index is country export share of sector / world export share of sector.

Source: calculations based on ITC data, www.intracen.org, downloaded 18 June 2015.

BOX 5.4 More countries, more goods, and more factors

The results discussed in this chapter on factor price equalization and Stolper–Samuelson are derived in a framework with two countries, two goods, and two factors of production. This raises the question, of course, whether these results also hold in a more general setting. Ignoring the rather complex

(continued...)

mathematical details of this more general setting, the answer is 'yes, sort of'. Factor price equalization (FPE), for example, does not hold in a strict sense (and it would also be immediately refuted by empirical evidence). Instead, it is possible to distinguish so-called 'cones of diversification' for which FPE holds, leading to groups of countries with similar factor prices. The Stolper–Samuelson result holds in a weaker sense; that is, a higher price for some final good 'on average' increases the rewards of the factors used intensively in the production of that good. The magnification effect (see Section 5.10.2) holds quite generally; that is, a higher price for some final good increases the relative reward to some factor of production (its 'friend') and reduces the relative reward of some other factor of production (its 'enemy'). Similarly, the Rybczynski result discussed in the next chapter holds in a weaker sense in a more general setting. An increase in the available amount of a factor of production 'on average' increases the production of goods using this factor intensively in the production process.

5.5 Production functions

As indicated in Section 5.4, there are two final goods, manufactures and food, with Cobb–Douglas production functions, different for the two sectors but identical in the two countries for each sector. We let M denote the production level of manufactures, K_m the amount of capital used in the manufacturing sector, and L_m the amount of labour used in the manufacturing sector, and similarly for food. Production is given by:

$$M = \underbrace{K_m^{\alpha_m}}_{\substack{capital\\input}} \underbrace{L_m^{1-\alpha_m}}_{\substack{labour\\input}} \; ; \quad F = \underbrace{K_f^{a_f}}_{\substack{capital\\input}} \underbrace{L_f^{1-a_f}}_{\substack{labour\\input}} \; ; \quad 0 < a_m, a_f < 1 \qquad\qquad 5.1$$

For reasons to be explained further below, the parameter α_m (α_f) is a measure of the capital intensity of the production process for manufactures (respectively food). Clearly, since we have assumed these two parameters to be strictly in between 0 and 1, both capital and labour are indispensable inputs for both final goods sectors; at least some of both inputs are required to produce any output.

An important implication of the neoclassical production function specified in equation 5.1 is the ability to substitute one input for another: that is, to produce the same level of output with different combinations of inputs. For example, if $\alpha_m = 0.5$, the entrepreneur is able to produce 1 unit of manufactures using 1 unit of capital and 1 unit of labour, or using 2 units of capital and 0.5 units of labour, or using 0.5 units of capital and 2 units of labour, etc. In principle, an infinite number of possible combinations are available to produce the same level of output. All possible efficient combinations of capital and labour able to produce a certain level of output is called an *isoquant* (see Box 5.5). This is illustrated for the isoquant $M = 1$ for three possible values of α_m in Figure 5.6. Note that, if very little of an input is used, it becomes harder to substitute this input for another input. The extent to which additional capital is needed to substitute for labour depends on the value of the parameter α_m.

BOX 5.5 Isoquants

If there are two or more inputs needed and/or available to produce a final good, we call the set of all efficient input combinations an *isoquant*: see Figure 5.6. The isoquant can be derived from the production function. Taking equation 5.1 as an example, the same level of output can be produced using many different combinations of capital and labour. Figure 5.6 illustrates this for the isoquant $M = 1$, where the shaded area shows all input combinations producing at least 1 unit of manufactures. The input combination at point A, therefore, enables the entrepreneur to produce 1 unit of manufactures. However, to produce 1 unit of manufactures the entrepreneur could use either less labour at point B than at point A, or less capital at point C than at point A, such that point A is not an efficient input combination to produce 1 unit of manufactures. As such, point A is not part of the $M = 1$ isoquant, in contrast to points B and C, which both are part of the $M = 1$ isoquant.

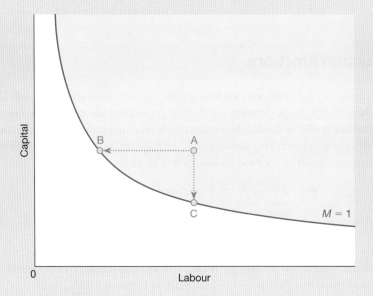

Figure 5.6 An isoquant.

5.6 Cost minimization

The objective function for the entrepreneurs inhabiting our economic models is quite simply profit maximization. Although some objections can be raised against this objective function, one of the strongest arguments in its favour is the fact that entrepreneurs not striving towards profit maximization tend to be driven out of business by those who do. This certainly holds in perfectly competitive economies characterized by constant returns to scale, as analysed here, where the best a firm can do is to ensure that it does not make a loss (a nicer term is 'excess profits are zero'). The entrepreneur can actually break down its production decision into two steps. First, for any arbitrary level of production determine how this output level is achieved at minimum cost. Second, taking the outcome of the first step into consideration, determine the optimum output level. This second step is discussed in Box 4.2. It is therefore time to analyse in somewhat more detail the first step, that of cost minimization. In this section we restrict attention to analysing the problem of producing 1 unit of output at minimum cost. Section 5.8 will discuss this problem for arbitrary levels of output.

The problem facing an entrepreneur in the manufacturing sector trying to minimize the costs for producing 1 unit of output is illustrated in Figure 5.7. Recall that the production function is given in equation 5.1, which implies that the entrepreneur can choose between two different inputs: capital K_m and labour L_m. Many different combinations of capital and labour are available to produce 1 unit of manufactures. This is illustrated by the isoquant $M = 1$ in Figure 5.7. There are three points (A, B, and C) explicitly stated in the figure. All three points can produce 1 unit of output. Point A, however, is not part of the isoquant $M = 1$, since the same level of output can be produced using either less labour or less capital (or a little less of both inputs) than the amount used at point A, which is therefore not an efficient input combination to produce 1 unit of output.[4]

Since the entrepreneur can choose between two different inputs, we first have to determine the level of costs associated with a certain input combination before we can determine how to minimize the level of these costs. In this respect the assumption of perfect competition, which also applies to the input markets, is most convenient. The entrepreneur simply takes the price level of labour, the wage rate w determined on the labour market, and the price level of capital, the rental rate r determined on the capital market, as given.

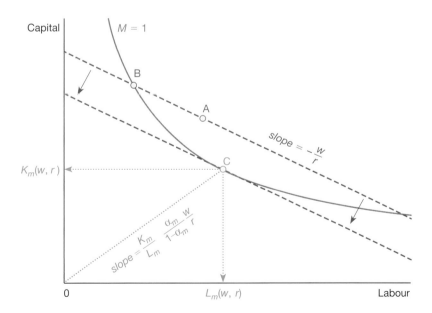

Figure 5.7 Unit cost minimization.

If the firm therefore hires L_m labour and K_m capital, total costs associated with this input combination are

$$costs = \underbrace{wL_m}_{\substack{labour \\ cost}} + \underbrace{rK_m}_{\substack{capital \\ cost}} \qquad\qquad 5.2$$

Obviously, different input combinations of capital and labour can give rise to the same cost level. From equation 5.2 it is clear that such isocost combinations are straight lines in labour–capital space, with a slope equal to $-w/r$. This is illustrated for two isocost lines in Figure 5.7, with points A and B part of the same isocost line. Graphically, the cost minimization problem facing the entrepreneur is quite simple: move the dashed isocost line down to the southwest (in the direction of the arrows) as far as possible, with the restriction that at least one of the input combinations on the isocost line is able to produce 1 unit of manufactures (part of the $M = 1$ isoquant). The solution to this procedure applied to Figure 5.7 gives point C as the optimal input combination, using $K_m(w, r)$ units of capital and $L_m(w, r)$ units of labour. This notation makes explicit the fact that the optimal input combination depends on the wage rate w and the rental rate r. Figure 5.7 also illustrates the optimal relative input combination K_m/L_m. This plays an important role in the next chapter. Technical Note 5.1 explicitly calculates the solutions $K_m(w, r)$ and $L_m(w, r)$ for the cost minimization problem, which gives the following optimal *relative* input combination (the capital–labour ratio) for manufactures and food:

$$\frac{K_m}{L_m} = \frac{\alpha_m}{1-\alpha_m}\frac{w}{r} \; ; \quad \frac{K_f}{L_f} = \frac{\alpha_f}{1-\alpha_f}\frac{w}{r} \qquad\qquad 5.3$$

It is important to note that the optimal capital–labour ratio depends on two factors:

- capital–labour ratio is higher if the capital intensity parameter α rises (see Box 5.6);
- capital–labour ratio is higher if the wage–rental ratio w/r rises (see Section 5.7).

For ease of exposition, and without loss of generality, we henceforth impose the following assumption:

> *Assumption: the production of manufactures is relatively more capital-intensive than the production of food for all w/r ratios, that is $\alpha_m > \alpha_f$.*

BOX 5.6 Capital intensity parameter and the cost share of capital

A simple and useful mnemonic for the capital intensity parameter α_m in the production function of equation 5.1 is the fact that it represents the share of total costs paid for the use of capital in the production process. This can be readily seen from equation 5.3, rewritten as $\frac{1-\alpha_m}{\alpha_m}rK_m = wL_m$. Using this in the definition of total costs gives

$$rK_m + wL_m = rK_m + \frac{1-\alpha_m}{\alpha_m}rK_m = \frac{rK_m}{\alpha_m} \Rightarrow \frac{\overbrace{rK_m}^{cost\ of\ capital}}{\underbrace{rK_m + wL_m}_{total\ cost}} = \alpha_m$$

Similarly, the total wage bill represents a share $1-\alpha_m$ of total costs. We will return to this when discussing the demand side of the neoclassical model in Chapter 6.

5.7 Impact of wage rate and rental rate

As argued above, and derived in Technical Note 5.1, the optimal input of labour and capital depends on the wage–rental ratio. Three issues are important. First, the cost-minimizing input combination depends only on the wage–rental *ratio*, not on their absolute levels. This is intuitively obvious, as an equiproportional change in the wage rate and the rental rate does not change the *slope* of the isocost lines in Figure 5.7, and therefore does not affect the cost-minimizing input combination. An equiproportional change in input prices does, however, change the cost level, as derived in Technical Note 5.2. Second, an increase in the price of an input reduces the demand for that input; that is, an increase in the wage rate reduces the demand for labour, while an increase in the rental rate reduces the demand for capital. Third, and linked to the previous two observations, if the price of an input factor rises there is a substitution away from the more expensive input towards the other input. Thus, if the wage rate rises, the demand for capital rises, and if the rental rate rises, the demand for labour rises.

These observations are explained in Figure 5.8, analysing the impact of a lower wage rate on the cost-minimizing input combination. Initially, the wage rate and rental rate are identical to those analysed in Figure 5.7, thus leading to the cost-minimizing input combination at point C. Now suppose that the wage rate falls from w_0 to w_1. As a result, the isocost line rotates counter-clockwise around point D. Consequently, production costs are no longer minimized at point C but, repeating the procedure described in Section 5.6, at point E, using $K_m(w_1, r) < K_m(w_0, r)$ units of capital and $L_m(w_1, r) > L_m(w_0, r)$ units of labour. Thus, there has been a substitution away from the now relatively more expensive capital towards the cheaper labour. This substitution effect is summarized in the lower capital–labour ratio at point E compared to point C. The actual cost level achieved for all possible combinations of wage rates and rental rates is derived in Technical Note 5.2.

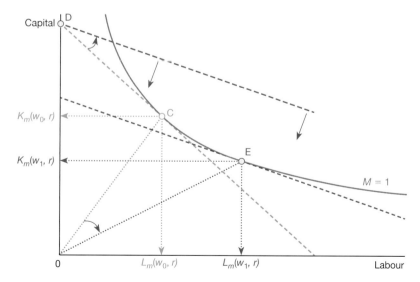

Figure 5.8 Impact of lower wage on cost-minimizing inputs.

5.8 Constant returns to scale

As mentioned in Section 5.5, the production processes are characterized by constant returns to scale; that is, if we increase the use of both factors of production by the same multiplicative factor κ, the output produced also increases by that factor κ:

$$\underbrace{(\kappa K_m)^{\alpha_m}}_{\substack{increase \\ capital}} \underbrace{(\kappa L_m)^{1-\alpha_m}}_{\substack{increase \\ labour}} = \kappa^{\alpha_m+1-\alpha_m} K_m^{\alpha_m} L_m^{1-\alpha_m} = \underbrace{\kappa}_{\substack{increase \\ production}} (K_m^{\alpha_m} L_m^{1-\alpha_m}) \qquad 5.4$$

Clearly, this results from the fact that we imposed the powers of the two inputs, capital and labour, to sum to unity in the production function $(\alpha_m + 1 - \alpha_m = 1)$.[5] The two main reasons for imposing constant returns to scale are ease of exposition (see Box 4.2 on the combination of perfect competition and constant returns to scale) and a replication argument; if the current mix of inputs produces four units of output, one should be able to double the output to eight units simply by replicating the current production process (thus doubling the use of all inputs). Imposing constant returns to scale in the production process gives us two important simplifications, namely (i) for the structure of the isoquants and (ii) for the cost minimization process.

5.8.1 Structure of the isoquants

For any constant returns to scale production process it suffices to derive only one isoquant. Quite literally, one can say 'if you have seen one isoquant you have seen them all'. This is illustrated in Figure 5.9 for $\alpha_m = 0.5$ and three isoquants. First, take an arbitrary point, such as point A, on the isoquant $M = 1$. By the constant returns to scale property of the production process we know that if we double the use of both inputs we double the output of the production process. Graphically, if we draw a straight line from the origin through point A, we can double the use of both inputs by measuring the distance from the origin to point A and adding this distance from point A along the line earlier drawn through the origin and

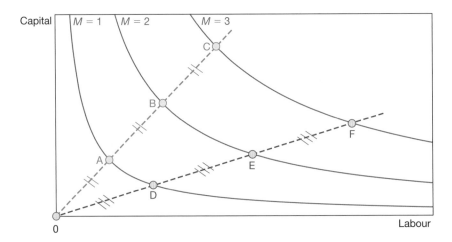

Figure 5.9 Constant returns to scale and isoquants, $\alpha_m = 0.5$.

point A. We thus arrive at point B. Since doubling the use of inputs doubles the output produced, point B must be part of the $M = 2$ isoquant. Similarly, by tripling the use of inputs from point A we arrive at point C, which must be part of the $M = 3$ isoquant. We can repeat this procedure for another point on the $M = 1$ isoquant, such as point D. Doubling the inputs leads to point E, which must be part of the $M = 2$ isoquant, and tripling the inputs leads to point F, which must be part of the $M = 3$ isoquant. Repeating this procedure for all other points on the $M = 1$ isoquant shows that all isoquants are radial blow-ups of the $M = 1$ isoquant. Thus, once we have drawn one isoquant, we have in principle drawn them all after rescaling the inputs.

5.8.2 Cost minimization

Imposing constant returns to scale in the production process considerably simplifies the cost minimization problem. In Technical Note 5.1 we solve the cost minimization problem for producing 1 unit of manufactures. Due to constant returns to scale, this suffices to determine the cost minimization problem for all levels of output. As argued above, all isoquants are radial blow-ups of one another. This implies in particular that the slope of an isoquant is the same for any ray through the origin. This is illustrated in Figure 5.10 and shown in Technical Note 5.3. Clearly, point A in Figure 5.10 minimizes the cost of producing 1 unit of manufactures for the wage–rental ratio drawn in the figure (equal to 1 in the example). Since a doubling of inputs (from point A to point B) doubles the output to 2 units of manufactures and the slope of the isoquant at point B is equal to the slope of the isoquant at point A, point B minimizes the cost of producing 2 units of manufactures. Similarly, point C minimizes the cost of producing three units of manufactures, etc. At the wage–rental ratio drawn in Figure 5.10, the cost-minimizing input combination is a radial blow-up from the origin through point A. An increase or decrease of the scale of production therefore takes place along the expansion path drawn in the figure. Thus, once we have solved the cost minimization problem for producing 1 unit of manufactures, we have automatically solved this problem for all other output levels.

5.9 Factor price equalization

Using the neoclassical production structure with two countries, two final goods, and two factors of production, Samuelson's (1948, 1949) result can most usefully be stated as follows.

Proposition 5.1 Factor price equalization (FPE)

In a neoclassical framework with two final goods and two factors of production, there is a one-to-one correspondence between the prices of the final goods and the prices of the factors of production, provided both goods are produced. This implies:
  if the factor rewards (w, r) are known the prices of the final goods (p_m, p_f) can be derived, and
  if the prices of the final goods (p_m, p_f) are known, the factor rewards (w, r) can be derived.

Reading the statement of the proposition above, the reader may justifiably wonder why it is called the factor price equalization (FPE) proposition, since there is no mention of any

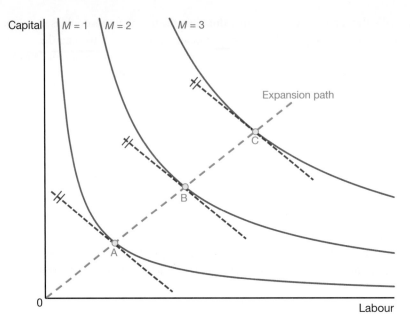

Figure 5.10 Constant returns to scale and cost minimization, $\alpha_m = 0.5$; $w = r = 1$.

equalization, or even of countries involved in such an equalization process. The reason is that a simple application of the above proposition leads to the following:

Corollary 5.1

> In a neoclassical framework with two countries, two final goods, and two factors of production, international trade of the final goods, which equalizes the prices of these goods in the two nations, also leads to an equalization of the rewards of the factors of production in the two nations, provided both final goods are produced in both nations and the state of technology in the two nations is the same.

The statement of the corollary makes two provisions, namely (i) both final goods must be produced in both nations, and (ii) the state of technology in the two nations must be the same. Provision (i) is also used in the FPE proposition. Clearly, if we want to apply that proposition, we also have to use the provision in the application. Why both goods must be produced in both countries will become clear in the discussion of the proposition in the sections below. Provision (ii), on the equality of the state of technology, is new because we now have the production functions in two countries to take into consideration. The reasoning in the corollary is quite simple. If international trade between the USA and the UK leads the prices of the final goods to be the same (recall that there are no transport costs or other impediments to trade), that is $p_{mA} = p_{mB}$ and $p_{fA} = p_{fB}$, then applying the FPE proposition leads us to conclude that the factor rewards, the wage rate and the rental rate, must also be equalized for the two countries; that is, $w_A = w_B$ and $r_A = r_B$, if both countries produce both

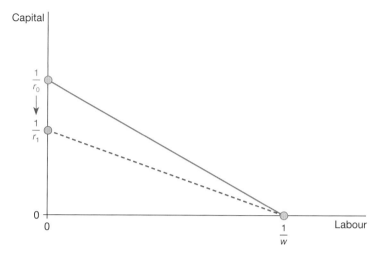

Figure 5.11 Unit value isocost line: effect of an increase in the rental rate.

goods and the state of technology is the same (otherwise the same set of final goods prices could lead to a different set of factor prices). Note, finally, that factor price equalization does not hold in the Ricardian model because technologies differ between countries.

5.9.1 The Lerner diagram

The FPE proposition makes two separate statements. It says that if the factor rewards (w, r) are known, the prices of the final goods (p_m, p_f) can be derived. It also says that if the prices of the final goods (p_m, p_f) are known, the factor rewards (w, r) can be derived. These two issues will be addressed in Sections 5.9.2 and 5.9.3. The tool of analysis used to derive this uses the unit value isocost line and the unit value isoquant, together forming the Lerner diagram. The unit value isocost line depicts all input combinations (L, K) giving rise to a cost level of 1 unit of measurement, taking the input prices (w, r) as given. This is illustrated in Figure 5.11. If you like big numbers, the unit of measurement could be \$1 million or \$1 billion, but this is simply a scale effect, so the same results are derived if the unit of measurement is \$1. The unit value isoquant for a final good, say manufactures, is a regular isoquant; that is, it depicts all efficient input combinations (L_m, K_m) giving rise to a certain production level of manufactures, with the provision that the value of this production level is 1 unit of measurement, taking the final goods price p_m as given: see Figure 5.12. Note that each final good gives rise to its own unit value isoquant, depending on the production function and its own price level. Combining these tools gives you Figure 5.13, which is known as the Lerner diagram, named after Abba Lerner (1952).

Figure 5.11 depicts two unit value isocost lines, namely for the factor prices (w, r_0) and for the factor prices (w, r_1). Note that by definition the isocost line is given by

$$rK + wL = 1 \qquad\qquad 5.5$$

From equation 5.5 the intercepts of the unit value isocost line are easily calculated as $1/w$ for the labour axis and $1/r$ for the capital axis. Figure 5.11 depicts a situation in which the rental rate of capital rises from r_0 to r_1, causing a counter-clockwise rotation of the unit value isocost line around the point $(1/w, 0)$.

Figure 5.12 depicts the unit value isoquant for food if the price is p_f and two unit value isoquants for manufactures, namely if the price is p_{m0} and p_{m1}. Note that by definition the unit value isoquant for manufactures and food is determined by

$$p_m M = 1; \quad p_f F = 1 \qquad\qquad 5.6$$

Thus, if you know the price p_m of the final good it is easy to determine the number of goods (and thus the isoquant) you have to produce, namely $1/p_m$, to ensure that this production level represents 1 unit of value (since $p_m \dfrac{1}{p_m} = 1$). Clearly, if the price level of the final good rises, fewer goods are needed to produce 1 unit of value. Thus a price rise results in an inward shift of the unit value isoquant, as illustrated for manufactures in Figure 5.12.

A final remark on Figure 5.12, depicting three different isoquants, may be useful. As drawn, the isoquants intersect at two locations, point A and point B. The reader will recall from the microeconomics class that two isoquants cannot intersect, since the same input combination cannot give rise to two different output levels if both combinations make efficient use of the resources. None the less, the isoquants in Figure 5.12 do intersect. Is there an error in the figure? No, there is not. Note that at the two points of intersection A and B an isoquant for manufactures intersects with an isoquant for food. Since these are two different goods, there is no contradiction. The points A and B have no special interpretation, other than that apparently the same input combination produces the same value of output, namely 1, for both goods.

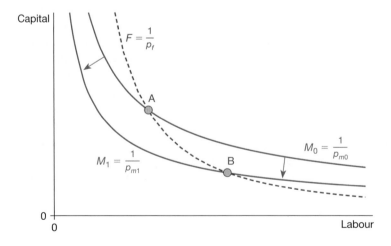

Figure 5.12 Unit value isoquants: effect of an increase in the price of manufactures.

5.9.2 From factor prices to final goods prices

Now that we have briefly discussed the unit value isocost line and the unit value iso-quants, we are in a position to derive the FPE proposition once we realize the connections between these tools in a perfectly competitive economy. As already discussed in Box 4.2, if a good is produced under perfect competition the price of the good is equal to the cost of production. In other words, there are no (excess) profits, such that if an entrepreneur can generate revenue of 1 unit of measurement, this entrepreneur also incurs a cost of 1 unit of measurement. The FPE proposition makes only one provision, namely that both goods must be produced. Thus for both final goods, 1 unit of revenue must be equal to 1 unit of costs.

The connections between costs and revenue are illustrated in Figure 5.13. If the price of manufactures is p_m and the wage-rental ratio is w/r, the entrepreneur minimizes produc-tion costs for the unit value isoquant of manufactures at point A. To be an equilibrium production point, the costs must be equal to the revenue, such that the unit value isocost line must be tangent at point A. Similar reasoning holds for the food sector at point B. Note also that the relative capital intensity is higher in the manufactures sector than in the food sector, that is $\dfrac{K_m}{L_m} > \dfrac{K_f}{L_f}$ because $\alpha_m > \alpha_f$.

With these preliminaries, it is relatively easy to show the first part of the FPE proposi-tion: that is, if the factor rewards (w, r) are known then the prices of the final goods (p_m, p_f) can be derived. Once the factor prices are known, the unit value isocost line is known and we only have to determine which isoquant for either good is tangent to this unit value isocost line:

$$(w, r) \Rightarrow isocost\ line \Rightarrow unit\ value\ isoquant \Rightarrow (p_m, p_f)$$

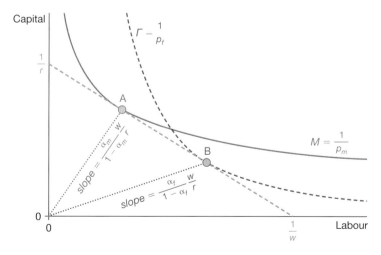

Figure 5.13 The Lerner diagram.

The calculations are performed in Technical Note 5.2: if the market is characterized by perfect competition and production by constant returns to scale, then *if* a good is produced in equilibrium the price of the good is equal to the unit costs of production:

$$p_m = \underbrace{\gamma_m}_{constant}\, r^{\alpha_m} w^{1-\alpha_m}; \quad p_f = \underbrace{\gamma_f}_{constant}\, r^{\alpha_f} w^{1-\alpha_f} \qquad 5.7$$

The constants γ_m and γ_f are defined in Technical Note 5.2. The relationship between the final goods prices and the input prices given in equation 5.7 shows that the price of food rises more quickly than the price of manufactures if the wage rate increases because $\alpha_m > \alpha_f$.

5.9.3 From final goods prices to factor prices

Showing the second part of the FPE proposition—that is, if the prices of the final goods (p_m, p_f) are known then the factor rewards (w, r) can be derived—is a little bit more complicated. Conceptually, we can reverse the logic of Section 5.9.2. First, the two unit value isoquants for manufactures and food can be determined from the identities $P_m M = 1$ and $P_f F = 1$. Second, the unit value cost line can then be determined by deriving the line tangent to both unit value isoquants:

$$(p_m, p_f) \Rightarrow unit\ value\ isoquant \Rightarrow isocost\ line \Rightarrow (w, r)$$

However, in this case it is easier to invert equation 5.7 above to get

$$w = \underbrace{\gamma_w}_{constant} (p_f^{\alpha_m} p_m^{-\alpha_f})^{1/(\alpha_m - \alpha_f)} ; \quad r = \underbrace{\gamma_r}_{constant} (p_m^{1-\alpha_f} p_f^{-(1-\alpha_m)})^{1/(\alpha_m - \alpha_f)} \qquad 5.8$$

See Technical Note 5.4 for a derivation of these equations and the definition of the parameter constants γ_w and γ_r. The structure of the equations is similar to those of the production functions and the unit cost functions. Note, however, that this time the difference in the capital intensity parameters $\alpha_m - \alpha_f$ plays a crucial role in determining the sign of the powers in the equation. Since we assumed that the production of manufactures is relatively more capital-intensive than the production of food, such that $\alpha_m - \alpha_f > 0$, equation 5.8 gives us a first indication that this assumption is important for the results that are to be derived and discussed below.

5.10 Stolper–Samuelson

Now that we have developed the economic tools to analyse factor price equalization, it is easy to derive the Stolper–Samuelson proposition, which relates the impact of a change in final goods prices to the rewards of the factors of production and the factor intensity of the production processes (see Box 5.7 for an alternative derivation). In retrospect the basic reasoning is quite simple and widely applicable. However, when summarizing the impact of international trade for goods and factor prices, production levels, and international trade flows, Bertil Ohlin (1933, Chapter II) argued:[6]

> goods containing a large proportion of scantily supplied and scarce factors are imported, the latter hence becoming less scarce . . . . The price even of the factors which are made relatively less scarce may well rise in terms of commodities, for the total volume of goods increases, owing to the more efficient use of the productive facilities made possible through trade, and the average price of productive factors consequently rises in all regions.

As we will see below, the conclusion Ohlin draws here, that the average price of productive factors rises in all regions, is wrong. At least, it is wrong if this statement is interpreted as an indication that both the wage rate and the rental rate will rise against a 'suitable' combination of the prices of manufactures and food. The precise consequences were analytically derived for the first time by Wolfgang Stolper and Paul Samuelson (1941). Ohlin's remark above may be salvaged, as we will see in Chapter 6, if the statement is interpreted as an

---

BOX 5.7 An alternative (dual) approach

The Stolper-Samuelson result can also be derived using the dual approach (see Technical Note 5.2), based on the fact that if food is produced in equilibrium the unit costs of production must be equal to its price, and similarly for manufactures.

Based on equation 5.7 we can draw isocost *curves* in (r, w)-space, that is combinations of rental rate and wage rate giving rise to the same costs for the production of one good. This is done in Figure 5.14 for both food and manufactures. Initially, the price of both goods is 1, leading to equilibrium at point E_0, the only combination of rental rate and wage rate at which both goods can be produced. Since the production of manufactures is relatively capital-intensive ($\alpha_m > \alpha_f$) the isocost curve for the manufactures sector cuts that of the food sector from above in E_0.[7] Now suppose that the price of manufactures rises from 1 to 1.25. This shifts the combinations at which price is equal to unit costs *up* in Figure 5.14. The equilibrium moves to E_1, such that the rental rate rises and the wage rate falls, in accordance with the Stolper-Samuelson result.

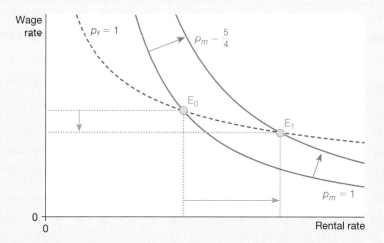

Figure 5.14 Stolper–Samuelson in the dual approach, $\alpha_m = 0.6$; $\alpha_f = 0.3$.

indication that the 'average' price of the wage rate and rental rate combined rises relative to the 'average' price of manufactures and food combined.[8] The formal link between the prices of final goods, the rewards to factors of production, and the relative intensity of the production process can be stated as follows.

Proposition 5.2 Stolper–Samuelson

> In a neoclassical framework with two final goods and two factors of production, an increase in the price of a final good increases the reward to the factor of production used intensively in the production of that good and reduces the reward to the other factor, provided both goods are produced.

Using the assumption that the relative capital intensity for manufactures is higher than for food, the proposition thus leads to the following conclusions:

- If the price of manufactures rises, the rental rate will rise (because the production of manufactures is relatively capital-intensive), and the wage rate will fall.
- If the price of food rises, the wage rate will rise (because the production of food is relatively labour-intensive), and the rental rate will fall.

These conclusions show that the first interpretation of the Bertil Ohlin quote above must be wrong. Suppose, for the sake of argument, that the price of manufactures rises as a result of international trade. Then the wage rate will fall. If we realize that the price of food has not changed, it is clear that the wage rate has fallen relative to the price of both final goods. The reward to labour has therefore unambiguously fallen; that is, a labourer can now buy less of both goods than before the change in the price of manufactures. Similarly, from the conclusions we know that the rental rate of capital has risen, such that capital owners can now buy more units of food (the price of which has not changed). Moreover, as we will see in Section 5.10.2, the rental rate of capital has also risen relative to manufactures, such that capital owners can also buy more units of manufactures. The reward to capital has therefore unambiguously risen relative to both final goods. These distribution aspects of the neoclassical production structure are interesting and receive considerable attention in applications. Whether or not the gains to the capital owners outweigh the losses to the labourers in our hypothetical example will be discussed in Chapter 6.

5.10.1 Graphical analysis

We analyse the impact of an increase in the price of manufactures for the factor rewards w and r using the Lerner diagram. We can do this because the Stolper–Samuelson proposition states that both final goods are produced, such that the price of both goods must be equal to the cost of production. Initially, the price of manufactures is equal to p_{m0}. As we know from the FPE proposition, the price p_{m0} for manufactures together with the price p_f for food, which does not change, determines the wage rate w_0 and the rental rate r_0 through the points of tangency at A and B in Figure 5.15.

If the price of manufactures rises from p_{m0} to p_{m1}, the unit value isoquant for manufactures shifts inward, as indicated by the straight arrows, because fewer goods are needed to generate 1 unit of value as a result of the price rise. Using the FPE proposition again, we

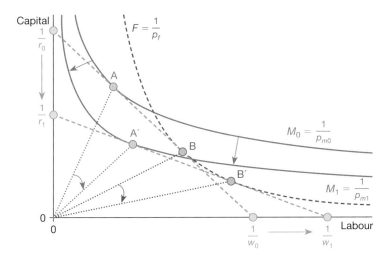

Figure 5.15 Analysis of an increase in the price of manufactures.

can derive the new wage rate w_1 and rental rate r_1 through the points of tangency at A′ for the new unit value isoquant of manufactures and B′ for the old unit value isoquant of food. It is clear from Figure 5.15 that the rental rate of capital r has increased (because $1/r$ has decreased) and the wage rate has fallen (because $1/w$ has risen).

Figure 5.15 is drawn in accordance with the assumption that the production of manufactures is relatively capital-intensive; the slope of the line $0A$, which is equal to the capital–labour ratio of manufactures, is steeper than the slope of the line $0B$, which is equal to the capital–labour ratio of food. Similarly, after the price change $0A′$ is steeper than $0B′$. Note that the capital–labour intensity falls for the production of both final goods, as indicated by the curved arrows; there is a substitution away from the more expensive capital towards the cheaper labour in both sectors of production. We can conclude that, as a result of the increase in the price of the relatively capital-intensive manufactures, the rental rate of capital rises and the wage rate falls, in accordance with the Stolper–Samuelson proposition. We get similar conclusions in accordance with this proposition, as the reader may verify, for all other possible combinations (for example by changing the price of food).

5.10.2 The magnification effect

The Stolper–Samuelson proposition says that if, for example, the price of manufactures rises, then the reward to the factor of production used relatively intensively in the production of manufactures, in our case capital, rises, and the reward to the other factor falls. Both the price of manufactures and the rental rate of capital rise, but there is no indication which rises faster. This issue is addressed by Ronald Jones (1965), who shows that the price of the factor of production rises more in relative terms than the price of the final good; that is, the rental rate rises faster than the price of manufactures. This can be seen in Figure 5.15 once we realize that the extent of the inward shift of the unit value isoquant is proportional to the price change of manufactures. The fact that the new unit value isoquant for manufactures cuts the line 0A strictly above the line from $1/r_1$ to $1/w_0$ indicates that the relative change of the rental rate is larger than the relative change of the price of manufactures. Analytically, this can be verified by totally differentiating equation 5.8, see Technical Note 5.5.

Jones magnification effect. In a neoclassical framework with two final goods, M and F, and two factors of production, K and L, with factor rewards r and w, respectively, changes in the final goods prices are magnified in the factor rewards. If we denote relative changes by ~ and assume that the production of manufactures is relatively capital-intensive, the following relationships hold:

(i) If $\tilde{p}_m > \tilde{p}_f$ then $\tilde{r} > \tilde{p}_m > \tilde{p}_f > \tilde{w}$.

(ii) If $\tilde{p}_m < \tilde{p}_f$ then $\tilde{r} < \tilde{p}_m < \tilde{p}_f < \tilde{w}$.

It is sometimes said that manufactures is a 'friend' of capital and an 'enemy' of labour, because a price increase for manufactures results in a higher factor price rise for capital and a relative factor price fall for labour. Similarly, food is a 'friend' of labour and an 'enemy' of capital. Textiles are a prime example of a labour-intensively-produced good, and are thus a 'friend' of labour: see Box 5.8.

BOX 5.8 Textile exports

As an example of an unskilled-labour-intensive product we discuss the main exporters of sector 61: 'Articles of apparel, accessories, knit or crochet'. We will refer to this sector as 'textiles' for short, but the reader should be aware that there is another two-digit sector of the Harmonized System which could also fall under this heading, namely sector 62: 'articles of apparel, accessories, not knit or crochet'. Rather than combining the two sectors we just focus on sector 61. Total world exports in this sector are $239 billion, which represents 1.3 per cent of all world exports.[9]

Table 5.5 provides an overview of the largest exporters in absolute and relative terms. On top of the list is China, with exports of $92 billion or 38.5 per cent of all exports in this sector. The gap with number two, Bangladesh (only $14 billion), is substantial. The list is completed by Hong Kong, Turkey, and Vietnam. As a large trader, Hong Kong is an outlier in this group of countries; the other countries are all relatively large and abundant in unskilled labour. Except for size, this also holds for the top countries in relative terms.

Table 5.5 Sector 61 exports: articles of apparel, accessories, knit or crochet, 2014

Top five in absolute terms			Top five in relative terms		
Country	% of world*	USD bn	Country	% of country	USD bn
China	38.5	92	Haiti	66.1	0.7
Bangladesh	6.0	14	Cambodia	49.6	6.0
Hong Kong	4.4	10	Bangladesh	43.2	14.3
Turkey	4.2	10	El Salvador	33.9	1.8
Vietnam	4.0	10	Lesotho	25.0	0.2
World	1.3	239			

Notes: * world flows are per cent of total world exports represented by sector 61; country flows are each country's per cent of sector 61 total world exports.
Source: calculations based on ITC data; www.intracen.org, downloaded 18 June 2015.

(continued...)

Despite exports of only $0.7 billion, Haiti depends on textile exports for more than 66 per cent of its export revenue.[10] Textile exports are also relatively important for Cambodia, Bangladesh, El Salvador, and Lesotho. Again, all these countries are relatively abundant in unskilled labour.

Figure 5.16 illustrates the top ten exporters in absolute and relative terms, where the latter is based on revealed comparative advantage as measured by the Balassa index (indicating revealed comparative advantage if the value is above 1; see Section 4.9). China is clearly by far the world's largest exporter of textiles, although it does not make it to the top in relative terms (in fact, it is number 24 in relative terms, with a Balassa index of 3.1). In absolute terms the list now also includes Germany, Italy, India, Cambodia, and the Netherlands. In relative terms textiles are also important for Sri Lanka, Mauritius, Nicaragua, Jordan, and Pakistan. For all these countries the Balassa index is above 7.5. It is even close to 52 for Haiti, which depends most heavily on textiles for its export revenue.

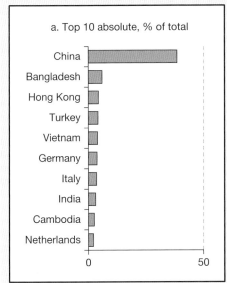 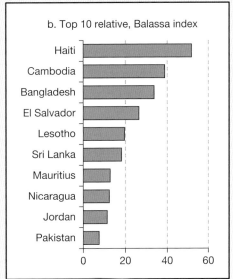

Figure 5.16 Sector 61 exports: articles of apparel, accessories, knit or crochet, 2014.

Notes: Balassa index is country export share of sector / world export share of sector.

Source: calculations based on ITC data, www.intracen.org, downloaded 18 June 2015.

5.11 Conclusions

This chapter briefly reviews the microeconomic foundations and main implications of the neoclassical production structure. There are two factors of production, capital and labour, that can be partially substituted for one another in the production process. As a result of constant returns to scale, the isoquants (depicting efficient combinations of capital and labour for producing a given output level) are radial blow-ups of one another. As a result, the final goods producer equiproportionally adjusts the cost-minimizing inputs of capital and labour to change the output level for a given wage rate and rental rate. The cost-minimizing capital–labour input mix depends on (i) the wage–rental ratio, and (ii) a parameter measuring the capital intensity of the production process. The latter parameter can therefore be used to classify the final goods based on the intensity with which they use capital (relative to labour) in the production process; we will assume that the production of manufactures is more capital-intensive than the production of food.

There is a one-to-one connection between the prices of final goods and the rewards to the factors of production; that is, if we know the price of food and manufactures we can derive the wage rate and the rental rate, and vice versa. If trade between nations equalizes the prices of food and manufactures, it therefore also equalizes the wage rate and the rental rate (factor price equalization). If the production of food is labour-intensive and the price of food rises, this raises the wage rate and reduces the rental rate. The opposite holds if the price of manufactures rises (Stolper–Samuelson). Moreover, the changes in the factor prices are larger in relative terms than the changes in the final goods prices (magnification effect).

 Technical Notes

Technical Note 5.1 Unit cost minimization

The problem for an entrepreneur who wants to minimize the cost of producing 1 unit of manufactures by choosing the input quantities of capital K_m and labour L_m, taking the rental rate of capital r and the wage rate of labour w as given, is specified as

$$\min_{K_m, L_m} w L_m + r K_m \quad \text{s.t.} \quad M = K_m^{\alpha_m} L_m^{1-\alpha_m} \geq 1 \tag{5.A1}$$

To solve this problem we define the Lagrangean Γ, using the Lagrange multiplier λ:

$$\Gamma = w L_m + r K_m + \lambda \left(1 - K_m^{\alpha_m} L_m^{1-\alpha_m}\right) \tag{5.A2}$$

Derive the two first order conditions $\partial \Gamma / \partial K_m = \partial \Gamma / \partial L_m = 0$ for an optimum, and note that

$$w = \left(1 - \alpha_m\right) \lambda K_m^{\alpha_m} L_m^{-\alpha_m} \text{ and } r = \alpha_m \lambda K_m^{-(1-\alpha_m)} L_m^{1-\alpha_m} \tag{5.A3}$$

Taking the ratio of these two conditions and simplifying determines the optimal capital–labour ratio K_m/L_m for the production of manufactures, which depends in a simple way on the wage–rental ratio w/r and the capital-intensity parameter α_m:

$$\frac{K_m}{L_m} = \frac{\alpha_m}{1 - \alpha_m} \frac{w}{r} \tag{5.A4}$$

This relationship between the optimal use of capital and labour can be substituted in the production function to derive the actual amount of capital and number of labourers you need to produce 1 unit of manufactures at minimum cost.

$$M = K_m^{\alpha_m} L_m^{1-\alpha_m} = \left(\frac{\alpha_m}{1 - \alpha_m} \frac{w}{r} L_m\right)^{\alpha_m} L_m^{1-\alpha_m} = 1 \tag{5.A5}$$

Simplifying this, denoting the optimal choice of labourers $L_m(w, r)$ since it depends on the wage rate w and the rental rate r, and repeating the procedure for the optimal choice of capital $K_m(w, r)$, gives

$$L_m(w, r) = \left(\frac{\alpha_m}{1-\alpha_m} \frac{w}{r} \right)^{-\alpha_m} \text{ and } K_m(w, r) = \left(\frac{\alpha_m}{1-\alpha_m} \frac{w}{r} \right)^{1-\alpha_m} \tag{5.A6}$$

The interpretation of these results is discussed in the main text. Replacing the index m with the index f in the above equations gives the demand for labour and capital in the food sector.

Technical Note 5.2 Duality

In Technical Note 5.1 we derived the optimal factor input mix of capital and labour to minimize the costs of producing 1 unit of manufactures. For the entrepreneur it is, of course, important to know how high these minimum costs for producing 1 unit of manufactures really are. We will denote these by $c_m(w, r)$, as they depend on the wage rate w and the rental rate r. They can be derived by substituting the *optimal* (cost-minimizing) factor inputs into the costs $wL_m + rK_m$:

$$c_m(w, r) = wL_m(w, r) + rK_m(w, r) = w\left(\frac{\alpha_m}{1-\alpha_m} \frac{w}{r} \right)^{-\alpha_m} + r\left(\frac{\alpha_m}{1-\alpha_m} \frac{w}{r} \right)^{1-\alpha_m} \tag{5.A7}$$

After some algebraic manipulations, the unit cost function can be simplified to

$$c_m(w, r) = \gamma_m r^{\alpha_m} w^{1-\alpha_m}, \text{ where } \gamma_m \equiv \alpha_m^{-\alpha_m}(1-\alpha_m)^{-(1-\alpha_m)} \tag{5.A8}$$

(The symbol $\equiv$ means 'is defined to be equal to'.) Replacing the index m by the index f gives the unit cost function of food. Note that the structure of the unit cost function is similar to the structure of the production function. Both are Cobb-Douglas functions, with α as the power for capital in the production function and for the *price* of capital in the unit cost function, and $1 - \alpha$ as the power of labour in the production function and for the *price* of labour in the unit cost function. This is no coincidence, but a phenomenon known as duality. Before we discuss this, note that

$$\frac{\partial c_m(w, r)}{\partial w} = \left(\frac{\alpha_m}{1-\alpha_m} \frac{w}{r} \right)^{-\alpha_m} = L_m(w, r); \quad \frac{\partial c_m(w, r)}{\partial r} = \left(\frac{\alpha_m}{1-\alpha_m} \frac{w}{r} \right)^{1-\alpha_m} = K_m(w, r) \tag{5.A9}$$

That is, if we differentiate the unit cost function with respect to the price of labour, the outcome is identical to the unit-cost-minimizing number of labourers; and if we differentiate the unit cost function with respect to the price of capital, the outcome is identical to the unit-cost-minimizing amount of capital. This result is known as *Shephard's lemma*.

We can thus arrive at the cost-minimizing input combinations in two different ways. First, we can specify a production function and explicitly derive the cost-minimizing input combination as we did in Technical Note 5.1. Second, we can use the dual approach: that is, we can specify a unit cost function as in (5.A8) above and simply differentiate with respect to the wage rate and the rental rate to derive the optimal combination of labour and capital.

Taking some technical restrictions into consideration, these two approaches, either specifying a production function or a cost function, are *equivalent*. Depending on the problem to be analysed, one approach may be more convenient than another. In this book we will not use the dual approach; see, however, Dixit and Norman (1980) and Brakman and van Marrewijk (1998) for various applications of the dual approach to international economics.

Technical Note 5.3 Slope of isoquants

By definition, an isoquant depicts all possible efficient input combinations to produce a certain level of output, say $M = \bar{M}$. Totally differentiating the production function shown in equation 5.1 for this level of output gives

$$\alpha_m K_m^{\alpha_m - 1} L_m^{1-\alpha_m} dK_m + (1-\alpha_m) K_m^{\alpha_m} L_m^{-\alpha_m} dL_m = d\bar{M} = 0 \tag{5.A10}$$

from which the slope on any point of the isoquant can be derived easily:

$$\frac{dK_m}{dL_m} = -\frac{1-\alpha_m}{\alpha_m} \frac{K_m}{L_m} \tag{5.A11}$$

Clearly, the slope of an isoquant depends only on the capital–labour *ratio*. Thus, if we change both inputs equiproportionally by the factor κ, the slope of the isoquant remains the same. The implications are discussed in the main text.

Technical Note 5.4 Factor prices as a function of final goods prices

We start by recalling the relationships between costs and prices:

$$p_m = \gamma_m r^{\alpha_m} w^{1-\alpha_m} \text{ and } p_f = \gamma_f r^{\alpha_f} w^{1-\alpha_f} \tag{5.A12}$$

Now write the rental rate r as a function of the final goods price and the wage rate for both equations, using the definition $\gamma_m \equiv \alpha_m^{-\alpha_m}(1-\alpha_m)^{-(1-\alpha_m)}$, and similarly for γ_f:

$$r = \alpha_m (1-\alpha_m)^{\frac{1-\alpha_m}{\alpha_m}} p_m^{\frac{1}{\alpha_m}} w^{-\frac{1-\alpha_m}{\alpha_m}} \text{ and } r = \alpha_f (1-\alpha_f)^{\frac{1-\alpha_f}{\alpha_f}} p_f^{\frac{1}{\alpha_f}} w^{-\frac{1-\alpha_f}{\alpha_f}} \tag{5.A13}$$

Since we have two equations determining the rental rate r, setting them equal to each other allows us to determine the wage rate w as a function of the final goods prices p_m and p_f; see below. A similar procedure gives the rental rate r as a function of the final goods prices.

$$w = \gamma_w p_f^{\frac{\alpha_m}{\alpha_m - \alpha_f}} p_m^{\frac{\alpha_f}{\alpha_m - \alpha_f}}; \quad \gamma_w \equiv \left(\frac{\alpha_m (1-\alpha_m)^{\frac{1-\alpha_m}{\alpha_m}}}{\alpha_f (1-\alpha_f)^{\frac{1-\alpha_f}{\alpha_f}}} \right)^{-\frac{\alpha_m \alpha_f}{\alpha_m - \alpha_f}} \tag{5.A14}$$

$$r = \gamma_r p_m^{\frac{1-\alpha_f}{\alpha_m - \alpha_f}} p_f^{\frac{-(1-\alpha_m)}{\alpha_m - \alpha_f}}; \quad \gamma_r \equiv \left(\frac{(1-\alpha_m)\alpha_m^{\frac{\alpha_m}{1-\alpha_m}}}{(1-\alpha_f)\alpha_f^{\frac{\alpha_f}{1-\alpha_f}}} \right)^{\frac{(1-\alpha_m)(1-\alpha_f)}{\alpha_m - \alpha_f}} \tag{5.A15}$$

Technical Note 5.5 Jones magnification

Quite frequently in economic analysis the relationships between different economic forces is rather complex when stated in levels, but surprisingly simple when stated in relative changes. This fact is, for example, fruitfully used in the Jones (1965) analysis of the neoclassical model in general. Suppose the relationship between the variables z and v is of the type $z = av^\eta$ for some constant a and parameter η. For any variable z, let $\hat{z}$ denote the relative change of z, that is $\hat{z} \equiv dz/z$. Total differentiation of

$z = av^\eta$ gives $dz = \eta av^{\eta-1}dv$. Dividing the left-hand side by z and the right-hand side by av^η (which is the same as z) gives

$$\frac{dz}{z} = \eta \frac{av^{\eta-1}dv}{av^\eta} \quad \text{or} \quad \tilde{z} \equiv \frac{dz}{z} = \eta \frac{dv}{v} \equiv \eta\tilde{v} \tag{5.A16}$$

In relative changes, the relationship $z = av^\eta$ therefore reduces quite simply to $\tilde{z} = \eta\tilde{v}$. Applying this result to equation 5.8 gives

$$\tilde{w} = \frac{\alpha_m}{\alpha_m - \alpha_f}\tilde{p}_f - \frac{\alpha_f}{\alpha_m - \alpha_f}\tilde{p}_m \quad \text{and} \quad \tilde{r} = \frac{1-\alpha_f}{\alpha_m - \alpha_f}\tilde{p}_m - \frac{1-\alpha_m}{\alpha_m - \alpha_f}\tilde{p}_f \tag{5.A17}$$

Now apply these relationships, for example if the price of manufactures rises ($\tilde{p}_m > 0$) and the price of food remains the same ($\tilde{p}_f = 0$):

$$\tilde{r} = \frac{1-\alpha_f}{\alpha_m - \alpha_f}\tilde{p}_m > \tilde{p}_m > 0 > -\frac{\alpha_f}{\alpha_m - \alpha_f}\tilde{p}_m = \tilde{w} \tag{5.A18}$$

Thus the rental rate of capital rises more than the price of manufactures, which uses capital intensively, which rises more than the price of food ($= 0$), which rises more than the wage rate (which actually falls relative to the price of both goods). This result, which holds more generally, is known as the *Jones magnification effect*.

 ## Notes

1 See Allen (1965, p. 173).
2 See Allen (1965, p. 185–6).
3 See the **online resources** for details: www.oup.com/uk/vanmarrewijk_it/.
4 It is part of another isoquant, producing a higher output level of manufactures (not illustrated).
5 If their sum exceeds unity, there are increasing returns to scale; see Part III of this book. If their sum falls short of unity, there are decreasing returns to scale.
6 See Allen (1965, p. 201–2).
7 Using Shephard's lemma, see Technical Note 5.2, it can be also be shown that the slope of the isocost curve is equal to the capital labour ratio.
8 It seems clear to me that this is not what Ohlin meant.
9 Total exports of sector 62 are slightly smaller at $235 billion and also represent 1.3 per cent of world exports. Taken together these two sectors thus represent 2.6 per cent of world trade.
10 It is the only country depending on this sector for more than 50 per cent of its export revenue. This contrasts with the 35 countries depending on oil revenue for more than 50 per cent; see Box 5.3.

 ## Questions

Question 5.1

Suppose there are two goods, buildings and necessities, in a neoclassical world with two factors of production, capital and labour. The production of necessities is relatively labour intensive.

a. *Draw* a (big) *Lerner diagram* which is *consistent* with the provided information.
b. *Explain* how this can be used to show that there is a one-to-one correspondence between factor prices and final goods prices as long as both goods are produced.

Question 5.2

Dwell produces desktop computers using high-skilled labourers (H) and low-skilled labourers (L) with constant returns to scale. To maximize profits, it wants to minimize its cost of production. Computers are relatively intensive in low-skilled labour production and Dwell is a price taker on the labour market. The market for computers is perfectly competitive.

a. Draw a production isoquant for computers and an isocost line. Indicate in your graph the number of high-skilled workers and the number of low-skilled workers involved in the production process.

Dwell forecasts an increase in demand for its newest model and doubles its production.

b. Draw the new situation in your graph of Question 5.2a.

c. What happens to the isocost line and production isoquant? Why? How many new labourers does Dwell hire?

d. What impact does the production change have on Dwell's profitability?

Question 5.3

Dwell computers has just doubled production. It wants to maintain its production level when it is confronted with a wage increase for high skilled-labour.

a. Draw the initial situation in a graph with a production isoquant and an isocost line. Indicate the change in the isocost line after the wage increase.

b. What implications does this have for Dwell's production process of computers? What happens to Dwell's demand for high-skilled labour?

Dwell does some research and development and manages to improve its production process. As a consequence, producing computers after the innovation becomes more low-skilled labour intensive.

c. Show in your graph the effect of this technological innovation. Does this alter the input mix of high- and low-skilled labour?

d. What would be the consequences of this kind of technological development for wages of skilled and non-skilled workers?

 *See the **online resources** for a Study Guide and questions:*
www.oup.com/uk/vanmarrewijk_it/

6 Factor abundance and trade

6.1 Introduction

After the discussion of the relationship between the prices of final goods and the rewards to factors of production in Chapter 5, we now turn to the relationship between the level of production of final goods (food and manufactures), the available production factors (labour and capital), and international trade flows.

The third main result in neoclassical trade theory is named after the Polish economist Rybczynski, who provided the first analysis in 1955 in a production equilibrium (such that all available inputs are employed). The Rybczynski result lies at the heart of the Heckscher–Ohlin proposition, which relates the direction of international trade flows to factor abundance. The tool used to demonstrate the Rybczynski effect is called the Edgeworth box.[1] Named after Francis Edgeworth, it elegantly combines various aspects of efficient production equilibrium in one graphical framework, and as such is a useful tool of analysis also in other areas of economics, such as microeconomics and game theory.

The fourth and last main result of the neoclassical trade model is the Heckscher–Ohlin proposition: countries tend to export goods making intensive use of the abundant factors of production. Although the principle of the result is not difficult to comprehend, a complete understanding does require knowledge of all aspects of the neoclassical trade model: that is, the production structure, the demand structure, and the equilibrium relationships between them. In short, it requires an understanding of the general equilibrium structure of the model. It is the only result that requires an assumption about the demand structure of the economy. As Ohlin (Box 6.1) remarked in his *Interregional and International Trade* (1933, Chapter I):[2]

> Australia has more agricultural land, but less labour, capital, and mines than Great Britain; consequently Australia is better adapted to the production of goods which require great quantities of agricultural land, whereas Great Britain has an advantage in the production of goods requiring considerable quantities of other factors. If both countries produced their own total consumption, agricultural products would be very cheap in Australia, but manufactured articles relatively dear, whereas the reverse would be the case in Great Britain, where owing to the scanty supply of land each acre would have to be intensely cultivated with much labour and capital to provide the necessary amount of food. The utmost economy would have to be exercised with land, and owing to the tendency to diminishing returns the yields of wheat, etc., from the last units of capital and labour would be very small. In Australia, on the other hand, the abundance of land would lead to an extensive method of cultivation, very little labour and capital being expended on each acre; hence the yield from each unit of capital and labour would be great.

BOX 6.1 Bertil Ohlin

Figure 6.1
Bertil Ohlin
(1899–1979).

Bertil Ohlin (Figure 6.1) was a Swedish economist who studied at Lund and Stockholm, worked mostly at the Stockholm School of Economics, and was politically active as a member of parliament for 33 years and as the leader of the Swedish liberal party. He became well known after his dispute with John Maynard Keynes on the transfer problem concerning German reparations payments after World War I. (It was Ohlin, not Keynes, who was right on most issues; see Brakman and van Marrewijk, 1998 and 2007.) His most important work, however, was on the theory of factor abundance, with the publication in 1933 of *Interregional and International Trade*, inspired by the work of his former teacher Eli Heckscher. The book won Ohlin the Nobel Prize in economics in 1977.

Ohlin therefore argues that in autarky, that is if there are no international trade flows, the price of agricultural goods in Australia will be low compared to Great Britain because the production of agricultural goods is relatively land-intensive (compared to the production of manufactured goods) and Australia has an abundant supply of agricultural land. The abundant supply of agricultural land in Australia leads to a low price for the factor services of land, which are a substantial part of the costs of production of agricultural goods, thus leading to low prices for those goods. Moreover, since the price of agricultural goods is lower in Australia than in Great Britain in autarky, Australia will export those goods if international trade is allowed.

The final result, which can be summarized as 'Australia will export those goods which intensively use the relatively abundant factor of production', is simple to comprehend and intuitively appealing. As is clear from the detailed analysis in this and Chapter 5, given the simplicity of the Heckscher–Ohlin proposition it is remarkable how much structure we have to impose on the economy before we can actually conclude that this connection between factor abundance, the capital–labour intensity in the production of final goods,

BOX 6.2 Precious stones exports

We have already discussed an example of natural-resource-intensive trade flows, namely the export of oil (see Box 5.3). This time we take a look at another example from this group, namely the exports of sector 71: 'pearls, precious stones, metals, coins, etc.' We will refer to this sector, which includes diamonds, as 'precious stones' for short. The reason to do so is to be able to distinguish between two types of activities. Total world exports in this sector are $615 billion, which represents 3.3 per cent of total world trade.

Table 6.1 provides an overview of the five largest countries in absolute and relative terms. In absolute terms the list is topped by Hong Kong with $82 billion (13.4 per cent of total exports in this sector), followed by the USA, China, the UK, and India. All these countries are important in the processing stage of precious stones, such as the cutting of diamonds. In relative terms, the list is topped by Botswana, which depends on precious stones trade for more than 85 per cent of its export revenue, followed by French Polynesia, Myanmar, Burkina Faso, and Lesotho. All these countries are hardly involved at all in the processing stages of precious stones. Botswana exports uncut diamonds, French Polynesia is well known for its cultured pearls, Myanmar for its jade and gems, Burkina Faso for its gold, and Lesotho for its diamonds.

Figure 6.2 illustrates the top ten in absolute and relative terms for the trade in precious stones. In absolute terms Belgium, United Arab Emirates, Israel, Canada, and Switzerland are added to the list. With the exception of Canada this is mostly related to the processing stages of precious stones. In relative terms, the British Virgin Islands, Israel (again), Zimbabwe, Namibia, and Guyana are added to the list, with Balassa indices (indicating revealed comparative advantage if above 1, see Section 4.9) above 8 for all countries. With the exception of Israel this is *not* related to the processing stages of precious stones. The discussion in this box thus serves as a good example that trade flows within the same sector can be related to quite different types of activities and stages of development.

Table 6.1 Sector 71 exports: pearls, precious stones, metals, coins, etc., 2014

Top five in absolute terms			Top five in relative terms		
Country	% of world*	USD bn	Country	% of country	USD bn
Hong Kong	13.4	82	Botswana	85.5	6.8
USA	10.5	65	French Polynesia	80.2	0.2
China	10.3	63	Myanmar	52.0	12.4
UK	8.7	54	Burkina Faso	51.4	1.5
India	6.6	41	Lesotho	40.3	0.4
World	3.3	615			

Notes: * world flows are per cent of total world exports represented by sector 71; country flows are each country's per cent of sector 71 total world exports.

Source: calculations based on ITC data: www.intracen.org, downloaded 18 June 2015.

(continued...)

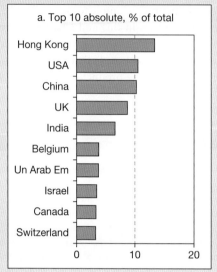

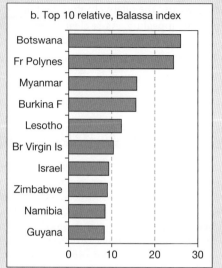

Figure 6.2 Sector 71 exports: pearls, precious stones, metals, coins, etc., 2014.

Notes: Balassa index is country export share of sector / world export share of sector.
Source: calculations based on ITC data, www.intracen.org, downloaded 18 June 2015.

and the direction of international trade flows actually exists. Examples of the connection between factor abundance and trade flows are discussed in Box 6.2 on precious stones and Box 6.3 on electronics exports.

BOX 6.3 Electronics exports

As an example of technology-intensive products we take a closer look at sector 85: 'Electrical, electronic equipment'. We will refer to this sector as 'electronics' for short. Total electronics exports are $2,382 billion, representing 12.8 per cent of all world exports (see Table 6.2). The technology-intensive electronics trade is thus one of the most important sectors in total trade flows, second only to the oil trade (sector 27: see Box 5.3).

With $571 billion, China is the world's largest electronics exporter, representing 24 per cent of all world electronics exports. It is followed by Hong Kong (a trading depot), the USA, Germany, and South Korea. In relative terms Hong Kong tops the list, since electronics exports represent about 46 per cent of Hong Kong's trade flows. It is followed by Taiwan, the Philippines, Malta, and Singapore. With the exception of Malta (with a small electronics trade of only $1 billion), all these countries are either in Southeast Asia or a technological leader (USA and Germany). In fact, there are intricate connections between these countries regarding electronics trade flows. This is discussed in further detail in Section 8.10.

Figure 6.3 illustrates the top ten electronics exporters in absolute and relative terms. In absolute terms Singapore, Taiwan, Japan, Mexico, and the Netherlands are added to the list. In relative terms Vietnam, Malaysia, and Tunisia are newcomers. Most of these countries are either in Southeast Asia or technological leaders (such as the Netherlands).

(continued...)

Table 6.2 Sector 85 exports: electrical, electronic equipment, 2014

Top five in absolute terms			Top five in relative terms		
Country	% of world*	USD bn	Country	% of country	USD bn
China	24.0	571	Hong Kong	45.8	240
Hong Kong	10.1	240	Taiwan	39.3	123
USA	7.2	172	Philippines	37.4	23
Germany	6.2	148	Malta	35.6	1
South Korea	5.8	138	Singapore	30.5	125
World	12.8	2,382			

Notes: * world flows are per cent of total world exports represented by sector 85; country flows are each country's per cent of sector 85 total world exports; # minimum export value must exceed $0.01 billion in order to be included.
Source: calculations based on ITC data: www.intracen.org, downloaded 18 June 2015

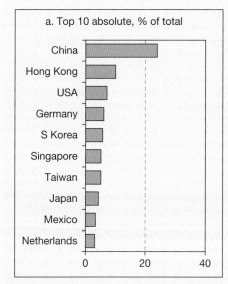

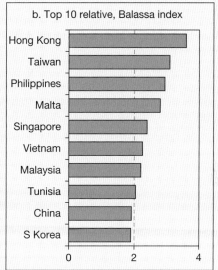

Figure 6.3 Sector 85: electrical, electronic equipment exports, 2014.
Source: calculations based on ITC data, www.intracen.org, downloaded 18 June 2015.

6.2 Rybczynski

The connection between the available factors of production, the output levels of final goods, and the relative intensity of the production processes for a given set of final goods prices with a neoclassical production structure can be stated as follows:

Proposition 6.1 Rybczynski

In a neoclassical framework with two final goods, two factors of production, and constant prices of the final goods, an increase in the supply of one of the factors of production results in an increase of the output of the final good that uses this factor of production relatively intensively and a reduction in the output of the other final good, provided both goods are produced in equilibrium.

Using the assumption made in Chapter 5 that the production of manufactures is relatively capital-intensive, this leads to the following conclusions:

- If the available amount of labour rises, the output of food increases (because its production is labour-intensive) and the output of manufactures falls.
- If the available amount of capital rises, the output of manufactures increases (because its production is capital-intensive) and the output of food falls.

There are at least two points to note with respect to the Rybczynski proposition. First, the statement is made for given values of the final goods prices p_m and p_f. This is important to realize, since in a full general equilibrium framework we would expect an increase in the amount of a factor of production, which leads to output changes, also to affect the (relative) price level of final goods. The Rybczynski proposition can then be used as an indication for the direction of the price changes of final goods. We return to this issue below. Second, the reader of course realizes that, starting from some initial equilibrium with concomitant production levels, an increase in the available amount of a factor of production in principle allows the economy to produce more of both goods, by allocating some of the extra input to one sector and the rest to the other sector. The Rybczynski proposition states, however, that this is not what happens; the output of one final good rises and the output of the other final good falls. We will show below why this is true. The analysis below assumes that capital is fully mobile between different sectors, while Box 6.4 analyses what happens if capital is sector-specific in the short run.

BOX 6.4 Sector-specific capital

A special case of the neoclassical model arises when we allow for sector-specific factors of production. Also adding a time dimension—a rapidly adjusting factor of production and a slowly adjusting factor of production—we can distinguish between the short term, the intermediate term, and the long term. Obviously, adjusting the allocation of factors of production after some exogenous change, say an increase in the price of manufactures, requires time to move capital and labour from one sector to the other. Let's assume that labour is easier to reallocate than capital, which we refer to as sector-specific (in the short run and intermediate run, but not in the long run). We discuss the reallocation of factors of production using Figure 6.4, which depicts the value marginal product of labour (VMPL) for manufactures (bottom left origin) and food (bottom right origin), given the distribution of capital. In equilibrium, a sector's VMPL is equal to the wage rate. The distance between the two origins is equal to the total labour force; the allocation of labour to manufactures is measured from the left-hand origin and the allocation of labour to food from the right-hand origin. In both sectors the VMPL declines as more labour is used.

- Point E_0 depicts the initial equilibrium, in which the wage rate for manufactures w_{m0} is equal to the wage rate in the food sector w_{f0}.

(continued...)

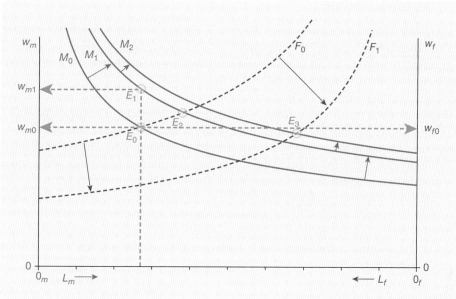

Figure 6.4 Sector-specific capital.

- Points E_0 and E_1 depict the short-term (Ethier) equilibrium, given the allocation of capital and labour to the two sectors, after an increase in the price of manufactures. Nothing changes for the food sector, such that the wage rate remains w_{f0}. The higher price of manufactures shifts the VMPL curve ($p \times MPL$) in that sector up, leading to a higher wage rate w_{m1} for manufactures than for food.

- Point E_2 depicts the medium-term (Neary, 1978) equilibrium. The higher short-term wage rate in the manufacturing sector leads to a reallocation of labour from food (where the wage rate starts to increase) to manufactures (where the wage rate starts to decline) until a new equilibrium (with equal wages) is reached. Obviously, this increases the production of manufactures and reduces the production of food.

- Point E_3 depicts the long-run (neoclassical) equilibrium. At the initial equilibrium point E_0 we implicitly assumed that the rental rate of capital was the same in the two sectors. However, after the price increase for manufactures (raising the value) and the reallocation of labour from food to manufactures (raising the marginal product of capital), the rental rate for manufactures is higher than for food. Over time, this will lead to a reallocation of capital from food to manufactures, leading to an upward shift of VMPL for manufactures and a downward shift of VMPL for food. These changes in turn require a reallocation of labour, which requires a reallocation of capital, etc. The process continues until both the wage rate and the rental rate are the same in the two sectors. Point E_3 depicts the ultimate long-run equilibrium. Note that in the intermediate term (point E_2) the wage rate is higher than at the initial equilibrium, while in the long run (point E_3) we have drawn the wage rate to be lower than at the initial equilibrium. When looking at Figure 6.4 this seems to be an arbitrary decision on our part, depending on the extent of the shifts in the VMPL curves as a result of the reallocation of capital. This is, however, not the case as the long-run equilibrium is determined by the neoclassical model and we know from the Stolper–Samuelson result that an increase in the price of manufactures (which is capital-intensive) raises the reward to capital (rental rate) and reduces the reward to labour (wage rate). For the labourers, the impact of the price change is therefore beneficial in the short run and intermediate run, but detrimental in the long run.

6.2.1 The Edgeworth box

In Chapter 5 we introduced the Lerner diagram to analyse the links between the prices of final goods and the prices of factors of production in an economic equilibrium in which both goods are produced. This time we want to analyse the connections between the available factors of production and the quantity of output produced, for which a different tool is suitable: the Edgeworth box.

Each production function generates a range of different isoquants for manufactures and food, as in Figure 5.9. Obviously, an increase in the available amount of capital or labour leads to an increase in the output of the sector to which it is allocated. The question arises as to how to allocate the available capital and labour over the two final goods sectors, and how to show this problem clearly in one picture. Drawing the isoquants for the two goods from the same origin, as we did in Figure 5.12, is not very useful as it does not help us to allocate the inputs efficiently. The important step in constructing the Edgeworth box (see Box 6.5) is the realization that in an economic equilibrium all available inputs must be used either in one sector or in the other: that is, both the capital market and the labour market must be in equilibrium.

$$K_m + K_f = K; \quad L_m + L_f = L \qquad\qquad 6.1$$

Once we know the total available amount of capital K, it suffices to know the capital input K_m to calculate the remaining use of capital $K_f = K - K_m$. Similarly, once we know how much labour L is available and the amount L_m used for manufactures, we also know how much is available for production of food, namely $L_f = L - L_m$. The Edgeworth box uses this principle by transposing the origin for the isoquants of one of the final goods onto the total amount of capital K and labour L available for production, as explained in Box 6.5.

Figure 6.6 illustrates the Edgeworth box for the Cobb–Douglas production functions of equation 5.1, assuming that $K = L = 5$. The origin for manufactures is in the southwest corner, as usual. The dashed lines in the figure give three different isoquants for manufactures, each having the well-known curvature. The origin for food is located exactly on top of the total available amount of capital and labour (in this case 5), and rotated 180°. The amount of labour used for food is thus measured from right to left, as indicated by the arrow in Figure 6.2, and the amount of capital used for food is measured from top to bottom, as indicated by the other arrow in Figure 6.2. There are also three isoquants for food drawn in the figure. At first sight, their curvature may seem strange and they may appear to be increasing in the wrong direction, but once it is realized that the axes for food are rotated (and the book is turned upside down), it is clear that these isoquants have the normal shape and production increases if more capital and labour is put into the production of food.

6.2.2 The contract curve

The Edgeworth box constructed in Section 6.2.1 depicts all possible distributions of capital and labour for the production of manufactures and food, and their concomitant output levels. We are interested, however, in finding efficient input combinations, that is,

BOX 6.5 Constructing the Edgeworth box

The Edgeworth box is constructed using the field of isoquants for manufactures and food illustrated on the left-hand side of Figure 6.5 (using the isoquants M = 2 and F = 1 as an example). The origin and axes of one of the goods, in this case food, is turned around 180° and placed exactly on the total amount of capital K and labour L available in the economy. The result is illustrated in Figure 6.6 and further discussed in the main text.

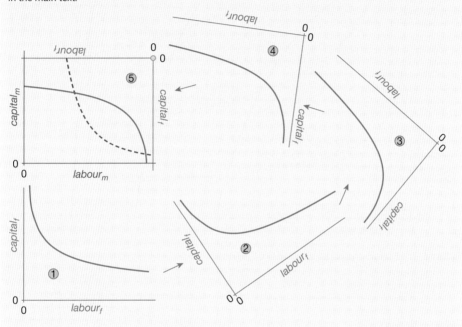

Figure 6.5 Construction of the Edgeworth box.

distributions of the allocation of capital and labour such that it is not possible to produce more of one good without reducing the production level of the other good. This concept is illustrated in Figure 6.7. Point A depicts an input combination of capital and labour that allows the economy to produce two units of manufactures. At the same time, this allocation of capital and labour allows the economy to produce three units of food.

Point A in Figure 6.7 is not an efficient input allocation. Keeping the output level of manufactures fixed, that is, restricting ourselves to the isoquant $M = 2$, we could produce more units of food. This is illustrated in Figure 6.7 by point B, where the economy produces two units of manufactures and simultaneously produces 3.4 units of food. If, starting from point B, we want to produce more units of food, we have to reduce the production of manufactures. Similarly, if we want to increase the production of manufactures, we have to reduce the production of food. Point B is thus an efficient input allocation. Graphically, it is characterized by the tangency of the isoquants for the production of manufactures and food. Point C in Figure 6.7 is another efficient input allocation. The curve connecting all efficient input combinations in the Edgeworth box is called the contract curve. It is analytically derived in Technical Note 6.1.

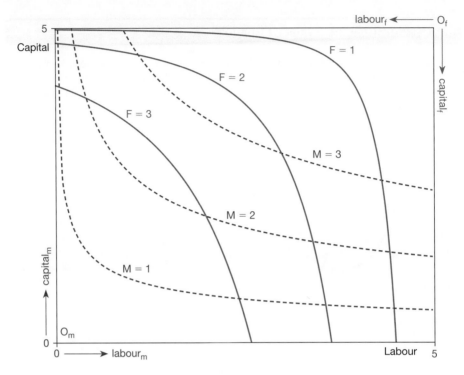

Figure 6.6 The Edgeworth box, $K = L = 5$; $\alpha_m = 0.7$; $\alpha_f = 0.3$.

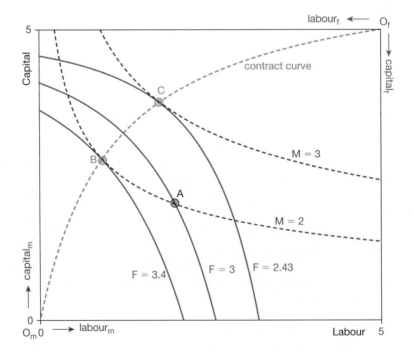

Figure 6.7 The contract curve, $K = L = 5$; $\alpha_m = 0.7$; $\alpha_f = 0.3$.

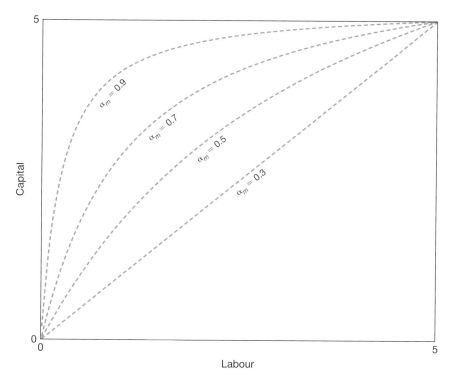

Figure 6.8 Contract curves for different capital intensities, $K = L = 5$; $\alpha_f = 0.3$.

In Figure 6.7 the contract curve is drawn above the diagonal connecting the two origins O_m and O_f. This is because the production of manufactures is relatively capital-intensive. The extent of the curvature of the contract curve depends on the difference in the degree of capital intensity. This is illustrated for four different cases in Figure 6.8. If the capital–labour intensity is the same for the two final goods, that is if $\alpha_m = \alpha_f$ (in which case the two production functions are identical), the contract curve coincides with the diagonal connecting the two origins. The larger the difference in capital intensity, the more pronounced the curvature of the contract curve (and the curvature of the production possibility frontier; see Section 6.5).

6.3 The distribution of labour and capital

We are now in a position to derive the distribution of capital and labour in the economy and the concomitant production levels of manufactures and food. Moreover, we can illustrate this graphically in the Edgeworth box and demonstrate the Rybczynski proposition stated in Section 6.2. The basic reasoning involves three main steps.

- Given the prices of the final goods p_m and p_f, we can determine the wage rate w and the rental rate r using the factor price equalization proposition of Chapter 5, provided both goods are produced in equilibrium.

- If we know the wage rate w and the rental rate r, we can derive the optimal (cost-minimizing) capital–labour ratios for both goods K_m / L_m and K_f / L_f. It is important to realize that these capital–labour ratios do not change as long as the final goods prices p_m and p_f do not change.
- Using the full employment conditions, equation 6.1, and the capital–labour ratios K_m / L_m and K_f / L_f we can derive the equilibrium allocation of capital and labour in the two sectors, and thus the production levels in both sectors.

This is illustrated in Figure 6.9. Once the final goods prices, and thus the wage–rental ratio, are known we also know the capital–labour ratios K_m / L_m and K_f / L_f in the two sectors. Output of manufactures will expand or contract along the optimal capital–labour ratio line with slope K_m / L_m. The further away from the origin O_m, the larger the output of manufactures. Similarly, output of food will expand or contract along its optimal capital–labour ratio line with slope K_f / L_f. The further away from the origin O_f, the larger the output of food. Finally, given this information and the total available amount of capital K and initially available labour L_0 there is one, and only one, allocation in which all capital and labour is employed, namely at point E_0. This point is on the contract curve connecting the origin O_m with the origin O_f in Figure 6.9 (not drawn). Technical Note 6.2 analytically derives the allocation of capital and labour, and thus the production levels of manufactures and food.

Figure 6.9 illustrates the Rybczynski proposition if there is an increase in the available amount of labour, rising from L_0 to L_1. The first thing to note is that the increase in the amount of labour shifts the origin of the isoquants for food from O_f to O'_f. Second, note that the final goods prices, and thus the wage–rental ratio, have not changed, and the expansion path for food is still along its optimal capital–labour ratio line with slope K_f / L_f, this time starting from the origin O'_f. Thus, as before, the allocation of capital and labour for the production of the two goods is determined by the intersection of the expansion paths, at point E_1. This point is on the contract curve (not drawn) connecting the origin O_m with the origin O'_f in Figure 6.9.

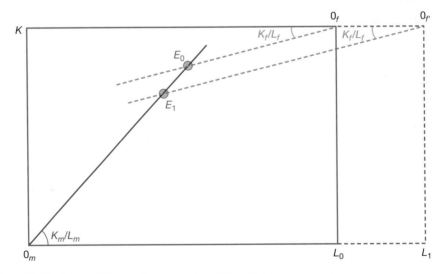

Figure 6.9 The Rybczynski proposition: expansion of labour force.

How can we conclude that the output level for food has increased and for manufactures has fallen, as required by the Rybczynski proposition? Quite simply, by measuring the distance of the allocation point from the origin. Since the line from O_m to E_0 is longer than from O_m to E_1, the output of manufactures has decreased. Similarly, since the line from O_f to E_0 is shorter than from O'_f to E_1, the output of food has increased. These conclusions are linked to the capital–labour intensity of the two sectors, as summarized in the Rybczynski proposition.

The proposition is also easy to understand if we let λ_m be the share of the labour force in manufactures, that is $\lambda_m = L_m / L$, and take the ratio of equation 6.1 (see Technical Note 6.2):

$$\underbrace{\frac{K}{L}}_{\substack{economy \\ cap.\,int.}} = \lambda_m \underbrace{\frac{K_m}{L_m}}_{\substack{manuf. \\ cap.\,int.}} + (1 - \lambda_m) \underbrace{\frac{K_f}{L_f}}_{\substack{food \\ cap.\,int.}} \qquad 6.2$$

Equation 6.2 shows clearly that the economy-wide capital–labour ratio K / L is equal to the weighted average of the sectoral capital–labour ratios K_m / L_m and K_f / L_f. Since the latter do not change for given final goods prices, a change in the available amount of one of the production factors, which changes the economy-wide capital–labour ratio K/L, can only be accommodated by changing the share of labour in manufactures λ_m. Obviously, an increase in the economy-wide capital–labour ratio must lead to an increase in the share of labour allocated to the capital-intensive sector, and vice versa for a decrease in the economy-wide capital–labour ratio. That, in a nutshell, is the Rybczynski proposition.

Finally, it is worthwhile to point out that Jones (1965) also shows that there is a magnification effect in output space, as was shown in Chapter 5 for the prices of factors of production. More specifically, given that the production of manufactures is capital-intensive, the following relationships hold:

(i)   if $\tilde{K} > \tilde{L}$ then $\tilde{M} > \tilde{K} > \tilde{L} > \tilde{F}$
(ii) if $\tilde{K} < \tilde{L}$ then $\tilde{M} < \tilde{K} < \tilde{L} < \tilde{F}$

6.4 Heckscher–Ohlin

We can state the main result of neoclassical trade theory, linking the available factors of production, the relative intensity of the production processes, and the direction of international trade flows, as follows.

Proposition 6.2 Heckscher–Ohlin

In a neoclassical framework with two final goods, two factors of production, and two countries which have identical homothetic tastes, a country will export the good which intensively uses the relatively abundant factor of production.

Using the assumption made in Chapter 5 that the production of manufactures is capital-intensive, this leads to the following conclusions.

- If a country is relatively capital-abundant, it will export manufactures (because its production is capital-intensive).
- If a country is relatively labour-abundant, it will export food (because its production is labour-intensive).

In the demonstration of the Heckscher–Ohlin result below we will use the previous results, in particular the factor price equalization proposition and the Rybczynski proposition. Evidently, the direction of international trade flows in the neoclassical trade model stems from the supply structure of the economy. Indeed, one can argue that the supply side of the economy over the centuries has received much more attention than the demand side of the economy, at least within international economics. None the less, as is evident from the Ohlin quote in Section 6.1, we must take the influence of the demand structure into consideration in a general equilibrium setting before we can draw any definite conclusions about the direction of international trade flows. Essentially, this problem is 'solved' by eliminating all demand bias.

6.4.1 Demand

Exports of goods and services from one country to another can be viewed as excess supply flows. After all, such exports can be defined as the difference between the quantities of goods produced and consumed within a nation.

exports = production − consumption   6.3

International trade flows therefore represent the outcome of the interplay between the supply structure and the demand structure of the economy. The supply structure determines the production level of goods and services in the economy. The demand structure of the economy determines the consumption level of goods and services in the economy. As is immediately evident from equation 6.3, a relationship between the supply structure of an economy and international trade flows can only be derived if we somehow eliminate differences in demand structure between nations. The neoclassical trade model therefore makes the following assumption:

Assumption: all consumers in all countries have identical homothetic preferences.

Rather than discussing what identical homothetic preferences are exactly, we will define a utility function for all consumers in accordance with the assumption above and briefly discuss the main implications of this function: see also Box 6.6. In economics we assume that consumers—that is you, I, and everyone else—try to maximize the utility derived from their income earned (through work or ownership of capital goods) by making a suitable choice of consumption of goods and services, in accordance with our preferences. Since we have to pay for our consumption goods and we have a limited income level, this problem can be stated mathematically as a maximization problem. Let C_m be the consumption level of manufactures, let C_f be the consumption level of food, and let I be the income level.

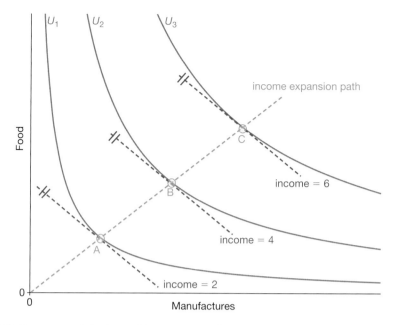

Figure 6.10 Consumer optimization problem, $p_m = p_f = 1$; $\delta_m = 0.5$.

Then the consumer's problem involves maximization of the utility function U below (with parameter δ_m), subject to the budget constraint $I = p_m C_m + p_f C_f$:

$$U = C_m^{\delta_m} C_f^{1-\delta_m}; \quad 0 \leq \delta_m \leq 1 \qquad\qquad 6.4$$

The problem is illustrated in Figure 6.10 for $p_m = p_f = 1$ and $\delta_m = 0.5$. The line 'income = 2' depicts the budget constraint for the consumer if her income level is 2. Any consumption combination on this line or below (to the southwest) is feasible from a budget point of view. The consumer chooses the consumption combination giving maximal utility. Graphically, this occurs at the point of tangency of the budget constraint with an iso-utility curve, that is, a curve depicting all consumption combinations giving rise to the same level of utility. In Figure 6.10 this occurs at point A, where the budget constraint is tangent to the U_1 iso-utility curve.

BOX 6.6 Homothetic demand

The utility function specified in equation 6.4 is an example of a homothetic utility function. As illustrated in Figure 6.10, it gives rise to iso-utility curves that are radial blow-ups of one another, just as the isoquants are radial blow-ups if the production function exhibits constant returns to scale. So why do we distinguish between these two different concepts? Because it is customary to think of preferences as an ordinal concept. It is meaningful to speak of a doubling in output, as is the case if we double all inputs in a constant returns to scale production process, but not of a doubling of utility if we double the consumption levels. We cannot say we are 'twice as happy' if we consume twice as many of all goods, just that we prefer this consumption level over some other consumption combination.

(continued...)

The concept of the utility function is therefore a tool for explaining the optimal choices of consumers; it is a translation of the consumer's preference structure. The numbers attached to the iso-utility curves depicted in Figure 6.11 are arbitrary; only their magnitude is important. More specifically, it must be true that $U_1 < U_2 < U_3$, which holds for the numbers 1, 2, and 3, but also for the numbers 1, 6, and 400. If a utility function is homothetic, the iso-utility curves are radial blow-ups, as in Figure 6.11, and the two conclusions emphasized in the main text (C_m / C_f is a function of p_m / p_f and the distribution of income is not important) still hold.

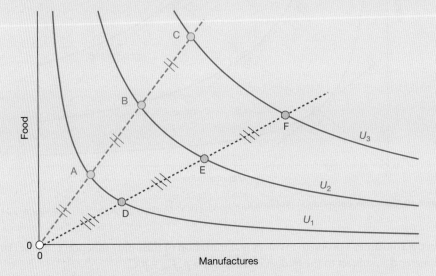

Figure 6.11 Homothetic iso-utility curves are radial blow-ups.

Remark 1: The marginal rate of substitution (MRS) is the absolute value of the slope of an iso-utility curve, that is $MRS = |dC_f / dC_m| = (\partial U / \partial C_m)/(\partial U / \partial C_f)$. It is a measure for the ease with which the consumer can substitute one good for another on the margin and still achieve the same utility level. If consumers take the final goods prices as given, utility maximization implies: $MRS = p_m / p_f$.

Since the utility function in equation 6.4 is of the Cobb–Douglas type, like the production functions shown in equation 5.1, the reader of course realizes that the consumer's maximization problem is quite similar to the producer's problem of cost minimization. In the former problem, the budget constraint is given and the solution is a tangent iso-utility curve. In the latter problem the isoquant is given and the solution is a tangent iso-cost line. In Chapter 5 it was shown that the parameter a_m in the production function for manufactures represents the share of total cost in the manufacturing sector paid to the capital owners. Similarly, the parameter δ_m in the utility function in equation 6.4 represents the share of income spent on manufactures as the solution to the maximization problem ($P_m C_m = \delta_m I$; see Technical Note 6.3).

Figure 6.10 also illustrates what happens if the consumer's income level increases from 2 to 4 or 6. Since the iso-utility curves are radial blow-ups of one another, any increase in the income level, for given final goods prices, leads to an equiproportional increase in the consumption of all goods, as illustrated by points B and C in Figure 6.10. This demand structure allows us to draw two main conclusions:

- The economy's optimal consumption ratio C_m / C_f is only a function of the final goods price ratio p_m / p_f. Obviously, an increase in p_m / p_f leads to a decrease in C_m / C_f. This is similar to the observation that under constant returns to scale the capital–labour ratios K_m / L_m and K_f / L_f depend only on the wage–rental ratio w / r.

- The economy's consumption level depends only on the final goods prices, and the aggregate income level I. The distribution of income over the different consumers in the economy is not relevant for determining the aggregate consumption levels.

The second observation is also clear from Figure 6.10. Suppose the aggregate income level is 8. If this income level is equally divided over two consumers, they both consume at point B. The aggregate consumption level is then 2B. If one of the consumers receives 6 income and the other consumer receives 2 income, then the first consumer consumes at point C and the second at point A. Aggregate income is then A + C = 2B. This holds similarly for any other distribution of income.

6.5 The production possibility frontier

We will illustrate and discuss the Heckscher–Ohlin proposition below using the production possibility frontier (PPF) introduced in Chapter 4. To do that we will first have to discuss some of the properties of the PPF in the neoclassical production structure. Recall that the frontier depicts all efficient production combinations in final goods space, that is, the maximum output of food for any given feasible production level of manufactures. Similarly, in Section 6.2.2 we showed that the contract curve in the Edgeworth box depicts all efficient input combinations. Since the contract curve was derived explicitly (see Technical Note 6.1), it is not hard to calculate all efficient output combinations, which is the PPF.[3] The result is depicted in Figure 6.12.

As the reader can see, in contrast to the Ricardian PPF of Chapter 4, which is a straight line, the PPF in the neoclassical trade model is curved. This arises from the difference in the degree of capital intensity between the two final goods sectors, which make one sector more responsive to changes in capital input and the other sector more responsive to changes in labour input. As with the contract curve in the Edgeworth box (illustrated in Figure 6.8), the larger the difference in capital intensity, the more pronounced the curvature of the PPF, as illustrated in Figure 6.13.

Remark 2: The marginal rate of transformation (MRT) is the absolute value of the slope of the production possibility frontier $|dF/dM|$. It is a measure of the ease with which the producers can technically substitute the production of one good for another on the margin. If factor markets are perfectly competitive, and MC denotes marginal costs of production, the following relationship holds: $MRT = MC_m/MC_f$.

The PPF of course also changes if the amount of the available inputs changes. Since the production of manufactures is capital-intensive, an increase in the capital stock K, for a fixed value of the labour stock L, has a larger impact on the maximum production of manufactures than on the maximum production of food. Indeed, if we let M_{max} and F_{max} be the

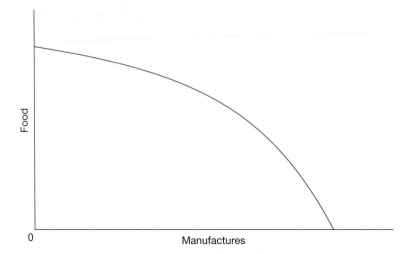

Figure 6.12 Production possibility frontier, $K = L = 5$; $\alpha_m = 0.8$; $\alpha_f = 0.1$.

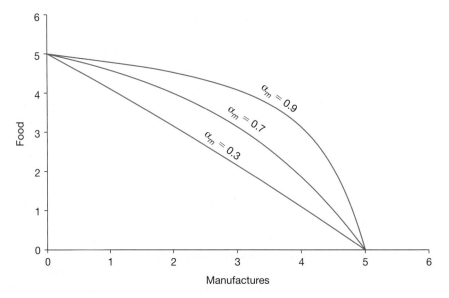

Figure 6.13 Production possibility frontiers: impact of changing capital intensity, $K = L = 5$; $\alpha_f = 0.1$.

maximum attainable levels of output for manufactures and food, and use relative changes (see Technical Note 5.5) for the production functions, we get

$$\tilde{M}_{max} = \alpha_m \tilde{K} + (1 - \alpha_m)\tilde{L}; \quad \tilde{F}_{max} = \alpha_f \tilde{K} + (1 - \alpha_f)\tilde{L} \qquad 6.5$$

Since $\alpha_m > \alpha_f$, the maximum production level for manufactures increases more rapidly than for food if the capital stock increases. Similarly, since $1 - \alpha_f > 1 - \alpha_m$ the maximum production level for food increases more rapidly than for manufactures if the labour stock

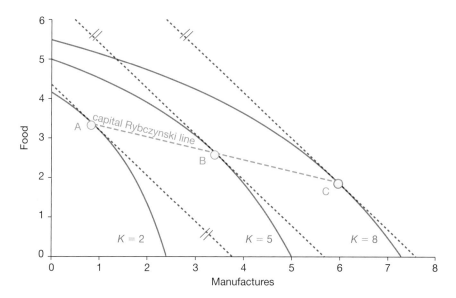

Figure 6.14 Impact of a change in capital on the PPF and the Rybczynski line, $L = 5$; $\alpha_m = 0.8$; $\alpha_f = 0.2$.

increases. The fact that an increase in the amount of an available factor of production leads to a biased shift of the PPF is illustrated for increases in the capital stock in Figure 6.14.

Figure 6.14 also illustrates another aspect of changes in output that will be useful in the discussion below. Recall that the Rybczynski proposition relates changes in the available amount of a factor of production and changes in output for given final goods prices. We can illustrate the proposition in final goods space, for example by increasing the capital stock, as in Figure 6.14. If the capital stock is 2, the economy produces at point A for some ratio of final goods prices. For the same final goods prices, but a higher capital stock of 5, the economy produces at point B. The output of the capital-intensive manufactures has increased, that of the labour-intensive food has decreased. Similarly, if the capital stock is 8 for that final goods price ratio, the economy produces at point C. Since the changes in the Rybczynski proposition are equiproportional, the points A, B, and C are on a straight line. It is called the capital Rybczynski line and traces out all changes in output for changes in the capital stock from 2 to 8, for given final goods prices and labour stock (equal to 5 in Figure 6.14). If we analyse changes in the labour stock, we can derive a similar labour Rybczynski line. Finally, note that the discussion above focuses on physical capital as a factor of production; human capital is also an important factor of production, see Box 6.7. We can therefore also derive a human-capital Rybczynski line.

BOX 6.7 **The importance of human capital**

The discussion in Chapter 5 and in this chapter relates factor abundance to differences in capital–labour intensity in the production process. We have seen in Box 5.2 that there are indeed enormous differences between countries in terms of available capital per worker. As discussed in Box 5.3, however, we can identify many more types of factors of production and thus many more types of factor intensity differences

(continued...)

in the production process. We discuss examples for specific products in various boxes: natural-resource-intensive products (oil in Box 5.3 and precious stones in Box 6.2), unskilled-labour-intensive products (textiles in Box 5.8), technology-intensive products (electronics in Box 6.3), and human-capital-intensive products (cars in Box 8.5). In many empirical applications the distinction between capital and labour is less relevant than the distinction between, for example, low-skilled workers and high-skilled workers. It is important to bear in mind that all the results we derive in Chapter 5 and Chapter 6 based on differences in capital–labour intensity also hold, of course, if we analyse a similar framework based on differences in, say, high-skilled workers and low-skilled workers. As in Box 5.2 (which discussed differences in capital per worker) the question thus arises to what extent human capital per worker differs between countries and how it is related to income per capita. The Penn World Table 8.1 provides an index of human capital per worker based on years of schooling and returns to education.

Table 6.3 provides information on the human capital per worker, income per capita, and population size for the same selection of countries as in Table 5.3. The ranking is based on human capital per worker from low to high (the ordering is quite different from that in Table 5.3). The variation in human capital per worker is substantial, ranging from 1.93 for India to 3.62 for the USA, or about twice as large. This is significantly less, however, than the variation in income per capita (which differs by a factor of 22). In general, countries with low human capital per worker, such as India, Tanzania, and Brazil, have low income per capita, while countries with high human capital per worker, such as Japan, Australia, and the USA, have high income per capita. The relationship is less clear-cut, however, than for capital per worker; examples of pairs of countries with lower income per capita despite higher human capital per worker are India and Tanzania, Brazil and China, China and the Philippines, and the UK and Russia.

Figure 6.15 illustrates the relationship between human capital per worker and the log of income per capita for 164 countries. It clearly shows the strong (but imperfect) positive association between these two variables. The estimated regression line shown in the figure explains 60 per cent of the variance in income per capita and has an estimated slope coefficient of 1.756. This implies that, on average, when the human capital per worker rises by 0.1 the income per capita level rises by about 18 per cent. Most big countries, such as India, China, and the USA, have observations close to the regression line. Some rich countries, such as Qatar (oil) and Macao (casinos), have higher income per capita levels than expected on the basis of human capital per worker only. Other countries, such as Zimbabwe and Tajikistan, have lower than expected income per capita (for a range of reasons). In any case, it is safe to conclude that human capital per worker is an important determinant of income per capita.

Table 6.3 Human capital per worker: selected countries, 2011

Country	Income per capita	Human capital per worker	Population (millions)
India	5,244	1.93	1,241.5
Tanzania	2,296	2.05	44.9
Brazil	14,555	2.45	196.7
China	11,525	2.58	1,324.4
Philippines	6,326	2.73	94.9
UK	36,931	2.82	62.4
Russia	23,564	3.24	142.8
Japan	35,614	3.27	126.5
Australia	42,834	3.39	22.6
USA	51,340	3.62	313.1

Notes: income per capita GNI PPP 2011 USD; human capital per worker is an index.
Source: Penn World Table 8.1 and World Development Indicators.

(continued...)

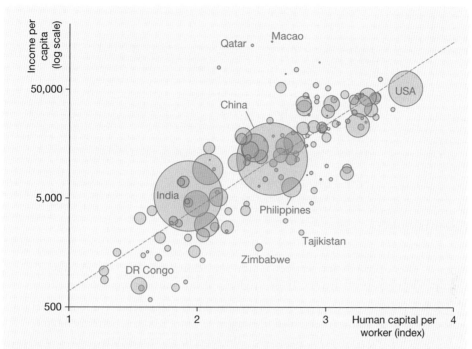

Figure 6.15 Income per capita and human capital per worker.

Notes: 134 countries included; bubbles proportional to population size; dashed line is a regression line.
Source: calculations based on sources mentioned in Table 5.3.

The relationship between capital per worker and income per capita (Box 5.3) is somewhat stronger than between human capital per worker and income per capita: the former explains 85.5 and the latter 57.9 per cent of the variance in log income per capita. We can, of course, look at the joint explanatory power of both log capital per worker and human capital per worker on log income per capita. This explains 88.7 per cent of the variance in log income per capita, only marginally better than the 85.5 per cent if we restrict attention to capital per worker only. The reason is, of course, the high correlation between the two explanatory variables: countries with a high stock of capital per worker also tend to have a high index of human capital per worker (the correlation coefficient is 0.77). The additional explanatory power of also knowing the human capital index per worker is thus limited.

6.6 Structure of the equilibrium

The Heckscher–Ohlin result concentrates on the structure of international trade flows in a trading equilibrium. It is therefore useful to review the general equilibrium structure of the neoclassical trade model, as summarized in Figure 6.16.

There are five types of economic agents: (i) labourers, (ii) capital owners, (iii) consumers, (iv) producers of manufactures, and (v) producers of food. Note that these are functional distinctions; the same person could be a producer of manufactures, a capital owner, and a consumer at the same time. Also note that Figure 6.16 distinguishes between two types of

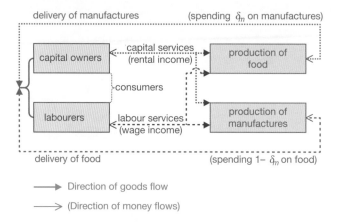

Figure 6.16 Equilibrium structure.

flows: the flows of goods and services, indicated by closed-point arrows, and money flows, indicated by open-point arrows. These two flows always move in opposite directions.

- The labourers supply their services to produce either manufactures or food. In return they receive a remuneration called the wage rate. Since labour is perfectly mobile between the two sectors, the wage rate is the same in the two sectors.
- The capital owners supply their services to produce either manufactures or food. In return they receive a remuneration called the rental rate. Since capital is perfectly mobile between the two sectors, the rental rate is the same in the two sectors.
- Both labourers and capital owners earn an income, which they use to spend on manufactures and food as consumers. Since production takes place under perfect competition and constant returns to scale, there are no profits generated in the economy. The only income available for consumption is therefore generated by supplying labour services and capital services.
- The producers of manufactures hire labour services on the labour market, for which they pay the wage rate, and capital services on the capital market, for which they pay the rental rate. They use these services in the most efficient way to produce manufactures, which they sell to consumers at the price p_m.
- The same applies for the producers of food.

The economy is in equilibrium if six conditions are fulfilled: (i) consumers maximize their utility, (ii) producers maximize their profits, (iii) all labourers are employed, (iv) all capital is used, (v) the supply of manufactures is equal to the demand for manufactures, and (vi) the supply of food is equal to the demand for food. In the next two sections we will distinguish between two types of equilibria.

- In the autarky equilibrium, the above six equilibrium relationships hold at the national level; there is no cross-border activity whatsoever.
- In the trade equilibrium, the above six relationships hold at the global level for the final goods markets, and at the national level for the factors of production. There is therefore no impediment to cross-border trade for final goods (at zero transport costs), while capital and labour services cannot move across borders.

6.7 **Autarky equilibrium**

Figure 6.17 illustrates the autarky equilibrium if there is an equal supply of capital and labour ($K = L = 5$), the cost share of capital in manufactures is 0.8 ($\alpha_m = 0.8$), the cost share of capital in food is 0.2 ($\alpha_f = 0.2$), and the share of income spent on manufactures is 0.6 ($\delta_m = 0.6$). As the figure shows, the PPF is tangent to the income line generated by the autarky production point; that is, the marginal rate of transformation (MRT) is equal to the final goods price ratio p_m / p_f because producers maximize profits and markets are perfectly competitive. Similarly, the iso-utility curve is tangent to the income line generated by the production point; that is, the marginal rate of substitution (MRS) is equal to the final goods price ratio p_m / p_f because consumers maximize utility and take prices as given. The autarky equilibrium is therefore characterized by (the sub-index '*au*' refers to autarky):

$$MRT_{au} = \left(\frac{p_m}{p_f} \right)_{au} = MRS_{au} \qquad\qquad 6.6$$

Clearly, given the restrictions facing the economy (no international contacts), the autarky equilibrium achieves the best possible outcome: at the equilibrium production point, which is also the equilibrium consumption point, welfare is maximized. The autarky equilibrium depends, of course, on the value of the parameters, the capital and labour stock available,

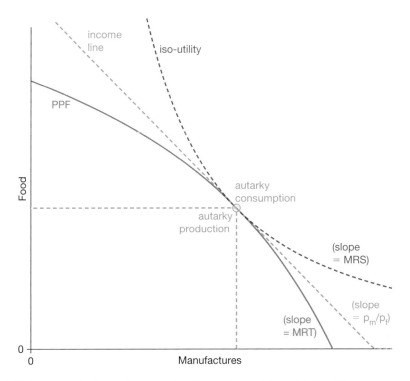

Figure 6.17 Autarky production and consumption, $K = L = 5$; $\alpha_m = 0.8$; $\alpha_f = 0.2$; $\delta_m = 0.6$.

the production functions, the utility function, and so on. Given the Cobb–Douglas production functions and utility function, the autarky equilibrium wage–rental ratio and final goods price ratio can be explicitly calculated: see Technical Note 6.4 (also for a definition of the parameter γ_{au}).

$$\left(\frac{w}{r}\right)_{au} = \gamma_{au} \frac{K}{L} ; \quad \left(\frac{p_m}{p_f}\right)_{au} = \frac{\gamma_m}{\gamma_f} \left(\frac{w}{r}\right)_{au}^{-(\alpha_m - \alpha_f)} \tag{6.7}$$

Both the wage–rental ratio and the final goods price ratio are simple functions of the *relative* factor abundance K/L of the economy. If the capital stock increases relative to the labour stock, the wage–rental ratio rises since labour becomes relatively scarcer. This, in turn, results in a decrease of the relative price of manufactures, which uses capital relatively intensively (see Chapter 5). If we look at two countries, say the USA (A) and the UK (B), and we assume that the USA has more capital per worker available than the UK (as in empirical Table 5.3), then it follows from equation 6.7 that the USA's wage-rental rate is *higher* in autarky then the UK's and that, as a consequence, the price of manufactures is *lower* in the USA in autarky than in the UK.

$$\text{To summarize: } \frac{K}{L} \uparrow \Leftrightarrow \frac{w}{r} \uparrow \Leftrightarrow \left(\frac{p_m}{p_f}\right) \downarrow$$

6.8 Trade equilibrium

The international trade equilibrium is also characterized by utility maximization and profit maximization. Since the former leads to equality of the marginal rate of substitution and the final goods price ratio, and the latter leads to equality of the marginal rate of transformation and the final goods price ratio, the international trade equilibrium is summarized by (the sub-index '*tr*' refers to trade):

$$MRT_{tr} = \left(\frac{p_m}{p_f}\right)_{tr} = MRS_{tr} \tag{6.8}$$

Since the same equalities between the marginal rate of substitution, the price ratio, and the marginal rate of transformation hold in the autarky equilibrium, the question may arise: what is the difference between the two equilibria? The answer is simple: international trade of final goods enables international arbitrage opportunities not previously available. The crucial aspect is to realize that although the autarky equilibrium is efficient given the imposed restriction of no trade, which leads to $MRT = p_m/p_f = MRS$ in both countries, it is not efficient if international trade is possible because the autarky prices are different in the two countries; more specifically: the autarky price of manufactures is lower in the USA than in the UK because the USA has more capital per worker available than the UK: see Section 6.7. Thus, in autarky $MRT = p_m/p_f = MRS$ holds within countries, but not between countries. It is this aspect that makes international trade and gains from trade possible.

The international trade equilibrium is illustrated in Figure 6.18.[4] International arbitrage opportunities arising from the costless trade of final goods ensures that the prices of food and manufactures must be the same in the two countries in the international trade equilibrium; the relative price with trade is in between the two autarky equilibrium prices:

$$\left(\frac{p_m}{p_f}\right)^A_{au} < \left(\frac{p_m}{p_f}\right)^{A=B}_{tr} < \left(\frac{p_m}{p_f}\right)^B_{au} \tag{6.9}$$

For the USA the relative price of manufactures rises in trade relative to autarky. The production of manufactures therefore increases (and that of food falls); the production shifts to point pr_A in Figure 6.18, the tangency point with the income line. Simultaneously, the higher relative price for manufactures in the USA results in a substitution away from manufactures on the consumption side; the consumption ratio C_f/C_m rises to the ratio in point CO_A. In the international trade equilibrium, the production point pr_A for the USA no longer coincides with the consumption point CO_A. There is, of course, a link between these two points, since the total value of the expenditures on consumption cannot exceed the total value of income generated by the production level in the economy.[5] That is, the consumption point must be on the income line generated by the production point of the USA, with a slope equal to the international price ratio p_m/p_f; see Figure 6.18. Clearly, the USA now produces more manufactures than it consumes. It will therefore export manufactures in exchange for imports of food. Finally, we note that the welfare level achieved by the USA rises; the new consumption point CO_A is on a higher iso-utility curve than in autarky.[6]

In the UK the opposite changes take place. The relative price of manufactures falls, such that Britain produces less manufactures and more food. Simultaneously, the consumption

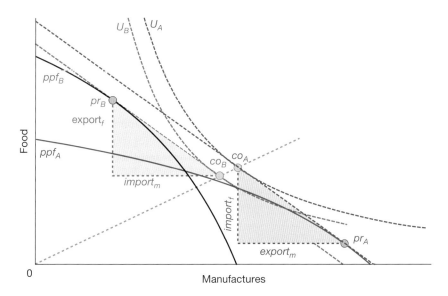

Figure 6.18 International trade equilibrium.

mix in the UK moves in the direction of manufactures. The UK therefore produces more food than it consumes, which it will export in exchange for imports of manufactures. This allows the UK also to reach a higher welfare level. On a global scale, international trade flows improve efficiency. The world production of manufactures rises by 5.7 per cent from 6.45 to 6.82, and the world production of food rises by 5.8 per cent from 4.97 to 5.26. Note also that the trade equilibrium requires that the excess demand for manufactures by the UK (its imports of manufactures) must be equal to the excess supply of manufactures by the USA (its exports of manufactures). The two trade triangles in Figure 6.18 must coincide.

We have seen that as a consequence of international trade flows the welfare level in both countries rises, while the USA (the relatively capital-abundant country) exports manufactures and the UK (the relatively labour-abundant country) exports food. Both countries thus export the good that uses the relatively abundant factor of production relatively intensively. This is the Heckscher–Ohlin proposition. The reader may want to verify this claim using capital and/or labour Rybczynski lines in Figure 6.18, starting from either production point.

6.9 Empirics: Leontief paradox and missing trade

The first empirical study of the neoclassical trade model was performed by Wassily Leontief (1956). Using trade data and factor intensities for the USA, Leontief computed the amount of capital and labour required to produce $1 million worth of US exports in 1951 and $1 million worth of US import-competing goods. Thinking that the USA was a capital-abundant country, he expected to show, on the basis of the Heckscher–Ohlin result discussed in this chapter, that US export production is more capital-intensive than US import-competing production. Instead, he found that the capital–labour ratio was roughly $13,000 per worker year in the export sector, which was lower than the $13,700 per worker year in the import-competing sector. It appeared, therefore, that the USA was, on balance, importing capital services from abroad through its trade of goods and services, a presumed contradiction of the Heckscher–Ohlin proposition. This has become known as the Leontief paradox.

Various explanations have been suggested to solve the Leontief paradox. First, it could be that there is a demand bias, in which case the USA would consume more capital-intensive products than other countries. Second, there could be a so-called factor-intensity reversal, in which case, for example, the production of manufactures is more capital-intensive in the rest of the world while the production of food is more capital-intensive in the USA, making it impossible to estimate the foreign factor intensities using US data, as Leontief did. Third, and more important, is the fact that a proper test should be based on the factor content of trade flows (Leamer, 1980). This is based on the work by Jaroslav Vanek (1959), who argued that the $2 \times 2 \times 2$ framework is too restrictive and we should distinguish between more types of goods and more factors of production (see Boxes 5.5, 5.8, 6.4, and 8.5). Theoretical work by Vanek showed that in a more general setting a weaker version of the Heckscher–Ohlin result holds; that is, a country tends to export goods and services which 'on average' make intensive use of the abundant factors of production.

Figure 6.19 illustrates the argument that we should take more factors of production into consideration. This figure and Boxes 5.8, 6.4, 6.7, and 8.5 discuss data distinguishing between five types of products: primary goods, natural-resource-intensive, unskilled-labour-intensive, technology-intensive, and human-capital-intensive. Figure 6.19 shows that

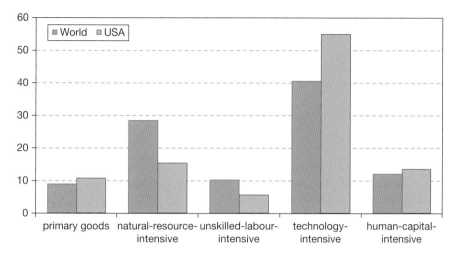

Figure 6.19 Share of USA and world trade in different types of goods, per cent.

Source: based on data for 2008 from www.intracen.org.

(i) by far the largest share of US exports are in technology-intensive products, and (ii) when compared to the world average the USA has a revealed comparative advantage in primary goods, technology-intensive products, and human-capital-intensive products. In view of its relatively large and fertile land per person and high levels of technology and human capital, none of these observations is controversial.

The first thorough analysis of the more general neoclassical trade model was performed by Bowen, Leamer, and Sveikauskas (1987). We now focus, however, on a more recent study by Daniel Trefler (1995), who analyses trade flows between 33 countries together accounting for 76 per cent of world exports and 79 per cent of world GNP. Trefler distinguishes nine factors of production: capital, cropland, pasture, and six labour categories (professional and technical workers, clerical workers, sales workers, service workers, agricultural workers, and production, transport, and unskilled workers).

The empirical success of the more general neoclassical trade model is modest: when the predicted sign of the net factor content of trade is weighted by size, the model explains about 71 per cent. As Trefler (1995, p. 1031) puts it, this is 'uncomfortably close to the coin-toss alternative of 50 per cent'. The important contribution of Trefler's work rests in the way he continues, by providing a detailed analysis of the deviations between empirical trade flows and predicted trade flows. He shows, in particular, that the factor service trade is much smaller than its factor-endowments prediction, a phenomenon referred to by him as 'the case of the missing trade'.

Trefler investigates several alternative hypotheses that may explain the case of the missing trade in conjunction with the neoclassical trade model, finding empirical support for two additions, namely (i) differences in technology and (ii) demand bias.

(i) The neoclassical model analysed in Chapter 5 and Chapter 6 assumes that countries have access to the same technology. Trefler argues, however, that there are technology differences between countries, and that incorporating these differences (in a neutral way) increases the goodness-of-fit from 71 to 78 per cent. Obviously, we have already discussed the impact of technology differences on international trade in Chapter 4 of this book.

(ii) It is generally observed that consumers display a bias toward domestically produced goods; see Armington (1969). Allowing for Armington-type demand bias in the neoclassical model increases the goodness-of-fit from 71 to 87 per cent. Incorporating both technology differences and Armington demand in the model increases the goodness-of-fit even further to 93 per cent.

6.10 Conclusions

We analyse the connection between the production levels of final goods and the available factors of production using the Edgeworth box. The set of all efficient allocation combinations, leading to maximum output of one good given the output level of the other good, is called the contract curve. The curvature of the contract curve is determined by the difference in capital intensity in the production processes of final goods. For given prices of the final goods, an increase in the available amount of capital leads to an increase in the production of (capital-intensive) manufactures and a reduction in the production of food. The opposite holds for an increase in the available amount of labour (Rybczynski effect). Next, we analyse the connection between the direction of international trade flows and the factor intensity of the production process. In autarky, countries with a high capital–labour ratio will have a high wage–rental ratio (since labour is relatively scarce) and a low relative price for the capital-intensive good. Allowing for free trade of final goods at no costs equalizes the final goods prices in the two countries, as well as the wage rate and the rental rate (provided both goods are produced in both countries: FPE proposition). Since the relative price of the capital-intensive good rises compared to autarky for the capital-abundant country (which raises the rental rate and reduces the wage rate: Stolper–Samuelson proposition), this country starts to produce more capital-intensive goods, which will be exported in exchange for the labour-intensive goods. The opposite holds for the labour-abundant country (Heckscher–Ohlin proposition). As a result of improved efficiency at the global level, welfare increases in both countries in the international trade equilibrium compared to autarky. The model performs reasonably well empirically, provided we also take into consideration technology differences and demand bias.

 Technical Notes

Technical Note 6.1 Determination of the contract curve

To determine the contract curve in the Edgeworth box it is clear that the slopes of the isoquants must be the same. For the Cobb–Douglas production functions of equation 5.1 these are (see Technical Note 5.3):

$$\frac{dK_m}{dL_m} = \frac{1-\alpha_m}{\alpha_m}\frac{K_m}{L_m}; \quad \frac{dK_f}{dL_f} = \frac{1-\alpha_f}{\alpha_f}\frac{K_f}{L_f} \tag{6.A1}$$

Setting these two slopes equal to each other and realizing that $K_f = K - K_m$ and $L_f = L - L_m$ gives the following relationship between K_m and L_m:

$$K_m = \frac{\alpha_m(1-\alpha_f)\, KL_m}{\alpha_f(1-\alpha_m)\, L + (\alpha_m - \alpha_f)\, L_m} \tag{6.A2}$$

This is the contract curve. Note that if the capital intensity is the same in the two final goods sectors, that is if $\alpha_m = \alpha_f$, the contract curve reduces to a straight line equal to the diagonal of the Edgeworth box.

Technical Note 6.2 The distribution of capital and labour

Given the total available factors of production capital K and labour L, and the prices of the final goods, and therefore of the wage rate and the rental rate, we can determine the share of labourers working in each sector as follows. Take the ratio of equation 6.1, and let λ_m be the share of the labour force in manufactures, that is $\lambda_m = L_m / L$:

$$\frac{K}{L} = \frac{K_m}{L} + \frac{K_f}{L} = \frac{L_m}{L}\frac{K_m}{L_m} + \frac{L_f}{L}\frac{K_f}{L_f} = \lambda_m \frac{K_m}{L_m} + (1-\lambda_m)\frac{K_f}{L_f} \tag{6.A3}$$

Now substituting the optimal capital–labour ratios in both sectors as a function of the wage–rental ratio gives:

$$\frac{K}{L} = \lambda_m \frac{\alpha_m}{1-\alpha_m}\frac{w}{r} + (1-\lambda_m)\frac{\alpha_f}{1-\alpha_f}\frac{w}{r} \tag{6.A4}$$

We use this equation to determine the share of labourers in manufactures λ_m:

$$\lambda_m = \frac{(1-\alpha_m)(1-\alpha_f)}{\alpha_m - \alpha_f}\frac{(K/L)}{(w/r)} - \frac{\alpha_f(1-\alpha_m)}{\alpha_m - \alpha_f} \tag{6.A5}$$

This completely determines the distribution of capital and labour over the two final goods sectors. Finally, this distribution of capital and labour can be used to determine the production level for manufactures:

$$M = K_m^{\alpha_m} L_m^{1-\alpha_m} = \left(\frac{K_m}{L_m}\right)^{\alpha_m} L_m = \left(\frac{\alpha_m}{1-\alpha_m}\frac{w}{r}\right)^{\alpha_m} \lambda_m L \tag{6.A6}$$

–and similarly for food.

Technical Note 6.3 Utility maximization

The problem for a consumer who wants to maximize utility, given the income level I and the prices of final goods p_m and p_f, by choosing the consumption levels C_m and C_f is

$$\max_{C_m, C_f} C_m^{\delta_m} C_f^{1-\delta_m} \quad \text{s.t.} \quad I = p_m C_m + p_f C_f \tag{6.A7}$$

To solve this problem we define the Lagrangean Γ, using the Lagrange multiplier λ:

$$\Gamma = C_m^{\delta_m} C_f^{1-\delta_m} + \lambda(I - p_m C_m - p_f C_f) \tag{6.A8}$$

Derive the two first order conditions $\partial \Gamma / \partial C_m = \partial \Gamma / \partial C_f = 0$ for an optimum, and note that

$$\lambda p_m = \delta_m C_m^{\delta_m - 1} C_f^{1-\delta_m} \quad \text{and} \quad \lambda p_f = (1-\delta_m) C_m^{\delta_m} C_f^{-\delta_m} \tag{6.A9}$$

Taking the ratio of these two conditions and simplifying determines the optimal spending ratio $(p_m C_m) / (p_f C_f) = \delta_m / (1 - \delta_m)$. Using this in the budget constraint gives

$$I = p_m C_m + p_f C_f = p_m C_m + \frac{1 - \delta_m}{\delta_m} p_m C_m = \frac{p_m C_m}{\delta_m} \quad \text{or} \quad p_m C_m = \delta_m I \tag{6.A10}$$

Thus, the share δ_m of income is spent on manufactures, and the share $1 - \delta_m$ on food.

Technical Note 6.4 Derivation of the autarky equilibrium

To derive the autarky equilibrium, we first note that the structure of the utility function ensures that the agents always want to consume a positive amount of both goods. Since these goods cannot be imported from abroad, both goods have to be produced in our own country. We can therefore use the Factor Price Equalization proposition, the Stolper–Samuelson proposition, and the Rybczynski proposition whenever convenient, all of which require the economy to produce both goods in equilibrium. The demand for manufactures is given in equation 6A.10 as a function of income I and price p_m. Since the only income generated in equilibrium derives from the supply of labour or capital, total income is given by

$$I = wL + rK = r\left(\frac{w}{r}L + K\right) \tag{6.A11}$$

Furthermore, in Chapter 5 it was shown that there is a one-to-one correspondence between the rewards to factors of production and the price of final goods. In particular, if the wage rate w and the rental rate r are known, equation 5.7 gives the prices p_m and p_f. Using this equation, it follows that

$$\frac{r}{p_m} = \frac{r}{\gamma_m r^{\alpha_m} w^{1-\alpha_m}} = \frac{1}{\gamma_m}\left(\frac{w}{r}\right)^{\alpha_m - 1} \quad \text{and} \quad \frac{p_m}{p_f} = \frac{\gamma_m r^{\alpha_m} w^{1-\alpha_m}}{\gamma_f r^{\alpha_f} w^{1-\alpha_f}} = \frac{\gamma_m}{\gamma_f}\left(\frac{w}{r}\right)^{-(\alpha_m - \alpha_f)} \tag{6.A12}$$

Using these results in the demand function for manufactures, we get

$$C_m = \delta_m \frac{I}{p_m} = \delta_m \frac{r}{p_m}\left(\frac{w}{r}L + K\right) = \delta_m \frac{1}{\gamma_m}\left(\frac{w}{r}\right)^{\alpha_m - 1}\left(\frac{w}{r}L + K\right) \tag{6.A13}$$

This gives us the demand for manufactures as a function of the wage-rental ratio w / r. If both goods are produced, the Rybczynski analysis and the full employment conditions determine the production level of manufactures, also as a function of the wage-rental ratio w / r: see Technical Note 6.2. Equating demand for and supply of manufactures gives us, after some algebra, the autarky equilibrium wage-rental ratio:

$$\left(\frac{w}{r}\right)_{au} = \gamma_{au} \frac{K}{L}; \quad \gamma_{au} \equiv \frac{(1 - \alpha_f) - \delta_m(\alpha_m - \alpha_f)}{\alpha_f + \delta_m(\alpha_m - \alpha_f)} \tag{6.A14}$$

 Notes

1   It is sometimes also called the Edgeworth–Bowley box.

2   See Allen (1965, p. 170).

3   The contract curve gives K_m as a function of L_m. The inputs for food can be calculated using $K_f = K - K_m$ and $L_f = L - L_m$. Using the production functions, the output levels can be determined. It is not possible to write the production possibility frontier as an explicit function.

4   We have made it easy for ourselves to calculate the equilibrium because both countries produce both goods in the trade equilibrium. This is not necessary.

5   At least if there is no international borrowing or lending in the period under consideration, or if the values are measured in present-value terms.

6   The same conclusion follows from revealed preference. Note that this utility level is strictly beyond reach in the autarky equilibrium.

 ## Questions

Question 6.1

Armenia is a small country (changes in endowments do not result in price changes for factor inputs or final goods prices). Suppose that it produces two goods, Manufactures and Food. It produces these goods in a Heckscher-Ohlin world using high-skilled labour (H) and low skilled labour (L). Manufactures make relatively intensive use of H and Food is relatively L intensive. About 3 million Armenians are high-skilled, while 1 million people are low-skilled.

a.   Draw the situation described above in an Edgeworth box. Put the origin of Food in the south-west corner and the origin of Manufactures in the north-east corner. Measure high-skilled labour (H) on the horizontal axis and low-skilled labour (L) on the vertical axis. Draw the contract curve, one efficient point of production, and the isoquants of both goods through the chosen efficient production point.

b.   What indicates in the Edgeworth box the level of output of a good?

c.   How can you determine the production levels of rice and clothes in full employment equilibrium?

After the fall of the Soviet Union and the declaration of Armenian independence, the socio-economic situation in Armenia deteriorates rapidly. As a consequence, people are voting with their feet. Estimates show that 2 million people have emigrated from Armenia since independence. It is the best (high-skilled) people who are emigrating.

d.   Show the effects of the Armenian emigration in the Edgeworth box you have drawn in Question 6.1a.

e.   What are the effects on the production of Manufactures and Food? What do we call this effect in theory?

Question 6.2

Suppose there are two countries (Cuba and India) in a neoclassical world with two factors of production (human capital and unskilled workers) able to produce two goods (merchandise and food). We will assume that the production of merchandise is relatively human capital intensive and that Cuba has 400 units of human capital and 800 units of unskilled workers while India has 300 units of human capital and 800 units of unskilled workers.

Draw a *production possibility frontier* for Cuba in international trade equilibrium *consistent* with the information above and illustrate clearly what happens in this diagram when the amount of human capital rises, *given that Cuba is a small country*. What happens to trade flows? Explain.

Question 6.3

Since Deng Xiaoping took over leadership of China in 1977, tariffs have decreased dramatically. In 2001, China even joined the WTO, sending a signal to the world that tariff reduction will continue in the future. The effects of the opening up of China to international trade are heavily debated within the media. Some commentators claim that trading with China is a good thing because products become cheaper. Others stress the negative effect it has on some Western sectors, such as the clothes industry.

Let's analyse the integration of China in the world economy with the Heckscher-Ohlin factor abundance model. Assume, to make things easy, that there are only two countries: China and the Western world (the Western world is considered to be one country). China is relatively labour abundant and the Western world relatively capital abundant. Furthermore, assume that only two goods are consumed and produced in China and the Western world. These are clothes (produced relatively labour intensively) and computers (produced relatively capital intensively).

a. Draw a consistent graph in which you indicate the autarky production and consumption points of China and the Western world with the help of production possibility frontiers and utility curves.

b. Explain intuitively whether the relative price of clothes in the Western world is higher or lower compared to the relative price of clothes in China when both China and the Western world are in autarky. How can you see this price difference in your graph?

c. Explain what will happen to the prices of clothes and computers in the Western world when the Western world and China start trading.

d. What effect will this have on the consumption of clothes and computers and on the production of clothes and computers in the Western world? Indicate the new consumption and production point in the graph with the help of a budget line and a new utility curve (if your graph becomes messy, please draw a new graph).

e. Is integration of China into the world economy a good thing for the Western world? Use the observations you made above in your analysis. Also comment on the distribution of welfare between industries and owners of production factors.

 See the **online resources** *for a Study Guide and questions:*
www.oup.com/uk/vanmarrewijk_it/

Part III

....

Competitive advantage

....

Part III of this book, which consists of three chapters, moves away from the classical and neoclassical world of perfect competition into the world of competitive advantages. We start in Chapter 7 with an overview of imperfect competition (monopoly, oligopoly, and monopolistic competition) and its main consequences for international trade flows. Chapter 8 provides empirical information on intra-industry trade and how to measure this, as well as theoretical explanations for such trade flows. Chapter 9 analyses international capital and labour mobility, with a focus on empirical information. The theoretical foundations for these flows, leading to foreign direct investments and multinational firms, is analysed in Part V of the book, which is on international firms.

7 Imperfect competition

Objectives

- To be able to identify imperfectly competitive markets.
- To understand how monopoly power leads to mark-up pricing.
- To understand how mark-up pricing leads to deviations between the marginal rate of substitution and the marginal rate of transformation, and thus to sub-optimal outcomes.
- To know what reaction curves are and how to derive the Cournot equilibrium.
- To understand how more competitors erodes market power; international competition may thus lead to pro-competitive gains from trade.
- To understand how costly trade of identical product may nonetheless increase welfare.

7.1 Introduction

So far we have analysed perfectly competitive markets: that is, markets in which the firms do not perceive they have any market power. More specifically, they do not think they can influence the price at which the market clears. All firms individually, therefore, take the market-clearing price as given in their profit maximization problem. Each firm determines how much it will produce at any given price level. The actions of all firms together determine the market supply. This is confronted with the demand of consumers, and that interaction determines the price at which the market actually clears. Collectively, the firms therefore do influence the market-clearing price. If there are many firms, the impact of any individual firm on the market-clearing price is negligible: hence the assumption that each firm takes this price as given.

In many cases the assumption of perfect competition is a reasonable approximation. At a Dutch flower auction, for example, each night hundreds of growers deliver the flowers cut, selected, and packed that day to the auction to be sold off early the next morning at whatever price will clear the market. In many other cases, however, perfect competition is not a reasonable approximation. There may, for example, be only one company that delivers water to your house, or only one telephone company, or only one electricity company, etc. If so, this company obviously has market power and will realize that an increase in its production level will reduce the market-clearing price. Or, equivalently, it will realize that if it raises the price level, the demand for its goods or services will fall. Alternatively, there may be only a few companies, rather than one. There are at the moment, for example, only two companies producing large wide-body commercial aircraft for the global market, namely the American Boeing company and the European Airbus consortium. Each of the two companies realizes that they have market power and that their actions will influence the other company. They take this into consideration when determining the optimal strategy; see also Chapter 11.

If a firm does not take the price level on the market as given, but strategically interacts with other firms and with the market to maximize its profits, we are no longer in the realm of 'perfect competition'. Instead, we say such a market is characterized by 'imperfect competition', a poorly chosen term indeed, certainly in those cases in which it gives a better description of the actual market interactions. The world of perfect competition is attractive: it is well defined, its behavioural assumptions are clear and easy to understand, it leads to powerful conclusions, and in most cases it is a concept that substantially increases our knowledge and understanding of the workings of an economy. In contrast, the world of imperfect competition is a mess. Since there is an unlimited number of ways in which one can deviate from the 'perfect' world, there are many different 'imperfect' models, some of astounding complexity, leading to many different outcomes and policy prescriptions. To top things off, imperfect competition is hard to model in a general equilibrium setting, certainly in conjunction with production under increasing returns to scale. No wonder (international) economists have shied away from examining imperfect competition for a long time.

This does not mean that there has been no attention paid to the connections between monopoly power and international trade flows. As early as in 1701 Henry Martyn wrote a clear and concise tract, entitled *Considerations upon the East India Trade*, opposing monopoly restraints on the East India trade and restrictions on manufactured imports from India. Instead, such trade should be open to all merchants, not just to those licensed by the government:[1]

> In an open trade, every merchant is upon his good behaviour, always afraid of being undersold at home, always seeking out for new markets in foreign countries; in the meantime, trade is carried on with less expense: This is the effect of necessity and emulation, things unknown to a single company.

Martyn therefore opposes monopoly power in trade flows, arguing that competition among companies improves efficiency. None the less, there may be good reasons why there are only a few firms, or one, in an industry. Many of the examples given above, such as power companies, telecommunications, or aircraft production, require large initial investments before production of goods and services can start: for example the construction of a power plant, the wiring of a city, or the development of new aircraft and the construction of a factory to build them. After the initial investment, which can be seen as a fixed cost, production can start, involving high or low production costs. The larger the firm, as measured by the production level, the lower the costs of production per unit of output, because the large initial fixed investment costs can be spread across more goods. In other words, there are increasing returns to scale at the firm level. As we will argue in Chapter 8, this is incompatible with perfect competition. The consequences of increasing returns to scale are analysed in more detail in the following chapters. Here we focus on the impact of market power, and not on the importance of increasing returns to scale, such that all production functions in this chapter still exhibit constant returns to scale. Box 7.1 provides some information on Joe Stiglitz, one of the main contributors to the analysis of imperfect competition, while Box 7.2 offers an overview of the structure of the type of trade flow we are trying to explain.

BOX 7.1 Joseph Stiglitz

Figure 7.1
Joseph Stiglitz (1942–).

Like Samuelson (see Box 5.1), Joe Stiglitz (Figure 7.1) was born in Gary, Indiana. He received his PhD from MIT when he was only 24 years old. He has moved around from one prestigious university to another, never staying very long. He was chief economist of the World Bank (1997–2000) and worked at several prestigious places before moving to Columbia University. His many contributions to economics focus on imperfect competition and the importance of costly information. Outside his own field, his most influential contribution has undoubtedly been 'Monopolistic competition and optimum product diversity', published jointly with Avinash Dixit in the *American Economic Review* in 1977 (see Box 8.1).

BOX 7.2 Regional trade intensity

In Section 5.2 we discussed the size of international trade flows at the country level (see Figure 5.3) and at the global regional level (see Table 5.2 and Figure 5.2). It is clear that trade flows are high in Europe (EUR), East Asia (EAS), and North America (NAM). This is shown again in Table 7.1, which lists the share of each region's trade flows as a percentage of total world trade. The table shows that taken together Europe, East Asia, and North America account for more than 70 per cent of world trade flows. In contrast, trade flows are low in the Pacific (PAC), Sub-Saharan Africa (SSA), and South Asia (SAS) regions: taken together they are less than 7 per cent of the world total.

To evaluate whether trade flows for a particular region are actually higher or lower than we might expect, we need a benchmark with which to compare these flows. Table 7.1 provides two such benchmarks for each of the ten global regions, namely the region's population level and the region's income level (corrected for PPP). The last two columns of the table show the intensity of trade flows relative to these two measures by dividing a region's percentage of world trade by either a region's percentage of world population or its income. The following points are noteworthy.

- There are only four regions with above-average trade flows when compared to the region's population level, namely Europe, Pacific, North America, and (barely) the Middle East and North Africa (MNA). We will analyse the connection this has with intra-industry trade (Chapter 8) and supply chains (Chapter 15).

- Two regions have particularly low trade flows when compared to the region's population level, namely South Asia and Sub-Saharan Africa (both less than 20 per cent of the world average). We will analyse the connection this has with supply chains (Chapter 15) and economic growth and competitiveness (Chapter 17).

(continued...)

- Only three regions have above-average trade flows when compared to the region's income level, namely Europe, Pacific, and Southeast Asia (SEA).
- Only one region, namely South Asia, has dramatically low trade flows compared to the region's income level (only 30 per cent of the world average).

Which trade intensity measure (relative to population or income) is more important? There are arguments for either measure. On the one hand we should, of course, expect people with higher income levels to trade more, so the income measure seems more relevant. In that case the trade performance of South Asia is particularly worrisome, while Europe and Pacific do rather well. On the other hand, there is, of course, an endogeneity issue. People intensively involved in trade flows (for whatever reason) will benefit from all the aspects associated with these trade flows as discussed in this book. Consequently, they can reach higher levels of income. From this point of view, people should be the centre of analysis because low trade flows per person are indicative of underlying economic problems. From that point of view, the performance of both South Asia and Sub-Saharan Africa is particularly worrisome, while Europe, Pacific, and North America are doing quite well.

Table 7.1 Relative intensity of regional trade flows

Region	Per cent of world total			Trade flows relative to	
	Trade	Population	GDP	Population	GDP
CAS	4.5	5.2	6.6	0.9	0.7
EAS	20.0	22.7	23.1	0.9	0.9
EUR	37.3	7.8	19.1	4.8	2.0
LAC	6.0	8.4	8.2	0.7	0.7
MNA	5.3	4.3	5.8	1.2	0.9
NAM	13.5	5.2	18.5	2.6	0.7
PAC	1.7	0.4	1.2	4.0	1.5
SAS	2.7	24.5	8.5	0.1	0.3
SEA	6.7	8.4	5.8	0.8	1.2
SSA	2.2	13.2	3.2	0.2	0.7
World	100	100	100	1.0	1.0

Notes: GDP in PPP; shaded areas have above world average intensity; for region abbreviations see Table 5.1 and the main text.
Sources: see Table 5.2 and Chapter 1.

7.2 Monopoly

Suppose that there is only one firm active on a specific market. This firm is called a monopolist. Like any other firm, it will be interested in maximizing its profits, an interest probably camouflaged in its brochures as commitment to efficiency, service to society, and eagerness to deliver high-quality goods and services to its customers. Since it is the only firm active in

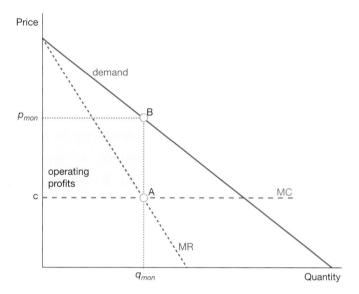

Figure 7.2 Optimal output for a monopolist.

the market, it will of course realize that its actions have a large impact on the market. In particular, the firm will realize that there is a negative relationship between the price charged for its products and the quantity sold on the market. The monopolist's profit maximization problem is therefore more sophisticated than the problem facing a perfectly competitive firm which treats the output price as a parameter. A monopolist must not only gather information about its own production processes and cost structure, but also about the market for its product and the responsiveness of this market to changes in the price charged by the monopolist. It is time for a quick review of the monopolist's profit maximization problem.

Figure 7.2 illustrates the monopolist's problem. The market demand curve is given by the downward-sloping solid line. It is assumed to be linear, which implies that the marginal revenue (MR) curve is also linear, with the same intercept and a slope twice as steep (see Box 7.3). The marginal revenue curve is steeper than the demand curve because the firm has to lower its price if it wants to sell more goods, which also lowers the revenue on the initially sold output. We assume that the firm's marginal costs (MC) are constant, as indicated by the dashed horizontal line in Figure 7.2.

To maximize its profits, the firm will set its marginal costs equal to its marginal revenue, as indicated by point A. It will therefore produce the monopoly output indicated by q_{mon} in Figure 7.2. To determine the price the firm will charge at this output level, we have to go back to the demand curve, see point B, which gives us price level p_{mon}. The most important thing to note about Figure 7.2 is that the price charged by the monopolist is *higher* than the marginal cost of production. In determining the optimal price for its products, the monopolist thus charges a *mark-up* over the marginal cost of production. This mark-up depends on the price elasticity of demand $\varepsilon(q) \equiv -(dq/dp)(p/q)$ as follows:

$$p\left(1 - \frac{1}{\varepsilon(q)}\right) = c(q) \qquad\qquad 7.1$$

BOX 7.3 Microeconomics and markets

The tools to be used in this chapter are taken from standard microeconomic theory. If a firm perceives it has market power, it will use this market power to the best of its advantage. We will analyse the case of a pure monopoly (one firm), of oligopoly (a few firms), and of monopolistic competition (many firms with individual market power, see Chapter 10). Let p be the price of a good and q the quantity produced. If the demand curve is linear, that is $p = a - bq$ for some positive parameters a and b, it follows that revenue R (price times quantity) equals $R = pq = (a - bq)q = aq - bq^2$. This, in turn, implies that marginal revenue MR (rise in total revenue if more output is produced) is equal to $MR = \dfrac{dR}{dq} = a - 2bq$.

We conclude, therefore, that if market demand is linear, then the marginal revenue curve is also linear; it has the same intercept and a slope twice as steep as the demand curve.

—where $c(q)$ is the marginal cost of production (see Technical Note 7.1). The deviation between price and marginal cost of production is in stark contrast to what is seen in a perfectly competitive market, in which the market clearing price is always equal to the marginal cost of production. The fact that a monopolist's market power enables the firm to charge a higher price than the marginal cost of production also implies that the firm is able to make a profit. Since we assumed the marginal cost of production to be constant, the firm's profits are represented by the shaded rectangle in Figure 7.2 as $(p_{mon} - c)q_{mon}$, that is, price minus cost times quantity sold.[2]

7.3 Monopoly in general equilibrium: autarky

As explained in Section 7.1, in this chapter we focus on the consequences of market power. Section 7.2 argued that in a partial equilibrium setting, the most important implication of monopoly power is the fact that the price charged on the output market is a mark-up over the marginal cost of production. We now discuss the impact of monopoly power in autarky in a simple general equilibrium setting, based on James Markusen's (1981) analysis. The main assumptions are as follows.

- There is a single producer of manufactures: this is a monopoly market.
- There are many producers of food: the market is perfectly competitive.
- The markets for factors of production (capital and labour) are also perfectly competitive (the monopolist of manufactures therefore has no monopsony power on its input markets).
- All firms maximize profits.
- All consumers maximize utility, taking the final goods prices as given.

Without going into any further detail as to how the autarky equilibrium is determined exactly, we can draw some important conclusions based on the properties that must hold in this equilibrium. First, we know that the marginal rate of transformation (MRT) must be equal to the ratio of marginal costs: see Chapter 6. Second, we know that the price charged by the monopolist is a mark-up over the marginal cost of production: see equation 7.1. Third, we know that the marginal rate of substitution (MRS) must be equal to the ratio of final goods prices: again, see Chapter 6. Fourth, we know that market clearing in autarky implies that production must be equal to consumption in equilibrium. Combining this information leads to the following important conclusion:

$$\text{MRT} = \frac{MC_m}{MC_f} = \frac{p_m\left(1 - \frac{1}{\varepsilon(q)}\right)}{p_f} < \frac{p_m}{p_f} = \text{MRS} \qquad 7.2$$

—where ε_m is the price elasticity of demand for manufactures.

The autarky equilibrium if there is a monopoly for manufactures is illustrated in Figure 7.3 at point mon. Note that point mon is in accordance with the four remarks made above. Perfect competition in the factor markets implies that the production point is efficient: that is, it must be on the production possibility frontier. Since the monopolist for manufactures charges a higher price than the marginal cost of production, the marginal rate of transformation deviates from the final goods price ratio, which in turn is equal to the marginal rate of substitution: see equation 7.2. Moreover, at the income level generated by the economy at point mon, consumers also want to consume at point mon, such that production equals consumption in both sectors.

As is clear from Figure 7.3, the fact that there is a monopoly in manufactures implies that the economy is not producing at the social optimum: the utility level achieved at point mon is equal to U_{mon}, which is strictly below the utility level U_{opt} which the economy can achieve in autarky at point opt. The monopoly in manufactures, leading to a mark-up of price over marginal costs, therefore leads to a sub-optimal autarky equilibrium in which the production level of manufactures is too low.

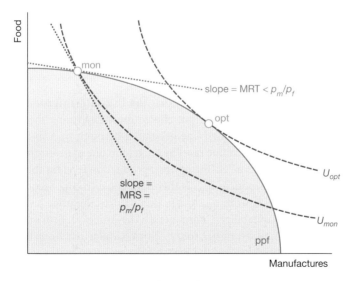

Figure 7.3 Autarky equilibrium with a monopoly for manufactures.

7.4 **Oligopoly**

Market power can, of course, also arise if there are only a few firms, rather than one, active in a market. This is called an oligopoly. If there are just two firms, say an American firm (sub-index A) and a British firm (sub-index B), the market is called a duopoly. That case has already been analysed by Augustin Cournot (1838). He assumes that the two firms produce identical goods, such that there is only one market demand curve, and that each firm maximizes its profits, given the demand curve and the output level of its opponent (see Chapter 11 on Bertrand-type price competition instead of quantity competition). Determining the equilibrium production levels, and concomitant price level, in this market is somewhat more involved than if there is only one firm. As in Section 7.2, we impose a linear demand curve; see, however, Technical Note 7.2.

Let p be the market price and $q = q_A + q_B$ be the total output in the market. We focus on the problem for the American firm. Similar observations hold for the British firm. The basic problem for the American firm is quite similar to the problem facing a monopolist. However, given the linear market demand $p = a - bq$ and the fact that total output is the sum of the American firm's and British firm's output, it follows that the American firm's profits π_A depend on the British firm's output level as follows:

$$\pi_A = (p - c)q_A = [(a - c) - b(q_A + q_B)]q_A \qquad 7.3$$

where c is the marginal cost of production. Observe that

(i)   given the output level q_{B0} of the British firm, the American firm maximizes profits π_A through a suitable choice of its output level, at say q_{A0};

(ii) if the British firm changes its production level from q_{B0} to q_{B1}, the American firm's profit maximization problem in point (i) is affected, which leads to a *different* optimal choice of its output level, say q_{A1};

(iii) in general, therefore, each different output level of the British firm leads to a different optimal output level for the American firm. The collection of all optimal output responses by the American firm to the British firm's output level is called the *American firm's reaction curve*.

This is illustrated in Figure 7.4. First, given that the British firm produces q_{B0} units of goods, the American firm's optimal output choice must determine the optimal output combination on the dashed horizontal line generated by point q_{B0}. Since the American firm maximizes profits, this dashed line must be tangent to one of its isoprofit curves, some of which are also drawn in Figure 7.4. The optimal production level for the American firm, given that the British firm produces q_{B0}, is therefore equal to q_{A0}. Second, if the British firm increases its output level from q_{B0} to q_{B1}, this reduces the price level in the market and the American firm's profitability. Consequently, the American firm's optimal response is then a reduction in output, from q_{A0} to q_{A1}. Third, similar reactions by the American firm to changes in the output level of the British firm are given by the dots in Figure 7.4. Connecting all such dots gives the *reaction curve* of the American firm. Fourth, note that if the output level of the British firm is equal to zero, the American firm's problem reduces to that of a monopolist. Clearly this leads to the maximum attainable profits for the American

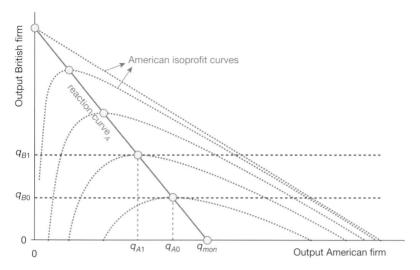

Figure 7.4 Derivation of the American firm's reaction curve, $a = 8$; $b = c = 1$.

firm, at point q_{mon} in Figure 7.4. The isoprofit curves of the American firm in Figure 7.4 thus increase as they approach q_{mon}.

As already remarked above, the British firm faces a similar problem to that of the American firm. This means that, taking the output level q_A as given, the British firm will derive its optimal (profit-maximizing) output level q_B. If we vary the American firm's output level, we can derive all optimal responses by the British firm, which then obviously gives the British firm's reaction curve. This is illustrated in Figure 7.5, which also gives the American firm's reaction curve and an isoprofit curve for each firm. Note that the isoprofit curve for the British firm is vertical at the point of intersection with its reaction curve because the British firm maximizes its profits at that point. The Cournot equilibrium is reached at the point of intersection of the two reaction curves, as indicated by point C in Figure 7.5. Why? Because, as the reader may wish to verify, it is the only point in the figure for which the American firm maximizes its profits given the output level of the British firm, while simultaneously the British firm maximizes its profits given the output level of the American firm. The duopoly price p_{duo} and quantity for each firm q_{duo} are derived in Technical Note 7.2:

$$q_{duo} = \frac{a-c}{3b} = q_A = q_B; \quad p_{duo} = \frac{a+2c}{3} < \frac{a+c}{2} = p_{mon}, \text{ since } a > c \qquad 7.4$$

Note, in particular, that the duopoly price is lower than the monopolistic price, which implies that the duopoly output level for the market ($2q_{duo}$) is higher than the monopoly output level. Apparently, more competition, as measured by an increase in the number of firms, leads to a lower price level. In fact, if the American firm operates in a market with more than one firm, the following result holds in general (again, see Technical Note 7.2):

$$p\left(1 - \frac{q_A}{q}\frac{1}{\varepsilon(q)}\right) = c(q_A) \qquad 7.5$$

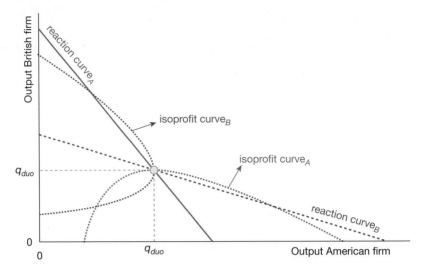

Figure 7.5 Cournot equilibrium.

Equation 7.5 indicates that the marginal-revenue-equals-marginal-cost rule which the American firm applies leads to a mark-up of price over marginal cost depending on:

- the price elasticity of demand $\varepsilon(q)$ prevailing in the market and
- the American firm's market share q_A/q.

More specifically, the higher the price elasticity of demand the lower the mark-up, and the lower the American firm's market share the lower the mark-up. In the limit, as the number of firms in the Cournot model becomes arbitrarily large and the American firm's market share becomes arbitrarily small, the mark-up disappears and the price becomes equal to the marginal cost of production, as in the perfectly competitive model. One of the main attractions of the Cournot model is therefore that it reduces to the monopoly model if there is only one firm and to the perfectly competitive model if there are arbitrarily many firms.

7.5 The pro-competitive effect of international trade

We are now in a position to illustrate another benefit of international trade flows, namely the increase in market competition, which lowers the mark-up of price over marginal costs, which in turn increases efficiency. This benefit is called the *pro-competitive gain from trade*. To discuss this effect we use the Markusen (1981) framework analysed in Section 7.3 above. That is, we assume that the factor markets are perfectly competitive, firms maximize profits, consumers maximize utility, and the food sector is perfectly competitive, while the market for manufactures has one monopoly producer.

In this section we want to analyse the impact of international trade flows. To do this, we assume that there are two identical countries; they have the same technology, the same homothetic tastes, the same stocks of capital and labour, etc. This has several advantages. First, it is easy to get our main point across. Second, we can illustrate the world economy by investigating only one country. Third, and most importantly, we neutralize any other reasons that may give rise to international trade flows, or that may lead to gains from trade. Since technology is the same, there is no Ricardian reason to trade. Since the capital–labour ratio is the same, there is no factor abundance (Heckscher–Ohlin) reason to trade.

The pro-competitive gains from trade are illustrated in Figure 7.6. In autarky both countries produce at the same distorted production and consumption point mon, as discussed in Section 7.3. In autarky, the manufactures firm is a monopolist, which implies that the marginal rate of transformation is below the marginal rate of substitution: see equation 7.5. If trade of final goods is allowed, however, the monopoly producers for manufactures in both countries are confronted with an extra competitor, namely the firm that had been a monopolist in the other country. The market for manufactures has therefore become a duopoly, rather than a monopoly, in both countries. As described in Section 7.4, and analogous to our reasoning in Section 7.3, we can therefore conclude:

$$MRT_{duo} = \frac{MC_m}{MC_f}\bigg|_{duo} = \frac{p_m(1-1/2\varepsilon_m)}{p_f} < \frac{p_m}{p_f}\bigg|_{duo} = MRS_{duo} \qquad 7.6$$

As in the autarky equilibrium with a monopoly summarized in equation 7.2, the marginal rate of transformation is below the marginal rate of substitution in the trade equilibrium with a duopoly. Note, however, that in a duopoly firms only take the effect of *their share of the market* into consideration when determining the optimal production level: see equation 7.5. The wedge between the marginal rate of transformation and the marginal rate of substitution has therefore *reduced* from $1-1/\varepsilon_m$ to $1-1/2\varepsilon_m$ (because each firm in our example controls half the market). Consequently, the Cournot international trade equilibrium is illustrated by point cou in Figure 7.6, in which the wedge between the marginal rate of transformation and the marginal rate of substitution has reduced, leading to more efficient production and higher welfare. This is known as the pro-competitive effect of international trade. Box 7.4 presents an empirical discussion of this effect.

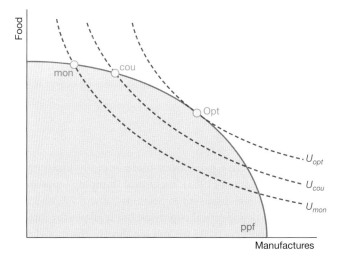

Figure 7.6 Pro-competitive gains from trade.

BOX 7.4 The Twaron takeover

Aramid fibres were made for the first time in the 1970s. These synthetic fibres are very strong and light, do not break or rust, and have a high chemical and heat resistance. They are used, for example, for friction and sealing, and in the production of tyres, protective clothing, optical cables, and bulletproof vests. Until fairly recently there were three firms producing aramid fibres, namely an American firm (DuPont, producing 18,000 tons annually under the brand name Kevlar), a Dutch firm (Acordis, producing 10,300 tons under the brand name Twaron), and a Japanese firm (Teijin, producing 1,400 tons under the brand name Technora). In 2000 the Japanese firm Teijin bought the aramid fibre component from the Dutch firm Acordis. The impact of the takeover in this oligopolistic market structure, which changed from three suppliers to two suppliers as a result of the takeover, can be estimated using the Cournot model of Section 7.4. This is indicated in Table 7.2 for a demand structure with constant price elasticity (rather than the linear demand discussed in Section 7.4). After calibrating the model to ensure that the result shows the above distribution of market shares (that is, DuPont has the lowest and Teijin the highest marginal costs), the table reports the impact of the takeover for two possible demand elasticities, namely $\varepsilon = 2$ and $\varepsilon = 1$.

The decrease in international competition as a result of the takeover increases the market-clearing price by about 2–6 per cent, depending on the price elasticity of demand. All suppliers in the market benefit from the higher price, and this leads to higher operating profits. These rise for Kevlar as a result of the higher price (an estimated effect of 6–8 per cent) and for the new combination Twaron/Technora as a result of the higher price and the better use of economies of scale (an estimated effect of 9–16 per cent).

Table 7.2 Implications of the Twaron takeover (%)

	Price elasticity of demand	
	$\varepsilon = 2$	$\varepsilon = 1$
Price rise after takeover	1.9	6.1
Rise in operating profits after takeover		
Kevlar	6.5	8.1
Twaron/Technora	9.5	15.6

Remark. Note that the monopoly firms in both countries have a strong incentive to lobby with their respective governments against international trade flows. If they are successful in producing barriers to such flows, their profits will rise.

7.6 'Reciprocal dumping'

The power of the pro-competitive gains from trade is nicely illustrated in the Brander (1981) and Brander and Krugman (1983) 'reciprocal dumping' approach. It is based on the Cournot competition model discussed in Sections 7.4 and 7.5, and therefore assumes a symmetric situation with two identical countries, but it allows for international trade to take place at positive transport costs. As we will see shortly, the model predicts that there is 'pointless' and costly trade in homogeneous products between the two countries, which none the less can increase welfare. The World Trade Organization (WTO, see Chapter 10) defines 'dumping' as the sale of export below normal value. The term 'normal value' is operationalized either as (i) the comparable price of the product in the exporting country, (ii) the comparable price for export to a third country, or (iii) the cost of production in the country of origin plus a reasonable addition for selling cost and profit.[3] Since the firms in the model to be developed below sell goods in the other country at the same price as at home and do not recuperate the costs of transportation, it is called the 'reciprocal dumping' model.

We illustrate the reciprocal dumping model for linear demand functions using 'iceberg' transport costs (see Box 7.5). The parameter $T \geq 1$ denotes the number of goods that need to be shipped to ensure that one unit of the good arrives in the other country. If the marginal cost of producing the good is c for both firms, the marginal cost of delivering the good in the other country is therefore $Tc > c$. Let q_{AA} be the American firm's supply in the USA and q_{BA} the British firm's supply in the USA. With a linear demand curve, the price p_A in the USA can be written as a function of the total quantity supplied:

$$p_A = a - b(q_{AA} + q_{BA}) \qquad\qquad 7.7$$

7.6.1 Autarky

In autarky, the American firm is a monopolist in the USA. As illustrated in Figure 7.7, the price is determined by the equality of marginal cost and monopoly marginal revenue at point A, leading to monopoly price p_{mon} and monopoly output q_{mon}.

7.6.2 Trade

With free international trade, the American firm faces competition from the British firm, despite the fact that the British firm has higher marginal costs of delivering goods to the market of the USA as a result of the transport costs T. This gives the American firm a natural advantage in the domestic market. Nonetheless, as long as the price in the USA is above the British firm's marginal costs inclusive of transport costs Tc, the British firm will make a profit by selling goods in the American market. As shown in Technical Note 7.3, the reciprocal dumping equilibrium is given by

$$q_{AA} = \frac{a + Tc - 2c}{3b}; \quad q_{BA} = \frac{a + c - 2Tc}{3b}; \quad p_{rec} = \frac{a + c + Tc}{3} \qquad 7.8$$

BOX 7.5 Iceberg transport costs

'Iceberg' transport costs, introduced by Paul Samuelson (1952), imply that only a fraction of the goods shipped between locations actually arrives at the destination. The fraction that does not arrive represents the cost of transportation. The parameter T, defined as the number of goods that need to be shipped to ensure that one unit arrives per unit of distance, represents the transport costs. Suppose, for example, that the unit of distance is equal to the distance from Naaldwijk (a small town in the centre of the Dutch horticultural agglomeration) to Paris, and that 107 flowers are sent from the Netherlands to France, while only 100 arrive unharmed in Paris and can be sold. Then $T = 1.07$. It is as if some goods have melted away in transit, hence the term 'iceberg costs'. This way of modelling the transport costs without introducing a transport sector is attractive in combination with the Chapter 8 price-setting behaviour of producers; see also Chapter 16.

Figure 7.7 Reciprocal dumping.

Note that $q_{AA} > q_{BA}$: that is, the American firm's market share in the USA is larger than the British firm's market share as a result of its lower marginal costs. The situation is illustrated in Figure 7.7. With imports equal to q_{BA} the domestic market demand curve for the American firm shifts inward (not drawn). The perceived marginal revenue curve therefore shifts down from MR_{mon} to MR_{rec}. The American firm's output level is determined by the equality of the new marginal revenue curve with the marginal cost of production at point B. The British firm's demand curve in the USA is shifted further inwards (by the extent of q_{AA}) and its output level is determined by equality of its perceived marginal revenue curve with its marginal costs inclusive of transport costs (not drawn). Since the British firm sells fewer units in the American market, its perceived elasticity of demand is higher than for the American firm, leading to a lower mark-up over marginal costs (which are higher for the British firm than for the American firm, leading to the same price in equilibrium).

7.6.3 Reciprocal dumping and welfare

Note that this symmetric model gives rise to 'reciprocal dumping' as a result of the difference in perceived elasticity of demand: the British firm incurs high transport costs to sell goods in the American market at a lower mark-up over marginal costs than at home,

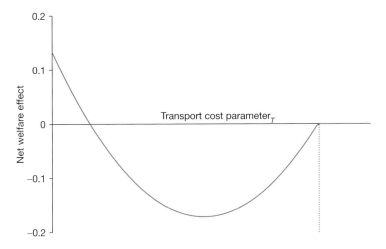

Figure 7.8 Trade and welfare in the reciprocal dumping model.

Note: The dashed line indicates prohibitive transport costs; $a = 3.25$; $b = 0.65$; $c = 0.75$.

and similarly for the American firm in the British market. Despite this seemingly point-less and costly international trade, the pro-competitive effect of trade, leading to lower prices, higher quantities, and smaller deviations between price and marginal costs, may increase the welfare levels of both countries. Figure 7.8 illustrates the welfare changes using the partial equilibrium tools developed in Chapter 10. Since trade reduces prices, there is an increase in consumer surplus. At the same time, the domestic firm's drop in profits at home is only partially compensated by an increase in profits abroad. In general, therefore, the welfare effect is ambivalent. As illustrated in Figure 7.8, however, for small and moderate transport costs the net welfare effects are positive. Only if transport costs are high (in this specific example if transport costs are 24 per cent; that is $T = 1.24$) is the net welfare effect negative. A further increase in transport costs eventually reduces this welfare loss as trade becomes too small and costly. Ultimately trade disappears (prohibi-tive transport costs).

7.7 Conclusions

Profit-maximizing firms in an imperfectly competitive market will charge a mark-up of price over marginal costs. The size of the mark-up depends on the price elasticity of demand and on the degree of competition, such that an increase in the number of firms reduces the mark-up. In a general equilibrium setting, imperfect competition leads to a sub-optimal outcome (a deviation between the marginal rate of substitution, MRS, and the marginal rate of transformation, MRT). Since international trade increases market competition, as foreign firms start to compete on the domestic market and vice versa, international trade improves economic efficiency (by diminishing the deviation between MRS and MRT): these improvements are the so-called pro-competitive gains from trade. This 'reciprocal' dumping may even increase welfare if international trade is costly.

Technical Notes

Technical Note 7.1 Monopolist profit maximization

If a market's demand curve is given by $p(q)$ and a monopolist's cost function is given by $C(q)$, where q is the quantity of output, then the firm's profits π are given by

$$\pi = p(q)q - C(q) \tag{7.A1}$$

The first-order condition for profit maximization is

$$p + \frac{dp}{dq}q = \frac{dC}{dq} \tag{7.A2}$$

If we let $c(q)$ denote the marginal cost of production and, as is customary, measure the responsiveness of demand to price changes in relative terms, that is using the elasticity of substitution $\varepsilon(q) \equiv -\left(\frac{dq}{dp}\right)\left(\frac{p}{q}\right) > 0$, the first-order condition can be rewritten as

$$p\left(1 - \frac{1}{\varepsilon(q)}\right) = c(q) \tag{7.A3}$$

If demand is linear ($p = a - bq$), we have $\varepsilon(q) = (a - bq)/bq$ resulting in

$$q_{mon} = \frac{a-c}{2b} \text{ and } p_{mon} = \frac{a+c}{2} > \frac{c+c}{2} = c, \text{ because } a > c. \tag{7.A4}$$

Technical Note 7.2 Cournot profit maximization

Suppose a market's demand curve is given by $p(q)$, where q is total output by all firms active in the market. If firm A is one of those firms, we can write market output as $q = q_A + q_{-A}$, where q_A is the output of firm A and q_{-A} is the output of all other firms. If firm A's cost function is given by $C(q_A)$, then firm A's profits π_A are given by

$$\pi_A = p(q)q_A - C(q_A) \tag{7.A5}$$

The first-order condition for profit maximization is

$$p + \frac{dp}{dq}q_A = c(q_A) \tag{7.A6}$$

where $c(q_A)$ is the marginal cost of production. Let $\varepsilon(q)$ be the price elasticity of demand; then the first-order condition can be rewritten as

$$p\left(1 - \frac{q_A}{q}\frac{1}{\varepsilon(q)}\right) = c(q_A) \tag{7.A7}$$

For a duopoly, linear demand curve $p = a - bq$, and $c(q) = c$, firm A's reaction curve is

$$\frac{\partial \pi_A}{\partial q_A} = 0 \Rightarrow q_A = \frac{a-c}{2b} - \frac{1}{2}q_B \tag{7.A8}$$

Similarly for firm B. The Cournot equilibrium is at the intersection of the reaction curves

$$q_A = q_B = \frac{a-c}{3b} \text{ and } p_{duo} = \frac{a+2c}{3} < \frac{a+c}{2} = p_{mon}, \text{ because } a > c. \tag{7.A9}$$

Technical Note 7.3 Reciprocal dumping model

Since the model is symmetric for the two countries, we concentrate on the USA. With a linear demand curve, the price p_A can be written as a function of firm A's supply in the USA q_{AA} and firm B's supply in the USA q_{BA}:

$$p_A = a - b(q_{AA} + q_{BA}) \tag{7.A10}$$

Assuming that marginal cost of production is equal to c for both firms, and that there are iceberg transport costs, such that marginal cost for firm B for delivery of goods in the USA is equal to Tc, the profit functions π are:

$$\pi_A = [a - b(q_{AA} + q_{BA})]q_{AA} - cq_{AA} \text{ and } \pi_B = [a - b(q_{AA} + q_{BA})]q_{BA} - Tcq_{BA} \tag{7.A11}$$

First order conditions for profit maximization, given the other firm's output level, are:

$$(a - bq_{BA}) - 2bq_{AA} = c \text{ and } (a - bq_{AA}) - 2bq_{BA} = Tc \tag{7.A12}$$

Solving these two linear equations gives:

$$q_{AA} = \frac{a + Tc - 2c}{3b}, \ q_{BA} = \frac{a + c - 2Tc}{3b}, \text{ and } p_{rec} = \frac{a + c + Tc}{3} \tag{7.A13}$$

Notes

1   See Irwin (1996, p. 57).

2   The shaded area represents operating profits. This may be required to recuperate the initial (fixed cost) outlays if there are increasing returns to scale: see Chapter 8.

3   The normal value minus the export price is the margin of dumping. It must exceed 2 per cent to be actionable, in which case the importing country can levy an anti-dumping duty if the imports cause, or are likely to cause, injury to the domestic industry.

Questions

Question 7.1

Briefly answer or comment on the questions and remarks below.

a.   What is, according to you, the main consequence of market power for firms? Why?

b.   In an oligopolistic setting with Cournot competition we derived firm A's *reaction curve*. Give a short definition of this reaction curve.

c.   Why is firm A's isoprofit curve *horizontal* at the point of intersection with its reaction curve, while firm B's isoprofit curve is *vertical* at the point of intersection with its reaction curve in Figure 7.5?

Question 7.2

Briefly comment on this statement: 'as explained in Section 7.3 of the book, the main welfare impact of a rise in firm market power in a sector of the economy is the creation of a sub-optimal economic outcome in autarky because of the deviation between the marginal rate of transformation (MRT) and the marginal rate of substitution (MRS) in equilibrium.' Hint: carefully look at equation 7.2.

Question 7.3

What are pro-competitive gains from trade? Briefly describe the main mechanism underlying these gains from trade under Cournot competition.

*See the **online resources** for a Study Guide and questions:*
www.oup.com/uk/vanmarrewijk_it/

8 Intra-industry trade

Objectives

- To know the difference between intra- and inter-industry trade.
- To be able to measure the extent of intra-industry trade using the Grubel–Lloyd index.
- To understand the relationships between increasing returns to scale and market power.
- To understand the main demand structure of the Dixit–Stiglitz model.
- To realize how increasing returns to scale limit the number of available varieties.
- To know what monopolistic competition is and how market size determines the number of available varieties.
- To understand how trade extends the market and increases the number of varieties.
- To know how trade in final goods leads to love-of-variety gains from trade (Krugman).
- To know how intermediate goods trade leads to production externality gains from trade (Ethier).

8.1 Introduction

We extend the analysis of imperfect competition by including economies of scale, which in conjunction with the size of the market determines the number of different types of goods and services available. Trade increases the extent of the market, thus making more types of goods available. This can be used to explain the empirical phenomenon of intra-industry trade (two-way trade in similar types of goods). This phenomenon is a prime example of a widely known and accepted empirical regularity for which a satisfactory theoretical foundation has been sought for many years. For a long time the empirical researchers were therefore clearly ahead of the theoretical researchers. What is intra-industry trade? It refers to the fact that many countries simultaneously export and import similar goods and services; intra-industry trade is therefore trade within the same industry or sector. Germany, for example, exports many cars to France and simultaneously imports many cars from France as well. Why does Germany do this? This chapter seeks to give an answer to this question based on aspects of a nation's demand structure, as well as its supply structure.

The intra-industry trade phenomenon was first noted empirically when a group of European countries formed the European Common Market, which has now grown into the European Union (EU) and currently consists of 28 countries; see Chapter 12. It was realized that most EU trade was with other EU countries and that it involved the simultaneous

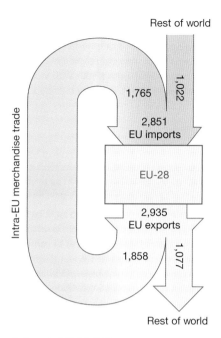

Figure 8.1 EU merchandise trade flows in 2014, in billion euros.

Source: calculations based on Eurostat data (http://ec.europa.eu/eurostat).

import and export of similar types of goods. Figure 8.1 illustrates that in 2014 about 63 per cent of the EU's merchandise exports of €2,935 billon were destined for other EU countries and about 63 per cent of the EU's imports of €2,851 billion came from other EU countries.[1] It was soon realized that intra-industry trade is a general characteristic of trade flows. Path-breaking empirical research in measuring the size and importance of intra-industry trade was performed by Pieter Verdoorn (1960), Bela Balassa (1966), and Herbert Grubel and Peter Lloyd (1975); see Section 8.3. One of the most important theoretical contributions was written by Avinash Dixit (see Box 8.1) together with Joe Stiglitz (see Box 7.1); see the discussion in Boxes 8.2 and 8.3 for further details.

Box 8.1 Avinash Dixit

Born in Bombay, India, where he studied mathematics and physics, Avanash Dixit (Figure 8.2) continued his studies at the University of Cambridge, where he got his BA, and at MIT, where he got his PhD, before moving to Princeton in 1981. His theoretical work, characterizing market equilibrium and designing policies, covers various areas of economics, including microeconomics, international economics, industrial organization, public economics, investment under uncertainty, and growth and

Figure 8.2
Avinash Dixit (1944–).

(continued...)

development. Influential contributions are 'Monopolistic competition and optimum product diversity', published jointly with Joseph Stiglitz (see Box 7.1) in the *American Economic Review* in 1977, and two books: *Theory of International Trade* (1980), with Victor Norman, and *Investment under Uncertainty* (1994), with Robert Pindyck.

Box 8.2 Dixit–Stiglitz monopolistic competition

There is only one way for competition to be 'perfect'. In contrast, there is a bewildering range of models describing 'imperfect' competition, investigating many different cases and assumptions regarding market behaviour, the type of good, strategic interaction, preferences of consumers, etc. This was also the case with monopolistic competition, until Avinash Dixit and Joseph Stiglitz (1977) published 'Monopolistic competition and optimum product diversity' in the *American Economic Review*. This article was to revolutionize model-building in at least four fields of economics: trade theory, industrial organization, growth theory, and geographical economics.[2]

The big step forward was to make some heroic assumptions concerning the symmetry of new varieties and the structural form, which allowed for an elegant and consistent way to model production at the firm level benefiting from internal economies of scale in conjunction with a market structure of monopolistic competition, without getting bogged down in a taxonomy of oligopoly models. These factors are responsible for the present popularity of the Dixit–Stiglitz model. Researchers in all fields now using the Dixit–Stiglitz formulation intensively were aware that imperfect competition is an essential feature of many empirically observed phenomena. The Dixit–Stiglitz model was therefore immediately accepted as the new standard for modelling monopolistic competition; its development was certainly very timely. In trade theory, its introduction enabled international economists to explain and understand intra-industry trade: see Krugman (1979, 1980). In industrial organization it helped to get rid of many ad hoc assumptions, which hampered the development of many models: see Tirole (1988). The Dixit–Stiglitz model was also used to explore the role of intermediate differentiated goods in trade models. This reformulation of the standard Dixit–Stiglitz model plays an important role in analysing the link between international trade and economic growth: see Grossman and Helpman (1991). Finally, the model is intensively used in geographical economics: see Brakman, Garretsen, and van Marrewijk (2009).

Box 8.3 The elasticity parameter as a measure of returns to scale?

The parameter ε is directly related to the consumer's preferences, as defined in equation 8.2. In equilibrium, however, it is also used as a measure of economies of scale. One specific measure of economies of scale is average costs divided by marginal costs: if marginal costs are lower than average costs, an increase in production will reduce the cost per unit. We can calculate this measure for the equilibrium

(continued...)

level of production. The production level is (see equation 8.9) $f(\varepsilon - 1)/m$, which requires $f\varepsilon$ labour, so the average costs are $f\varepsilon/[f(\varepsilon - 1)/m] = m\varepsilon/(\varepsilon - 1)$. The marginal labour costs are simply m, so this measure of scale economies reduces to average costs/marginal costs = $\varepsilon/(\varepsilon - 1)$. For a low value of ε this measure of scale economies is high, and vice versa. In equilibrium it depends only on the elasticity of substitution parameter ε, and not on the parameters f and m of the production function. This peculiar result, in which the measure of scale economies is related to parameters not of the production function but of the utility function, is an artefact of the Dixit–Stiglitz model of monopolistic competition, which makes average costs over marginal costs an unsuitable measure of scale economies.

8.2 Theoretical issues

Why did the realization that there is intensive intra-industry trade between nations embarrass theoretical economists? Because the theories of comparative advantage developed until then, based on Ricardian technology differences or Heckscher–Ohlin factor abundance, cannot explain this type of trade. Both types of models assume that firms in the same industry produce identical goods, such that consumers do not distinguish between the goods produced by different firms, nor care which firm produced the goods in making their demand decisions. A country will therefore either only export goods within a particular sector, or only import such goods, but will not simultaneously export and import goods within the same sector.

It was, of course, immediately realized that the goods and services produced by firms in the same sector are, in fact, not identical. Taking the simultaneous German exports of cars to France and imports of cars from France as an example, everyone acknowledges that a Volkswagen Golf is not the same as a Peugeot 308. They are similar products, delivering similar services and produced using a similar technology, such that they are classified in the same sector, but they are not the same. A satisfactory theoretical explanation should therefore be able to distinguish between goods and services that are close, but imperfect, substitutes. This requires a change in the demand structure of the economic model, such that consumers demand many different varieties of similar, but not identical, products in the same sector.

Suppose that we are able to change the demand structure of the economic model such that consumers have a preference for different varieties of similar products. Are we then able to explain intra-industry trade? Not yet, because we still have to explain why the domestic industry does not provide an arbitrarily large number of varieties to cater to the preferences of consumers. Going back to the Germany–France car example, it is clear that Volkswagen has the ability and technology available to produce a car virtually identical to the Peugeot 308, and is thus able to fulfil demand for that type of product. Large initial investment costs, spread over several years, are required, however, before such a new type of car is designed, developed, tested, and produced. These large investment costs, giving rise to increasing returns to scale, are the primary reason for Volkswagen, or other German car manufacturers, to produce only a limited number of varieties. This also implies that a car manufacturer, being the only producer of a particular variety, has considerable market power, which it takes into consideration when maximizing profits.

These considerations clarify why it took some time, and considerable ingenuity, to provide a solid theoretical explanation of intra-industry trade flows, since such an explanation has to incorporate:

- consumer preferences with a demand for different varieties of similar products;
- increasing returns to scale in production, limiting the diversity in production that the market can provide;
- a market structure of imperfect competition consistent with the phenomenon of increasing returns to scale.

The challenge is to incorporate these features in a simple general equilibrium setting, for which the industrial organization literature provided the most important stimulus with the Dixit and Stiglitz (1977) paper: see Box 8.2. The American economist Paul Krugman (1979, 1980) used the Dixit–Stiglitz variety specification combined with internal increasing returns to scale to analyse intra-industry trade in a model of monopolistic competition (Chamberlin, 1933). Simultaneously, Lancaster (1979) introduced consumer heterogeneity, where consumers are distinguished by their most preferred product characteristics, in which differentiated products cater to different tastes. In both cases, increasing returns to scale limit the extent of diversity that the market can provide. We restrict attention to the Krugman variety approach, not only because it is the easiest framework to work with, but also because it has had a bigger impact on the rest of the trade literature and serves as a good introduction to geographical economics (Chapter 16) and trade and growth (Chapter 17). A disadvantage of this choice is that the analysis of trade does not eliminate some domestic varieties from the market (see Sections 8.8 and 8.9), something that is behind a lot of protests against globalization.

8.3 Measuring intra-industry trade: Grubel–Lloyd

How do we measure intra-industry trade, the extent of trade in similar goods? Although various options are available, the measure most often used is the Grubel–Lloyd index, which is simple and intuitively appealing. Let Ex_i be the exports of industry i and let Im_i be the imports of industry i; then the Grubel-Lloyd index GL_i for industry i is defined as

$$GL_i = 1 - \frac{|Ex_i - Im_i|}{Ex_i + Im_i} \qquad 8.1$$

If a country only imports or only exports goods or services within the same industry, such that there is no intra-industry trade, the second term on the right-hand side of equation 8.1 is equal to 1 (since $Ex_i/Ex_i = 1$ or $Im_i / Im_i = 1$), such that the whole expression reduces to zero. Similarly, if the exports of goods or services are exactly equal to the imports of those goods or services within the same industry ($Ex_i = Im_i$), the second term on the right-hand side of equation 8.1 is equal to zero, such that the whole expression reduces to 1. The Grubel–Lloyd index therefore varies between zero, indicating no intra-industry trade, and 1, indicating only intra-industry trade.

Which share of international trade is intra-industry trade? We illustrate this question using data for France's top ten export sectors as given in Table 8.1. (We report the results of a more detailed study below—Table 8.2 and Figure 8.3—and we present a case study of China's trade flows in Section 8.10.) International trade data are grouped at the 'digit' level. Table 8.1 gives exports and imports of France at the two-digit level (ten out of 96 two-digit sectors are listed). With an export value of $65.2 billion, France's largest export sector in 2013 is HS84 'nuclear reactors, machinery'.[3] Now note that France's import value for sector 84 is $74.5 billion; applying equation 8.1 shows that according to the Grubel–Lloyd index 93.3 per cent of the trade in HS84 is intra-industry trade: see the last column in Table 8.1. Similar observations hold for most sectors reported in Table 8.1: the percentage of intra-industry trade is about 69 for aircraft, 88 for cars, 94 for plastics, and so on. It is the lowest in Table 8.1 for mineral fuels and oils and for beverages, but still a substantial 34 and 37 per cent, respectively. The lowest overall score is still 17.1 per cent for HS10 cereals, of which France exports almost $11 billion and imports $1 billion (not listed in Table 8.1). France's trade-weighted average Grubel–Lloyd index for all sectors is no less than 75.9 per cent. Based on this information we conclude that intra-industry trade is very important for France.

So what goods are classified in sector HS84 nuclear reactors, machinery? At the four-digit level it includes such diverse products as nuclear reactors (HS8401), compression-ignition internal combustion piston engines (HS8408), air conditioning machines (HS8415), machine tools for honing or finishing metal (HS8460), and so on. The calculation in Table 8.1 groups all of this together at the two-digit level. The Grubel–Lloyd index of 93.3 per cent calculated above thus classifies trade of nuclear reactors in exchange for air conditioners as intra-industry trade. This seems a bit far-fetched and obviously leads to artificially high intra-industry trade estimates, such that it is preferable to analyse the

Table 8.1 France: top ten export sectors, 2013

Code	Sector (simple names)	export	import	GL index
84	Nuclear reactors, machinery	65.2	74.5	93.3
88	Aircraft, spacecraft	56.5	29.5	68.7
87	Cars	46.4	58.8	88.2
85	Electrical machinery	44.7	55.4	89.3
30	Pharmaceutical products	37.0	26.1	82.6
27	Mineral fuels and oils	22.2	110.1	33.6
39	Plastics	22.1	24.9	94.1
22	Beverages	18.4	4.2	37.1
90	Optical and medical instruments	18.0	19.3	96.5
33	Perfumery	16.6	5.6	50.3
Total	(all sectors)	567	669	

Notes: two-digit HS code; top ten export sectors listed; trade value in billion USD; GL = Grubel–Lloyd index in per cent.

Source: calculations based on UN Comtrade data, extracted 23 April 2015.

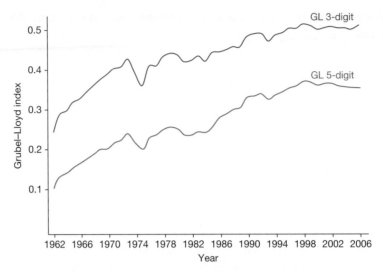

Figure 8.3 Evolution of intra-industry trade: global weighted average, 1962–2006.

Source: figure based on Brülhart (2008) data at SITC (third revision) three-digit and five-digit level.

goods classification and intra-industry trade at a more detailed level. This is done below (see Table 8.2 and Figure 8.3) using the SITC (Standard International Trade Classification) methodology, the forerunner of the Harmonized System. The trade-weighted average GL index for France then reduces from about 76 per cent at the two-digit level to about 60 per cent at the three-digit level and about 42 per cent at the five-digit level. This suggests that analysing international trade flows at a lower, or more detailed, level of aggregation leads to a reduction in the estimated extent of intra-industry trade. The phenomenon of intra-industry trade, however, does not disappear if we do this, and its development over time is similar at different levels of aggregation, as will be discussed further.

Table 8.2 summarizes the extent of intra-industry trade in 2006 at the five-digit SITC level for all global regions in the world. Take western Europe, the largest trading block, as an example (see WEUR in the bottom row of the table). The table indicates that the weighted-average level of intra-industry trade for western Europe is high in western Europe (45.7%), relative to North America (40.5%), and eastern Europe and Russia (30.8%), which are all regions containing high-income or nearby middle-income countries. Intra-industry trade for western Europe is particularly low relative to Middle Africa (0.3%), Western Africa (0.6%), East Africa (3.2%), and North Africa (4.9%), which are regions containing low-income countries. Similarly, North American intra-industry trade is high relative to itself (55.3%), western Europe (40.5%), and Central America and the Caribbean (38.1%), which again comprise high-income countries or nearby middle-income countries, and low again relative to African regions. In addition, note that for North Africa, Middle Africa, and Western Africa the degree of intra-industry trade relative to other regions never exceeds the 5 per cent level (all other regions exceed at least the 10 per cent level). Evidently, the degree of intra-industry trade is both related to the level of development (where higher income is associated with more intra-industry trade) and being in the neighbourhood of a high-income region (Central America relative to North America and eastern Europe relative to western Europe).

Table 8.2 Intra-industry trade and global regions, 2006

	AUS	CAC	CACT	EAF	EEUR	MAF	NAF	NAM	NEAS	SAF	SAM	SAS	SEAP	WAF	WAS	WEUR
AUS	0.448															
CAC	0.128	0.118														
CACT	0.008	0.037	0.012													
EAF	0.005	0.004	0.002	0.027												
EEUR	0.047	0.119	0.080	0.006	0.204											
MAF	0.001	0.001	0.000	0.000	0.001	0.022										
NAF	0.007	0.016	0.018	0.004	0.005	0.000	0.003									
NAM	0.194	0.381	0.073	0.017	0.142	0.001	0.004	0.553								
NEAS	0.042	0.110	0.022	0.003	0.053	0.000	0.014	0.208	0.270							
SAF	0.142	0.092	0.021	0.021	0.054	0.000	0.011	0.149	0.092	0.002						
SAM	0.050	0.119	0.033	0.002	0.028	0.000	0.001	0.101	0.024	0.062	0.202					
SAS	0.049	0.054	0.070	0.005	0.056	0.000	0.010	0.153	0.119	0.083	0.045	0.006				
SEAP	0.114	0.128	0.029	0.010	0.059	0.001	0.026	0.251	0.305	0.046	0.038	0.134	0.357			
WAF	0.001	0.002	0.000	0.003	0.000	0.001	0.003	0.000	0.000	0.001	0.000	0.000	0.001	0.003		
WAS	0.010	0.024	0.024	0.005	0.035	0.000	0.037	0.087	0.016	0.009	0.007	0.030	0.017	0.000	0.033	
WEUR	0.112	0.157	0.182	0.032	0.308	0.003	0.049	0.405	0.229	0.126	0.097	0.201	0.208	0.006	0.103	0.457

Notes: GL index, weighted average, five-digit SITC level; AUS = Australia and New Zealand; CAC = Central America and Caribbean; CACT = Central Asia, Caucasus and Turkey; EAF = East Africa; EEUR = eastern Europe and Russia; MAF = Middle Africa; NAF = North Africa; NAM = North America; NEAS = Northeast Asia; SAF = Southern Africa; SAM = South America; SAS = Southern Asia; SEAP = Southeast Asia and Pacific; WAF = Western Africa; WAS = Western Asia; WEUR = western Europe

Data source: Brülhart (2008).

Figure 8.3 depicts the global, weighted average evolution of the Grubel–Lloyd index over a period of 45 years (1962–2006), measured at both the three-digit and the five-digit level. It is clear that the measured degree of intra-industry trade falls if we identify more sectors (the five-digit line is below the three-digit line). Nonetheless, it is equally clear that the evolution over time is similar using either measure, where in both cases intra-industry trade is becoming more important over time, rising from about 10 per cent in 1962 to about 35 per cent in 2006 at the five-digit level and from about 25 per cent in 1962 to about 52 per cent in 2006 at the three-digit level. The 'dip' in both lines at around 1973–5 shows that the large rise in oil prices at that time shifted the balance from intra- to inter-industry trade temporarily.

8.4 Dixit–Stiglitz demand

The Dixit–Stiglitz model of monopolistic competition acknowledges that consumers demand a large range of different varieties of similar, but not identical products. Think, for example, of the range of varieties for mobile telephones, automobiles, televisions, etc. Although each producer of any individual variety has monopoly power in supplying its own variety, there is of course strong competition between firms in producing varieties of similar products. The demand structure of the Dixit–Stiglitz model allows for this strong competition. Let c_i be the level of consumption of a particular variety i of manufactures, and let N be the total number of available varieties. The Dixit–Stiglitz approach uses a constant elasticity of substitution (CES) function for the utility U derived from the consumption of manufactures as a function of the consumption c_i of the N varieties:[4]

$$U = \left(\sum_{i=1}^{N} c_i^{\rho} \right)^{1/\rho}, \ 0 < \rho < 1 \qquad 8.2$$

Note that the consumption of all varieties enters equation 8.2 symmetrically. This greatly simplifies the analysis in the sequel. The parameter ρ, discussed further below, represents the love-of-variety effect for consumers. If $\rho = 1$ then equation 8.2 simplifies to $U = \sum_i c_i$ and variety as such does not matter for utility (100 units of one variety gives the same utility as one unit of 100 varieties). Products are then perfect substitutes (one unit less of one variety can exactly be compensated by one unit more of another variety). We therefore need $\rho < 1$ to ensure that the product varieties are imperfect substitutes. In addition, we need $\rho > 0$ to ensure that the individual varieties are substitutes (and not complements) for each other, which enables price-setting behaviour based on monopoly power: see Technical Note 8.1.

It is worthwhile to dwell a little longer on the specification of equation 8.2. Suppose all c_i are consumed in equal quantities, that is $c_i = c$ for all i. We can then rewrite equation 8.2:

$$U = \left(\sum_{i=1}^{N} c^{\rho} \right)^{1/\rho} = \left(N c^{\rho} \right)^{1/\rho} = N^{\left(\frac{1}{\rho} \right) - 1} (Nc) \qquad 8.3$$

In many models, as in the model discussed here and in the endogenous growth model of Chapter 17, the term Nc in equation 8.3 corresponds to a claim on real resources, requiring labour (and/or capital) to be produced. The number of available varieties N therefore represents an externality, or the extent of the market. The term $N^{\left(\frac{1}{\rho} \right) - 1}$ denotes love-of-variety, since $(1/\rho)-1$ is larger than zero. This implies that an increase in the extent of the market N, which requires a proportional increase in the claim on real resources Nc, increases utility U derived from consumption of N varieties by more than the increase in the claim on real resources (because the term $N^{\left(\frac{1}{\rho}\right)-1}$ rises, it represents a bonus for large markets). In this sense an increase in the extent of the market, which increases the number of varieties N the consumer can choose from, more than proportionally increases utility, hence the term 'love-of-variety effect'.

Now that we have briefly digressed on the love-of-variety effect it is time to go back to the problem at hand: how does the consumer allocate spending on manufactures over the different varieties? Let p_i be the price of variety i for $i = 1, \ldots, N$. Naturally, funds $p_i c_i$ spent on variety i cannot be spent simultaneously on variety j, as given in the budget constraint with income I in equation 8.4:

$$\sum_{i=1}^{N} p_i c_i = I \qquad\qquad 8.4$$

In order to derive a consumer's demand, we must now solve a somewhat more complicated optimization problem, namely maximize utility derived from the consumption of manufactures given in equation 8.2, subject to the budget constraint of equation 8.4. The solution to this problem is (see Technical Note 8.1):

$$c_j = p_j^{-\varepsilon}\left[P^{\varepsilon-1}I\right], \text{ where } P = \text{price index}, U = \frac{I}{P}, \varepsilon \equiv \frac{1}{1-\rho} > 1 \qquad\qquad 8.5$$

Note that the definition of the price index P apparently implies that $U = I/P$. The price index P thus gives an exact representation of the utility level derived from the consumption of manufactures; this utility increases if, and only if, the income level I increases faster than the price index P. Such a price index is called an exact price index; see Diewert (1981) for further details.

8.5 Demand effects: income, price elasticity, and the price index

Section 8.4 derived the demand for manufacturing varieties. The demand for variety 1, for example, is influenced by four variables (see equation 8.5):

(i)   the income level I;

(ii)   the price p_1 of good 1;

(iii)   some parameter ε; and

(iv)   the price index P.

Let's go over these points in more detail.

Point (i) is straightforward. The higher the income level, the more the consumer spends on variety 1. In fact, this relationship is equiproportional: other things being equal, a 10 per cent rise in the income level results in a 10 per cent increase in the demand for all varieties of manufactures.

Point (ii) is also straightforward, but important. It is straightforward in the sense that we obviously expect that the demand for variety 1 is a function of the price charged by the firm producing variety 1. It is important in view of *how* demand for variety 1 depends on the price p_1. Note that the last part of equation 8.5 is written in square brackets. It depends on the price index for manufactures P and the income level I. Both are macroeconomic entities which the firm producing variety 1 will take as given: that is, it will assume that it has no control over these variables (as will be further discussed). In that case, we can simplify the demand for variety 1, defining $\gamma \equiv [P^{\varepsilon-1}I]$, as $c_1 = \gamma p_1^{-\varepsilon}$. This in turn implies that the price elasticity of demand for variety 1 is constant and equal to the parameter $\varepsilon > 1$, that is, $-(\partial c_1/\partial p_1)(p_1/c_1) = \varepsilon$. This simple price elasticity of demand is the main advantage of the Dixit–Stiglitz approach, as it simplifies the price-setting behaviour of monopolistically competitive firms: see Section 8.7.

Point (iii) becomes clear after the discussion of point (ii). We have defined the parameter ε not only to simplify the notation of equation 8.5 as much as possible, but also because it is an important economic parameter as it measures the price elasticity of demand for a variety of manufactured goods. In addition, this parameter measures the elasticity of substitution between two different varieties: that is, how difficult it is to substitute one variety of manufactures for another variety of manufactures. Evidently, the price elasticity of demand and the elasticity of substitution are related in the Dixit–Stiglitz approach, a point which has been criticized in the literature. Be that as it may, our intuitive explanations of some phenomena in the remainder of this book will sometimes be based on the price elasticity of demand interpretation of ε, and sometimes on the elasticity of substitution interpretation, using what we feel is easiest for the problem at hand.

Point (iv), finally, indicates that the demand for variety 1 depends on the price index P. If the price index P increases, implying that on average the prices of the manufacturing varieties competing with variety 1 are rising, then the demand for variety 1 is increasing (recall that $\varepsilon - 1 > 0$). The varieties are therefore economic substitutes of one another (if the price of a particular variety increases, its own demand falls and the demand for all other varieties rises).

To finish our discussion of the demand structure of the core model we want to make a final remark concerning point (ii) above, where we argued that the (own) price elasticity of demand for the producer of variety 1 is equal to ε. Recall the specification of the demand function: $c_1 = p_1^{-\varepsilon} [P^{\varepsilon-1} I]$. We argued that the term in square brackets is treated as a constant by the producer because these are macroeconomic entities. Although this is true, it overlooks a tiny detail: one of the terms in the specification of the price index of manufactures P is the price p_1. Thus, a truly rational producer would also take this minuscule effect on the aggregate price index into consideration.[5] For that reason it is often assumed that if the number of varieties N produced is large, for example if our producer is one of 80,000 firms, we can safely ignore this effect. This is illustrated in Figure 8.4, where we have plotted the demand curve facing the producer of a variety if she assumes she cannot influence the price index of manufactures, and the true demand taking this effect on the price index into consideration (details below Figure 8.4). Clearly, the assumption is a bad approximation if there are just two firms (panel a.), but then nobody suggests you should use monopolistic competition in a duopoly. If there are 20 firms the approximation is already much better (panel b.); if there are 200 firms the deviation is virtually undetectable (panel c.); while it is

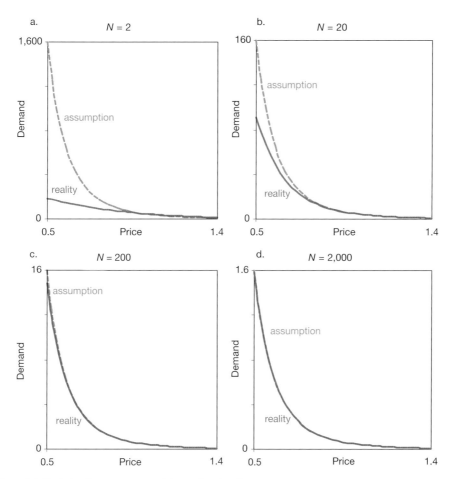

Figure 8.4 Deviation between assumed demand and reality.

Notes: spending on manufactures = 100; price of other firms = 1; $\varepsilon = 5$.

unobservable if there are 2,000 firms (panel d.). We can thus safely ignore this detail for a reasonably large number of varieties.

8.6 Increasing returns to scale

The Dutch ASM Lithography company (ASML) dominates the global market for chip machines (together with the Japanese companies Nikon and Canon at some distance), the vital tools for producing computer chips. The newest technology uses extreme ultra-violet lithography, with a wavelength shorter than 15 nanometres. In April 2015 ASML announced the delivery of 15 such machines to one client in the coming years. It did not disclose the customer, but it is generally known to be Intel Corporation, which became actively involved in the production process in 2012. The value of the deal was also not disclosed, but the price of one machine is estimated at $75 million, which places the order at around $1.1 billion. The development of such advanced and complex technology takes many years of high-risk investment and research. For that reason, in 2012 AMSL persuaded three of its main customers, namely Intel, Samsung, and TSMC, to participate in a co-investment programme worth $1.5 billion over a five-year period. With these large investment costs, chip makers are operative in a market with increasing returns to scale, implying that total costs increase, but costs per unit of output fall, as output expands. Numerous other sectors of the economy are also characterized by increasing returns to scale, usually because of initial investment costs before production can start; think of the automobile sector, the shipping industry, the aircraft industry, or setting up an internet site or a law firm (where an initial investment in knowledge is required before legal services can be produced), and so on.

We distinguish between external and internal increasing returns to scale: see Box 8.4. If there are increasing returns to scale, as in the examples given above, the firm will realize that its costs per unit of output fall if output expands. Internal returns to scale are therefore incompatible with perfect competition.[6] If you think returns to scale are important in a particular sector, you must necessarily analyse a market of imperfect competition. In order not to overestimate the firm's power at the macroeconomic level, we will focus on a market of monopolistic competition.

Box 8.4 External and internal economies of scale

The term 'economies of scale' or 'increasing returns to scale' refers to a situation in which an increase in the level of output produced implies a decrease in the average costs per unit of output for the firm. It translates itself into a downward-sloping average cost curve: see Figure 8.5. To identify the source of the fall in average costs Scitovsky (1954) distinguished between internal and external economies of scale. With internal economies of scale the decrease in average costs is brought about by an increase in the production level of the firm itself. The more the firm produces, the better it can profit from scale

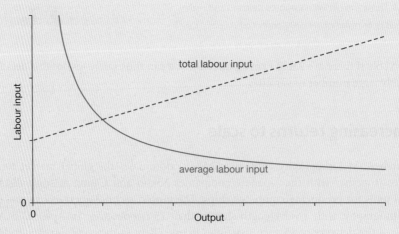

Figure 8.5 Production function for a variety of manufactures.

Note: Fixed labour requirement $f = 3$, marginal labour requirement $m = 1$.

(continued...)

economies, and the higher its cost advantage over smaller firms. The market structure underlying inter-nal scale economies must necessarily be one of imperfect competition as internal economies of scale imply market power. With external economies of scale, the decrease in average costs comes about through an output increase at the level of the industry as a whole, making average costs per unit a function of industry-wide output. Scitovsky distinguished here between pure and pecuniary external economies.

With pure (or technological) external economies an increase in industry-wide output alters the techno-logical relationship between input and output for each individual firm. It therefore has an impact on the firm's production function. A frequently used example (dating back to Alfred Marshall) concerns informa-tion spillovers. An increase in industry output increases the stock of knowledge through positive informa-tion spillovers for each firm, leading to an increase in output at the firm level. The market structure can then be perfectly competitive since the size of the individual firm does not matter.

Pecuniary external economies are transmitted by the market through price effects for the individual firm, which may alter its output decision. Two examples, again based on Marshall, are the existence of a large local market for specialized inputs, and labour market pooling. A large industry can support a mar-ket for specialized intermediate inputs and a pool of industry-specific skilled workers, which benefits the individual firm. Unlike pure external economies these spillovers do not affect the technological relation-ship between inputs and output (the production function). The price effects that are crucial to pecuniary externalities can come about only with imperfect competition.

Suppose, therefore, that production in the manufacturing sector is characterized by internal economies of scale, which means that there is imperfect competition in this sec-tor (see Box 8.4). The varieties in the manufacturing sector are all produced with the same technology. Internal economies of scale mean that each variety is produced by a single firm; the firm with the largest sales can always outbid a potential competitor. The economies of scale are modelled in the simplest way possible:

$$l_i = f + mx_i \qquad\qquad 8.6$$

where l_i is the amount of labour necessary to produce x_i of variety i. The parameters f and m describe, respectively, the fixed and marginal labour input requirement. The fixed labour input f in equation 8.6 ensures that as production expands, less labour is needed to produce a unit of x_i, which means that there are internal economies of scale. This is illustrated in Figure 8.5, showing the total labour required to produce a certain amount of output, and the average amount of labour required to produce that amount of output.

8.7 Optimal pricing and zero profits

Each manufacturing firm produces a unique variety under internal returns to scale. This implies that the firm has monopoly power, which it will use to maximize its profits. We will therefore have to determine the price-setting behaviour of each firm. The Dixit–Stiglitz monopolistic competition model makes two assumptions in this respect. First, it is assumed that each firm takes the price-setting behaviour of other firms as given; if firm 1 changes its price it assumes that the prices of the other $N-1$ varieties will remain the same. Second, it is assumed that the firm ignores the effect of changing its own price on the price index P of manufactures. Both assumptions seem reasonable if the number of varieties N is large, as also discussed in Section 8.5. For ease of notation we will drop the sub-index for the firm in this section. Note that a firm which produces x units of output using the production function in equation 8.6 will earn profits π given in equation 8.7 if the wage rate it has to pay is W.

$$\pi = px - W(f + mx) \tag{8.7}$$

Naturally, the firm will have to sell the units of output x it is producing: that is, these sales must be consistent with the demand for a variety of manufactures derived in Section 8.4. Although this demand was derived for an arbitrary consumer, the most important feature of the demand for a variety, namely the constant price elasticity of demand ε, also holds when we combine the demand from many consumers with the same preference structure. If the demand x for a variety has a constant price elasticity of demand ε, maximization of the profits given in equation 8.7 leads to a simple optimal pricing rule, known as mark-up pricing: see Technical Note 8.1.

$$p(1 - 1/\varepsilon) = mW \tag{8.8}$$

The situation is illustrated in Figure 8.6. The marginal revenue curve associated with the iso-elastic demand function is an inward-shifted version of the demand curve itself (by the fraction $1 - 1/\varepsilon$). It intersects the horizontal marginal cost curve at point C. This determines the optimally produced quantity q, while the concomitant point on the demand curve determines the optimal price level p. The difference between price and marginal costs multiplied by the produced quantity gives the operating profits op. The term 'mark-up pricing' is obvious. The marginal costs of producing an extra unit of output is equal to mW, while the price

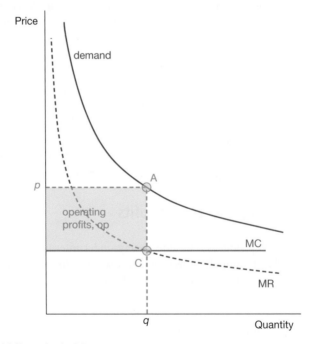

Figure 8.6 Dixit–Stiglitz optimal pricing.

p the firm charges is higher than this marginal cost. How much higher depends crucially on the price elasticity of demand. If demand is rather inelastic, say $\varepsilon = 2$, the mark-up is high (in this case 100 per cent). If demand is rather elastic, say $\varepsilon = 5$, the mark-up is lower (in this case 25 per cent). Note that the firm must charge a higher price than marginal cost in order to recuperate the fixed costs of labour fW. Because the price elasticity of demand ε is constant, the mark-up of price over marginal cost is also constant, and therefore invariant to the scale of production.

Now that we have determined the optimal price a firm will charge to maximize profits, we can actually calculate those profits. This is where another important feature of monopolistic competition comes in. If profits are positive (sometimes referred to as excess profits) it is apparently attractive to set up shop in the manufacturing sector. One would then expect that new firms would enter the market and start to produce different varieties. This implies, of course, that the consumer will allocate her spending over more varieties of manufactures, as illustrated in Figure 8.7 by the inward shift of the demand curve and the marginal revenue curve. Thanks to the peculiarities of the Dixit–Stiglitz model, this inward shift does not affect the price charged by the firm but reduces the produced quantity (from q to q'), and thus the operating profits. This process of entry of new firms will continue until profits (that is, operating profits minus fixed costs) in the manufacturing sector are driven to zero. A reverse process, with firms leaving the manufacturing sector, would operate if profits were negative. Monopolistic competition in the manufacturing sector therefore imposes as an equilibrium condition that profits are zero. If we do that in Figure 8.7 we can calculate the scale at which a firm producing a variety in the manufacturing sector will operate: see Technical Note 8.2.

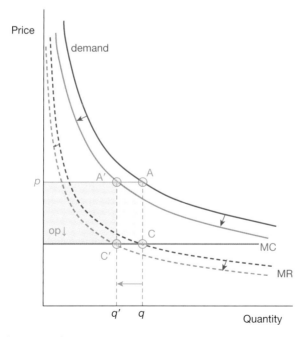

Figure 8.7 Entry in the Dixit–Stiglitz model.

$$x = \frac{f(\varepsilon-1)}{m} \qquad\qquad 8.9$$

Equation 8.9, which gives the scale of output for an individual firm, may seem strange at first sight. No matter what happens, the output per firm is fixed in equilibrium. The constant price elasticity of demand in conjunction with the production function is responsible for this result. It implies that the manufacturing sector as a whole only expands and contracts by producing more or fewer varieties, as the output level per variety does not change. Since the scale of production is constant, as given in equation 8.9, it is easy to determine (i) how much labour is needed to produce this amount of output using the production function, and (ii) how many varieties N are produced in the economy by dividing the total labour force L by the amount of labour required per variety (which gives $N = L/f\varepsilon$): see Technical Note 8.2. Evidently, a larger market, as measured by the available amount of labour L, is able to support a larger number N of varieties, thus giving consumers more varieties to choose from.

8.8 Explaining intra-industry trade

How does all of the above help us to understand intra-industry trade flows, and possible gains from such trade flows? Let us first summarize the main conclusions derived above:

- Consumers demand different varieties of similar goods. Other things being equal, the more varieties are available to cater to specific needs of the consumer, the higher the derived utility level.

- Consumer demand for any particular variety increases if (i) the price of the variety falls (with a constant price elasticity of demand ε), (ii) the price of any other variety increases, and (iii) the income level increases.

- Producers supply many different varieties of similar goods. Before production of any particular variety can start, an initial investment cost is necessary (for invention of the variety, or to set up a production plant), such that there are internal increasing returns to scale. This gives market power to the individual producers.

- Producers maximize profits by choosing the optimal price level. Since the price elasticity of demand is constant, the mark-up of price over marginal costs is also constant.

- Firms enter and exit the market for producing new varieties until (excess) profits are equal to zero. In this setting, this results in a constant production level for each variety of manufactures, such that a change in total market supply is equivalent to a change in the number of varieties produced.

Given these preliminary results, it is straightforward to put two and two together and explain how intra-industry trade may arise, and what its benefits are. Consider two countries, Belgium and the Netherlands, with a demand and supply structure as laid out in sections 8.4–8.7. We will assume these countries are identical in all respects, except in the size of their labour force; more specifically, we assume Belgium has 5 million labourers, and the Netherlands has 7 million labourers. Since technology is the same for the two countries, there is no Ricardian basis for international trade. Since there is only one factor of production (labour) it is impossible even to identify relative factor abundance, such that there is no Heckscher–Ohlin basis for international trade. Nonetheless, international trade, of the intra-industry type, will arise in this model, and it will lead to gains from trade for both countries.

We start with a brief discussion of the autarky equilibrium. If we let the wage rate be the numéraire, all firms face the same marginal costs and the same price elasticity of demand. They therefore all charge the same price. If all workers are employed, the total income level is identical to the number of labourers, because firms enter and exit the market until profits are zero and the wage rate is the numéraire. As explained at the end of Section 8.7, and emphasized above, the number of varieties produced in each country is proportional to the size of the market (as measured by the total labour force):

$$N_B = \frac{L_B}{f\varepsilon}; \quad N_{NL} = \frac{L_{NL}}{f\varepsilon} \qquad\qquad 8.10$$

Suppose that the fixed costs f and the elasticity of substitution ε are such that 500 labourers are required in equilibrium for the production of one variety. As illustrated in Figure 8.8, Belgium will then produce and consume 10,000 varieties in autarky and the Netherlands will produce and consume 14,000 varieties in autarky.

What changes if these two countries start to trade with one another (at zero transport costs and in the absence of any other impediment to trade)? The answer is: virtually nothing and very much at the same time. The 'virtually nothing' part refers to the fact that the price for a variety does not change, nor does production size for any variety, or the number of varieties produced. The 'very much' part refers to the fact that we now have intensive trade flows between the two nations, because the consumers have a preference for variety and therefore want to consume all varieties produced in both countries. The total number of varieties consumed therefore increases from 10,000 in Belgium and 14,000 in

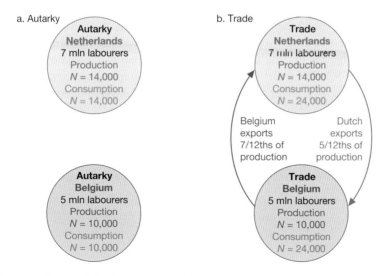

Figure 8.8 Intra-industry trade in the Krugman model.

the Netherlands to 24,000 in both countries. Since demand is proportional to the size of the market, a Belgian producer will export 7/12ths of total production to the Netherlands, while a Dutch producer will export 5/12ths of total production to Belgium. These intensive trade flows of similar types of goods, produced using similar technologies in both countries, can be classified as intra-industry trade.

In the Ricardian model, as in the Heckscher–Ohlin model, there are gains from trade through more efficient production at a global scale. In Chapter 7, where we discussed the pro-competitive gains from trade, the pressure of international competition reduces the domestic distortions and therefore leads to efficiency gains. In the Krugman model, none of these factors is operative. The reader will have noticed that the production levels have not changed at all in either country. Since the Dutch are exporting 5/12ths of their production level of each variety, the level consumed of those varieties falls by 5/12ths. In exchange the Dutch are now consuming 7/12ths of the Belgian production level of the varieties produced in Belgium. The total consumption level has not changed ($10,000 \times 7/12 - 14,000 \times 5/12 = 0$). All we are doing is exporting manufactures in exchange for the import of an equal amount of manufactures. Are there any gains from these trade flows? The answer is: yes. Two remarks are in order.

First, note that the wage rate, and thus the consumer's income level, has not changed in trade relative to autarky, nor has the price of domestically produced varieties. If trade is possible, therefore, the consumer can still consume the same combination of goods as in autarky. The utility level cannot possibly decrease, while the fact that the consumer decides to consume a different basket of goods indicates that the utility level must rise.

Second, note that the varieties are imperfect substitutes for one another. Other things being equal, the marginal utility from consuming an extra unit of any particular variety falls. Recall that the consumer will equate the marginal utility per dollar for all goods in equilibrium. If trade is possible, therefore, the consumer will benefit by reducing the consumption level of domestically produced varieties with low marginal utility, in exchange for an increase in foreign-produced varieties with a high marginal utility.

International trade in this set-up thus leads to an increase in welfare because it allows consumers to enjoy the benefits of a larger market, which is able to sustain a large variety of goods and services produced to cater to specific preferences. Indeed, it is straightforward to show that the derived utility is a power function of the size of the market: see Technical Note 8.3. The trade flows of cars and car components provide an important empirical example of a sector where both factor abundance arguments (see Chapter 6) and intra-industry trade arguments (as analysed in this chapter) play an important role: see Box 8.5.

Box 8.5 Car exports

As an example of human-capital-intensive trade flows we now focus on exports in sector 87: 'Vehicles other than railway, tramway'. We will refer to this as 'car exports' for short. With a total export value of $1,391 billion, or 7.8 per cent of world total exports, the car sector is important in world trade flows. In fact, it is the fourth largest sector, after oil (discussed in Box 5.3), electronics (Box 6.3), and machinery (sector 84).

(continued...)

Table 8.3 provides an overview of the five largest car exporters, both in absolute terms and in relative terms. As might be expected, Germany tops the list with an export value of $268 billion, representing 19.2 per cent of total car exports. It is followed by Japan, the USA, Mexico, and South Korea, in that order. With the exception of Mexico, there are many well-known global car brands originating from these countries. So what is the role of Mexico? Some more perspective is provided when we look at the top five in relative terms. In that case Slovakia tops the list as one-quarter of all its exports is related to cars, followed by Mexico, Japan, Georgia, and the Czech Republic. As discussed in this chapter, many of these countries play a role in the trade of intermediate products in the car sector and in the final processing stage. Germany, for example, ships important high-tech car components to Slovakia and the Czech Republic, where these components are used in the final car-assembly stage of production. The

Table 8.3 Sector 87 exports: vehicles other than railway, tramway, 2014

Top five in absolute terms			Top five in relative terms		
Country	% of world*	USD bn	Country	% of country	USD bn
Germany	19.2	268	Slovakia	25.0	21
Japan	10.3	143	Mexico	21.6	86
USA	9.8	136	Japan	20.9	143
Mexico	6.2	86	Georgia	19.6	1
South Korea	5.3	73	Czech Rep	19.0	33
World	7.8	1,391			

Notes: * world flows are per cent of total world exports represented by sector 87; country flows are each country's per cent of sector 87 total world exports.
Source: calculations based on ITC data: www.intracen.org, downloaded 18 June 2015.

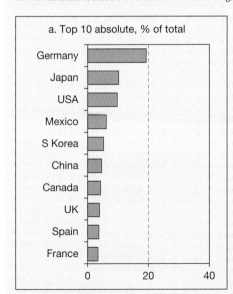
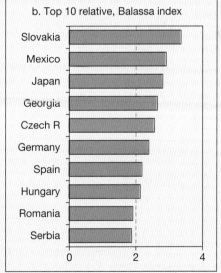

Figure 8.9 Sector 87 exports: vehicles other than railway, tramway, 2014.
Notes: Balassa index is country export share of sector / world export share of sector.
Source: calculations based on ITC data, www.intracen.org, downloaded 18 June 2015.

(continued...)

same arrangment applies to the USA and Mexico. Section 8.10 discusses a similar example for the electronics sector in more detail.

Figure 8.9 illustrates the top ten car exporters in absolute and relative terms. In absolute terms China, Canada, UK, Spain, and France join the list. In relative terms, based on the Balassa index (indicating revealed comparative advantage if the index is above 1, see Section 4.9), Germany, Spain, Hungary, Romania, and Serbia join the list.

8.9 An alternative interpretation: intermediate goods

So far, we have discussed the Krugman model of intra-industry trade, that is, trade between countries of similar goods and services within the same industry, which is becoming more important, as measured by the Grubel–Lloyd index. The gains from trade in the Krugman setting derive from the ability to sustain a wider variety of goods and services in a larger market as a result of increasing returns to scale. A larger market therefore is better able to fulfil the preferences of consumers, who like variety. In short, the entire discussion and interpretation of the model is in terms of production and trade of final goods and services for the consumer market.

The Krugman interpretation of the model is illustrated in Figure 8.10. In autarky, country A produces N_A different varieties under increasing returns to scale and monopolistic competition. The same applies to country B. If the two countries engage in international trade with one another, the consumers in both countries purchase some goods from all domestic producers and import some goods from all foreign producers. The resulting trade flows are therefore intra-industry trade flows of final goods from producers to consumers.

The American economist Wilfred Ethier (1982) came up with an entirely different, and influential, interpretation of the same model. He pointed out (1982: 950–52) that 'the largest and fastest growing component of world trade since World War II has been the exchange of manufactures between the industrialized economies. . . . (I cannot resist the temptation to point out that producers' goods are in fact much more prominent in trade than are consumer's goods)'. One of the objectives of the Ethier article is therefore to explain the large intra-industry trade flows of intermediate goods: that is, trade flows from one producer to another, rather than from producer to consumer.

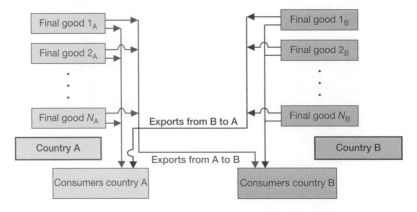

Figure 8.10 The Krugman interpretation: trade extends the market, love-of-variety gains.

Figure 8.11 illustrates how Ethier was able to explain those trade flows through a reinterpretation of the Krugman model. Instead of interpreting the various varieties produced in both countries as different final goods, he interpreted them as different, and new, intermediate goods in a complex final goods production process. This can refer to different types of capital goods, such as cars, printing machines, copiers, presses, etc., or to different types of services, such as accounting, engineering, cleaning, etc. The providers of intermediate goods, produced under increasing returns to scale, have market power and are operating in a market of monopolistic competition.

There is only one final good delivered to the consumers. The producers of the final good, say Y, combine the intermediate inputs from all variety producers in a perfectly competitive market, that is, taking the prices of the intermediate goods providers as given, into the single output. The final good production function is similar to the utility function in the Krugman approach (compare with equation 8.2):

$$Y = \left(\sum_{i=1}^{N} x_i^\rho \right)^{1/\rho}$$

8.11

In this interpretation, the x_i refers to intermediate goods deliveries. The price elasticity of demand for intermediate goods by final goods producers is, of course, again a constant, equal to $\varepsilon = 1/(1 - \rho)$. Once we impose a well-behaved utility function $U(Y)$ on top of this structure, the outcome is essentially the same as in the Krugman model. This time, as displayed in Figure 8.11, we have active international intra-industry trade flows of *intermediate goods* between nations.

It is also important to understand the difference in interpretation of an increase in the extent of the market in the Ethier model. First, recall that a larger market enables an increase in the number N of varieties produced. Second, remember that the increase in the number of varieties leads to higher utility levels in the Krugman model through a love-of-variety effect. In a similar way, a larger market leads to an increase in the number of intermediate goods available to final goods producers, which increases their total output level through a positive production externality. The different intermediate goods are imperfect substitutes

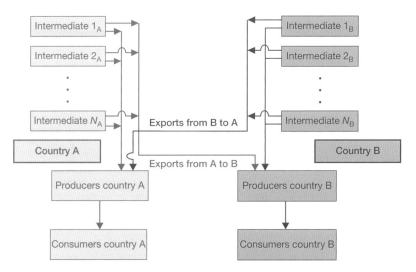

Figure 8.11 The Ethier interpretation: trade extends the market, production externality gains.

for one another. Therefore, the more there are available to the final goods producer, the more efficiently the production process is organized, and the higher the production level.

8.10 Case study: China and 'electrical, electronic equipment'

With an export value of $2,209 billion, or about 12.7 per cent of the world total, China was the world's largest exporter in 2013. So what was China exporting? At the Harmonized System two-digit level, the United Nations Comtrade website identifies 96 different sectors. Figure 8.12 provides an overview of China's ten largest export sectors, together accounting for 68 per cent of China's total exports. By far the largest export sector, with a value of $561 billion which accounts for more than 25 per cent of China's exports, is number 85: Electrical, Electronic Equipment. Other important export sectors include machinery (84), textiles (61, 62), furniture (94), and optical instruments (90).

Figure 8.12 also shows the size of the import flows into China for the top ten export sectors. In some sectors, such as textiles (61, 62), furniture (94), and footwear (64), imports are very low. Using the Grubel–Lloyd (GL) index, which ranges from zero to 100 per cent and measures the extent of *intra*-industry at the two-digit level, these are clear examples of *inter*-industry trade flows (GL index below 10 per cent): the good is exported, but not imported. Similarly, there are examples of inter-industry trade sectors where the good is imported but not exported, such as (not shown) ores, slag, and ash (26) and pulp of wood (17). On the other hand, as also illustrated in Figure 8.12, there are many sectors where the measure of intra-industry trade is very high: the good is exported and imported at the same time. A prime example is the largest export sector, electrical, electronic equipment (85), where imports are $439 billion and the GL index is 89 per

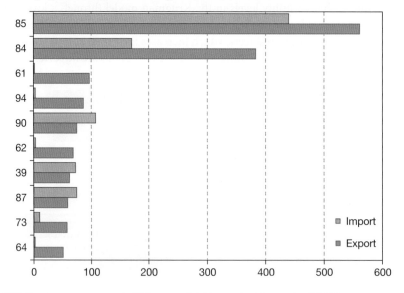

Figure 8.12 Top ten export sectors in China: two-digit Harmonized System level, 2013.

Notes: billion USD; short description: 64 = footwear; 73 = articles of iron and steel; 87 = vehicles other than railway or tramway; 39 = plastics; 62 = apparel and clothing, not knitted or crocheted; 90 = optical and medical instruments; 94 = furniture; 61 = apparel and clothing, knitted or crocheted; 84 = nuclear reactors, boilers, and machinery; 85 = electrical, electronic equipment.
Source: based on UN Comtrade data.

cent. Similar high intra-industry trade flows at the two-digit level (GL index above 60 per cent) in Figure 8.12 are observed for machines (84), optical instruments (90), plastics (39), and vehicles (87).

Panel a. of Figure 8.13 illustrates how rapidly China's trade flows have increased over time. Measured in constant 2013 dollar, China's exports increased 17-fold since 1992, from $128 billion to $2,209 billion, while its imports increased 16-fold, from $122 billion to $1,950 billion. In both cases the compounded growth rate is above 14 per cent per year. Trade flows for sector 85 increased even more spectacularly, with a 31-fold increase in imports from $14 to $439 billion and a 45-fold increase in exports from $12 billion to $561 billion, with respective compounded growth rates of about 18 and 20 per cent per year. As a consequence, as illustrated in panel b. of Figure 8.13, the share of sector 85 in China's total

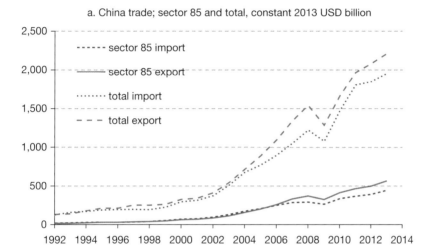

a. China trade; sector 85 and total, constant 2013 USD billion

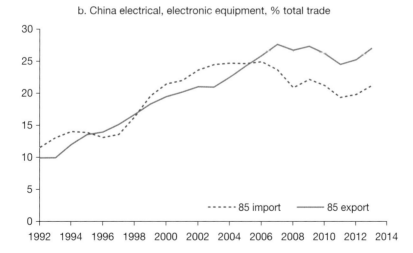

b. China electrical, electronic equipment, % total trade

Figure 8.13 China total trade and sector 85 trade, 1992–2013.

Notes: in billion constant 2013 USD (using GDP deflator); China total trade in a given year is the average of exports and imports.
Source: based on UN Comtrade data.

trade flows (measured as the average of exports and imports in a given year) increased from 11 to 21 per cent for imports and from 10 to 27 per cent for exports.

There are two main types of intra-industry trade, namely *horizontal* intra-industry trade, which involves simultaneously importing and exporting goods in the same stage of the production process, and *vertical* intra-industry trade, which involves simultaneously importing and exporting goods in different stages of the production process. To get an indication regarding the type of trade flows in China's electrical, electronic equipment sector, we look in more detail at the 48 sub-sectors into which these trade flows can be divided at the four-digit level of the Harmonized System. Figure 8.14 shows the net exports (as a per cent of total trade) of the largest three sub-sectors (in absolute terms): 8517, 8528, and 8542. For ease of reference we label these telephones, televisions, and chips and components, respectively.

We note that China has been a net exporter of televisions since 1992. These net exports reached a peak of more than 3 per cent of total trade in 2007, after which the percentage declined to about 1.3 per cent in 2013. We also note that China was initially a net importer of telephones from 1992 (except for 1997) until 2002, after which it became a large exporter of telephones, with a sharp increase in 2007 (the year of the introduction of the first iPhone) and rising above 6 per cent of total trade in 2013. To enable the net exports of televisions and telephones, China has been a net importer of chips and components since 1992. These net imports rose particularly fast after 1997 to reach a peak of 9.7 per cent of total trade in 2006 and then gradually declined below 7 per cent of total trade in 2013. This information thus shows that China imports chips and components to be used in the relatively labour-intensive assembly of final electric and electronic goods, such as televisions and telephones, which are subsequently exported to other countries.

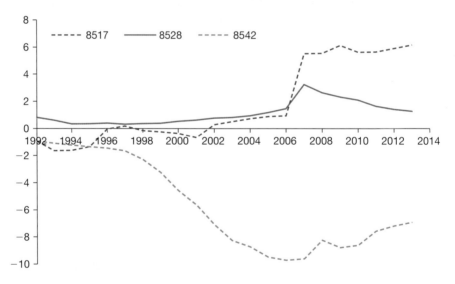

Figure 8.14 China: net exports in sub-sectors of electronics, per cent of total trade.

Notes: China total trade in a given year is the average of exports and imports; 8517 = electric apparatus for line telephony, telegraphy; 8528 = television receivers, video monitors, projectors; 8542 = electronic integrated circuits and micro assemblies. *Source:* based on UN Comtrade data.

Figure 8.15 provides an indication of where the chips and components are imported from (panel a.) and where the telephones are shipped to (panel b.). Japan was initially the largest supplier of chips and components to the Chinese electric, electronic equipment sector. After a peak of almost 2 per cent of total trade in 2003, however, Japan's influence declined gradually to about 0.6 per cent in 2013. South Korea is currently the largest supplier of chips and components, taking over from Japan in 2005 and with a current import value of 2.3 per cent of total trade. For some time the role of the Philippines as a supplier of chips and components was quite strong as well, but as with Japan its influence declined after 2007, when imports peaked at more than 1.4 per cent of total trade. Other important suppliers are the USA and Singapore. It should be noted that the substantial influence of

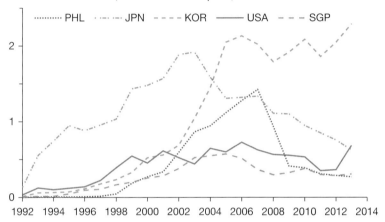

a. China; subsector 8542 imports, % total trade

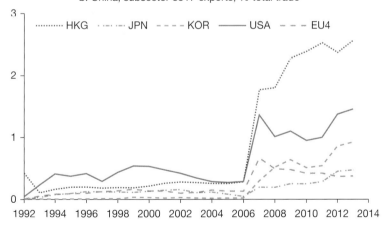

b. China; subsector 8517 exports, % total trade

Figure 8.15 China: imports of chips and exports of telephones, per cent of total trade.

Notes: China total trade in a given year is the average of exports and imports; 8517 = electric apparatus for line telephony, telegraphy; 8542 = electronic integrated circuits and micro assemblies; EU4 = Britain, Germany, France, and Italy.
Source: based on UN Comtrade data.

Taiwan on China's electric, electronic equipment sector is not visible in panel a. of Figure 8.15 as these data are not provided by Comtrade, which is part of the United Nations and thus does not include information on Taiwan. Taken together, this illustrates that China imports chips and components mostly from nearby countries, such as Japan, Korea, Taiwan, the Philippines, and Singapore, and from the world's technological leader: the USA.

The most important destination countries for the export of telephones are given in panel b. of Figure 8.15. For a long time the USA has been the main trading partner, also for telephones, with direct exports rising to 1.5 per cent of total trade in 2013. On paper the role of leading destination country for telephones was taken over by Hong Kong in 2007, rising to 2.6 per cent of total trade in 2013. This is only on paper, however, as Hong Kong's role as a trading hub implies that it re-exports the imported telephones to other countries, such as those listed in Figure 8.15. The other main destination countries are all economically advanced countries, such as South Korea, Japan, and the European Union (represented in the figure by EU4: the UK, Germany, France, and Italy). We thus observe that China imports chips and components, mostly from nearby countries, uses these to assemble final goods such as televisions and telephones, and then ships these goods to advanced markets in Asia, North America, and Europe. Since the final assembly stage of the production process is relatively labour-intensive, and under the assumption that China is a relatively labour-abundant country, we thus note that China specializes in the part of the production process in accordance with its comparative advantage, as discussed in Chapter 6. We also note that the gross export data is not adequate to be used to identify and measure these trade flows.

This example illustrates how modern supply chains operate. Different parts and components are produced in different countries. These components are imported to a large extent not to be consumed locally but to be processed and re-exported, with additional domestically produced value added on top of what was imported. Countries at different stages of development are cooperating together in a (firm-coordinated) fashion to produce final goods, where each country specializes in producing part of the production process in accordance with its comparative advantage. This is a very important sector for China. Being part of this supply chain has been crucial for China's rapid economic development since the turn of the twenty-first century.

8.11 Conclusions

The empirically observed prevalence of intra-industry trade (two-way trade in similar products measured using the Grubel–Lloyd index) is hard to explain on the basis of differences in factor abundance or technology. Using the Krugman model, an extension of the Dixit–Stiglitz model, we provide an analysis of imperfect competition under economies of scale, which in conjunction with the size of the market determines the number of different varieties of goods and services available to consumers (or firms in the intermediate product interpretation of Ethier). International trade increases the extent of the market, thus making more types of goods available. This raises welfare through a love-of-variety effect for final goods or raises production through increased specialization leading to positive production externalities. In both cases the model can be applied to better understand intra-industry trade of final goods and intermediate goods. The general structure of this model will be the basis of more applications in the next parts of the book.

Technical Notes

Technical Note 8.1 Dixit–Stiglitz demand

To maximize equation 8.2 subject to the budget constraint 8.4 we define the Lagrangean Γ, using the multiplier κ:

$$\Gamma = \left(\sum_{i=1}^{N} c_i^{\rho} \right)^{\frac{1}{\rho}} + \kappa \left(I - \sum_{i=1}^{N} p_i c_i \right) \qquad (8.A1)$$

Differentiating Γ with respect to c_j and equating to 0 gives the first-order conditions:

$$\left(\sum_{i=1}^{N} c_i^{\rho} \right)^{\left(\frac{1}{\rho}\right)-1} c_j^{\rho-1} = \kappa p_j \text{ for } j=1,\dots, N \qquad (8.A2)$$

Take the ratio of these first-order conditions with respect to variety 1, note that the first term on the left hand side cancels (as does the term κ on the right hand side), and define $\varepsilon = 1/(1-\rho)$ as discussed in the main text. Then:

$$\frac{c_j^{\rho-1}}{c_1^{\rho-1}} = \frac{p_j}{p_1} \text{ or } c_j = p_j^{-\varepsilon} p_1^{\varepsilon} c_1 \text{ for } j=1,\dots, N \qquad (8.A3)$$

Substituting these relations in the budget equation gives:

$$\sum_{j=1}^{N} p_j c_j = \sum_{j=1}^{N} p_j \left(p_j^{-\varepsilon} p_1^{\varepsilon} c_1 \right) = p_1^{\varepsilon} c_1 \sum_{j=1}^{N} p_j^{1-\varepsilon} = I$$

or

$$c_1 = p_1^{-\varepsilon} P^{\varepsilon-1} I, \text{ where } P \equiv \left(\sum_{j=1}^{N} p_j^{1-\varepsilon} \right)^{\frac{1}{1-\varepsilon}} \qquad (8.A4)$$

This explains the demand for variety 1 as given in equation 8.5. The demand for the other varieties is derived analogously. The question remains why the price index P was defined as given in equation (8.A4). To answer this question we have to substitute the derived demand for all varieties in equation 8.2, and note along the way that $-\varepsilon\rho = 1-\varepsilon$ and $\frac{1}{\rho} = -\frac{\varepsilon}{1-\varepsilon}$:

$$U = \left(\sum_{i=1}^{N} c_i^{\rho} \right)^{\frac{1}{\rho}} = \left(\sum_{i=1}^{N} \left(p_i^{-\varepsilon} P^{\varepsilon-1} I \right)^{\rho} \right)^{\frac{1}{\rho}}$$

$$= IP^{\varepsilon-1} \left(\sum_{i=1}^{N} p_i^{-\varepsilon\rho} \right)^{\frac{1}{\rho}} = IP^{\varepsilon-1} \left(\sum_{i=1}^{N} p_i^{1-\varepsilon} \right)^{\frac{-\varepsilon}{(1-\varepsilon)}}$$

Using the definition of the price index P from equation (8.A4) this simplifies to:

$$U = IP^{\varepsilon-1} P^{-\varepsilon} = I/P \qquad (8.A5)$$

Technical Note 8.2 Equilibrium scale of production

Put profits in equation 8.7 equal to zero and use the pricing rule $p\left(1 - \dfrac{1}{\varepsilon}\right) = mW$:

$$px - W(f + mx) = 0 \quad \text{or} \quad px = fW + mWx \quad \text{or}$$

$$\left(\frac{\varepsilon}{\varepsilon - 1} mW\right) x = fW + mWx \quad \text{or} \quad \left(\frac{\varepsilon}{\varepsilon - 1} - 1\right) mWx = fW \quad \text{or} \quad x = \frac{f(\varepsilon - 1)}{m} \tag{8.A6}$$

This explains equation 8.9. Now use the production function 8.6 to calculate the amount of labour required to produce this much output:

$$l_i = f + mx = f + m\frac{f(\varepsilon - 1)}{m} = f + f(\varepsilon - 1) = f\varepsilon \tag{8.A7}$$

Determining the number of varieties N produced follows, simply by dividing the total number of manufacturing workers by the number of workers needed to produce 1 variety: $N = \dfrac{L}{l_i} = \dfrac{L}{f\varepsilon}$

Technical Note 8.3 Intra-industry trade and welfare

Since the price of all varieties is the same in equilibrium, the consumption level is the same for all varieties in equilibrium. From equation 8.2 it follows that the utility level is then equal to $U = N^{1/\rho}c$. The production level for any variety is given in equation 8.9 as $x = f(\varepsilon-1)/m$. Dividing this by the number of people L gives the per capita consumption c. Finally, recall that the number of varieties is proportional to the labour force, that is, $N = L/f\varepsilon$, and combine the above information to get:

$$U = N^{\frac{1}{\rho}}c = \left(\frac{L}{f\varepsilon}\right)^{\frac{1}{\rho}} \frac{f(\varepsilon - 1)}{mL} = \gamma_U L^{\frac{1}{\varepsilon - 1}}, \text{ where } \gamma_U \equiv \frac{\varepsilon - 1}{m}\left(\frac{1}{f\varepsilon}\right)^{\frac{1}{\rho}} \tag{8.A8}$$

 Notes

1   The reader may note the slight statistical discrepancy between the exported value to other EU countries (€1,858 billion) and the imported value from other EU countries (€1,793 billion).

2   The paper by Spence (1976) on a similar topic slightly pre-dates Dixit and Stiglitz (1977), but had considerably less influence. See Neary (2001) for a discussion of monopolistic competition.

3   Table 8.1 uses simplified sector names; the formal name for sector 84 is 'nuclear reactors, boilers, machinery and mechanical appliances; parts thereof'.

4   Many textbooks discuss the properties of the CES function. See also Brakman and van Marrewijk (1998), who compare it with the properties of other utility functions.

5   In fact the exact price elasticity of demand for a specific variety can be derived. Illuminating in this respect is the analysis in the neighbourhood of p if $p_i = p$ for all other varieties, in which case $-\left(\dfrac{\partial c}{\partial p}\right)\left(\dfrac{p}{c}\right) = \varepsilon\left(1 - \dfrac{1}{N}\right)$. The second term on the right-hand side is inversely related to the number of varieties N, approaching 1 if N becomes large.

6   If a firm takes the price of output p as given and the costs per unit of output c fall as output expands, the firm would want to make an infinite amount of goods if c falls below p, which cannot be an equilibrium.

 **Questions**

Question 8.1

Table 8.4 International trade flows in 2013 (USD billion, rounded).

World total export	18,000	
Sector 85 Electrical Electronic Equipment world export		2,000
China total export	2,200	
Sector 85 Electrical Electronic Equipment China export		550
China total import	2,000	
Sector 85 Electrical Electronic Equipment China import		450

a. What does the Grubel-Lloyd index measure? On the basis of the empirical information in the table above: calculate the Grubel-Lloyd index for sector 85 for China. Provide a suitable interpretation.

b. What does the Balassa index measure? On the basis of the empirical information in the table above: calculate the Balassa index for sector 85 for China. Provide a suitable interpretation.

c. In light of your answer to Question 8.1a, is the Balassa index you calculated in Question 8.1b for sector 85 in China a good indicator or not? Provide a suitable interpretation.

Question 8.2

Chapter 8 introduces the Constant-Elasticity-of-Substitution (CES) utility function, which provided a breakthrough for intra-industry trade theory. Suppose that a consumer with this type of utility function (see equation 8.2) consumes three goods: coffee, tea, and milk.

a. Use a numerical example to show that if $\rho = 1$ the consumer is indifferent to consuming three units of coffee or three units of a mix of the goods.

b. Use a numerical example to show that if $0 < \rho < 1$, the consumer prefers to purchase a combination of goods.

For the rest of this question we assume that each good is consumed in the same quantity. Section 8.3 then rewrites the utility function to distinguish between a love-of-variety effect and a claim on real resources (see equation 8.3). Suppose that $\rho = 0.5$ and assume that one unit of each good is consumed.

c. Rewrite the utility function for coffee, tea, and milk to mimic equation 8.3. How large is the claim on real resources? How large is the love-of-variety effect?

d. Use an example to illustrate how the love-of-variety effect represents a multiplier-like role in the utility function (use equation 8.3).

Question 8.3

'One definition of an economist is somebody who sees something happen in practice and wonders if it will work in theory.'

a. How does this joke relate to the theory of intra-industry trade?

Though the theory of intra-industry trade was an important breakthrough, much remains to be done. Several economists take issue with the parameter ε in the model.

b. Give two reasons why economists might be concerned about this parameter.

The merits of globalisation are subject to fierce debates. One of the issues that anti-globalization advocates raise is the perceived decrease in the amount of variety in the world. Everybody buys the same brands and shops at the same stores.

c. What can the theory of intra-industry trade say about this issue?

 See the **online resources** for a Study Guide and questions:
www.oup.com/uk/vanmarrewijk_it/

9 Investment and migration

Objectives

- To get an overview of the size of international investment and migration flows.
- To observe the volatility of investment flows relative to trade and income flows.
- To understand the distribution of investment flows (main sources and main destinations) and how this distribution has changed over the past four decades in favour of developing nations.
- To understand the difference between greenfield investments and mergers and acquisitions.
- To observe the size of multinational firms and how their importance is rising over time.
- To understand the main welfare gains from international investment and migration flows.
- To observe the current and expected future size and direction of migration flows, largely from developing to economically advanced nations.
- To understand the cumulative long-run impact of migration flows over the past five centuries for the Americas and the Pacific, originating from Europe and (to a lesser extent) Africa.

9.1 Introduction

Chapters 4–8 discussed the underlying reasons for international trade flows based on differences in technology (Chapter 4), differences in factor abundance (Chapters 5 and 6), market power of firms (Chapter 7), and love-of-variety or production externalities (Chapter 8). Throughout this analysis we assumed that inputs in the production process (capital and labour) can flow freely between sectors within a country but cannot move between countries. This contrasts with the assumed free flow of goods and services between countries. It is time, therefore, to analyse to what extent factors of production are mobile between countries. This chapter focuses on the size and direction of such flows, with limited attention for theoretical explanations and economic consequences; these are analysed in more detail in Chapters 13–17.

We start our analysis with a discussion of international capital mobility through foreign direct investment (FDI) flows, which can be either through greenfield investments (setting up a new production plant) or through cross-border mergers and acquisitions (M&As:

merging with or taking over all or part of an existing company in another country). We emphasize the volatility of investment flows relative to trade and income flows. We also analyse the direction of the investment flows by pointing out the main source and destination countries. In addition, we show how the role of developing nations as destinations of FDI has grown in the past four decades.

When engaging in FDI, a firm controls by means of ownership productive assets in more than one country and thus becomes a multinational firm. Such multinational firms represent perhaps the most visible part of the 'globalization' phenomenon and as such attract a lot of media attention. We analyse the structure and economic effects of multinational firms in Chapters 13–15. In this chapter, we simply give examples of large multinational firms (location, sector, and size) and discuss the rising importance of multinational firms for production, trade, investment, and employment since the late twentieth century.

Based on the national income accounting framework discussed in Chapter 3, Section 9.7 analyses the main welfare gains from capital mobility for both source and destination countries. The same framework can be used to analyse the welfare gains from international migration flows. The last part of this chapter discusses the size and direction of migration flows. These flows can be either voluntary or involuntary. Voluntary migration is primarily based on differences in real wage rates and the direction of the flow is from developing to advanced countries (in this text we use the term 'advanced' as a shorthand for 'economically advanced'). Involuntary migration is related to violence, (civil) war, and catastrophes, the migrants being refugees and internally displaced persons. Involuntary migration is largely concentrated in the Middle East, Africa, and Latin America. Adam Smith (see Box 9.1) provided an early analysis of migration flows in the eighteenth century. We conclude the chapter with a discussion of the long-run, cumulative impact of migration flows over a period of 500 years.

BOX 9.1 **Adam Smith**

Figure 9.1
Adam Smith (1723–1790).

Adam Smith (Figure 9.1) was a Scottish philosopher. He is considered by many to be the founder of modern economic science as we know it. His most famous ideas are that of the 'invisible hand', which denotes the way that people pursuing their own self-interest actually benefit society as a whole, and that of the advantages of increasing 'specialization' (the pin factory example). His major publications are *The Theory of Moral Sentiments* (1759) and *An Inquiry into the Nature and Causes of the Wealth of Nations* (1776). Adam Smith considered poverty and unemployment to be push factors for migration and sufficiently high wages a pull factor (Rauhut, 2010). Free mobility of labour through migration tends to reduce unemployment, decrease wage differences, and improve the allocation of labour.

9.2 **Foreign direct investment (FDI)**

A firm becomes a multinational if it controls by means of ownership productive assets in more than one country. This requires foreign direct investment (FDI) either through greenfield investments (setting up a new production plant or part of one) or through cross-border mergers and acquisitions (buying or merging with an existing company or part of one). How important are FDI flows? To get some idea about the size and relevance of these flows we take a closer look at data from the United Nations Conference on Trade and Development (UNCTAD), the most important source of information on FDI flows. In 2014 total world inward FDI flows were estimated to be $1,228 billion. Total world outward FDI flows were estimated to be $1,354 billion. By now we should be used to the fact that at the aggregate level there are discrepancies between incoming and outgoing flows for all sorts of reasons. For illustration purposes we therefore take the average of inward and outward FDI flows, which was a total of $1,291 billion in 2014. This is, indeed, a substantial number; it is equivalent to more than 30 per cent of the world's trade flows and amounts to 1.9 per cent of the world's income level.

Figure 9.2 illustrates the evolution over time (since 1970) for world income, trade, and FDI flows, measured in constant 2014 USD billion. The figure uses a log scale to more easily depict these variables in one graph and at the same time provide information on the differences in growth rates, which can be measured by looking at the slope of a variable at a point in time. A number of observations can be made.

- The evolution of the world's income level is rather stable over time: the slope varies little over time and the average compounded growth rate is almost 3 per cent per year. Consequently, the world's income level increased 3.6 times in the period 1970–2014.

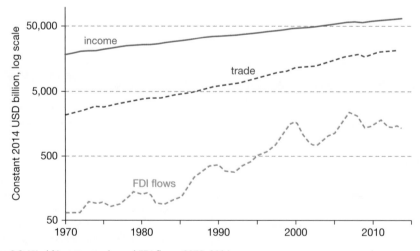

Figure 9.2 World income, trade, and FDI flows, 1970–2014.

Notes: all variables converted to constant 2014 USD billion using US GDP deflator, log scale; income is GDP (constant 2005 USD); trade is export of goods and services (constant 2005 USD); FDI flows is average of world inward and outward FDI.
Sources: calculations based on data from UNCTAD (downloaded 9 September 2015) and World Investment Report 2015 and World Development Indicators.

- The evolution of the world's trade flows varies a bit more over time than the world's income level but except for some special cases (see Chapter 2) is also rather stable. Moreover, trade flows grow faster than income levels; over the period 1970–2014 trade flows increased 10.2-fold, or 2.8 times faster than income.

- The evolution of FDI flows is volatile and FDI flows come in waves: periods of rapid expansion are followed by periods of collapse. In the longer run, however, FDI rises more rapidly than both trade and income; in the period 1970–2014 FDI increased 22.2 fold, or 6.1 times faster than income and 2.2 times faster than trade.

Figure 9.3 illustrates the dynamics of trade and FDI flows as a percentage of world income. Trade levels are depicted on the left-hand scale of the graph and (except for the clear dip in 2009) mostly increased during the whole period, from 11.5 per cent of world income in 1970 to 32.4 per cent in 2013. FDI flows are depicted on the right-hand scales and are much more volatile. FDI did not seem to increase relative to world income in the period 1970–1985. Since then, however, FDI has been increasing more rapidly, with two noteworthy collapses after 2000 (with a peak of 3.7 per cent of income) and 2007 (with a peak of 4.0 per cent of income). For the period as a whole, FDI increased from 0.4 per cent of income in 1970 to 1.9 per cent in 2014.

9.3 Distribution of FDI

Now that we have established that FDI flows are substantial and volatile and that, in the long run, they rise more rapidly than income levels and trade flows, we will provide information on the distribution of FDI: where do the flows come from and where do they go to? We address this question in three steps. First, we provide information on the ten countries with the largest stock of FDI, both in absolute terms and in relative terms, before providing a graphical distribution for the world as a whole. Second, we provide information on the

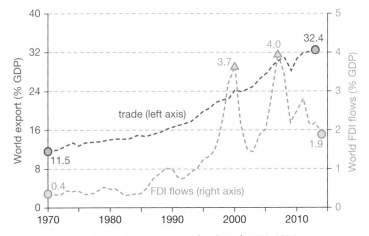

Figure 9.3 World trade and FDI flows relative to income (% of GDP), 1970–2014.

Source: see Figure 9.2

distribution of FDI flows for three large groups of countries: advanced countries, developing countries, and transition countries. Third, we look at the regional distribution of the FDI stocks and FDI intensity relative to income and population.

FDI changes rapidly from year to year. This even holds for the world as a whole (see Section 9.2), and it certainly holds for individual countries. This implies that if we analyse the distribution of FDI the conclusions we reach may be sensitive to the choice of year. We will deal with this problem in two ways.

First, we will look at the stock of FDI rather than the flow of FDI. In principle the relationship between stocks and flows is simple: $FDI_{stock,\, t} = FDI_{stock,\, t-1} + FDI_{flow,\, t}$. The FDI stock at a particular point in time is thus the accumulation of all FDI flows from the past. In practice, however, things are more complicated, since we have to deal with valuation and re-valuation issues, changes in exchange rates relative to all countries, previous flows that become more or less valuable, and so on. The experts at UNCTAD do this difficult job for us by providing estimates of the inward and outward stock of FDI for every country.

The second way to deal with FDI volatility is to look at FDI flows over a longer time period. We will do this below by analysing five-year moving averages. The advantage of this approach is that it allows us to analyse changes in the distribution of FDI flows over time.

Table 9.1 shows the ten countries with the largest stock of inward FDI (investments into the country from other countries) and outward FDI (investments from the country to other countries), both in absolute terms (panel a.) and in relative terms (panel b.). Not surprisingly, the largest absolute destination country is the USA, with an estimated inward stock of FDI of $5,007 billion, or about 20.2 per cent of the world total inward stock of FDI. It is also the largest source country, with an estimated outward stock of FDI of $6,442 billion, or 25.1 per cent of the world total. The USA has thus, on net, invested more in other countries than other countries have invested into the USA: it is a net source of FDI. The same holds for the number two spot on both lists: the UK is also a net source of FDI. Other large source countries are Germany, France, and Japan. The small country of Hong Kong is the world's third largest destination for FDI, not only because it is an important financial and trade centre but also because it provides access to the large Chinese markets (which itself is a large destination of FDI). Other important sources or destinations of FDI are small open economies, such as Switzerland, the Netherlands, Belgium, Singapore, and Canada. The top ten countries in the table together account for 57 per cent of inward FDI and 71 per cent of outward FDI. In relative terms (panel b.) Luxembourg and Hong Kong stand out as source and destination countries, with a per capita inward and outward FDI stock of more than $190,000, or more than 50 times the world average. Apart from Hong Kong and Singapore, all other relatively large source countries are located in Europe. The same ten countries make it to the top destination list, except for Denmark and Norway which are replaced by the Bahamas and Bermuda for tax reasons.

The distribution of the stock of FDI is shown in more detail in Figure 9.4 for 166 countries, classified in global regions (see Table 9.2); panel a. shows inward FDI (the countries as destinations of FDI) and panel b. shows outward FDI (the countries as sources of FDI). A closer look at the figure and a comparison with similar figures on land area (Figure 1.1), population (Figure 1.2), and income (Figure 1.4) immediately shows that there are five main regions active in FDI (certainly as a source), namely: Europe, North America, East Asia,

Table 9.1 Countries with largest absolute and relative FDI stocks, 2013

a. Largest total FDI stocks (billion 2014 USD)

Country	Inward FDI	Per cent[#]	Country	Outward FDI	Per cent[#]
USA	5,007	20.2	USA	6,442	25.1
UK	1,629	6.6	UK	1,912	7.4
Hong Kong	1,465	5.9	Germany	1,735	6.7
France	1,097	4.4	France	1,661	6.5
China	971	3.9	Hong Kong	1,372	5.3
Belgium	937	3.8	Switzerland	1,278	5.0
Germany	864	3.5	Netherlands	1,087	4.2
Singapore	850	3.4	Belgium	1,024	4.0
Switzerland	758	3.1	Japan	1,007	3.9
Brazil	735	3.0	Canada	743	2.9

b. Highest FDI stocks per capita (2014 USD)

Country	Inward FDI	Multiple*	Country	Outward FDI	Multiple*
Luxembourg	263,994	72.5	Luxembourg	339,106	89.9
Hong Kong	203,828	55.9	Hong Kong	190,899	50.6
Singapore	157,407	43.2	Switzerland	157,983	41.9
Switzerland	93,763	25.7	Ireland	110,975	29.4
Belgium	83,834	23.0	Singapore	93,559	24.8
Ireland	83,350	22.9	Belgium	91,544	24.3
Bahamas	46,123	12.7	Netherlands	64,712	17.2
Bermuda	41,567	11.4	Denmark	46,280	12.3
Netherlands	40,459	11.1	Norway	46,156	12.2
Sweden	39,959	11.0	Sweden	46,074	12.2

Notes: [#] per cent of world total stock; * multiple of world average stock.
Sources: as Figure 9.2.

Southeast Asia, and Pacific. The role of other regions in global FDI is minimal, particularly as a source. The importance of Hong Kong and Singapore in global FDI, both as source and destination, is noteworthy. The largest net source FDI countries (measured as the difference in the per cent of global outward FDI and the per cent of global inward FDI) are the USA (4.9 per cent), Germany (3.3 per cent), Japan (3.2 per cent), and France (2.0 per cent). The largest net destinations FDI countries (measured similarly) are Brazil (−1.8 per cent), China (−1.5 per cent), Singapore (−1.5 per cent), and Mexico (−1.0 per cent).

Figure 9.5 illustrates the distribution of FDI flows for three large groups of countries (in panel a. for inward FDI and in panel b. for outward FDI). The three groups are the advanced countries (largely OECD members: Europe, North America, Japan, and so on), the transition countries (Southeast Europe, the Commonwealth of Independent States, and Georgia), and the developing countries (all other countries). The figure mitigates the annual fluctuations in three ways: (i) by calculating annual percentages, (ii) by depicting five-year moving averages, and (iii) by aggregating for groups of countries. The figure clearly illustrates a number of developments over time.

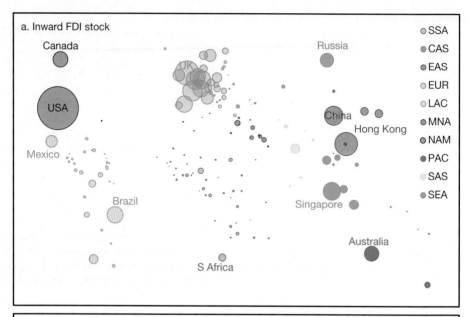

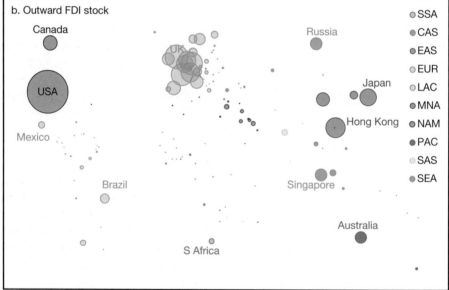

Figure 9.4 World distribution of FDI stock, 2013.

Source: UNCTAD (downloaded 9 September 2015); 166 countries; see Table 9.2 for the World Bank region abbreviations.

- The role of advanced countries as virtually the only sources of FDI flows (more than 99 per cent in 1975) has gradually (but not monotonically) diminished over time (to about 65 per cent in 2014).
- The role of advanced countries as dominant destinations of FDI flows has gradually eroded over time (from 76 per cent in 1975 to 44 per cent in 2014).

Table 9.2 Regional distribution of FDI stock and FDI intensity, 2013

a. Per cent of world total

Region	Code	FDI stock Inward	FDI stock Outward	Pop*	GDP
Central Asia	CAS	4.1	2.3	5.2	6.6
East Asia	EAS	11.3	12.5	22.7	23.1
Europe	EUR	39.0	47.8	7.8	19.1
Latin America and Caribbean	LAC	7.4	2.5	8.4	8.2
Middle East and North Africa	MNA	3.3	1.2	4.3	5.8
North America	NAM	22.8	27.9	5.2	18.5
Pacific	PAC	2.8	1.9	0.4	1.2
South Asia	SAS	1.1	0.5	24.5	8.5
Southeast Asia	SEA	6.3	2.8	8.4	5.8
Sub-Saharan Africa	SSA	1.9	0.5	13.2	3.2
World		100	100	100	100

b. FDI intensity

Region	Inward FDI	Outward FDI	Inward FDI	Outward FDI
	Relative to population		Relative to GDP	
CAS	0.8	0.4	0.6	0.4
EAS	0.5	0.6	0.5	0.5
EUR	5.0	6.1	2.0	2.5
LAC	0.9	0.3	0.9	0.3
MNA	0.8	0.3	0.6	0.2
NAM	4.4	5.4	1.2	1.5
PAC	6.4	4.5	2.4	1.6
SAS	0.0	0.0	0.1	0.1
SEA	0.8	0.3	1.1	0.5
SSA	0.1	0.0	0.6	0.2
World	1.0	1.0	1.0	1.0

Notes: GDP in PPP (2014 dollars); * pop = population; shaded areas have above world average intensity.
Sources: based on UNCTAD data (downloaded 9 September 2015), World Investment Report 2015, and World Development Indicators.

- The role of transition countries as sources and destinations of FDI flows was absent before the fall of the Iron Curtain (0 per cent up to 1991) and has since increased, but remains modest (less than 5 per cent as source and less than 6 per cent as destination in 2014).

- The share of developing countries as destinations of FDI flows has fluctuated substantially over time, with a long-run upward trend (from 24 per cent in 1975 to 50 per cent in 2014).

- The role of developing countries as sources of FDI flows has increased dramatically, particularly in the new millennium (from 9.3 per cent in 2002 to 30.2 per cent in 2014).

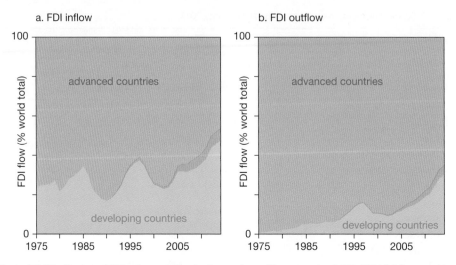

Figure 9.5 Distribution of FDI: advanced, developing, and transition countries, 1975–2014 (pink = transition countries).

Notes: data in 1975 are based on five-year moving average for 1971–1975, and so on; the small area in between advanced countries and developing countries is for transition countries; developing countries excludes financial centres in the Caribbean. *Source:* see Figure 9.2.

Table 9.2 summarizes the regional involvement in the global stock of FDI in absolute terms (panel a.) and in relative terms (panel b.). Europe and North America are the most important players in global FDI, together accounting for 76 per cent of the outward and 62 per cent of the inward stock of FDI. East Asia plays a substantial, and as we have seen increasingly important, role in global FDI with more than 11 per cent of the world total. The absolute role of the other regions is modest.

Table 9.2 also provides information on the intensity of FDI by relating the stock of FDI to either the population size or the income level (panel b.: the FDI stock percentage is divided by either the population percentage or the GDP percentage). Relative to their populations, Europe, North America, and Pacific are the most active players for both inward and outward FDI. Note that there is basically no role for South Asia and Sub-Saharan Africa in global FDI measured relative to population size. More or less the same conclusions hold when we relate FDI to the income level, with Europe, North America, and Pacific as the main players, joined by Southeast Asia as an important destination for FDI. Again, the role of South Asia and, to a lesser extent, Sub-Saharan Africa is limited.

Recall that we arrived at similar conclusions regarding the most active and least active global participants for international trade flows in Box 7.2. Indeed, the entire discussion in this section has illustrated that countries heavily involved in international trade flows, such as Hong Kong, Singapore, and the small open European economies, are also heavily involved in global FDI. In contrast, regions that are less active in international trade, such as South Asia and Sub-Saharan Africa, are also less active in global FDI. We will get back to this link between trade and FDI in our theoretical modelling of heterogeneous firms (Chapter 13), multinationals (Chapter 14), and offshoring (Chapter 15).

9.4 Greenfield FDI and mergers and acquisitions

As indicated in Section 9.2, FDI can take place through (i) *greenfield* investments, where a firm participates in setting up a new production plant or part of one; or (ii) cross-border *mergers and acquisitions* (M&As), where a firm merges with or acquires a firm, or part of a firm, already operative in another country. We briefly discuss both aspects in this section.

Regarding cross-border M&As, UNCTAD focuses on the *net* value, which is the difference between M&A gross sales (all multinational cross-border acquisitions) and divestment of sales (the sales from multinationals to domestic entities or to other multinationals). Measured in net values, the sales and purchases thus reflect the M&A component of FDI flows.[1] We can distinguish between three types of M&As.[2]

- Horizontal M&As between competing firms in the same industry: by consolidating their resources, the merging firms aim to achieve synergies and often greater market power. Typical sectors are pharmaceuticals, automobiles, petroleum, and several services sectors.

- Vertical M&As between firms in client–supplier or buyer–seller relationships: the firms seek to reduce uncertainty and transaction costs as regards forward and backward linkages in the production process. Typical sectors are electronics and automobiles.

- Conglomerate M&As between companies in unrelated activities. The firms seek to diversify risk and deepen economies of scope.

Figure 9.6 provides information on the net sales (panel a.) and net purchases (panel b.) from cross-border M&As, distributed over advanced, developing, and transition countries. The panels show that M&As come in waves and their total value rises and falls quickly, roughly ranging from $300 to $700 billion. For example, global cross-border M&As fell by

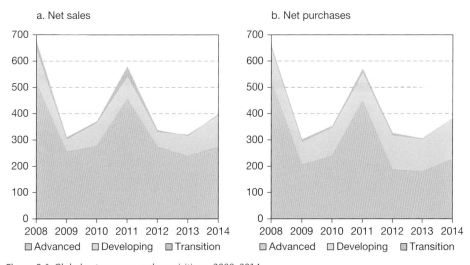

Figure 9.6 Global net mergers and acquisitions, 2008–2014.

Notes: values in 2014 USD billion; developing economies excludes financial centres in the Caribbean; net sales by region of the acquired company; net purchases by region of the ultimate acquiring company.

Sources: calculations based on UNCTAD World Investment Report 2015 and World Development Indicators.

more than 50 per cent in 2009 as a result of the Great Recession (from $674 to $311 billion), then bounced back by more than 50 per cent in 2011 (from $371 to $580 billion), only to decline again by more than 40 per cent in 2012 (as a result of the European crisis).

Most of the net sales (acquired companies, panel a.) and most of the net purchases (acquiring companies, panel b.) were from the advanced countries, namely on average 77 and 67 per cent, respectively. The average share of developing countries in net sales was 21 per cent and in net purchases 31 per cent. Firms from developing countries thus on net acquired firms from advanced countries in this period (which is in contrast to the overall distribution flows discussed in Section 9.3). The remaining net sales and purchases of around 2 per cent are for the transition countries, which thus play a minor role in cross-border M&As.

Figure 9.7 provides an overview of the value of announced greenfield FDI projects by source (panel a.) and by destination (panel b.), distributed over advanced, developing, and transition countries. When comparing with Figure 9.6 on cross-border net M&As, we note that (i) greenfield investments have mostly declined in the period 2008–12 as a result of the Great Recession (in contrast to M&As and in contrast to the long-run trend described in Section 9.2) and (ii) the value of greenfield investments is larger than the value of net M&As. In 2008 the value of greenfield FDI was $1,478 billion, compared to $674 billion for net M&As. By 2014 these values had declined to $696 billion for greenfield FDI and $399 billion for net M&As. For the period as a whole, roughly one-third of total FDI consisted of M&As and two-thirds consisted of greenfield investments (with the share of M&As varying from 23 to 39 per cent).

In accordance with our discussion in Section 9.3, the advanced economies are the primary source of greenfield FDI (about 70 per cent of the total) and an important, but significantly smaller, destination for greenfield FDI (about one-third of the total). The developing

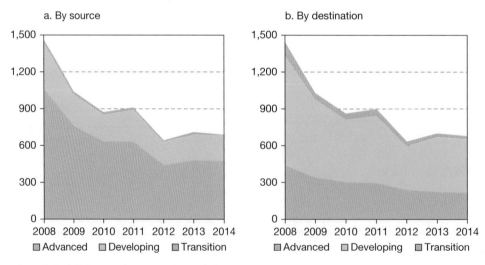

Figure 9.7 Global value of announced greenfield FDI projects, 2008–2014.

Notes: values in 2014 USD billion; developing economies excludes financial centres in the Caribbean; net sales by region of the acquired company; net purchases by region of the ultimate acquiring company.

Sources: calculations based on UNCTAD World Investment Report 2015 and World Development Indicators.

countries provide a mirror image of this picture: they are the primary destination for greenfield FDI (about 61 per cent of the total) and an important, but significantly smaller, source of greenfield FDI (about 28 per cent of the total). Regarding greenfield investments, therefore, advanced economies are on net investing in developing countries in this period. Since the greenfield flows are larger than the net M&A flows, the overall effect is a net investment from advanced to developing countries (see Section 9.3). The remaining green-field FDI shares are for the transition countries, which are the source of about 2 per cent of greenfield FDI and the destination for about 5 per cent of greenfield FDI. They are thus net recipients of greenfield FDI from advanced countries.

9.5 The size of multinationals

One of the reasons for FDI volatility over time, certainly at the country level, is the enor-mous value of some of the investments, particularly for M&As. In 2014, for example, UNCTAD counted 54 different M&As with a value of more than $3 billion. Table 9.3 pro-vides an overview of the ten largest cross-border M&As in 2014. On top of the list, with a value of more than $130 billion, is the takeover in the radiotelephone communications sector of 45 per cent of Verizon Wireless Inc. in the USA by Verizon Communications Inc., also in the USA. Note that as long as the ultimate host economy is different from the ultimate home economy, M&A deals on the surface undertaken within the same country are still considered cross-border M&As. This was the case with the top deal and imme-diately draws our attention to an important data problem: it may be hard to disentan-gle particular investment flows and discern their direction because a company may have its formal headquarters in some country, perhaps for tax reasons, even if its activities are mostly located in another country. Note that the deal is also somewhat incestuous, as some Verizon company is taking over part of some other Verizon company.

The second-largest cross-border M&A, with a value of more than $42 billion, concerns the complete takeover in the investment advice sector of CITIC Ltd in China by CITIC

Table 9.3 Top ten cross-border M&As, 2014

Value	Acquired firm	Host ec	Sector	Acquiring firm	Home ec
130.3	Verizon Wireless	USA	Radiotel	Verizon Comm	USA
42.2	CITIC	China	Inv adv	CITIC Pacific	Hong Kong
23.1	Soc Fr Radiotel	France	Telecom	Numericable Group	France
15.3	Alliance Boots	Switz	Drug store	Walgreens	USA
14.2	Merck & Co Care	USA	Pharmac	Bayer	Germany
13.9	Beam	USA	Wine etc.	Suntory Hold	Japan
13.4	Tim Hortons	Canada	Eating	Burger King	USA
11.2	E-Plus Mobilfunk	Germany	Radiotel	Telefonica	Germany
10.0	Grupo Corporativo	Spain	Telecom	Vodafone Hold	Spain
9.1	Concur Tech	USA	Software	SAP America	USA

Notes: value in billion USD; ec = economy; Switz = Switzerland; sector names and firm names are shortened.
Source: UNCTAD, World Investment Report 2015.

Pacific Ltd from Hong Kong. There is a similar incestuous flavour, but at least it involves more or less two different countries.[3] Similar observations can be made for the other deals in Table 9.3, involving activities in telecommunications, drug stores (chemists), pharmaceuticals, eating, and software from and to North American, European, and East Asian countries. The number ten deal is still worth more than $9 billion.

Table 9.4 lists the 20 largest multinational firms, ranked by foreign assets. The largest firm is General Electric, based in the USA. It has $338 billion foreign assets out of $685 billion total assets, $76 billion foreign sales out of $145 billion total sales, and 171,000 foreign employees out of 305,000 total employees. The last column in Table 9.4 lists the Transnationality Index (TNI), an indicator of the relative degree of the firm's global activities, which is the average of the three ratios just mentioned. For General Electric the TNI is thus:

$$TNI_{GE} = \frac{1}{3}\left(\frac{338}{685} + \frac{76}{145} + \frac{171}{305}\right) \times 100\% = 52.5 \qquad 9.1$$

The TNI for General Electric is much lower than for the second- and third-largest firms, the oil firms Shell (76.6 per cent) and BP (83.8 per cent). The highest TNI, however, is achieved by the Swiss food and drinks firm Nestlé (97.1 per cent, ranked twelfth). In the top 100 list (not shown) the lowest TNI is achieved by the diversified Chinese firm CITIC Group (18.4 per cent, ranked thirty-sixth).

Table 9.4 Top 20 non-financial multinationals, ranked by foreign assets

Company	Home	Sector	Assets	Sales	Empl	TNI
1 General Electric	USA	El and electronic	685	145	305	52.5
2 Royal Dutch Shell	UK	Petroleum	360	467	87	76.6
3 BP	UK	Petroleum	300	376	86	83.8
4 Toyota	Japan	Motor vehicles	377	266	333	54.7
5 Total	France	Petroleum	227	234	97	78.5
6 Exxon Mobil	USA	Petroleum	334	421	77	65.4
7 Vodafone	UK	Telecom	217	70	86	90.4
8 GDF Suez	France	Utilities	272	125	219	59.2
9 Chevron	USA	Petroleum	233	223	62	59.5
10 Volkswagen	Germany	Motor vehicles	409	248	533	58.2
11 Eni SpA	Italy	Petroleum	185	164	78	63.3
12 Nestlé SA	Switzerland	Food and drink	138	98	339	97.1
13 Enel SpA	Italy	Utilities	227	109	74	56.6
14 E.ON AG	Germany	Utilities	186	170	72	65.0
15 Anheuser–Busch InBev	Belgium	Food and drink	123	40	118	92.8
16 Arcelor Mittal	Luxembourg	Metal products	115	84	245	91.1
17 Siemens	Germany	El and electronic	139	102	369	77.9
18 Honda	Japan	Motor vehicles	145	119	187	73.4
19 Mitsubishi	Japan	Wholesale	153	243	63	40.6
20 EDF SA	France	Utilities	331	93	155	30.8

Notes: assets and sales in billion USD; Empl = Employment (in thousands); TNI = Transnationality Index, see main text.
Source: UNCTAD, World Investment Report 2013.

The top 20 list in Table 9.4 contains three firms each from the USA, the UK, France, Germany, and Japan, as well as two firms from Italy and one each from Switzerland, Belgium, and Luxembourg. Taken together, Europe thus dominates this list with 14 out of 20 firms. However, some caution in allocating firms to countries seems warranted. For example, the table lists Royal Dutch Shell as a British firm, rather than a British–Dutch firm. Similarly, it lists Arcelor Mittal as a firm from Luxembourg rather than India, and it lists Anheuser–Busch InBev as a Belgian firm rather than a Belgian–American firm. The top 100 list (not shown) has a similar geographic distribution: it contains 60 firms from Europe, 25 firms from North America, 13 firms from East Asia, and two firms from the rest of the world (one each from Australia and Brazil).

From a sector perspective, the top 20 list in Table 9.4 contains six oil firms, four utilities firms, three car firms, two each of electrical and electronic equipment and food and drink firms, and one each of wholesale, telecommunications, and metal products firms. In the top 100 list there are 11 motor vehicles firms, 11 petroleum firms, 10 pharmaceutical firms, nine telecommunications firms, and seven firms each in electrical and electronic equipment; food, beverages, and tobacco; and utilities (electricity, gas, and water). The remaining 38 firms are in 16 different sectors.

9.6 The importance of multinationals

In the long run, FDI rises more rapidly than both income levels and trade flows (see Section 9.2). As a consequence of these investment flows we expect multinational activity, which is associated with FDI, to become more important in the global economic system. Figure 9.8 provides six indicators of this rising importance at four points in time, namely 1990 (a long time ago), 2006 (actually, the average of 2005–7, just before the Great Recession), 2012 (briefly after the Great Recession), and 2014 (the most recently available information). Remarkably, five of the six indicators are rising over time despite the impact of the Great Recession. The only exception is FDI relative to total investments (panel d.). We briefly discuss each panel.

a. The sales of foreign affiliates relative to income rose from 21 per cent in 1990 to 47 per cent in 2014, or by about 1.1 percentage point per year. This is a substantial increase, even if we realize that sales are a value measure and income is a value-added measure (see also point c. below). The growth rate slowed down in the period 2006–12 (at 0.3 per cent per year), but accelerated in the period 2012–14 (at 2.0 per cent per year).

b. The global stock of FDI relative to income rose from 10 per cent in 1990 to 34 per cent in 2014, or by about 1.0 percentage point per year. Again, the growth rate slowed down in the period 2006–12 (at 0.4 per cent per year), but accelerated in the period 2012–14 (at 1.6 per cent per year).

c. The value added by foreign affiliates relative to income rose from about 4 per cent in 1990 to 10 per cent in 2014, or about 0.3 percentage points per year. In this case we are comparing value added with value added, so about 10 per cent of all production in the world is taken care of by foreign affiliates.[4] Growth stagnated in the period 2006–12 (at 0.0 per cent per year), but returned to the long-run average in the period 2012–14 (at 0.3 per cent per year).

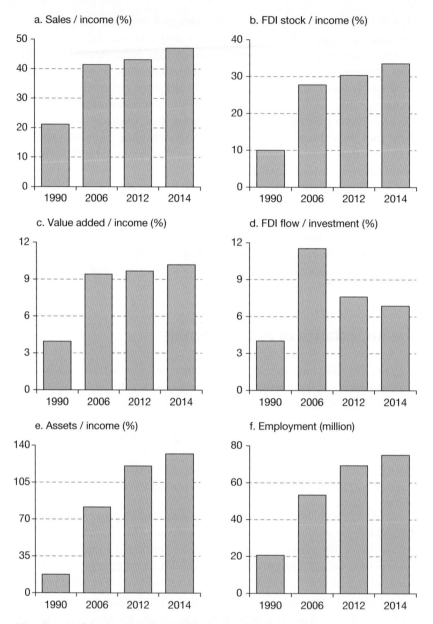

Figure 9.8 Indicators of the rising importance of multinationals.

Notes: world totals; 2006 values are average of 2005–07; a. sales of foreign affiliates/GDP; b. FDI stock[#]/GDP; c. value added of foreign affiliates/GDP; d. FDI flow*/gross fixed capital formation; e. assets of foreign affiliates/GDP; f. employment of foreign affiliates; [#]FDI stock is average of inward and outward stock; *FDI flow is average of inflows and outflows.
Source: calculations based on UNCTAD and World Bank (2015).

d. FDI flows relative to investment (measured as gross fixed capital formation) rose from about 4 per cent in 1990 to about 7 per cent in 2014, or by about 0.1 percentage points per year. FDI flows relative to investment reached a peak (of 11.5 per cent) before the Great Recession. They have not recovered since, but recovery is thought to be imminent (UNCTAD, 2015).

e. The assets of foreign affiliates relative to income rose from 17 per cent in 1990 to132 per cent in 2014, or by about 4.8 percentage points per year. This increase has not slowed down but accelerated after the Great Recession (to 6.3 per cent per year).

f. Employment by foreign affiliates rose from 20.6 million in 1990 to 75.1 million in 2014, or by about 2.3 million per year. As in point e., this increase has not slowed down but accelerated after the Great Recession (to 2.7 million per year).

9.7 Simple gains from capital mobility

Building on our discussion of the Balance of Payments (see Chapter 3), we now provide a simple macroeconomic model to illustrate one aspect of the gains from capital mobility associated with FDI flows. From our analysis in Chapter 3 we know that a current account surplus (deficit) has to be matched by a capital outflow (inflow). This is why the current account is a useful indicator for (net) international capital flows between a country and the rest of the world. From national income accounting (see again Chapter 3) we also know that the current account balance CA is equal by definition to the difference between national savings S and investments I: that is $CA \equiv S - I$. The term 'national' indicates that both the private and the government sector are included.

From this accounting identity it becomes clear that a national savings surplus, $S - I > 0$, has to be invested abroad. This is reflected in a corresponding capital outflow. In other words, when exports are larger than imports, the excess capital has to go somewhere. It becomes part of the national savings, and these savings can be used to finance investments. If the domestic investment opportunities are limited, it would be beneficial to use (part of) the savings to invest abroad. Similarly, if national savings fall short of national investment, there has to be a capital inflow to match this difference. But what causes these capital inflows or outflows?

Although the basic workings of our model are similar to the trade models discussed in Chapters 4 through 8, we have to keep in mind that financial transactions are different from goods transactions. The main difference is the degree of risk that is involved. Savings are channelled directly through capital markets or indirectly through financial intermediaries (such as banks) towards investment opportunities in the expectation that the investments will yield a positive return or future income stream. To induce agents to save more and reduce current consumption, the interest rate r has to increase. Also, when the risk of financial transactions increases, the interest rate has to increase to compensate savers for the higher risk involved. This suggests the savings functions S for our two-country world, consisting of the USA (index A) and the UK (index B), see equation 9.2. In other words, the savings in either country increases if the interest rate rises.

$$S_A = S_A(r_A), \text{ with } S'_A > 0; \quad S_B = S_B(r_B), \text{ with } S'_B > 0 \qquad 9.2$$

Turning next to investment I, the interest rate is important again. Each investment project increases the existing capital stock. This raises the productivity of capital, but each new addition to the capital stock makes a smaller contribution to the productivity of capital due to the law of diminishing marginal returns. What is the optimal or equilibrium level of investment in this case? Investment takes place until the contribution of the latest, or marginal, investment project to productivity equals the cost of capital. The cost of capital, or the cost of financing an investment project, is equal to the interest rate r. Investment will thus take place until the (declining) marginal productivity of capital is equal to the cost of capital. This suggests the investment functions I for the two countries given in equation 9.3. In other words, investment declines in either country if the interest rate rises.

$$I_A = I_A(r_A), \text{ with } I'_A < 0; \quad I_B = I_B(r_B), \text{ with } I'_B < 0 \qquad\qquad 9.3$$

Figure 9.9 illustrates what happens in the absence of international capital mobility (panel a. for the USA and panel b. for the UK), in which case national savings must equal national investment in both countries: $S_A = I_A$ and $S_B = I_B$. We have assumed that the American equilibrium interest rate r_{A0} (which is achieved at point A) is higher than the British equilibrium interest rate r_{B0} (which is achieved at point B), but this is not important for the reasoning below.

What changes if we allow for international capital mobility? The most important change is that we no longer require that national savings is equal to national investment. Instead, we now require that total world savings is equal to total world investment: $S_A + S_B = I_A + I_B$. As a consequence, we no longer have two different interest rates for the two countries but one interest rate for the world as a whole (we implicitly assume that there is no country-specific risk). Figure 9.9 illustrates this equilibrium for the interest rate $r_{A1} = r_{B1}$, which is in between r_{B0} and r_{A0}. The interest rate thus rises in the UK, where savings go up and investments go down, and falls in the USA, where investments go up and savings go down. The equilibrium interest rate is characterized by the fact that the British savings surplus $S_{B1} - I_{B1}$ is equal in absolute value to the American investment surplus $I_{A1} - S_{A1}$.

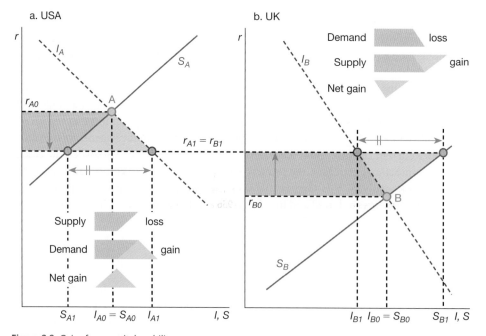

Figure 9.9 Gains from capital mobility.

Despite the fact that the interest rate rises in the UK and falls in the USA, both countries gain from international capital mobility. The area in between a demand or supply curve and the vertical axis is a welfare measure derived in standard microeconomics courses (see also Chapter 10). In the USA, the fall in the interest rate causes a larger increase in the investor surplus (the area in between the investment schedule and the change in interest rates) than the decrease in savings surplus (the area in between the savings schedule and the change in interest rates), leading to a net welfare gain as indicated in Figure 9.9. The opposite holds in the UK, where the increase in the savings surplus is larger than the decrease in the investment surplus, also leading to a net welfare gain as indicated in Figure 9.9. International capital mobility thus does not make everyone better off: investors gain in the USA and savers gain in the UK, while savers lose in the USA and investors lose in the UK. The net welfare effects, however, are positive in both countries. In principle, therefore, the losers can be completely compensated for their loss, even if this does not occur in practice.

9.8 Migration

So far, the discussion in this chapter has concentrated on the international mobility of one factor of production: capital.[5] In reality there is, of course, also international mobility of other factors of production, in particular of labour through international migration flows. Indirectly, migration also implies international mobility of other inputs, such as many different types of human capital and skills. These inputs are embodied in the migrating population and acquired through years of schooling, studying, practice, training, and on-the-job learning-by-doing. The remainder of this chapter briefly discusses the (relative) size of international migration flows.

People mainly migrate for one of two reasons.

First, fighting and other violence associated with (civil) war, persecution of minorities, drugs trade, and so on may force people to leave their homes and seek safety and shelter elsewhere. See Box 9.2 for a brief discussion of this type of migration.

BOX 9.2 UNHCR, refugees, and internally displaced persons

The United Nations High Commissioner for Refugees (UNHCR), the UN's refugee agency, was established in 1950 to help Europeans displaced by World War II, initially for a period of three years. The never-ending arrival of new conflicts and humanitarian crises has unfortunately made UNHCR necessary up to this day. Initial examples are the Hungarian crisis in 1956 and the decolonization of Africa in the 1960s. Later examples are the displacement crises in Asia and Latin America in the 1970s and 1980s, the 30-year-old refugee crises in Afghanistan, and the turmoil in the Middle East (Syria and Iraq) in the twenty-first century.

The UNHCR website provides regular updates of 'populations of concern to UNHCR' for 16 different global regions, see Figure 9.10. At the beginning of 2015 the total number of people of concern was 42.9 million. Only a minority of these (about 27 per cent) are (international) refugees (11 million) or people in a refugee-like situation (0.7 million). The largest group concerns Internally Displaced Persons (IDPs): that

(continued...)

is, people who are migrating in search of safety and shelter but who have not crossed an international border, consisting of IDPs protected/assisted by UNHCR (23.9 million) and returned IDPs (1.4 million). Other groups consist, for example, of asylum seekers (1.2 million), stateless persons (3.5 million), and various other people of concern to whom UNHCR extends protection and/or assistance. For simplicity, Figure 9.10 distinguishes only between the three main groups: Refugees (27 per cent), IDPs (59 per cent), and Others (14 per cent). Note that from a migration perspective we should discuss only (international) refugees. From a humanitarian perspective, however, we should also include internally displaced persons.

By far the largest number of refugees and IDPs are in the Middle East (10.8 million, or more than 25 per cent of the world total). Almost 8 million of these people are internally displaced persons as a result of the conflicts in Iraq, Syria, and Turkey. Other large concentrations of displaced persons, with a majority of IDPs, are in Latin America (5.8 million), East Africa and Horn of Africa (5.8 million), and Central Africa (5.4 million). Southwest Asia has 4.3 million displaced persons, of which the majority (58 per cent) are refugees. Although much media attention has been focused on the European refugee crisis (see Box 9.3), the total number of displaced persons in all European regions taken together is 4.2 million persons, fewer than in any of the other regions mentioned so far and less than 10 per cent of the world total. The numbers are even lower for North America and for East Asia and the Pacific. The conclusion is, therefore, that the displaced person problem is largely a problem in developing economies, concentrated in the Middle East, Africa, and Latin America. Taken together these regions account for more than 30 million (or more than 70 per cent) of globally displaced persons.

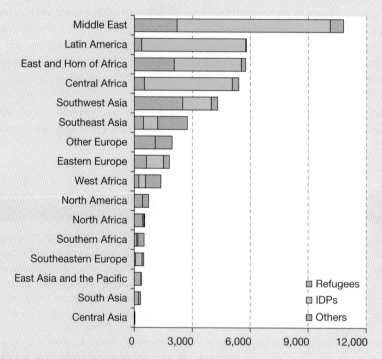

Figure 9.10 Refugees and internally displaced persons, 2015.

Notes: persons in thousands; 'Refugees' includes people in refugee-like situations; IDPs = internally displaced persons; 'Others' includes asylum-seekers and various.

Source: UNHCR Global Appeal 2015 update.

BOX 9.3 Syrian refugees in Europe

The Syrian refugee crisis started in 2011 when the initially peaceful demonstrations against the Assad regime (inspired by the Arab Spring) were met with torture and violence by the police and the military, and civil war erupted. There are many different rebel groups involved in the fighting, including the notorious so-called Islamic State (IS, or Islamic State of Iraq and the Levant). By 2015 the fighting has resulted in more than 200,000 casualties. Various foreign nations are involved in the conflict, providing support for the rebels from the USA, France, and the UK and support for the Assad regime from Iran, Iraq, and Russia.

As usual when violence erupts, a stream of refugees appears: people who try to find safety and shelter elsewhere. A large number of these have tried to seek asylum in European countries, travelling by various dangerous routes in order to get there. Many drown, particularly when they try to cross the Mediterranean to get from Libya to Italy. The Syrian refugee crisis became the centre of media attention in Europe during 2015. As Figure 9.11 shows, a large number of Syrian nationals had already applied for asylum in 2014, with a peak of more than 18,000 per month in September and October of 2014. These numbers were dwarfed, however, by the number of asylum-seekers in 2015, with about 51,000 applications in July 2015 and more than 73,000 in August 2015. The total number of applications has reached more than 440,000 by August 2015.

A source of friction is the distribution of the Syrian refugees across the European countries. As Table 9.5 shows, in absolute terms (left-hand part of the table) almost 109 thousand (25 per cent) have sought asylum in Germany, followed by Serbia (17 per cent), Sweden (16 per cent), and Hungary (12 per cent). All the other countries together have taken care of the remaining 132 thousand (30 per cent). Note that, with the exception of Germany, all the countries in the top ten in absolute terms are small countries in terms of population. Each of them has more asylum applications than the large countries such as the UK, France, Spain, and Italy. In response to this uneven distribution, the European Union decided to redistribute 120,000 refugees in September 2015. On the basis of the absolute number of refugees who applied for asylum from Syria alone reported in Table 9.5, this is a modest redistribution only, unlikely to solve this problem in the long run.

Our picture of the uneven distribution of Syrian refugees across Europe changes only modestly when we look at the top ten recipients in relative terms (per million population of the receiving countries).

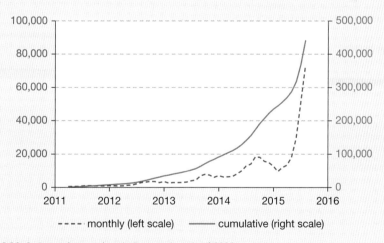

Figure 9.11 Syrian asylum-seekers in Europe since April 2011.

Notes: number of asylum applications by Syrian nationals for 37 European countries (excludes East Europe, such as Russia, Belarus, and Ukraine).

Source: based on UNHCR data (downloaded 10 October 2015).

(continued...)

Table 9.5 Distribution of Syrian refugees in Europe, August 2015

Top ten absolute		Top ten relative	
Country	Asylum applications	Country	Applications/million
Germany	108,897	Serbia (and Kosovo)	10,777
Serbia (and Kosovo)	77,207	Sweden	7,232
Sweden	69,427	Hungary	5,471
Hungary	54,125	Montenegro	4,767
Austria	20,877	Cyprus	2,601
Netherlands	18,096	Austria	2,462
Bulgaria	15,714	Denmark	2,356
Denmark	13,230	Malta	2,249
Switzerland	8,683	Bulgaria	2,163
Belgium	8,230	Germany	1,350
Other 27 countries	47,228	Other 27 countries	185
Total	441,714	Total	822

Notes: number of asylum applications by Syrian nationals for 37 European countries, cumulative April 2011–August 2015; relative: per million population.
Source: based on UNHCR data (downloaded 10 October 2015).

Again, Germany is the only large country involved, with 1,350 applications per million (compared to 822 for the European countries on average). Germany is again accompanied by nine relatively small countries, where Montenegro, Cyprus, and Malta are new on the list (replacing the Netherlands, Switzerland, and Belgium).[6] The highest relative number of applications is in Serbia (13 times the European average), followed by Sweden (9 times) and Hungary (7 times).

The influx of such a large number of refugees and the rapid increase during 2015 to more than 73 thousand in one month clearly puts pressure on the absorption capacity of European countries and the willingness of populations to accommodate these refugees. In addition, there are migrants from other countries (such as Somalia, Afghanistan, and Nigeria) also entering Europe, some as refugees and some for economic reasons.[7] The problems associated with distinguishing between different types of migrants also create tensions. Germany, for example, estimated in September 2015 that about one-third of the asylum-seekers in Germany who claim to be Syrian are not actually from Syria (*De Volkskrant*, 2015). The flows depicted in Figure 9.11 are thus both overestimating the problem (as they include non-Syrians) and underestimating the problem (as they exclude many other refugees).

Keeping the above observations in mind, it is still useful to put the European Syrian refugee problem in proper perspective. To do that, Figure 9.12 repeats the cumulative graph of European asylum-seekers from Figure 9.11 and combines it with a graph of the number of *regional* Syrian refugees registered in Turkey, Lebanon, Jordan, Iraq, Egypt, and North Africa. The total number of regional Syrian refugees exceeded four million by September 2015, no less than nine times the total number of Syrian asylum-seekers in Europe. Turkey alone hosted close to two million Syrian refugees (more than four times all of Europe combined), while Lebanon hosted more than one million (more than twice the European total). Notwithstanding the fact that a large number of these refugees might still find their way to Europe and apply for asylum there, this indicates that the Syrian refugee problem in Europe is dwarfed by the regional problems created in Turkey, Lebanon, and Jordan. It is also dwarfed by the humanitarian problems the refugees themselves are facing every day.

(continued...)

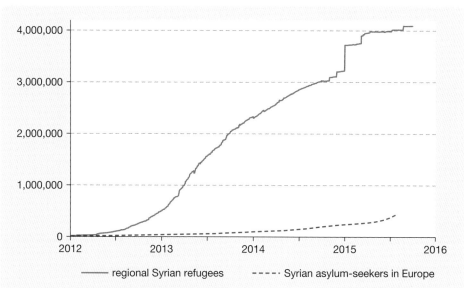

Figure 9.12 Regional versus European Syrian refugees.

Notes: regional Syrian refugees is number of registered Syrian refugees in Turkey, Lebanon, Jordan, Iraq, Egypt, and North Africa; asylum seekers in Europe is number of asylum applications by Syrian nationals for 37 European countries. *Source:* based on UNHCR data (downloaded 10 October 2015).

Second, there may be differences in the reward to specific types of labour in different locations. In principle, this creates an incentive for people to migrate from locations with low real wages to locations with high real wages. In view of the enormous differences between countries in terms of income per capita (see Chapter 1), the real-wage-difference migration incentive is strong.

Note that the main economic consequences of migration flows based on real wage differences can be analysed using a similar framework as that discussed in Section 9.7 for the gains from international capital mobility. In principle, therefore, migration flows enhance welfare.

There are three main obstacles to migration flows based on real wage differences. First, one needs to actually have the (educational) skills required to benefit from the real wage difference and be aware of its existence. In many cases, people do not have the required skills or lack information regarding opportunities in other countries. Second, there are many legal obstacles to migration flows, both within and between countries. Many advanced countries, for example, have a quota system, which limits the number of people that can legally enter the country. Third, there are large costs and uncertainties associated with international migration. Many people in Africa, for example, simply lack the resources or financial security needed in order to engage in migration efforts.

United Nations (UN) evidence indicates that although the absolute numbers have increased, world migrants—i.e. foreign-born—comprise only about 3.1 per cent of the world population.[8] This low number seems inconsistent with popular opinion that the level of migrants is much larger, primarily as a result of the low number of migrants in developing

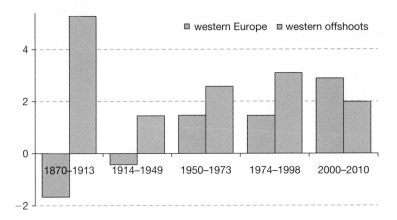

Figure 9.13 Relative migration flows: western Europe and western offshoots, 1870–2010.

Note: data for 1999 not included; net migration in the period (Maddison, 2001, table 3.4) is divided by the (simple) average population and length of the period, normalized per 1,000 inhabitants; updated for the period 2000–2010 with data from UN Population Division, Migration Section; western Europe consists of Belgium, France, Germany, Italy, Netherlands, Norway, Sweden, Switzerland, and UK.

Data source: Beugelsdijk et al. (2013).

countries. Indeed, in some individual countries these numbers are much larger. The share of foreign-born as a percentage of the labour force is relevant, as this number gives an impression of competition on the labour markets. In Australia, for example, 26.5 per cent of the labour force in 2008 was foreign-born, in the USA this number was 16.5 per cent, in the UK 12.6 per cent, in the Netherlands 11.4 per cent, and in Denmark 6.8 per cent.[9]

Historians have identified two modern 'waves' of migration (see Figure 9.13). The first took place between 1820 and 1913. More than 50 million migrants departed (mostly) from Europe to Australia, Canada, South America, and the USA. Almost 60 per cent of the migrants went to the USA. Most were young and relatively low-skilled. After 1850, most migrants came from Ireland.

The second 'wave' started after World War II, and has not yet ended. Between 1913 and 1950 migration was only a fraction of what it had been during the nineteenth century. The USA remained the main destination country. Immigration grew from a low of 252,000 per year in the 1950s to 916,000 in the 1990s, but the source countries changed dramatically. Before the 1950s most immigrants came from Europe; in the 1990s most came from Asia and, from 1990 onwards, also from the former Soviet bloc countries. During this second wave, immigration regulations became more restrictive than before. Many countries use a quota, and allow in migrants only for reasons such as a family reunion or specific labour needs. Within Europe, most migration flows are in the form of intra-EU migration. From 1990 to 2010 the stock of migrants in Europe increased from 49 million to 70 million, compared to an increase from 28 to 50 million in North America. In general, labour markets are less globally integrated than trade and capital markets.

To give an idea of the expected size of future migration flows, Figure 9.14 provides predictions of each global region's total change in population, both absolute and as a percentage, as a result of migration flows over the period 2013–50. The graph is based on the

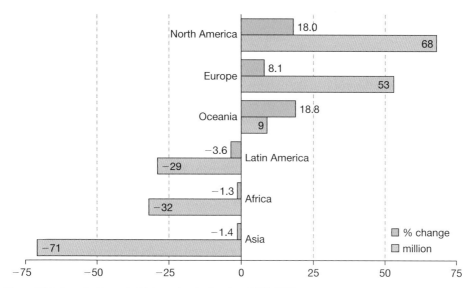

Figure 9.14 Expected impact of international migration, 2013–2050.

Notes: million indicates expected increase in a region's total population (medium variant) as compared to a zero migration scenario; % change indicates the change in per cent of a region's total population relative to the zero migration scenario.
Source: based on data from UN International Migration Report (2013).

UN International Migration Report 2013 and compares the predicted population size of a global region in 2050 (medium variant) with the predicted population size of that region if there were no international migration (zero migration variant).

The largest net recipient of people is North America, which is predicted to have a 68 million higher population as a result of international migration flows by 2050. The relative impact is also substantial, with an expected increase in population of 18 per cent. The second-largest net recipient is Europe, with a 53 million higher expected population or an 8 per cent increase. The third net recipient is Oceania. In absolute terms the rise in population is more modest (9 million), but in relative terms it is the largest (19 per cent). All three net recipient regions consist largely of advanced countries.

The migration flows come from mostly developing regions, namely 71 million from Asia, 32 million from Africa, and 29 million from Latin America. In relative terms these flows are more modest, namely 1.3 per cent for Africa, 1.4 per cent for Asia, and 3.6 per cent from Latin America. In general, these expected migration flows support the idea that people tend to move towards locations with higher real wages. In terms of change in total population, the impact is modest for developing regions, but quite substantial for the advanced regions.

9.9 Impact of migration flows since 1500

Section 9.8 discussed the size of migration flows since 1870 and the expected size and impact of such flows up to 2050. This section takes a much longer-run perspective on the impact of migration flows by analysing how migration flows that took place a long time ago affect the current population structure of a country or region. We do this by looking at the migrating people, the descendants of the migrating people, the descendants of the descendants of the migrating people, and so on.

Putterman and Weil (2010) were the first to provide a structural and detailed account of migration flows in the world in the past five centuries. They use information for 172 countries, together comprising almost the entire world population. We are interested in determining to what extent the current population living in a particular country are descended from people who already lived there in 1500 and what percentage are descended from ethnicities from other countries. The 1500 benchmark date is taken as the starting point of the era of European colonization of other continents, which resulted in large-scale population movements. We refer to both the direct and indirect consequences of these movements as 'migration' flows; the term therefore includes voluntary migration as well as the transport of slaves and forced relocation. If a person migrated recently from one country to another, the direct consequence for the current population is just one additional person. If a person migrated from one country to another several decades or even centuries ago, the consequences for the current population add up indirectly as well through their offspring (their children, grandchildren, and so on). Putterman and Weil use detailed country-level studies and genetic information to estimate both the direct and the indirect consequences of migration flows.

To analyse the consequences of the main migration flows since 1500, we (i) use the detailed data on 172 countries, which we (ii) combine with the current population size for these countries, and then (iii) group together in larger global regions for illustration purposes. Our grouping uses the World Bank's seven global regions, which are defined on the basis of geography, history, and development. We further subdivide two of those regions. First, we subdivide the large East Asia and Pacific region (31.3 per cent of the world population) into three parts: East Asia (including China, Korea, and Japan), Southeast Asia (including Indonesia and the Philippines), and Pacific (including Australia and New Zealand). Second, we subdivide the Europe and Central Asia region into two parts: Central Asia (including Russia) and Europe. We thus have ten different global regions. These regions are listed in Table 5.1 in Section 5.2, where we discussed intra- and interregional trade flows.[10]

Figure 9.15 illustrates the consequences of migration flows since 1500 for the ten global regions, while further detail is provided in Table 9.6. First, we note that the population of only three global regions currently consists largely of people of non-indigenous descent, namely North America (97 per cent), Pacific (94 per cent), and Latin America (68 per cent). Of the 351 million people currently living in North America, for example, only 11 million descend from people who lived there in 1500. For the remaining seven global regions the non-indigenous population is less than 6 per cent (even zero per cent for East Asia). To the extent that migration flows have an impact on current development levels, this impact will therefore be present only in the Americas and the Pacific. There are a few exceptions at the country level. In contrast to the largely non-indigenous population in the Pacific and Latin America, more than half of the population *is* indigenous in Fiji, Bolivia, Ecuador, Guatemala, Honduras, Mexico, and Peru. With the exception of Mexico, which benefits from being in the neighbourhood of North America, all these countries with a

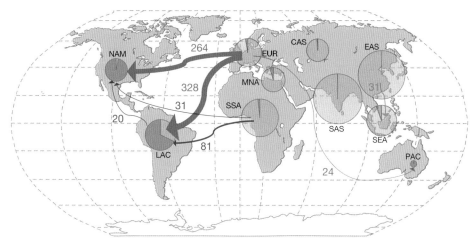

Figure 9.15 Current population size, indigenous population, and migration since 1500.

Notes: region abbreviations: see Table 5.1; bubbles proportional to population size in 2013; light-shaded area is indigenous population (descended from people who lived in the region in 1500); dark-shaded area is non-indigenous population; weight of migration line is proportional to size of population flow (in millions); only flows of 15 million or more people are shown, see Table 9.5 for further details.

Source: own calculations based on data from Putterman and Weil (2010) and World Bank Development indicators.

Table 9.6 Global migration flows in the past five centuries

Region-wide global migration flows in the past five centuries (millions of people)										
					Originates from					
Lives in	CAS	EAS	EUR	LAC	MENA	NAM	PAC	SAS	SEA	SSA	sum
CAS	352	1	3	0	1	0	0	0	0	0	357
EAS	0	1,593	0	0	0	0	0	0	0	0	1,593
EUR	7	0	524	0	4	0	0	2	1	1	540
LAC	1	2	328	196	3	0	0	1	0	81	613
MENA	4	0	5	0	378	0	0	3	0	7	398
NAM	6	8	264	20	2	11	0	4	5	31	351
PAC	0	1	24	0	1	0	2	1	1	0	28
SAS	4	0	0	0	0	0	0	1,666	0	0	1,670
SEA	0	31	0	0	0	0	0	4	589	0	624
SSA	0	0	12	0	1	0	0	2	0	909	925
Origin	375	1,636	1,160	216	389	11	2	1,684	596	1,030	7,099
In per cent of total world population										
Origin	5.3	23.0	16.3	3.0	5.5	0.2	0.0	23.7	8.4	14.5	100

Notes: calculations based on migration matrix and population in 2013; 172 countries included; CAS = Central Asia; EAS = East Asia; EUR = Europe; LAC = Latin America and Caribbean; MENA = Middle East and North Africa; NAM = North America; PAC = Pacific; SAS = South Asia; SEA = Southeast Asia; SSA = Sub-Saharan Africa.

high indigenous population have a lower income per capita than their region average.[11] Similarly, in contrast to the largely indigenous population in their region, there are only two countries where the non-indigenous population is more than half, namely Mauritius and Singapore. Both these countries have a (substantially) higher income level than their region average.

Second, we note that by far the largest global regional migration flows originate from Europe. Of the 1,160 million people currently alive originating from Europe in 1500, only 524 million live within Europe: see Table 9.6. The remaining 636 million moved to Latin America (328 million), North America (264 million), Pacific (24 million), and other regions. Sub-Saharan Africa is a distant second global region for the origin of migration flows. Of the 1,030 million people currently alive who originate from Sub-Saharan Africa in 1500, most live within Sub-Saharan Africa (909 million), while 81 million migrated to Latin America and 31 million to North America. This was, of course, to a large extent forced migration through the slave trade. The only remaining migration flow we would like to mention is from East Asia to Southeast Asia (31 million).

9.10 Conclusions

We analysed the size and direction of the international mobility of production factors through investment and migration flows. We discussed a simple framework to analyse the main welfare gains from the mobility of factors of production for both source and destination countries.

Foreign direct investment (FDI) flows take place through either greenfield investments or cross-border mergers and acquisitions (M&As). FDI flows are more volatile than trade and income flows. In the long run, however, FDI rises faster than both trade and income flows. As a result of FDI, firms control productive assets in more than one country and become multinational firms. We gave examples of large multinational firms (location, sector, and size) and discussed their rising importance over time (since FDI rises faster than trade and income flows in the long run) for production, trade, investment, and employment since the 1990s.

Advanced nations are still the main source of FDI, although their importance is gradually decreasing over time. As a destination of FDI, developing countries have become as important as advanced countries over the past four decades.

We also discussed the size and direction of migration flows. Voluntary migration is primarily based on differences in real wage rates and flows from developing to advanced countries. Involuntary migration by refugees and internally displaced persons is largely concentrated in the Middle East, Africa, and Latin America.

Finally, we showed that the long-run, cumulative impact of migration flows over a period of 500 years is particularly important for the Americas and the Pacific, which are largely populated by descendants from Europe and (to a lesser extent) Africa.

This concludes our discussion of comparative and competitive advantages. We now continue with a discussion of government trade policies before investigating the complex role of firms and multinationals in the current economic system.

Notes

1   Van Marrewijk (2002), Chapter 15, provides an indication of the distribution of greenfield and M&A FDI based on *gross* rather than *net* values for M&As, using UNCTAD data for 1999 from the *World Investment Report 2000*. In that case the relative importance of M&As in total FDI is about twice as high, as will be discussed in this section. The new net value data is to be preferred.

2   See UNCTAD (2000, p. 101).

3   The phrase 'more or less' draws attention to the special nature of Hong Kong within China.

4   Note that the importance of multinationals in global production is larger than 10 per cent since it also includes the output of the parent companies.

5   This section is partially based on Chapter 1 of Beugelsdijk et al. (2013).

6   Note that the Netherlands, Switzerland, Norway, and Macedonia are also above the European average.

7   The European Agency for the Management of Operational Cooperation at the External Borders of the Member States of the European Union (Frontex: http://frontex.europa.eu) reported that about 540,000 migrants entered the EU in the period January–August 2015, with the largest share coming from Syria. The data shown in Figure 9.12 add up to slightly more than 219,000 Syrian asylum-seekers in that period, or about 41 per cent of the total. Note that the Frontex numbers may include some double counting.

8   Based on UN Population Division, Migrant Section data, 2011.

9   Based on OECD labour force statistics.

10 As a United Nations organization, the World Bank does not include Taiwan in its global regions. We have included it in the East Asia region.

11 GDP per capita in 2013 (measured in constant 2011 PPP dollars).

 Questions

Question 9.1

Briefly answer the questions below.

a. Rank world income, world trade, and world FDI flows since 1970 in terms of (long run) growth rate and volatility.

b. Which parts of the world are most active in terms of outward and inward FDI flows since 1970 if we distinguish between advanced, developing, and transition countries? What has been the main change in this distribution?

c. What is the difference between greenfield FDI and cross-border M&As?

Question 9.2

Is multinational activity becoming more or less important since 1990? Briefly illustrate using some appropriate measures and comment on their suitability.

Question 9.3

a. Are international migration flows today (since the year 2000) in *relative* terms larger or smaller than a century ago (the period 1870–1913) for western Europe and the western Offshoots? How about the direction of these flows?

b. If we look to the future (up to 2050) and the continents (Asia, Africa, Latin America, Oceania, Europe, and North America), where do we expect large migration flows in absolute and relative terms? How about the direction of these flows? Why?

c. Which regions of the world are most affected as source and destination of refugees?

 See the **online resources** for a Study Guide and questions:
www.oup.com/uk/vanmarrewijk_it/

Part IV

· ·

Trade policy

· ·

Part IV on international trade policy consists of three chapters. We start in Chapter 10 by providing a brief overview of the international economic order (the World Trade Organization—WTO—and so on) before analysing the main possibilities and implications of trade restrictions (tariffs, quotas, and so on) under perfect competition. Chapter 11 analyses different types of WTO trade disputes and the possibilities and limitations of strategic trade policy under imperfect competition. Chapter 12 concludes with an overview of different types of regional trade agreements (which are becoming more popular) and the economic consequences and limitations of such agreements, with special attention for the European Union.

10 Trade organizations and policy

 Objectives

- To understand the basic developments that have led to the current international economic order.

- To appreciate the role of the General Agreement on Tariffs and Trade (GATT), which later became the World Trade Organization (WTO), in multilateral trade negotiations and understand why these negotiations are so difficult and take so much time.

- To know and understand the three main GATT/WTO principles.

- To understand the size and complexity of the United Nations institutions and the role UNCTAD plays in this framework.

- To know what the OECD is and what it does.

- To understand the many ways in which trade restrictions can be imposed, through tariffs, quotas, voluntary export restraints, and so on.

- To know what an effective tariff is and how it should be calculated.

- To understand the basic partial equilibrium welfare effects of tariffs for consumers, producers, and the government, both for small and large countries.

- To understand the basic general equilibrium welfare effects of tariffs, how to measure opportunity costs, and how tariffs lead to a double distortion.

- To be able to derive an offer curve and to know what a trade indifference curve is.

- To be able to derive the 'optimal' tariff rate using offer curves and to understand the damaging role of international retaliation in determining this tariff rate.

10.1 Introduction

In the previous six chapters we have presented and analysed various economic forces giving rise to international flows of goods, services, and inputs. We also demonstrated that these flows are beneficial for all countries involved, leading to efficiency gains from trade based on technology differences (Chapter 4) or differences in factor abundance (Chapters 5 and 6), to pro-competitive gains from trade (Chapter 7), to love-of-variety and production externalities gains from trade (Chapter 8), and to welfare gains from more efficient allocations (Chapter 9).

This view of trade and input flows benefiting society and increasing efficiency contrasts with a variety of different views from pressure groups frequently popularized in the media, blaming international economics, globalization, international trade, and international factor movements for virtually anything a specific group may dislike either at home or abroad, such as unemployment, low wages, environmental degradation, low development levels, unfair competition, and so on.

It is not possible to evaluate precisely the quality of the arguments of all pressure groups leading to a specific position and policy recommendation. Such arguments may simply not exist, may be inconsistent, and may be contradicted even within the same group.[1] More importantly, new pressure groups pop up and old ones disappear at a rate that is hard to keep up with. It is clear, however, that these pressure groups give rise to a demand, whether successful or not, for action by government officials to impose trade restrictions, to limit 'unfair' competition, to save domestic jobs or the environment, and so on.

This chapter provides some reasons for the existence of pressure groups or lobby groups by analysing the consequences of imposing trade restrictions for production, consumption, and international trade flows. Arnold Harberger (1954), for example, argued that the monopoly power distortions in the USA impose a cost on society in the order of a few tenths of a per cent of income. A couple of years later, he estimated the costs of trade restrictions for the Chilean economy to be about 2.5 per cent of income, see Harberger (1959). How did he arrive at these estimates, and how accurate are they? Before we start our analysis, however, we briefly discuss the history and functioning of the main international trade organizations. The econometrician Jan Tinbergen (see Box 10.1) was a strong advocate of using international cooperation to solve global problems.

BOX 10.1 Jan Tinbergen

Figure 10.1
Jan Tinbergen
(1903–1994).

The Dutch economist Jan Tinbergen (Figure 10.1) was the first to receive the Nobel Prize in economics in 1969 (together with Ragnar Frisch). He studied physics at the University of Leiden and wrote his thesis on extremum problems in physics and economics. Tinbergen was one of the founding fathers of econometrics in the 1930s. While working at the League of Nations, the predecessor of the United Nations, he wrote *Statistical Testing of Business Cycle Theories* (1939). The book's second volume constructed the first complete macroeconomic model for the USA.[2]

After World War II, Tinbergen became the first director of the Dutch CPB (a think-tank on economic problems for the government) and focused on policy making, which resulted in his book *Economic Policy: Principles and Design* (1956). Tinbergen argued that a government can only achieve several quantitative policy targets if it has an equal number of quantitative policy instruments available, the so-called 'Tinbergen rule'. Tinbergen held a position at the Netherlands School of Economics (now Erasmus University Rotterdam) from 1933, eventually focusing on development problems. He gave advice to many countries and UN agencies and lectured all over the world, which led inter alia to *Reshaping the International Order* (1976), a report to the Club of Rome coordinated by Tinbergen.

10.2 International economic order

The basis of the present international economic order was laid during and immediately after World War II. The primary concern in the consultations was not to repeat the disastrous experience of the international economic relations of the inter-war period. During the Great Depression in the 1930s, the 'beggar-thy-neighbour' policies, in which each country tried to transfer its economic problems to other countries by depreciating its own currency and imposing high tariffs (see for example the Hawley–Smoot Act put in place in the USA in 1930), led to an almost complete collapse of the international trade system, further exacerbating and prolonging the economic crisis. The impact of the beggar-thy-neighbour policies on international trade is aptly illustrated by the 'spider web spiral', measuring the size of world imports in each month by the distance from the origin: see Figure 10.2. In a period of only four years world trade flows dropped to one-third of their previous level (from January 1929 to January 1933, world imports fell from 2,998 to 992 million US gold dollars per month).

The signing of the Charter in 1945 in San Francisco laid the foundations of the United Nations (UN) as an international organization. The system of international bodies that developed afterwards is known as the United Nations family. Although consultations took place within the UN, arguably the most important international organizations—the

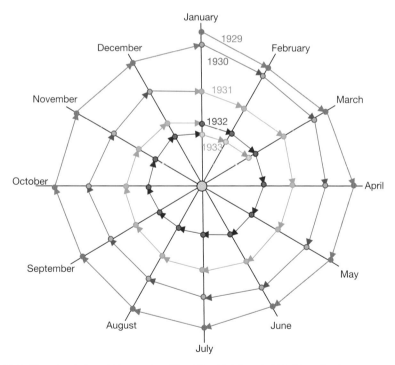

Figure 10.2 Spiderweb spiral: world imports in million US gold dollars, 1929 (2,998 million) to 1933 (992 million).

Source: League of Nations (1933).

International Monetary Fund (IMF) and the World Bank (WB) dealing with financial issues and the General Agreement on Tariffs and Trade (GATT), later to become the World Trade Organization (WTO), dealing with international trade issues—were eventually located outside the UN. The post-war international economic order is therefore sometimes called the GATT/WTO—IMF/WB order. The next section briefly discusses international organizations dealing with trade and trade policies. Karns and Mingst (2009) and Barkin (2006) provide overviews of the workings of international organizations.

10.3 World Trade Organization

The original intention in the post-war period was to set up the International Trade Organization (ITO) to deal with international trade issues (Havana Charter, 1948). In the end, the ITO was not set up, primarily because it was not ratified by the American Congress. As a result, the General Agreement on Tariffs and Trade (GATT), which was signed in 1947 in Geneva in anticipation of the formation of the ITO, evolved into a de facto international organization with a secretariat in Geneva. Much later, on 1 January 1995, the GATT was converted to the World Trade Organization (WTO), thus becoming an official international organization.

The international GATT agreement is based on three principles.

1. Non-discrimination; this is expressed in two sub-principles.
   Most favoured nation (MFN) treatment: if a GATT country grants a trade concession to another GATT country, this concession automatically applies to all other GATT countries as well.
   National treatment of foreign products: apart from trade policy measures, imported goods must be treated the same as home-produced goods.

2. Reciprocity: if one GATT country makes a trade concession, other GATT countries should make equivalent concessions to balance the advantages and disadvantages of trade liberalization. As explained throughout this book, taking all static and dynamic gains of trade liberalization into consideration, it is probably optimal to allow free trade regardless of whether other countries do the same. In practice, however, countries regard trade liberalization as a concession that should be reciprocated by other countries. The most important exception to this principle is for developing countries, which are not required to reciprocate.

3. Prohibition on trade restrictions other than tariffs: in principle, trade restrictions other than tariffs, such as quotas, are prohibited. The main reason is that, although the imposition of a tariff influences the market, its operation does not affect the market mechanism. Moreover, it is easier to negotiate on tariff reductions than on the removal of other trade measures, which are more difficult to quantify. The most important exception to this principle applies in the case of balance-of-payments problems.

There are two main exceptions to the non-discrimination principle.

- Free trade areas and customs unions: if two or more countries decide to form a free trade area or a customs union, such as the European Union, discriminatory treatment is allowed, essentially because it is viewed as a move in the right direction towards free trade. This is discussed in Chapter 12.
- Developing countries: preferential treatment for imports is allowed to assist developing countries since part IV, 'Trade and development', was added to the GATT in 1965. This enables the Generalized System of Preferences; see Section 10.4 on UNCTAD.

After the establishment of the GATT as an agreement, a series of trade liberalization rounds followed. Their success in terms of the large reductions of imposed tariff rates was illustrated in Figure 10.5. Initially, the trade liberalization rounds rapidly succeeded each other, took a limited amount of time, and involved a limited number of countries, as illustrated in Figure 12.3. As time passed, more countries became members of the GATT, such that the negotiations became more complicated and took several years to complete: see Table 10.1.

The Kennedy Round (1964–7) is often taken as the dividing line, as it involved a change in negotiating technique. In the first five rounds, negotiations took place according to the principal-supplier rule; that is, there were bilateral negotiations for each product involving the principal suppliers to one another's markets. Under the MFN clause the results of the bilateral negotiations also apply to the GATT partners. This connection between the bilateral negotiations made it difficult to get an overall picture of the

Table 10.1 GATT/WTO rounds

Round	Start	Duration	Principal concern	No. of participants
Geneva	Apr. 1947	7 months	Tariffs	23
Annecy	Apr. 1949	5 months	Tariffs	13
Torquay	Sep. 1950	8 months	Tariffs	38
Geneva II	Jan. 1956	5 months	Tariffs, admission Japan	26
Dillon	Sep. 1960	11 months	Tariffs	26
Kennedy	May 1964	37 months	Tariffs, anti-dumping	62
Tokyo	Sep. 1973	74 months	Tariffs, NTBs, framework	102
Uruguay	Sep. 1986	87 months	Tariffs, NTBs, services, dispute settlement, textiles, agriculture, WTO	123
Doha	Nov. 2001	?	Tariffs, NTBs, labour standards, environment, competition, investment, transparency, patents	153

Note: NTBs = non-tariff barriers.
Source: Neary (2004).

granted and received concessions, which were meant to be balanced under the principle of reciprocity. The Kennedy Round therefore started with the aim of achieving linear tariff reductions, making it necessary to negotiate only on the exceptions. In the end, the average tariff reduction was about 35 per cent, somewhat below the target of 50 per cent, primarily because countries whose tariffs were already low in absolute terms were not willing to apply the same percentage reduction as countries whose tariffs were high in absolute terms.

To avoid the difficulties of linear tariff reductions that became apparent in the Kennedy Round, the Tokyo Round (1973–1979) used the so-called 'Swiss formula' for tariff reduction, which leads to higher tariff reductions for initially high tariffs (and thus to a more rapid tariff harmonization). In addition, the Tokyo Round (which was called the Nixon Round until Nixon was forced to resign as president of the USA) involved negotiations on tropical products (concessions for some products, but not for sugar), non-tariff measures (agreement on codes of conduct), agriculture (restraint on export subsidies), specific sectors (total trade liberalization for civil aircraft), and safeguards (no agreement).

Attention in the negotiations clearly shifted towards the importance of non-tariff barriers. Initially, this was thought to be a result of the success of the achieved tariff reductions. As Lanjouw (1995, p. 12) puts it:

> The metaphor applied here was of trade liberalisation representing the draining of a swamp. The reduction in tariffs symbolised letting the water level fall, uncovering what was below the surface in the form of non-tariff barriers. However, it gradually became clear that protection by non-tariff measures was steadily increasing, so the expression 'new protectionism' became commonplace.

A clear example of the new protectionism is a 'voluntary' export restraint (VER), where a country limits the number of goods exported to another country, usually as a result of the pressure exerted by the government of the importing country. VERs are against GATT rules, but they do not lead to complaints to the GATT as they are imposed by the exporting country.

The complications arising from the desire to stop the rise of protectionism and the increased number of countries involved in the GATT negotiations implied that the last completed GATT round (Uruguay Round) lasted for seven years, from 1986 to 1993. In the end, substantial agreements were reached in several areas.

First, the negotiations on liberalization of trade in services, an increasingly important part of world trade flows, led to the General Agreement on Trade in Services (GATS: see Box 10.2), a framework of principles and rules such as MFN treatment of foreign suppliers and, for some sectors, national treatment of foreign suppliers. Some sub-sectors were excluded (e.g. audio-visual, telecommunications, and maritime transport), for example because France feared impairing its 'cultural identity' if it had to liberalize its television programming.

Second, the negotiations for the agricultural sectors eventually resulted in (i) conversion of non-tariff barriers to equivalent tariffs, (ii) tariffs to be reduced on average by 36 per cent in the next six years, (iii) a minimum foreign market share of 5 per cent after the

BOX 10.2 General Agreement on Trade in Services

The General Agreement on Trade in Services (GATS) came into force in January 1995 (as a result of the GATT Uruguay Round) and is the first and only set of multilateral rules covering international trade in services. The total value of trade in services was about $4,645 billion in 2013, or about 20 per cent of total trade flows. It is generally agreed that this underestimates the true value of services trade, since a large share of this trade takes place through establishment in the export market and is not recorded in balance-of-payments statistics.

The largest component of trade in services is travel services (tourism), estimated to be $1,185 billion in 2013, or about one-fourth of all services trade, see Figure 10.3. Another important category is transport services ($905 billion), or about one-fifth of all services trade. Three roughly equally sized components take care of another one-fifth, namely financial services ($335 billion), royalties and licence fees ($310 billion), and computer and information services ($285 billion). The remaining categories are other[3] business services ($1,245 billion, 27 per cent) and other[4] services ($380 billion, 8 per cent).

The GATS defines four ways (modes of supply) in which a service can be traded:

- cross-border supply – services supplied from one country to another, such as telephone calls;
- consumption abroad – consumers from one country making use of a service in another country, such as tourism;
- commercial presence – a company from one country setting up subsidiaries or branches to provide services in another country, such as banking services;
- movement of natural persons – individuals travelling from one country to supply services in another country, such as consultants or maids.

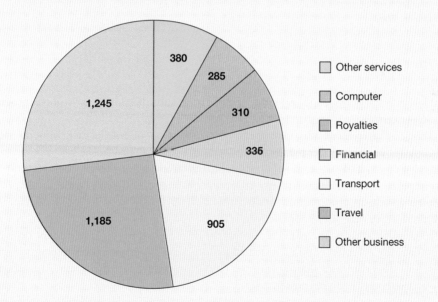

Figure 10.3 Components of world trade in services: USD billion, 2013.

Notes: royalties = royalties and licence fees; computer = computer and information services.
Source: based on data from World Trade Report 2014.

(*continued...*)

The GATS covers all services with two exceptions, namely services provided in the exercise of governmental authority and air traffic rights (and all services directly related to air traffic rights). The negotiations regarding the liberalization of services trade were quite complex and led to a north–south controversy in the early years of the Uruguay Round. In the end these issues were resolved by agreeing to a minimal and flexible set of rules.

The GATS consists of two parts, namely (i) the framework agreement containing the general rules and principles and (ii) the national schedules, which list individual countries' specific commitments on access to their domestic markets by foreign suppliers. The latter provides the required flexibility as follows.

- Each member chooses service sectors or sub-sectors on which they will make commitments to guarantee foreign suppliers the right to provide the service. There is no minimal coverage requirement.

- For the committed sectors, governments may set limitations regarding market access and the degree of national treatment.

- Governments may limit commitments to one or more of the above-listed modes of supply and they may withdraw or renegotiate commitments.

- Although the MFN treatment (see Section 10.3) applies to all services (whether scheduled or not), governments may take exemptions and provide more favourable treatment to certain trading partners for a maximum of up to ten years.

It is clear that this flexibility, which was necessary in order for the parties to come to an agreement, also limits the impact of GATS on those countries willing to liberalize their trade in services. A new round of trade negotiations to further liberalize trade in services was therefore started in January 2000.

implementation period, and (iv) reduction of export subsidies for 17 agricultural products by 36 per cent.

Third, an agreement was reached on the protection of intellectual property rights (patents for 20 years and copyright for 50 years).

Fourth, the GATT was converted to a full-fledged international organization: the WTO. An important practical consequence of the establishment of the WTO was the improved dispute settlement procedure to be used after a complaint is made to the WTO. Not only are there strict time limits for each stage in the procedure, but also the system is virtually automatic: that is, the panel report on the dispute written by independent experts is automatically accepted within a specified period, unless there is a consensus in favour of rejection. This contrasts sharply with the GATT procedure in which, rather remarkably, the accused party had veto power.

The current round of negotiations is called the Doha Round and started in November 2001. It discusses many issues, such as tariffs, non-tariff barriers, labour standards, environment, competition, investment, transparency, and patents, with many participating countries. Not surprisingly, therefore, progress is slow and the Doha Round is still not finished, nor does it seem likely to finish soon. The WTO is located in Geneva, Switzerland. By April 2015 it had 161 member countries. See www.wto.org for details.

10.4 The United Nations and UNCTAD

The signing of the Charter in 1945 in San Francisco laid the foundations of the United Nations (UN) as an international organization; it became operative in October of the same year after ratification by sufficiently many countries. As of October 2015 the UN has 193 member states (see www.un.org for details). Under the guidance of the secretary general and the secretariat located in New York, the large UN system deals with many aspects of human life and organization, such as human rights, international justice, security, military and peacekeeping operations, and economic, social, cultural, and development issues. In the economic sphere, the most important body is ECOSOC, the Economic and Social Council, which coordinates work in the economic and social fields. In this respect, and to give an idea of the size of the UN family of organizations, ECOSOC's main involvement can be subdivided as follows.

- Programmes and funds, such as the UN Conference on Trade and Development (UNCTAD), the UN Development Programme (UNDP), the Office of the UN High Commissioner for Refugees (UNHCR), and the UN Children's Fund (UNICEF)

- Functional commissions, such as the Commission for Social Development, the Commission on Human Rights, the Commission on Sustainable Development, and the Commission on the Status of Women

- Regional commissions, such as the Economic Commission for Africa (ECA), the Economic Commission for Europe (ECE), the Economic Commission for Latin America and the Caribbean (ECLAC), the Economic and Social Commission for Asia and the Pacific (ESCAP), and the Economic and Social Commission for Western Asia (ESCWA)

- Specialized (independent) agencies, such as the International Labour Organization (ILO), the Food and Agriculture Organization of the UN (FAO), the UN Educational, Scientific and Cultural Organization (UNESCO), the World Health Organization (WHO), the World Bank group, and the International Monetary Fund (IMF)

For various reasons, the developing countries became increasingly dissatisfied with their role in the world economy during the 1950s and 1960s. One reason, forwarded by the development economists Raul Prebisch and Hans Singer, was the argument that over longer periods of time the terms of trade are turning against the developing countries, as these countries tend to be dependent for their export earnings on a limited number of primary products with falling relative prices. According to this argument, developing countries are forced to produce and export ever-increasing quantities of their primary products to finance the imports of manufactured goods from developed countries (see Box 10.3). Many empirical studies have tried to test the Prebisch–Singer hypothesis of deteriorating terms of trade for developing countries. All in all, it is fair to say that the hypothesis is far from proven.

A second reason for the dissatisfaction of developing countries with their role in the world economy was the phenomenon of 'tariff escalation', referring to the fact that

BOX 10.3 Terms of trade: are high export prices good or bad?

The ratio of export prices to import prices of a country is called the terms of trade. Now, ask yourself: is it good or bad to have high export prices? If you have the interests of a firm in mind, you may be inclined to go along with the popular reasoning of businessmen in the newspaper: the dollar is overvalued, which implies that our export prices are too high, so that we can no longer compete effectively with foreign firms (followed by threats that factories will be closed down and jobs will be lost). The suggestion is that high export prices are bad.

In Chapter 1, however, we argued that an important characteristic of international economics is the general equilibrium approach. We have to look at the complete picture, in which 'high' export prices reflect the interplay of economic forces on the supply side and the demand side, perhaps caused by the fact that we produce high-quality goods in popular demand. In this interpretation, high export prices are good, as they lead to higher welfare levels. This is illustrated in Figure 10.4 in a neoclassical equilibrium framework in which the country (which exports manufactures) initially reaches welfare level U_0. If the price of manufactures, the export good, rises, the economy is able to reach the higher welfare level U_1. A simple analogy is to think of yourself as a country: you want the price of your export goods (labour services) which earns you an income to be as high as possible, and the price of your import goods (all goods and services you consume) to be as low as possible.

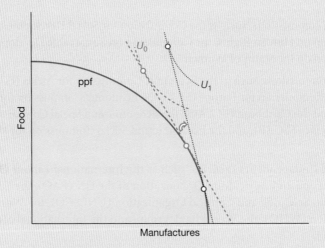

Figure 10.4 Impact of a rise in export prices.

developed countries tend to levy low tariffs for the imports of primary products necessary in the early stages of the production process, and high tariffs for the imports of processed goods, leading to high effective rates of protection for the later stages of the production process.

A third reason for dissatisfaction was the GATT principle of non-discrimination, as the developing countries argued that they needed preferential treatment because they are less developed, a variant of the infant-industry argument.

The developing countries, united in the Group of 77 (now containing more countries), wanted to set up an organization concentrating on their interests. This aim was realized at the first UNCTAD session in Geneva in 1964, establishing UNCTAD as a permanent international organization, with a secretariat and a secretary general (a post first held by Raul Prebisch). Plenary UNCTAD sessions take place every three or four years.

As an organization, UNCTAD does not have executive power. Instead, UNCTAD conference resolutions are recommendations for the UN General Assembly. After the confrontational approach at the first UNCTAD conference, which did not lead to any substantial results, the second UNCTAD conference at New Delhi in 1968 was more consensus-based and led to the Generalized System of Preferences (GSP). Under this system, OECD countries apply non-reciprocal preferential tariffs to imports of (primary) products from developing countries to raise export earnings and stimulate growth. To provide a legal basis for GSP, an addition (Part IV) was made to the GATT system in 1965. UNCTAD and the GATT/WTO are therefore both concerned with trade and development issues, the main difference being that the GSP of UNCTAD is based on a unilateral decision by OECD countries (which can also be unilaterally withdrawn), while the GATT agreements are binding contractual obligations.

Accounts of the history and activities of UNCTAD can be seen on the UNCTAD website (www.unctad.org). Since both UNCTAD and the WTO are active in the fields of international trade and development, they work together in the International Trade Centre, located in Geneva, Switzerland. The ITC website (www.intracen.org) contains trade documentation, detailed trade statistics per country, and the ITC magazine.

Multinational, or transnational, corporations, which have active branches in several countries, have become increasingly important in the world economy since World War II; see also Chapter 15. To analyse the impact of multinationals on international trade and investment flows and their general influence on the economic and social structure of (developing) nations, ECOSOC set up the Commission on Transnational Corporations in 1974, followed by the UN Centre on Transnational Corporation (UNCTC) in 1975 to support the work of the Commission. Over the years, there has been a shift in the appreciation of the impact of multinationals on the economic system, from a hostile and negative view in the 1960s and 1970s to a much more positive view since the 1980s and 1990s. The earlier negative picture was partly due to the political meddling of multinationals in the host countries. The more recent positive picture on the impact of multinationals arises from the realization that the large investments by these companies, and the local knowledge and productivity spillovers created as a result of these activities, can be of vital importance for a successful development process. Since 1991, UN research in this area has been summarized annually in UNCTAD's *World Investment Report*, at present arguably UNCTAD's most important publication.

10.5 Organization for Economic Cooperation and Development

The final international body to be briefly discussed in this chapter is the Organization for Economic Cooperation and Development (OECD), which was established in 1961 as the successor to the Organization for European Economic Cooperation (OEEC). The latter organization, comprising western European countries and Turkey, was established in 1948 to implement the Marshall Aid programme, through which the USA was assisting post-war recovery in Europe. By the end of the 1950s, the OEEC had attained its objectives. Its transformation into the OECD, in part to coordinate aid to developing countries, allowed Canada and the USA to become full members. In the 1970s, membership was extended to Japan, Finland, Australia, and New Zealand. As of October 2015, the OECD had 34 member states. It is based in Paris (see www.oecd.org).

The OEEC played an important role in the 1950s in reducing quantitative trade barriers (quotas) in Europe, leaving the reduction of tariffs to the GATT. Plans to form a free trade area were not successful, as there was a division between the countries that later formed the European Economic Community (EEC) and the countries that later formed the European Free Trade Area (EFTA). Eventually, many EFTA countries joined the EEC and formed the European Union (EU): see Chapter 12.

The OECD's Development Assistance Committee (DAC) plays an important role in coordinating national aid programmes to developing countries. The DAC strives for a reduction of tied aid, in which the recipient country is obliged to spend the development assistance in the donor country or in a group of countries linked to the donor country. In general, the effectiveness of development assistance diminishes if aid is tied rather than untied; see Brakman and van Marrewijk (1998) for a general overview of (unilateral) international transfers and tied aid.

The OECD plays an important role as a consultation forum on trade policy issues for the developed nations, without the necessity of coming to any direct agreements, which is a matter for the GATT/WTO. The OECD thus serves a mediating role in this respect. An example of this role was provided in October 2015 when the OECD announced significant progress on its Base Erosion and Profit Shifting (BEPS) project, which intends to limit international tax avoidance by multinationals. Such tax avoidance is particularly painful for developing nations and is estimated by the OECD to be in between $100 and $240 billion annually. As OECD secretary general Gurría phrased it, the new rules 'will put an end to double non-taxation, facilitate a better alignment of taxation with economic activity and value creation, and when fully implemented, these measures will render BEPS-inspired tax planning structures ineffective'.

10.6 Tariffs, quotas, and other trade restrictions

Once a government body is convinced, for whatever reason, of the necessity to impose trade restrictions, there is an endless list of policy options to choose from. Suppose the European Commission decides that the domestic production of computers is of vital interest to the European Union, perhaps for security or strategic reasons, and decides to protect the computer industry from the hard and cold winds of global competition. Here are some options available to the European Commission:

- Impose a 100 euro tax per imported computer (specific tariff)
- Impose a 12 per cent tax per imported computer (ad valorem tariff)
- Restrict the number of imported computers (quota)
- Subsidize the production of European computers

- Subsidize the export of European computers
- Require a 'minimum content' before a computer may be labelled 'European'
- Prohibit the sale or import of computers to or from certain countries for safety reasons

All these policy measures will affect production, consumption, and trade flows in a different way. Clearly we cannot provide an in-depth analysis of each policy measure in this introductory textbook. Instead, we restrict ourselves to providing a rather detailed analysis of the impact of tariffs on the international economic system, dealing more cursorily with the impact of some other trade restrictions (see Box 10.4 for further discussion).

Despite frequent trade disputes, trade restrictions, such as tariffs, have been falling on a global scale for a long time (see Box 10.5 on American tariffs). This has undoubtedly contributed to the rapid increase in international trade and capital flows. To a large extent, the fall in trade restrictions can be attributed to the work of the World Trade Organization (see Section 10.3). Figure 10.5 illustrates the falling of tariff rates on a global scale since 1996. The figure depicts three different rates. The first is the simple mean of applied tariffs

BOX 10.4 Quota equivalence and the attractiveness of VER

The discussion in this chapter focuses attention on the analysis of tariffs. There are three reasons for this. First, there are many different types of trade restrictions and we cannot analyse them all in the same detail. Second, tariffs continue to present an important and visible obstacle to international trade flows, despite the reductions achieved over the years as a result of WTO efforts. Third, and most importantly, the impact of other trade restrictions, such as quota and voluntary export restraints (VERs), is largely *equivalent* to the impact of tariffs, at least in the framework analysed in this chapter.[5]

Consider, for example, the impact of imposing an import quota in the partial equilibrium framework analysed in Figure 10.7 below. If the size of this quota is equal to $q_{tar}^d - q_{tr}^s$ the domestic market will clear at the price $p_{ft} + T$ and it is argued that the impact of a quota is equivalent to imposing a tariff T. This holds clearly for the loss in consumer surplus, the rise in producer surplus, and the net efficiency loss (the two Harberger triangles). The only distribution effect where the equivalence between tariffs and quota breaks down is regarding the government revenue. Who collects this revenue if a quota is imposed, rather than a tariff? To save the equivalence argument, it is argued that the government can auction the import quota, and thus collect all this revenue. In practice, this does not occur, such that entrepreneurs who, through lobbying, historical accident, or otherwise, are able to get the licence to import the good with the quota restriction can earn large profits.

The distribution of the tariff revenue can also explain the attractiveness of a so-called voluntary export restraint for an exporting country. Suppose this country (say China) is convinced that a large importing country (say the USA) is about to impose trade restrictions on the import of one of its goods. Obviously, China will be opposed to any trade restrictions. Convinced of the inevitability of American action, however, China may decide to 'voluntarily' limit the export of the goods to the American market. The effect is equivalent to the USA imposing an import quota, except for the fact that the Chinese exporters are able to reap the tariff-equivalent government revenue. This makes a VER more attractive than a tariff or an import quota.

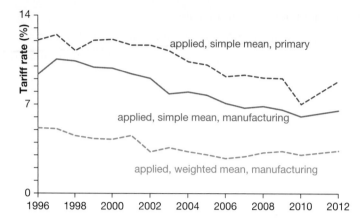

Figure 10.5 Worldwide applied tariff rates.

Source: World Development Indicators online.

for manufacturing, which declined from about 10 per cent to 6.5 per cent. Second is the simple mean of applied tariffs for primary products, which declined from about 12 per cent to 9 per cent. This illustrates that tariffs on primary products tend to be higher (see the discussion below on effective tariffs). Third is the weighted mean of applied tariffs for manufacturing, which declined from about 5 to 3.4 per cent. Since it is below the simple mean, this illustrates that the tariff rates for intensively traded products tends to be lower than for less traded products.

BOX 10.5 Tariffs in the USA

For some countries, such as the USA, the average tariff rate has reached historically low levels, as illustrated in Figure 10.6. At the beginning of the nineteenth century the tariff revenue was high at about 50 per cent of the value of imports. In this period the southern part of the USA wanted to import cheap foreign manufactures (from Britain) while the northern part of the USA demanded protection of the domestic industry. The controversy over tariffs peaked in 1828 with the Tariff of Abominations, when the southern congressmen made a strategic mistake by amending a bill to include high tariffs on raw materials in the hope that their northern colleagues would reject it (because northern manufacturers used those raw materials). They did not.

   With a compromise law in 1833 the average American tariff rate started to decline, although not coming down as far as European tariffs. The decline stopped in 1861 when the Morrill tariff was passed, raising rates on iron and steel products, followed by other duties in 1862 and 1864, also designed to finance the Civil War. At the beginning of the twentieth century, tariff rates came down considerably when the Wilson administration put many items on the 'free list'. This was reversed in the first recession after World War I, when the Fordney–McCumby tariff was passed in 1922, intended to help the farmers. It was followed by the Hawley-Smoot tariff in 1930, which as Kenen (2000, p. 213) put it was 'once called the "Holy-Smoke Tariff" by a student with keener insight than memory'. After World War II a series of multilateral GATT negotiations, for example in the American-inspired Kennedy Round, eventually resulted in the current low average tariff rate of about 1.5 per cent.

(continued...)

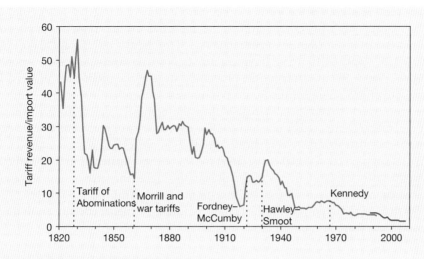

Figure 10.6 USA average tariffs, 1820–2014.

Note: Total tariff revenue/total imports, 1998–2014: weighted average applied tariff (all goods).

Calculating an average tariff rate, as is done in the data underlying Figure 10.5, is actually quite complicated. We will not go into too much detail here, but an obvious first candidate for calculating an average tariff is, of course, weighing the imports of the various goods and services into the country by the value of the import flows. There are at least two disadvantages to that method. First, if a tariff on a specific good, say cheese, is very high, this may completely stop all imports of cheese into the country. This is called a prohibitive tariff. When import shares are used to calculate the average tariff, the prohibitive tariff for cheese imports receives a weight of zero, thus leading to a low estimate of average tariffs despite the fact that the tariff on cheese is so high as to stop all imports of cheese. Second, we should be careful to specify which activity we are protecting when calculating the impact of a combination of tariff rates. For this purpose, the effective tariff rate can be calculated: see Table 10.2.

Suppose the production of a final good is a simple process, requiring only the availability of some raw material and a processing stage to make the finished product. If the value of the finished product on the world market is $100 and our country imposes a 20 per cent tariff on the import of finished products, one could say that the tariff protection

Table 10.2 Calculating the effective tariff rate

Good	World price	Tariff (%)	Domestic price
Finished product	$100	20	$120
Raw material	$60	10	$66
Available for processing stage	$40	$100 \times (54 - 40)/40 = \underline{35}$	$54

is 20 per cent. However, if the world market price for the raw material is $60, and our country imposes only a 10 per cent tariff on the import of raw materials, this implies that the entrepreneurs in our country can be remunerated for the processing stage to the extent of $100 × 1.20 − $60 × 1.10 = $54. If our country imposes no tariffs at all, there would be only $100 − $60 = $40 available for the processing stage of the production process. The effective rate of protection for the production process is therefore 100 × (54 − 40)/40 = 35 per cent, which is considerably higher than the nominal rates of 10 per cent and 20 per cent officially imposed by our country. The effective rate of protection is more cumbersome to calculate in a more complicated production process. In general, however, the effective rate of protection is higher the larger the share of raw materials in the production process, the lower the tariff on raw materials, and the higher the tariff on finished goods. Advanced countries indeed have a tendency to put lower tariffs on the imports of raw materials than on the imports of finished products, leading to higher effective tariffs for the processing stage than the nominal tariffs suggest.

10.7 Tariffs and partial equilibrium

10.7.1 Small country

We start our analysis of tariffs with an explanation of the estimate of the costs of trade restrictions as calculated by Harberger (1959). The basic consequences of imposing a tariff on a specific good within a partial equilibrium framework is illustrated in Figure 10.7, which gives the domestic demand and supply schedule for a specific good. We assume that the country is small, that its (net) demand is so small that the country is not able to influence the price for the good on the world market, such that the world price is given. Moreover, we assume that the country imposes a specific tariff T.

If the home country engages in free trade, the price is equal to the world market price p_{ft}. At that price, the quantity supplied q^s_{ft} is lower than the quantity demanded q^d_{ft}, such that the difference must be imported from abroad. What happens if the country imposes a tariff T? First of all, since the country is small and cannot affect world prices, the world price p_{ft} remains unchanged. When goods are imported from abroad, however, the tariff has to be paid, which increases the domestic price level to $p_{ft} + T$. Second, as a result of the increase in the domestic price, home production increases from q^s_{ft} to q^s_{tar}, and consumer demand falls from q^d_{ft} to q^d_{tar}. Imports from abroad thus decline. Since domestic production has increased and imports have fallen, some people might argue that the imposition of the tariff has the desired effect of protecting home production and jobs. It is better, however, to address these issues in a general equilibrium setting (see Section 10.8). Is the imposition of the tariff, within the structure of the partial equilibrium model, a good idea? No, it is not. To arrive at this conclusion, we have to investigate the welfare effects of the tariff, where we will distinguish between three types of agents, namely the producers, the government, and the consumers.

- Welfare for the domestic producers, as measured by the producer surplus, has increased. The size of this increase is measured left of the supply curve from the old price to the new price: see area A in Figure 10.7.

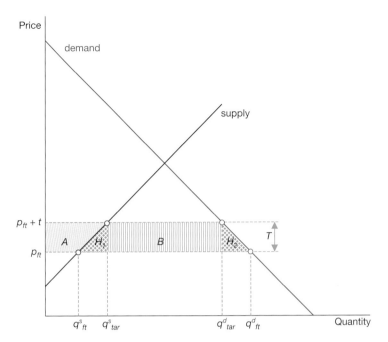

Figure 10.7 Impact of a tariff: partial equilibrium, small country.

- Welfare for the government, as measured by government revenue, has increased. The size of government revenue is equal to the difference between the domestic price and the world price, multiplied by the size of the imports: see area B in Figure 10.7.
- Welfare for the consumers, as measured by the consumer surplus, has decreased. The size of this decrease is measured left of the demand curve from the old price to the new price: see area $A + B + H_1 + H_2$ in Figure 10.7.

This analysis clarifies that there are winners and losers within the home country as a result of the imposition of the tariff, creating a conflict of interests within the country and thus explaining the frequently heated debates on imposing trade restrictions. The domestic producers are in favour of the tariff, as it increases the producer surplus. This explains why producers organize themselves into lobbying groups trying to convince government officials of the need to impose trade restrictions. Focusing attention strictly on revenue, the government is also in favour of the tariff. Within a broader perspective, the government will, of course, have to weigh the interests of the various groups within the country. The big losers are the consumers, who are faced with a large decrease in the consumer surplus. The consumers more than completely finance the increase in producer surplus and the increase in government revenue. The difference is a net welfare loss to the home country, as measured by the so-called Harberger triangles H_1 and H_2 in Figure 10.7. Note that the loss caused by the imposition of the tariff is spread across many consumers, while the benefits are enjoyed by a limited number of producers and the government. This makes it much harder for consumers to organize themselves and defend the benefits of free trade than it is for the producers to organize vocal lobbying groups. There is thus a lobbying bias against free trade.

10.7.2 Large country

The arguments above specifically stipulated that the tariff-imposing country is small. Apparently this is important, but why? The essential point is to realize that the imposition of a tariff *reduces* imports of the good into the home country (see Figure 10.7). If the tariff-imposing country is 'large' this reduction in imports, which is a decrease in net demand on the world market, results in a *lower* price for the good on the world market. In Figure 10.8 this fall in the world price level as a result of the imposition of the tariff is indicated by the decline from p_{ft} to p_{tar} (see the arrows in the figure). Essentially, then, the imposition of the tariff implies that the tariff-imposing country uses its monopsony power to improve its terms of trade, as it can now import the good more cheaply. The rest of the analysis is similar.

- Producer welfare increases, as indicated by area A in Figure 10.8.
- Government revenue increases, as indicated by area $B_1 + B_2$ in Figure 10.8.
- Consumer welfare falls, as indicated by area $A + B_1 + H_1 + H_2$ in Figure 10.8.

The main difference from the preceding analysis, in which the country was small and could not influence the terms of trade, is that *part* of the government revenue, namely the area B_2 in Figure 10.8, is paid for not by the domestic consumers but by the foreign producers. The net welfare gain for the home country is therefore the difference between this area B_2 of government revenue paid for by the foreign producers and the efficiency loss triangles H_1 and H_2. This difference is potentially positive, in which case the partial equilibrium welfare effect is positive for the tariff-imposing country. Under these circumstances it is certainly positive for a sufficiently small tariff.

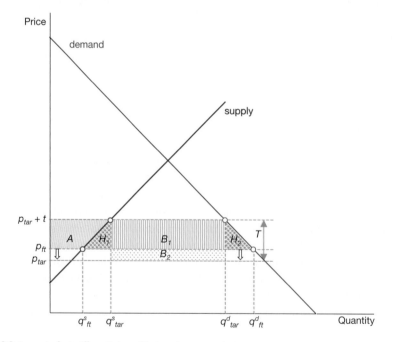

Figure 10.8 Impact of a tariff: partial equilibrium, large country.

10.8 **Tariffs and general equilibrium**

We will now analyse the impact of a tariff in a general equilibrium setting. To do that, we use the neoclassical model explained in Chapters 5 and 6. We assume that the tariff-imposing country is relatively labour-abundant, such that under free trade it will import the capital-intensive manufactures and export the labour-intensive food. Moreover, we assume in this section that the home country is small and cannot influence its terms of trade. The price of manufactures relative to the price of food is therefore given. Section 10.9 analyses the general equilibrium impact of imposing a tariff if the country is large. If the country engages in free trade, the analysis in Chapter 6 shows that the equilibrium of production, consumption, and trade is characterized by:

$$MRS_{trade} = \frac{p_m}{p_f} = MRT_{trade} \qquad\qquad 10.1$$

The (given) world price of manufactures relative to food—that is, the ratio at which the economy can trade with the rest of the world—is therefore equal to both the marginal rate of substitution on the consumption side of the economy and the marginal rate of transformation on the production side of the economy. If the country imposes an ad valorem tariff t on the imports of manufactures, however, this raises the domestic price of manufactures above the world price of manufactures. Producers and consumers in the home economy, facing domestic prices, therefore equate the marginal rate of transformation and the marginal rate of substitution to the tariff-ridden relative price level, which exceeds the ratio at which the economy can trade with the rest of the world:

$$MRS_{tariff} = \frac{(1+t)p_m}{p_f} = MRT_{tariff} > \frac{p_m}{p_f} \qquad\qquad 10.2$$

This equation characterizes the equilibrium if a tariff on the import of manufactures is imposed once we realize that the tariff-imposing country can still trade with the rest of the world at the world relative price ratio p_m/p_f, and *not* at the domestic price ratio $(1 + t) p_m/p_f$. The tariff-ridden consumption point of the economy must therefore be on the income line generated by the tariff-ridden production point, evaluated at world prices.[6]

The impact of the tariff is illustrated in Figure 10.9, where Q^* is the production point under free trade, C^* is the consumption point under free trade, Q_2 is the production point under the tariff, and C_2 is the consumption point under the tariff. Let's summarize the main conclusions.

- As in the partial equilibrium approach of Section 10.7, the production of manufactures increases because the relative price of manufactures rises, but it is clear that there is a simultaneous *reduction* in the production of food. This represents the opportunity costs of trade restrictions, as already identified by Adam Smith; see Chapter 4.
- There is a reduction of income generated by the economy (evaluated at world prices).
- The income loss and the deviation from world prices lead to a reduction in welfare (this is further explained below).
- The tariff leads to a reduction in the volume of trade.

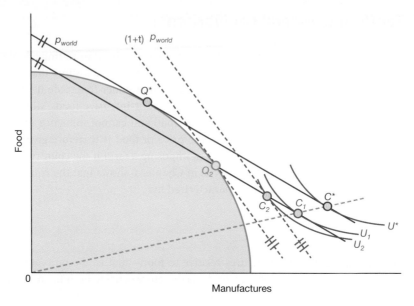

Figure 10.9 Impact of a tariff in general equilibrium.

The imposition of the tariff actually imposes a double distortion on the economy, as is implicit in equation 10.2 and made explicit in Figure 10.9. First, because the domestic price level deviates from the price level at which the economy can trade with the rest of the world, the economy produces at a sub-optimal production point, leading to an income loss. This reduction in income leads, of course, to a lower welfare level. Note, however, that at the income level generated by the tariff-ridden production point, the economy could consume at point C_1 in Figure 10.9, lowering the welfare level from U^* to U_1. Second, the tariff also leads to a sub-optimal consumption point because the domestic price level deviates from the world price level, leading to consumption at point C_2 and further reducing the welfare level from U_1 to U_2.

10.9 The 'optimal' tariff and retaliation

We can use offer curves (see Box 10.6) to derive the free trade equilibrium. To illustrate this, we combine the USA's offer curve derived in Figure 10.11 with the offer curve for the UK (representative of the rest of the world) in Figure 10.12. To do this we have to derive the offer curve for the UK using the procedure explained in Box 10.6. To depict these two offer curves in one figure we must measure the UK's imports in the same direction as the USA's exports (and vice versa for the UK's exports). This switches the orientation of the UK's offer curve relative to the USA, as illustrated in Figure 10.12. The free trade equilibrium is now simply given by the point of intersection of the two offer curves at point E, where the USA's offer of exports in exchange for imports exactly matches the UK's offer of imports in exchange for exports. The world markets for both goods are thus in equilibrium. The slope of the line from point E to the origin gives the free trade relative price.

We can now analyse the impact of imposing a tariff if the tariff-imposing country is large. If the country is able to benefit from imposing a tariff, this benefit must arise from the ability to influence its terms of trade: as demonstrated in Section 10.7, for any *given* terms of trade imposing a tariff always leads to a welfare loss. It also showed that for any given terms of trade, imposing a tariff reduces the volume of trade. Since (i) the offer curve depicts the combination of exports and imports for all possible terms of trade and (ii)

BOX 10.6 Offer curve

Before we can continue with analysing the impact of imposing a tariff if the home country is large, such that it has market power and can influence its terms of trade, we have to introduce another economic tool of analysis, namely the *offer curve* (as used by Alfred Marshall). Figure 10.10 depicts free trade production and consumption combinations for six different relative price levels of manufactures.[7] Going from panel a. to panel f., we see that, as the relative price of manufactures increases, the economy will produce more and more manufactures until the economy is completely specialized in the production of manufactures. Simultaneously, we see that the consumption ratio of food to manufactures increases from top to bottom, because the relative price of manufactures is rising, and that the distance from the origin is determined by the income level of the economy generated by the production point.

Figure 10.10 also draws the trade triangles at the different price levels, which make possible the inequality between production and consumption at the national level. Going again from panel a. to panel f., we see that the economy initially exports food in exchange for the import of manufactures if the relative price of manufactures is low. Once the relative price level of manufactures exceeds the autarky price (0.695), the economy starts to export manufactures in exchange for the import of food. The figure clearly demonstrates the connections that exist between the relative price of manufactures and the export–import combination the economy is willing to offer to the rest of the world at that price level.

Figure 10.11 translates these observations to the offer curve for a country which we have labelled USA for convenience. The horizontal axis depicts the USA's exports. The vertical axis depicts the USA's imports.[8] At a world relative price p the USA can trade with the rest of the world at any point along a line from the origin with slope p (reflecting trade balance at that price). Consumers and producers will choose the best option available at that price (see Figure 10.10), which results in offering the export–import combination depicted by point C in Figure 10.11. We also show a trade indifference curve U_p in the figure, depicting all combinations of exports and imports leading to the same welfare level in the USA (see van Marrewijk, 2012, Chapter 8 for a derivation). Such a curve must be tangent at point C because that is the best possible choice that consumers and producers can make given relative price p.

If the relative world price changes to p', all options from the origin on a line with slope p' are available for the USA (and guarantee balanced trade). In this case, the USA's best choice is at point D in Figure 10.11, which must be a point of tangency for trade indifference curve $U_{p'}$. Relative to curve U_p we note that for a given level of exports the USA receives more imports, so $U_{p'}$ must generate higher welfare than U_p and welfare increases for the USA in the direction of the arrow. Points C and D depict two specific export levels the USA is willing to offer in exchange for two specific import levels for two possible relative prices. As such they are two points on the USA's offer curve, which simply connects all possible export offers in exchange for imports for all possible relative prices.

(continued...)

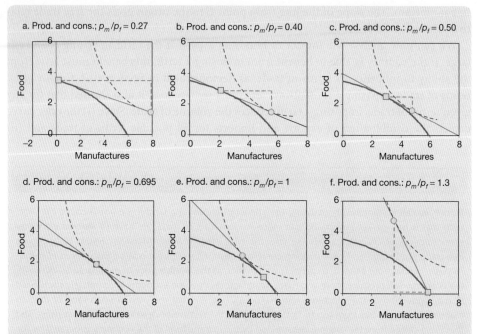

Figure 10.10 Production (square), consumption (circle), and relative price.

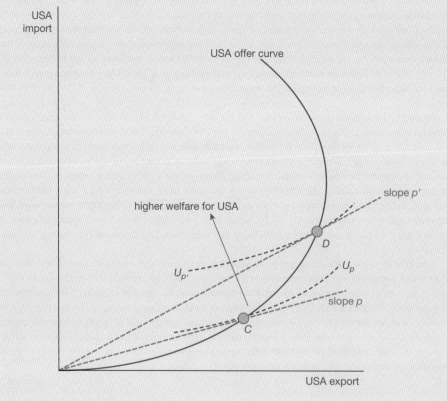

Figure 10.11 The USA's offer curve.

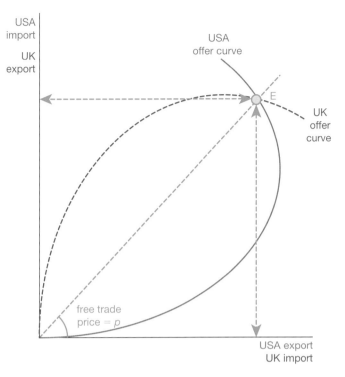

Figure 10.12 Free trade equilibrium with offer curves.

imposing a tariff reduces the volume of trade for any given terms of trade, we can conclude that the imposition of a tariff leads to an inward rotation of the offer curve. This inward rotation is illustrated in Figure 10.13, showing what happens if the USA imposes a tariff on its imports from the UK. The imposition of the tariff would then shift the trade equilibrium from point *E* to point *F*. The tariff thus leads to a higher relative export price for the USA, representing an improvement in the USA's terms of trade.

To what extent can the USA manipulate the international economic conditions and improve its terms of trade? The answer is given in Figure 10.13. By carefully choosing its tariff rate, the US government can in principle ensure that its tariff-ridden offer curve intersects the UK's offer curve at point *F*. Given the offer curve of the UK, the highest possible welfare level the USA can achieve is at this point, where the USA's trade indifference curve is tangent to the UK's offer curve. The tariff rate that ensures that the USA's tariff-ridden offer curve intersects the UK's offer curve at point *F* is therefore known as the 'optimal' tariff. It is derived formally in Technical Note 10.1. If the country is large, in the sense that it can influence its terms of trade, this optimal tariff is always positive within this framework.

In the analysis above, the government of the USA is clever. In fact, the government knows a lot and is able to perform extremely complicated calculations. It knows the production structure of its own economy, the preferences of its consumers, and the economic behaviour of its inhabitants. This allows it to calculate the production and consumption points for all possible relative prices of manufactures, and thus the concomitant export and import decisions at those prices. Using all this information, the government of the USA

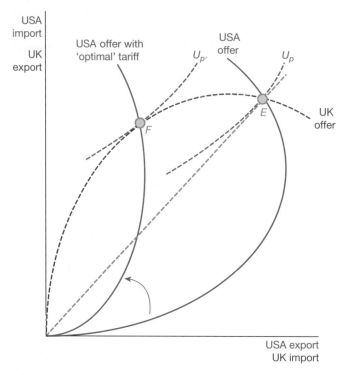

Figure 10.13 The 'optimal' tariff.

can then derive its own offer curve. In addition, the government can manipulate this offer curve by calculating the impact of imposing a tariff on imports for the above production, consumption, export, and import decisions. But that is not all. The government of the USA also knows all of this information on production, technology, preferences, consumption, exports, and imports for the economy of the UK, which allows it to derive the UK's offer curve. Finally, then, the government of the USA is able to combine all of this information into determining the point of tangency of its own trade indifference curves with the UK's offer curve, which enables it to calculate the 'optimal' tariff.

These observations on the formidable informational requirements and supposed ability of the government of the USA to process detailed economic information in determining the optimal tariff raises two important questions. First, do we really think any government in the world has this information available, and is capable at the same time of performing the required calculations? The answer undoubtedly must be negative, which calls into question the entire reasoning process of a country attempting to determine the optimal tariff. Second, even if we allow the government of the USA, within the setting of this economic structure, to be so clever as to calculate the optimal tariff, why shouldn't the same hold for the government of the UK?

The second question is addressed in Figure 10.14. If both countries engage in free trade, the trade equilibrium occurs at point E, the intersection of the two offer curves if neither country imposes a tariff on imports. As explained above, if the USA is clever it can calculate the point of tangency of the UK's offer curve and its trade indifference curves to determine the optimal tariff which will rotate its own offer curve inwards to ensure that the trade equilibrium moves from point *E* to point *F* to maximize its own welfare. If the government of the UK is equally clever, however, it will follow a similar procedure to calculate its own optimal tariff, which will rotate its own offer curve inwards to ensure that its own welfare is maximized at the point of tangency of its own trade indifference curves and the USA's offer curve. In Figure 10.14 this is given by point *G*. The UK's optimal tariff is therefore calculated to rotate the UK's offer curve inward to move the trade equilibrium from point *E* to point *G*.

What is the end result of this cleverness? The USA performs complicated calculations to try to move the international equilibrium from point *E* to point *F*. The UK performs complicated calculations to try to move the international equilibrium from point *E* to point *G*. The end result is that neither country gets what it wants, because the intersection of the two tariff-ridden offer curves occurs at point *H*. As drawn in Figure 10.14, this leads to lower trade and welfare levels for both countries. One can imagine that numerous game-theoretic manoeuvres have been analysed by international economists within this framework, assuming that both countries move simultaneously in calculating 'optimal' tariffs in a sequence of steps, or that one country moves before the other country retaliates in a series of alternating steps in calculating 'optimal' tariffs, and so on. In all cases, the end result of all this cleverness is the same. The international equilibrium moves in the wrong direction, leading to lower welfare levels for both countries than is achieved at the free trade equilibrium at point *E* in Figure 10.14. This identifies an important role for

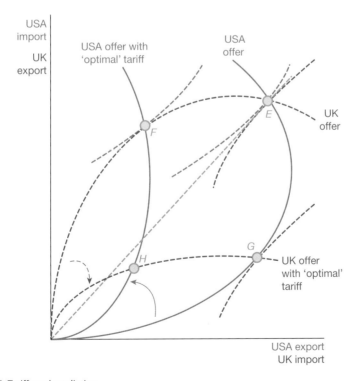

Figure 10.14 Tariffs and retaliation.

multilateral trade negotiations in the WTO: moving the international economy into the direction of free trade (which improves welfare) and away from retaliation and trade wars (which reduce welfare).

10.10 Conclusions

First, we briefly discuss the history and functioning of the main international trade organizations. The GATT/WTO deals most directly with international trade problems and has been successful in reducing trade barriers in a series of complicated negotiation rounds. The UN consists of many organizations. We emphasize the role of UNCTAD, which focuses on the problems of developing nations. The OECD, in contrast, is a club of advanced nations, but it also coordinates interactions with developing countries.

Second, we analyse the impact of trade policy on the size of trade flows and the distribution of welfare effects. In general, there are both winners and losers when trade restrictions are imposed, which makes the demand for protection (lobbying) understandable. Among the winners are protected domestic producers and, in terms of tariff revenue, the government. The main losers are domestic consumers, who pay for the increased profits of domestic producers and the tariff revenue for the government. The country as a whole suffers an efficiency loss (Harberger triangles). Foreign producers also suffer. The main difference between tariffs and quota rests in the question of who receives the tariff-equivalent government revenue. The foreign country can try to reap this benefit by establishing a 'voluntary' export restraint.

Imposing a tariff always leads to a net welfare loss for a small country, which cannot influence its terms of trade. Within a neoclassical framework, a large country, which can influence its terms of trade, might benefit from a net welfare gain by imposing an 'optimal' tariff based on its monopoly power. This argument breaks down under a system of retaliation leading to tariff wars, which clarifies the necessity of multilateral trade negotiations as organized by the WTO.

 Technical Note

Technical Note 10.1 Derivation of the 'optimal' tariff

Using the standard optimal pricing rule for a monopolist $p(1 - 1/\varepsilon) = MC$, see Technical Note 7.1, the 'optimal' tariff t_A for the USA can quite easily be derived as a function of the foreign excess demand elasticity ε_B^d once we realize that the USA acts as a monopolist, its marginal costs is its own price p_A, the price it charges indirectly through the tariff it imposes is the foreign price p_B, with elasticity $\varepsilon = \varepsilon_b^d$, and the two prices are related through $p_B = (1+t_A)p_A$. Simple substitution gives:

$$\left. \begin{array}{c} p_B\left(1-1/\varepsilon_B^d\right)=p_A \\ p_B =(1+t_A)p_A \end{array} \right\} \Rightarrow t_A = \frac{1}{\varepsilon_B^d -1} \qquad \text{('optimal' tariff)}$$

Notes

1   The American economist Paul Krugman analyses the arguments of many influential pressure groups in an accessible style: see www.nytimes.com/column/paul-krugman.

2   Tinbergen had earlier made a smaller model for the Netherlands. John Maynard Keynes did not like this work, as is evident from his book review in the *Economic Journal* (Keynes, 1939). Tinbergen politely replied that Keynes had totally misunderstood his econometric methods.

3   The word 'other' indicates that it excludes, for example, financial, computer, and insurance services.

4   This includes, for example, communications, construction, insurance, and personal services.

5   This remark does not hold for the retaliation analysis at the end of this chapter.

6   To be precise, this requires either a lump sum redistribution of the government tariff revenue to the consumers, or government consumption preferences identical to those of private consumers.

7   The structure of the economy is explained in Chapters 5 and 6; $\alpha_m = 0.8$; $\alpha_f = 0.2$; $\delta_m = 0.6$; $K = 7$; and $L = 3$.

8   Note that which good is on the export and import axis depends on the relative price of manufactures, as shown in Figure 10.9. More precisely, the figure only shows part of the USA's offer curve.

 Questions

Question 10.1

'If economists ruled the world, there would be no need for a WTO.'

a.   Do you agree with the statement above? Explain.

b.   Throughout the book we illustrate the benefits of free trade. Yet international trade negotiations are still steeped in terms such as concessions received and granted. Can you explain why this is so?

c.   What is a beggar-thy-neighbour policy?

d.   How is this related to the set-up of international trade organizations after World War II?

e.   On which three main principles is the GATT based?

f.   Two main exceptions are given for the non-discrimination principle. Can you explain why these have been created?

g.   Why did the successive trade rounds change their negotiating technique at the Kennedy Round?

h.   Why do international trade negotiations give particular attention to non-tariff barriers?

i.   What is the new protectionism?

j.   Which concerns gave rise to the foundation of UNCTAD?

Question 10.2

We investigate trade policy in this question from a purely neoclassical perspective.

a.   Draw a *partial equilibrium* diagram for Britain on the effects (for consumers, producers, and the government) of imposing a *tariff* on wheat (which is on net imported into Britain) on the assumption that *Britain is a large country* and is able to benefit in this framework from the fact that it is a large country. Explain.

b.   Briefly discuss and illustrate (for example using offer curves) why or how a trade policy which leads to a *partial equilibrium welfare gain* for Britain (for example if Britain imposes a tariff and is a large country) may be *reversed* in a general equilibrium framework.

Question 10.3

Suppose that Hong Kong is a small, open economy in a neoclassical world. It can produce two types of goods, machines and agricultural products, using two inputs, capital and labour. Assume that Hong Kong is relatively capital abundant. Hong Kong is currently engaged in free trade, but it is contemplating whether to impose a 50 per cent import tariff.

Assume you are an advisor to the Hong Kong government. *Draw* a (big) consistent production possibility frontier illustrating *trade flows* under free trade and show what happens if an import tariff is imposed (general equilibrium framework). *Explain* to the government how imposing a tariff creates a welfare loss through a double distortion.

 See the **online resources** for a Study Guide and questions:
www.oup.com/uk/vanmarrewijk_it/

Strategic trade policy

⊙ Objectives

- To have an understanding of the number of WTO trade disputes (about 20–25 per year).
- To know that most disputes are about anti-dumping and countervailing duties, other issues being safeguards and sanitary barriers.
- To know that large advanced countries and some large emerging markets are most actively involved in trade disputes, both as respondent and as claimant.
- To know that small Caribbean nations and developing nations tend to be involved in disputes as third parties.
- To understand the heterogeneity of disputes in terms of global versus partial policies, size of trade flows involved, and the estimated changes (value and volume) of disputed new policies.
- To understand how market powers affect the consequences of imposing a tariff, in particular how raising a tariff if no goods are imported may still have negative welfare effects.
- To understand why quotas are more restrictive than tariffs if firms have market power.
- To know the fundamentals of the Brander–Spencer model and understand how an export subsidy may provide a strategic advantage within this model.
- To know the fundamentals of the Eaton–Grossman model and understand how an export tax may provide a strategic advantage within this model.
- To understand the main limitations of strategic trade policy in terms of competition for resources, entry and exit, retaliation, and informational requirements.

11.1 Introduction

In Chapter 10 we discussed the effects of trade policy—that is, tariffs, quotas, and the like—in a classical or neoclassical world of perfect competition. We concluded that trade restrictions are detrimental for small countries unable to influence the world price level, in both a partial and a general equilibrium setting. The analysis was somewhat less clear-cut for large countries, since their ability to influence the terms of trade suggested that a suitable restriction of trade (the 'optimal' tariff) would enable them to increase their welfare, albeit at the cost of a deterioration in welfare in other countries of the world. In a more general setting, taking into consideration the possibility of retaliation from other countries making a suitable choice of their 'optimal' tariffs, we concluded again that free trade is the true optimal policy.

The optimal tariff argument is based on market power at the country level. Chapters 7 and 8 discussed market power at the firm and sector level in a world of imperfect competition (monopoly, oligopoly, and monopolistic competition), sometimes based on increasing returns to scale. This suggests, of course, that the analysis of trade policy in a world based on imperfect competition is more involved and potentially leaves more room for beneficial government intervention. As we will elaborate below, both suggestions are true in principle. An omniscient government could indeed potentially make the right 'strategic' choices by promoting the interests of certain sectors. This so-called strategic trade policy argument received a lot of attention for a fairly brief period of time. We explain why this attention did not last very long and give a number of reasons why the strategic trade policy arguments are not important in practice.

Before addressing these problems, we examine two issues. First, in Sections 11.2 and 11.3, we provide a brief overview of the size and frequency of actual trade disputes between countries, based on WTO data. We also discuss which type of countries are involved, the heterogeneity of the trade flows, and the heterogeneity of policies and economic changes. Second, in Sections 11.4 and 11.5, we explain the main economic implications of imposing a tariff to protect a domestic industry characterized by market power, in particular how welfare may be negatively affected even if imports are zero. We also discuss why quotas are more restrictive, and thus lead to larger welfare losses, in imperfectly competitive markets.

11.2 **WTO trade disputes**

One of the main advantages of the WTO is the improved dispute settlement process compared to the GATT procedures (see Section 10.3). Bown and Reynolds (2015) are the first to provide a detailed structural overview of the main characteristics of WTO disputes since 1995 (when the WTO was formed). This section and the next are based on their work, classifications, and data.

Figure 11.1 displays the evolution of the cumulative number of WTO disputes by date of request for consultation by the complainant country. Up to 2011 there had been 427 disputes in total, or slightly more than 25 per year on average. In the initial phase this number was a bit higher, reaching a peak in 1998 of slightly above 40 disputes per year on average from the founding of the WTO. Since the new millennium the average number of disputes has been slightly above 20 per year.

Figure 11.2 provides an overview of the main types of disputes and the main respondents (countries accused of WTO violations) involved in those disputes. Panel a. of Figure 11.2 shows that more than 25 per cent of the disputes involve anti-dumping and countervailing duties and procedures, followed by 10 per cent disputes on safeguards, and about 7 per cent each for disputes involving sanitary and phytosanitary barriers, national treatment on internal taxation, and export subsidies. Other important causes for disputes are other subsidies, intellectual property rights, customs valuation, and quantity restrictions. The remaining 18 per cent of the disputes are caused by ten other, more minor topics.

Panel b. of Figure 11.2 shows that more than 26 per cent of the disputes have involved the USA as the respondent (accused party), followed by the European Union (EU) with 16 per cent, China and India with about 5 per cent each, Canada and Argentina with 4 per cent each, and Japan, Mexico, and South Korea with about 3 per cent each. The main

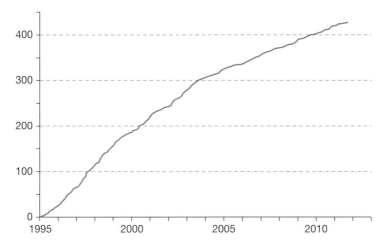

Figure 11.1 Cumulative number of WTO disputes since 1995.

Source: based on Bown and Reynolds (2015) data, by date of request for consultations by complainant.

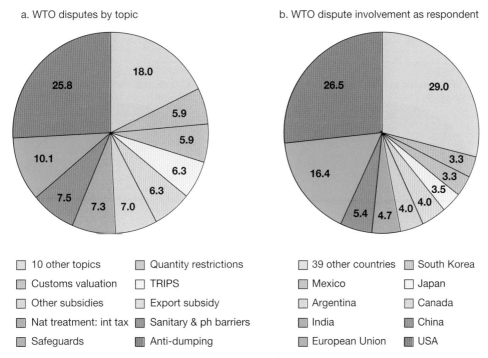

Figure 11.2 Trade disputes by topic and respondent (per cent).

Notes: data are for 1995–2011; nat treatment: int tax = national treatment: internal taxation; TRIPS = WTO intellectual property rights agreement; ph = phytosanitary; antidumping = antidumping and countervailing duties cases and procedures. *Source:* based on data from Bown and Reynolds (2015).

respondents are thus the advanced countries combined with some large emerging markets (China, India, Argentina, and Mexico). The remaining 29 per cent of the disputes involve 39 different countries.

Figure 11.3 provides an overview of the main complainants and of the countries involved indirectly in the dispute as third parties. Panel a. of Figure 11.3 shows that the USA is not only the biggest respondent but also the biggest complainant (26 versus 21 per cent of the disputes). Similarly, the EU is also a big respondent as well as a big complainant (16 versus 19 per cent of the disputes). Some other advanced countries are also large complainants, such as Canada (7 per cent), South Korea (3 per cent), and Japan (3 per cent). The other big complainants are again some large emerging markets, such as Brazil (5 per cent), Mexico (5 per cent), India (4 per cent), and Argentina (3 per cent). The fact that virtually the same country names appear as the most actively involved both as respondent and as complainant is already indicative of the type of games these countries play by mutually accusing each other of violating WTO rules.

Panel b. of Figure 11.3 shows the main countries involved in the dispute not as respondent or complainant but as third party (as described in the WTO dispute settlement documents). Here we see a rather more diluted and different list of countries. The small Caribbean islands of St Kitts and Nevis (about 55,000 people) are most frequently involved as third party (8 per cent), followed by other small Caribbean states, such as Grenada (8 per cent), St Vincent and the Grenadines (6 per cent), Jamaica (6 per cent), and Barbados (4 per cent), and some developing countries, such as Congo (6 per cent), Malawi (5 per cent), and Tanzania (4 per cent). The only advanced nation listed is Canada (5 per cent). The remaining 46 per cent of third-party involvement is shared across 37 different nations.

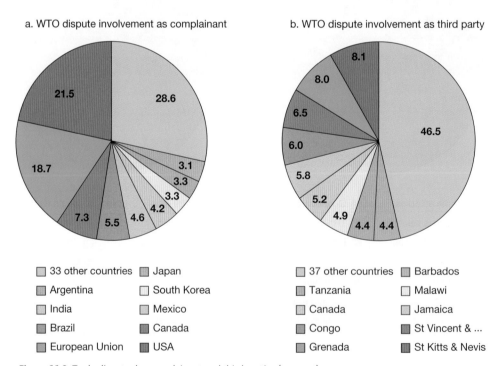

a. WTO dispute involvement as complainant

b. WTO dispute involvement as third party

Figure 11.3 Trade disputes by complainant and third parties (per cent).

Notes: data are for 1995–2011; St Vincent & ... = St Vincent and the Grenadines.

Source: based on data from Bown and Reynolds (2015).

One reason these small nations are involved only as third parties is related to tax evasion. Another reason is related to the high costs associated with filing a complaint at the WTO. Bown and Reynolds (2015, p. 158) note that the minimum private sector fees for litigating even a simple case range from $250,000 to $750,000.

11.3 Analysis of WTO disputes

In their analysis of WTO disputes Bown and Reynolds focus on disputes related to imports that can be connected to particular products. They thus ignore the 41 disputes related to exports, the 11 disputes related to services imports (which cannot be mapped to product-level trade data), and the 67 disputes that affect general imports (which cannot be mapped to a particular product). This leaves 308 disputes (72 per cent of the total) to analyse. A fair number of these disputes (68) are based on the failure to reform policies so as to bring them into WTO compliance. In these cases there is no new policy imposed and we cannot perform a 'before' and 'after' comparison. The remaining 240 disputes are classified into two types of policies:

- 95 'global' policy disputes—respondent policies that negatively affect all trading partners: for example, the application of an internal tax or subsidy imposed on a most-favoured-nation conforming basis inconsistently with WTO principles.

- 145 'partial' policy disputes—respondent policies that negatively affect only selected trading partners: for example, the application of an anti-dumping or countervailing duty or trade preference scheme inconsistently with WTO principles.

The next step is to relate these types of policies to detailed trade data. This is done at the Harmonized System six-digit (HS6) level, the most detailed level that is consistently defined across countries, which consists of about 5,000 different products.

- On average, for all disputes, there are 84 products involved at the HS6 level. This number is significantly higher for disputes based on no policy change (169 products: an index of 200, see Figure 11.4a.) than for disputes based on new policies.

- On average, for all disputes, the value of bilateral imports in disputed products is about $743 million (constant 2005 dollars). This is the same for no policy change and policy change.

- On average, for all disputes, the complainant's market share in the respondent's disputed import market is 21 per cent. This share is significantly lower for disputes based on no policy change (15.3 per cent: an index of 73, see Figure 11.4a.) than for disputes based on new policies.

- The distribution of all these variables is skewed: see the scale of the index values in Figure 11.4b. The median number of involved products is 6.5 (compared to the average of 84.2), the median value is $66 million (compared to the average of $743 million), and the median market share is 11.7 per cent (compared to the average of 21 per cent). At median values the number of products involved is again higher for no policy change and the market share is again lower (Figure 11.4b.).

From this classification we observe substantial heterogeneity. A large number of disputes are small in terms of number of products, value, and market share involved. Indeed, more

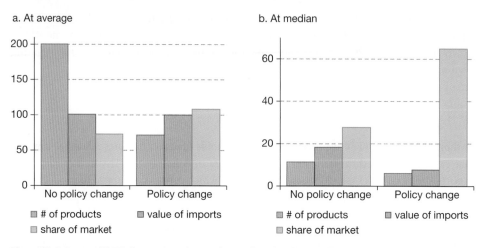

Figure 11.4 Scope of WTO disputes: products, value, and market share, index.

Notes: data for 1995–2011; to display in one figure and be able to compare the two panels, all values are indexed to the average number of products, value of imports, and share of market for all disputes; value of bilateral imports in disputed products in constant 2005 dollar; market share of complainant in respondent's disputed product imports in per cent.
Source: based on data from Table 2, Bown and Reynolds (2015).

than 17 per cent of the disputes involve only one product and 14 per cent involve bilateral trade of less than one *million* dollars per year. This is remarkable in terms of the high costs of litigation mentioned above. On the other hand, more than 19 per cent of the disputes involve more than 50 products and almost 15 per cent involve bilateral trade flows of more than one *billion* dollars per year.

We expect, of course, that a country will file a dispute at the WTO if a new policy alleged to be inconsistent with WTO principles is negatively affecting trade flows of the disputed products. Some indication that this is indeed the case is provided by looking at the change in affected trade flows in the year after the new policy was imposed relative to trade flows before it was imposed. Note that this is a weak indicator only, as annual trade flows tend to be volatile at the detailed HS6 level and trade flows may change over time for many other reasons (in particular, they tend to increase over time as the economy grows). Nonetheless, for disputes involving new policies we can observe the following average per cent changes:

- −21.5 per cent of the value of imports;
- −24.1 per cent of the volume of imports;
- −0.6 per cent of prices/unit values received by the exporter;
- −2.2 per cent of the complainant's share of the respondent's disputed product import market.

On average, therefore, there is indeed an indication that new policies disputed at the WTO are harmful for trade flows through their effects on value, volume, prices, and the complainant's market share.[1] Please note, however, that there is enormous variation in these variables, as is illustrated by the estimated density functions in Figure 11.5 for volume

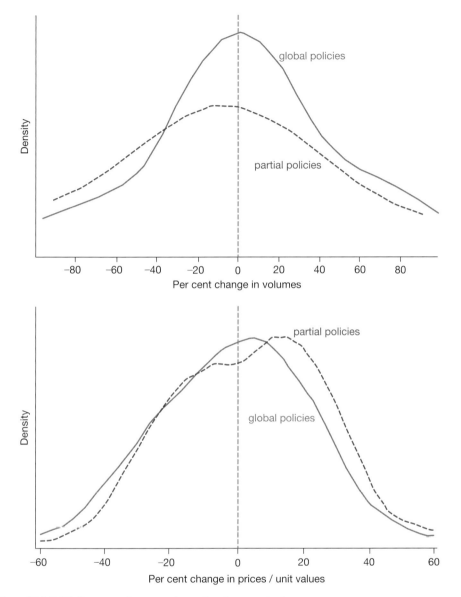

Figure 11.5 WTO disputes and per cent change in volumes and prices.

Notes: per cent change in volume and in prices/unit values of the respondent's bilateral import of the disputed product from the complainant; year after the imposition of the alleged WTO violating policy compared to the year before the imposition of the policy.
Source: based on Bown and Reynolds (2015).

and prices. The figure shows global policies and partial policies separately. Regarding the volume of trade, the average per cent change is negative for partial policies and positive for global policies (and this difference is significant; similarly for the per cent change in value of imports). The per cent change in prices is negative for global policies and positive for partial policies (but this difference is not significant).

11.4 Market power and tariffs

The analyses and discussions in Chapters 7 and 8 show that international trade reduces the market power of domestic firms. Conversely, therefore, we expect protection to increase domestic market power. In contrast to the perfect competition analysis of Chapter 10,

---

BOX 11.1 Jagdish Bhagwati

Figure 11.6
Jagdish Bhagwati (1934–).

Born and raised in India, Jagdish Bhagwati (Figure 11.6) studied at Cambridge, MIT, and Oxford before returning to India in 1961 to work at the Indian Statistical Institute and the Delhi School of Economics. In 1968 he went back to MIT, where he worked for 12 years before moving to Columbia University. Currently, he is Special Adviser on Globalization to the United Nations and External Adviser to the World Trade Organization. Jagdish Bhagwati has published numerous articles and books on virtually all subfields of international economics, notably on trade, development, and trade policy. In 1971 he founded the *Journal of International Economics*, the foremost journal in the field today. Among his better-known books are *Protectionism* (1988) and *The World Trading System at Risk* (1991).

---

however, the effects of protection depend on the form it takes. In general, as first shown by Jagdish Bhagwati (1965; see Box 11.1) and demonstrated in this section and the next, quantitative restrictions such as quotas create larger distortions and generate more domestic market power than tariffs.

Figure 11.7 illustrates the case considered by Bhagwati. There is a single producer in the domestic market facing a downward sloping demand curve, with concomitant marginal revenue curve (MR), and an upward sloping marginal cost curve (MC). In the absence of international trade, the domestic supplier is a monopolist and output would be determined by equality of marginal cost and marginal revenue at point C, such that the firm would charge the monopoly price p_{mon}. Recall that, if this were a competitive industry, output would be determined by equality of price and marginal cost, that is at point B leading to price p_{pc}. If there is free international trade, and assuming that this is a small country facing competition from price-taking foreign suppliers[2] at the price p_{world}, the domestic firm would produce at the point where marginal cost is equal to the world price level, that is at point D. The difference between domestic demand at point E and domestic supply at point D would be imported from abroad.

11.4.1 Imposing a tariff such that $p_{world} + t < p_{pc}$

If the government decides to protect the domestic firm by imposing a specific tariff t, the (welfare) consequences are initially similar to those shown in the analysis in Chapter 10. As long as the world price plus the tariff is below the perfect competition price, as illustrated in Figure 11.7 for tariff t_0, the domestic firm increases output from point D to D', domestic demand falls from point E to E', and imports from abroad also decrease.

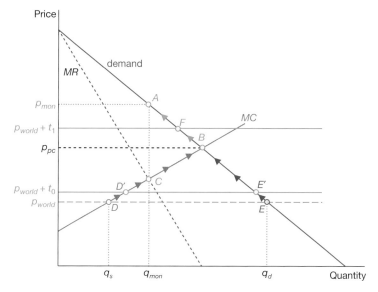

Figure 11.7 Market power and tariff.

11.4.2 Imposing a tariff such that $p_{pc} < p_{world} + t < p_{mon}$

The analysis starts to deviate from the competitive analysis in Chapter 10 once the government imposes a 'prohibitive' tariff, such that the world price plus the tariff is above the perfect competition price, as illustrated for tariff t_1 in Figure 11.7. If the domestic market were competitive, any tariff increase above the competitive price would have no further effects. The price equilibrium would remain at point B, price and quantity would be constant, and imports would be zero. If there is a single domestic firm, however, an increase of the tariff beyond the perfect competition price level enables the domestic firm to use its monopoly power by lowering output and increasing price and profits, up to the level $p_{world} + t_1$, that is at point F. Note that the *threat* of imports keeps the monopolist from exercising its monopoly power fully, even when no imports actually occur, such that raising an already prohibitive tariff leads to a domestic price increase and reduces domestic output.

11.4.3 Imposing a tariff such that $p_{mon} < p_{world} + t$

If the government raises the prohibitive tariff even further, such that the world price plus the tariff exceeds the monopoly price, the domestic firm maximizes profits at the monopoly price and does not raise the price any further: that is, the equilibrium remains at point A.

Note that, as the tariff level increases from 0 to $p_{mon} - p_{world}$, the domestically produced quantity and price combination first moves from point D to point B, and then from point B to point A. Similarly, the domestically demanded quantity and price combination first move from point E to point B, and then from point B to point A. After point B, therefore, the domestically produced and demanded quantities coincide and nothing is imported from abroad. Any further tariff increases beyond the price level at point A have no effect.

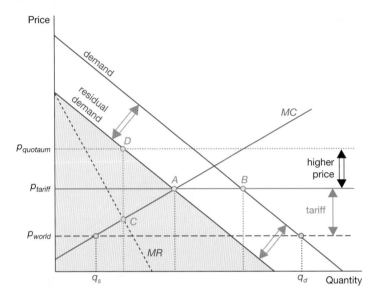

Figure 11.8 Market power and quota.

11.5 The non-equivalence of tariffs and quotas

In Chapter 10 we briefly discussed how the imposition of a tariff and a quota leading to the same level of imports results in the same welfare effects and price level, as discussed in Box 10.4. This so-called equivalence between tariffs and quotas no longer holds if there is domestic market power (see also Box 11.2 on non-tariff measures). This is illustrated in Figure 11.8 for the Bhagwati framework explained in the previous section (one domestic firm and price-taking foreign suppliers). First, suppose the country imposes a tariff such that the world price plus the tariff is below the competitive price. As explained in Section 10.7 and illustrated in Figure 11.8, this leads to domestic production at point A, domestic demand at point B, and imports equal to the difference between points B and A. Second, suppose that instead of imposing a tariff, the government decides to impose a quantitative import restriction equal to the import level under the tariff (the difference between points B and A). Does this change the domestic equilibrium? Yes, it does. To understand this, we have to consider the strategic possibilities available to the domestic firm if either tariffs or the quota are imposed, as indicated by marginal revenue.

Under the tariff, the marginal revenue curve for the domestic supplier is equal to $p_{world} + t$. As a result of the quota, however, the domestic firm's demand curve essentially shifts to the left by the extent of the quota, as indicated by the arrows in Figure 11.8. Consequently, the domestic firm's marginal revenue curve is generated by this residual demand curve. After allowing for the restricted foreign imports, the domestic firm can again exercise its monopoly power, leading to the equality of marginal revenue and marginal cost at point C and the price p_{quotum}, as determined by point D. Clearly, if domestic firms enjoy some market power, protection of the domestic industry with a quota rather than a tariff leads to higher prices and lower output. Using a similar partial equilibrium welfare analysis as in Chapter 10, quotas therefore lead to larger welfare losses. The clear policy message is therefore: if you must protect the domestic industry, use a tariff rather than a quota.

BOX 11.2 Non-tariff measures (written by Koen Berden)

Since World War II we have seen a long-term decrease in the height of tariffs, in part because of multilateral efforts (through GATT and WTO) and in part through bilateral or regional trade agreements (RTAs). What has been—and, maybe because of the success of tariff reductions, is becoming—an increasingly important challenge, however, to free trade and a truly globalised world, are non-tariff measures (NTMs).

Non-tariff measures are defined as all non-price and non-quantity restrictions on trade in goods, services, and investment, at federal and state level. This includes border measures (customs procedures, and so on) as well as behind-the-border measures flowing from domestic laws, regulations, and practices.

This NTM definition is broader than the more commonly known one of NTBs—non-tariff barriers—in that they are WTO-compliant and NTBs are not. Two examples of NTMs are:

- Differences in testing requirements for new cars in different countries that have the purpose of creating safety for passengers. These differences also cause multinational car producers to bear costs of having to test the same car in various different ways: these costs add to the cost of production and are (in part) passed on to consumers via the price of the final product; such costs are deadweight losses to society.

- Differences in rules regarding animal testing in the cosmetics industry. In the EU, a ban on animal testing for cosmetics has been passed, while in the US cosmetics may be tested on animals before they are approved for human use. This discrepancy is posing challenges for the cosmetics industry; it disrupts the industry's global supply chain and limits market access, causing economic rents to those with market access.

Ecorys, a large consulting firm based in Rotterdam, provides an economic analysis on the effects of eliminating NTMs for EU–US trade and investment (Berden et al., 2009). The study finds that regulatory differences—though fully legitimate—add significantly to the cost of doing business and increase prices for consumers. The main results of the study are presented in Table 11.1.

Effects on GDP: the ambitious scenario could push EU GDP to be 0.7 per cent higher in 2018 compared to the baseline scenario (i.e. doing nothing), which would represent an annual potential gain of $158 billion. For the US GDP the same operation could yield a 0.3 per cent gain per year in 2018 (compared to the baseline), which would represent an annual potential gain of $53 billion. The different results over time are the consequences of a dynamic investment effect that occurs in the long-run scenario but not the short-run scenario. As a comparison: this research also shows that full elimination of all remaining tariff barriers between the EU and the US would yield $12 billion for both economies combined.[3] The difference in the estimated impact between the EU and the US stems from the different volumes of affected trade and investment flows, different comparative advantages, and a mixed picture on differences in the values of measures for specific sectors, whereby the EU would gain more from cheaper imports while both the EU and the US would gain from lower costs of production. Economic gains would be achieved through different channels. First of all, cheaper prices for imported products would increase consumer welfare. Second, exports and production for competitive sectors would increase. Third, production costs would be lower for companies due to more aligned regulation and lower levels of NTMs. Fourth, investment flows would increase due to more harmonized investment regimes.

Effects on wages for high- and low-skilled workers: dismantling NTMs would raise wages for both low- and high-skilled workers in the EU and the US, making wage-earning households better off. This effect is caused by the productivity gains that would result from dismantling NTMs. The increase in wages in the US would be around 0.4 per cent per year while in the EU this increase would be around 0.8 per cent annually.

Effects on imports and exports: exports would be expected to go up for both the EU and the US, but the percentage increase in exports would be higher for the US (6.1 per cent) than for the EU (2.1 per cent), even though in absolute terms the increases would be similar in magnitude. The results predict that net exports would increase in all scenarios, implying that both EU and US trade balances would improve. This is an indication that bilateral liberalization (regulatory alignment) would improve the global competitiveness of both the EU and the US economies.

(Continued)

Table 11.1 Impact of liberalization of EU–US non-tariff measures

	Ambitious scenario (full liberalization)		Limited scenario (partial liberalization)	
	Short run	Long run	Short run	Long run
Real income, billion $				
United States	24.7	53.0	10.1	23.8
European Union	59.7	158.0	25.2	69.7
Real income, % change				
United States	0.13	0.28	0.05	0.13
European Union	0.27	0.72	0.11	0.32
Real wages % change, unskilled workers				
United States	0.24	0.35	0.11	0.16
European Union	0.40	0.82	0.17	0.36
Real wages % change, skilled workers				
United States	0.26	0.38	0.11	0.17
European Union	0.36	0.78	0.16	0.34
Value of exports, % change				
United States	6.12	6.06	2.72	2.68
European Union	1.69	2.07	0.74	0.91
Value of imports, % change				
United States	3.97	3.93	1.76	1.74
European Union	1.63	2.00	0.72	0.88

Notes: The results depend to some extent on the assumption of actionability of NTMs in about 50 per cent of the cases overall. The ambitious scenario assumes that all NTMs that are actionable are addressed (50 per cent of all NTMs). The limited scenario assumes that 50 per cent of all actionable NTMs are aligned (25 per cent of all NTMs).
Source: Berden et al. (2009).

11.6 Strategic trade policy

One of the most controversial topics in the new trade literature is the suggestion that active government intervention, through tariffs, quotas, subsidies, or otherwise, may be able to raise domestic welfare by shifting oligopoly profits from foreign to domestic firms. The debate started in the 1980s, when there was great concern about American international competitiveness, with a series of papers by James Brander and Barbara Spencer (1983, 1985). The general idea is that government intervention can serve the 'strategic' purpose of altering the incentives of firms, thus deterring foreign competitors.

The main idea is conveyed quite easily in the Brander–Spencer analysis, which is based on the Cournot model discussed in Section 7.4, by simplifying the international trade aspects of the model. There are two firms, an American firm (index A) and a British firm (index B), producing a homogeneous good. Both firms export to a third market and do not face any domestic demand. Since there are no distortions in this partial equilibrium analysis other than the monopoly power in the industry, the marginal cost of each firm is also the social cost of the resources it uses. As a result, national welfare for each country can be measured by the profits earned by its firm. Details on the discussion below are given in Technical Note 11.1 at the end of this chapter.

In the absence of government intervention, the American firm maximizes its profits taking the output level of the British firm as given; the British firm does similarly. As explained in Section 7.4, this leads to two 'reaction curves' in (q_A, q_B)-space, giving the optimal response of each firm to the other firm's output level. The Cournot equilibrium is determined by the point of intersection of the reaction curves, where neither firm has an incentive to change its output decision: see Figure 11.9.

Does the Cournot equilibrium lead to the highest possible profits for the American firm? No. As indicated in Figure 11.9, the American firm's isoprofit curve is horizontal at the Cournot equilibrium, since it is the optimal response (maximizes profits) given the output level of the British firm. Taking the British firm's reaction curve as a restriction, the American firm's profits are maximized at a point of tangency of the British firm's reaction curve with the American firm's isoprofit curve: see the Brander–Spencer square in Figure 11.9.[4] Why does the American firm not produce this level of output? Because it is lacking a credible pre-commitment. Given the output level of the British firm at the Brander–Spencer equilibrium, the American firm has an incentive to produce a smaller level of output, which would raise its profits even further.

The potential for beneficial active government intervention now becomes clear. If the American government is somehow able to shift the American firm's reaction curve to the right, such that it precisely intersects the British firm's reaction curve at the Brander–Spencer

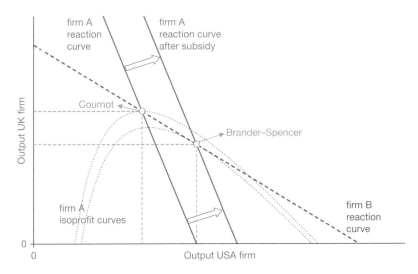

Figure 11.9 Brander–Spencer equilibrium.

equilibrium, it will have made this point a credible equilibrium. In essence, the American government would then give its firm a strategic advantage. Several options are available, but Technical Note 11.1 shows that one strategy that works for the American government is giving an export subsidy of exactly the right amount to the production of goods in the USA. Technical Note 11.1 also shows that American welfare (firm profit minus government outlays) is indeed maximized at the Brander–Spencer equilibrium.

11.7 The nature of competition

The Brander–Spencer model discussed in the previous section, leading to an export subsidy as the government's optimal policy, is based on strong assumptions (two firms exporting to a third market using Cournot competition). Naturally, this led to a series of responses from other economists investigating different strategic settings, based on price competition, more firms, domestic sales, entry and exit, differentiated goods, and so on. The most important contribution in this respect is by Jonathan Eaton and Gene Grossman (1986). Before making a more general argument, they discuss the impact of a small change in the Brander–Spencer setting: rather than analysing Cournot-type quantity competition they analyse Bertrand-type price competition in an identical framework.

Consider, therefore, an American and a British firm exporting to a third market, not facing any domestic demand. Since the firms are engaged in price competition we assume that the goods are imperfect substitutes to facilitate the analysis.[5] If the American firm raises its price, this increases the demand for the British firm, and vice versa. The absence of other distortions ensures that the marginal cost of each firm is also the social cost of the resources it uses, such that national welfare for each country is equal to the profits earned by its firm. Technical details on the discussion below are given in Technical Note 11.2 at the end of this chapter.

In the absence of government intervention, the American firm maximizes its profits by choosing its price and taking the price level of the British firm as given, and similarly for the British firm. This leads to two 'reaction curves' in (p_A, p_B)-space, giving the optimal response of each firm to the other firm's price level. In contrast to the scenario discussed in Section 11.6, these reaction curves are upward sloping: if the British firm raises its price, the demand for the American firm's product increases, which allows the American firm to raise its price as well. Analogous to the analysis in Section 11.6, the Bertrand equilibrium is determined by the point of intersection of the reaction curves, where neither firm has an incentive to change its pricing decision; see Figure 11.10.

The Bertrand equilibrium does not lead to the highest possible profit level for the American firm, which is determined by the point of tangency of the British firm's reaction curve with the American firm's isoprofit curve: see the Eaton–Grossman square in Figure 11.10. This time, however, the American government can ensure that the American firm's reaction curve is shifted to the right to intersect at the Eaton–Grossman point by levying an export *tax* of exactly the right amount. As Krugman (1990, p. 251) put it:

> So what Eaton and Grossman show is that replacing the Cournot with a Bertrand assumption reverses the policy recommendation. Given the shakiness of any characterization of oligopoly behaviour, this is not reassuring.

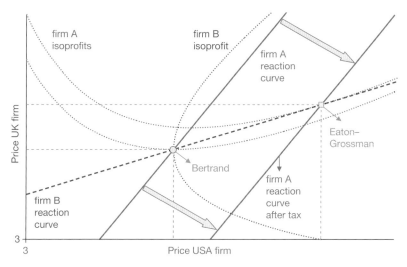

Figure 11.10 Eaton-Grossman equilibrium.

Why do we have this reversal of the policy recommendation? Using terms introduced by Bulow, Geanokoplos, and Klemperer (1985), it is because with Cournot competition the choice variables are 'strategic substitutes' (higher output leads to lower marginal profitability of similar moves by the firm's rival), while with Bertrand competition the choice variables are 'strategic complements' (a higher price raises the marginal profitability of similar moves by the firm's rival). Eaton and Grossman show in a more general setting that the optimal policy recommendation depends on the choice variables being strategic substitutes (export subsidy) or strategic complements (export tax). Leaving aside the willingness of government officials who want to be re-elected to impose an export tax on an industry should the structural details demand such a policy response, it is time to evaluate the contribution of strategic trade policy.

11.8 Evaluation of strategic trade policy

For a fairly brief time period the idea of strategic trade policy, building on the framework of new trade theory, received a lot of attention, both from the international economics profession and from outside. The main reason for the outside attention is that any intellectually respectable case for intervention will quickly find support for the wrong reasons, namely as an excuse to impose arbitrary trade restrictions to protect sectors under competitive pressure from abroad. The special interest boxes in this chapter (Boxes 11.3 and 11.4) may give an idea how the Brander–Spencer idea can be misused in view of the 'strategic' importance of some protected sectors. The attention from the international economics profession is a response primarily based on this outside pressure for protection, namely to carefully scrutinize any idea that seems to support protection under some circumstances. Since the game-theoretic nature of the strategic trade policy argument makes the analyses of the

---

BOX 11.3 The strategic importance of sugar

After months of negotiations, the EU Council (as represented by the Ministers for Agriculture: see Chapter 12) decided in May 2001 to reduce EU support for the production of sugar. Because sugar was one of the most protected sectors in Europe, it had been virtually impossible for developing countries to export it to the EU, with the exception of ex-colonies, which were given preferential treatment. The €300 million annual subsidy for the storage of sugar was to be abolished. The EU had been buying sugar for €632 per tonne, almost three times the world price, and was levying import tariffs to keep foreign, more efficiently produced cane sugar from the market. Consequently, the European consumer was heavily subsidizing the 'strategically' important European sugar industry. In June 2005 the European Commission announced a drastic change in this system; they reduced the price of sugar by 39 per cent in 2009, allocating subsidies to farmers to mitigate their losses. In addition, the EU began to pay factories to stop producing sugar (starting with €730 per not-produced tonne initially, and a falling rate each subsequent year).

Source: NRC Handelsblad (2001) and The Economist (2005).

BOX 11.4 The strategic importance of bananas

After nine years of trade warfare the USA and the EU, with teams led by the US trade representative Robert Zoellick and the EU trade commissioner Pascal Lamy, reached an agreement in April 2001 on a new regime for importing bananas into the EU. The warfare began in 1993 when the EU set up a mix of tariffs and quotas to help exports from former colonies. This system discriminated against bananas from Latin America, most of which are shipped by American companies, and was therefore ruled illegal by the WTO. The new system consisted of a tariff-only regime by 2006 (in line with WTO 'tariffication'; see Chapter 10). In the transitional period, starting 1 July 2001, quotas were based on the import volume of 1994–6. This benefited the struggling, near-bankrupt Chiquita company relative to its rival Dole, which had diversified its sourcing of bananas. Personal contacts seem to be important in striking strategic trade deals, not only because Robert Zoellick and Pascal Lamy are personal friends, but also behind the scenes, as suggested by The Economist (2001):

> If the banana accord survives it will also be a victory for Trent Lott, the Republican Leader of the Senate. Last year Mr Lott, who has received tens of thousands of campaign dollars thanks to the efforts of Chiquita's chief executive, made it clear that he would oppose any deal that hurt the company. This week Mr Lott is touring Europe. In Brussels, he should drop a thank-you note into Mr Lamy's letter box.

Source: The Economist (2001).

---

scrutiny rather complex (involving the number of players, the number of time periods, the choice of strategic variables, who moves first, second, or third, the credibility of commitments, and so on), we will only briefly describe the main results in general terms.

11.8.1 Competition for resources

The arguments in Sections 11.6 and 11.7 are based on a partial equilibrium framework. By now we have become accustomed in this book to value a general equilibrium framework for investigating international trade and trade policy, as it forces us to express our ideas in a consistent way and sometimes identifies the misleading nature of partial equilibrium results. As Dixit and Grossman (1986) argue, the export subsidy in the Brander–Spencer model works because it reduces the marginal costs for the American firm in the subsidized sector, which deters exports to the third market by the British firm. In a general equilibrium framework, however, the subsidized sector can only expand by bidding away resources from other sectors, thus driving up the marginal costs in those sectors. This leads to reverse-deterrence in non-targeted sectors. Constructing a tractable general equilibrium model, Dixit and Grossman show that a subsidy to a specific sector raises national income only if the deterrent effect is higher in the subsidized sector than in the sectors that are crowded out as a result of the subsidy. Optimal policy therefore requires detailed knowledge of all sectors in the entire economy.

11.8.2 Entry and exit

The arguments in Sections 11.6 and 11.7 are based on the possibility of firms earning supernormal profits over which firms (and countries) can compete. As argued in Chapter 8, the potential for supernormal profits will entice new firms to enter the market. This eliminates not only such profits but also the arguments for strategic trade policy based on them. This line of reasoning is followed by Horstmann and Markusen (1986), who extend the Brander–Spencer framework by allowing for entry and exit of firms. The number of firms is determined by fixed costs leading to economies of scale. The authors show that a subsidy provided by a country leads to a welfare loss through a reduction in scale economies or a worsening in the terms of trade.

11.8.3 Retaliation

There is an asymmetry in cleverness on the part of the governments in the Brander–Spencer model: the American government gathers a lot of information and performs detailed calculations to determine the optimal export subsidy for its firm, while the British government does not. In an extended framework, many variants of which are analysed by Dixit and Kyle (1985), it is reasonable to assume that the British government is able to undertake similar Brander–Spencer policies. In this case the two countries end up in a prisoner's-dilemma-type subsidy war, leading to a welfare loss for both countries (and a welfare gain for the third country).

11.8.4 Informational requirements

From a practical point of view, the most important objection to the ideas underlying strategic trade policy is the enormous amount of information required to carry out such a policy, certainly if the above objections are taken into consideration. Even in the partial equilibrium framework, the American government must gather information about the production structures of the home and foreign firms, about market demand in the third country, about the type of competition in the industry (Cournot or Bertrand), and about the interaction between firms. Then it must accurately undertake detailed calculations to determine the optimal policy. If it makes a mistake, either in the scale or the direction of the policy, national income will fall rather than rise. In a more general setting, it must gather all of this information not only for the countries directly involved in this sector, but for all countries, all sectors, and all firms in the world. It must determine the nature of competition for all these sectors and countries, it must correctly weigh and calculate the benefits of taxing or subsidizing each sector, and it must correctly predict and evaluate the response for all sectors by governments from all countries in the world. Needless to say, all of this is quite impossible. Making mistakes along the way will reduce, rather than increase, national income. Moreover, it is evident that the entire process of gathering and processing so much information would put a claim on real resources that could have been used to produce goods and services.

11.9 The aircraft industry: from AB to ABC?

The civil aircraft industry is a prime example of an industry characterized by increasing returns to scale.[6] Kenneth Arrow (1962), for example, cites the empirical regularity that after a new aeroplane design has been introduced, the time required to build the frame of the marginal aircraft is inversely proportional to the cube root of the number of aeroplanes of that model that have already been built. The aircraft industry is also a prime example of an industry that has been (mis)used for strategic trade policy reasons.

In view of the importance of economies of scale in the production process (attributed to learning-by-doing effects), large companies enjoy a vital competitive advantage as they are able to produce and sell a large number of aircraft. At the same time, the development and implementation of a newly designed type of aeroplane is extremely costly, as will be described, which makes it doubly difficult to enter the market. In the late 1960s Boeing invented the 747 jumbo jet and the European politicians were worried that the big three American firms (Boeing, McDonnell Douglas, and Lockheed), which enjoyed the benefit of a huge home market, would close down the smaller and divided European industry, so they joined forces and began to pour government money into the Airbus group, a consortium with four parent companies (France's Aérospatiale, Germany's Daimler-Benz Aerospace, British Aerospace, and CASA of Spain).

For a long time it looked like money down the drain. Eventually, however, Airbus group has become successful enough to present the only challenge to Boeing's dominance (Lockheed stopped producing civil aircraft in 1981 and McDonnell Douglas has merged with Boeing). Over the years, the battle between Boeing and Airbus has caused heated disputes between the American and European governments. The Americans see the struggle as a battle against subsidized competition, while the Europeans are fighting the American hegemony in a 'strategic' industry and argue that Boeing's aircraft are subsidized indirectly by the American defence budget. As *The Economist* (1997) put it: 'Any account of the civil-aircraft industry must begin with the caveat that it has never had free and fair competition. The civil-aircraft industry is the most politicised in the world—apart from the defence industry, to which it is joined at the hip.' A striking example occurred shortly after the Gulf War when the newly installed American president Bill Clinton called King Fahd of Saudi Arabia, urging him to buy $12 billion worth of Boeing and McDonnell Douglas aircraft (rather than Airbuses) made in the country that saved his hide. He did.

There have been two major attempts to force Boeing and Airbus to fight purely commercial battles. First, there was a special section written in the GATT's Tokyo Round in

1979, forbidding uneconomic pricing for airliners: see Chapter 10. Second, there was a bilateral European–American deal in 1992 limiting 'launch aid' (money to help develop a new model) to 33 per cent of the total development costs, to be repaid with interest within 17 years. This put an end to most existing arguments on subsidized aircraft, opening up new problems for the super-jumbo market instead.

For decades Airbus looked enviously at Boeing's 747 jumbo jets, which represented a very lucrative share of the civil aircraft market, where Boeing holds a monopoly. As *The Economist* (1997) put it: 'Boeing's jumbo jet has been a licence to print money: the company makes $45m on each of the $150m jets that it produces.' Since Boeing realized that Airbus was keen to develop an alternative to its ageing 747 jumbo jet, it came up with a rather successful delaying tactic in 1992 by starting talks with the four parent companies of Airbus about jointly developing a huge super-jumbo (to carry around 800 passengers). In 1995 the cooperation fell apart and Airbus started in earnest to develop the A380, as a (larger) direct competitor for the 747. The total development costs for the A380 were about $10 billion, of which, in line with the 1992 agreement, the European governments financed 33 per cent.

The first flight of the A380 was in 2005 and, thanks to several delays, the first delivery to launch customer Singapore Airlines was in 2007. By 2015, revenue from the new aircraft was still hardly able to cover its production costs, let alone recover the development costs. On 30 June 2010 the World Trade Organization (WTO) ruled on an American complaint that Airbus received illegal subsidies by concluding that some of the repayable 'launch aid' was illegal. A few months later, the WTO ruled that Boeing had also received illegal hand-outs, in the form of subsidies channelled through the Department of Defence and NASA.[7] Unless the EU and the USA come to some negotiated agreement, these mutual claims on illegal subsidies and intermediate WTO victories are likely to continue, primarily at the benefit of lawyers's pockets.

The global market for full-sized commercial planes is enormous. In 2015 it was predicted to be around $4,600 billion for the period 2015–2035 (*The Economist*, 2015). No wonder other companies would like to enter this market. Some rather unsuccessful attempts were made by Bombardier of Canada and Irkut of Russia, the latter with considerable government support. One reason for this lack of success is the enormous development costs for new planes. After Airbus decided to develop the A380, Boeing started to develop the 787 Dreamliner from scratch. The estimated research and development costs are about $28 billion. For that reason alone the duopoly has long remained a duopoly. This may change, however, in the near future. China has been working hard to break into this market with a state-owned plane maker. This competitor for the Airbus A320 and Boeing 737 (the two most popular planes in the sky) is labelled C919; it is scheduled to have its maiden flight in 2016 and to go into service in 2019. The Chinese government conveniently named the company COMAC, such that if successful we will go from AB (Airbus–Boeing) competition to ABC (Airbus–Boeing–Comac) competition. *The Economist* doubts whether COMAC will be successful in view of the costs and demanding technical specifications involved. My feeling is that this is the only firm likely to break the duopoly: the Chinese domestic market is enormous, China's technical capabilities are rapidly improving, and the Chinese government is probably the only government in the world for which $28 billion in development costs is no problem at all.

11.10 Conclusions

First, we provided an overview of the main types of WTO trade disputes, as well as the main countries involved as either respondent, complainant, or third party. We then analysed the heterogeneity of these disputes, with on the one hand a substantial share focusing on rather small trade flows (less than $1 million, which makes one wonder if the dispute is worth the litigation costs) and on the other hand a substantial share focusing on rather large trade flows (more than $1 billion). When the dispute involves a new policy, we find that on average the complainant seems to have been negatively affected by this policy. Here again, however, the heterogeneity is large.

Second, we analysed the impact of trade policy in a world characterized by imperfect competition. Tariffs and quantitative restrictions are no longer equivalent. The imposition of tariffs in general leaves the forces of foreign competition intact, albeit at a lower level. This contrasts with the imposition of quantitative limitations, which restrict more severely the strategic possibilities of foreign firms. It is therefore generally acknowledged that quotas are more restrictive than tariffs, which is one of the main reasons for the World Trade Organization to strive for 'tariffication' (the other being the clarity of the imposed trade restrictions).

Third, and finally, we discussed the so-called strategic trade policy, which tries to provide a competitive advantage to domestic firms by providing a credible pre-commitment. When evaluating the potential for this type of strategic trade policy we emphasized its weakness in a general equilibrium setting, the fragility of policy recommendations (type of strategic interactions, who moves first, strategic games, etc.), and most importantly from a practical perspective the enormous informational requirements for accurately carrying out such a policy.

 Technical Notes

Technical Note 11.1 The Brander–Spencer model

The American firm produces quantity q_A and the British firm produces quantity q_B. This production is exported to a third country, with price p and a linear demand curve:

$$p = a - b(q_A + q_B) \tag{11.A1}$$

Both firms have marginal production costs c, but the American government may give a production subsidy s per unit to the American firm. The profit functions π are therefore:

$$\pi_A = pq_A - (c-s)q_A \text{ and } \pi_B = pq_B - cq_B \tag{11.A2}$$

Both firms maximize profits taking the output level of the other firm as given, which leads to the following reaction curves (see Chapter 7):

$$\text{firm } A: q_B = \frac{(a-c+s)}{b} - 2q_A \text{ and firm } B: q_B = \frac{(a-c)}{2b} - \frac{q_A}{2} \tag{11.A3}$$

The intersection of the two reaction curves determines the equilibrium:

$$q_A = \frac{(a-c+2s)}{3b} \text{ and } q_B = \frac{(a-c-s)}{3b} \tag{11.A4}$$

Taking the British firm's reaction curve into consideration, the American government now has to decide how high the subsidy s should be. The government's objective is to maximize the American firm's profits minus the subsidy it pays:

$$\pi_A - sq_A = pq_A - cq_A \tag{11.A5}$$

Note that this is equivalent to maximizing the American firm's profits net of subsidies. The American government should therefore ensure that the British firm's reaction curve is tangent to the American firm's isoprofit curve net of subsidies, as illustrated in Figure 11.9. Note that for a given profit level $\bar{\pi}_A$ the American firm's isoprofit curve net of subsidies is given by all combinations q_A and q_B such that

$$(p-c)q_A = (a-c-bq_B)q_A - bq_A^2 = \bar{\pi}_A, \text{ so } q_B = \frac{a-c}{b} - q_A - \frac{\bar{\pi}_A}{bq_A} \tag{11.A6}$$

The slope of an isoprofit curve is therefore $-1 + \bar{\pi}_A / bq_A^2$. Setting this equal to $-1/2$, the slope of the British firm's reaction curve gives: $\bar{\pi}_A = bq_A^2 / 2$. Substitute this in the equation equalizing the American firm's isoprofits and the British firm's reaction curve:

$$\frac{(a-c)}{2b} - \frac{q_A}{2} = \frac{(a-c)}{b} - q_A - \frac{\bar{\pi}_A}{bq_A} = \frac{(a-c)}{b} - q_A - \frac{bq_A^2 / 2}{bq_A} \tag{11.A7}$$

Solving this equation in q_A and substituting for the other variables in the other equations determines the Brander–Spencer optimum:

$$q_A = \frac{(a-c)}{2b}; q_B = \frac{(a-c)}{4b}; s = \frac{(a-c)}{4}; \bar{\pi}_A = \frac{(a-c)^2}{8b} \tag{11.A8}$$

Technical Note 11.2 The Eaton–Grossman model

We discuss a simple version of this model, in which an American firm and a British firm export to a third market and compete in prices, rather than quantities. The goods produced by the two firms are imperfect substitutes for one another, in which the demand for the good rises if the other firm raises its price. Naturally, the own price effect is negative. Taking linear demand curves and constant marginal costs c, we get:

$$q_A = a - p_A + p_B; \quad q_B = a - p_B + p_A \tag{11.A9}$$

$$\pi_A = (p_A - c)q_A; \quad \pi_B = (p_B - c)q_B \tag{11.A10}$$

The remainder of this Technical Note follows the procedure of Technical Note 11.1. Maximizing profits, taking the competitor's price as given, leads to a firm's reaction curve in (p_A, p_B)-space. The intersection of the reaction curves gives the Bertrand equilibrium:

$$p_A = p_B = a + c \tag{11.A11}$$

The American government, strategically maximizing domestic welfare, will decide to *tax* the production of the American firm, leading to the Eaton–Grossman equilibrium:

$$p_A = \frac{3a}{2} + c; p_B = \frac{5a}{4} + c; \bar{\pi}_A = \frac{9a^2}{8}; tax = \frac{3a}{4} \tag{11.A12}$$

Notes

1   There is no statistically significant difference for the reported per cent changes between high-income and low-income countries as complainants. As respondents, however, the average per cent change is significantly more negative for volume for high-income countries and for market share for low-income countries.

2   It is not explained why the market structure at home and abroad is different.

3   We will argue in Chapter 17 that estimates of the benefits of reducing obstacles to trade, as presented in this box, substantially *under*estimate the true cost of trade restrictions.

4   From your microeconomics course you may recognize this as the equilibrium that results if the American firm is the Stackelberg leader.

5   With homogeneous goods, Bertrand price competition would drive the price down to marginal costs, leaving no possibility of strategically transferring profits and effectively eliminating market power.

6   The information in this section is based on *The Economist* (1997, 2000, 2001, 2015).

7   See *The Economist*, 16 September 2010, 'Another nose in the trough'.

 Questions

Question 11.1

The rapid economic growth in China is accompanied by rapid growth in air travel, creating opportunities for Boeing (an American firm) and Airbus (a European firm) to sell their planes in China. We use the Cournot framework as in the Brander–Spencer model for our analysis. Figure 11.11 gives possible reaction curves and isoprofit curves for both Airbus and Boeing.

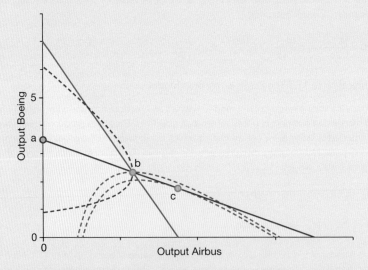

Figure 11.11 Possible reaction curves and isoprofit curves for both Airbus and Boeing.

a. Make clear for each of the different curves in Figure 11.11 if it is a reaction curve or an isoprofit curve and to which of the two firms it belongs. Where is the Cournot equilibrium (or Cournot–Nash equilibrium) without government intervention? Explain.

b. Suppose that the European Commission (EC) would like to give Airbus a strategic advantage in China. It therefore gives an optimal (total welfare-maximizing) subsidy for every airplane Airbus sells to China. What does the EC do and how does it affect the curves in your figure? Explain.

Question 11.2

We could also imagine that Airbus and Boeing (see Question 11.1) are competing with each other in a Bertrand framework (price competition), rather than a Cournot framework (quantity competition). Again the European Commission wants to stimulate the sales of Airbus in China.

a. Draw the reaction curves and some isoprofit curves for both Airbus and Boeing in a Bertrand framework. Put the price of an Airbus aircraft on the horizontal axis and the price of a Boeing aircraft on the vertical axis.

b. Should the European Commission subsidize or tax the aircraft Airbus sells to China? Draw the new situation in the figure when the European Commission optimally employs the instrument. How does the price demanded for aircraft change for both Airbus and Boeing?

c. What will the US government think of the EU policy?

d. Explain whether the Cournot or Bertrand framework is more appropriate to analyse competition between Airbus and Boeing.

Question 11.3

Table 11.2 X = Policies affecting rice prices, 2007–2013.

	Tariffs of 15% or more	Import subsidies	Minimum farm price	Consumer subsidies	Export restrictions	Gov't trading	Gov't stockpiling	Import restrictions
Cambodia		X			X	X		
China	X	X	X			X	X	X
India	X	X	X	X	X	X	X	
Indonesia	X	X	X	X	X	X	X	X
Myanmar		X			X			
Pakistan		X				X		
Philippines	X		X	X		X	X	X
Thailand		X	X		X		X	
Vietnam	X	X	X		X	X	X	

Source: USITC.

Rice is extremely important for Asian countries. The information in Table 11.2 is taken from *The Economist*, 14 November 2015. It depicts information on intervention in the domestic rice market for a range of Asian countries for eight different types of policies. Indonesia, for example, uses all eight policies for its rice market, while Pakistan uses only two policies (import subsidies and government trading). China uses six policies; all *except* consumer subsidies and export restrictions.

Choose *one* of the nine countries listed in the table and write a brief *essay* regarding the *economic and policy implications* of this country's intervention in the rice market relative to the eight other countries and possibly non-listed countries. Give brief associated *advice to the government* of your country regarding rice market intervention.

 *See the **online resources** for a Study Guide and questions:* www.oup.com/uk/vanmarrewijk_it/

12 Regional trade agreements

◎ Objectives

- To know that the number of regional trade agreements (RTAs) has risen rapidly since 1993.
- To understand that this rise is hard to grasp from a tariff-based preferential perspective.
- To appreciate the complicated nature of current RTAs, involving many different competition issues.
- To be aware of some of the most important RTAs in different parts of the world.
- To know the main types of RTAs, understand the evolution of these types over time, and understand the scale from shallow integration to deep integration.
- To understand the link between the increasing RTA activity of developing and emerging markets and global supply chains.
- To appreciate the heterogeneity of RTAs in terms of coverage and the implications this has for policy analysis.
- To know the most important welfare effects of RTAs and understand the difference between trade creation and trade diversion.
- To understand how the popularity of RTAs (regionalism) might be welfare-reducing in a new trade theory analysis.
- To know the main steps in the development of the European Union (EU), the four freedoms, and the main institutions of the EU.
- To have an idea of the enlargement process of the EU (from 6 to 28 countries), the diversity of its member states, and the size of the EU relative to powerful nations.
- To have an understanding of the possible consequences of the UK leaving the EU (Brexit).
- To understand how we can analyse the hypothetical impact of a proposed new RTA, such as the Transatlantic Trade and Investment Partnership (TTIP) between the EU and the US.

12.1 Introduction

There are many regional trade agreements (RTAs) in the world, whereby countries give each other's products preferential treatment in their markets.[1] Important examples are the North American Free Trade Agreement (NAFTA), which involves Canada, Mexico, and the USA, and the European Union (EU), which involves 28 different European nations. Because an

RTA gives preferential treatment to the members of the agreement, but not equal treatment to non-members as would be in line with the most favoured nation (MFN) clause of the WTO, any such agreement violates the non-discrimination principle of the WTO. As explained in Chapter 10, however, RTAs can be exempted from the non-discrimination principle, either because a move towards uninhibited trade flows among a group of countries is seen as a step in the right direction of free trade, or because a preferential trade agreement provides an impulse to the growth and development process of less developed countries.

According to Maggi (2014) there are two main motives for governments to sign trade agreements. First, they can provide governments with an escape from an international prisoners' dilemma which is caused by international externalities from trade policy. These include the terms-of-trade externalities discussed in Chapter 10 and the new trade (imperfect competition) externalities discussed in Chapter 11. Second, it can provide governments with a commitment device relative to domestic agents, such as lobby groups and big investors. According to Whalley (1998), this commitment played a central role in Mexico's negotiations of the North American Free Trade Agreement (NAFTA). According to Bajona and Chu (2010), China's accession to the WTO should be viewed as a method of locking in the agenda for fundamental domestic reforms.

We start our discussion by describing the development of the number of RTAs (Section 12.2), the differences between the main types of RTAs (Section 12.3), and an indication regarding the many different topics covered by RTAs, including export taxes, the movement of capital, services, state aid, and so on (Section 12.4). The diversity in the types of RTAs makes us realize there is a sliding scale from 'shallow integration' to 'deep integration'. Next we turn to the main theories of the economic impact of RTAs, in which trade creation and trade diversion as developed by Jacob Viner (see Box 12.1 and Section 12.5) play an important role. We also analyse the impact of the abundance of RTAs, the so-called 'regionalism', in a new trade framework (Section 12.6). We continue by discussing the development and main institutions of the EU, the world's most influential RTA, in Sections 12.7 and 12.8. We analyse the possible first cracks in the EU framework after the inhabitants of the UK voted to leave the EU (the decision known as Brexit) in Section 12.9. We conclude the chapter with a case study on the potential implementation of the

---

BOX 12.1 Jacob Viner

Born in Montreal, Canada, of Romanian immigrant parents, Jacob Viner was, according to Mark Blaug (1985, p. 256), 'a leading interwar price and trade theorist and quite simply the greatest historian of economic thought that ever lived'. He received his PhD in 1915 at Harvard University, having written his dissertation under the supervision of Frank Taussig, and worked at the University of Chicago, where he became editor of the *Journal of Political Economy*, before moving to Princeton in 1946. Viner's *Studies in the Theory of International Trade* (1937) provides the basis for much of our current views and knowledge on the history

Figure 12.1
Jacob Viner (1892–1970).

(continued...)

of international economics, particularly on the pre-scientific fallacies of the mercantilists in the seventeenth and eighteenth centuries. In 1950 Viner wrote *The Customs Union Issue*, identifying the trade-creation and trade-diversion effects, which became the basis for all subsequent work on RTAs.

Transatlantic Trade and Investment Partnership (TTIP), an RTA between the EU and the US, in Section 12.10.

12.2 Number of RTAs

The WTO allows regional trade agreements (RTAs)—despite the fact that they violate the most favoured nation (MFN) principle—as they view each new agreement as a step towards further free trade. Looking at the number of existing RTAs, this policy could be considered a success. As Figure 12.2 indicates, the number of RTAs increased rapidly from the 1990s onward and the total number of RTAs—as acknowledged by the WTO—is now close to 300; the average number of RTAs that a typical WTO member is part of is around 13. The WTO calculated that the share of intra-RTA trade in world trade increased from 18 per cent in 1990 to 38 per cent in 2008 (in terms of exports). As of 28 June 2016 the total number of RTAs still in force as notified to the WTO is 280. Figure 12.2 shows that their number has increased rapidly since about 1993 (from fewer than 30). One of the longest still active agreements is the EC Treaty, which entered into force on 24 April 1957: nearly 60 years at the time of writing. However, the average agreement that is still active has been in force for about 13 years and the median agreement 10.5 years. Figure 12.2 also provides an indication regarding the extent to which the European Union (EU) and the United States (US) are involved in the active RTAs, by date of entry into force. It shows that both countries were involved early on in active RTAs. As a consequence the average duration of the active RTAs for the US is almost twice as long as the average and for the EU more than four times as long.

Figure 10.6 already illustrated that the WTO, in combination with country initiatives, has been successful in lowering average tariff levels around the world. As explained above, one of the most visible direct effects of an RTA is to give preferential treatment to participating countries. The question then arises why RTAs have become so popular since the 1990s, as illustrated in Figure 12.2, since the preferential treatment of participating countries in terms of tariff levels is declining over time. For advanced countries in particular the imposed tariffs on a large range of products is zero per cent, so there is little room for preferential treatment from a tariff perspective. This argument is illustrated in Figure 12.3, which provides estimates of the de facto margin of preference, which is the difference between the tariff applied to imports from RTA partners as opposed to non-RTA partners, for a large range of countries. Panel a. of Figure 12.3 illustrates this for the EU (both internally and externally), the USA, China, and Japan, and panel b. for Korea, Canada, Mexico, Singapore, and Taiwan. For all countries (except for Mexico and the EU internally) the share of imports for which the margin of preference is actually zero exceeds 60 per cent

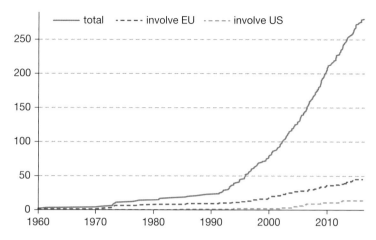

Figure 12.2 Number of RTAs still in force in 2016, by date of entry into force.

Source: based on WTO data, 28 June 2016.

of all imports. For a modest share of imports the margin of preference is in the positive-but-lower-than-5-per-cent range. The share for which the margin of preference is higher than 10 per cent or 20 per cent is very low for all countries, except Mexico. To understand why signing RTAs has become so popular despite these small margins of preference we take a closer look at the type of RTAs that have been negotiated on in the twenty-first century.

We discuss the European Union, arguably the world's strongest RTA, separately in Section 12.7. The remainder of this section briefly reviews important RTAs in the rest of the world.

12.2.1 Africa

The most important regional trade agreement in Africa is the Common Market for Eastern and Southern Africa (COMESA), which was established in December 1994 and replaced a former preferential trade area that had been operative since 1981. Egypt and Ethiopia are the most populous nations, while oil-rich Libya and tourist-attractive Egypt (at least until the terrorist attack in 2015) are the largest trading nations. COMESA's task is to promote peace and security in the region and enhance economic prosperity through economic integration. It is therefore implementing a free trade area, and it is planning to introduce a common external tariff schedule for third parties.

12.2.2 Asia

The most important regional trade agreement in Asia is the Association of South-East Asian Nations (ASEAN), established by five countries in 1967, but currently consisting of ten countries. The ASEAN countries work together in several areas (political, economic, cultural, and social). Indonesia is by far the most populous nation of ASEAN, followed by the Philippines and Vietnam. The small city-state of Singapore, on the other hand, is the largest trading nation of ASEAN, followed by Thailand and Malaysia.

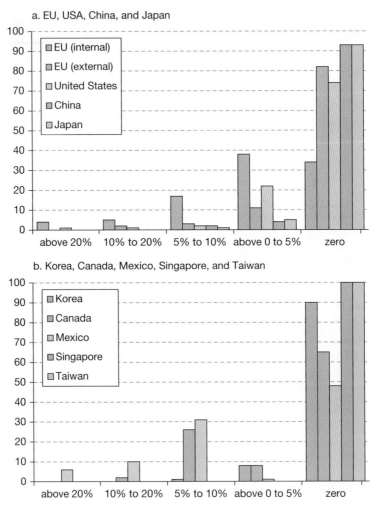

Figure 12.3 Share of imports according to margin of preference (per cent), 2008.

Source: based on data from Baldwin (2014) and Brakman et al. (2015).

12.2.3 The Americas

The American continents have been very active in the formation of regional trade agreements, starting with Latin America in the 1950s. In the drive towards industrialization by import substitution, and realizing that for many countries in the region the domestic market was too small to allow for efficient production, regional free trade agreements were set up to increase the size of the local market. This resulted in, for example, the Central American Common Market (CACM), the Caribbean Community (CARICOM), the Andean Pact (ANDEAN), and the Mercado Commun del Sur (MERCOSUR), although some of these agreements were not energetically implemented. In North America, the agreements started in 1965 with the USA–Canada Auto Pact, involving tariff-free trade in motor vehicles and parts. A few years later the maquiladores in Mexico, processing or assembling parts imported from the USA and subsequently exported to the USA, started to expand and develop, in part because import duties were only charged on the value added and not on the total value. After some years of negotiations these three countries, Canada, Mexico, and the USA, launched the North American Free Trade Agreement (NAFTA).

12.3 Types of RTAs

The WTO provides information on four main types of RTAs, namely, in order of increasing economic integration: (i) partial scope agreements, (ii) free trade areas, (iii) customs unions, and (iv) economic integration agreements. Figure 12.4 shows that from the 1990s there was a sharp rise in the number of free trade areas. Since the new millennium, however, there has been a sharp increase in the more complicated and more detailed economic integration agreements. Modern RTAs therefore look beyond margins of preference towards other important aspects.

Issues that play a role in the deeper EIAs include, for example, customs, export taxes, the movement of capital, trade in services, state aid, state trading enterprises, intellectual property rights, technical barriers to trade, competition policy, and so on. Baldwin argues that the changes over time in the prevalent types of RTAs reflect the developments in global supply chains (see Chapter 15), which requires (i) coordinating internationally dispersed facilities (a continuous two-way flow of goods, people, ideas, and investments) and (ii) producing abroad (limiting exposure to international risks for capital and technical, managerial, and marketing know-how; Baldwin, 2014). As a consequence of these changes, the role of developing and emerging markets in global supply chains is increasingly reflected in the number of RTAs, as illustrated in Figure 12.5. The new entrants in the 1990s mainly involved developing nations and least developed countries (LDCs). This has set the stage for an explosion in the number of trade agreements involving advanced and developing countries and also involving only developing countries. Interestingly, the relative decrease

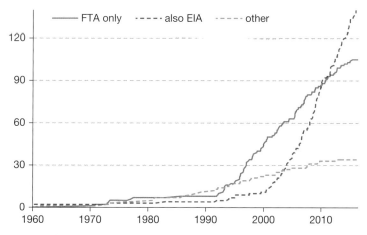

Figure 12.4 Numbers of RTAs still in force in 2016: by type and date of entry into force (FTA = free trade area; EIA = economic integration agreement).

Notes: FTA = Free Trade Area; EIA = Economic Integration Agreements.

Source: based on WTO data, 28 June 2016.

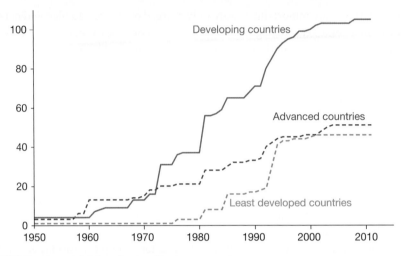

Figure 12.5 Development status of regional trade agreements.

Source: Brakman et al. (2015); labels based on World Bank classification.

in agreements between advanced countries suggests that these agreements have been expanded to include developing members. However, plurilateral agreements with members from all levels of development are scarce, as are agreements between advanced countries and LDCs.

To summarize: we find that the period leading up to the 1990s can be characterized by intra-regional agreements that are plurilateral in nature and that involve mainly advanced countries. Since the 1990s, the picture has become much more complex. Some countries are engaged in several agreements of various sizes; others have only one or two agreements. Although plurilateral agreements are growing, approximately 60 per cent of all trade agreements are bilateral. With almost all countries having had at least a small taste of having a trade agreement, trade agreements are becoming more diverse in terms of their participants' development status.

12.4 Shallow versus deep integration and RTA heterogeneity

Trade agreements can include much more than just simple border measures (such as tariffs) by also including objectives related to political economy considerations: for example, agreements on intellectual property rights, investment policies, product standards, competition policies, dispute settlements, and so on. This is now part of a growing body of literature in which 'shallow integration', usually referring to border measures only, is distinguished from 'deep integration', which affects not only border measures but also domestic policies. Table 12.1 illustrates the sliding scale from shallow to deep integration by distinguishing between six different types of agreements, namely:

FTA ↔ FTA + ↔ Customs Union ↔ Common Market ↔ Monetary Union ↔ Fiscal Union

Empirical evidence indeed shows that the extent to which RTAs affect trade flows is related to the type of agreement: deeper integration agreements yield stronger trade-promoting effects (Baier et al., 2014).

Recent trade studies go one step further by emphasizing the heterogeneity of trade agreements within the types of RTAs distinguished in Table 12.1, particularly regarding non-tariff measures. A customs union, for example, may or may not involve provisions regarding competition policy, sanitary measures, and so on; the same may be the case for an FTA+ agreement. Figure 12.6 illustrates the extent of variation in coverage for a sample of 96 RTAs regarding measures that go beyond simple tariff measures. Almost all RTAs (more than 60 per cent of the agreements) include aspects of customs and export taxes. A substantial share of RTAs (between 40 and 60 per cent of the agreements) include the movement of capital, services, state aid, state trading enterprises, intellectual property rights, investment, technical barriers to trade, and competition policy. Aspects of minor importance (between 10 and 40 per cent of the agreements) include sanitary measures, visas and asylum, labour market regulation, environmental laws, and social matters. Other matters such as terrorism and cultural cooperation are included in only a few agreements.

A more detailed description (using three groups of agreements) is provided in Table 12.2 (Kohl et al., 2015). It is based on a dataset of 296 trade agreements for the period 1948–2011 and accounts for 26 trade-related policy domains. It distinguishes between provisions that *can* and *cannot* be considered to be legally enforceable commitments in a court of (international) law. The trade agreement data are from the World Bank's Global Preferential Trade Agreements Database.

- The first group of agreements consists of the so-called WTO$^+$ provisions that are within the current mandate of the WTO. Among the provisions are agriculture, anti-dumping and countervailing measures, customs administration, export restrictions, import restrictions, intellectual property rights, investment, public procurement, sanitary and phytosanitary measures, services, state aid, state trading enterprises, and technical barriers to trade.

Table 12.1 Shallow versus deep integration

Level	Type of RTA	Features	Example
Shallow integration	Free trade agreement (FTA)	Members liberalize internal trade but retain independent external tariffs	US–Israel FTA
	FTA+	An FTA that harmonizes some beyond-border standards (e.g. environmental standards)	NAFTA
	Customs union	Members liberalize trade within the union and adapt common external tariff against rest of world	SACU
	Common market	Establishment of free movement of all factors of production within the RTA including labour and capital	EU
	Monetary union	Establishment of a common currency and completely integrated monetary and exchange rate policy	Euro area
Deep integration	Fiscal union	Establishment of a common fiscal policy	US

Source: WTO (2011), *World Trade Report 2011*, WTO, Geneva, p. 110.

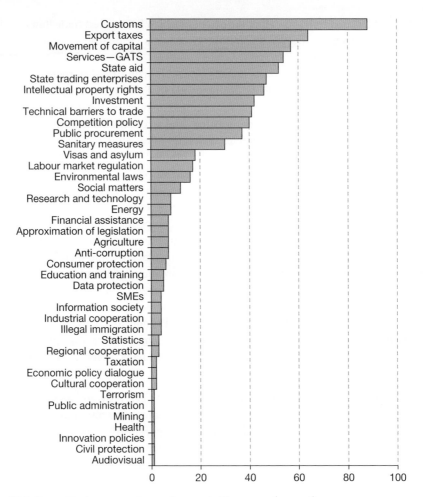

Figure 12.6 Share of trade agreements covering non-tariff measures (per cent).

Notes: GATS = General Agreement on Trade in Services; SMEs = small and medium-sized enterprises; sanitary measures include phyto-sanitary measures.

Source: based on data from World Trade Report (2014, Table C9).

- The second group of policy areas is not yet part of WTO negotiations and labelled WTO$^\times$ provisions: capital mobility, competition, environment, and labour.
- The third group of provisions relate to institutional quality (IQ). These describe how an agreement should be implemented and enforced and, for example, refer to information about consultations, definitions, dispute settlement, duration and termination, an evolutionary clause, an institutional framework, objectives, plan and schedule, and transparency.

An important conclusion from this categorization of RTAs is that there is significant variation in their composition. Table 12.2 shows that 292 out of 296 trade agreements provide

Table 12.2 Characterization of provisions: coverage and legal enforceability

Type	Provision	(1) Number covered	(2) Number enforceable	(3) Sample covered (%)	(4) Sample enforceable (%)	(2)/(1) (%)
WTO+	Agriculture	189	188	64	64	99
	Anti-dumping and countervailing measures	220	217	74	73	99
	Customs administration	216	214	73	72	99
	Export restrictions	256	256	86	86	100
	Import restrictions	292	292	99	99	100
	Intellectual property rights	191	180	65	61	94
	Investment	162	85	55	29	52
	Public procurement	172	103	58	35	60
	Sanitary and phytosanitary measures	182	163	61	55	90
	Services	168	86	57	29	51
	State aid	190	187	64	63	98
	State trading enterprises	162	149	55	50	92
	Technical barriers to trade (TBT)	187	138	63	47	74
WTO×	Capital mobility	212	212	72	72	100
	Competition	209	181	71	61	87
	Environment	89	66	30	22	74
	Labour	48	43	16	15	90

(Continued)

Table 12.2 *Continued*

Type	Provision	(1) Number covered	(2) Number enforceable	(3) Sample covered (%)	(4) Sample enforceable (%)	(2)/(1) (%)
IQ*	Consultations	238	238	80	80	100
	Definitions	152	152	51	51	100
	Dispute settlement	242	242	82	82	100
	Duration and termination	218	218	74	74	100
	Evolutionary clause	235	235	79	79	100
	Institutional framework	273	273	92	92	100
	Objectives	267	267	90	90	100
	Plan and schedule	128	128	43	43	100
	Transparency	162	162	55	55	100

Note: *IQ = institutional quality.
Source: Kohl et al. (2015).

some coverage of commitments on import restrictions, while only 48 agreements deal with labour issues. Columns (2) and (4) refer to provisions that are legally enforceable. Countries make legally enforceable commitments on export restrictions in 256 out of 296 agreements while only half of the agreements make credible commitments on state trading enterprises. Column (5) shows the share of provisions that are legally enforceable, conditional on the provision being covered in a trade agreement. Note that the provisions on institutional quality always have a score of 100 per cent in column (5) because these provisions are 'strong' commitments by definition.

Many of the items listed in Table 12.2 deal with barriers to trade in different ways. It can be expected that they also affect trade in different ways or intensity. A number of scholars have started opening this black box of RTA heterogeneity (Horn et al., 2010, and Orefice and Rocha, 2014). These studies account for heterogeneity in the design of particular RTAs, such as provisions on dispute settlement, investment, services, or trade remedies. Indicative findings from this literature tell us that recognizing the design of trade agreements is necessary and that describing participation in an RTA using a simple binary variable no longer seems sufficient.

12.5 Neoclassical theory of RTAs

Jacob Viner (1950) provided the first rigorous analysis of the ways in which a customs union can affect trade flows and resource allocations. He identified trade-creation and trade-diversion effects, as will be discussed in this section, and argued that if trade creation is dominant, the customs union raises welfare for the members of the customs union and world welfare. The main consequences of economic integration in a partial equilibrium framework are illustrated in Figure 12.7 and Figure 12.8, depicting the demand and supply schedule for a specific good for the USA. We assume that the USA is a small country on the world market. There are two possible import sources, the UK and China. The price for the good in the UK is equal to p_B; in China it is equal to p_C. We also assume that the USA initially imposes a specific tariff T on imports of the good from both the UK and China. We analyse the impact of economic integration if the USA decides to form a customs union with the UK, in which case the specific tariff T for imports from the UK is eliminated. Relative to China, for which the tariff is still in place, the UK therefore gets preferential treatment within the customs union with the USA.

12.5.1 Customs union with the most efficient producer: trade creation

Figure 12.7 depicts what happens if the UK is a more efficient producer than China, in which case p_B is lower than p_C. Before the formation of the customs union, the USA imports $q_{in}^d - q_{in}^s$ goods from the UK ('in' for initial), and the price in the USA is equal to $p_B + T$. After the formation of the customs union, the tariff T between the USA and the UK is eliminated, such that the price in America falls to p_B, quantity demanded increases from q_{in}^d to q_{cu}^d ('cu' for customs union), quantity domestically supplied falls from q_{in}^s to q_{cu}^s, and imports from the UK rise from $q_{in}^d - q_{in}^s$ to $q_{cu}^d - q_{cu}^s$, hence the term trade creation.

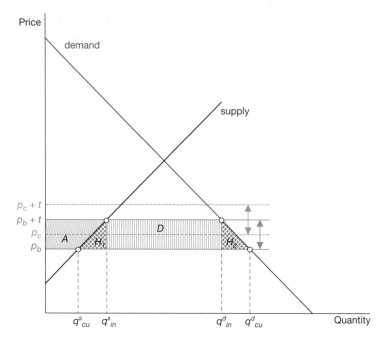

Figure 12.7 Customs union and welfare I: trade creation.

- Welfare for the producers in the USA, as measured by producer surplus, falls by area A in Figure 12.7.
- Welfare for the government in the USA, as measured by government revenue, decreases by the area D in Figure 12.7.
- Welfare for the consumers in the USA, as measured by consumer surplus, increases by the area $A + H_1 + D_1 + H_2$ in Figure 12.7.
- The net welfare effect for this particular good is therefore a gain for the USA equal to the area $H_1 + H_2$ in Figure 12.7.

12.5.2 Customs union with an inefficient producer: trade diversion

Figure 12.8 depicts what might happen if the UK is a less efficient producer than China, in which case p_B is *higher* than p_C. Before the formation of the customs union, the USA imports $q_{in}^d - q_{in}^s$ goods from China, the more efficient producer, and the price in the USA is equal to $p_C + T$. After the formation of the customs union, the tariff T between the USA and the UK is eliminated. Since imports from China are still subject to the tariff T and p_B is lower than $p_C + T$, this implies that the price falls from $p_C + T$ to p_B, quantity demanded increases from q_{in}^d to q_{cu}^d, quantity domestically supplied falls from q_{in}^s to q_{cu}^s, and imports rise from $q_{in}^d - q_{in}^s$ to $q_{cu}^d - q_{cu}^s$. As we saw above, this results in positive welfare effects through trade creation. This time, however, there is a second, negative welfare effect operative, called trade diversion. Since the customs union with the USA gives the UK preferential treatment, the USA

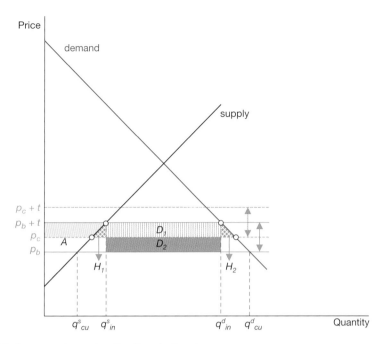

Figure 12.8 Customs union and welfare II: trade diversion.

now starts to import goods from the UK rather than from China: that is, trade is diverted from the more efficient producer to the less efficient producer.

- Welfare for the producers in the USA, as measured by producer surplus, falls by the area A in Figure 12.8.
- Welfare for the government in the USA, as measured by government revenue, decreases by the area $D_1 + D_2$ in Figure 12.8. Note that this area consists of two parts: part D_1 performs the same role as area D in Figure 12.7 and benefits domestic consumers, while part D_2 benefits foreign producers.
- Welfare for the consumers in the USA, as measured by consumer surplus, increases by the area $A + H_1 + D_1 + H_2$ in Figure 12.8.
- The net welfare effect for this particular good for the USA could either be positive or negative; it is equal to the area $H_1 + H_2$ minus the area D_2 in Figure 12.8.

12.5.3 The welfare effects of a customs union: general equilibrium

In the above partial equilibrium analysis, the positive welfare effects arise from the Harberger triangles measuring the efficiency gains from trade creation. The negative welfare effects arise from the reallocation of resources from the more efficient to the less efficient producer as a result of trade diversion. As mentioned above, Jacob Viner therefore argued that the net welfare effect of creating a customs union is positive if the trade-creation effects dominate the trade-diversion effects. The potential positive welfare benefits of the formation of a customs union, which after all eliminates artificial barriers to trade, was convincingly demonstrated by Murray Kemp and Henry Wan Jr (1976).

Proposition 12.1 Kemp–Wan: customs union

Consider any competitive world trading equilibrium with a neoclassical production structure, with any number of countries and commodities, with no restrictions whatever on the tariffs and other commodity taxes of individual countries, and with cost of transport fully recognized. Now let any subset of the countries form a customs union. Then there exists a common tariff vector and a system of lump-sum compensatory payments involving only members of the union, such that each individual, whether a member of the union or not, is not worse off than before the formation of the union.

The formal proof of the proposition is based on a fundamental theorem of neoclassical general equilibrium theory and is beyond the scope of this book; see Debreu (1959).[2] This theory is able to derive general results with respect to the number of goods and countries involved because it is based on two strong assumptions: perfect competition and a neoclassical production structure. This means that imperfect competition, economies of scale, knowledge spillovers, and so on are ruled out. Note that the partial equilibrium analysis above suggests that there may be negative welfare effects if trade diversion dominates trade creation, which requires a decline of international trade flows for the countries forming the customs union relative to the rest of the world. To rule out this possibility Kemp and Wan argue that it is possible for the countries forming the customs union to impose a common tariff vector that leaves world prices, and therefore the trade and welfare of non-members, at their pre-union prices. The elimination of trade barriers within the union then leads to efficiency gains, which in principle enables welfare gains for each union member through a system of lump-sum transfers.

12.6 Regionalism and new trade theory

In the course of the twentieth century, after World War II, the process of trade liberalization through multilateral negotiations within the GATT/WTO framework became increasingly difficult and time-consuming as more countries joined the WTO. At the same time, RTAs (such as in western Europe and North America) became increasingly popular and more powerful as many countries organized themselves in such agreements, a phenomenon that became known as 'regionalism'. The success of RTAs may have been at the expense of the multilateral WTO negotiations (Aggarwal and Evenett, 2015).

On the basis of the Kemp–Wan proposition (Section 12.5.3) one might think that this process, the apparent shift away from multilateralism towards regionalism, would be seen as a step in the right direction by trade policy experts, although worldwide liberalization would be better still. Instead, at the end of the 1980s and the beginning of the 1990s many trade policy experts and trade economists were worried about the shift from multilateralism towards regionalism for three reasons. First, there is a fear that countries that join a regional trade agreement might be more protectionist towards countries outside the trading bloc than they were before. Second, there was concern because the Kemp–Wan proposition in which no individual country is made worse off after the formation of a customs union is based on (i) the imposition of external tariffs that keep world prices and trade with non-members fixed, and (ii) a complicated internal transfer scheme among the members of the customs union, both of which are not observed in reality. Third, there was worry because the Kemp–Wan proposition is based on perfect competition and neoclassical production, such that it does not allow for imperfect competition, increasing returns to scale, and external effects.

Paul Krugman (1991) developed a simple, tractable, general equilibrium model based on an intra-industry trade framework (Chapter 8) to substantiate the fears of the trade policy experts regarding the shift from multilateralism to regionalism. His work illustrates the main issues involved and became the starting point of subsequent analysis and discussion (De Melo and Panagariya, 1993). In his first contribution Krugman assumes that a group of countries forming a trading bloc uses its monopoly power with respect to the rest of the world by imposing the 'optimal' tariff, as derived in Chapter 10. As a result, the tariff rate increases as the number of trading blocs falls. Since we do not observe increasing tariff rates in reality after the formation of a new trade bloc, which might start a process of retaliation, we discuss Krugman's model in this section for a *given* tariff rate, which is eliminated for those countries forming a trade bloc. This is not only closer to what we observe in reality, it also does not affect the main results and insights of the analysis and is easier to derive analytically; see also Krugman (1993).

Suppose the world consists of a large number N of 'provinces', each producing one unit of a unique good or variety.[3] Whether or not production takes place under increasing returns to scale or imperfect competition is unimportant. A collection of provinces may form a country, such that a large country may contain more provinces, each producing a unique good, than a small country, but the country level is basically irrelevant in the analysis below. The price charged domestically is 1. If c_i is the consumption level for a good produced in province i, the identical utility function for all economic agents is given by:

$$U = \left(\sum_{i=1}^{N} c_i^{\rho} \right)^{1/\rho} \; ; \quad \varepsilon \equiv \frac{1}{1-\rho} > 1 \qquad\qquad 12.1$$

As explained in Chapter 8, this specification implies that consumers have a love-of-variety and that goods produced in different provinces are imperfect substitutes for one another, with the parameter ε as the elasticity of substitution. The world is divided into b symmetric trading blocs. There is free trade for all provinces within each trading bloc, such that the price charged for a good produced within the trading bloc is 1. Each trading bloc imposes a uniform ad valorem tariff t on all imports from outside the trading bloc, such that the price charged for such goods is $1 + t$. We are interested in the welfare effects in this simple set-up of the formation of a smaller number of larger trading blocs:, that is, we are interested in the welfare effects of a fall in b.

Suppose, for example, that the world is initially divided into ten trading blocs of equal size. The inhabitants of any trading bloc then have access to 10 per cent of the world's varieties produced inside the trading bloc and freely traded at the price 1, and 90 per cent of the world's varieties imported from outside the trading bloc, subject to the tariff t, at the price

$1 + t$. The income available to the inhabitants of a trading bloc derives from the income generated by the production of varieties inside the trading bloc and the tariff revenue levied on imports from outside the trading bloc.

A reduction of the number of trading blocs in the world, say from ten to eight, implies that the inhabitants of any trading bloc have access to 12.5 per cent of the world's varieties produced inside the trading bloc and freely traded at the price 1, and 87.5 per cent of the world's varieties imported from outside the trading bloc at the price $1 + t$. At first sight this might seem beneficial as a larger fraction of goods is available at a lower price. However, we have seen that the total welfare effect depends on the balance between the trade-creation and trade-diversion effects. Note that the term trade-diversion is not entirely appropriate in this set-up, since all goods are imperfect substitutes for one another. Instead, it should be interpreted in this framework as a diversion away from consumption of goods produced outside the trading bloc towards goods produced inside the trading bloc: that is, the increase from 10 to 12.5 per cent of the share of goods produced inside the trading bloc can be viewed as an increase in the fraction of goods whose *relative* price is distorted compared to the rest of the world. The latter interpretation makes the main effects derived in this model readily understandable. It can be shown, see Technical Note 12.1, that total welfare (normalized to 1 for total free trade, that is if there is only one trading bloc) as a function of the tariff t, the elasticity of substitution between varieties ε, and the number of trading blocs b is equal to:

$$welfare = \frac{\left[b^{-1} + (1-b^{-1})(1+t)^{1-\varepsilon} \right]^{\varepsilon/(\varepsilon-1)}}{b^{-1} + (1-b^{-1})(1+t)^{-\varepsilon}} \qquad 12.2$$

Figure 12.9 illustrates the total welfare level given in equation 12.2 as a function of the number of trading blocs b; in the first panel for different values of the tariff rate and in the second panel for different values of the elasticity of substitution. The main conclusions are:

1. Total welfare falls as the number of trading blocs b decreases for a large range of parameter settings. Only if the number of trading blocs is already fairly small, in Figure 12.9 ranging from three to six, is a further reduction in the number of trading blocs welfare improving.[4]

2. Total welfare is, of course, maximized if there is free trade (only one trading bloc). This welfare level is also approached in this set-up if the number of trading blocs becomes very large because then the relative price distortion disappears (the share of goods produced within the trading bloc then approaches zero).

3. An increase in the tariff rate t imposed on imports from outside the trading bloc leads to (i) a reduction in the welfare level and (ii) an increase in the number of trading blocs where the minimum welfare level is reached, see Figure 12.9a. To some extent the connection between high tariffs and regionalism is ambivalent, where part (i) is the bad news and part (ii) is the good news (as a fall in b implies that the minimum is reached sooner if tariffs are high).

4. An increase in the elasticity of substitution ε leads to (i) a reduction in the welfare level and (ii) an increase in the number of trading blocs where the minimum welfare

level is reached, see Figure 12.9b. These results can be understood by realizing that if it is easier to substitute one variety for another the distortive effect of the tariff is stronger. The connection between the elasticity of substitution and regionalism is therefore, like the connection between tariffs and regionalism, also ambivalent.

The advantage of the model in this section is that it highlights in a simple framework the main issues involved in the move towards regionalism and provides a clear warning signal that this move could be detrimental to world welfare. Moreover, it shows how these issues depend on the elasticity of substitution between different goods and the tariff level imposed in the world economy. It should be noted that the picture of the move toward regionalism emerging from the analysis in this section is somewhat too gloomy, as it does not take into consideration the costs of transporting goods and services. As repeatedly pointed out by Krugman (1991, 1993), in reality large trading blocs are formed between *neighbouring* countries. The trade bloc thus accounts for a large share of a country's trade flows as the cost of transportation is low for neighbouring countries. Eliminating trade barriers within such 'natural' trading blocs therefore removes distorted relative prices to a larger extent than estimated on the basis of the share of income in the world economy of the countries in the trading bloc, therefore more rapidly leading to an increase in world welfare than suggested by the analysis in this section.

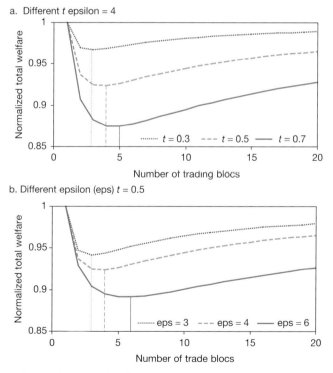

Figure 12.9 Regionalism model and total welfare.

Note: thin lines indicate where the minimum level is reached.

12.7 **RTA example: European Union (EU)**

The European economic integration process started after World War II with the European Coal and Steel Community, established in 1951 by the Treaty of Paris. As the name indicates, the ECSC was a sectoral agreement, establishing free trade among the member countries for the (at that time vital) coal and steel sectors only. Following the devastating experiences of World War I and World War II, which cost the lives of millions of people and destroyed the economic, social, cultural, and historical fabric of many countries in Europe, one of the underlying ideas of strengthening the economic integration process of the major countries on the continent was to reduce the probability of future wars, particularly between France and Germany. Fortunately, there has been peace among the current EU member countries ever since, although the extent to which the economic integration process can take credit for this fact is of course open for discussion. Table 12.3 gives an overview of the European economic integration process.

The Treaties of Rome in 1957 continued the sectoral integration process with the establishment of the European Atomic Energy Community (EURATOM), and started the total economic integration process with the establishment of the European Economic Community (EEC). The three organizations (ECSC, EEC, and EURATOM) were combined in the European Community (EC) in 1967. The Treaty of Maastricht (1991) established the European Union (EU, 1993) and provided the criteria for monetary integration in the Economic and Monetary Union (EMU, 1999). Over the years, the number of countries participating in the European integration process has increased from 6 to 28, see Figure 12.10. Seventeen EU countries had introduced the euro as their single currency by 2011 (making up what is known as the Eurozone).

Table 12.3 Overview of European economic integration

1951	ECSC	European Coal and Steel Community
	Membership	Belgium, France, Luxembourg, the Netherlands, Italy, West Germany
1957	EURATOM	European Atomic Energy Community
1957	EEC	European Economic Community
1967	EC	European Communities: combining ECSC, EEC, EURATOM
1973	Membership	+ United Kingdom, Ireland, Denmark
1981	Membership	+ Greece
1986	Membership	+ Spain, Portugal
1990	Membership	+ East Germany (reunification of West and East Germany)
1993	EU	European Union
1995	Membership	+ Finland, Austria, Sweden
1999	EMU	Economic and Monetary Union
2002	Euro	Introduction of the euro
2004	Membership	+ Cyprus, Czech Republic, Estonia, Hungary, Latvia, Lithuania, Malta, Poland, Slovenia, Slovakia
2007	Membership	+ Bulgaria, Romania
2013	Membership	+ Croatia

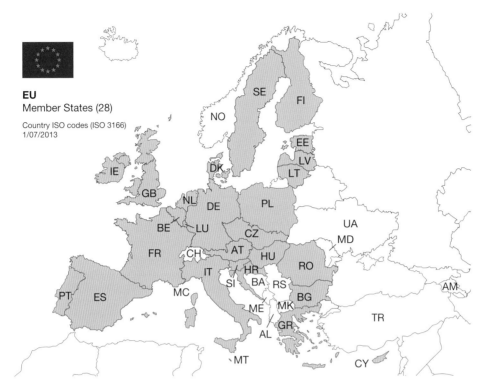

EU
Member States (28)

Country ISO codes (ISO 3166)
1/07/2013

Figure 12.10 The European Union in 2016.

Source: Data from http://europa.eu.

The objective of the EEC Treaty was the establishment of a common market, which also allows for the 'four freedoms'.

1. *Free movement of goods*: the common market requires not only the removal of tariffs and quantitative restrictions, but also the dismantling of other obstacles to free movement of goods. Most important in this respect was the Cassis de Dijon case in 1979. According to German regulations, Cassis de Dijon, a French fruit liqueur, did not contain enough alcohol (17 per cent rather than the minimum 32 per cent), and was therefore forbidden. The European Court of Justice ruled that a product legally brought to the market in one country of the EU also has to be accepted in another country. This principle ensures that different national regulations are mutually recognized, except for hazardous products, or for health, safety, or environmental reasons.

2. *Free movement of persons*: workers have a right to work anywhere else in the EU (right of free movement) and individuals have the right to establish businesses anywhere else in the EU (right of establishment).

3. *Free movement of services*: the Cassis de Dijon verdict also holds for services, such that services offered in one EU country can also be offered in another EU country. The free movement of persons and that of services are related, as the export of services frequently requires physical presence in the customer country.

4. *Free movement of capital*: although capital controls were still operative in some countries until the late 1980s, restrictions on capital flows between EU countries have now been eliminated.

The main institutions of the European Union are as follows.

- The *Council of the European Union*: also known as the Council of Ministers, this central decision-making body meets in many different forms (bringing together heads of state or ministers for foreign affairs, agriculture, transport, etc.). It is not to be confused with the European Council (quarterly summits where EU leaders meet to set the broad direction of EU policy making) or the Council of Europe (not an EU body at all).

- The *European Commission* administers and initiates policy in the EU; it mediates between the member states and represents the EU in international negotiations.

- The *European Parliament*: this body, involved in decision and law making, is democratically chosen by the people of the EU member countries every four years. The number of members per country depends on population, but is not less than six and not more than 96.

- The *European Court of Justice* provides judicial safeguards and is concerned with the interpretation of EU law, including actions brought before the court between member states and between the Commission and a member state.

- The *European Central Bank* (ECB) is a largely independent institution responsible for the monetary policy of the euro area, with price stability as the primary objective.

Two other European economic integration agreements outside the EU should be mentioned in this section. First, the Stockholm Convention established the European Free Trade Association (EFTA) in 1960. In the course of the twentieth century, many EFTA countries joined the EU, such that EFTA currently consists only of Iceland, Norway, Liechtenstein, and Switzerland. Second, the Central European Free Trade Area (CEFTA) was established in 1993 to reduce tariffs and other trade barriers and increase intra-regional trade. All CEFTA countries have now joined the EU, which brings us to the next section on recent EU enlargement.

12.8 Enlargement of the EU

Soon after the fall of the Berlin Wall in 1989, the EC established diplomatic relations with the countries of central Europe, removed import quotas on a number of products, extended the Generalized System of Preferences, and concluded trade and cooperation agreements with many central European countries. In 1993 at the Copenhagen European Council, the member states agreed that 'the associated countries in central and eastern Europe that so desire shall become members of the European Union'—provided the candidate country met the Copenhagen Criteria: that is, the country

- has achieved stability of institutions guaranteeing democracy, the rule of law, human rights, and respect for and protection of minorities;

- has achieved the existence of a functioning market economy as well as the capacity to cope with competitive pressure and market forces within the Union;

- has achieved the ability to take on the obligations of membership, including adherence to the aims of political, economic, and monetary union;

- has created the conditions for its integration through the adjustment of its administrative structures, so that European Community legislation transposed into national legislation is implemented effectively through appropriate administrative and judicial structures.

As summarized in Table 12.3, ten countries joined the EU in 2004, two more in 2007, and one more in 2013. The prospects of the remaining candidate countries (Iceland, Macedonia, Montenegro, and Turkey) are less clear, for Turkey this is partially because of concerns about its sheer (population) size and its Muslim cultural background. The short-hand term EU15 is used to denote the EU members joining before 2004. These countries also joined at different stages, implying that the EU integration process has involved a pro-longed increase in the number of member states. This resulted in a gradual and jump-wise increase in the EU's total population, which now consists of more than 500 million people: see the historical overview in Figure 12.11. The projected decline in 2019 is related to Brexit (see Section 12.9).

As suggested by the Copenhagen Criteria, there are substantial differences between the EU15 countries and the new entrants, which also differ substantially among themselves.

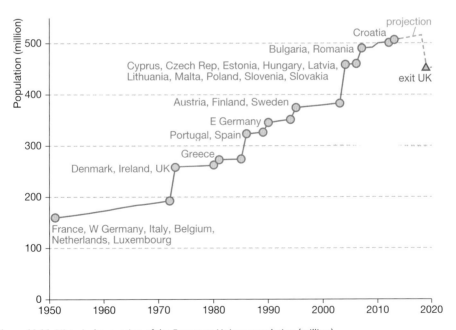

Figure 12.11 Historical expansion of the European Union: population (million).

Notes: the jumps reflect expansion of EU population resulting from new entrants (as indicated) or re-unification (in the case of East Germany); the projected fall in population around 2019 depends on the UK exit after the Brexit referendum, see Section 12.9. *Source:* based on population data from World Development Indicators.

Table 12.4 provides details regarding the size in terms of land area, population, and income for the EU member countries, for the EU candidate countries, and (for comparison purposes) for China, India, Japan, and the USA. In terms of land area, France is the largest EU country, followed by Spain, Sweden, and Germany, while Malta is the smallest EU country. In terms of population, Germany is the largest EU country, followed by France, the UK, and Italy, while Malta is again the smallest EU country. In terms of total income, Germany is again the largest EU country, this time followed by the UK, France, and Italy, while Malta is once more the smallest EU country. In terms of income per capita, the differences between the EU countries are quite large. Luxembourg has by far the highest income per capita, followed by Ireland, the Netherlands, and Sweden. Of the new entrants Cyprus has the highest income per capita, but it is lower than those of all EU15 countries except for Greece and Portugal. Bulgaria has the lowest income per capita level, namely about half the EU28 average. The diversity is illustrated in Figure 12.12.

As a whole, the EU28 represents a formidable economic power. Total EU28 income is about 3 per cent larger than China's income level and 6 per cent larger than that of the USA. The EU28 population is 508 million inhabitants, which is about 4 times larger than Japan's population and 60 per cent more than the USA's, but only about 40 per cent of the populations of China and India. The EU28's income per capita is only about two-thirds of that of the USA, about the same as that of Japan, almost three times that of China, and more than six times that of India.

In 2007 the EU countries signed the Treaty of Lisbon, which entered into force on 1 December 2009. The objective is to make the EU more democratic, efficient, and transparent. The main changes are:

Table 12.4 Statistics for EU countries and selected other countries, 2014

Name	Code	GDP/capita	GDP	Land area	Population
EUnew					
Bulgaria	BGR	16,363	118	109	7.2
Croatia	HRV	20,033	85	56	4.2
Cyprus	CYP	29,673	25	9	1.2
Czech Republic	CZE	28,715	302	77	10.5
Estonia	EST	26,612	35	42	1.3
Hungary	HUN	23,735	234	91	9.9
Latvia	LVA	22,076	44	62	2.0
Lithuania	LTU	25,813	76	63	2.9
Malta	MLT	28,822	12	0	0.4
Poland	POL	23,976	911	306	38.0
Romania	ROM	19,098	380	230	19.9
Slovak Republic	SVK	26,471	143	48	5.4
Slovenia	SVN	28,153	58	20	2.1

(Continued...)

Table 12.4 *Continued*

Name	Code	GDP/capita	GDP	Land area	Population
EU15					
Austria	AUT	43,908	375	83	8.5
Belgium	BEL	40,823	458	30	11.2
Denmark	DNK	42,758	241	42	5.6
Finland	FIN	38,535	211	304	5.5
France	FRA	37,214	2,464	548	66.2
Germany	DEU	43,602	3,527	349	80.9
Greece	GRC	24,372	267	129	11.0
Ireland	IRL	48,431	223	69	4.6
Italy	ITA	33,039	2,026	294	61.3
Luxembourg	LUX	91,408	51	3	0.6
Netherlands	NLD	45,691	770	34	16.9
Portugal	PRT	26,184	272	92	10.4
Spain	ESP	31,802	1,476	500	46.4
Sweden	SWE	44,034	427	407	9.7
UK	GBR	38,178	2,463	242	64.5
EU total	EU	34,771	17,675	4,238	508
China	CHN	12,599	17,189	9,388	1,364
India	IND	5,439	7,045	2,973	1,295
Japan	JPN	35,635	4,530	365	127
USA	USA	52,118	16,618	9,147	319
index EU28 = 100					
China	CHN	36	97	222	268
India	IND	16	40	70	255
Japan	JPN	102	26	9	25
USA	USA	150	94	216	63

Notes: GDP in PPP constant 2011$, billion; land area in 1,000 km^2; population in million.

Source: World Bank: *World Development Indicators online*.

- Single legal personality: the European Community was replaced by the European Union, which succeeds it and takes over all its rights and obligations.

- President of the European Council: there is a fixed full-time president of the European Council, with a term of two-and-a-half years, renewable once. The president at the time of writing is Donald Tusk (up to May 2017).

- High Representative of the Union: this person is the Council's representative for the common foreign and security policy, the president of the Foreign Affairs Council, and vice-president of the Commission.

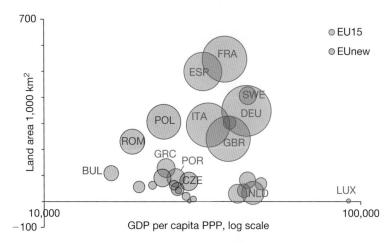

Figure 12.12 EU diversity in size, population, and income per capita, 2014.

Notes: GDP per capita PPP in constant 2011 USD; see Table 12.4 for country abbreviations; bubbles proportional to population size.
Data source: World Development Indicators.

- Double (qualified) majority voting in the Council: starting in 2014 a large majority of the decisions in the Council (except those that expressly require unanimity or a simple majority) will require a double majority to be adopted, with the support of at least 55 per cent of the member states and at least 65 per cent of the population of the EU. A blocking minority must include at least four member states.

- Number of seats in the European Parliament: cannot exceed 751.

- Citizens' right of initiative: a million citizens may sign a petition inviting the Commission to submit a proposal on any area of EU competence.

Figure 12.13 provides an overview of the number of seats each country has in the European Parliament (equal to 751 in total), as well as the relative weight of the vote of an inhabitant of each country (normalized to ten for the EU average). The figure is ordered from left to right in rising relative weight. The inhabitants of France, which has 74 seats in the European Parliament, have the *lowest* relative weight in casting their votes: 7.57, which is 24 per cent below the EU average of ten. The inhabitants of Malta, which has six seats in the European Parliament, have the *highest* relative weight: 95, which is 850 per cent above the EU average. This makes an inhabitant of Malta about 12.6 times more important than an inhabitant of France. To some extent this is inevitable. According to population-based proportionality Malta would be entitled to 0.6 seats in the European Parliament, which has to be rounded upward to the integer one. The minimum number of six seats per country in the European Parliament significantly magnifies the over-representation of small countries.

Figure 12.13 also illustrates a consistency problem. If the number of seats in the European Parliament were in principle proportional to population taking the minimum and maximum per country into consideration, then this number (the blue bars in Figure 12.13) would be monotonically declining from left to right. This is not the case. Among the larger countries Spain, for example, is under-represented compared to its right-hand neighbour. Among the smaller countries this holds, for example, for the Netherlands,

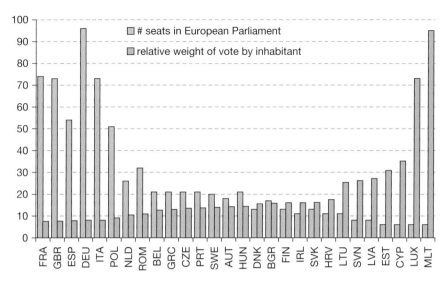

Figure 12.13 Distribution of power in the European Parliament, 2014.

Notes: ordered by rising relative weight of vote by inhabitant, which is normalized to ten for the EU average.
Source: based on WDI and europa.eu.

Austria, Denmark, and Ireland. From a European perspective only the six largest countries (France, UK, Spain, Germany, Italy, and Poland) are under-represented (have a relative weight below ten). All 22 other countries are over-represented. The democratic principle of one person, one vote is violated to an even greater extent in the Council of Ministers and the committees. From this perspective there is room for democratic improvement within the EU.

12.9 Brexit: start of the decline of the EU?

Early in the morning on 24 June 2016 it became clear that David Cameron, the prime minister of the UK, had made *a big mistake* three years earlier. The UK had voted in a referendum the day before to leave the European Union: a *Brexit* outcome (Britain exits the EU) rather than the more widely expected *Bremain* outcome (Britain remains in the EU). It was a costly mistake, not just for Cameron (he had to step down as prime minister) but also for more than 64 million inhabitants of Britain and, to a lesser extent, for people elsewhere in Europe and in the rest of the world. The referendum was the result of David Cameron's decision in 2013 to pledge to hold a vote on the UK's EU membership. He had not needed to, but was trying to silence the backbenchers in his own party; he was confident that the people would vote to remain in the EU (as Cameron wanted), without giving sufficient consideration to the risks of such a promise.

On referendum day about 52 per cent of the votes were for Brexit, compared to 48 for Bremain. As this margin suggests, in the months and weeks before the referendum the outcome was hard to predict. The Bremain campaign, with Cameron (leader of the Conservative Party) and Jeremy Corbyn (leader of the Labour Party) as its main supporters, focused on the economic gains coming from EU membership (see Sections 12.5 and 12.6). The Brexit campaign, with Boris Johnson (a member of the Conservative Party and former mayor of London) and Nigel Farage (leader of the UK Independence Party) as its main supporters, focused on immigration issues and British independence. In light of this uncertainty the British pound had gradually declined in value. It reached a low of around 1.41 USD per pound on 15 June, eight days before the election. From that point the pound then regained most of its value in reaction to reports and polls that the Bremain campaign would win, briefly exceeding 1.50 USD per pound on referendum day. British gambling businesses also reported confident spreads for a Bremain outcome just prior to the referendum.

Most of the media reports on referendum day were pointing to a Bremain outcome by the time most people were going to sleep. The Brexit outcome when they woke up the next day thus came as a big surprise and caused a financial shock. The pound plunged about 11 per cent in the first two trading days after the referendum (see Figure 12.14), which was the biggest drop since the pound was floated in 1971 (*The Economist*, 2016a). The FTSE 100, the UK's main stock market index, fell 5.6 per cent and the broader FTSE 250 index declined even more (by 7.2 per cent), the largest drop since the stock market crash of 1987 (*The Economist*, 2016a). Smaller, but substantial, declines were recorded in the rest of the world. On Monday 27 June, Standard & Poor lowered the UK's credit rating by two steps, from AAA+ to AA.

The referendum has left the UK divided and uncertain about its future.[5] The majority of the population in London and Scotland voted for Bremain, while most of the rest of the country voted for Brexit. The majority of the younger population voted for Bremain, while the majority of the older population (most of whom actually voted, in contrast to the younger population) voted for Brexit. In the days following the referendum open hostility against foreigners was more widely reported, while millions of migrants are unsure about their future within the UK. At the time of writing (29 June 2016) there was talk of a second referendum (supported at that point by more than 3.5 million people), but that seems highly unlikely. There was also talk of organizing a referendum on Scotland

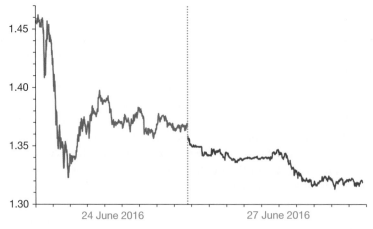

Figure 12.14 Value of the British pound in USD: 24 and 27 June 2016.

Source: based on Datastream.

becoming independent, thus leaving the UK and remaining in the EU. Scotland had organized a referendum earlier (in 2014), when they voted to stay in the UK. On the one hand, a new referendum might make voting for independence more likely, since the majority of Scots supported Bremain and want to stay in the EU. On the other hand, a new referendum might make voting for independence less likely given that oil prices have fallen significantly since 2014, which hurts the case for independence. The outcome thus remains uncertain, and uncertainty hurts the economy.

So what's next? The UK will only leave the EU if it invokes Article 50 of the Lisbon treaty, which starts a two-year timetable to agree on the terms of departure; the time period can be extended only if all member states agree. Although David Cameron said he would invoke Article 50 immediately, he did not do so; it will be up to Theresa May, his successor as prime minister, to start the process and the ticking clock. Figure 12.11 indicates that this means that the UK is likely to leave the EU at the end of 2018, at which time the EU will have a population size of about 450 million people. There are several possible outcomes of the negotiations.

1. *WTO option*: the UK leaves the EU and gets access to the EU market under the same conditions as all other WTO members. This is a fall-back option.

2. *Norway option*: the UK has full access to the internal EU market, including the four freedoms (free movement of goods, capital, services, and persons). It also contributes to the EU budget, but it has no role in the decision-making process. The UK is unlikely to go for this outcome.

3. *Norway-plus option*: the UK has full access to the internal EU market, including three of the four freedoms (free movement of goods, capital, and services), but excluding the free movement of persons. It also contributes to the EU budget and has no role in the decision-making process. The EU is unlikely to go for this outcome.

4. *Compromise option*: something in between the Norway-plus option and the WTO option.

One of the main obstacles in the negotiating process is the future of international banking in London outside of the EU. At the moment the UK benefits from the EU's 'passport' rules, under which financial firms in one member state can serve customers in another member state without setting up local operations. As a consequence, British subsidiaries of non-EU banks (from USA, Japan, China, and so on) are able to serve all of Europe from London, such that in 2016 London had about 70 per cent of the market for euro-denominated interest rate derivatives and 90 per cent of European prime brokerage (*The Economist*, 2016c). A deal regarding passport rights seems unlikely, since the EU member states would like to take over part of London's financial sector. A range of international banks have already announced plans to relocate parts of their businesses inside the EU if the UK leaves. Bank share prices have taken the hardest hits, both on 24 June and on 27 June.

Other countries have their own anti-EU resentments. According to a recent poll in France, only 38 per cent of the population still hold a favourable view of the EU (*The Economist*, 2016e). The weaker economies of Greece and Italy are suffering from austerity measures imposed by the stronger German economy. Central and eastern European nations are opposed to 'cosmopolitan' values such as approval for gay marriage. And so on. Some people therefore argue that Brexit may be the start of the decline of the EU. The silver lining of the Brexit outcome may be that the economic advantages are now more clearly highlighted,

---

BOX 12.2 Unsuccessfully fighting European Union myths

The UK has a long tradition of fabricating facts about Europe, and the Brexit campaign and its supporting tabloids have done their best to add to this tradition. The claims made are absurd, ridiculous, silly, or based on misunderstandings. Some examples of ridiculous claims? Fishing boats will be forced to carry condoms. Zippers on trousers will be banned. The speed of children's playground roundabouts will be limited (a guideline not suggested by the EU but by another organisation with 'Europe' in its name). The Queen will have to make her own tea (not only inaccurate, but also referring to laws enacted by the UK itself in 1993). Bananas must not be excessively curved. Euro coins will make you sick. Euro notes will make you impotent. And so on.

In response to all these myths, the European Commission even set up a website decades ago to debunk the lies.[6] The Commission has already responded to more than 400 myths, many of which are related to food, public services, and jobs. A large share of the myths originate from daily newspapers (*Daily Mail, Daily Telegraph*, and *Daily Express*), but even the BBC contributes. Unfortunately, as pointed out by *The Economist* (2016b), the Commission's myth-debunking work is hardly read: 'The average rebuttal is read about 1,000 times. The *Daily Mail*'s website, by contrast, garners 225m visitors each month.'

It seems many people were not well-informed and based their vote on different sentiments. As CNN's Christiane Amanpour pointed out on 29 June (Amanpour, 2016, also for the other quotes below), 'Remain was dubbed "Project Fear" by the Leavers, but never has there been a case so one-sided—Remain having been supported by a majority in parliament, the overwhelming number of business, science, and academic leaders, all of the UK's major allies, and international institutions.' According to Justice Minister Michael Gove, however: 'People in this country have had enough of experts.' Instead, many people apparently based their opinion on tabloids such as *The Sun*, which actively campaigned for Brexit, leading Martin Fletcher (former editor of *The Times*) to point out in an article for the *New York Times* (Fletcher, 2016):

> British newspapers have offered their readers an endless stream of biased, misleading and downright fallacious stories about Brussels. ... I was appointed Brussels correspondent for *The Times* of London in 1999, a few years after Mr [Boris] Johnson reported from there for another London newspaper, *The Telegraph*. I had to live with the consequences. Mr Johnson, fired from *The Times* in 1988 for fabricating a quotation, made his name in Brussels not with honest reporting but with extreme euroskepticism, tirelessly attacking, mocking and denigrating the European Union. He wrote about European Union plans to take over Europe, ban Britain's favorite potato chips, standardize condom sizes and blow up its own asbestos-filled headquarters. These articles were undoubtedly colorful but they bore scant relation to the truth.

Source: The Economist (2016b).

---

thus making it less attractive for other countries to follow suit. After all, *The Economist* (2016d) summarized the consequences of Brexit as follows: 'The unexpected outcome will be a Britain poorer, more isolated, less influential and more divided.' Perhaps this is more effective than anything else in debunking myths about the European Union: see Box 12.2.

12.10 RTA case study: TTIP

While I was working on this chapter (end of 2015 and early 2016) two major RTAs were in the process of formation and received wide media coverage. The first was the Trans-Pacific Partnership (TPP), involving 12 countries bordering the Pacific Ocean, namely Australia, Brunei, Canada, Chile, Japan, Malaysia, Mexico, New Zealand, Peru, Singapore, the USA, and Vietnam. Some large countries bordering the Pacific Ocean are conspicuously absent from this list, in particular China, Indonesia, South Korea, the Philippines, Taiwan, and Colombia. The second agreement is the Transatlantic Trade and Investment Partnership (TTIP), which involves the USA and the 28 nations of the EU. We briefly discuss some aspects of the potential implementation of TTIP in this section.

After the official announcement in February 2013, the TTIP negotiations started in July 2013; they are still ongoing.[7] If successful, TTIP will be the largest RTA to date, as illustrated in Table 12.5. The TTIP countries represent 47.3 per cent of the world's imports, 43.2 per cent of the world's exports, 35.6 per cent of the world's total income (PPP), and 12.1 per cent of the world's total population. The economic importance of the TTIP countries for income and trade flows is therefore substantial. The non-participating 'rest of world' (RoW) countries represent almost 90 per cent of the world's population and a little more than half of the world's trade flows. These countries are subdivided into five different income groups in Table 12.5.

The aims of TTIP are

- to eliminate or reduce tariffs and tariff-rate quotas;
- to eliminate, reduce, or prevent barriers to trade in goods and services;
- to eliminate, reduce, or prevent barriers to investment;
- to enhance compatibility of regulations and standards;
- to eliminate, reduce, or prevent unnecessary 'behind the border' Non-Tariff Barriers (NTBs);
- to apply to trade in all categories;
- to enhance cooperation for the development of rules and principles on global issues;
- to achieve shared global economic goals of common concern.

Table 12.5 The power of TTIP countries, 2011

Country group	Share of country group in world total (per cent)			
	Import	Export	Income	Population
TTIP countries	47.3	43.2	35.6	12.1
EU countries	34.0	34.2	18.3	7.4
USA	13.3	9.0	17.3	4.6
RoW countries	52.7	56.8	64.4	87.9
ADV countries	21.7	24.8	14.0	4.6
HiMID countries	4.5	4.9	6.9	4.5
MID countries	17.8	20.0	27.5	31.5
LoMID countries	7.1	6.2	14.0	33.5
LOW countries	1.6	0.8	2.0	13.8

Notes: world total is based on 168 countries (with a total population of 6.825 billion people, representing 96 per cent of the true world total); TTIP = Transatlantic Trade and Investment Partnership; RoW = rest of world; ADV = advanced / high-income countries; HiMID = countries in transition from MID to ADV; MID = average income countries; LoMID = countries in transition from LOW to MID; LOW = low-income countries.
Source: Brakman, Kohl, and van Marrewijk (2015).

The European Commission expects positive welfare effects for the members of TTIP (François et al., 2013). This conclusion is based on a gravity analysis taking modern developments regarding price effects into consideration and is largely corroborated by other studies (for a survey, see Felbermayr et al., 2015). The impact may be less positive for non-TTIP members, so-called third countries. On the one hand these countries may be hurt by trade diversion effects, as analysed in Section 12.5. On the other hand they may benefit from trade creation, from positive total income effects, and from the partial removal of non-tariff barriers, which will make it easier for third countries to trade with the EU and the US. In the case of TTIP most third countries are developing countries and TTIP might potentially frustrate the EU development agenda. Brakman, Kohl, and van Marrewijk (2015) analyse these issues using the Egger and Larch (2011) methodology, taking the heterogeneity of RTAs (Sections 12.3 and 12.4) into consideration. Instead of the standard method, which uses a dummy variable to indicate whether an RTA is present or not and then calculates the hypothetical impact of an RTA between countries, they take the heterogeneity in terms of institutional design, content, and legal enforceability of RTAs into consideration before calculating the hypothetical impact of TTIP.

To better demonstrate the impact of TTIP on different countries Figure 12.15 illustrates the relationship between the level of economic development, as measured by income per capita PPP using a log scale, and a country's total dependence on the TTIP countries for its exports (in per cent: the sum of EU and USA export percentages). The graph clearly shows the high dependence of the EU countries themselves on the TTIP countries for their exports. The graph also illustrates the wide variation in the dependence of third countries on the TTIP countries for their exports: the minimum is 1.6 per cent, the maximum is 90.9 per cent, the mean is 38.6 per cent, and the standard deviation is 24.6 per cent. Moreover, there is virtually no relationship between the level of economic development and this trade

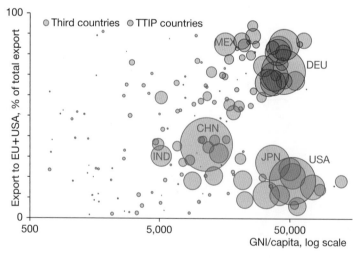

Figure 12.15 Economic development and EU+US export dependence: per cent of total.

Notes: data for 2011; bubbles proportional to size of total exports; 166 countries in total.
Source: Brakman, Kohl, and van Marrewijk (2015).

dependence: the correlation coefficient between the log of income per capita and the per cent of exports going to the TTIP countries is a modest 0.05. Indeed, the figure shows that also for the poorest countries (the left side of the figure) there is enormous variation in export dependence. The 77 countries in the LOW and LoMID income groups include the minimum and maximum, while the mean and standard deviation is virtually the same as for the third country group as a whole.

Figure 12.16 illustrates the hypothetical impact of TTIP on the trade flows for each country (exports plus imports). These are essentially the result of two effects, namely a substitution effect based on estimated changes in relative prices and accessibility and an income effect based on estimated changes in income levels for the country and all its trading partners. The US estimated trade effect is a modest increase of 1.6 per cent. The population-weighted average trade effect for the EU28 countries is a 4.2 per cent increase. This is understandable: as shown in Figure 12.15, trade flows with the TTIP countries are higher for the EU than for the US. There is considerable variation within the EU, from a low of 1.1 per cent for Croatia to a high of 12.7 per cent for Ireland.[8] The effects are most pronounced for the TTIP countries themselves and less dramatic for third countries. Countries close to the EU or that trade a lot with the EU, such as Russia and Ethiopia, tend to benefit from trade creation/income growth effects of TTIP. Countries close to the US or that trade a lot with the US, such as Mexico, Canada, and Chad, tend to be hurt by the trade diversion effects of TTIP. This also holds for important middle-income countries, such as China. The overall suggestion from Figure 12.16 is that the lower-income third countries are relatively better off as a result of TTIP than the higher-income third countries.[9]

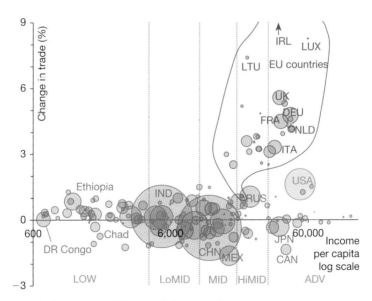

Figure 12.16 Hypothetical impact of TTIP on trade flows: relative change in per cent.

Notes: bubbles proportional to population; 166 countries in total; the vertical lines indicate the cut-off points for the income groups.

Source: author, based on Brakman, Kohl, and van Marrewijk (2015) analysis.

Table 12.6 Impact of TTIP on trade flows per income group: relative change in per cent

Group	Mean		Median	Standard deviation	No. of countries	Population (million)
	normal	pop wgh				
TTIP countries	4.24	3.18	3.79	2.20	29	823
Third countries	0.10	−0.04	0.09	0.62	137	5,994
ADV	0.12	−0.30	0.03	0.64	18	316
HiMID	0.10	0.65	0.18	0.65	13	308
MID	−0.05	−0.35	−0.06	0.69	29	2,143
LoMID	0.07	0.07	0.03	0.65	33	2,288
LOW	0.22	0.26	0.23	0.53	44	939

Note: pop wgh = population weighted.
Source: Brakman, Kohl, and van Marrewijk (2015).

Table 12.6 provides summary statistical information on the TTIP trade effects for the TTIP countries themselves and the third countries, where the latter are subdivided into five income classes. The effect is clearly positive for the TTIP countries, with an average increase of 4.2 per cent, a median of 3.8 per cent, and a standard deviation of 2.2 per cent. The effect for the TTIP countries is somewhat smaller if we use a population-weighted average, namely 3.2 per cent instead of 4.2 per cent. There are 29 TTIP countries with a total population of 823 million people. The population-weighted average impact of TTIP for the trade flows of the 137 third countries with a total population of 6 billion people is *zero* (note that the median is a modest 0.1). All in all, therefore, the trade effects are negligible or small for third countries. When we look at the different income classes, we see that the population-weighted competitive impact of TTIP on third countries is only mildly negative for other advanced economies, such as Canada and Japan, and for middle-income countries, such as China and Mexico.

12.11 Conclusions

Regional trade agreements (RTAs) have become increasingly popular since the 1990s, a movement away from the multilateral WTO framework known as regionalism. Trade agreements are becoming more complex, cover a larger and more varied range of policy issues, and increasingly involve developing and emerging economies that are linked to advanced countries through global supply chains. Although a trade agreement in general raises welfare through increased trade flows (trade creation), the discriminatory nature of the agreement which benefits insiders at the expense of outsiders may reduce welfare through a shift towards less efficient producers (trade diversion). The European Union (EU) presents the most powerful and successful economic integration scheme to date. Its future is seriously challenged by the decision of the UK to leave the EU (Brexit). Finally, we briefly discuss the potential trade implications of an EU–US RTA (TTIP).

Technical Note

Technical Note 12.1 Regionalism model

Using the exact price index P defined in equation (8.A4), we get

$$P \equiv \left(\sum_{i=1}^{N} p_i^{1-\varepsilon} \right)^{\frac{1}{1-\varepsilon}} = \left(\sum_{i=1}^{\frac{N}{b}} 1 + \sum_{i=\frac{N}{b}+1}^{N} (1+t)^{1-\varepsilon} \right)^{\frac{1}{1-\varepsilon}} = N \left[\frac{1}{b} + \left(1-\frac{1}{b}\right)(1+t)^{1-\varepsilon} \right]^{\frac{1}{1-\varepsilon}} \tag{12.A1}$$

Thus, once we know the income level I in a trading bloc, equation (8.A4) gives us the demand for a particular variety, namely:

$$c_j = p_j^{-\varepsilon} P^{\varepsilon-1} I = \begin{cases} \dfrac{I}{N\left[\frac{1}{b}+\left(1-\frac{1}{b}\right)(1+t)^{1-\varepsilon}\right]}, \text{ for } j \in \text{trading bloc} \\[3ex] \dfrac{(1+t)^{-\varepsilon} I}{N\left[\frac{1}{b}+\left(1-\frac{1}{b}\right)(1+t)^{1-\varepsilon}\right]}, \text{ for } j \notin \text{trading bloc} \end{cases} \tag{12.A2}$$

The income level I of a trading block is the sum of the production value N/b and the tariff revenue t levied per unit on the c_j goods sold of the $N(1-1/b)$ varieties imported from outside the trading bloc. Using the equation above, this implies:

$$I = \frac{N}{b} + \frac{N\left(1-\frac{1}{b}\right) t(1+t)^{-\varepsilon} I}{N\left[\frac{1}{b}+\left(1-\frac{1}{b}\right)(1+t)^{1-\varepsilon}\right]} \tag{12.A3}$$

Solving this equation for the income level I gives

$$\left(1 - \frac{\left(1-\frac{1}{b}\right) t(1+t)^{-\varepsilon}}{\frac{1}{b}+\left(1-\frac{1}{b}\right)(1+t)^{1-\varepsilon}} \right) I = \frac{N}{b} \tag{12.A4}$$

$$\left(\frac{\frac{1}{b}+\left(1-\frac{1}{b}\right)(1+t)^{1-\varepsilon} - \left(1-\frac{1}{b}\right)t(1+t)^{-\varepsilon}}{\frac{1}{b}+\left(1-\frac{1}{b}\right)(1+t)^{1-\varepsilon}} \right) I = \left(\frac{\frac{1}{b}+\left(1-\frac{1}{b}\right)(1+t)^{-\varepsilon}}{\frac{1}{b}+\left(1-\frac{1}{b}\right)(1+t)^{1-\varepsilon}} \right) I = \frac{N}{b}$$

$$I = \frac{N}{b} \left(\frac{\frac{1}{b}+\left(1-\frac{1}{b}\right)(1+t)^{1-\varepsilon}}{\frac{1}{b}+\left(1-\frac{1}{b}\right)(1+t)^{-\varepsilon}} \right)$$

As shown in Chapter 8, the welfare of a trading bloc is equal to I/P. Since there are b trading blocs in the world, and using the above, total world welfare is equal to

$$b\frac{I}{P} = b\frac{N}{b}\left(\frac{\frac{1}{b}+\left(1-\frac{1}{b}\right)(1+t)^{1-\varepsilon}}{\frac{1}{b}+\left(1-\frac{1}{b}\right)(1+t)^{-\varepsilon}}\right)\frac{1}{N^{1/(1-\varepsilon)}\left(\frac{1}{b}+\left(1-\frac{1}{b}\right)(1+t)^{1-\varepsilon}\right)^{1/(1-\varepsilon)}} = \tag{12.A5}$$

$$= N^{\varepsilon/(\varepsilon-1)}\frac{\left(\frac{1}{b}+\left(1-\frac{1}{b}\right)(1+t)^{1-\varepsilon}\right)^{\varepsilon/(\varepsilon-1)}}{\frac{1}{b}+\left(1-\frac{1}{b}\right)(1+t)^{-\varepsilon}}$$

The figures in the text depict this total welfare level, normalized to unity if there is one trading bloc (global free trade).

 Notes

1   This chapter is partially based on previous work (Brakman, Kohl, and van Marrewijk, 2015).

2   In this literature the weak phrase in the proposition that an individual 'is not worse off' after the formation of the customs union actually means that in general there is room for welfare improvement.

3   One 'unit' could, of course, refer to 1 billion, or 4 billion, or whatever the number of goods produced.

4   In Krugman (1991), which is based on the 'optimal' tariff approach, the minimum was reached at three trading blocs for a large range of elasticities of substitution.

5   On top of it all, England lost to Iceland in the European Cup on 27 June 2016.

6   See http://blogs.ec.europa.eu/ECintheUK/euromyths-a-z-index/.

7   See http://ec.europa.eu/trade/policy/in-focus/ttip and https://ustr.gov/ttip for details.

8   The effect for Ireland is so large we did not include it in the figure.

9   A formal regression of the relative change in trade flows on the log of GNI per capita is negative, but not statistically significant. See the discussion in the main text.

 Questions

Question 12.1

Briefly answer the following questions.

a.   What happened to the number of regional trade agreements (RTAs) since 1960?

b.   Which (type of) countries were initially (1960s to 1980s) more active in RTAs and which (type of) countries have become more active since the 1990s?

c.   What is shallow versus deep integration and how does it relate to the development of RTAs over time?

Question 12.2

The European Union has some minor grapefruit producers (mostly in Cyprus, Italy, and Greece) and imports most grapefruit from the USA. On all imports of grapefruit the European Union levies a common tariff. Recently, Turkey has expressed ambitions to conquer the European grapefruit market by planting many new grapefruit trees. These new farms are not yet as productive as their US counterparts (even when transport costs are taken into account) but will be cheaper once Turkey establishes a customs union with the European Union in agricultural products. Officials from the European Union worry about what will happen with the European grapefruit market and ask for your advice.

a. Draw a partial equilibrium framework of the European grapefruit market. Draw the demand and supply of grapefruit within Europe and the supply curves of the USA and Turkey. Indicate clearly the price of grapefruit in Europe, European production, and European imports of grapefruit.

b. What happens to the imports, the production, and the price of grapefruit in Europe once it establishes a full customs union with Turkey?

c. What are the welfare effects of a full customs union with Turkey for consumers, producers, and the EU governments? What is the total welfare effect?

d. If the European Union still wants to pursue a full customs union with Turkey, is there a loophole to increase welfare on the grapefruit market?

Question 12.3

Briefly answer the following questions.

a. What are the European Union's (EU) four freedoms?

b. Briefly describe the history of EU integration.

c. What are two main challenges for the EU?

See the **online resources** *for a Study Guide and questions:*
www.oup.com/uk/vanmarrewijk_it/

Part V

. . . .

International firms

. . . .

Part V of this book focuses on the role of international firms in international trade flows and consists of three chapters. We start in Chapter 13 by providing an overview of the enormous differences between firms (in size, productivity, and so on) before analysing the economic trade consequences of this heterogeneity. Chapter 14 analyses the rising importance of (heterogeneous) multinational firms in international trade flows, with a focus on horizontal foreign direct investment. Chapter 15 concludes with an overview of global supply chains and offshoring, examining the role of multinationals in vertical foreign direct investment.

13 Heterogeneous firms

◎ Objectives

- To know that in many sectors only a fraction of firms engage in trading activities.
- To know that exporting firms are larger, employ more workers, use more capital, pay higher wages, use more skilled workers, and are more productive.
- To know that similar observations hold for importing firms and multinational firms.
- To understand the main structure of the heterogeneous firms model in which the least productive firms (below the viability cut-off level) exit the market.
- To understand that more productive firms charge lower prices and have higher production, revenue, and profits than less productive firms.
- To understand how (costly) firm entry determines the viability cut-off level endogenously.
- To understand how trade raises competition and thus increases the viability cut-off level.
- To know why only the most productive firms self-select in export activities and expand production; to understand why only the most productive exporting firms have higher profits.
- To know that trade raises welfare through two novel welfare effects: (i) the least productive firms exit the market and (ii) production volume shifts toward the most productive firms.
- To know and understand the productivity ranking of firms: exiting firms— domestic firms—exporting firms—multinational firms.

13.1 Introduction

Casual observation shows that firms differ in many aspects. What they produce, how they are organized, how much they sell, for which markets they produce, and how productive they are vary substantially from one firm to another. Since the late twentieth century the activities and characteristics of the firm and how firms differ in many relevant aspects have become central concerns in international economic analysis. This shift of emphasis was made possible by a much wider availability of detailed micro-level data (first in the US and then in many other countries) which allowed empirical economists (led by Bernard and Jensen, 1995, 1999) to analyse firm characteristics for different types of firms. As we will emphasize throughout this part of the book, these differences between firms are astoundingly large, a fact that calls into question the relevance of the hitherto dominant models in which firm size is indeterminate (and unimportant; see Chapters 4 to 6) or there is a representative firm (see Chapter 7 and Chapter 8).

Section 13.2 reviews empirical evidence on the heterogeneity of firms: how they differ in size, productivity, and organization. We will see that even in a country's strong sectors only a small share of all firms engage in export activities. These exporting firms tend to be larger, employ more workers, use more capital, pay higher wages, use more skilled workers, and have higher productivity than firms that are active only in the domestic market. Similar observations hold for firms that engage in multinational activities or importing activities (see Section 13.3).

Melitz (2003; see Box 13.1) provided the first thorough (and enormously influential) theoretical analysis of the consequences of international trade between countries when firms differ in terms of productivity. We analyse the main structure and outcomes of his approach, which is based on the monopolistic competition model of Chapter 8, in Sections 13.4–13.6. In this analysis, differences in firm productivity are not explained at the firm level, as it is the outcome of a random draw after firms pay a fixed entry cost. In contrast, average firm productivity at the firm level is explained *endogenously* at the *country* level, since a minimum viability cut-off level below which firms are forced to exit the market is determined endogenously, which in turn determines average productivity. This is one of the most important contributions of the Melitz model. Moreover, if firms engage in trading activities there are two important new welfare gains from trade. First, the rising firm competition from trade raises the minimum viability cut-off level and thus forces the least efficient firms out of the market. This raises average productivity. Second, for the remaining firms there is a redistribution of output from the less efficient to the more efficient firms, which again raises average productivity. Regarding the variety gains from trade analysed in Chapter 8, the Melitz model behaves like the representative firm model analysed in that chapter with the important qualifications that the productivity of the representative firm is determined endogenously and underlies a wide distribution of firms with different productivity levels.

A wide range of theoretical work building on the Melitz model has appeared: see Melitz and Redding (2014) for a recent overview. In this chapter we restrict attention to the link between comparative advantage and heterogeneous firms (in Box 13.2, based on the work of Bernard, Redding and Schott, 2007) and determining the mode of entering a foreign market for heterogeneous firms through either exports or multinational activity (based on

---

BOX 13.1 Marc Melitz

Figure 13.1
Marc Melitz (1968–).

Born in New Orleans and the son of an economist, Marc Melitz grew up in France (outside Paris) and has dual French–US citizenship. He returned to the US to study mathematics and attend business school (University of Maryland). While working as a management consultant in business logistics and visiting many production facilities he became interested in productivity issues. He decided to go back for a PhD in economics at the University of Michigan and since then has worked at Harvard University (with an interlude at Princeton University). His article on firm heterogeneity published in 2003 in *Econometrica* was the start of a flourishing literature with the aim of better understanding the macroeconomic implications of microeconomic firm differences.

BOX 13.2 Firm heterogeneity and comparative advantage

In this book we discuss a country's comparative advantage in certain sectors (based on factor abundance or technology differences) as a source of trade flows and gains from trade. This obviously raises the question of how firm heterogeneity as a source of gains from trade interacts with the previously discussed comparative advantages. In an ingenious exposition, Bernard, Redding, and Schott (2007) answer this question based on a model that combines insights from both literatures by having heterogeneous firms in two different sectors (both consisting of a range of varieties produced by individual firms), where production requires two inputs (skilled labour and unskilled labour) and factor abundance determines in which sector a country has a comparative advantage.

The key results of the paper are illustrated in Figure 13.2. Suppose the two sectors have a similar autarky cut-off productivity level A (so in autarky firms with lower productivity exit the market). Then with costly trade (that is: with transportation costs) the heterogeneous firms trade selection effect is *stronger* for the firms in the sector with *comparative* advantage: the trade cut-off productivity level shifts more to the right ($B > B'$). At the same time (other things equal) a larger share of surviving firms in the strong sector (with comparative advantage) will engage in exporting activities as the export cut-off productivity level (beyond which firms start to export) is higher for firms in the sector with comparative disadvantage ($C' > C$). The two sources of trade flows and gains from trade thus reinforce each other, since the authors show that average firm output increases, but more so in the sector with comparative advantage.

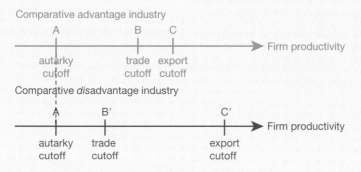

Figure 13.2 Comparative advantage, trade, and firm heterogeneity.

the work of Helpman, Melitz, and Yeaple, 2004, in Section 13.7). This framework is able to explain the empirical ranking of firms, in which the least productive firms exit the market, the less productive firms produce for the domestic market, the more productive firms also export, while the most productive firms become multinationals (see Chapter 14 for more on multinational activity).

13.2 Firm heterogeneity in exports

We begin this chapter by providing some basic empirical information on firm heterogeneity and trade, largely based on data from Bernard et al. (2015).[1] Figure 13.3 shows on the horizontal axis that, on average, only 35 per cent of US manufacturing firms export their products. This differs widely for the 21 manufacturing sectors identified in the figure (bubbles proportional to the number of firms in the sector), ranging from 15 per cent for printing and related support to 75 per cent for computer and electronic products. We make four observations. First, on average it is relatively rare to be an exporting firm, as only one in three firms engage in exporting activities. Second, the share of exporting firms differs per sector. Third, assuming that the US has a 'traditional' (technology or factor-abundance based) comparative advantage in computers, the share of exporting firms is positively related to traditional sources of comparative advantage. Fourth, firm heterogeneity is substantial: even for the strongest sectors not *all* firms are exporting, while for the weak sectors there are still some firms that *do* export.

Figure 13.3 also indicates (on the vertical axis) mean exports as a share of total shipments. The average export share is only 17 per cent, considerably less than the 35 per cent of firms that engage in exporting activities. The lowest share of export revenue is for paper manufacturing (6 per cent) and the highest share for electrical equipment, appliance (47 per cent). Beverages and tobacco products is the only sector where the mean exports as a share of total shipments (30 per cent) is not less than the fraction of firms in the sector that exports (also 30 per cent). For the majority of firms the domestic market seems to be more important, but there is substantial variation among the different sectors.

Since not all firms engage in exporting activities it is worthwhile to investigate to what extent exporting firms differ from non-exporting firms. One way to do this is to analyse information for thousands of firms using regression analysis to estimate the size of the differences. This is done in Figure 13.4, which reports exporter premia over non-exporters in per cent. Let's first focus on the simple regressions (the 'none' bars). Panel b. of the figure

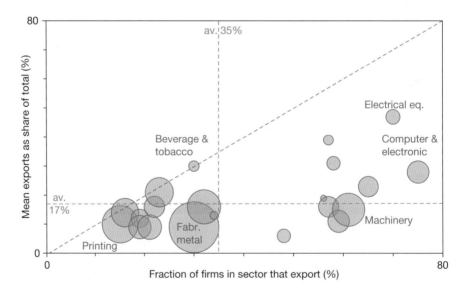

Figure 13.3 Exporting activities in different sectors: USA, 2007.

Notes: 21 sectors; averages refer to aggregate manufacturing; bubble size proportional to the percentage of firms in total manufacturing for that sector.

Source: based on data in Bernard et al. (2015).

shows that exporting firms are larger than non-exporters: they employ about 128 per cent more people and shipments are about 172 per cent larger. Panel a. shows that they have other characteristics as well: the skill per worker is about 6 per cent higher, the capital per worker about 28 per cent higher, the wages they pay about 21 per cent higher, the value added per worker about 33 per cent higher, and the firm's total factor productivity is about 3 per cent higher.[2] The simple regressions lump all firms in all sectors together. To control for differences between sectors we should look at the 'FE' bars, which allow for sector-specific fixed effects. In general, the estimated premia are a little bit lower (except for total factor productivity), but all still strong and highly significant (except for skill per worker). Finally, we can also control for the size of the firm by looking at the 'FE+Empl' bars, which control for sector fixed effects and employment size. As expected, this reduces the estimated shipment premium (from 135 to 24 per cent, see panel b.). All other estimated firm characteristic premia in panel a., however, become larger and are highly significant (including skill per worker).

To conclude this section we illustrate the extent to which different firms are heterogeneous regarding their productivity levels. This is done for total factor productivity in

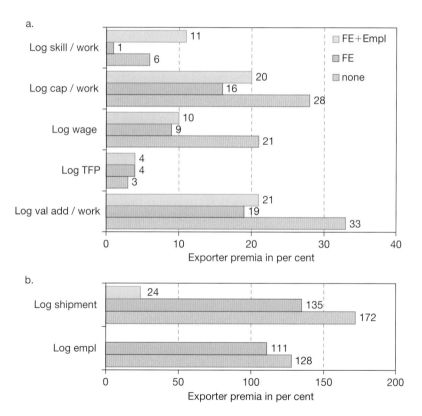

Figure 13.4 Exporter premia in per cent: USA, 2007.

Notes: legend identifies additional covariates in bivariate OLS regressions; FE = Industry Fixed Effects; FE+Empl = Industry Fixed Effects and Log Employment; Skill/Work = Skill per Worker; Cap/Work = Capital per Worker; TFP = Total Factor Productivity; Val Add/Work = Value Added per Worker; Empl = Employment; all significant at 1 per cent except log skill/work FE.
Source: based on data in Bernard et al. (2015).

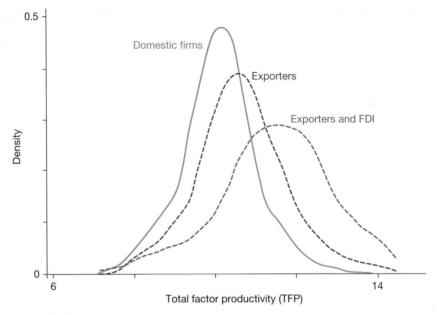

Figure 13.5 Differences in total factor productivity: Belgium, 2004.

Source: based on Mayer and Ottaviano (2007).

Belgium in Figure 13.5 for three different types of firms, namely firms producing only for the domestic market (domestic firms), firms that also engage in export activity (exporters), and firms that, in addition, also engage in foreign direct investment (exporters and FDI). The figure clearly illustrates two main empirical regularities. First, there are large productivity differences between firms, even within the same type of firm. Second, there is a ranking of firm level productivity. On average, firms engaging in exports *and* FDI are the most productive, domestic firms are the least productive, and exporting firms are in between these two types of firms. The theoretical analysis in this chapter explains why this is the case and what the welfare consequences of international trade flows are in a setting that incorporates firm heterogeneity.

13.3 Firm heterogeneity in imports

As larger and more detailed data sets on firms became available, economists first focused on the characteristics of exporting firms, as discussed in Section 13.2. Only at a later stage was attention also given to the characteristics of importing firms. As we will discuss in Chapter 15, firms may be able to increase their productivity if they import parts or components from elsewhere, for example because they are part of a global supply chain. This section therefore briefly analyses firm heterogeneity in imports.

Figure 13.6 analyses three dimensions of firm heterogeneity. In panel a. the horizontal axis shows the share of firms in a sector that exports (as in Figure 13.3), while the vertical axis shows the share of firms in a sector that imports. On average, fewer firms engage in importing activity than in exporting activity (20 versus 35 per cent). Apparel manufacturing is the

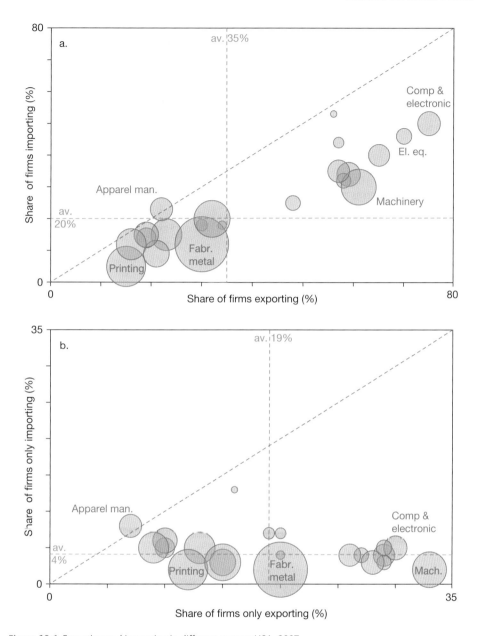

Figure 13.6 Exporting and importing in different sectors: USA, 2007.

Notes: 21 sectors; averages refer to Aggregate Manufacturing; bubble size proportional to the per cent of firms in total manufacturing for that sector.

Source: based on data in Bernard et al. (2015).

only sector where the share of importing firms is larger than the share of exporting firms (23 versus 22 per cent). There are, again, substantial differences between sectors, ranging from 5 per cent importing firms for printing to 53 per cent for leather and allied product. We also notice the positive association between the share of firms that export and import;

on average, the share of firms importing rises by about two-thirds of a per cent if the share of firms exporting rises by 1 per cent.

We should realize, of course, that some firms may be engaged in both exporting and importing activity, while other firms engage only in exporting or only in importing activity. In fact, the average number of firms engaging in both exporting and importing activity is 16 per cent, slightly below the 20 per cent of firms that import. If we created a panel (not shown) with exporting firms on the horizontal axis and importing and exporting firms on the vertical axis it would look very similar to panel a. of Figure 13.6 (slightly shifted downward; the share of firms exporting and importing also rises by about two-thirds of a per cent if the share of firms exporting rises by 1 per cent). Instead, we created panel b., which shows the share of firms only exporting on the horizontal axis (on average 19 per cent) and the share of firms only importing on the vertical axis (on average 4 per cent). This shows that there is no relationship between these two variables. It also shows that just a few firms only import, while a substantial number of firms only export.[3]

Figure 13.7 shows trade premia relative to domestic firms for three different groups of firms, namely exporters, importers, and exporter–importers (see Box 13.3 for European

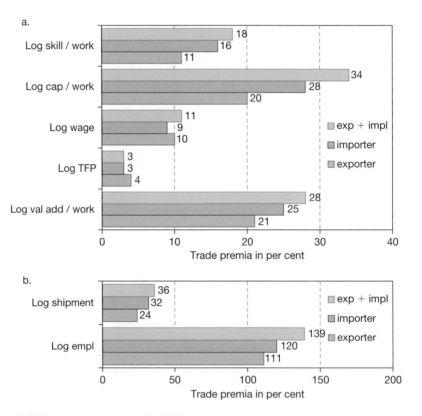

Figure 13.7 Trade premia in per cent: USA, 2007.

Notes: exp+imp = exporter and importer; all bivariate OLS regressions with Industry Fixed Effects and Log Employment (except Log Employment itself); Skill/Work = Skill per Worker; Cap/Work = Capital per Worker; TFP = Total Factor Productivity; Val Add/Work = Value Added per Worker; Empl = Employment.
Source: based on data in Bernard et al. (2015).

evidence). All premia control for sector fixed effects and employment size (except, of course, employment itself, which has only sector fixed effects). All premia are highly significant. The trade premia for importers are higher than for exporters (except for total factor productivity and wages), while the trade premia for exporter–importers are higher than for importers (except for total factor productivity, which is the same). In any case, we can conclude that firms engaging in international trade activity have significantly higher employment, shipments, value added per worker, total factor productivity, capital per worker, and skills per worker and they also pay higher wages than domestic firms.

BOX 13.3 European exporter and FDI premia

Mayer and Ottaviano (2008) provide an empirical overview of firm heterogeneity for firms engaged in exports and foreign direct investments (FDI) for a selection of European countries. For three countries (France, Belgium, and Norway) information is available for both exporting firms and firms engaged in FDI regarding four firm characteristics (employment, value added, wage rates, and capital intensity; see Figure 13.8). The premia are defined as the ratio of a variable for exporters relative to non-exporters or for firms engaging in FDI relative to non-FDI firms. It is clear that firms engaged in exports or FDI have substantial employment and value added premia.[4] In addition (less clear from the figure), they pay somewhat higher wages and are more capital-intensive.[5] This is in line with the more detailed American information reported in Sections 13.2 and 13.3.

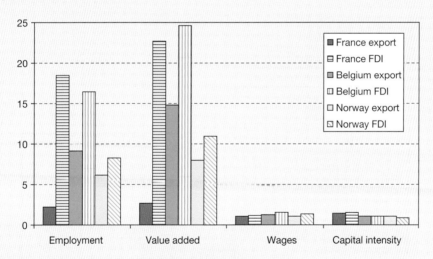

Figure 13.8 Exporter and FDI premia: France, Belgium, and Norway.

Source: figure based on data from Mayer and Ottaviano (2008, Table 4).

13.4 Main structure and firm behaviour

Building on Hopenhayn's (1992a, 1992b) work on endogenous selection of heterogeneous firms in a sector and Krugman's (1979, 1980) model of trade under monopolistic competition with increasing returns to scale, Melitz (2003) develops an ingenious dynamic model in which (i) less productive firms exit the market, (ii) intermediately productive firms produce only for the local market, and (iii) the most productive firms both export and produce for the local market. The Melitz approach is based on the monopolistic competition model of intra-industry trade discussed in Chapter 8 with one important difference: instead of all firms having identical technology, a firm may now be identified by its productivity level φ (which differs among firms). As in Chapter 8 there is increasing returns to scale at the firm level due to a (per period) fixed cost f, which we assume to be the same for all firms. Firm productivity heterogeneity arises from differences in marginal production costs. More specifically, for a firm with productivity level φ the labour costs involved in producing q units of a good are $f + q/\varphi$. As we will see, firms with different productivity levels charge different prices, produce different quantities, and so on. We denote these variables with a sub-index φ.

The main structure of the model is illustrated in Figure 13.9. There is a large number M of active firms in the economy, each producing a differentiated good under monopolistic competition. Since the firms differ in their productivity levels φ, they have different levels of operating profits.[6] Firm exit at this stage occurs with an exogenous probability of 'bad luck' δ, identical for all firms. In each period δM active firms therefore exit the market. The prospective of earning positive operating profits entices M_{en} firms, out of an unlimited pool of potential entrants, to try to enter the market. Each of these firms incurs a fixed entry cost f_{en} for their attempt (note that these entry costs differ from the per-period fixed costs f).

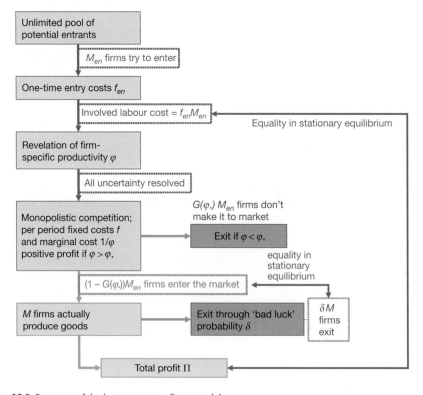

Figure 13.9 Structure of the heterogeneous firms model.

In equilibrium, the total entry costs $f_{en}M_{en}$ are equal to the total operating profits. The only uncertainty in the model involves the *ex ante* firm productivity level, which is resolved upon investing the one-time entry costs. Once the firm productivity level is known, the entrepreneur can determine if it is possible to earn positive operating profits. If not—that is, if the productivity level is below a certain threshold φ_*—the potential entrant will immediately exit the market with probability $G(\varphi_*)$. The remaining $1 - G(\varphi_*)$ firms do in fact enter the market succesfully. In the stationary equilibrium, the number of entrants is equal to the number of active firms that exit the market δM and the total number of active firms does not change.

We already saw in Chapter 8 that the demand for a particular variety of a good is iso-elastic with elasticity parameter $\varepsilon > 1$, such that $q_\varphi = Ap_\varphi^{-\varepsilon}$ (see equation 8.5).[7] We also noted that this leads to a constant mark-up $\varepsilon/(\varepsilon - 1)$ of price over marginal costs (see equation 8.8). Setting the wage rate as numéraire ($w = 1$), this implies that a firm with productivity level φ which has marginal costs $1 / \varphi$ charges an optimal price $p_\varphi = \left(\dfrac{\varepsilon}{\varepsilon-1}\right)\left(\dfrac{1}{\varphi}\right)$.

This is illustrated in Figure 13.10 for two firms with different productivity levels; firm 1 is more productive than firm 2 and thus has lower marginal costs ($c_1 < c_2$). The left-hand graph of Figure 13.10 illustrates iso-elastic demand and the associated marginal revenue curve (MR). Firm 1 equates marginal revenue and marginal costs at point a_1, charges optimal price p_1, and earns operating profits equal to area $p_1b_1a_1c_1$. Firm 2 equates marginal revenue and marginal costs at point a_2, charges a higher optimal price p_2, and consequently earns lower operating profits equal to area $p_2b_2a_2c_2$. The right-hand graph of Figure 13.10 depicts these two operating profit levels for the two different marginal costs levels. If we

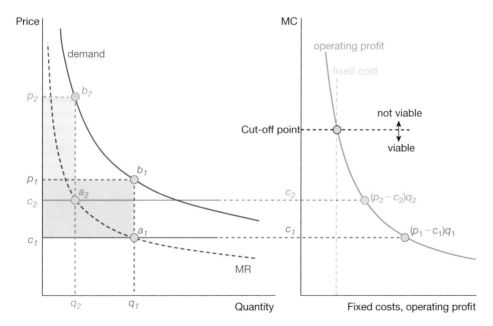

Figure 13.10 Firm heterogeneity, prices, and profits.

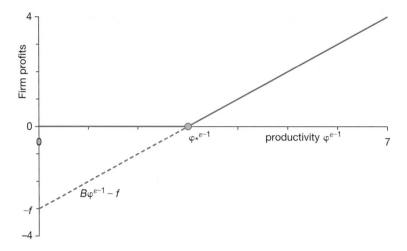

Figure 13.11 Firm productivity and firm profits.

repeat this exercise for all possible different marginal cost levels we can derive the optimal profit curve for all possible combinations also shown in the right-hand graph. If we substitute the optimal price information in the demand function we can derive the firm's total revenue r_φ and profits π_φ (see Technical Note 13.1, also for a definition of the constant B):

$$r_\varphi = p_\varphi q_\varphi = \varepsilon B \varphi^{\varepsilon-1}; \quad \pi_\varphi = B\varphi^{\varepsilon-1} - f \tag{13.1}$$

So far we have identified firm productivity by the variable φ. Equation 13.1 shows that if we identify firm productivity instead by the monotonic transformation $\varphi^{\varepsilon-1}$, then firm revenue and firm profits are *linear* in firm productivity. Figure 13.11 illustrates the relationship between this measure of firm productivity and firm profits. If firm productivity is close to zero then the firm makes a per-period loss equal to the fixed costs f if it decides to produce. As a consequence, the best this firm can do is exit the market and have zero profits. As productivity rises, firm profits rise as well. Once firm productivity passes a certain threshold level, equal to $\varphi_*^{\varepsilon-1}$ in Figure 13.11, profits become positive and non-zero production is possible (the firm becomes viable in the market). This point is also illustrated in Figure 13.10. The firm takes this cut-off point as given, but it is determined endogenously in the general equilibrium of this model through entry, exit, and the mass of firms.

13.5 Entry, exit, and equilibrium

To construct a minimalist dynamic model, we impose an exogenous probability of firm exit (through some shock or bad luck) equal to δ and common for all firms. In each period δM firms therefore exit the market. This is confronted with an endogenous determination of firm entry. The active firms in the market are earning positive operating profits as given in equation 13.1. This makes it attractive for potential entrants to enter the market. There are two caveats. First, they do not yet know their productivity level. Second, they have to incur a one-time fixed cost (in terms of labour), equal to f_{en}, in order to enter the market. These issues are connected, as we assume that all uncertainty is resolved once the entry costs are paid.

The firm's entry problem is illustrated in Figure 13.12, which shows the *ex ante* probability density function (pdf, see Box 13.4) of a firm's productivity draw φ which becomes known once the entry costs f_{en} are paid. The probability that the firm is not viable (and does not produce) after paying the entry costs depends on the location of the cut-off level φ_*: more specifically, the probablity that $\varphi < \varphi_*$ is equal to the area under the pdf. In all those cases the firm will have zero operating profits and make an *ex post* loss equal to f_{en}. If productivity is above the cut-off level ($\varphi > \varphi_*$), the firm makes a positive operating profit each period it survives in the market. Per period the operating profit is ($B\varphi^{\varepsilon-1}- f$), see equation 13.1. Since the probability of exit in any period is equal to δ, the probability that the firm is still operative after t periods is $(1 - \delta)^t$. Ignoring discounting for simplicity, the net present value of the operating profits is therefore equal to $(B\varphi^{\varepsilon-1}- f) / \delta.$[8] If this value is less than the entry costs f_{en} the entrant will still make an *ex post* loss; only if this value is larger than the entry costs will the entrant make an *ex post* expected profit. The probability of any particular outcome occurring is, of course, given by the pdf $g(\varphi)$. The *free entry condition* for potential entrants ensures that the ex ante expected value of discounted profits is equal to the entry costs f_{en}:

$$\int_{\varphi_*}^{\infty} [(B\varphi^{\varepsilon-1} - f)/\delta]g(\varphi)d\varphi = f_{en} \qquad 13.2$$

We can now combine the free entry condition with the zero profit condition regarding viability to endogenously (and uniquely) determine the cut-off productivity level φ_* in autarky:

$$h(\varphi_*) = \frac{\delta f_{en}}{f} \qquad 13.3$$

—where the monotonically declining function $h(\varphi_*)$ is as defined in Technical Note 13.2. Note that the free entry condition determines the average profits (and revenue)

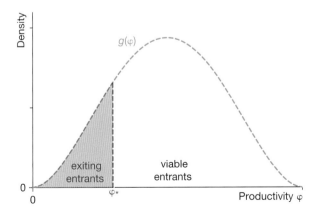

Figure 13.12 Firm entry problem.

BOX 13.4 Uncertainty: density and distribution

When you flip a coin the outcome is uncertain. If the coin is fair the chance that 'tails' will appear is 50 per cent, indicating that if you flip the coin infinitely many times, half of the outcomes will be tails. The other outcomes will be 'heads' because these are the only two possibilities. We can represent this mathematically by defining the (discrete) random variable $x = 1$ if heads occurs and $x = 0$ if tails occurs. For the fair coin we then write $P(x = 1) = 0.5$ and $P(x = 0) = 0.5$ to indicate the probability P of an outcome. If the coin is not fair, say $P(x = 1) = 0.6$, then we know that $P(x = 0) = 0.4$ because the total probability must be unity (*some* outcome must occur).

The variable x of outcomes may also take on a continuum of possibilities, say any value in the interval [0,1]. Rather than focusing on a particular outcome, we now focus on the probability that the outcome falls in a certain range as dictated by the *probability density function* (pdf), say $g(x)$. The probability that the outcome is then below a certain value x, referred to as the *cumulative distribution function* (cdf), say $G(x)$, is given by $G(x) \equiv P(X \leq x) = \int_0^x g(x)dx$. This is illustrated in Figure 13.13, where the area under the curve of $g(x)$ between 0 and x gives the probability that the outcome is below the value x, which is equal to the value of the cdf. Note that $G'(x) = g(x)$, the probability that the outcome is in between the values x_0 and x_1, is given by the area under the pdf between those points $\int_{x_0}^{x_1} g(x)dx = G(x_1) - G(x_0)$ and the probability that the outcome is equal to a specific value is zero.[9]

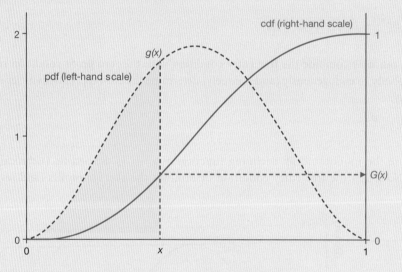

Figure 13.13 Cumulative distribution (cdf) and probability density (pdf).

of active firms, say $\bar{\pi} = \delta f_{en}/(1 - G(\varphi_*))$. If we denote by $\bar{\varphi}$ the productivity level associated with this average profit level it can be shown that the economy behaves *similarly* to the representative firm monopolistic competition model discussed in Chapter 8 with that average level of firm productivity (see, for example, Melitz and Redding, 2014). In particular, the number of firms active in the economy is proportional to the market size of the country and the love-of-variety effect is reflected in higher welfare levels for larger markets. The important difference is, of course, that this productivity level is determined *endogenously* within the model and is the appropriate representative of an underlying distribution of heterogeneous firms with many different levels of firm productivity.

13.6 Firm heterogeneity, trade, and productivity

What will happen in the economy described in Sections 13.4 and 13.5 when it is confronted with another, identical[10] economy with which it is able to trade? Based on overwhelming empirical evidence, we will make two crucial assumptions.[11] First, the firm must pay a per-unit trade cost and ship $\tau > 1$ units in order to ensure that one unit arrives in the destination country. This elegant way to model trade costs was introduced by Samuelson (1952) to avoid the need for explicitly modeling a transport sector. Since it is as if part of the product melts away in transit, it is called *iceberg* transportation costs. Second, the firm faces significant entry costs to get acquainted with the export market, to learn about the foreign legal system, to set up a foreign distribution channel, to adapt the product to foreign standards, and so on (see Roberts and Tybout, 1977). We model these export cost as a per period fixed investment cost $f_x > 0$, independent of the firm's export volume.[12] Each firm therefore faces the decision whether or not it is worthwhile to pay the fixed export costs and sell goods in the foreign market. We assume that the firm makes this export decision when it knows its productivity level and that the per period fixed production costs f are the same irrespective of export status.

The symmetry assumption ensures that the two countries have the same wage rates (normalized to unity) and the same aggregate variables. We have seen in Section 13.5 that in autarky the viability cut-off productivity level φ_* is determined endogenously by the condition $B\varphi_*^{\varepsilon-1} = f$. We have seen in Section 13.4 that the constant B, which determines a firm's demand and profitability, is determined endogenously and depends, in particular, on the economy-wide price index P. As a consequence, when the two identical countries engage in international trade under the conditions specified above this means that this constant differs in the trade equilibrium relative to the autarky equilibrium. We denote this by B_{tr}, where the sub-index *tr* refers to trade. In the discussion below we will analyse a trade equilibrium in which a fraction of firms export goods to the other country. As a consequence, more firms are active on a country's market under trade than in autarky, which increases competition and lowers the price index P. This, in turn, implies that the firm's demand and profitability constant is lower under trade than in autarky: $B_{tr} < B$.[13]

The optimal pricing rule is the same constant mark-up over marginal costs, so a firm with productivity level φ charges price $p_\varphi = \left(\dfrac{\varepsilon}{\varepsilon-1}\right)\left(\dfrac{1}{\varphi}\right)$ in the domestic market and price τp_φ in the foreign market to cover the higher marginal costs, provided exports are positive. Since the price charged in the foreign market is τ times as high and demand is iso-elastic with elasticity ε, the revenue in the foreign market is $\tau^{1-\varepsilon}$ times the revenue in the domestic markets (equal to $\tau^{1-\varepsilon}\varepsilon B_{tr}\varphi^{\varepsilon-1}$, see equation 13.1). Since operating profits are $1/\varepsilon$ times revenue and a firm will engage in exporting activity if the associated operating profits are larger than the fixed exporting costs f_x, this means a firm will export if $\tau^{1-\varepsilon}B_{tr}\varphi^{\varepsilon-1}-f_x>0$. We will denote this export productivity cut-off level by φ_{*x}. In line with the empirical observations discussed in Section 13.2, we will assume that the export cut-off level is higher than the viability cut-off level. This means that all firms are active in the domestic market and only a fraction of firms engages in export activity; this implies that the fixed export costs must be sufficiently large, namely $f_x>\tau^{1-\varepsilon}f$.

The trade situation relative to autarky is illustrated in Figure 13.14. In autarky, the profit line intercepts the vertical axis at $-f$ and has a slope equal to B. Firms become viable at the cut-off productivity level φ_* (the square in the figure). Under trade, firms that are active in the domestic market also have a profit line that intercepts the vertical axis at $-f$. This time, however, the slope is equal to B_{tr} which is smaller than B, hence the profit line rotates clockwise around the point $(0,-f)$ and firms become viable at a *higher* productivity level than under autarky: $\varphi_{*tr}>\varphi_*$. An important consequence of engaging in international trade is therefore that the least efficient firms are forced to exit the market; this holds for all firms in between productivity levels φ_* and φ_{*tr}. Figure 13.14 also shows the profit line for firms that want to engage in exporting activity. This profit line intercepts the vertical axis at $-f_x$ and has a slope equal to $\tau^{1-\varepsilon}B_{tr}$, which is strictly lower than the slope of the domestic profit line B_{tr} because $\varepsilon>1$. As a consequence, the export profit line is rotated clockwise relative to the domestic profit line and shifted along the vertical axis.[14] This implies that only the most productive firms engage in exporting activities. Finally, the green solid line in the figure shows the firm's profits under trade, which has two kinks. The first kink occurs at the viability point $\varphi_{*tr}^{\varepsilon-1}$: profits are zero for all firms below this cut-off point. The second kink occurs at the export viability point $\varphi_{*x}^{\varepsilon-1}$: export profits are positive for all firms beyond this cut-off point and these profits are added to the domestic profits.

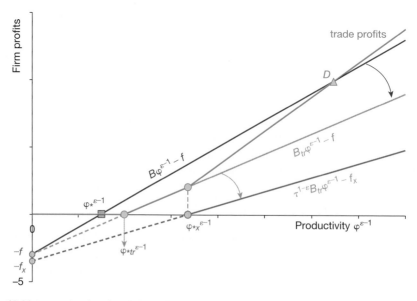

Figure 13.14 International trade viability and profits.

All firms in between these two cut-off points produce only for the domestic market. Note that profits under trade increase only for the most efficient firms with the highest productivity levels (above point D).

The main effects of trade for the firms are illustrated in Figure 13.15. The *ex ante* probability of a firm's productivity draw after paying the entry costs f_{en} is given by the pdf $g(\varphi)$. Under autarky the viability cut-off productivity is equal to φ_* and all firms below this productivity level are forced to exit the market (exit autarky). Under trade the viability cut-off productivity level increases to φ_{*tr} (as indicated by the arrow in the figure) and all least productive firms (those with productivity levels in between φ_* and φ_{*tr}) are forced to exit the market (exit trade). The export cut-off productivity level is given by φ_{*x}; only the most productive firms (with productivity levels beyond this cut-off value) will engage in export activities (exporting firms) and expand their production level (see Box 13.5). All firms in between these two productivity levels will produce only for the domestic market (domestic firms); these firms will contract their production level (see again Box 13.5). As noted by Melitz (2003, p. 1,712):

> The result that the modelling of fixed export costs explains the partitioning of firms by export status and productivity level is not exactly earth-shattering. This can be explained quite easily within a simple partial equilibrium model with a fixed distribution of productivity levels.

What such a partial equilibrium approach cannot explain, and what is thus the main contribution of the Melitz model, is the endogenous impact of trade flows on the distribution of productivity levels. It allows us to explain which firms gain or lose from trade competition, which firms exit the market, which firms produce only for the domestic market, and which firms export. In addition, we now understand that the shift of production towards the more efficient firms creates an additional and hitherto unexplored welfare gain.

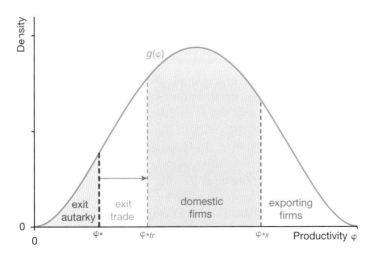

Figure 13.15 Impact of trade and distribution of firms.

BOX 13.5 Firm revenue

A firm's profit as a function of productivity is continuous with non-differentiable kinks at the viability and export cut-off points, as illustrated in Figures 13.11 and 13.14. This box points out that a firm's production and revenue level is not continuous and has 'jumps' at these cut-off points. This is illustrated for firm revenue in Figure 13.16. In autarky, firm revenue is (i) zero below the viability cut-off level $\varphi_*^{\varepsilon-1}$, (ii) jumps to εf at this cut-off level (since $B\varphi_*^{\varepsilon-1} = f$ and revenue is $\varepsilon B\varphi_*^{\varepsilon-1}$, see equation 13.1), and (iii) then rises at the rate εB. Under trade, firm revenue is (i) zero up to the higher viability cut-off level $\varphi_{*tr}^{\varepsilon-1}$, then (ii) jumps to εf at this cut-off level (for the same reason), then (iii) rises at the lower rate εB_{tr} up to the export viability cut-off level $\varphi_{*x}^{\varepsilon-1}$, followed by (iv) a jump of size εf_x (for similar reasons), and finally (v) a continued rise in revenue at the (higher) rate $(1 + \tau^{1-\varepsilon})\varepsilon B_{tr}$ beyond this cut-off level. The figure clearly shows that revenue expands only for the most productive firms that engage in export activities and contracts for all other firms, some of which are even forced to exit the market. As a consequence, there is a shift in total output towards the most productive firms.

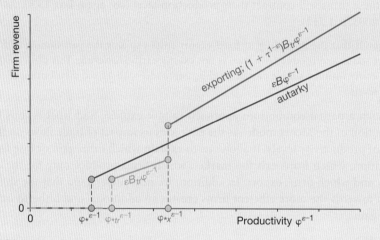

Figure 13.16 Firm productivity and firm revenue.

13.7 Firm heterogeneity and mode of entry

The analysis so far has been helpful in determining whether or not a firm will enter the foreign market under firm heterogeneity. It is time to go one step further and determine not only under which conditions a firm will enter the foreign market, but also how it will be active on that market, namely through trade or through (horizontal) foreign direct investment (FDI). We base our exposition on the Helpman, Melitz, and Yeaple (2004) approach and distinguish between three types of firms, namely (i) domestic firms (producing only for the domestic market), (ii) exporting firms (serving also the foreign market through trade flows), and (iii) multinationals (serving also the foreign market through a subsidiary). It is vital, of course, to have an idea about the main empirical differences between these three types of firms. This is provided in Table 13.1, which shows that (other things equal) exporting firms are about 39 per cent more productive than domestic firms (see also Section 13.2), while multinationals are about 54 per cent more productive than domestic firms. Consequently (third row of Table 13.1), multinational firms are about 15 per cent more productive

Table 13.1 Productivity advantage of multinationals and exporters

	coefficient	t-statistic
Multinationals*	0.537	14.432
Non-multinational exporters*	0.388	9.535
Advantage of multinationals over non-multinational exporters	0.150	3.694
Number of firms	3,202	

Notes: labour productivity (log of output per worker) differences, controlling for capital intensity and four-digit industry fixed effects, 1996; all results significant at the 1 per cent level; * = relative to domestic firms.
Source: Helpman, Melitz, and Yeaple (2004, Table 1).

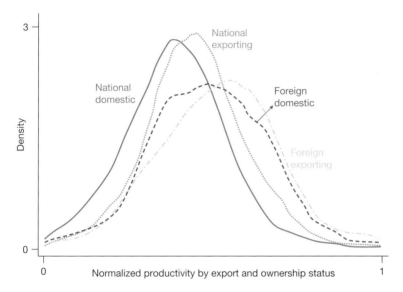

Figure 13.17 Productivity distributions in Latin America, 2006.
Source: Chang and van Marrewijk (2013).

than exporting firms. There is, therefore, a clear productivity hierarchy: domestic firms are the least productive, multinationals the most productive, and in between are exporting firms.

Figure 13.17 illustrates the findings of Table 13.1 for a somewhat more detailed distinction of four types of firms for Latin America, namely national firms producing for the domestic market, national firms that also export, foreign firms producing for the domestic market, and foreign firms that also export. Although there is considerable overlap between the different types of firms, the figure clearly shows that the national firms producing for the domestic market are the least productive, while the foreign firms (FDI) engaged in exporting are the most productive.

Inspired by the Melitz model explained above, Helpman, Melitz, and Yeaple (2004) analyse a world with many countries and many sectors and a homogeneous good.[15] A sector produces differentiated goods using labour as the only input. As above, a firm incurs a fixed cost to be able to start production and then learns its productivity parameter drawn from an *ex ante* distribution function. It may then either exit (if productivity is not high enough) or start production, in which case it is faced with a fixed overhead cost. A producing firm can either not serve the foreign markets (in which case it is a *domestic* firm)

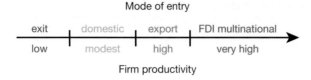

Figure 13.18 Firm productivity and mode of entry.

or serve the foreign markets in one of two ways, namely either through *exports* (in which case it incurs an additional fixed cost in each market as well as [iceberg] per unit transport costs) or through FDI (in which case it incurs higher additional fixed cost in each market than exporting firms but does not have to pay for transport costs). The fixed costs for firms engaged in FDI are higher per market than for firms engaged in exports because the exporters have to pay only for establishing a distribution and servicing network while the FDI firms also have to pay for establishing a foreign subsidiary.

Firms with higher productivity can charge lower prices and thus sell more goods, and they have higher revenue and higher operating profits. Firms with very low productivity cannot earn high enough operating profits to cover the fixed costs and thus exit the market. Similarly, firms with modest productivity cannot recover the additional fixed cost to export to other countries and produce only for the domestic market. For firms with high productivity it is worthwhile to export to other countries as they recover the fixed export cost, but only firms with very high productivity are able to recover the very high fixed costs involved in establishing a foreign subsidiary. Figure 13.18 summarizes the theoretical implications of this model, which is in line with the empirical regularities observed in Section 13.2 and Figure 13.17. We return to this problem in the next chapter: see Section 14.8.

13.8 Conclusions

For a long time the international economics literature focused attention mostly on the aggregate level: that is, on sector-wide or country-wide outcomes. We have to keep in mind, however, that it is ultimately not countries but *firms* that export to and invest in other countries. These firms differ from one another enormously in terms of the amount of capital, labour, and technology used in their production processes and in terms of their size and productivity level. Over the past decades much more detailed data sets on firm characteristics have become available in many countries, allowing us to explore the empirical characteristics of different types of firms.

Thanks to the work of Melitz (2003) and many of his followers we are now able to better understand the consequences of international trade for heterogeneous firms that differ in their productivity levels. The main contribution of this work is (i) to *endogenously* determine average firm level productivity at the country level, (ii) to understand how rising firm competition from trade forces the least efficient firms out of the market (thus raising average productivity), and (iii) to understand how total output is redistributed among the remaining firms from less efficient to more efficient (exporting) firms (again raising average productivity). Similar observations and models can be constructed from an importing firm's perspective. We return to this issue in Chapter 15, after analysing other aspects of multinational firms in Chapter 14.

Technical Note

Technical Note 13.1 Firm revenue and profits

For a firm with productivity φ we substitute the optimal price $p_\varphi = \left(\dfrac{\varepsilon}{\varepsilon-1}\right)\left(\dfrac{1}{\varphi}\right)$ in the demand function $q_\varphi = Ap_\varphi^{-\varepsilon}$ and multiply by p_φ to get revenue r_φ:

$$r_\varphi = p_\varphi q_\varphi = \left[\left(\frac{\varepsilon}{\varepsilon-1}\right)\left(\frac{1}{\varphi}\right)\right]A\left[\left(\frac{\varepsilon}{\varepsilon-1}\right)\left(\frac{1}{\varphi}\right)\right]^{-\varepsilon} = \varepsilon(\varepsilon-1)^{\varepsilon-1}\varepsilon^{-\varepsilon}A\varphi^{\varepsilon-1} = \varepsilon B\varphi^{\varepsilon-1} \qquad (A13.1)$$

—where the constant B is defined as $B \equiv (\varepsilon-1)^{\varepsilon-1}\varepsilon^{-\varepsilon}A$. Using this to determine profits π_φ gives

$$\pi_\varphi = p_\varphi q_\varphi - \left(f + \frac{q_\varphi}{\varphi}\right) = \frac{p_\varphi q_\varphi}{\varepsilon} - f = \frac{r_\varphi}{\varepsilon} - f = B\varphi^{\varepsilon-1} - f \qquad (A13.2)$$

—where the second equality uses the optimal pricing rule and the third and fourth equality use equation (A13.1).

Technical Note 13.2 Autarky equilibrium

The cut-off viability condition is given in equation (A13.3). Substituting this in the free entry condition (A13.4) to eliminate the constant B gives equation (A13.5). It can be shown that the function $h(\varphi_*)$ monotonically declines from ∞ to zero and thus uniquely determines the autarky equilibrium cut-off productivity given by equation (13.3).

$$B\varphi_*^{\varepsilon-1} - f = 0 \qquad (A13.3)$$

$$\int_{\varphi_*}^{\infty} \left[\left(B\varphi^{\varepsilon-1} - f\right)/\delta\right]g(\varphi)d\varphi = f_{en} \qquad (A13.4)$$

$$\int_{\varphi_*}^{\infty} \left(\varphi^{\varepsilon-1}\varphi_*^{1-\varepsilon} - 1\right)g(\varphi)d\varphi \equiv h(\varphi_*) = \delta f_{en}/f \qquad (A13.5)$$

Notes

1   See also Mayer and Ottaviano (2007, 2008), Bernard and Wagner (1997), and Aw and Hwang (1995).

2   See Chapter 17 on total factor productivity; for the firm this is based on Caves et al. (1982).

3   About half the exporting firms also import, while about four-fifths of the importing firms also export.

4   Value added is almost 25-fold for Belgian FDI firms.

5   The (not statistically significant) exception is capital intensity for Norwegian FDI firms, where the premium is slightly below unity.

6   This chapter analyses a very large (continuum) number of firms, hence we do not use a sub-index i to identify different firms but instead use the continuous parameter φ for this purpose.

7   The constant A is thus defined as $A \equiv IP^{\varepsilon-1}$, where I is the income level and P is the price index: see equation 8.5.

8   Since $\sum_{t=0}^{\infty}(1-\delta)^t = 1/\delta$.

9   We exclude continuous–discrete combinations with 'mass points' from our discussion.

10   The identical economy precludes wage differences between countries, so we can focus exclusively on the links between heterogeneity, trade, and productivity.

11   In the absence of these assumptions, trade has only a size-of-market (positive variety) welfare effect, as in Krugman (1980).

12 In our set-up this is equivalent to a one-time export investment cost equal to f_x / δ. See Romer (1994) and van Marrewijk and Berden (2007) for heterogeneity in the fixed entry costs.

13 This condition is intuitively obvious and is formally derived in Melitz (2003).

14 It is not necessary that $f_x > f$ as drawn in Figure 13.14, as long as $f_x > \tau^{1-\varepsilon} f$.

15 The homogeneous good sector is a catch-all numéraire sector, eliminating all income effects. The disadvantage of this approach, which is a common modeling trick, is that all rises in income are absorbed by this sector and have no impact at all on any of the other sectors. In contrast, the analysis itself usually focuses completely on these other sectors.

 ## Questions

Question 13.1

Figure 13.19 shows a productivity distribution of firms in Somewheria.

a. Briefly discuss how Melitz's model of firm heterogeneity under autarky and free trade identifies three types of firms under these different situations; illustrate these three firm types in a copy of the above figure with additional information.

b. What are the additional gains from trade identified by Melitz? Relate your discussion to your copy of the figure.

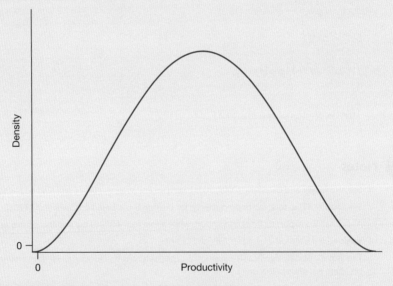

Figure 13.19 Productivity distribution of firms in Somewheria.

Question 13.2

Figure 13.20 illustrates a demand schedule confronted by three types of firms, namely a firm with marginal cost level c_1, c_2, and c_3.

a. Make a (large) copy of the figure. Draw in the marginal revenue curve. For each of the three firms determine (*explain and draw in the figure*):

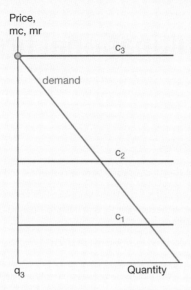

Figure 13.20 A firm with marginal cost level c_1, c_2, and c_3.

- The quantity produced
- The price charged
- The operating profits received

b. *Explain* briefly how the information from question a. can be useful for determining which firms are engaged in export activity and which firms are not.

Question 13.3

Suppose the economic conditions in Mirandia are perfectly described by the Melitz model of sections 13.4 to 13.6 and the *ex ante* productivity distribution function is *uniform* from 0 to 5. Moreover, assume that in autarky only 80 per cent of the entrepreneurs who invest in setting up a new firm actually succeed.

a. What is the autarky cut-off productivity level?

b. What is the *ex ante* average productivity? What is the *ex post* average productivity in autarky?

The government of Mirandia opens up international trade possibilities with Marconia. As a consequence, only 60 per cent of the entrepreneurs who invest in setting up a new firm actually succeed. Of the viable firms only one-third become exporters.

c. What is the trade cut-off productivity level?

d. What is the export cut-off productivity level?

e. What is the *ex post* average productivity with trade?

f. What is the average productivity for exporting firms?

g. What do you consider the best indicator of the new source of gains from trade explained in this chapter using (a combination of) your answers to the questions above?

 *See the **online resources** for a Study Guide and questions:*
www.oup.com/uk/vanmarrewijk_it/

14 Multinational firms

Objectives

- To be able to distinguish between extensive and intensive margins of trade.
- To understand the enormous size differences between firms in trade flows.
- To know the increasingly dominant role played by multinationals in trade flows.
- To understand the main stylized facts of multinationals in trade and investment flows.
- To know the difference between parents and affiliates and between source and destination countries.
- To understand the basic requirements of the OLI framework for becoming a multinational.
- To understand how transport costs and plant-level fixed costs create a proximity–concentration trade-off which determines how firms service foreign markets.
- To understand why multinational firms are particularly active if countries are similar in size and factor endowments and why exporting is dominant if they are very different.
- To understand how differences in firm productivity creates firms that produce only for the domestic market, firms that also export, and firms that become multinationals.
- To know that empirical evidence supports the proximity–concentration trade-off.

14.1 Introduction

We have seen in Chapter 9 how foreign direct investment (FDI) flows create multinationals through greenfield investments or mergers and acquisitions (M&As) and in Chapter 13 that there are enormous size and productivity differences between firms. We now combine and analyse this type of information by investigating the role of multinational firms in international production. Peter Neary is an important contributor to this type of research: see Box 14.1.

BOX 14.1 Peter Neary

Figure 14.1
Peter Neary (1950–).

Born in Ireland and educated at University College Dublin and Oxford, Peter Neary (Figure 14.1) returned to both places during his career and has been stationed at the University of Oxford since 2006. He seems to be indefatigable in his economic analysis, organizational enthusiasm, and travel explorations. Virtually all economists you meet know him (and like him). Amazingly, he also knows all of them personally. One of the first papers he published, on sector-specific capital, turned into a classic contribution almost instantly. Since then he has worked together with many economists on, for example, the Dutch disease, policy choice, strategic commitment, and multinational firms. Neary (2001) provides an excellent overview of the geographical economics literature, while Neary (2003) manages to successfully tackle the problem of strategic interaction among firms in a general equilibrium setting.

We start in Section 14.2 by providing information on multinationals in trade flows. We do this by analysing the *extensive margin* of trade, which refers to the number of products a firm trades and the number of trade origins or destinations. It contrasts with the *intensive margin*, which refers to the value of trade per product per country. We also do this by analysing within-firm trade transactions (related party trade). Together this information shows that large multinationals dominate international trade flows, particularly for advanced countries.

Section 14.3 provides additional information on multinational activities and combines this with information from Section 14.2 and Chapter 9 into a list of six stylized facts on multinational activity that need to be explained theoretically. The minimum requirements for explaining multinationals are provided in Section 14.4. The remainder of the chapter then supplies a theoretical framework for *horizontal* multinational activity (replicating a production process in another country). Chapter 15 will concentrate on analysing the sources and consequences of *vertical* multinational activity (fragmentation of the production process in supply chains).

The main insights into the forces underlying horizontal FDI decisions are clearly analysed in Section 14.5 using a simple one-production-factor model with differentiated goods and symmetric countries. We argue that the combination of transportation costs and plant-level scale economies leads to a proximity–concentration trade-off that explains why firms service some markets through exporting and other markets through multinational activities. Subsequently, Section 14.6 extends this framework by allowing for two factors of production, two types of goods, and two countries which may differ in relative size and factor endowments. It turns out that country differences are important for explaining exporting versus multinational activities and the proximity–concentration trade-off, as discussed empirically in Section 14.7. Using our analysis from Chapter 13 on heterogeneous firms,

Section 14.8 provides a second extension of the simple model analysed in Section 14.5 to incorporate differences in firm productivity. This allows us to derive a clear ranking of firms in terms of productivity levels, in which low-productivity firms produce for the domestic market, intermediate-productivity firms also engage in exporting activities, and only the most productive firms become multinationals.

14.2 Trade and multinationals

We have already found in Chapter 13 on firm heterogeneity that exporting firms tend to be larger and more productive. We now continue this discussion in two steps. First, we will analyse the extent to which trading firms differ regarding the number of products they trade and the number of countries they trade with, the so-called extensive margin of trade flows. Second, we analyse the extent to which trade involves within-firm transactions, so-called related party trade, where a firm in one country trades with a parent or affiliate in another country. We base our discussion on evidence for American firms, but similar observations hold for the structure of trade flows for other advanced countries.

Recall that only about a third of all American manufacturing firms are active in exporting activities (see Section 13.2). The differences between these exporting firms regarding the number of products they export, the number of countries they export to, and the value of these exports are enormous, as illustrated in Figure 14.2.

Panel a. of Figure 14.2 shows the distribution of the share of exporting firms over the number of products and the number of countries. By far the largest number of exporting firms (35 per cent of the total) export only one product to one other country, visualized in panel a. by the high bar in the left corner. Less than 9 per cent of the firms export one product to two countries, less than 4 per cent of the firms export one product to three countries, and only about 1 per cent of the firms export one product to 11 or more countries. In total, about 53 per cent of the exporting firms export only one product. In the other dimension,

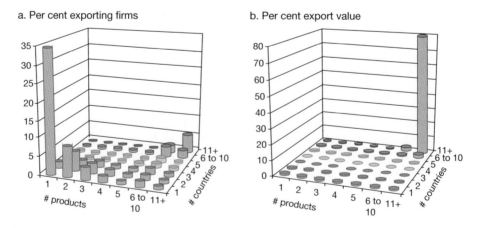

Figure 14.2 Export distribution by product and country: USA, 2007.

Source: based on data in Bernard et al. (2015).

about 2 per cent of the firms export two products to one country and less than 1 per cent of the firms export three products to one country, four products to one country, and so on. In total, about 38 per cent of the exporting firms export only to one country. In the upper right corner of panel a. we see the share of firms that export many products to many countries. About 16 per cent of the firms export six or more products to six or more countries. We thus observe a clear distinction in this panel: the majority of firms (more than 51 per cent) export one or two products to one or two countries (lower left corner), while only a small fraction of firms (less than 6 per cent) export 11 or more products to 11 or more countries.

Panel b. of Figure 14.2 shows the distribution of the export value over the number of products and the number of countries. This panel is clear: there are only four entries above 1 per cent of export value and they are all in the top right corner for firms that export six or more products to six or more countries; taken together these 16 per cent of firms account for more than 86 per cent of all export value (about seven times higher than the average value for exporting firms). By far the highest bar in panel b. is for the superstar firms that export more than 10 products to more than 10 countries; taken together these 5.5 per cent of firms account for about 80 per cent of all export value (about 15 times higher than the average value for exporting firms). A small fraction of very large firms is thus responsible for the large majority of export revenue. Most of these firms are multinationals, as we discuss below.

Figure 14.3 provides information regarding the distribution of imports rather than exports with respect to the number of products and the number of countries. Panel a. again shows the distribution of the number of firms. The picture is similar to that of exporting firms: a large share of firms (46 per cent) import one or two products from one or two countries, while a small fraction of firms (less than 9 per cent) import six or more products from six or more countries.

Panel b. of Figure 14.3 provides information on the per cent of employment rather than the per cent of import value. The reason is simple: a graph of the distribution of import value looks very similar to panel b. of Figure 14.2 on export value. The reader can thus simply look at that graph to get an impression; about 86 per cent of all import value is

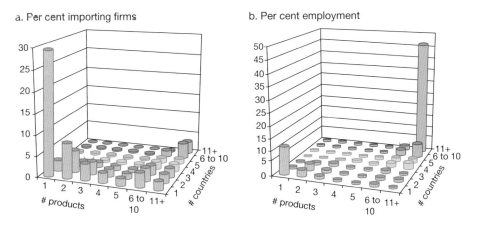

Figure 14.3 Import distribution by product and country: USA, 2007.

Source: based on data in Bernard et al. (2015).

located in the top right corner for firms that import six or more products from six or more countries and the largest bar is for the superstars, where 3 per cent of the firms import more than 76 per cent of import value. Regarding employment the position of the superstars is less prominent, as shown in panel b. of Figure 14.3. The share of employment for the 46 per cent of firms importing only one or two products from one or two countries is about 18 per cent (considerably more than the share of import value, which is less than 2 per cent). The share of employment for the 9 per cent of firms that import six or more products from six or more countries is 'only' about 56 per cent (considerably less than the 86 per cent of import value). The distribution of employment is thus in between the distributions of the number of firms and the trade value. The same holds for exports.

Now that we have established that a few large firms are responsible for a large share of the value of international trade flows (both for exports and imports) we take the next step by analysing the extent to which multinational firms are involved in these trade flows. As an indication of their importance we show in Figure 14.4 the size of total trade (panel a. for imports and panel b. for exports) and the size of related party trade. Note that related party trade underestimates the importance of multinationals in total trade flows as it only records within-firm flows between parents and affiliates and not trade flows between multinationals and other firms.

In real terms (constant 2014 USD), total import value rose from $1,471 billion in 2002 to $2,314 billion in 2014 (an increase of 57 per cent), with a substantial dip in 2009 (of more than $600 billion) as a result of the Great Recession, see panel a. of Figure 14.4. The related party imports follow the same pattern but show a more pronounced effect: they rose from $700 billion in 2002 to $1,179 billion in 2014 (an increase of 68 per cent), also with a substantial dip (of more than $260 billion) in 2009 as a result of the Great Recession. We thus note that, as a consequence of these developments, the share of related party trade in total imports is substantial (about half of all imports) and rose from about 48 per cent in 2002 to about 51 per cent in 2014 (see Figure 14.5).

Panel b. of Figure 14.4 depicts the same information for export value. Total export value rose from $802 billion in 2002 to $1,402 billion in 2014 (an increase of 75 per cent), with a dip of more than $260 billion in 2009. Note that total exports are considerably less than total imports as the USA has a large trade deficit (in these data of about $670 billion in 2002 and more than $900 billion in 2014). The related party exports follow the same pattern but with a *less* pronounced effect: they rose from $251 billion in 2002 to $408 billion in 2014 (an increase of 62 per cent), with a dip of $74 billion in 2009. We thus note that, as a consequence of these developments, the share of related party trade in total exports is substantial (around 30 per cent of all exports), but considerably less than their share in total imports (see Figure 14.5). Related party trade is thus particularly important for US imports. The share of related party exports in total exports declined slightly from about 31 per cent in 2002 to about 29 per cent in 2014 (see again Figure 14.5).

14.3 Stylized facts of multinationals

Multinationals differ from other firms in many aspects. An important objective of this chapter and the next is to better know and understand how and why multinationals are different. As a framework for their analysis of multinational firms in the most recent

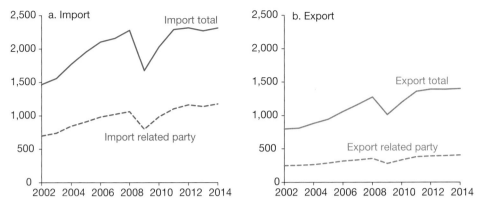

Figure 14.4 US total and related party imports and exports, 2002–2014.

Source: based on US Census Related Party Database; values in constant 2014 USD billion.

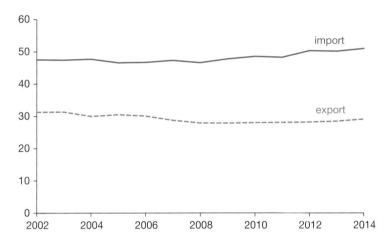

Figure 14.5 US related party trade: per cent of total import or export, 2002–2014.

Source: based on US Census Related Party Database.

Handbook of International Economics, Antràs and Yeaple (2014) therefore identify the following stylized facts:[1]

1. Multinational activity is primarily concentrated in advanced countries, where it is mostly two-way. Developing countries are more likely to be the destination of multinational activity than the source.

2. The relative importance of multinationals in economic activity is higher in goods that are intensive in capital and in research and development (R&D), and a significant share of two-way foreign direct investment (FDI) flows is intra-industry in nature.

3. The production of the foreign affiliates of multinationals falls off in distance, but at a slower rate than either aggregate exports or parent exports of inputs to their affiliates.

4. Both the parents and the affiliates of multinational firms tend to be larger, more productive, more R&D-intensive, and more export oriented than non-multinational firms.

5. Within multinational firms, parents are relatively specialized in R&D while affiliates are primarily engaged in selling goods in foreign markets, particularly in their host market.

6. Cross-border mergers and acquisitions (M&As) make up a large fraction of FDI and are a particularly important mode of entry into advanced countries.

We have already analysed FDI in Chapter 9, where we showed that advanced countries are the largest source and destination of FDI flows (resulting in two-way investments) and that developing countries are more active as destinations than as source of FDI, in line with stylized fact 1 above.[2] We also noted the importance of M&As in total FDI, particularly for entry into advanced countries, in line with stylized fact 6 above. Antràs and Yeaple provide and discuss some evidence for the other stylized facts listed above, partially illustrated here as well.[3]

Figure 14.6 provides some information on the size of US affiliates relative to other firms in six destination countries (Finland, France, Ireland, the Netherlands, Poland, and Sweden) for four different variables (employment, sales, R&D expenditure, and exports). The share of affiliates in the total economy is typically small (around 6 per cent on average for the included countries).[4] The figure depicts the size of a variable (per cent of total) relative to the number of affiliates (per cent of total). A value above one thus depicts a larger-than-average value of that variable for affiliates relative to all firms. All variables in the figure are above one, ranging from a minimum of 1.3 for R&D expenditure in Poland to a maximum of 19.8 for exports in France. On average, affiliates are about eight times larger in employment, ten times larger in sales and R&D expenditure, and 13 times larger in exports. All of this is in line with stylized fact 4 above.

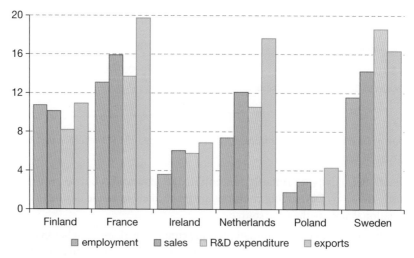

Figure 14.6 Size of US affiliates relative to local firms.

Notes: data shows the percentage of a variable accounted for by affiliates divided by the percentage of affiliates in the number of firms in that country.

Source: calculations based on data from Antràs and Yeaple (2014).

Figure 14.7 provides some information on the involvement of different sectors in related party trade flows, where the bubbles in the figure are proportional to the size of a sector's trade flow and the sectors are identified using the four-digit North American Industry Classification System (NAICS). In line with our discussion in Section 14.2, the trade-weighted average of related party trade for the included sectors is 51 per cent for imports and 31 per cent for exports. For most sectors (79 out of 103) the related party trade import percentage is larger than the export percentage (most observations are below the diagonal). The difference tends to be small for the 24 exceptions where the share of related party exports is larger than related party imports. It is, for example, six percentage points for plastics (NAICS 3261, plastics products), the largest exception sector with a trade value (average of exports and imports) of $25 billion. It is highest (25 percentage points) for lime (NAICS 3274, lime and gypsum products), with a trade value of only $0.2 billion.

Figure 14.7 shows that there is a positive relationship between related party trade import and export percentages; on average, an increase of one percentage point in related party imports results in an increase of 0.43 percentage points in related party exports for that sector (see the trend line in the figure; this explains about 33 per cent of the variance). Related party imports are particularly high for cars (NAICS 3361, motor vehicles), namely 99 per cent, and for pharma (NAICS 3254, pharmaceuticals and medicines), namely 84 per cent. These sectors are capital-intensive, R&D-intensive, and intra-industry-trade-intensive, in line with stylized fact 2 above.

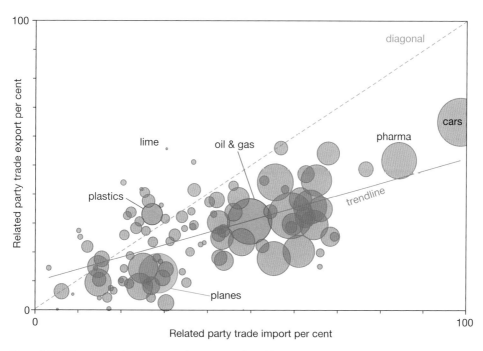

Figure 14.7 US sectoral related party trade: per cent of total import or export, 2014.

Notes: 103 NAICS4 sectors (excludes the 9000 classifications); bubbles proportional to trade size of sector (average of export and import).

Source: based on US Census Related Party Database.

Figure 14.8 illustrates the destination of US affiliate sales for eight large sector groups and for total manufacturing. The figure distinguishes between three types of sales markets for these affiliates, namely (i) the USA (parent country), (ii) the host country, and (iii) other foreign countries. Only a relatively small share of affiliate sales (11 per cent on average) is destined for the USA (the source country). This ranges from a minimum of 6 per cent for chemicals (and plastics) to a maximum of 19 per cent for cars (transport equipment) and textiles (and apparel). The largest share of affiliate sales (on average 55 per cent) is sold in the host country. This ranges from a minimum of 40 per cent for computers (and electronics) to a maximum of 66 per cent for other manufacturing. A considerable share of affiliate sales (on average 34 per cent) is sold in other foreign countries. This ranges from a minimum of 26 per cent for other manufacturing to a maximum of 43 per cent for computers (and electronics). By far the largest share of affiliate sales (on average 89 per cent) is thus sold in foreign markets (either the host country or other foreign markets) and not in the source country, in line with stylized fact 5.

14.4 Explaining multinationals

We have seen in Chapter 9 and in Sections 14.2 and 14.3 that multinationals are important in the global system of production, trade, and investment. A multinational firm controls and manages production facilities (plants) in at least two countries. We briefly analyse some taxation difficulties associated with multinationals in Box 14.2. In principle, we distinguish between *parents* and *affiliates*, where a parent in a *source* country controls the

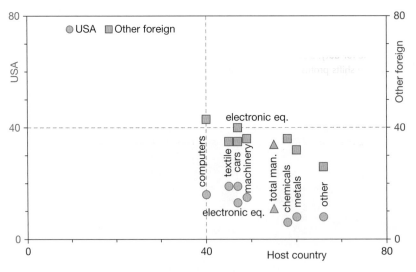

Figure 14.8 Destination of US affiliate sales by sector (per cent).

Notes: the figure is a combination of two scatter plots, namely host country = USA and host country = other foreign, such that sectors are horizontally the same, the total adds to 100 per cent, and sectors can be identified vertically (except for electronic equipment, which is listed twice to distinguish it from cars); triangle = total manufacturing.
Source: calculations based on data from Antràs and Yeaple (2014).

production facilities of an affiliate in a *host* country. Control is usually associated with ownership, which can be acquired through FDI either by taking over another firm (M&As) or by building a new plant (greenfield investments): see Chapter 9. In view of the difficulties of organizing production facilities in multiple countries we can pose the question why multinationals arise at all. In this respect, Bowen, Hollander, and Viaene (1998, p. 463) remark:

> That such a question is raised in the first place attests to the belief that familiarity with local business practices, consumer preferences and labour market conditions is an important asset which gives local firms an advantage over foreign transplants. From this it follows that a foreign firm, less familiar with the local terrain, must, in order to sustain the rivalry of local enterprises, possess some other advantages, not shared by local firms.

The modern approach to answering this question starts with Hymer (1960), who argues that some firms own special assets which give them an advantage over other firms in foreign markets. This culminated in Dunning's (1977, 1981) ownership–location–internalization (OLI) framework, which suggests that three conditions need to be satisfied for a firm to become a multinational.

- *Ownership advantages* allow a firm to overcome the disadvantages of a foreign location; such advantages can take the form of a product or a production process to which other firms do not have access, such as a patent or a trademark.

BOX 14.2 Transfer pricing

When firms are operative in more countries, each having different tariffs and different corporate income taxes, this raises the possibility of 'transfer pricing': that is, the setting of prices on intrafirm transactions to minimize tax and tariff payments and maximize corporate profits; see Horst (1971). Although, according to international principles, the dutiable value of these transactions should be the arm's-length price—that is, the price that would be charged to an outside buyer—exporters have some manoeuvring space when declaring a value for duty. Declaring a high import value increases the tariff payments to be made and at the same time shifts profits from the importing country to the exporting country. The latter will be beneficial if the importing country has a higher corporate tax rate than the exporting country. The overall payments of the firm therefore depend on the tariff duty relative to the difference in taxation rates.

In a small partial equilibrium model, Bowen, Hollander, and Viaene (1998, pp. 474–9) show that transfer pricing may also influence the firm's location decision. Assuming that the marginal production costs are the same in a home-country plant and a foreign-based plant, that the transfer prices may vary in a range with a minimum and a maximum, and allowing for the possibility to set up a production plant either in the home country only or in both the home country and a foreign country, they show that a home-country plant alone is optimal if the taxation of profits is low compared to the taxation of profits in the foreign country. Otherwise, as the taxation rates become more equal, it is optimal to establish two production plants. Empirical studies, for example by Grubert and Mutti (1991), who study US multinational activity in 33 countries, have found ample evidence of income shifting into countries with low tax rates. Moreover, host-country corporate taxes have a negative impact on export sales of local subsidiaries, but not on local sales. A study by Bartelsman and Beetsma (2003, p. 2,238) for the OECD countries argues that an 'increase in the tax rate leads to only a minor increase in the corporate tax revenue, because by far most of the additional revenue vanishes through income shifting ... at the margin, the share of the revenue increase that is lost because of the fall in the amount of reported income is estimated at 0.73'. They therefore estimate that about three-quarters of the potential revenue increase is lost as a result of transfer pricing.

- *Location advantages*, such as input costs, strategic interaction, or trade policy, make it more profitable to produce in a country than to export to it.

- *Internalization advantages* make it more profitable for a firm to undertake foreign production itself, rather than dealing with a foreign partner more familiar with the local environment.[5]

These ideas entered the international economics literature only after the tools for analysing market power under increasing returns to scale with monopolistic competition were developed (Chapter 8). The development of the heterogeneous firm model (Chapter 13) also enables us to take the large differences between firms into consideration in our analysis. The discussion in the remainder of this chapter therefore builds upon the main insights already derived in these chapters. As explained in Section 14.1, we focus attention in the remainder of this chapter on horizontal FDI and thus try to answer the questions about how and why firms serve different markets in different ways. We proceed in three steps. First, we provide a simple framework that allows us to analytically derive a condition under which multinational activity arises. Second, we analyse a richer general equilibrium environment and characterize the types of national firms and multinational firms that arise under different circumstances. Third, we analyse the mode of entry of foreign markets when firms differ in their productivity levels.

14.5 Proximity–concentration trade-off

As our starting point, we take the Krugman (1980) monopolistic competition model using one factor of production (labour) in a symmetric setting with two countries of equal size (see Chapter 8). We discuss the impact of asymmetric countries at the end of this section. Since the two countries are identical we can normalize the wage rate to 1 in both countries. A firm produces a unique variety of a good (the ownership advantage in the OLI framework) and faces identical iso-elastic demand for its product in both markets. A firm with marginal productivity φ charging price p_φ thus sells quantity $q_\varphi = A p_\varphi^{-\varepsilon}$, where ε is the price elasticity of demand.

On the cost side, there are increasing returns to scale of production as a result of fixed production costs and constant marginal production costs. All firms have the same productivity level φ and thus the same marginal production costs. As a consequence they charge the same price for their goods if the organizational structure is the same. We analyse firm heterogeneity in Section 14.8. There are two types of fixed costs:

- *Firm-level* costs f_{en}: these fixed costs represent the costs for entering the market. They are incurred only once per firm.

- *Plant-level costs* f_{pl}: these fixed costs represent the costs for setting up a production facility. They are incurred for each production facility of the firm and can thus occur more than once.

We will assume that each firm always has a production facility in its home market. The firm can serve the foreign market in two ways. First, it can *export* to the foreign market by shipping goods from the production facility in the home market. In this case it has only one production facility and its total fixed costs are $f_{en} + f_{pl}$. Second, it can become a *multinational* firm and set up a production plant in the foreign market to serve its foreign consumers from that location. In this case it has two production facilities and its total fixed costs are $f_{en} + 2f_{pl}$.

The exposition above indicates that multinationals have a disadvantage over exporting firms as they have higher fixed costs, since they have two production facilities instead of one. We call this the *concentration advantage* of exporting firms: concentrating production in one location allows exporting firms to take better advantage of scale economies. To offset this disadvantage and allow for the possibility of multinational activity we need to provide firms with a location advantage according to the OLI framework.[6] We do this by providing them with a *proximity advantage*: being close to the foreign market allows multinational firms to avoid transportation costs to deliver goods to the foreign consumers. As in Chapter 7 and Chapter 13 we model transportation costs using the iceberg approach: a firm needs to ship $\tau > 1$ units of a good from one country to make sure that one unit of a good arrives to sell in the other country. These costs could also represent tariffs or other obstacles to trade flows. The marginal costs of selling goods in the foreign market are thus τ times higher for exporting firms than for multinationals. As a consequence, exporting firms charge a price that is τ times higher than multinational firms, sell $\tau^{-\varepsilon}$ less goods (since the price elasticity of demand is $-\varepsilon$) and earn $\tau^{1-\varepsilon}$ times lower revenue (τ times higher price multiplied by $\tau^{-\varepsilon}$ lower quantity). The decision to serve the foreign market either by exporting or by becoming a multinational is thus determined by a tug-of-war between the proximity advantage of multinationals versus the concentration advantage of exporting firms, the so-called proximity–concentration trade-off.

Figure 14.9 illustrates the proximity–concentration trade-off by evaluating the two options the firm has available.

First, a firm may decide to supply the foreign market by exporting (left part of the figure). It then has lower fixed costs in total and higher marginal costs in the foreign market. We found in Chapter 13 that a firm with productivity level φ confronted with iso-elastic demand for its product charges a constant mark–up $\varepsilon/(\varepsilon-1)$ of price over marginal costs. We also analysed how the operating profits in the domestic market (where marginal costs are $1/\varphi$) are equal to $B\varphi^{\varepsilon-1}$ and how operating profits in the foreign market (where marginal costs are τ/φ) are equal to $B\tau^{1-\varepsilon}\varphi^{\varepsilon-1}$, where B is some constant (see Technical Note 13.1). Total profits for the exporting firm are given in the bottom left panel of the figure.

Second, a firm can decide to set up a production plant abroad and become a multinational. It then has higher fixed costs and the same marginal costs at home and abroad. Operating profits are thus equal to $B\varphi^{\varepsilon-1}$ in both markets. Total profits for the multinational firm are given in the bottom right panel of the figure.

When evaluating these opportunities we also have to take into consideration the general equilibrium aspects of the model through entry and exit of firms. This imposes restrictions on the constant B in Figure 14.9. It turns out that exporting is attractive compared to multinational activity if, and only if, the following condition holds:

$$f_{pl} > \alpha f_{en} \qquad\qquad 14.1$$

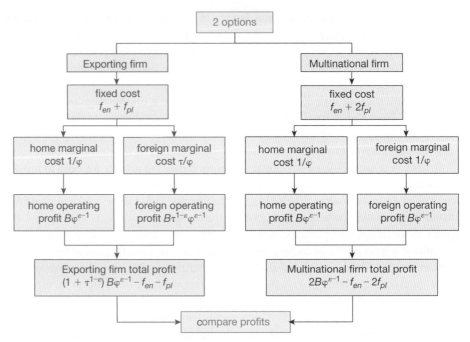

Figure 14.9 Horizontal FDI proximity–concentration trade-off.

—where $\alpha \equiv (1 - \tau^{1-\varepsilon})/\tau^{1-\varepsilon}$: see Technical Note 14.1. The consequences of the firm's decision problem are illustrated in Figure 14.10. If the plant-level fixed costs are relatively high (above αf_{en}) the firm supplies the foreign market through exporting. If the plant-level fixed costs are relatively low (below αf_{en}) the firm supplies the foreign market by becoming a multinational. Other things equal, an increase in transport costs τ or an increase in the price elasticity of demand ε rotates the line in Figure 14.10 counter-clockwise and thus makes exporting as the mode of entry less likely.

The discussion so far has analysed a symmetric equilibrium with identical countries. In this case the wage rate in the two countries is the same and all firms are either exporters or multinationals. What happens if we allow for asymmetric countries: that is, for countries of different size? A few remarks are in order. First note that size is not the same as the number of people within a country. We should interpret country size in an economic sense, reflecting a country's economic power not only through the number of persons but also through the productivity of workers. Second, the analysis of the asymmetric case is surprisingly cumbersome: we therefore refer the reader to Antràs and Yeaple (2014) for details. Third, as a result of country asymmetry the wage rate in the two countries is not the same. More specifically, the wage rate in the large country will be higher than in the small country, an example of Krugman's (1980) home market effect. Fourth, the condition in equation 14.1 is still relevant, but no longer necessary *and* sufficient. In other words, if this condition does not hold, multinational activity will not arise. More specifically, if the condition is reversed, multinational activity *may* arise, depending on the circumstances. Fifth, in general the incentive for a firm to deviate from an exporting equilibrium and become a multinational is highest when the difference in factor prices is lowest, that is when the

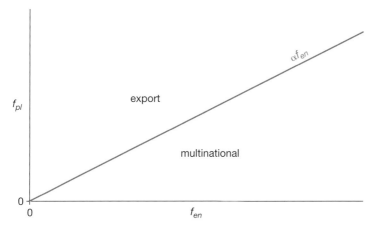

Figure 14.10 Export or multinational decision with symmetric countries.

Note: $\alpha = (1 - \tau^{1-\varepsilon})/\tau^{1-\varepsilon}$.

two countries are more similar. Sixth, in contrast to the symmetric case, there are no pure multinational equilibria: if multinationals do arise there are still exporting firms active in the market as well. We now take up the discussion of country asymmetry in more detail, allowing for two different types of goods and two factors of production.

14.6 Horizontal FDI and country differences

The previous section analyses the decision problem of becoming a multinational firm if there is just one type of good (manufactures) and a single factor of production (labour). The end of the section discusses asymmetric countries within this framework. This section takes three more steps in addressing the multinational problem by analysing two types of goods (food F and manufactures M), produced using two factors of production (capital K and labour L), for two countries (the USA A and the UK B) that may differ in size or relative factor abundance. Our discussion is based on the work of Markusen and Venables (1998, 2000).[7]

The food sector produces a homogeneous good under constant returns to scale, using capital and labour as inputs, in a perfectly competitive market. There are no transport costs for food, which will be used as numéraire. The production function for food in the USA is:

$$F_A = K_A^{\alpha_f} L_{Af}^{1-\alpha_f} \quad 0 < \alpha_f < 1 \tag{14.2}$$

—and similarly for food production in the UK (with sub-index B). Recall that α_f measures the capital intensity of the production process. Also note that the capital used in the production process of food in equation 14.2 does not have a sub-index f, in contrast to the labour used. This will be explained below. If we know the amount of capital and labour used in the food sector, we can derive the wage rate and the rental rate by equating them to the marginal product of labour and capital, respectively.[8]

Multinationals may arise in the production of manufactures, which is also a homogeneous good produced in a framework of imperfect competition using the Cournot model (see Chapter 7). Since multinational production is labour-intensive, we assume that the production process of manufactures uses no capital.[9] The entire capital stock in both countries is therefore employed in the production of food, such that there is no need for a sub-index f in equation 14.2. As in Section 14.5, there are increasing returns to scale in the production process of manufactures because of firm-level fixed costs f_{en} and plant-level fixed costs f_{pl}. In both countries the marginal production costs in terms of labour is c units, which has to be multiplied by the country's wage rate (w_A or w_B) for actual costs. In addition, there are transportation costs of t units of labour needed to transport one unit of manufactures from the USA to the UK or vice versa.

We can now distinguish between four different types of manufacturing firms, as summarized in the decision process of Figure 14.11. First, the firm must decide in which country, the USA or the UK, it will establish its headquarters. In conjunction with the wage rate, this determines the level of the firm-specific and plant-specific fixed cost in the country of establishment. Second, the firm can decide whether or not to establish a production plant in the other country.[10] As in Section 14.5, there is a proximity–concentration trade-off. Setting up a production plant in the other country avoids the transportation costs of exporting goods at the expense of additional plant-level fixed costs. If the firm does *not* establish a production plant in the other country we will call it a *national* firm: n_A if it is established in the USA and n_B if it is established in the UK. If the firm *does* establish a production plant in the other country we will call it a *multinational* firm: m_A if the headquarters are in the USA and m_B if the headquarters are in the UK; see Figure 14.11.

Let M_{AA}^n be the sales of manufactures in the USA of a national firm established in the USA, M_{AB}^n the sales in the UK of a national firm established in the USA, M_{AA}^m the sales in the USA of a multinational firm with headquarters in the USA, and so on. The cost function for an American firm is then given by $(f_{en} + f_{pl})w_A + cw_A M_{AA}^n + (c+t)w_A M_{AB}^n$ for national firms and $(f_{en} + f_{pl})w_A + f_{pl}w_B + cw_A M_{AA}^m + cw_B M_{AB}^m$ for multinational firms. The remainder of the model is familiar from previous chapters. The utility function in both countries is Cobb–Douglas, with δ_M as the share of income spent on manufactures. This implies that the price elasticity of demand is equal to 1, such that the optimal pricing rule for a firm is equal to its market share: see Technical Note 7.2 for details. Firms will enter the market for manufactures in both countries until profits are equal to zero. Finally, general equilibrium obviously requires full employment of labour and capital, as well as market clearing for food and manufactures in both countries.

The main strong point of this type of multinational models is the ability to *endogenously* determine the market structure. Firms may or may not decide to establish headquarters in a country. Similarly, they may or may not decide to establish another production plant in the other country. Whether or not they make these decisions is determined within the model, thus determining the nature of market competition endogenously. The market equilibrium outcome depends, of course, on the parameters and the size and distribution of the capital and labour stock.

Unfortunately, the main strong point of this type of models also constitutes its main weakness, as illustrated in Figure 14.12. The flexibility of the model, which enables a firm in manufactures to be a national firm in either country, or a multinational firm with headquarters in either country, opens up four logical possibilities: n_A, n_B, m_A, and m_B This implies, in

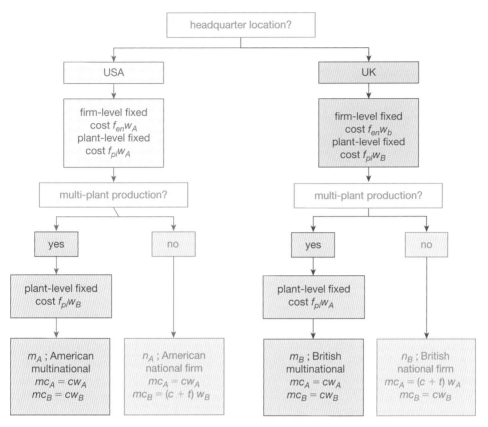

Figure 14.11 Decision process and firm types.

Note: mc refers to marginal costs.

turn, that there are $2^4 = 16$ possible equilibrium market structures, of which we can delete only one (there has to be at least one firm): see Figure 14.12. The reader will of course realize that it is tiresome, if not virtually impossible, to analyse 15 different regimes for a large range of parameter values or endowment distributions. Imagine the possibility of distinguishing between national firms, horizontal multinationals, *and* vertical multinationals, as some models do, in a world of five countries; it would increase the range of possible firms to $3 \times 5 = 15$, and the range of possible regimes to more than 30,000. It is clear that such a number of possibilities cannot be analysed without powerful tools to assist the researcher.

To present the main results of the model more clearly, we group the 15 regimes of Figure 14.12 into three aggregate types (see the figure for the regime numbers). First, we have three regimes with only national firms (regimes 6, 8, and 14). Second, we have three regimes with only multinational firms (regimes 11, 12, and 15). Third, the remaining nine mixed regimes have both national firms and multinationals. To adequately illustrate the main findings of the model we use an Edgeworth box (see Figure 14.13) which allows us to determine the differences between countries regarding their size and factor intensities. In the centre of the box the capital–labour ratio is the same in the two countries and they are exactly equal in size. Going from this point to the northeast corner does not affect the

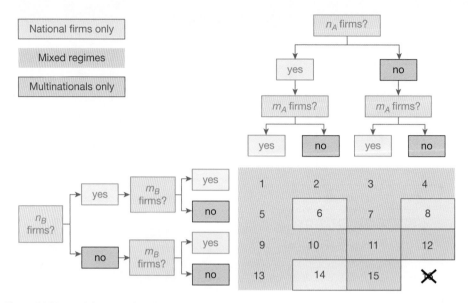

Figure 14.12 Possible national/multinational regimes.

capital–labour ratio in either country, but implies that the USA becomes larger than the UK. The reverse holds if we go in the opposite direction, to the southwest corner. Similarly, going from the centre to the northwest corner implies that capital becomes more abundant in the USA and labour becomes more abundant in the UK. Again, the reverse effect holds if we go into the opposite direction.

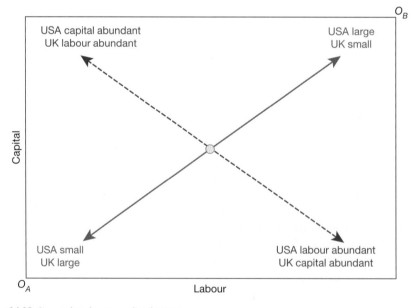

Figure 14.13 Size and endowment distributions.

Figure 14.14 shows the impact of all possible distributions of the world endowment of capital and labour between the two countries for the three main types of endogenous market equilibria of the multinational model in a base scenario.[11] The following observations are evident.

- If the two countries are similar in size and capital–labour ratio (in the neighbourhood of the centre of the box), the production equilibrium is dominated by multinational firms.

- If the two countries are different in size and capital–labour ratio (in the corners of the box), the production equilibrium is dominated by national firms.

- For intermediate endowment distributions, the production equilibrium is mixed, with both *national firms and multinational firms.*

All three observations are in accordance with the stylized facts discussed in Section 14.3. How can we explain these results? Recall that the decision to start multinational production (set up a second production plant in the other country) depends on the size of the extra fixed plant costs relative to the size of the transport costs. Now suppose that we are close to one of the corners of the Edgeworth box; either (a) the endowment ratio is very different between the two countries or (b) one country is very small and the other country is very large.

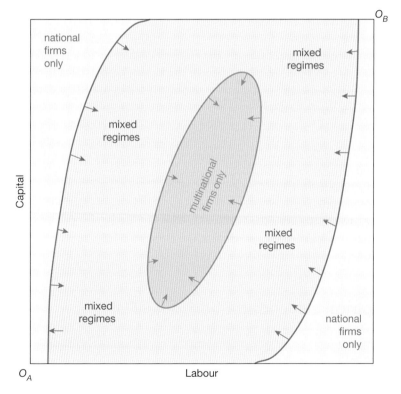

Figure 14.14 Characterization of main horizontal FDI regimes.

Notes: the arrows in the figure point in the direction of changes in the main regime distribution if (i) countries are smaller, (ii) transport costs decrease, and (iii) fixed costs of multinationals rise.

Source: based on Markusen and Venables (1998).

a) The endowment ratio is very different, there is a strong incentive for Heckscher–Ohlin type (factor abundance) inter-industry trade. The labour-rich country will specialize in the production of the labour-intensive manufactures. Since labour is expensive in the capital-abundant country it will be too expensive to incur the additional fixed costs of setting up an extra production plant, such that the production equilibrium is characterized by national firms producing manufactures in the labour-abundant country only.

b) One of the countries is very small, it is important to realize that there are economies of scale associated with the production of manufactures. This makes the small country unattractive as a home base for production (as it will be impossible to recuperate the fixed costs domestically) and as the basis for a foreign affiliate (the small market implies that the transport costs are fairly low if this market is serviced from abroad). The production equilibrium is therefore characterized by national firms producing manufactures in the large country only.

In both case (a) and case (b) the countries are very different and the production equilibrium is characterized by national firms. At the same time, the above reasoning explains why multinationals arise if countries are similar, because similar countries imply similar wage rates (no specialization incentive) and similar market size (large transport costs to the other market which can be avoided by setting up a subsidiary abroad). The intermediate cases with the mixed regimes represent the transition from one extreme to the other.

The economic reasoning in cases (a) and (b) also enables us to understand the main impact of changing some of the parameters in the model, as illustrated by the arrows in Figure 14.14. Since economies of scale are important for the production of manufactures, a decrease in the size of the global economy makes it more difficult to recuperate fixed-cost investments. As fixed costs are larger for multinational firms than for national firms, a reduction in the size of the economy will reduce the range of endowment distributions in which multinationals arise and will increase the range of endowment distributions in which national firms arise. Growth in the world economy, as we have witnessed for many recent decades, therefore leads to the opposite effect of increasing the importance and occurrence of multinationals. Similarly, a decrease in transport costs makes it relatively less attractive to incur the extra fixed costs of setting up a subsidiary abroad and therefore reduces the range of endowments in which multinationals arise, as does a rise in the fixed costs of multinational firms relative to national firms.

14.7 Empirical evidence for horizontal FDI

The proximity–concentration trade-off explained above is intuitively plausible and has various implications for the cross-country and cross-sector structure of trade and FDI flows. Brainard (1997) provides an evaluation of the empirical relevance of this trade-off. In this section we briefly discuss Antràs and Yeaple's (2014) updated version of this work using more complete and more recently available data. Essentially, we try to explain as well as possible the extent to which firms service foreign markets through exporting. The analysis is based on data for American multinationals servicing 42 different destination countries for a range of manufacturing sectors. Let X_i^j be the exports from the US to country i in sector j, let S_i^j be the sales of American affiliates in sector j located in country i, and let $s_{x,i}^j$ be the share of exports in serving country i for sector j, defined as $s_{x,i}^j = X_i^j / (X_i^j + S_i^j)$. The variable $s_{x,i}^j$ is taken as indication of the extent to which a foreign market is serviced through exports rather than affiliate sales.

The top part of Table 14.1 provides a direct estimate of the impact of the theoretical variables on the attractiveness of exports for servicing foreign markets. The variables 'freight costs' and 'tariffs' are the logs of the value estimates of shipping costs and tariffs in sector j from the US to country i. They represent the variable τ in Section 14.5 and the variable t in Section 14.6. In accordance with the model, a rise in both types of shipping costs makes exporting significantly less attractive. The variables 'firm-level costs' and 'plant-level costs' are logs of the number of nonproduction workers per representative firm and of production workers per representative plant. They represent the variables f_{en} and f_{pl}, respectively. Again in accordance with the model, the attractiveness of exporting as a means to service foreign markets significantly falls if firm-level costs rise or plant-level costs decline.

The bottom part of Table 14.1 provides estimates of the degree to which country differences can explain the proximity–concentration trade-off as illustrated in Figure 14.14. The variable 'GDP difference' is the log of the absolute value of the difference in GDP for the US and country i. In accordance with the model, large differences in country size make exporting significantly more attractive. The variables 'schooling difference' and 'capital–labour ratio difference' are the logs of differences in the years of schooling and capital–labour ratios for the US and country i. These variables try to measure differences in factor endowments for the relative attractiveness of exports. Unfortunately, neither of the variables is statistically significant, which suggests that differences in factor endowments are not important. Note, however, that the specification assumes that the role of endowments for the proximity–concentration trade-off is the same for all sectors. We will return to this issue in Chapter 15 when we analyse the role of comparative advantage in more detail and allow factor abundance to interact with a sector's factor intensity.

Table 14.1 Proximity–concentration empirics for American multinationals, 2009

Dependent variable log($s_{x,i}^j$), see main text for details		
Variable	Coefficient	Standard error
Freight costs	−0.13**	0.04
Tariffs	−0.29**	0.06
Firm-level costs	−0.32**	0.04
Plant-level costs	0.14*	0.05
GDP difference	0.39*	0.17
Schooling difference	0.07	0.09
Capital–labour ratio difference	0.08	0.06
Number of observations	2,315	

Notes: ** and * indicate significant at 1 per cent and 5 per cent level; 42 countries included in the analysis; no sector or − country fixed effects; additional controls not reported.
Source: Antràs and Yeaple (2014), Table 2.3 column 4.

14.8 Horizontal FDI and firm heterogeneity

We started our discussion in this chapter by pointing out the enormous differences between firms regarding trade and investment flows in terms of differences in size, productivity, and the number of markets they service. In contrast, the analysis in Sections 14.5 and 14.6 is based on representative firms with the same productivity level for each sector and country. Fortunately, with the tools developed above and in Chapter 13 we can easily alleviate this shortcoming.

To simplify the exposition, we return to the assumption of differentiated goods and symmetric countries also used in Section 14.5. As a consequence, the wage rate is the same in the two countries and we can use it as numéraire. As in Chapter 13, a firm has to pay a cost to enter the market (similar to the cost f_{en} analysed in Sections 14.5 and 14.6) and observe its firm-specific productivity level φ, which is drawn from some underlying distribution. A firm can enter the domestic market if it pays a fixed cost f_{pl} (similar to the costs f used in Chapter 13). It will do so only if its operating profits will cover these fixed costs. As in Section 14.5, the operating profits are equal to $B\varphi^{\varepsilon-1}$ so all firms with a productivity level below some viability cut-off level φ_* will exit the market, where φ_* is determined by $B\varphi_*^{\varepsilon-1} = f_{pl}$ (see Figure 14.15).

As discussed in Section 14.5, if a firm decides to service the foreign market it can do so either by exporting or by setting up a production facility in the other country.

If the firm exports to the other country it has to pay iceberg-type transport costs $\tau > 1$, so τ units have to be shipped to make sure that one unit arrives. Since the marginal costs for exporting are τ times higher, the firm charges a τ times higher price in the foreign market, sells $\tau^{-\varepsilon}$ fewer goods, and earns $\tau^{1-\varepsilon}$ lower revenue. As a consequence, its operating profits from exports are equal to $\tau^{1-\varepsilon} B\varphi^{\varepsilon-1}$. Note that the constant B, which represents the size of the foreign market, is the same as for the domestic market since the two countries are symmetric. To enter the foreign market the firm has to pay a fixed cost f_x, representing for example a marketing budget to introduce the product. The firm will only engage in exporting activity if its operating profits from exporting are at least as high as these fixed costs f_x. Only firms above some second cut-off productivity level φ_{*x} might therefore engage in exports, where φ_{*x} is determined by $\tau^{1-\varepsilon} B\varphi_{*x}^{\varepsilon-1} = f_x$. If the fixed costs for exporting are large enough (more specifically, if $f_x > \tau^{1-\varepsilon}f_{pl}$) then the exporting cut-off level is higher than the viability cut-off level ($\varphi_{*x} > \varphi_*$) and only the more productive firms might engage in exporting activity, as illustrated in Figure 14.15.

A second way to service the foreign market is by setting up a production facility abroad and becoming a multinational. In this case the marginal costs are the same as those for the domestic market, so the operating profits $B\varphi^{\varepsilon-1}$ are identical to those of the domestic market as well. This time, however, the additional fixed costs of servicing the foreign market consist of the plant-level costs f_{pl} and the foreign market entry costs f_x. If the firm services the foreign market its net profit from doing so is thus equal to $B\varphi^{\varepsilon-1} - f_{pl} - f_x$. It will compare these net profits to those generated by exporting to the foreign market, which is equal to $\tau^{1-\varepsilon} B\varphi^{\varepsilon-1} - f_x$. This generates a third, multinational cut-off productivity level φ_{*m}. A firm will service the foreign market by becoming a multinational if its productivity level is higher than this cut-off level φ_{*m}.

The illustration in Figure 14.15 puts the multinational cut-off level φ_{*m} to the right of the export cut-off level φ_{*x}. In this case we can identify four productivity ranges: the least

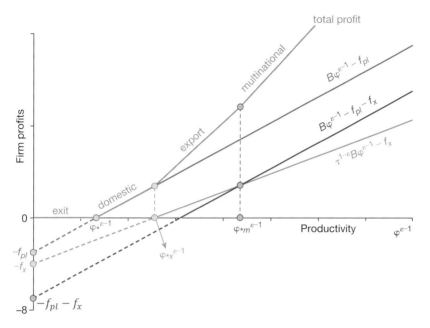

Figure 14.15 Firm heterogeneity and horizontal FDI.

productive firms exit the market, the second range of firms produces only for the domestic market, the third range of firms also engages in exporting, and the fourth, most productive range of firms becomes a multinational. This ordering is in accordance with empirical observations (see Section 13.7), but it requires a range of exporting firms to exist, which is equivalent to assuming $\varphi_{*x} < \varphi_{*m}$. Technical Note 14.2 shows that this holds if, and only if, the following condition is met:

$$f_{pl} > \alpha f_x \qquad\qquad 14.3$$

—where α is as defined in Technical Note 14.1. This condition is *the same* as that derived in Section 14.5, with the costs of entering the foreign market f_x replacing the firm entry costs f_{en} (see equation 14.1). So if we allow for firms with different productivity levels in a world with symmetric countries we empirically observe both methods of servicing the foreign market (exporting and multinational activity), provided that becoming a multinational is not a dominant strategy as given in the condition shown in equation 14.3.

14.9 Conclusions

The analysis in this chapter first provides evidence that there are large differences between firms in terms of their involvement in international trade flows, which are dominated by a relatively small number of large multinationals, particularly for advanced countries (Section 14.2). Next, we discuss six stylized facts on multinational activities regarding trade and investment flows that need to be explained theoretically (Section 14.3). After discussing some minimum requirements in the OLI framework (Section 14.4), we concentrate on explaining horizontal multinational activity. This is done in three steps: (i) provide a simple framework to introduce and analyse the proximity–concentration trade-off which determines market entry through either exports or FDI in a symmetric country setting (Section 14.5); (ii) extend this analysis by allowing for more goods, more factors of production, and country asymmetry in terms of size and factor endowments (Section 14.6); and (iii) extend this analysis by allowing for heterogeneous firms (Section 14.8). We provide empirical information regarding the proximity–concentration trade-off in Section 14.7. This supports the analysis in this chapter, except regarding the influence of differences in factor abundance. As already pointed out in Section 14.7, to understand the role of comparative advantage in multinational activity we must allow factor abundance to interact with sector intensities. We do this in the next chapter, where we analyse the consequences of offshoring and supply chains (vertical FDI).

 ## Technical Notes

Technical Note 14.1 Proximity–concentration trade-off

Figure 14.9 analyses how total profits for an exporting firm are $(1 + \tau^{1-\varepsilon})B\varphi^{\varepsilon-1} - f_{en} - f_{pl}$. If this is the only type of firm organizational structure available, entry and/or exit of firms until profits are zero will ensure that

$$(1+\tau^{1-\varepsilon})B\varphi^{\varepsilon-1} = f_{en} + f_{pl} \quad \text{or} \quad B\varphi^{\varepsilon-1} = (f_{en} + f_{pl})/(1+\tau^{1-\varepsilon}) \tag{A14.1}$$

Taking this as our starting point we now want to determine if becoming a multinational firm is attractive or not. This is not the case if multinational profits are lower than the profits for an exporting firm, which in light of the above is zero. From Figure 14.9 this implies:

$$2B\varphi^{\varepsilon-1} - f_{en} - 2f_{pl} < 0 \quad \Leftrightarrow \quad 2B\varphi^{\varepsilon-1} < f_{en} + 2f_{pl} \tag{A14.2}$$

Substituting for $B\varphi^{\varepsilon-1}$ from (A14.1) above gives

$$2\frac{(f_{en} + f_{pl})}{(1+\tau^{1-\varepsilon})} < f_{en} + 2f_{pl} \quad \Leftrightarrow \quad 2f_{en} + 2f_{pl} < (1+\tau^{1-\varepsilon})(f_{en} + 2f_{pl})$$

$$\Leftrightarrow \quad \frac{1-\tau^{1-\varepsilon}}{\tau^{1-\varepsilon}}f_{en} < f_{pl} \quad \text{or} \quad f_{pl} > \alpha f_{en}, \text{ where } \alpha = \frac{1-\tau^{1-\varepsilon}}{\tau^{1-\varepsilon}}.$$

Technical Note 14.2 Positive range of exporting firms

To ensure that a positive range of exporting firms exists in the model discussed in Section 14.8 requires the export cut-off level to be below the multinational cut-off level: $\varphi_x < \varphi_m$. The export cut-off level is determined by the condition

$$B\tau^{1-\varepsilon}\varphi_x^{\varepsilon-1} = f_x \tag{A14.3}$$

The multinational cut-off level is determined by the equality of net profits for servicing the foreign market through either exporting or multinational activity:

$$B\varphi_{*m}^{\varepsilon-1} - f_{pl} - f_x = B\tau^{1-\varepsilon}\varphi_{*m}^{\varepsilon-1} - f_x \qquad \text{(A14.4)}$$

From equation (A14.3) we see that $\varphi_{*x}^{\varepsilon-1} = f_x / B\tau^{1-\varepsilon}$ and from equation (A14.4) we see that $\varphi_{*m}^{\varepsilon-1} = f_{pl} / B(1-\tau^{1-\varepsilon})$. The condition $\varphi_{*x} < \varphi_{*m}$ is thus equivalent to

$$\frac{f_x}{B\tau^{1-\varepsilon}} < \frac{f_{pl}}{B(1-\tau^{1-\varepsilon})} \quad \Leftrightarrow \quad f_{pl} > \alpha f_x, \text{ where } \alpha = \frac{1-\tau^{1-\varepsilon}}{\tau^{1-\varepsilon}}. \qquad \text{(A14.5)}$$

Notes

1 In line with our terminology we have replaced their use of 'developed economies' with 'advanced economies' as it more easily distinguishes between the two types of countries.

2 We also noted that developing nations are becoming more important over time as a source of investments, a fact not emphasized by Antrás and Yeaple.

3 The gravity equation (stylized fact 3) is discussed in Chapter 16.

4 The percentage of the total number of firms that are affiliate firms is 1.6 for Finland, 2.0 for France, 13.4 for Ireland, 3.4 for the Netherlands, 16.0 for Poland, and 2.8 for Sweden.

5 The internalization problem is briefly analysed in Section 15.10 on the firm's boundaries.

6 The internalization advantage of the OLI framework is taken for granted for now.

7 The complete specification of the model is a bit too involved for this book, so we refer the reader for details to Markusen and Venables (1998).

8 Which is equal to the value marginal product of labour and capital because food is the numéraire.

9 To emphasize the distinction between high-skilled versus low-skilled labour, the reader may reinterpret the capital stock in this chapter as low-skilled labour and the labour stock as high-skilled labour. The production of food is then relatively low-skilled labour-intensive.

10 The logical possibility of incurring firm-specific fixed costs in one country and one plant-specific fixed cost in the other country (vertical multinationals) is analysed in Chapter 15.

11 In the base scenario transport costs are 15 per cent as a proportion of marginal costs and (if the wages in the two countries are equalized) the fixed costs for a multinational firm are 60 per cent higher than for a national firm.

Questions

Question 14.1

Briefly answer the questions below.

a. For *exporting* firms, briefly comment on the distribution of these firms regarding:

- The number of products exported.
- The number of countries exported to.
- The value of exports.

b. Do the same for importing firms.

c. Briefly list three of Antrás and Yeaple's six stylized facts.

Question 14.2

Several academics have wondered why a firm establishes a production plant abroad since this involves extra costs compared to home production (think, for example, of the cost of transferring people to a foreign country, of acquiring information, of overcoming language barriers, and of fighting cultural differences).

a. What is required, according to Dunning, before firms establish or purchase production plants abroad? Describe all the conditions carefully.

b. Give an example of every condition that is not mentioned in the main text.

c. How are the conditions modelled in the multinational model of Markusen and Venables (see Section 14.6)?

d. Why do all conditions have to be satisfied before a firm becomes a multinational?

Question 14.3

The Markusen-Venables general equilibrium model on national and multinational firms explains how the distribution of endowments—that is (human) capital and labour, over two countries A and B—and the economic size of these countries can help to explain why we have (i) only national firms, (ii) only multinational firms, or (iii) a mix of national and multinational firms. It analyses both inter- and intra-industry trade.

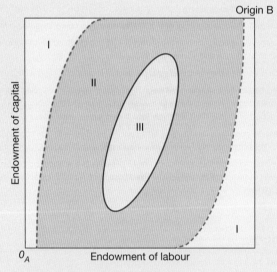

Figure 14.16 Distribution of endowments.

Figure 14.16 identifies three areas, namely I, II, and III. Indicate which area belongs to (i), (ii), and (iii) mentioned above and explain why.

 See the **online resources** for a Study Guide and questions:
www.oup.com/uk/vanmarrewijk_it/

Offshoring and supply chains

◎ Objectives

- To know the difference between offshoring and outsourcing.
- To understand that supply chains, also called global value chains, involve the fragmentation of production into separate value-added stages in different countries.
- To understand why it is hard to determine nationality of supply chain production and why supply chains are difficult to measure empirically.
- To know why the increasing role of supply chains lowers value-added trade relative to gross trade.
- To understand why vertical FDI offshoring is attractive only if factor prices are sufficiently different between countries.
- To understand why there are no simple and robust links between fragmentation and wage inequality between the source country and the destination country.
- To know why only the most productive firms will offshore part of the production process.
- To understand why an empirical test of vertical FDI requires the interaction of factor intensity of the fragmented part with factor intensity of the destination country.
- To know the difference between forward and backward linkages in value-added trade.
- To understand that using intra-industry trade to identify supply chains shows that participation tends to increase with income levels and that the poorest countries of the world essentially do not participate.
- To know that transaction costs (rent dissipation and hold-up inefficiencies) and property rights are important for determining the boundaries of the firm (internalization advantage).

15.1 Introduction

After our analysis of heterogeneous firms in Chapter 13 and horizontal foreign direct investment (FDI) in Chapter 14 we now complete our analysis of international firms by discussing vertical FDI. As a result of ever-lower transportation and interaction costs and ever-improving communication possibilities it is now possible for firms to reorganize their production process in different locations, taking into consideration the specific advantages of these locations for certain upstream or downstream parts of the process. A low-skilled, labour-intensive part of the production process may be moved to a country with relatively low wage rates. Similarly, an advanced and technology-intensive part of the production process may be moved to a country abundant in human capital, and so on.

Various colourful names have been given to these developments, such as fragmentation, slicing-up-the-value-chain, global value chains, and supply chains. Since the various parts of the production process need to be fitted together at some point in time it is often better to locate the various plants in each other's vicinity and not on the other side of the globe. As a consequence some supply chains combine the advantages of countries at different stages of economic development that are near to each other, such as Germany and the Czech Republic or the USA and Mexico. Other supply chains use the differences in technical expertise of countries at similar levels of economic development, such as Japan, the USA, and the UK.

Although a firm may fragment the production process domestically, we focus attention on the international dimension of the fragmentation process. The proper term for locating part of the production process in another country is *offshoring*. Firms can decide to organize offshoring activities either within the firm boundaries (integration) or by *outsourcing* to another firm. In the media the terms offshoring and outsourcing are sometimes confused. Joseph Schumpeter is an important pioneer regarding the importance of entrepreneurship and (multinational) firm activity for global welfare gains: see Box 15.1.

We begin our analysis in Section 15.2 with a supply-chain example of hard-disk drives involving many different countries. Each part of a fragmented production process is responsible for only a part of the value added for the final product. Section 15.3 therefore

BOX 15.1 Joseph Schumpeter

Figure 15.1
Joseph Schumpeter
(1883–1950).

Born in Austria, where he was briefly minister of finance after World War I, Joseph Schumpeter (Figure 15.1) emigrated to the USA in 1932, where he worked at Harvard University. At the early age of 28 he wrote *Theory of Economic Development* (1912), which gave a pivotal role to the dynamic, innovating entrepreneur in achieving technical progress and a positive rate of profit on capital. As Blaug (1985, p. 215) puts it, Schumpeter 'stressed the fact that scientific and technical inventions amount to nothing unless they are adopted, which calls for as much daring and imagination as the original act of discovery by the scientist or engineer'. Moreover, Schumpeter emphasized that economic progress consists not only of new machines and products, but also of new sources of supply, new forms of organization, and new methods of production. Schumpeter distinguished sharply between the entrepreneur, doing things in a new way and earning 'profit', and the capitalist, providing the capital required to finance a new venture and earning 'interest'. In 1942 he wrote *Capitalism, Socialism, and Democracy*, a book predicting the growth of socialism. Another Schumpeter must-have for any economist's bookshelves is *History of Economic Analysis* (1954). Published four years after his death, this history of economic thought holds many important remarks scattered about in hundreds of footnotes.

briefly discusses gross trade flows versus value-added trade flows. Next we show that vertical FDI essentially requires differences in factor prices (Section 15.4), how fragmentation is related to wage inequality between source and destination countries (Section 15.5), and how to incorporate heterogeneous firms (Section 15.6). We present empirical evidence on vertical FDI in Section 15.7. Supply chains involve many countries responsible for different parts of an ever more complicated production process. This makes supply chains hard to measure empirically. We analyse these issues in Section 15.8 using value-added trade flows and in Section 15.9 using the Grubel–Lloyd index of intra-industry trade. We conclude by discussing the boundaries of the firm in Section 15.10.

15.2 Hard-disk drive supply-chain example

The manufacture of hard-disk drives, an essential component for the computer business, is a dynamic industry, with high revenues, product life cycles of less than eighteen months, and rapidly falling prices.[1] In 1980 about 80 per cent of all drive production and assembly was done by American firms in the USA. Within two decades less than 5 per cent of drives were still assembled in the USA. Figure 15.2 gives a simplified picture of the main steps in the hard-disk drive value chain: the sequence and range of activities that go into making a final product. Ignoring research and development (R&D), there are four major steps in the value chain: (i) electronics—this includes semiconductors, printed circuit boards (PCBs) and their assembly; (ii) heads—devices that read and write the data, which are manufactured in stages with labour-intensive subassembly activities, such as head-gimbal assembly (HGA) and head-stack assembly (HSA); (iii) media—the material on which the information is stored;[2] and (iv) motors—which spin the media with extreme precision.

Producers locate the production of the many discrete steps in the value chain around the world for various reasons. The final assembly of the disk, which gives it the 'Made in Singapore' or 'Made in Thailand' label, is only one (and not necessarily the most important)

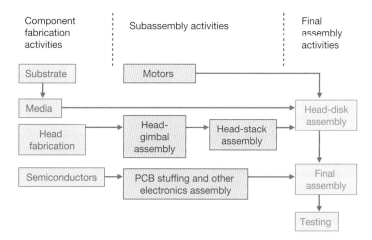

Figure 15.2 The hard-disk drive value chain.

Source: Simplified version of Gourevitch et al. (2000).

aspect of this process. As Gourevitch, Bohn, and McKendrick (2000) put it in their discussion of the structure of Seagate, the world's largest manufacturer of hard-disk drives:

> Although Seagate has kept control over almost all production, it has globally dispersed its operations to an extraordinary degree. A single component may be worked on in five countries and cross two oceans while Seagate is building it up through its value chain. Seagate develops new products (and processes) at seven locations in the United States and Singapore. It assembles disk drives in Singapore, Malaysia, Thailand, and China. In heads, the company fabricates its wafers in the United States and Northern Ireland, and cuts them into bars and assembles them into HGAs in Thailand, Malaysia, and the Philippines. It makes media in Singapore and motors in Thailand. It manufactures printed circuit cables in Thailand and assembles the electronics onto printed circuit boards in Indonesia, Malaysia, and Singapore. It is the largest nongovernment employer in Thailand and Singapore.

Table 15.1 gives four different indicators of nationality of production for the hard-disk drive industry. The large majority (88.4 per cent per unit of output) of hard-disk drives is made by US firms. In sharp contrast, only 4.6 per cent of the final assembly is done in the USA. Most final assembly of disks now takes place in Southeast Asia (64.2 per cent), which means the bulk of employment is in Southeast Asia (44 per cent), rather than in the USA (19.3 per cent), although the value of wages paid is much higher in the USA (39.5 per cent) than in Southeast Asia (12.9 per cent). Essentially, the hard-disk drive industry currently has two concentration clusters. The first is Silicon Valley in the USA, with a substantial share of research, design, development, marketing, and management (with a smaller counterpart in Japan). The second is in Southeast Asia, which dominates final assembly, most labour-intensive subassemblies, and low-tech components such as baseplates.

Figure 15.3 illustrates how involved the supply chain network is within Southeast Asia. To do so, the figure shows the sources of parts of a disk drive that is assembled in Thailand by a Japanese affiliate. A range of components, such as the spindle motor and the flex cable, are sourced locally (from Thailand). Many other components are sourced from a range of other countries, most of which are in Southeast Asia. The filter cap comes from Hong Kong, the damping plate from the Philippines, the top clamp from Taiwan, Japan, or Malaysia, the disks themselves from the USA, Japan, or Malaysia, and so on. Each of the listed parts may, of course, consist of other parts and components. Each of these other parts and components may again be sourced from different countries. Trying to complete the interlinkage picture by tracing out the ultimate source of each and every component is basically impossible.

Table 15.1 Hard-disk drives: indicators of nationality of production

Measure*	USA	Japan	SE Asia	Other Asia	Europe	Other
Nationality of firm	88.4	9.4	0.0	2.2	0.0	0.0
Final assembly	4.6	15.5	64.2	5.7	10.0	0.0
Employment	19.3	8.3	44.0	17.1	4.7	6.5
Wages paid	39.5	29.7	12.9	3.3	8.5	6.1

Notes: numbers as per cent of world total; *nationality of firm (% of unit output), location of final assembly, employment in value chain, and wages paid in value chain.
Source: Gourevitch et al. (2000), Table 2.

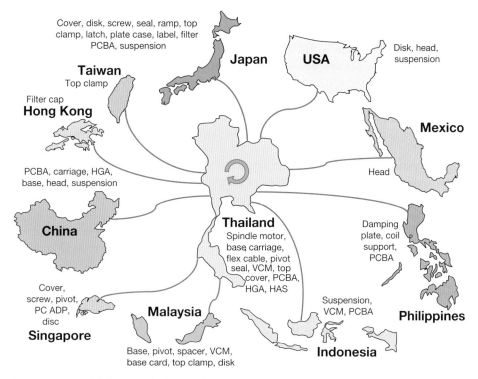

Figure 15.3 Hard-disk drive supply chain in Thailand.

Source: van Marrewijk (2009), adapted from Baldwin (2008) and Hiratsuka (2005).

Finally, we should realize that once the hard-disk drive is finished it does not stay in Thailand but serves as a component in another production process. It could, for example, be part of a computer assembled in China that is subsequently sold as a final good to a consumer in Switzerland or as an intermediate input to a consulting firm in Canada. At each next export step only part of the value of the product represents value added for the exporting country. The next section thus investigates value-added trade flows in more depth.

15.3 Trade in value added

Traditionally, international trade is analysed by using data on gross exports and imports.[3] This is the trade that crosses national borders and is registered by custom officials.[4] The assumption is that gross trade flows provide sufficient information to analyse the structure of international trade and, for example, comparative advantage. As long as international fragmentation is limited, gross trade flows do indeed provide this information. This is, however, no longer the case. International fragmentation of the production process has become a salient characteristic of the world economy and international trade flows no longer, or to a lesser extent than they used to, reflect what a country is producing and exporting (see Brakman, van Marrewijk, and Partridge, 2015).

There have been several recent attempts to remedy this shortcoming by constructing estimates of value-added trade flows, as opposed to gross export flows, across countries. This section focuses on the World Input–Output Data (WIOD) database. Section 15.8 will discuss the OECD-WTO Trade in Value Added database. The WIOD trade data identify 40 individual countries and a 'Rest of World' (RoW) group of countries to characterize global trade flows in the period 1995–2009.[5] The countries are the 27 countries of the EU (as of 1 January 2007) combined with Australia, Brazil, Canada, China, India, Indonesia, Japan, Mexico, Russia, Taiwan, Turkey, and the USA. Together these countries represent about 85 per cent of world GDP. The data cover 35 sectors and are constructed by combining national input–output tables with international trade data.

Expressed in constant 2009 US dollars, global gross trade flows increased by about 94 per cent in this period (see Figure 15.4), from $7,305 billion in 1995 to $14,160 billion in 2009.[6] Global gross trade flows peaked in 2008 at $18,315 billion (the drop in 2009 was almost 23 per cent). Measured in value-added terms, global trade flows increased in the same period by about 82 per cent, from $5,722 billion in 1995 to $10,397 billion in 2009. As illustrated in Figure 15.4, value-added trade and gross trade move up and down quite closely, although the gap between these flows gradually increased over the period because value-added trade rises more slowly. As a consequence, the *ratio* of value-added trade to gross trade gradually declined over time, from 78 per cent in 1995 to 73 per cent in 2009 (see Figure 15.4, where this ratio is depicted on the right-hand scale of the figure).[7]

There are substantial differences between countries regarding the ratio of value-added export flows to gross export flows. This is illustrated in Figure 15.5, where the countries are ranked from low to high value added as a per cent of gross exports. The size of the bubbles is proportional to the size of value-added flows, while the horizontal line depicts the median value (equal to 71 per cent).[8] The minimum value of 38.7 per cent is reached

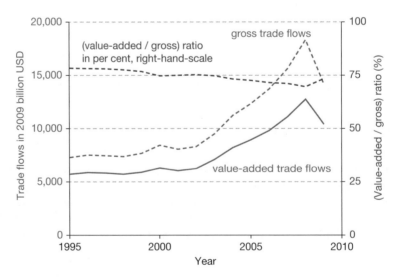

Figure 15.4 Global trade flows and ratio of value-added trade to gross trade, 1995–2009.

Source: Brakman and van Marrewijk (2015).

for Luxembourg, a small open economy which depends heavily on intermediate inputs from other countries for its exports. The maximum value of 93.9 per cent is reached for the Russian Federation, which makes only limited use of intermediate inputs from other countries. A closer look at Figure 15.5 shows that Luxembourg is rather exceptional in this group of countries since its value-added share of gross exports is more than 18 percentage points smaller than the second-ranked country (Taiwan). This is partially related to the WIOD selection of countries, which includes Luxembourg only because it is a member of the European Union (which paid for the construction of the WIOD database) and not because of the size of its economy, population, or export flows. The share of value-added exports in gross exports is close to the median country value for Germany and China; it is fairly high for the USA and fairly low for South Korea.[9]

As a method for identifying countries heavily involved in global supply chains on the basis of low value-added trade flows relative to gross export trade flows (indicating exports that heavily depend on importing value-added components), the data presented in Figure 15.5 is only slightly useful. At the lower-left end of the graph we indeed identify some countries that are intensively involved, such as Taiwan, Ireland, Hungary, the Czech Republic, Belgium, and South Korea (most of them not shown separately in the figure). On the other hand we do not identify other countries that are also heavily involved in other parts of the graph, such as Germany, China, France, USA, UK, and Japan (also not all shown separately in the figure). This problem is related to two main issues.

First, the value-added data is based on rather aggregate data. This is necessary since the construction uses input–output tables that are only available on a rather coarse scale. This contrasts with the detailed information involving thousands of goods for gross exports at the five-digit or six-digit level. Actual supply chains are based on this much more minute

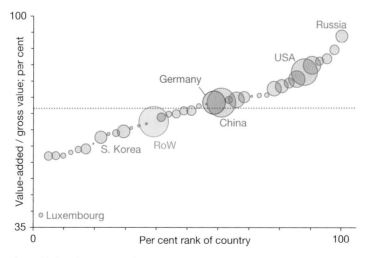

Figure 15.5 Value-added trade: per cent of gross export, 2009.

Notes: size of bubbles proportional to the size of value-added flows; the horizontal line depicts the median country value (71 per cent); 41 countries plus Rest of World (RoW).

Source: Brakman and van Marrewijk (2015).

detail. As a consequence, the ratio of value-added export to gross export does not adequately identify the large countries involved in global supply chains, as listed above.

Second, and related to this, the number of countries is limited. The data requirements for constructing value-added trade flows are high. As a consequence, only a small number of mostly advanced countries are included in the analysis. This makes it difficult to adequately assess the performance of the included countries relative to the excluded countries. It also means that countries with a lower level of economic development are excluded from the analysis. Indeed, none of the least developed countries is included in the WIOD database.

We return to the discussion of measuring supply chains in Sections 15.8 (also analysing forward linkages) and 15.9 (analysing an alternative measure of supply chains).

15.4 Vertical FDI (fragmentation)

We start our discussion of vertical FDI with a simple $2 \times 2 \times 2$ framework of two countries (the USA A and China C), two types of goods (food and differentiated manufactures), and two factors of production (capital K and labour L).[10] As in the factor abundance models used in Chapters 5 and 6, we assume that the two countries have identical technologies and that all firms are equally productive. We relax both assumptions later in this chapter. To avoid the incentive for horizontal FDI activity analysed in Chapter 14 we assume that there are no transport costs.

In line with our case study on hard-disk drives (Section 15.2), the key new modelling aspect is that we allow for fragmentation of the production process into different stages that are geographically separated. More specifically, the production process of manufactures consists of two stages:

- *Headquarter services*: think of the fixed entry costs for firms, such as R&D, marketing, development of specialized machines, financing, and so on. These services are firm-specific, performed under increasing returns to scale, nonrival within the firm, and performed with relatively intensive use of (human) capital.

- *Manufacturing*: this uses capital, labour, and headquarter services to produce final output under increasing returns to scale. Production costs fall if the supply of headquarter services rises.

The manufacturing firm's decision process is now simple, as illustrated in Figure 15.6. Since both stages of the production process have increasing returns to scale, there will be only one location for headquarter services and one manufacturing location. Headquarter services tend to be located in the country with the ownership advantage, so for an American firm headquarter services will be located in the USA. This firm then has to decide whether the manufacturing location is in China or also in the USA. Based on this location decision, the firm then determines the production levels for both stages of the production process to maximize profits.

The key insight of Helpman (1984) is that there is *no* incentive for vertical FDI if the factor prices are the *same* in the two countries. After all, the incentive to relocate the manufacturing stage of the production process to China must be based on the ability to achieve lower costs by doing so. Since manufacturing is relatively labour-intensive, this will be possible if, for

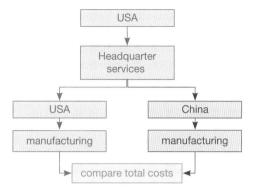

Figure 15.6 Vertical FDI decision process.

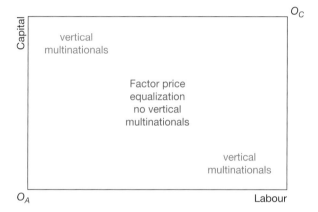

Figure 15.7 Characterization of main vertical FDI regimes.

example, the wage rate is lower in China than in the USA. In the case of factor price equalization, both the wage rate and the rental rate are the same in the two countries and there is no cost advantage associated with vertical FDI at all. Any arbitrarily small costs associated with organizing a production process in two separate countries would thus preclude vertical FDI from being feasible if factor price equalization holds.

Recall from the analysis in Chapters 5 and 6 that international trade leads to factor price equalization in the centre of the Edgeworth box (if the distribution of factor endowments is not too different). The same holds in this setting, so if factor endowments are similar, factor price equalization occurs and there will be no vertical multinationals (in the centre of the Edgeworth box in Figure 15.7).[11] On the other hand, if factor endowments differ substantially between countries, firms can lower total costs by fragmenting the production process into two separate stages and locating part of the production process in the other country such that vertical multinationals arise (in the corners of the Edgeworth box in Figure 15.7). In our example, if labour is sufficiently abundant in China compared to the USA such that the Chinese wage rate is sufficiently low compared to the American wage rate, it is advantageous for American firms to become vertical multinationals and locate manufacturing production in China. Moreover, in this setting fragmentation tends to work in the direction of restoring factor price equalization.

The observant reader will note that this prediction of the occurrence of vertical multinational activity as illustrated in Figure 15.7 is the mirror image of the prediction for horizontal multinational activity as illustrated in Figure 14.14. This poses some challenge in distinguishing the appropriate empirical prediction regarding factor endowments and multinational activity, as already noted in Section 14.7. We deal with this problem in Section 15.7.

15.5 Vertical FDI and wage inequality

As discussed in Chapter 2, there is an ongoing debate about the links between globalization and income inequality, both within and between countries. Regarding the economic consequences of vertical FDI, the focus of attention is on within-country income inequality. This section briefly discusses some possible consequences of fragmentation for within-country wage inequality. To do so we distinguish between two types of workers: high-skilled workers (sub-index H) and low-skilled workers (sub-index L). Relative to Section 15.4 one can think of high-skilled workers as being represented by (human) capital K and low-skilled workers by labour L. Regarding factor prices it is most appropriate to refer to these as wages in this setting, so we let w_{HA} denote the wage rate of high-skilled workers in the USA, w_{LC} the wage rate of low-skilled workers in China, and so on.

We assume that the USA is relatively abundant in high-skilled labour and take for granted that the wage rate for high-skilled workers is higher than for low-skilled workers within a country, thus providing an incentive for workers to become high-skilled workers (although we do not model this process).[12] We focus attention on analysing whether w_{HA}/w_{LA}, the wage rate of high-skilled workers relative to low-skilled workers in the USA, rises as a consequence of fragmentation, or not. If w_{HA}/w_{LA} rises we conclude that fragmentation leads to higher wage inequality in the USA. If not, the reverse holds. We also look at this question from China's perspective. At the end of this section we conclude that 'anything goes', which means that there are no simple and robust predictions regarding the links between fragmentation and wage inequality.

15.5.1 Rising wage inequality in the USA and lower wage inequality in China

We start our discussion with the model analysed in Section 15.4, where the variable K is re-interpreted as high-skilled workers, as explained above. The predictions of the effect of fragmentation in this model are straightforward along the neoclassical lines of the Stolper–Samuelson theorem (see Chapter 5). Fragmentation occurs only outside the factor price equalization area of the Edgeworth box. If fragmentation does occur it works in the direction of restoring factor price equalization, since fragmentation increases the relative demand for and reward of the relatively abundant factor of production in each country. Since the USA is abundant in high-skilled workers, this means that w_{HA}/w_{LA} *rises* and offshoring leads to higher wage inequality in the USA. Since China is abundant in low-skilled workers this means that w_{HC}/w_{LC} *falls* and offshoring leads to lower wage inequality in China. The impact is thus rising wage inequality in the source country and lower wage inequality in the destination country.

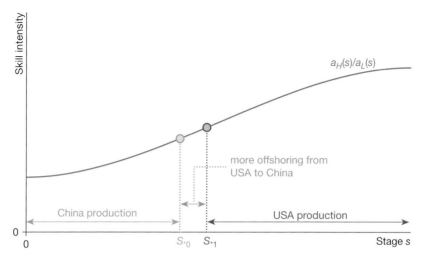

Figure 15.8 Stage offshoring and wage inequality.

15.5.2 Offshoring tasks and rising wage inequality in both countries

We now analyse a model based on Feenstra and Hanson (1996) as discussed in Antràs and Yeaple (2014). Suppose that instead of only two production stages for manufactures there is a continuum of stages indexed by s, ranging from 0 to 1. The marginal cost for stage s is determined by the use of high-skilled and low-skilled labour at this stage: $a_H(s)w_H + a_L(s)w_L$. We order the stages in terms of rising skill intensity $a_H(s)/a_L(s)$: see Figure 15.8. The stages are combined into final goods using a Cobb–Douglas production function. There is also a fixed cost at each stage in terms of final output (such that the relative cost ordering is not affected). Fragmentation is frictionless. Finally, assume for simplicity that the production of food uses only low-skilled labour.

In some sense this model leads to the same conclusions as discussed in Section 15.4: namely (i) if endowment differences are small there is factor price equalization and no incentive for fragmentation of the production process, and (ii) for larger but 'not too big' factor endowment differences fragmentation occurs and restores factor price equalization. More interestingly, the model also leads to different conclusions. If factor endowments are sufficiently different between countries there is a critical stage s_* such that all stages with low skill intensity (stage 0 to s_*) are produced in China and all stages with high skill intensity (stage s_* to 1) are produced in the USA: see Figure 15.8. Since technology is assumed identical in the two countries this equilibrium implies that the low-skilled wage is higher in the USA than in China ($w_{LA} > w_{LC}$) while the high-skilled wage is higher in China than in the USA ($w_{HC} > w_{HA}$).

Suppose that we are in a situation with large endowment differences such that there is no factor price equalization, as illustrated by the critical stage s_{*0} in Figure 15.8. Next, assume that the supply of both high-skilled and low-skilled workers increases proportionally in China. This increases the range of tasks outsourced to China, say from s_{*0} to s_{*1} in Figure 15.8. The key observation to make is that this raises the demand for high-skilled workers in both countries. The newly outsourced tasks (in the range from s_{*0} to s_{*1}) are *more* skill-intensive than the range of tasks (from 0 to s_{*0}) that were already performed in China, so the relative demand for high-skilled workers increases in China. Similarly, the newly outsourced tasks (in the range from s_{*0} to s_{*1}) are *less* skill-intensive than the range of tasks (from s_{*1} to 1) that continue to be performed in the USA, so the relative demand for high-skilled workers also increases in the USA. As a consequence, wage inequality rises in both countries.

15.5.3 Offshorability of tasks and lower wage inequality in the USA

We now continue with a discussion of a model by Grossman and Rossi-Hansberg (2008) in which the degree of offshorability of tasks plays a role: see Antràs and Yeaple (2014). We return to the benchmark model of Section 15.5.1 with headquarter services and manufacturing. This time, however, China is $\gamma < 1$ times less productive than the USA. We focus on a situation with *conditional* factor price equalization (such that $w_{LC} = \gamma w_{LA}$ and $w_{HC} = \gamma w_{HA}$) in which China is so large it produces food, headquarter services, and manufacturing, while the USA only produces headquarter services and manufacturing. Moreover, suppose headquarter services and manufacturing are both produced from a continuum of tasks involving high-skilled workers and a continuum of tasks involving low-skilled workers (similar to Section 15.5.2), with headquarter services relatively more skill-intensive. Finally, suppose that all high-skilled labour tasks cannot be outsourced while all low-skilled tasks can be outsourced to China using the superior American technology at an offshorability cost requiring $\beta t(s) \geq 1$ units of labour for task s.

If we now order the low-skilled labour tasks in terms of rising offshorability costs we get a picture similar to Figure 15.8 with a critical task s_* such that alls tasks below s_* are offshored to China and the remaining tasks are performed in the USA. The critical task is implicitly defined by the equality of costs for the low-skilled worker for that task: $w_{LA} = \beta t(s_*)w_{LC}$. A fall in the parameter β can now be interpreted as an increase in the offshorability of low-skilled tasks. This raises the range of outsourced low-skilled tasks, similar to Figure 15.8. This time, however, the wage costs are essentially pinned down by China. This implies that the high-skilled wage rate in the USA does not change, while the increase in offshorability for low-skilled workers in the USA is similar to low-skilled-labour-biased technological change and raises the low-skilled wage rate. As a consequence, an increase in offshorability lowers wage inequality in the source country.

15.5.4 Conclusion

We have briefly analysed three different models of vertical FDI leading to different implications regarding the link between offshoring and wage inequality. In one model offshoring leads to higher wage inequality in the source country and lower wage inequality in the destination country. In another model offshoring leads to higher wage inequality in both countries. In yet another model offshoring leads to lower wage inequality in the source country. This implies to some extent that 'anything goes', indicating that there are no simple and robust predictions regarding the links between fragmentation and wage inequality. A more detailed look at the construction of the models shows that we simply have too many different model construction possibilities to lead to robust conclusions. This suggests that from an empirical point of view the impact of fragmentation depends on the specific circumstances for the country, time period, and sector under investigation. A broader discussion on globalization and income inequality is provided in Chapter 2.

15.6 Heterogeneous firms and vertical FDI

In Chapters 13 and 14 we analysed the enormous differences between firms in terms of size, productivity, and the number of markets they service. So far in this chapter, however, the analysis in Sections 15.4 and 15.5 is based on representative firms with the same productivity level for each sector and country. As we did in Chapter 14 we can easily alleviate this shortcoming using the tools developed in Chapter 13.

To do this, we return to the two-sector model from Section 15.4, but this time using only one type of labour as the factor of production. We assume that both countries produce food (under constant returns to scale) and that the USA is more productive in food production. This implies that the American wage rate is higher than the Chinese wage rate ($w_A > w_C$) and that the producers of manufactures face a perfectly elastic supply of labour at these wage rates. Manufacturing firms produce headquarter services h one-to-one with labour in the USA because the USA is assumed to have a sufficiently large technological advantage for producing these services. Both countries can produce manufacturing m one-to-one with labour, which means China has a comparative advantage in manufacturing since its wage rate is lower.

To produce final output, manufacturing firms combine h and m using a Cobb–Douglas technology. Since firms differ in their productivity *level* φ (drawn from some underlying distribution after paying a fixed cost), total output for a firm is proportional to $\varphi h^\eta m^{1-\eta}$, where η is the intensity of headquarter services. We continue to assume that the transport of final goods is frictionless. Firms have two location choices.

- *Domestic firm*: produce both headquarter services and manufacturing in the USA. In this case there is a fixed cost f associated with headquarter services provision and the marginal production costs are proportional to the American wage rate w_A.

- *Multinational firm*: produce headquarter services in the USA and manufacturing in China. In this case there is a higher fixed cost $f_m > f$ reflecting both the headquarter services provision and the costs associated with organizing the fragmentation of the production process. In addition, there is an iceberg transport cost $\tau > 1$ associated with shipping the manufacturing input m from China back to the USA. The marginal costs of production thus depend on both the American and Chinese wage rate and are proportional to $w_A^\eta (\tau w_C)^{1-\eta}$.

As in Chapter 13, producers of a variety of manufactures face iso-elastic demand, where ε is the price elasticity of demand. They thus charge a constant mark-up of price over marginal cost. Operating profits depend on the price charged for final goods and the size of the American and Chinese markets. For a domestic firm with productivity level φ and marginal costs w_A, operating profits are equal to $Bw_A^{1-\varepsilon}\varphi^{1-\varepsilon} - w_A f$, where B is some constant (see Technical Note 13.1). A domestic firm will only produce if it is able to recover its fixed

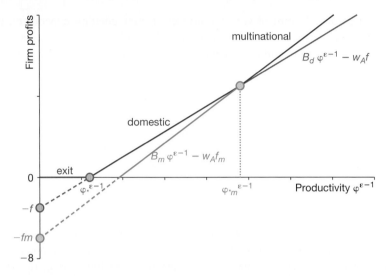

Figure 15.9 Firm heterogeneity and vertical FDI.

Note: $B_d \equiv Bw_A^{1-\varepsilon}$ and $B_m \equiv B(w_A^{\eta}(\tau w_C)^{1-\eta})^{1-\varepsilon}$.

costs f. All firms with a productivity level below some viability cut-off level φ_* will thus exit the market, where φ_* is determined by $Bw_A^{1-\varepsilon}\varphi_*^{\varepsilon-1} = f$ (see Figure 15.9).

For a multinational firm with productivity level φ and marginal costs $w_A^{\eta}(\tau w_C)^{1-\eta}$, operating profits are equal to $B(w_A^{\eta}(\tau w_C)^{1-\eta})^{1-\varepsilon}\varphi^{1-\varepsilon} - w_A f_m$: see Figure 15.9. As drawn, the intercept for multinational profits on the vertical axis is lower than for domestic firms (which requires $f_m > f$), while the slope of the multinational profit line is steeper than for domestic firms, which requires $w_A > \tau w_C$ (see Technical Note 15.1). If the American wage rate is sufficiently high compared to the Chinese wage rate, the profits of becoming a vertical multinational are higher than for a domestic firm if the firm is sufficiently productive. See Box 15.2 for empirical evidence from Spain. In Figure 15.9 the switching point is given by

---

BOX 15.2 Domestic and foreign sourcing in Spain

In Chapter 13 we reviewed empirical information on productivity differences between firms. We also illustrated differences in the productivity distribution for different types of firms, such as the distinction between domestic firms, exporters, and exporters also using FDI in Belgium (Figure 13.5) and the distinction between national domestic, national exporting, foreign domestic, and foreign exporting firms in Latin America (Figure 13.17). We now use data from Spain to illustrate that the selection of firms into domestic and foreign sourcing is also relevant, see Figure 15.10. The data allows us to distinguish between firms that buy inputs only from other Spanish producers and firms that buy inputs from foreign producers. The distribution of foreign sourcing is shifted to the right compared to the distribution of domestic sourcing firms. On average, therefore, foreign sourcing firms in Spain are more productive than domestic sourcing firms. This is in line with expectations if the fixed cost of sourcing from foreign firms tends to be higher than for domestic firms, which is compensated by some other advantage, such as higher productivity or quality.

(continued...)

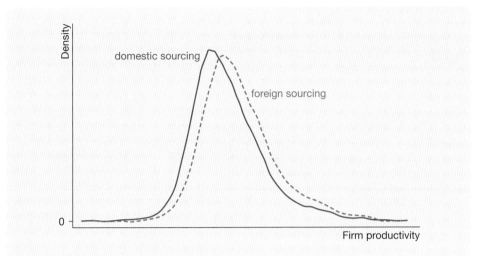

Figure 15.10 Domestic and foreign sourcing in Spain.

Source: based on Antràs and Yeaple (2014, Figure 2.9); data for 2007.

φ_{*m}. All firms above φ_{*m} become vertical multinationals. All firms below φ_* exit the market. All firms in between these two levels are domestic firms (that export to the Chinese market). Note that, in accordance with empirical observations, there is a range of domestic firms active in the market in Figure 15.9; if the multinational profit line is sufficiently steep this range may not exist (see Technical Note 15.1 for the exact condition).

15.7 Empirical evidence for vertical FDI

When discussing empirical evidence for horizontal FDI for US multinationals in Section 14.7 we noted that differences in capital–labour ratios and schooling did not seem to have significant explanatory power. When we take a closer look at the most actively involved countries we see that the top five countries for US affiliate exports back to the USA are (in this order) Canada, Mexico, Ireland, UK, and Singapore. These countries differ substantially in their characteristics and development level, indicating that strict adherence to a $2 \times 2 \times 2$ framework does not do justice to the rich empirical connections between countries. Evidently, some American firms find it worthwhile to outsource part of the production process to an advanced country such as Canada while other firms choose to outsource to a middle-income country such as Mexico. At the same time, some firms outsource to neighbouring countries (Canada and Mexico) while other firms outsource to countries further away (UK, Ireland, and Singapore). The comparative advantage of fragmentation for a particular production process depends, of course, on the production process itself and the factor intensity of the fragmented part. In short, we need to interact a country's factor abundance with the factor intensity of the production activity.

To allow for flexibility in our empirical evaluation we interact endowments with skill intensity. As in Chapter 14, let X_i^j be the exports from the US to country i in sector j, let S_i^j

Table 15.2 Skill interactions for American multinationals, 2009

Dependent variable log($s^j_{x,i}$); see main text for details				
Variable	(1)	(2)	(3)	(4)
Skill endowment	−0.03	1.57*	1.57*	
	(0.29)	(0.63)	(0.64)	
Skill endowment ×		−10.5**	−9.83**	08.77**
skill intensity		(3.57)	(3.38)	(2.68)
Skill intensity		13.7**		
		(2.74)		
Observations	2,315	2,315	2,315	2,482

Notes: ** and * indicate significant at 1 per cent and 5 per cent level; standard errors in parentheses; 42 countries included in the analysis; country fixed effects only in column (4); sector fixed effects only in columns (3) and (4); additional controls not reported.
Source: Antràs and Yeaple (2014), Table 2.4.

be the sales of American affiliates in sector j located in country i, and let $s^j_{x,i}$ be the share of exports in serving country i for sector j, defined as: $s^j_{x,i} = X^j_i / (X^j_i + S^j_i)$. This indicates the extent to which a foreign market is serviced through exports rather than affiliate sales.

We now extend the analysis from Section 14.7 by taking skill interactions into consideration. All variables analysed before are now used as control variables in this specification, which allows us to focus on skill endowments, skill intensity, and skill interactions: see Table 15.2. From the vertical FDI analysis in this chapter, the crucial prediction is that the impact of the interaction term should be negative: skill-intensive parts of the production process should tend to be located in skill abundant countries. Column (1) confirms that skill endowments are not significant if the interaction term is absent. Column (2) includes the interaction term and confirms that American firms tend to export more to skill scarce countries in skill-intensive sectors. Columns (3) and (4) show that this result is robust to including sector and country fixed effects.

15.8 Measuring supply chains: value added

As already noted in Section 15.1, measuring global supply chains is notoriously difficult. A closer look at the examples we discussed for China's electronics sector (Section 8.10) or Thailand's hard-disk drive production (Section 15.2) shows why: supply chains usually involve the simultaneous importing and exporting of goods and components at different stages of the production process in the same broader sector. It tends to involve locations in a range of different countries. The streams are usually coordinated at the firm level, involving large multinational enterprises. The interdependencies are important, as are the logistic problems. As a consequence, supply chains tend to involve multiple countries at different stages of economic development (which allows for differences in comparative advantages between the countries), but these countries have to be relatively close together in space in order to manage the logistics and coordination problems. Many large supply chains therefore involve advanced countries and nearby middle-income countries, such as the USA and Mexico, Germany and the Czech Republic, or Japan and China. Indeed, it is not too far-fetched to argue that some middle-income countries became precisely that

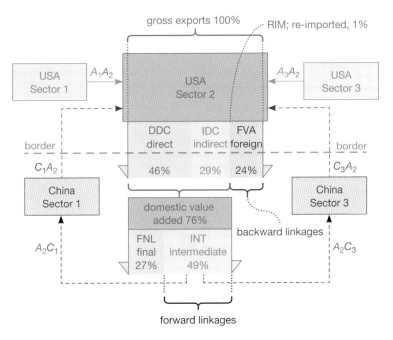

Figure 15.11 Backward and forward linkages in value-added trade.

Notes: percentages are global averages for 2011 based on OECD–WTO database.

(middle-income countries) because they benefited from being at the right stage of economic development in the neighbourhood of advanced countries at the right time.

One way to identify supply chains is by looking at the simultaneous trade of products across the border in the same sector. We do this in the next section. Another way to identify supply chains is by looking at the value added at each step of the production process. We do that in some detail in this section using the OECD-WTO Trade In Value Added database (it is thus a continuation of the analysis in Section 15.3 using the WIOD database). The most recent version of this database identifies 61 different countries plus a Rest of World combination of other countries and provides information up to 2011. We start by discussing the main concepts involved.

Suppose the American economy consists of three sectors, labelled 1, 2, and 3. For simplicity we assume that all American exports consist of sector 2 exports to China, which is taken to be the only other country in the world. The Chinese economy consists of two sectors, labelled 1 and 3. We focus attention on domestic value added and so-called backward and forward international linkages in our discussion below. We use gross exports from the USA (equated to 100 per cent) as our frame of reference: see Figure 15.11 for details.

Backward linkages. Not all value incorporated in the USA's gross exports is created in the USA, since part of it is created in so-called upstream sectors that supply intermediate goods to sector 2. More specifically, both China sector 1 and China sector 3 supply intermediate products to the American producers in sector 2; we identify these flows by the arrows C_1A_2 and C_3A_2 in Figure 15.11. As a consequence, part of gross exports represents value added imported from abroad. It is identified as FVA (foreign value added) in Figure 15.11

and consists of the (international) backward linkages of global supply chains. The global average backward linkages were 24 per cent of gross exports in 2011, as listed in the figure.

Domestic value added. All value incorporated in the USA's gross exports that is not created abroad is domestic value added. In view of the above, the global average domestic value-added share in 2011 was 76 per cent, since the foreign value-added share was 24 per cent. Not all of this value is added in sector 2, however, since both the USA sector 1 and the USA sector 3 supply intermediate products to the American producers in sector 2; we identify these flows by the arrows A_1A_2 and A_3A_2 in Figure 15.11. As a consequence, we can identify three different types of domestic value-added flows.

- DDC—direct domestic contribution. This is the value added incorporated in the gross exports that is created in the exporting sector itself (in this case sector 2); the global average direct contribution was 46 per cent of gross exports in 2011.

- IDC—indirect domestic contribution. This is the value added incorporated in the gross exports that originates from domestic upstream sectors (in this case sectors 1 and 3). The global average indirect contribution was 29 per cent of gross exports in 2011.

- RIM—re-imported domestic value-added content of exports. A small percentage of domestic value added incorporated in the gross exports of a sector consist of value added that was first exported from the country to be used as an intermediate input by foreign sectors (in this case China sectors 1 and 3), which is then subsequently re-imported into the country as an intermediate input in the production process. The global average re-imported domestic value-added share was about one per cent of gross exports in 2011.

Forward linkages. The domestic value added incorporated in gross exports can be used to satisfy the demand for final goods or it can be used as an intermediate input in the production process of a foreign sector. In this case, the USA sector 2 supplies intermediate goods to both China sector 1 and China sector 3; we identify these flows by the arrows A_2C_1 and A_2C_3 in Figure 15.11. These substantial deliveries of intermediate goods to international downstream sectors represent the forward linkages in global supply chains. The global average forward linkages were 49 per cent of gross exports in 2011, which implies that the global average domestic value added incorporated in the demand for final goods was 27 per cent of gross exports in 2011.

Figure 15.12 provides an overview of domestic value added as a share of gross exports in 2011. It is the counterpart of Figure 15.5 which used WIOD data for 2009. The general tendency regarding the country classification in the two data sets is similar: Luxembourg ranks low, Russia ranks high, Germany is close to the world average, and USA is above the world average. There are, however, also some differences: the average domestic value-added share is higher for OECD-WTO (this also holds in 2009), China has moved below the world average, the Rest of the World has moved above the world average, and Saudi Arabia has the highest domestic value-added share of the included countries (97 per cent). The differences arise both from slightly different methodologies and from including more countries (61 instead of 41). Saudi Arabia, for example, was not included in the WIOD data. Its main export is domestically produced oil, hence the high score on domestic value added. The same holds for Brunei with the second-highest score on domestic value added (96 per cent: the small circle close to Saudi Arabia).

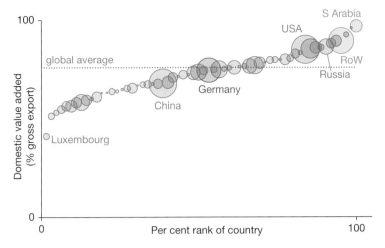

Figure 15.12 Domestic value added as share of gross exports (%), 2011.

Notes: 61 countries plus Rest of World (RoW); global average is 75.8 per cent; bubbles proportional to gross export value.
Source: based on data from OECD–WTO trade in value added database (EXGR-DVASH).

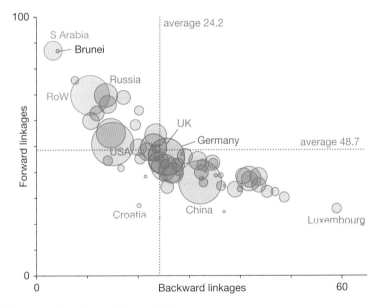

Figure 15.13 Backward and forward linkages, 2011.

Notes: 61 countries plus Rest of World; EXGR-FVASH and EXGR-INTDVASH; bubble size proportional to gross exports.
Source: based on data from OECD–WTO trade in value added database (EXGR-DVASH).

Regarding the participation in global supply chains the OECD-WTO identifies two important international linkages, as explained above. An overview of the backward and forward linkages in 2011 is provided in Figure 15.13. The countries with the highest-scoring forward linkages are the oil exporting nations Saudi Arabia and Brunei (87 per cent of gross exports). This reflects the fact that most of the exported oil is subsequently used as an

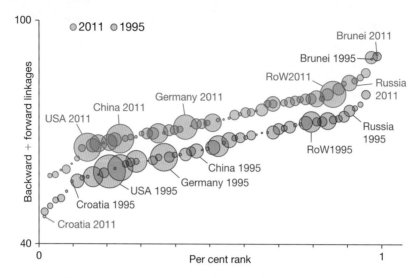

Figure 15.14 Sum of backward and forward linkages in 1995 and 2011.

Notes: 61 countries plus Rest of World; bubbles proportional to percent of gross exports in the respective year.
Source: based on data from OECD–WTO trade in value added database (sum of EXGR-FVASH and EXGR-INTDVASH).

intermediate input in virtually all sectors of the importing countries. Other high-scoring forward linkages are those of Russia and Rest of World (70 per cent of gross exports). The global average forward linkage is 49 per cent of gross exports, which is about equal to the value for the UK and close to the values for USA (51 per cent) and Germany (46 per cent).

The highest backward linkage by far is provided by Luxembourg (59 per cent). This reflects the fact that many sectors in Luxembourg intensively use imported intermediate inputs in the production process. The backward linkages are, of course, already illustrated in Figure 15.12, since these linkages are equal to 1 minus the domestic value-added share, as analysed in Figure 15.11. This implies that the countries scoring high in domestic value added, such as Saudi Arabia, Brunei, and Russia, score low in backward linkages. The global average backward linkage is 24 per cent, which is close to the value for the UK, India, and Canada (the latter two are not identified separately in the figure). The USA has clearly lower backward linkages (15 per cent), while Germany and China have higher backward linkages (26 and 32 per cent, respectively), reflecting the fact that German and Chinese sectors more intensively use imported components from other countries in their production processes than do the UK or the USA.

The sum of the backward and forward linkages is generally taken as an indication of the intensity with which a country participates in global value chains: see Koopman et al. (2010).[13] Figure 15.13 illustrates that for most countries there is a clear trade-off: higher backward linkages come at the expense of lower forward linkages. In fact, a simple regression of Figure 15.13 gives a slope of −0.95 and explains about 65 per cent of the variance in forward linkages. There are, nonetheless, substantial differences between countries. The global average sum of backward and forward linkages is 73 per cent, ranging from a low of 47 for Croatia to a high of 91 for Brunei.

To conclude our discussion of value-added measures of global supply chains, Figure 15.14 shows the sum of backward and forward linkages for both 1995 and 2011. This clearly shows that participation in global value chains is rising over time: the values for the 2011 score tend to be above those for the 1995 score. In fact, the global average sum of backward and forward linkages increased from 65 per cent in 1995 to 73 per cent in 2011. The values were higher for all individual countries except for Saudi Arabia (minus 0 per cent), Cambodia (minus 1 per cent), and Croatia (minus 10 per cent). The rise was above ten percentage points for 12 countries, with an increase of 15 percentage points for Hungary and Iceland and of 16 percentage points for India. The large drop for Croatia clearly puts it in a rather special (low) position in 2011 compared to the other countries. The ranking tends to be rather persistent over time, with Germany and Rest of World moving up a bit while USA and China are moving down. Also note the increase in bubble size for China and Rest of World, indicating their rapidly rising importance in global trade flows.

15.9 Measuring supply chains: Grubel–Lloyd

The value-added supply chain indicators discussed in Section 15.8 are informative and based on data that became available only recently. These indicators, however, also have some important shortcomings.[14]

First, the informational requirements for constructing the data are large, which means that a large number of countries are still excluded from the analysis. This holds, in particular for low income countries. Brakman, Kohl, and van Marrewijk (2015), for example, divide nations into five income classes relative to the world average per capita income level as follows: LOW (below 30 per cent), LoMID (between 30 and 70 per cent), MID (between 70 and 130 per cent), HiMID (between 130 and 220 per cent), and ADV (for Advanced, above 220 per cent). We use this classification also for our discussion below. Of the 61 countries in the OECD-WTO database only one country (Cambodia) belongs to the LOW income class and only five countries (Tunisia, Vietnam, India, Philippines, and Indonesia) belong to the LoMID income class. Not a single Sub-Saharan African developing nation is included.[15] This creates a substantial bias in our value-added view of global supply chains.

Second, the construction of the data is based on internationally comparable input–output data, which means that the number of sectors is limited. The OECD-WTO database identifies 34 sectors (including 16 manufacturing and 14 services sectors). The WIOD database covers 35 sectors. This contrasts sharply with the thousands of sectors for which gross export data is available for basically all countries of the world. (A disadvantage of gross export data is that information on services trade is limited.)

Third, the supply chain indicators analysed in Section 15.8 probably do not actually identify participation in global value chains in the way we think is most appropriate. It is, for example, true that Saudi Arabia's oil exports are used as an intermediate input in many countries in the world. This does not mean that Saudi Arabia is part of supply chains in the sense discussed in examples so far. Its input is specialized only to a limited extent and a disruption in oil supply by Saudi Arabia can rather easily be replaced by oil supply from another source. In contrast, a disruption in, for example, the supply of the taptic engine for the Apple watch had immediate and important consequences (see Box 15.3). In some sense the involvement of Saudi Arabia in supply chains is 'too distant'. Brunei and Russia also score high in the value-added index shown in Figure 15.14, but their involvement in global

> **BOX 15.3 Supply chain dependencies: Apple Watch and the taptic engine**
>
> Being part of a supply chain also creates dependencies within the chain. A good example is provided by the taptic engine of the Apple Watch. This device creates a subtle feeling on the wrist if a new notification arrives. Apple was forced to delay the introduction of the Apple Watch in early 2015 because of technical problems with the taptic engine. At this stage of development two manufacturers were able to supply the taptic engine, namely AAC Technologies from China and Nidec from Japan. During the long-term testing phase Apple realized that some of the watches did not function properly if the taptic engine was supplied by the Chinese manufacturer. Before delivery started it thus had to dispose of all watches that had been produced with this component. It is clearly hard to substitute for this component as now the Japanese firm is the only one able to make the component (a substitutability problem that does not arise, for example, when delivery of a supply of raw materials is interrupted). Apple's dependence on the Japanese Nidec firm, which was able to only gradually increase production of its components, thus resulted in a delay of the introduction of the Apple Watch.
>
> *Source:* rtlnieuws.nl, 30 April 2015.

supply chains mimics that of Saudi Arabia and is rather limited.[16] At the other end of the picture the USA, China, and Germany score relatively low on the value-added supply chain index of Figure 15.14, whereas we know that all three countries play an important role in many global supply chains. Their low score seems related to the size of their trade flows rather than their actual involvement.

What we need, therefore, is an alternative measure of global supply chains such that (i) information is available for almost all countries, (ii) information is available for many more sectors, and (iii) the index measures actual involvement in supply chains rather than more distant involvement. Since supply chains involve two-way trade in the same sector, an indicator of a country's involvement in international supply chains might be based on determining the extent of such trade. In fact, we already developed such an index in Chapter 8, namely the trade-weighted average of the Grubel–Lloyd index of intra-industry trade. Under the assumption that most intermediate trade—within a supply chain—is trade within the same sector we can use it as a method for measuring supply chains; the higher the index, the more important are supply chains. It solves the 'too distant' value-added problem of Saudi Arabia discussed above by excluding trade flows with other sectors. The index is easy to calculate based on gross export data, which is available for thousands of sectors for virtually all countries in the world. To get a proper view, we analyse data at the detailed five-digit level based on the work of Marius Brülhart (2008).

Figure 15.15 shows that many of the world's largest trading sectors have a high Grubel–Lloyd index. This holds, for example, for instruments (and apparatus, 7 per cent of world trade), cars (road motor vehicles, 7.6 per cent of world trade), nonelectric machines (14.6 per cent of world trade), and electrical machinery (10.5 per cent of world trade). This is, of course, partially an inflated impression of the real importance of these sectors precisely because of the intensive two-way trade flows (which put the focus on gross exports and not on value-added exports). The highest scoring sector is electrical power machines and switchgear (with a Grubel–Lloyd index of 52.7 per cent, representing 0.5 per cent of world trade). Two large sectors are below the global average, namely organic chemicals

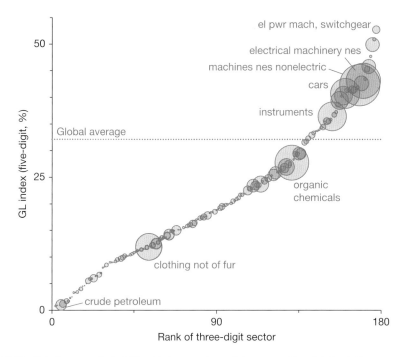

Figure 15.15 Global average Grubel–Lloyd index, per three-digit sector at five-digit level, %.

Notes: bubbles proportional to the size of global trade flows; sectors ranked from low to high index, 177 sectors; nes is not elsewhere specified; el pwr mach is electrical power machines; global trade weighted average is 31.9 per cent.
Source: figure based on Brülhart (2008) data for 2006 at SITC (3rd rev) five-digit level.

(10.3 per cent of world trade and very close to the global average) and clothing not of fur (6.1 per cent of world trade).

Figure 15.15 makes clear that if your country specializes in the production of goods in sectors with a low Grubel–Lloyd index globally, then your country is likely to score low on the Grubel–Lloyd index at the country level as well. This holds, for example, for countries specializing in the export of uranium; cotton; silk; jute; crude petroleum; non-ferrous base metal ore; rice; coal, coke and briquettes; and iron ore. These are the eight lowest-scoring sectors in the bottom left part of Figure 15.15 (not identified separately, except for petroleum). Countries specializing to a large extent in these types of sectors do not for the most part participate in global supply chains.

Our next task is to identify the countries that are intensively involved in global supply chains based on the five-digit Grubel–Lloyd index and to identify the countries that are not. To do so we calculate each country's trade-weighted average Grubel–Lloyd index. To illustrate the connection with different levels of economic development and country size, we plot the results relative to income per capita (log scale) for each of the income groups using bubbles proportional to population size. Our findings are depicted in Figure 15.16 and Figure 15.17 and our analysis is summarized in Table 15.3 and Table 15.4.

We now have information for a large group of countries (176 in total), including a substantial number of LOW income countries (47 in total). One look at Figure 15.16 immediately illustrates three important points.

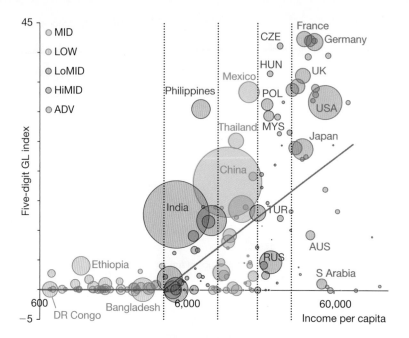

Figure 15.16 Grubel–Lloyd index per country: trade-weighted average, five-digit level.

Notes: income per capita PPP in constant 2011 international $ (log scale); trade-weighted Grubel–Lloyd index at SITC (third revision) five-digit level per country; 176 countries; the solid line is a regression line for LOW countries, combined with a regression line for all other countries, see Table 15.3 for details.

Source: figure based on Brülhart (2008) data combined with World Development Indicators.

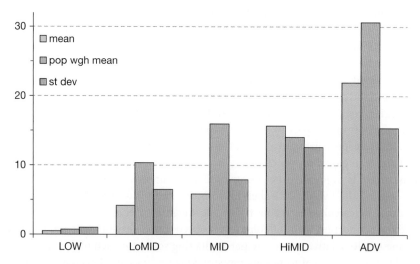

Figure 15.17 Grubel–Lloyd index by income group: trade-weighted, five-digit level.

Notes: see Table 15.4 for details; average trade-weighted Grubel–Lloyd index at SITC (third revision) five-digit level per country; mean is unweighted country average within the income group; pop wgh mean is population-weighted country average within the income group; st dev is standard deviation within the income group.

Source: figure based on Brülhart (2008) data combined with World Development Indicators.

Table 15.3 Intra-industry trade (five-digit) and income per capita, OLS estimates

| Endogenous variable: trade-weighted five-digit Grubel–Lloyd index | | | | |
| Exogenous variable: log of income per capita | | | | |
Country group	intercept	slope	R^2	no. obs
All countries	−44.15***	5.78***	0.33	176
	(0.0000)	(0.0000)		
Excluding LOW countries	−69.57***	8.34***	0.25	129
	(0.0000)	(0.0000)		
LOW countries only	−1.02	0.20	0.01	47
	(0.6595)	(0.5139)		

Notes: p-values in parentheses; *** indicates significance at 1 per cent.
Source: author's calculations, see Figure 15.15.

First, the five-digit trade-weighted Grubel–Lloyd index is able to adequately identify all countries at different levels of economic development that we *know* are intensively involved in global supply chains. This holds, for example, for the Philippines for the LoMID countries, for Mexico, Thailand, and China for the MID countries, for the Czech Republic, Hungary, Poland, and Malaysia for the HiMID countries, and for France, Germany, UK, USA, and Japan for the ADV countries. The geographical component of these links is also noticeable, as is illustrated for the low score for Australia, which is too far away from most other countries to be a successful link for most types of global supply chains.

Second, there is a strong positive association between the level of economic development and the degree of participation in global supply chains. The first line of Table 15.3 illustrates this using a simple regression for all countries of Figure 15.16, leading to a highly statistically significant coefficient of 5.78 for the effect of log income per capita on the Grubel–Lloyd index.

Third, and most striking: the *poorest* countries in the world *do not* participate in global supply chains. There are 47 LOW income countries included in Figure 15.16. They all have a low Grubel–Lloyd index, the variation in these scores is minimal, and there is no discernible increase within this group as income per capita rises. The last line of Table 15.3 makes this clear, as a regression using only the LOW income countries leads to insignificant results for both slope and intercept.

Excluding the LOW countries from the sample, as is done in the second row of Table 15.3, thus increases the slope of the estimated coefficient for the remaining countries from 5.78 to 8.34, indicating an overall stronger positive association between the level of economic development and the participation in global supply chains once a critical income per capita level is reached. The estimated intercept for this critical level on the horizontal income per capita axis is at 4,185 PPP international dollars, which is essentially *on* the cut-off level for LOW versus LoMID countries ($4,204; the deviation is less than 0.5 per cent).

Table 15.4 provides summary statistics on intra-industry trade for the world as a whole and for each income group. The most important results are illustrated in Figure 15.17. For the LOW income group there is basically no participation in global supply chains. The score is low for both the unweighted and the population-weighted mean. Moreover, there is almost no variation, leading to a very low standard deviation for this income group

Table 15.4 Intra-industry trade (five-digit) and income per country statistics

	mean		median	st dev	min	max	no. co	pop
	normal	pop wgh						
World	8.6	14.1	1.9	12.2	0.0	42.4	176	6,828
LOW	0.5	0.7	0.0	1.0	0.0	4.0	47	948
LoMID	4.2	10.3	1.5	6.5	0.0	30.5	31	2,250
MID	5.9	16.0	2.4	7.9	0.0	33.4	39	2,210
HiMID	15.7	14.1	13.0	12.6	0.0	41.2	27	408
ADV	21.9	30.6	23.9	15.3	0.0	42.4	32	1,012

Notes: normal mean is unweighted average; pop wgh = population-weighted average; st dev = standard deviation; min = minimum; max = maximum; no. co = number of countries; pop = population (in millions).
Source: author's calculations, see Figure 15.15.

(1 per cent). The maximum score for the LOW income group is only 4 per cent. For the remaining income groups all indices rise as the level of economic development rises. The mean, the median, and the standard deviation all go up consistently. The only exception is the minimum, which remains at zero for all income groups, and a small decrease for the population-weighted average when going from the MID to the HiMID group. The maximum score is reached for France at 42.4 per cent. Other countries scoring above 40 per cent are: Czech Republic, Germany, Canada, and Austria.

We conclude that LOW income countries do not participate actively in global supply chains. Most of these countries are in Africa, namely 34 out of 47 (or 72 per cent). Another five countries are in Southeast Asia and the Pacific, three are in Southern Asia, two are in Central Asia and Caucasus, two in Central America and the Caribbean, and one in Western Asia. Indeed, when analysing his results, Brülhart (2008) discusses in detail how there is essentially no intra-industry trade at the five-digit level for the countries of the Central African Economic and Monetary Community (CEMAC), the West African Economic and Monetary Union (WAEMU), the East African Community (EAC), and the Southern Africa Customs Union (SACU).

15.10 Firm boundaries

So far the analysis of horizontal FDI (Chapter 14) and vertical FDI (this chapter) has ignored the internalization advantage that is necessary for creating multinationals according to the OLI framework (see Section 14.4). This advantage is identified in order to answer the question of when a firm should set up a new facility integrated within the firm boundaries (integration) and when it should buy inputs from another firm outside of the firm boundaries (outsourcing). In conjunction with setting up facilities at home (domestic) or abroad (foreign), we can thus distinguish between four types of organizational inputs: domestic outsourcing, foreign outsourcing, domestic integration, and foreign integration. This section briefly discusses some of the issues that play a role in determining the firm's boundaries.

If it would be possible to have complete and perfect contracting available which specifies in an enforceable way what to do under any circumstances that may arise for the contracting parties, the firm boundaries would be indeterminate and irrelevant (Coase, 1937). Since this is clearly not possible, as we cannot foresee all possible future circumstances nor do we have the time available to specify a contract under all such circumstances, the boundaries of the firm tend to be based on the limits of contracting and enforceability. There are two main strands of literature, namely the transaction-cost approach and the property-rights approach.

1   The *transaction-cost theory* argues that a firm will internalize transactions within the firm if the transaction costs of doing so through the market are higher than doing this internally. Two main issues play a role, namely rent dissipation and hold-up inefficiencies.

   a   *Rent dissipation* occurs when a firm that licenses the production of a good to another firm through a market transaction cannot fully capture the net surplus of selling these goods. In practice, the firm will end up sharing the rents with licensees. Issues involved with this problem include the partial transfer of technology to the other firm and the partially nonexcludable nature of this technology (see the discussion in Chapter 17). In modelling this problem a firm must usually weigh the advantages of market transactions through licensing, such as lower costs, against the rent dissipation from doing so.

   b   *Hold-up inefficiencies* occur when two parties engage in relation-specific investments prior to determining the *ex post* distribution of returns from these investments (Williamson, 1985). The distribution is (partially) determined ex post because of the limited enforceability of *ex ante* contracts. Once the firm has made the relation-specific investment, meeting for example certain quality, weight, or dimension requirements, the produced goods are worth more inside the relationship than outside. On the one hand this means that the investing party has power inside the relationship which it can use to (re-)negotiate a deal on the distribution of rents (the hold-up problem). On the other hand this means that it has an incentive to under-invest, as it can only receive part of the associated benefits. In modelling this problem a firm must usually weigh the advantages of market transactions through outsourcing (lower costs) against the disadvantages of hold-up inefficiencies.

2   The *property-rights approach* focuses on the idea that ownership of assets is a source of power when contracts are incomplete (Grossman and Hart, 1986). It starts with the idea that the transaction cost difficulties analysed above (rent dissipation and hold-up inefficiencies) are also important for within-firm transactions, and not just for market transactions. Internalization therefore does not really solve these problems, and in that sense it is hard to determine the boundaries of the firm based on transaction cost theory. The property-rights approach focuses on ownership of assets, such as machines, buildings, patents, and the like. When two parties arrive at a situation unforeseen in some incomplete initial contract the owner of the assets naturally holds *residual* rights of control and uses this to maximize her profits. This idea is then crucial for determining when and how a firm decides to integrate a facility or to outsource.

The ideas above can be used in developing theoretical models determining whether a firm should integrate or outsource and whether it should do so domestically or abroad. These models are similar to the ones already analysed in Chapter 14 and this chapter, also taking firm heterogeneity (Chapter 13) into consideration: see Antràs and Yeaple (2014).

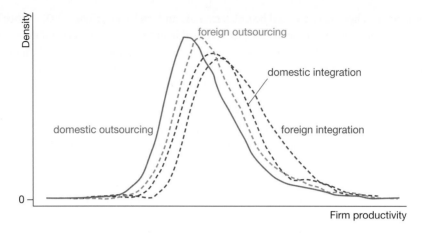

Figure 15.18 Organizational sorting in Spain.

Source: based on Antràs and Yeaple (2014, Figure 2.11); data for 2007.

We conclude this section with an empirical evaluation of the sorting of firms into different types of organizations using Spanish data, see Figure 15.18. This suggests that, on average, domestic outsourcing firms are the least productive and foreign integrated firms are the most productive. The other two firm types are in between, with domestic integrated firms being on average more productive than foreign outsourcing firms. Further empirical research in this area is needed to confirm these relationships.

15.11 **Conclusion**

Supply chains fragment parts of the production process into separate value-added stages in different countries. One way, therefore, to analyse the rising importance of supply chains is to note the declining share of domestic value added in gross export flows. We show that vertical FDI associated with the fragmentation process is attractive only if factor prices are sufficiently different between countries. Empirical evidence of vertical FDI therefore focuses on the interaction between the factor intensity of the fragmented part of the production process and the factor abundance of the destination country. We explain why there is no simple and robust link connecting fragmentation with wage inequality between the source and destination countries and why only the most productive firms engage in vertical FDI activities. Firms have to decide to organize fragmentation through outsourcing or within the firm boundaries. Transaction costs (rent dissipation and hold-up inefficiencies) and property rights are important for this decision process. Supply chains are notoriously hard to measure empirically and no measure is perfect. In value-added trade flows we focus on forward linkages (the use of our value-added exports as an intermediate input) and backward linkages (the use of foreign added value as an intermediate input for our exports). The Grubel–Lloyd index focuses on two-way trade flows within the same sector as an identifier. In general, supply chain activity rises as income per capita rises (although the variance rises too). There seems to be a minimum income level before countries start to engage in supply chain activities. The poorest countries, particularly in Africa, therefore hardly play a role in global supply chains.

Technical Note

Technical Note 15.1 Vertical FDI

As explained in the main text in Section 15.6, operating profits are equal to $Bw_A^{1-\varepsilon}\varphi^{1-\varepsilon} - w_A f$ for a domestic firm and $B(w_A^{\eta}(\tau w_C)^{1-\eta})^{1-\varepsilon}\varphi^{1-\varepsilon} - w_A f_m$ for a firm engaging in vertical FDI. To make it possible to have vertical FDI and a distribution of firms into domestic firms and multinationals, three simple conditions need to be fulfilled. First, we must make sure that the vertical intercept of the profit function is lower for multinationals than for domestic firms. This requires that $f < f_m$, such that the fixed costs are larger for multinationals than for domestic firms. Second, we must ensure that the slope of the profit function is steeper for multinationals than for domestic firms. This requires:

$$w_A^{1-\varepsilon} \langle (w_A^{\eta}(\tau w_C)^{1-\eta})^{1-\varepsilon} \Leftrightarrow w_A \rangle w_A^{\eta}(\tau w_C)^{1-\eta} \Leftrightarrow w_A > \tau w_C \qquad \text{(A15.1)}$$

—where the inequality reversal in the first step arises from the fact that $\varepsilon > 1$. This implies that it is attractive to become a multinational firm only if the wage rate paid in the USA is sufficiently high compared to the wage rate paid in China, taking the transportation costs τ into consideration. Third, we must ensure that the viability threshold for domestic firms occurs before that of multinational firms is reached, or equivalently that the point where the two profit levels are the same is reached after the viability threshold is reached. If this third condition is not met, we will only observe multinational firms in equilibrium and no domestic firms. We can determine this threshold by equating the profit functions above to zero, which gives:

$$\varphi_*^{\varepsilon-1} = \frac{w_A f}{B w_A^{1-\varepsilon}}; \qquad \varphi_m^{\varepsilon-1} = \frac{w_A f_m}{B(w_A^{\eta}(\tau w_C)^{1-\eta})^{1-\varepsilon}} \qquad \text{(A15.2)}$$

—where $\varphi_*^{\varepsilon-1}$ is the threshold for domestic firms and $\varphi_m^{\varepsilon-1}$ is the threshold for multinationals. The third condition is therefore met if $\varphi_*^{\varepsilon-1} < \varphi_m^{\varepsilon-1}$, which means:

$$\frac{w_A f}{B w_A^{1-\varepsilon}} < \frac{w_A f_m}{B(w_A^{\eta}(\tau w_C)^{1-\eta})^{1-\varepsilon}} \Leftrightarrow \frac{f}{w_A^{1-\varepsilon}} < \frac{f_m}{(w_A^{\eta}(\tau w_C)^{1-\eta})^{1-\varepsilon}} \Leftrightarrow (w_A^{\eta}(\tau w_C)^{1-\eta})^{1-\varepsilon} f < w_A^{1-\varepsilon} f_m \qquad \text{(A15.3)}$$

 ## Notes

1 This section is based on Brakman, Garretsen, and van Marrewijk (2001).

2 According to Gourevitch, Bohn, and McKendrick (2000, p. 304): 'Typically, aluminum blank substrates are nickel-plated and polished before the platters are sputtered and finished. As with heads, media are a very high-technology aspect of HDD production.'

3 This section is largely based on Brakman and van Marrewijk (2016).

4 Except for intra-EU trade, where it is estimated.

5 See www.WIOD.org

6 Based on WIOD data; we converted current dollars to constant dollars using the US GDP deflator.

7 The exception is the rise in the ratio of value-added trade flows to gross trade flows in 2009 as a consequence of the Great Recession. This rise appears to have been only temporary: see Brakman, van Marrewijk, and Partridge (2015) and Los, Timmer, and de Vries (2015).

8 The un-weighted average is 70.8 per cent and the weighted average is 73.4 per cent.

9 It is better not to pay too much attention to RoW in Figure 15.5, as this is an artificial construct combining all other countries in the world.

10 The analysis in this section is based on Helpman (1984) and Helpman and Krugman (1985).

11 We are skipping over some technical details here, but Helpman (1984) shows that for a given relative size of countries the share of intra-firm trade in total trade is rising in differences in factor endowments. He also shows that for some factor endowment regions fragmentation may restore factor price equalization.

12 Note that we can always assure that $w_H > w_L$ within a country by redefining the units in which high-skilled and low-skilled workers are measured.

13 Taking $\log(1 + backward) + \log(1 + forward)$ as an indicator does not affect our discussion below.

14 This section is partially based on Brakman, Kohl, and van Marrewijk (2015).

15 South Africa, a MID income country, is included.

16 Norway and Luxembourg also score high, but this may reflect actual involvement in supply chains.

 Questions

Question 15.1

Briefly answer the following questions.

a. What are global supply chains?

b. What is an indicator for the rise of global supply chains if we look at trade data? Why?

c. How are global supply chains related to offshoring?

d. What are 'backward linkages' in trade flows?

e. What are 'forward linkages' in trade flows?

Question 15.2

Figure 15.19 is taken from the *World Trade Report 2014*.

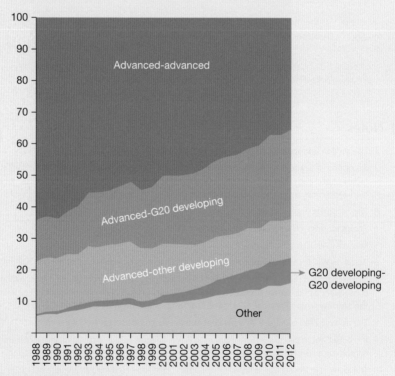

Figure 15.19 Share of imports in parts and components, 1988–2012 (per cent).

Source: World Trade Organization, World Trade Report 2014.

Briefly explain the connection of Figure 15.19 with global value chains and the two main issues that (according to you) the figure illustrates, and why.

Question 15.3

a. Explain why a (detailed) Grubel–Lloyd index can be used as an indicator of supply chains?

b. Which types of countries (in terms of income per capita) are most involved in global supply chains if we use the Grubel–Lloyd index as an indicator, and which type of countries are not?

 See the **online resources** *for a Study Guide and questions:*
www.oup.com/uk/vanmarrewijk_it/

Part VI

....

International interactions

....

Part VI concludes our analysis of international trade with a discussion of international interactions, consisting of two chapters. We start in Chapter 16 with two empirical regularities (Zipf's Law and the gravity equation) and explain how a proper mix of the insights we have learned about throughout the book helps us to understand these regularities in terms of three variations of geographical economics models. Chapter 17 analyses the dynamic aspects of international economics through the accumulation of physical and human capital, endogenous growth, and knowledge spillovers. Through this analysis, we provide insights into the changing role of global competitiveness as countries mature from factor-driven economies in their early stages, to efficiency-driven economies in their intermediate stages, to innovation-driven economies in their most advanced stages of economic development.

16 Geography and gravity

Objectives

- To know Zipf's Law, a regularity for the distribution of cities across space.
- To know the gravity equation, a regularity for the interaction between economic centres.
- To understand the basic geographical economics model, which leads to core–periphery distribution patterns if transport costs are sufficiently low.
- To be able to distinguish between short-run and long-run equilibrium.
- To understand the difference between stable and unstable equilibria.
- To know how the tomahawk diagram summarizes the implications of geographical economics models, including the alternative models (human capital and intermediate goods).
- To know the three types of gravity equations (general, structural, and naïve) and understand that many different theoretical models give rise to structural gravity.
- To understand how bilateral accessibility between two locations can be influenced by the price elasticity of demand or an inverse measure of (consumer, sector, or firm) heterogeneity.

16.1 Introduction

One of the most remarkable aspects of the global economic system is the unequal distribution of population and economic activity across the earth: see also Chapter 1. Millions of people are living close together in New York, Moscow, and Beijing. At the same time, there are large, virtually empty spaces available in the USA, Russia, and China. The distribution of people and economic activity across space is not only remarkably unequal, it is also remarkably regular, both in terms of a pattern across space (Zipf's Law) and in terms of the interaction between economic centres (the gravity equation): see Section 16.2. The question arises, obviously, why economic activity is so unequally distributed, and why these regularities occur.

It has long been evident that these aspects cannot be adequately explained using a neoclassical framework. In particular, economies of scale and imperfect competition, interacting with some form of local advantages, are essential. This implies that it is rather complicated to endogenously determine the size of economic activity in different locations in a general equilibrium framework. Such a framework was only fairly recently developed, as it is based on tools that needed to be developed first in other fields of economics (tractable scale economies and monopolistic competition). The path-breaking contribution of the American economist Paul Krugman appeared in 1991 (see Box 16.1). Since then many prominent researchers have published work on refinements, generalizations, and applications in this field now known as 'geographical economics' or 'new economic geography', which combines elements from international economics, industrial organization, economic geography, spatial economics, urban economics, and endogenous growth.[1] The body of this chapter describes Krugman's original 'core' model. More recent alternative specifications (based on input–output linkages and factor abundance) are also available and lead essentially to the same conclusions: see Section 16.6. We conclude with an overview in Section 16.8 of the three types of gravity equations, how these can be based on many different types of economic models, and some of the main empirical geographical implications for bilateral trade flows.

BOX 16.1 Paul Krugman

Figure 16.1
Paul Krugman (1953–).

Krugman (Figure 16.1) was born in a suburb of New York City and received his BA from Yale (1974) and his PhD from MIT (1977). He worked at Yale, MIT, Stanford, and MIT (again), before moving to Princeton. He is probably, and deservedly, the most influential international economist around today, well known both in the academic world and, thanks to his lucid prose, outside. As he puts it: 'There are several different ways of doing good economics ... But what has always appealed to me, ever since I saw Nordhaus practice it on energy, is the MIT style: small models applied to real problems, blending real-world observation and a little mathematics to cut through to the core of an issue.' He has used the MIT style splendidly to start off various new fields of study: new trade theory, geographical economics, target zone models, and financial crises. For the source of the quote, see the Collier laudatio on the internet when Paul Krugman received his honorary doctorate in Berlin (Collier, 1999)

16.2 Zipf's Law and the gravity equation

This section discusses two regularities in the unequal distribution of people and economic activity across space, namely (i) regarding the distribution pattern of centres of economic activity and (ii) regarding the interactions between these centres of activity.

16.2.1 Distribution pattern (Zipf's Law)

The regularity in the distribution pattern, known as Zipf's Law, is most easily illustrated using a concrete example. Take the largest city in India. In 2010, the most recent year for which we have reliable data, this was Mumbai (formerly known in English as Bombay), with about 13.8 million inhabitants. Give this city rank number 1. Then take the second largest city (Delhi, with about 12.6 million inhabitants) and give this rank number 2. The third largest city (Bangalore, with 5.4 million inhabitants) is given rank number 3, and so on. The data above are derived from the 2011 Indian census, which concluded that there are more than 1.2 billion Indians. Arranging the data for the 180 largest Indian cities this way, you now take the natural logarithm of the population size and of the city (rank-0.5).[2] When the latter are plotted in a scatter diagram, the outcome is an almost perfect straight line; see Figure 16.2.[3] Obviously, there is a negative relationship between population size and rank by construction. The puzzling feature is why this is an almost perfect log-linear straight line. A simple linear regression of the data plotted in Figure 16.2 gives

$$ln\left(rank - \frac{1}{2} \right) = 20.66 - 1.24 ln(population) \qquad 16.1$$

The coefficient is highly significant and the regression explains 98.3 per cent of the variance in city size. Based on this estimate, we would predict the size of the population of urban agglomeration number 100, for example, to be 437,000 people. This is very close to the actual size of number 100 (Jhansi), with a population of 449,000. This regularity in the distribution of city sizes holds not only for India, but also for the USA, Brazil, France, China, Russia, and many other countries. Apparently, hitherto poorly understood economic forces play an important role in determining the size distribution of cities, regardless of the economic structure, organization, wealth, and history of a nation. Ever since George Kingsley Zipf (1949) presented evidence on this regularity, scientists have been searching for an adequate explanation.[4]

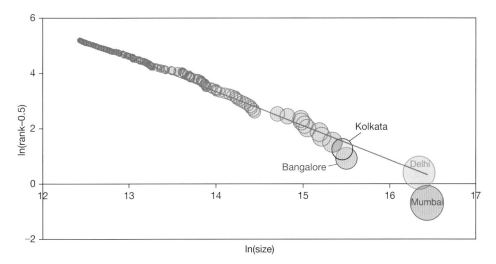

Figure 16.2 Zipf's law for India, 2010.

Source: calculations based on www.censusindia.gov.in 2011; bubbles proportional to population size.

16.2.2 Interaction (gravity equation)

There is also a pattern in the interaction between centres of economic activity. It is known as the 'gravity equation', and is related to Zipf's Law. The gravity equation, too, is most easily illustrated using a concrete example, for which we focus on the trade flows of Germany, the dominant European economy. Trade is measured as the sum of exports from and imports to Germany in billion US dollars. In 2015 the Netherlands was the largest trade partner for Germany, with a value of $216 billion. The second largest trade partner was France ($194 billion), followed by the USA ($177 billion), China, the UK, Italy, Poland, Austria, Belgium, Switzerland, and the Czech Republic.

The 'local' flavour of this top trade partner list is immediately evident. With the exception of the USA and China (the world's largest economies) the most important German trade partners are in its vicinity. Germany has eight direct neighbours, seven of which are listed above.[5] All of these neighbours, some of which are tiny in terms of economic size, are more important for German trade flows than the mighty Japanese economy, which only ranks seventeenth as trade partner with a trade value of $35 billion. This is only one step up from Germany's last direct neighbour, Denmark, which is ranked eighteenth with a trade value of $33 billion. Indeed, Denmark is about as important for German trade flows as Japan despite the fact that the Japanese economy is about 19 times larger than the Danish economy. Similarly, the Netherlands is more important for German trade than the USA or China, despite the fact that these economies are about 21 times larger than the Dutch economy.

The trade of goods and services from one country to another involves time, effort, and hence costs. Goods have to be physically loaded and unloaded, transported by truck, train, ship, or plane, packed, insured, traced, etc. before they reach their destination. There they have to be unpacked, checked, assembled, and displayed before they can be sold to the consumer or as intermediate goods to another firm. A distribution and maintenance network has to be established, and the exporter will have to familiarize herself with the (legal) rules and procedures in another country, usually in another language and embedded in a different culture. All of this involves costs, which tend to increase with 'distance'. As indicated above, this can be both physical distance, which may be hampered or alleviated by geographical phenomena such as mountain ranges or easy access to good waterways, and political, cultural, or social distance, which also require time and effort to cover before one can successfully engage in international business.

We use the term 'transport costs' as a shorthand notation for both types of distance described above. As these costs increase it will become more difficult to trade goods and services between nations. As a proxy for transport costs we calculated the 'weighted distance to Germany' for all German export markets, using the average distance between the main population centres in both countries. Also taking into consideration the economic size of the trade partner as measured by a country's income level (GDP PPP), a simple regression yields the following result:[6]

$$ln(trade) = 3.9925 + 1.0605 \times ln(GDP) - 1.0613 \times ln(distance) \qquad 16.2$$

This simple relationship, which explains 88.4 per cent of the variance in German export size, is illustrated with respect to the distance to the German market in Figure 16.3—that

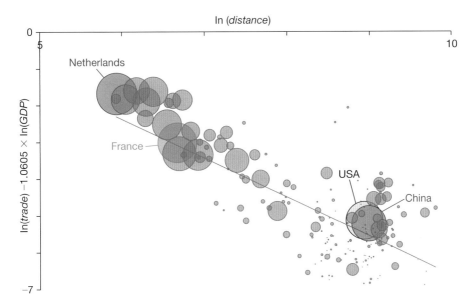

Figure 16.3 German trade and distance, 2015.

Source: author's calculations based on data from International Trade Centre www.intracen.org; *trade* = (*export* + *import*) in USD billion, World Bank (GDP PPP, current USD billion), and CEPII www.cepii.fr; weighted distance km; bubbles proportional to share of trade flows; 184 trade partners included; the slope of the line is −1.0613.

is, after correcting the size of the trade flow for the size of the destination market using the estimated coefficient of equation 16.2. The top left corner is dominated by neighbours and other countries close to Germany. The slope of the regression line in the figure is −1.0613 as given in equation 16.2. This empirical relationship known as the 'gravity equation' was first applied to international trade between nations by Jan Tinbergen (1962) and holds quite generally for all countries. The relationship is influenced by wealth and development level, as well as cultural, political, and social organization, and history, such as whether trading partners share a common language or a common border, have a colonial history together, and so on. One of the main objectives of geographical economics is to provide a better understanding of the unequal distribution of economic activity across space and its regularities in terms of distribution pattern and interaction. We first discuss geographical economics models in Sections 16.3 to 16.7 and then return to the gravity equation in Section 16.8.

16.3 **Geographical economics**

This section gives a non-technical overview of the structure of the geographical economics model, as illustrated in Figure 16.4 (with so-called 'callouts' a–g). There are two regions (1 and 2) and two sectors in the economy (food and manufactures). Consumers in region 1 consist of farm workers and manufacturing workers; similarly for region 2. The farm workers earn their income by working for the farmers in their region. If they own the farm, it is as if they hire themselves. They then play a dual role, as both farmers and farm

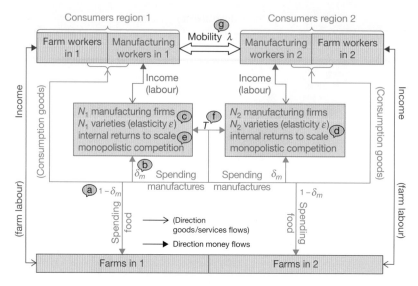

Figure 16.4 Structure of the geographical economics model.

workers. The income stream of the farm workers is part of a bilateral transfer: they receive an income from the farmer (the farm wage rate) and in return they supply labour services to the farmer. All such bilateral transfers are indicated with double-headed arrows in Figure 16.4. The closed-headed arrows refer to the direction of money flows, that is of income and spending. What the flow represents exactly is indicated along the lines connecting the arrow heads. The open-headed arrow refers to the direction of goods flows. These are indicated in parentheses along the lines connecting the arrow heads. The farmers in region 1 use the labour services of the farm workers from region 1 to produce food under constant returns to scale and perfect competition. They sell this food to the consumers, either in region 1 or in region 2. There are no transport costs for food.

The manufacturing sector consists of N_1 firms in region 1 and N_2 firms in region 2. Each manufacturing firm produces a differentiated good; that is, it produces a unique variety of manufactures, using only labour under internal economies of scale. This implies that the firms have monopolistic power, which they use in determining the price of their product. There are transport costs involved in selling a manufactured good in another region. These costs do not arise if the manufactured good is sold in the region in which it is produced. As a result of the transport costs involved in exporting manufactured goods, firms will charge a higher price in the other region than at home. The manufacturing workers earn their income (the manufacturing wage rate) by supplying labour to the firms in the manufacturing sector of their region.

16.3.1 Demand

Consumers spend their income on food and manufactures. Since food is a homogenous good, they do not care if it is produced in region 1 or in region 2. As there are no transport costs for food, it fetches the same price in both regions (implying that farmers earn the same wage in both regions). The optimal spending of income *I* is determined in two stages. At the first stage the consumers decide how much to spend on food and manufactures in general. Using a Cobb–Douglas utility function (Section 6.4.1), we already know the outcome: a constant share δ_m of income is spent on manufactures and $1-\delta_m$ on food (callout a). At the second stage the consumers decide how much of their income to spend on a particular variety of manufactures. Using the Dixit–Stiglitz approach of Chapter 8 gives demand as in equation 8.5, with $\delta_m I$ as the income term since $(1-\delta_m)I$ is spent on food (callout b). As discussed in Chapter 8, this results in a constant price elasticity of demand ε (callout c).

16.3.2 Supply

Food production is characterized by constant returns to scale and is produced under conditions of perfect competition. Workers in the food sector, which is used as numéraire, are assumed to be immobile. Given the total labour force, which we will normalize to 1, a fraction $1-\delta_m$ works in the food sector.[7] Production in the food sector equals, by choice of units, food employment: $F = 1-\delta_m$. Since farm workers are paid the value of marginal product, their wage is 1. Production in the manufacturing sector is characterized by internal economies of scale (Chapter 8), such that $l_i = f + mx_i$, where l_i is the amount of labour necessary to produce x_i units of variety *i*. The parameters *f* and *m* are the fixed and marginal labour input requirements (callout d). The market structure for manufactures is monopolistic competition (Chapter 8), leading to a constant mark-up of price over marginal costs. Entry and exit into the manufacturing sector until (excess) profits are zero gives a constant optimal scale of production for each variety, see Technical Note 8.2. This production size per variety determines the number of varieties produced in a region (callout e).

16.3.3 Transport costs

Transport costs (see Box 16.2) are of the *iceberg* type (see Box 7.5); the parameter $T \geq 1$ denotes the number of goods that need to be shipped to ensure that one unit of a variety of manufactures arrives per unit of distance (equal to the distance between regions 1 and 2). We assume that the distance from a location to itself is zero (callout f).

BOX 16.2 The relevance of transport costs

Adam Smith noted the importance of locations near the coast with lower costs of transport: 'so, it is upon the sea-coast, and along the banks of navigable rivers, that industry of every kind naturally begins to subdivide and improve itself, and it is frequently not till a long time after that those improvements extend themselves to the inland part of the country.'

Many measures, such as travel time, have been constructed to estimate transport cost.[8] The most straightforward measure in international trade is the difference between the so-called CIF (cost, insurance, and freight) and FOB (free on board) quotations of trade. CIF measures the value of imports from the point of entry, while FOB measures the value from a carrier in the exporting 'port'. The difference between these two values is a measure of the cost of getting an item from the exporting country to the importing country. The ratio [(CIF/FOB) − 1] × 100% thus provides an indication of the transport costs, although it clearly underestimates the actual transport costs of international trade (note that products

(continued...)

with very high transport costs are not traded at all). Different goods have, of course, different transport costs. Goods with a high value added have a relatively low CIF/FOB ratio, while perishable goods have a higher ratio.

Figure 16.5 provides a rough indication of the ranking of countries in terms of CIF/FOB ratios by calculating the simple average of these rates relative to three markets, namely Australia, Brazil, and the USA. The average trade costs for all countries is 6.3 per cent, ranging from a low of 1.6 per cent for Ireland to a high of 19 per cent for Burkina Faso. Shipping costs tend to be lower for countries close to the world market, such as Germany in Europe, and higher for countries far away, such as Australia and large parts of Africa. China is slightly above the world average, while the USA is slightly below.

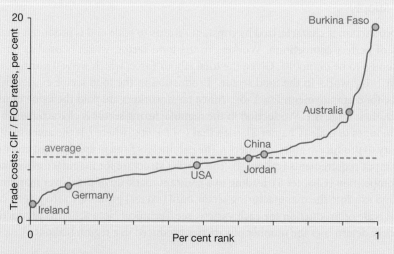

Figure 16.5 Indication of trade costs: based on CIF-FOB rates (per cent), 2008.

Notes: simple average of cif/fob rates relative to Australia, Brazil, and USA in 2008; average for all countries is 6.3 per cent; 134 countries included.

Source: based on data from Sourcin and Pomfret (2012).

To give an indication of how trade costs differ by transportation mode and decline over time, Figure 16.6 depicts the simple average for four countries (Australia, Brazil, Chile, and the USA) for all trade, air trade, and sea trade after first calculating import-weighted averages for each country separately. Trade costs declined on average from 7.8 per cent in 1990 to 5.5 per cent in 2008. The relative costs tend to be lower for trade by air (used for more valuable products) than for trade by sea (used for more bulky products), but the decline has been lower for air trade than for sea trade.

16.4 Multiple locations and equilibrium

Now that we have introduced two regions and transport costs it is important to know where the economic agents are located. We therefore have to (i) specify a notation to show how labour is distributed over the two regions and (ii) investigate what the consequences are for some of the demand and supply equations discussed in Section 16.3. To start with

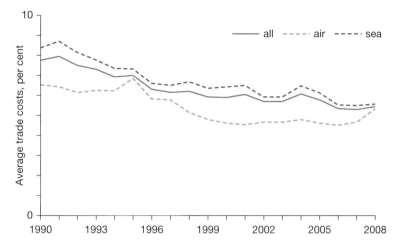

Figure 16.6 Average trade costs for Australia, Brazil, Chile, and USA, 1990–2008.

Notes: import-weighted average cif/fob rates are calculated for Australia, Brazil, Chile, and USA; reported values are simple averages of these four countries.

Source: based on data from Sourcin and Pomfret (2012).

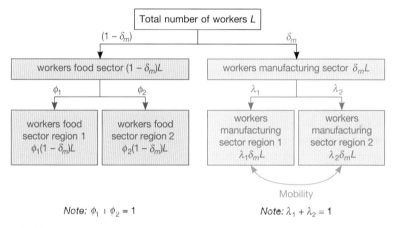

Figure 16.7 Division of labour over the regions.

point (i), we have already introduced the parameter δ_m to denote the fraction of the labour force in the manufacturing sector, such that $1-\delta_m$ is the fraction of labour in the food sector. We now assume that of the labourers in the food sector a fraction ϕ_i are located in region i, and of the labourers in the manufacturing sector a fraction λ_i are located in region i. Figure 16.7 illustrates the division of labour. The manufacturing sector in a region can increase or decrease as a result of the mobility of manufacturing workers.

Point (ii) involves a little more work. We concentrate on region 1. Similar remarks hold for region 2. It is easiest to start with the producers. Since there are $\phi_1(1 - \delta_m)$ farm workers in region 1 and production is proportional to the labour input, food production in region 1 equals $\phi_1(1 - \delta_m)$, which is equal to the income generated by the food sector in region 1.

The wage rate paid to manufacturing workers in region 1 differs in general from the wage rate paid to manufacturing workers in region 2 (identified by W_1 and W_2). From now on, whenever we speak of 'the wage rate' we refer to the manufacturing wage rate. If we know the wage rate W_1 in region 1, we know from mark-up pricing that the price charged in region 1 by a firm located in region 1 is equal to $mW_1(\varepsilon-1)/\varepsilon$. The price this firm will charge in the other region is T times higher as a result of the transport costs. This holds for all N_1 firms located in region 1. Since there are $\lambda_1\delta_m$ manufacturing workers in region 1, and the number of firms in region 1 is proportional to the number of workers, we get $N_1 = \lambda_1\delta_m/f\varepsilon$ (see Chapter 8).

The price a firm charges to a consumer for a unit of a variety depends both on the location of the firm (which determines the wage rate the firm will have to pay to its workers) and on the location of the consumer (which determines whether or not the consumer will have to pay for the transport costs of the good). As a result, the price index of manufactures P differs between the two regions. More specifically, substituting the price a firm will charge in each region and how many firms there are in each region in the demand function gives (see Technical Note 16.1)

$$P_1 = \left\{ \underbrace{\lambda_1 W_1^{1-\varepsilon}}_{\substack{locally \\ produced}} + \underbrace{\lambda_2 T^{1-\varepsilon} W_2^{1-\varepsilon}}_{imported} \right\}^{1/(1-\varepsilon)} \qquad 16.3$$

Thus, the price index in region 1 is essentially a weighted average of the price of locally produced goods and imported goods from region 2. The impact of location on the consumption decisions of consumers requires us to know their income level, which brings us to the determination of equilibrium below. To determine equilibrium relationships we proceed in three steps. First, we explain the *short-run* equilibrium relationships in Section 16.4.1, that is for a *given* distribution of the manufacturing labour force. Second, we discuss the dynamics in Section 16.4.2, which determines how we move over time through a sequence of short-run equilibria (without factor mobility) to a *long-run equilibrium* (with factor mobility). Third, we *analyse* both short-run and long-run equilibria in Section 16.5.

16.4.1 Short-run equilibrium

In the short run, the distribution of the manufacturing work force over the regions is given and cannot be changed instantaneously. We therefore first determine the equilibrium relationships for an arbitrary distribution of the labour force. There are no profits for firms in the manufacturing sector (because of entry and exit), nor for the farmers (because of constant returns to scale and perfect competition). This implies that all income earned in the economy derives from the wages earned in the two sectors. The income I_i in region i is thus the sum of farm wages (with wage rate 1) and manufacturing wages (with wage rate W_i); for region 1 this is equal to (L is normalized to 1)

$$I_1 = \underbrace{\lambda_1\delta_m W_1}_{\substack{manufacturing \\ income}} + \underbrace{\phi_1(1-\delta_m)}_{\substack{food \\ income}} \qquad 16.4$$

Demand in region 1 for products from region 1 is the sum of all individual demands by local consumers. It depends on the aggregate income I_1, the price index P_1, and the price $mW_1(\varepsilon-1)/\varepsilon$ charged by a producer from region 1 for locally sold varieties. Similarly, demand in region 2 for products from region 1 depend on aggregate income I_2, price index P_2, and the price $mTW_1(\varepsilon-1)/\varepsilon$ charged by a producer from region 1 for a good sold in region 2. Total demand for a producer in region 1 is the sum of local and foreign demand, which depends on income in *both* regions, transport costs, and the price charged relative to the price index. Equating demand and supply determines equilibrium in the manufacturing sector (see Technical Note 16.2):

$$W_1 = \left(I_1 P_1^{\varepsilon-1} + I_2 T^{1-\varepsilon} P_2^{\varepsilon-1} \right)^{1/\varepsilon}$$ 16.5

Intuitively, the equation makes perfect sense: wages in region 1 can be higher if this region is located close to large markets. The attractiveness of a region is related to the purchasing power of all regions and relative to the distance from the market. The advantage of using an equilibrium approach is that the price indices and income levels, which play a crucial role, are determined endogenously. Given the distribution of the manufacturing work force λ_i, we have now derived the short-run equilibrium equations for region 1: namely equation 16.3 for the price index, equation 16.4 for the income level, and equation 16.5 for the wage rate. Together with their counterparts for region 2, these equations determine the short-run equilibrium: see Section 16.5.

16.4.2 Dynamics and long-run equilibrium

The introduction of factor mobility implies that the size of a region's manufacturing work force can change over time, as indicated in Figure 16.4 and Figure 16.7. This, in turn, implies that the short-run equilibrium changes. Recall that labour is the only factor of production. We assume that the mobile workers react to differences in the *real* wage w, which perfectly measures the utility level achieved; for region i the real wage is $w_i = W_i P_i^{-\delta_m}$, see Technical Note 16.1. The adjustment of the short-run equilibrium over time is simple. If the real wage for manufacturing workers is higher in region 1 than in region 2, we expect manufacturing workers to move from region 2 to region 1. If the real wage is higher in region 2 than in region 1, we expect the reverse to hold. We let the parameter γ denote the speed with which manufacturing workers react to differences in the real wage, and use the simple dynamic system:

$$\frac{d\lambda_1}{\lambda_1} = \underbrace{\gamma}_{\substack{change \\ labour\ 1}} \underbrace{(w_1 - \bar{w})}_{\substack{wage \\ difference}}; \quad \bar{w} = \underbrace{\lambda_1 w_1 + \lambda_2 w_2}_{\substack{average \\ real\ wage}}$$ 16.6

Note that $\bar{w}$ denotes the average real wage in the economy. A similar equation holds for region 2. Although this is essentially an ad hoc dynamic specification, it can be grounded in evolutionary game theory, see Weibull (1995), or otherwise justified, see Brakman, Garretsen, and van Marrewijk (2001). Now that we have specified how the manufacturing work force reacts to differences in the real wage between regions, we can also note when

Table 16.1 When is a long-run equilbrium reached?

Possibility 1	Possibility 2	Possibility 3
If the real wage for manufacturing workers in region 1 is the same as the real wage for manufacturing workers in region 2	All manufacturing workers are located in region 1 (agglomeration in region 1)	All manufacturing workers are located in region 2 (agglomeration in region 2)

a long-run equilibrium is reached. This occurs when one of three possibilities arises, as summarized in Table 16.1: namely (i) if the distribution of the manufacturing work force between regions 1 and 2 is such that the real wage is equal in the two regions, (ii) if all manufacturing workers are located in region 1, or (iii) if all manufacturing workers are located in region 2.

16.5 Simulation analysis

Now that we have determined the short-run equilibrium equations and the dynamic adjustment over time, we need to analyse the economic implications of the geographical model in more detail. To do this we assume that the two regions are identical in all respects, except possibly regarding the distribution of the manufacturing labour force. In particular, we assume that the farm workers are equally divided over the two regions: $\phi_1 = \phi_2 = 0.5$. This implies that neither region has an inherent advantage over the other region. Any asymmetric outcome we derive below is thus the result of the *economic* forces active within the model. We are able to derive the short-run equilibrium analytically for only three special cases.

- *Spreading*: suppose the two regions are identical in *all* respects, that is, the manufacturing work force is also evenly distributed $\lambda_1 = \lambda_2 = 0.5$. Naturally, we then expect the wage rates of the short-run equilibrium to be the same for the two regions. In fact, one can verify that $W_1 = W_2 = 1$ solves the short-run equilibrium equations. Obviously, the real wage rate is the same for the two regions in the spreading equilibrium.

- *Agglomeration in region 1*: suppose now that all manufacturing activity is agglomerated in region 1 such that there are no manufacturing labourers in region 2 ($\lambda_1 = 1$ and $\lambda_2 = 0$). One can now verify that $W_1 = 1$ is a solution for the short-run equilibrium.

- *Agglomeration in region 2*: this is the mirror image of the second situation described above.

Unfortunately, these are the only three cases that we can solve analytically. In all other cases (recall that λ_1 can vary all the way from 0 to 1, so there are infinitely many other cases) we cannot derive the short-run equilibrium analytically. So we have to find another way to determine these equilibria, and explain what they mean in economic terms. We do so numerically using computer simulations, see Box 16.3. We want to use simulations to learn about the structure of the model. In this case, we do so by investigating how the short-run equilibrium changes if the distribution of the manufacturing workers changes. Varying λ_1 between 0 and 1 gives a complete description of all possible distributions of the mobile workforce. We focus attention on the real wage in region 1 relative to the real wage in region 2, as this determines the dynamic forces operating in the model through migration flows. Once we find a short-run equilibrium for a distribution of the mobile labour force, it is easy to calculate the relative real wage w_1/w_2.

BOX 16.3 Computer simulations

In a two-region setting, Section 16.4.1 provides six equations to determine the short-run equilibrium for a given distribution of manufacturing workers. In general, we cannot solve these equations analytically. We can, however, use numerical solutions based on computer simulations to get a better understanding of the economic forces of the model. We briefly explain how computer simulations are performed.

- We must be clear *what* it is we are solving for. The short-run equilibrium determines the *endogenous* variables: income I_i, price index P_i, and wage rate W_i for regions $i = 1,2$ (and in doing so also gives us the real wages, as will be discussed). So we must determine numeric values of I_i, P_i, and W_i for which the short-run equilibrium equations hold.

- The solutions for the endogenous variables depend on the values of λ_i (the distribution of the mobile labour force, fixed in the short run) and the *parameters* (δ_m, ε, and T). This implies that we must specify these values before we can start to find solutions for the endogenous variables. Table 16.2 lists these for the 'base-scenario', in which the share of income spent on manufactures is fairly low at 0.4, the elasticity of substitution is 5, and transport costs are 1.7. The parameter σ will be discussed below.[9]

- We must find a *solution method*: that is, a well-specified procedure that will lead us to solving the short-run equations for numeric values of the endogenous variables, given the choice of parameters. Several options are available at this point, but in this case the order of equations readily suggests a solution method, labelled sequential iterations. It works as follows:

  (i)   Guess an initial solution for the wage rate in the two regions, say $(W_{1,0}, W_{2,0})$, where 0 indicates the number of the iteration (we will use $W_{1,0} = W_{2,0} = 1$).

  (ii) Using $(W_{1,0}, W_{2,0})$, calculate the price indices $(P_{1,0}, P_{2,0})$ and the income levels $(I_{1,0}, I_{2,0})$ as implied by equations 16.3 and 16.4.

  (iii) Using the values $(P_{1,0}, P_{2,0})$ and $(I_{1,0}, I_{2,0})$ as calculated in step (ii), determine a new possible solution for the wage rate $(W_{1,1}, W_{2,1})$ as implied by equation 16.5.

  (iv) Repeat steps (ii) and (iii) until a solution is found.

- We must specify a *stopping criterion*. In the above description of the solution method, step (iv) casually instructs us to 'repeat steps (ii) and (iii) until a solution is found', but when is a solution found? How close do we want get to be satisfied that the numeric values we have found are indeed a short-run equilibrium? We use as a stopping criterion the condition that the absolute value of the relative change in the wage rate should not exceed some small value σ (see Table 16.2) for all regions i from one iteration r to the next:

$$\left| \frac{W_{i,r} - W_{i,r-1}}{W_{i,r-1}} \right| < \sigma \qquad \qquad 16.7$$

- Finally, we must choose a *programming language* and write a small program to actually perform the above calculations. Again, several options are available, but we use Gauss$_{TM}$, a widely used mathematical programming language, for our simulations.[10]

Table 16.2 Base-scenario parameter configuration

$\delta_m = 0.4$	$\varepsilon = 5$	$T = 1.7$	$\sigma = 0.0001$

Figure 16.8 illustrates how the relative real wage in region 1 varies as the share of the mobile workforce in region 1 varies. It is the result of a range of simulations in which the value of λ_1 is gradually increased from 0 to 1. Each time, the short-run equilibrium is calculated using the procedure described in Box 16.3. The implied relative real wage is then plotted in the figure. What can we learn from this exercise?

First, we can identify the location of long-run equilibria. Mobile workers move to regions with a higher real wage, such that a short-run equilibrium is also a long-run equilibrium if the real wage for the mobile workforce is the same in the two regions. A long-run equilibrium therefore requires that the relative real wage is 1 if there are mobile workers in both regions, such as at points B, C, and D in Figure 16.8. When a long-run equilibrium implies complete agglomeration (one region ends up with all mobile workers) the relative real wage is not equal to 1 (see points A and E).[11]

Second, there are three types of long-run equilibria: (i) equal spreading of manufacturing production over the 2 regions (point C), (ii) complete agglomeration of manufacturing production in either region (points A and E), or (iii) partial agglomeration in one of the two regions (points B and D). This leads to a total of five long-run equilibria. We can only find equilibria B and D as a result of our simulations.

Third, we can determine adjustment over time and the stability of long-run equilibria. Suppose, for example, that $\lambda_1=F$ in Figure 16.8. The mobile workforce is then smaller in region 1 than in region 2. As illustrated, the associated short-run equilibrium implies $w_1/w_2 >1$. The higher real wage in region 1 gives mobile workers an incentive to move from region 2 to region 1. This migration process represents an increase of λ_1 in the figure. Migration continues until the spreading equilibrium at point C is reached, where the real wages are equalized. Similar reasoning leading to point C holds for any arbitrary initial distribution of the mobile labour force in between points B and D. The spreading equilibrium is a stable equilibrium in the sense that a small deviation of the mobile labour force away from point C activates economic forces to bring us back to point C. Similar reasoning holds for the two agglomeration equilibria (points A and E). In contrast, the partial agglomeration long-run equilibria (points B and D) are *un*stable. If, for whatever reason,

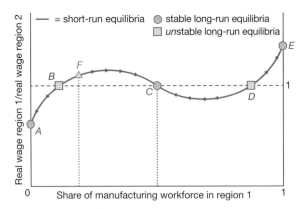

Figure 16.8 Relative real wage, base-scenario.

we are initially at point *B* or *D*, a long-run equilibrium is reached in the sense that the real wages are equal for the two regions. However, any small perturbation of this equilibrium will set in motion a process of adjustment leading to a *different* long-run equilibrium. For example, a small negative disturbance of λ_1 at point *B* leads to complete agglomeration of manufacturing activity in region 2 (point *A*), while a positive disturbance leads to equal spreading (point *C*).

16.5.1 **Stability**

The most important parameter in geographical economics models is transport cost, assumed to be zero within a region and positive between different regions. The term 'transport costs' is a shorthand notation for many different types of obstacles to trade between locations, such as tariffs, language, and culture barriers, and indeed the costs of actually getting goods or services at another location (see Box 16.2). An important question is thus what the impact is of a change in transport costs. To answer this question we repeat the simulation procedure of Figure 16.8 for both higher ($T = 2.1$) and lower ($T = 1.3$) transport costs, see Figure 16.9. Note the following points.

- If transport costs are large, the spreading equilibrium is the only stable equilibrium. It makes intuitive sense that if manufactures are difficult to transport from one region to another, the dynamics of the model will lead to the spreading of manufacturing activity; distant provision of manufactures is too costly such that they need to be provided locally.

- If transport costs are small, the spreading equilibrium is unstable while the two agglomerating equilibria are stable. An initial share of the mobile workforce λ_1 in between 0 and ½ serves as the basin of attraction for complete agglomeration in region 2, while an initial λ_1 in between ½ and 1 serves as the basin of attraction for complete agglomeration in region 1. Again this makes sense intuitively. With very low transport costs, the immobile market can be provided effectively from a distance,

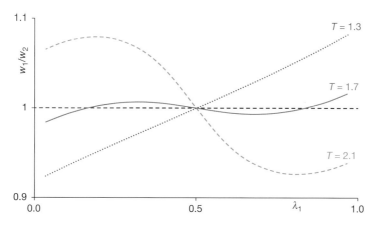

Figure 16.9 The impact of transport costs.

which therefore does not pose a strong enough force to counter the advantages of agglomeration.

- For a range of intermediate values of transport costs (here for example if $T = 1.7$) there are five long-run equilibria. Three of those five, namely spreading and the two agglomeration equilibria, are stable. The other two equilibria are unstable. In this situation, the transport costs are high enough to allow for the local provision of manufactures (spreading). At the same time, transport costs are low enough to allow for the provision of the immobile market from a distance (agglomeration).

The suggestions of the impact of a change in the transport costs on the stability of agglomeration and spreading in the geographical economics model, as discussed on the basis of Figure 16.9, hold in fact quite generally (Fujita, Krugman, and Venables, 1999, and Neary, 2001).

- For all transport costs *below* a critical level, labelled the *sustain point*, complete agglomeration of manufacturing activity in one region is a stable long-run equilibrium. If the transport costs exceed the critical sustain point level, agglomeration is not 'sustainable': that is, agglomeration is an unstable equilibrium.

- For all transport costs *above* another critical level, labelled the *break point*, the spreading of manufacturing activity over the two regions is a stable equilibrium. If the transport costs are lower than the critical break point level, the spreading equilibrium 'breaks': that is, spreading is an unstable equilibrium.

- The sustain point occurs at a higher level of transport costs than the break point. There is thus *always* an intermediate level of transport costs at which agglomeration of manufacturing activity is sustainable while simultaneously the spreading of

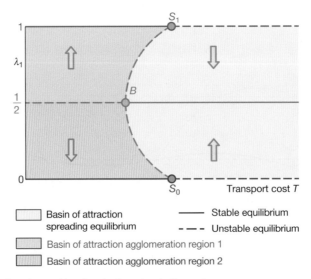

Figure 16.10 Sustain points and break point (tomahawk diagram).

manufacturing activity is a stable equilibrium. Note that the transport cost level chosen in Table 16.2 ($T = 1.7$) lies in between the break point and the sustain point, such that (i) the spreading equilibrium is stable, and (ii) the agglomeration equilibria are sustainable.

The analysis can be neatly summarized in the so-called tomahawk diagram of Figure 16.10, where B is the break point, S_0 and S_1 are the sustain points, and the arrows indicate the direction of migration of mobile workers as a result of differences in the relative real wage. For each of the three stable equilibria the 'basin of attraction' is indicated: that is, the area of initial parameter settings which will converge to this equilibrium, as shown at the bottom of Figure 16.10.

It is important to point out the *hysteresis* or path-dependency aspect of the model: history matters. Suppose that transport costs are initially high, say $T = 2.1$ in Figure 16.9. Then spreading of manufacturing activity is the only stable long-run equilibrium. Now suppose that, given that the spreading equilibrium is established, transport costs gradually start to fall to $T = 1.7$. This will have no impact on the equilibrium allocation of manufacturing production, since spreading remains a stable equilibrium. Only after the transport costs have fallen even further, below the break point B in Figure 16.10, will the spreading equilibrium become unstable. Any small disturbance will then result in complete agglomeration of manufacturing production in one region. It is not possible to predict beforehand which region this will be, but suppose that agglomeration takes place in region 1. Given that region 1 contains all manufacturing activity, assume now that the transport costs start to rise again, perhaps because of the imposition of trade barriers, say back to $T = 1.7$. What will happen? The answer is: nothing! Agglomeration of manufacturing activity remains a stable equilibrium. So for the same level of transport costs ($T = 1.7$), the equilibrium that becomes established depends on the way this level of transport costs is reached, on history. Obviously, predictions of what will happen if parameters change are considerably harder in models characterized by path-dependency.

16.6 Alternative models: human capital and intermediate goods

The description of the geographical model in Sections 16.3 to 16.5 uses Krugman's (1991) original specification, frequently referred to as the 'core' model. The nice aspect of this model is that it can endogenously explain the creation of core–periphery structures as transport costs fall beyond a certain critical level, as elegantly summarized in the tomahawk diagram of Figure 16.10. A potential drawback in an international setting is that this model relies on labour mobility between locations to generate core–periphery structures, whereas empirically labour mobility between different countries is low. Partially in response to this problem, the literature has developed two alternative approaches which do not rely on labour mobility to generate core–periphery patterns. These approaches have been so successful that they are now considered alternative 'core' models of geographical economics. In this section we briefly discuss these models; see Brakman, Garretsen, and van Marrewijk (2009) for a general description.

Figure 16.11 illustrates the general structure of the (human) capital model, also termed the 'solvable' model because its equilibrium can be derived analytically. It is based on the work by Forslid and Ottaviano (2003). There are two main changes relative to Krugman's (1991) approach. First, there is inter-sectoral mobility of labour within the region between food workers and manufacturing workers. Second, the fixed cost part of the manufacturing production process requires human capital rather than raw labour as an input. The model assumes that there is inter-regional human capital mobility, which is in accordance with the stylized fact that high-skilled workers are more mobile between countries than low-skilled workers. It turns out that the analytic structure of this model gives rise to the *exact same* tomahawk diagram summarizing the workings of the Krugman (1991) model, thus also explaining core–periphery patterns (with human capital mobility only).

Figure 16.12 illustrates the general structure of the intermediate goods model, based on the work of Krugman and Venables (1995). This time the main difference is that the manufacturing sector itself uses two types of input, namely labour and manufacturing output, as intermediate input. Producers of manufacturing goods thus like to be agglomerated close to each other as this allows for cheaper inputs (avoiding the transportation costs) into the production process. As before, if transport costs are sufficiently low, agglomeration of manufacturing production in one location is the resulting outcome. The model makes this agglomeration possible because of inter-sectoral labour mobility between food workers and manufacturing workers in the same region. Inter-regional

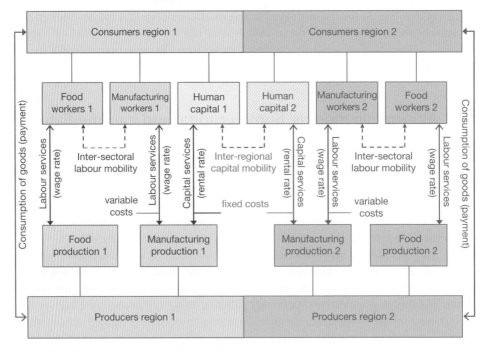

Figure 16.11 Human capital: the solvable model.

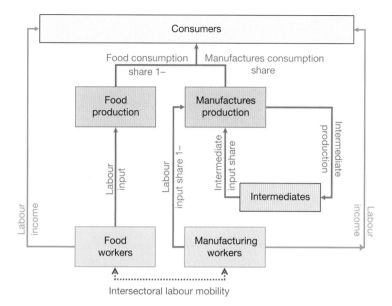

Figure 16.12 Intermediate goods model.

labour mobility is not necessary to generate the core–periphery structure. Remarkably, this model too gives rise to the *exact same* tomahawk diagram of Figure 14.9, which therefore is representative of the underlying structure for three different types of core–periphery models.[1] In all three core models, therefore, a rise in transport costs can have large welfare consequences, particularly for the affected regions (see Box 16.4 for an example).

BOX 16.4 Somali pirates, transport costs, trade, and welfare (written with Koen Berden)

Declining transport and communication costs have resulted in more complicated and more internationally connected production processes (so-called fragmentation, see Chapter 15). As a consequence—and despite declining transport costs—the *share* of transport costs in total production costs for final products has increased. The return of old-fashioned piracy in some locations of the world is a danger for these transport routes and for the trade flows they represent. The International Maritime Bureau points out that piracy has occurred more and more frequently since the year 2000, which forces liner-shipping companies to take into consideration the probability of becoming a target for this profitable underground 'business' run by specialized criminal organizations.

Figure 16.13 illustrates the range of operations in 2011 for the most prominent Somali pirates, who have become a major threat for the Europe-Asia trade route. These pirates started with small-scale operations just off the coast of Haradeere (with a maximum range of about 165 nautical miles in 2005), but expanded quickly to cover the northeast coast of Africa up to the Mozambique channel, the sea of Aden, into the Red Sea, and into the Gulf of Oman (with a maximum range of about 1,300 nautical miles in 2011).

(continued...)

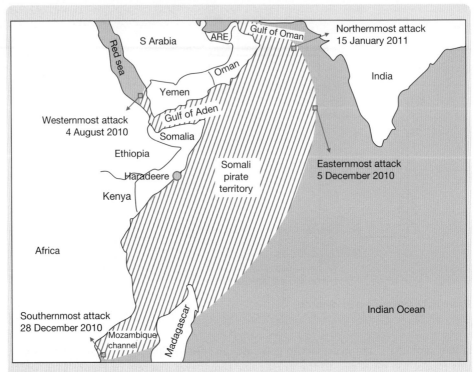

Figure 16.13 Somali pirate territory, 2011.

Source: based on BBC News (2011).

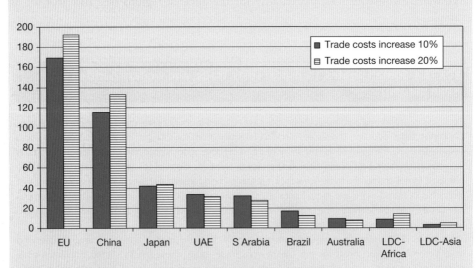

Figure 16.14 Welfare loss of Somali piracy for selected countries (USD billion).

Source: based on data from Berden (2011).

To estimate the impact of Somali piracy on international trade flows and welfare we use the Global Simulation Model (GSIM, a global partial equilibrium model developed by Francois and Hall, 1997). Somali pirates have an economic effect in the model because of higher insurance premiums for vessels sailing through the affected area (in 2008, for example, they were 1,000 per cent higher than five years earlier), expenses made for paying ransom for sailors held hostage, costs for keeping naval forces in the area to patrol, costs for legal prosecution, costs for equipping vessels with security on board (weapons or armed guards), and additional costs from diverging routes away from the affected area. Two scenarios are analysed. In the first scenario trade costs increase by 10 per cent as a result of the piracy factors mentioned above (a low estimate). In the second scenario trade costs increase by 20 per cent (a more likely case).

Figure 16.14 illustrates the total welfare loss for these two scenarios for different countries or regions (in billion US dollars). Piracy clearly has large negative welfare effects, particularly for the European Union (EU) and China, with a loss of $193 billion and $133 billion in the 20 per cent scenario. Brazil is also negatively affected, as part of its iron ore exports to Asia pass through the affected area. Table 16.3 depicts the effect of Somali piracy on changes in maritime trade flows. Evidently, as outlined in this chapter, trade is in part diverted to other routes (which flourish), while the countries with heavy trade routes through the Somali area are hurt most. EU trade, for example, shifts away from Asia towards Brazil and the Rest of the World (USA). For China, trade within Asia and to Australia gets a boost, while trade to Europe, the Middle East, and Brazil is diminishing. Saudi Arabia and the United Arab Emirates (ARE) are hurt badly since all their seaborne trade passes through the affected area. Clearly, the personal gains to some pirates on the eastern coast of Africa (the few who get away with it) are at the expense of significant global welfare losses and diverging, sub-optimal transport routes.

Table 16.3 Shipping trade effects of Somali piracy for selected countries (per cent change)

From	Destination									
	EU	CHN	JPN	BRA	AUS	SAU	ARE	L-AF	L-AS	ROW
EU	0	-36	-43	48	-46	-22	-26	15	-40	9
CHN	-36	0	39	-42	35	-30	-33	-28	48	2
JPN	-42	41	0	-50	27	-32	-35	-35	39	-5
BRA	44	-3	-57	0	25	-36	-39	-37	-55	-7
AUS	-45	37	27	32	0	-37	-40	-39	35	-8
SAU	0	-7	-12	-9	-17	0	-1	7	-11	-7
ARE	0	-7	-12	-8	-16	3	0	8	-10	-7
L-AF	14	-38	-47	-43	-51	-26	-28	71	-41	7
L-AS	-44	44	33	-54	29	-38	-40	-35	42	-5
ROW	7	1	-9	-3	-12	14	10	16	-3	-3

Notes: shaded cells indicate declining trade flows; EU = European Union (27), CHN = China, JPN = Japan, BRA = Brazil, AUS = Australia, SAU = Saudi Arabia, ARE = United Arab Emirates, L-AF = LDCs Africa, L-AS = LDCs Asia, ROW = Rest of World.
Source: Berden (2011).

16.7 Predicting the location of European cities

The geographical economics model has been successfully modified in various ways to explain empirical phenomena, such as Zipf's Law and the gravity equation. A nice application by the Dutch economist Dirk Stelder (2000) makes only a slight modification to the model described in this chapter to see to what extent it can be used to predict the location of European cities. Stelder defines a large grid of square locations on a truncated map of Europe. The distance between two locations is in principle calculated as the shortest path (that is 1 for horizontal and vertical neighbours, $\sqrt{2}$ for diagonal neighbours). Stelder's grid of western Europe has more than 2,800 locations. Sea transportation is made possible at a few places, which are part of the network but do not act as potential locations for cities. The model allows for specific costs for transportation across land, across sea, and in hubs where (un)shipping can take place. The grid is also extended with a third dimension (height) to take the extra transportation costs into account when goods have to cross mountains.

The Stelder model starts with a flat initial distribution in which all locations on the grid are of equal size. The model simulations then calculate the re-distribution of economic activity based on differences in real wages, given the parameter configuration. The location

Figure 16.15 Simulated location of European cities.

and size of the cities which emerge in the long-run equilibrium depend on the chosen parameter values and on the geographical shape of the economy. Figure 16.15 shows a model run that produces an equilibrium of 94 cities with $\delta_m = 0.5$, $\varepsilon = 5$, and $T = 1.57$.[13] The open circles are the simulated outcomes, and the closed circles represent the 94 largest actual cities in 1996. As was to be expected with a flat initial distribution, the model produces an optimal city distribution that is more evenly spread than in reality. Large agglomerations such as Paris, London, Madrid, and Rome are not correctly simulated, because population density is for historical reasons higher in the north than in the south. The model predicts too many large cities in Spain and too few cities in the UK, the Netherlands, and Belgium. The results are nevertheless relatively good for Germany. The Rurhgebiet, Bremen, Berlin, Frankfurt, Stuttgart, and Munich are not far from the right place. Vienna is on target and in the periphery of various countries some cities also appear correctly, such as Lille, Rouen, Nantes, Bordeaux, and Nice in France, Lisbon and Porto in Portugal, and Seville and Malaga in Spain.

Stelder points out that these kinds of model results of course *should be* wrong. A good fit would mean 'total victory of economics over all other social sciences because then the whole historical process of city formation would be explained with the three parameters δ_m, ε, and T'. One of his objectives of the model is to clarify to what extent pure economic factors have contributed to the city formation process, concluding that even the basic model can produce city hierarchies if applied in spaces closer to geographic reality.

16.8 The gravity equation

The gravity equation illustrated in Section 16.2.2 for German trade flows has played an important role in theoretical developments in the past 15 years, as summarized by Head and Mayer (2014) in the *Handbook of International Economics*. This section briefly reviews these developments based on their work. Head and Mayer identify three types of gravity equations: general gravity, structural gravity, and naïve gravity.

$$X_{ni} = GS_i M_n \theta_{ni} \qquad\qquad 16.8$$

General gravity models are of the type given in equation 16.8. In this specification, X_{ni} represents exports from country i to country n as the main interaction flow between the two countries. The size of this flow is explained by

- S_i—supplier i capabilities for exports to all locations
- M_n—destination market n characteristics promoting imports from all sources
- θ_{ni}—bilateral accessibility of country n from country i; this variable ($0 \leq \theta_{ni} \leq 1$) combines trade costs and elasticity to measure the overall impact on trade flows
- G—a gravitational constant (in cross-section)

The two main restrictions imposed by the general gravity specification are that all terms enter multiplicatively (in analogy with the gravity equation in physics) and that any third-country effects are mediated via the i and n multilateral terms (S_i and M_n).

$$X_{ni} = \underbrace{\frac{Y_i}{A_i}}_{S_i}\underbrace{\frac{X_n}{B_n}}_{M_n}\theta_{ni} \; ; \; B_n = \sum_l \frac{\theta_{nl}Y_l}{A_l} \; ; \; A_i = \sum_l \frac{\theta_{li}X_l}{B_l}$$ 16.9

Structural gravity models are of the type given in equation 16.9. Such models are a subset of general gravity models that impose consistency requirements on the terms S_i and M_n. The variable Y_i represents the exporter's value of production $\left(Y_i = \sum_n X_{ni} \right)$ and the variable X_n represents the importer's value of expenditure $\left(X_n = \sum_i X_{ni} \right)$. In practice, GDP is often used as a proxy for both Y_i and X_n. The variables A_i and B_n are so-called 'multilateral resistance' terms which must meet certain consistency requirements imposed by theory as indicated in equation 16.9; see also Technical Note 16.3.

$$X_{ni} = GY_i^a Y_n^b \theta_{ni}$$ 16.10

Naïve gravity models are of the type given in equation 16.10. This specification was used in Section 16.2.2 (because it is 'pedagogically useful'; see Head and Mayer, 2014, p. 139). It is slightly more general than structural gravity because the parameters a and b do not have to be equal to 1. It does not include the multilateral resistance terms identified by Anderson and van Wincoop (2003) and therefore is no longer used in empirical work.

Most theoretical foundations for gravity equations predict unit elasticities for the impact of income on trade flows. This restriction can, of course, be empirically tested; most empirical

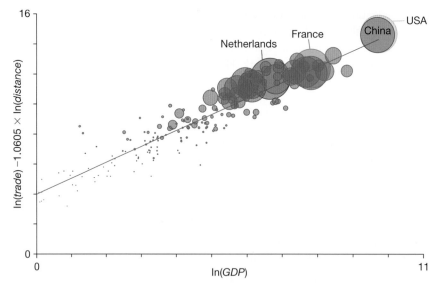

Figure 16.16 German trade and income, 2015.

Source: author's calculations based on data from International Trade Centre www.intracen.org; *trade* = (*export* + *import*) in USD billion, World Bank (GDP PPP, current USD billion), and CEPII www.cepii.fr; weighted distance km; bubbles proportional to share of trade flows; 184 trade partners included.

research indicates that the income elasticity is close to unity, as illustrated for distance-corrected German trade flows in Figure 16.16, where the slope of the regression line is 1.0605.

So what is the 'bilateral accessibility' term θ_{ni} in equations 16.8 to 16.10? Head and Mayer analyse nine different theoretical foundations for the gravity equation. All of these are based on trade costs of the iceberg type, so T_{ni} units have to be shipped from the origin to ensure that one unit arrives at the destination and $T_{ni}-1$ is the ad valorem equivalent of trade costs. Of the nine models, seven lead to structural gravity and two lead to general gravity. Many different theoretical models thus give rise to the gravity equation. The bilateral accessibility terms in the underlying models are essentially of two types:

- $\theta_{ni} = T_{ni}^{1-\varepsilon}$, where ε is the *price elasticity of demand*. These models can be based on some Armington (1969) type of national product differentiation (see Chapter 6) or on some (Dixit-Stiglitz type) monopolistic competition (see Chapter 8). Note that bilateral accessibility θ_{ni} approaches 0 if trade costs T_{ni} become arbitrary large (since $\varepsilon > 1$) and approaches 1 if trade costs T_{ni} become arbitrary small (since 1 to some power is 1). This type of interaction is illustrated in equations 16.3 and 16.5 of the geographical economics model.

- $\theta_{ni} = T_{ni}^{-\eta}$, where η is an *inverse measure of heterogeneity*. These models can be based on heterogeneous consumers, heterogeneous sectors, or heterogeneous firms (see Chapter 13). Again, bilateral accessibility θ_{ni} approaches zero if trade costs T_{ni} become arbitrary large and approaches one if trade costs T_{ni} become arbitrary small.

Note that for any given level of trade costs T_{ni} the bilateral accessibility θ_{ni} *falls* if the elasticity of demand ε rises in the first type of model or if the inverse measure of heterogeneity η rises in the second type of model. The economic implications are thus quite similar, since a

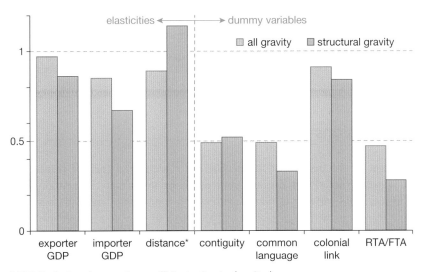

Figure 16.17 Typical gravity equation coefficient estimates (median).

Notes: data; * -distance coefficient; see main text for details.

Source: based on Head and Mayer (2014, Table 3.4).

rise in ε implies that goods are becoming more homogeneous, while a rise in η implies that consumers, sectors, or firms are becoming less heterogeneous.

So what are typical empirical estimates for gravity equation variables? To get an indication, Head and Mayer (2014) collected 2,509 estimates from 159 papers and calculated median coefficients. Figure 16.17 summarizes this information for 'all gravity' (which includes all estimates of the relevant coefficients) and 'structural gravity' (which includes only estimates based on structural gravity equations). On average, the all-gravity medians are based on 765 estimates and the structural gravity medians are based on 147 estimates. The left-hand side of the graph reports elasticity estimates and the right-hand side reports coefficients for dummy variables.

The elasticity estimates focus on exporter and importer GDP and (minus) the impact of distance. For all gravity, the elasticity of exporter GDP is close to 1, and for importer GDP somewhat lower than 1 (0.97 and 0.85, respectively). This is in line with most theoretical models, which assume that trade flows rise proportionally with income levels. Both estimates are somewhat lower for structural gravity (0.86 for exporter GDP and 0.67 for importer GDP). The lower estimate for importer GDP might be indicative of a home market effect. The elasticity of distance for all gravity is −0.89, which indicates that trade flows fall by about 8.9 per cent if the distance between exporter and importer rises by 10 per cent. The distance elasticity is −1.14 for structural gravity, which suggests that controlling for the multilateral resistance terms is important.

The dummy variables indicate whether exporter and importer share a common border (contiguity), a common language, or a former colonial link, or engage in a regional or free trade agreement (RTA/FTA). The most powerful impact on trade flows is sharing a colonial link; with coefficients of 0.84 to 0.91 this means that trade flows are about 130 to 150 per cent higher than without such a link. The all-gravity coefficients for contiguity, common language, and a trade agreement are about half this size, which implies that trade flows are about 60 per cent higher if the trading partners share a common border or language or if they have a trade agreement. In structural gravity models, the estimated impact of a common language or trade agreement is smaller (about 30 per cent higher trade flows).

We conclude this section by pointing out that gravity-type equations and gravity-type models are increasingly used for other types of flows and interactions, such as service offshoring, migration flows, commuting flows, stocks and flows of foreign direct investment, and tourism flows.

16.9 Conclusions

Blending some of the insights of the neoclassical trade model (perfect competition and constant returns to scale) with the new trade model (monopolistic competition, increasing returns to scale, and varieties of manufactures) and combining these with factor mobility (migration to regions with high real wages) allows us to provide a simple theory of location and agglomeration. The dynamic migration process implies that we distinguish between short-run equilibria (in which the distribution of manufacturing activity is given) and an adjustment path leading to a long-run equilibrium (either spreading of manufacturing activity or complete agglomeration). Using computer simulations to gain further insights into the model, we show that for high transport costs the spreading of manufacturing activity is a stable outcome, while for low transport costs agglomeration is a stable outcome. In an intermediate range both agglomeration and spreading are stable outcomes, which points to some problems in predicting the effect of policy changes in view of the hysteresis aspect of the model (history matters). The model has been modified to explain some important empirical observations and regularities (such as Zipf's Law concerning the distribution of city sizes, and the gravity equation concerning the size and direction of international trade flows). Applying the basic model to predict the location of European cities, taking the geographical context into account, turns out to be mildly successful. Note that the model predicts that regions of similar size (spreading) will be involved in intra-industry trade and regions of different size (agglomeration) will be involved in inter-industry trade, roughly in line with empirical observations (see Chapter 8). We conclude with an overview of the three types of gravity equations and observe how these can be based on many different types of economic models.

Technical Notes

Technical Note 16.1 Derivation of the price index

Some preliminary equations are given below. The first equation gives spending on food and manufactures, the second gives the demand for a particular variety, the third defines real income and wage, and the fourth gives the notation for transport costs between regions r and s, depending on the parameter T and the distance D_{rs} between regions r and s.

$$F = (1 - \delta_m)I \; ; \; PM = \delta_m I \tag{16.A1}$$

$$c_j = p_j^{-\varepsilon}(P^{\varepsilon-1}\delta_m I) \; ; \; P = \left(\sum_{i=1}^{N} p_i^{1-\varepsilon}\right)^{1/(1-\varepsilon)} \tag{16.A2}$$

$$y = IP^{-\delta_m}; \; w = WP^{-\delta_m} \tag{16.A3}$$

$$T_{rs} = T^{D_{rs}}; \; T_{rs} = T_{sr} \text{ and } T_{rr} = T^0 = 1 \tag{16.A4}$$

The number of firms in region s equals $\lambda_s \delta_m / f\varepsilon$. The price a firm located in region s charges in region r equals $mW_s T_{rs}(\varepsilon-1)/\varepsilon$. Substituting these two results in the price index for manufactures, see equation (16.A2), and assuming that there are $R \geq 2$ regions, gives the price index for region r.

$$P_r = \left(\sum_{s=1}^{R}\left(\frac{\lambda_s \delta_m}{f\varepsilon}\right)\left(\frac{mW_s T_{rs}(\varepsilon-1)}{\varepsilon}\right)^{1-\varepsilon}\right)^{\frac{1}{1-\varepsilon}} =$$

$$= \left[\left(\frac{m(\varepsilon-1)}{\varepsilon}\right)\left(\frac{\delta_m}{f\varepsilon}\right)^{1/(1-\varepsilon)}\right]\left(\sum_{s=1}^{R}\lambda_s W_s^{1-\varepsilon} T_{rs}^{1-\varepsilon}\right)^{1/(1-\varepsilon)} \tag{16.A5}$$

It can be shown (Brakman, Garretsen, and van Marrewijk, 2001, Chapter 4) that the parameter normalization $m = (\varepsilon-1)/\varepsilon$ and $f = \delta_m/\varepsilon$ does not essentially affect the dynamic behaviour of the model, although it does affect the welfare level. Applying this normalization considerably simplifies notation as it reduces the awkward constant in square brackets on the right-hand side of equation (16.A5) to 1. Using that normalization implies that equation 16.3 is a special case for two regions $(R = 2)$, applied to the first region $(r = 1)$.

Technical Note 16.2 Derivation of manufacturing equilibrium

Equation (16.A2) gives the demand for an individual consumer in a region. Replacing the income level I with the income level I_s of region s, the price index P with the price index P_s of region s, and the price p_j of the manufactured good with the price $mW_s T_{rs}(\varepsilon-1)/\varepsilon$ which a producer from region r will charge in region s, we get the demand in region s for a product from region r:

$$\delta_m I_s \left(\frac{mW_s T_{rs}(\varepsilon-1)}{\varepsilon} \right)^{-\varepsilon} P_s^{\varepsilon-1} = \delta_m \left(\frac{m(\varepsilon-1)}{\varepsilon} \right)^{-\varepsilon} I_s W_r^{-\varepsilon} T_{sr}^{-\varepsilon} P_s^{\varepsilon-1} \tag{16.A6}$$

To fulfil this consumption demand in region s, note that T_{sr} units have to be shipped and produced. To derive the total demand in all $R \geq 2$ regions for a manufactured good produced in region r, we must sum production demand over all regions (that is, sum over the index s in the above equation and multiply each entry by T_{sr}):

$$\delta_m \left(\frac{m(\varepsilon-1)}{\varepsilon} \right)^{-\varepsilon} \sum_{s=1}^R I_s W_r^{-\varepsilon} T_{sr}^{-\varepsilon} P_s^{\varepsilon-1} = \delta_m \left(\frac{m(\varepsilon-1)}{\varepsilon} \right)^{-\varepsilon} W_r^{-\varepsilon} \sum_{s=1}^R I_s T_{sr}^{-\varepsilon} P_s^{\varepsilon-1} \tag{16.A7}$$

In equilibrium, this total demand for a manufactured good from region r must be equal to its supply $(\varepsilon-1)f/m$ (see Chapter 8). Equalizing these two gives

$$\frac{(\varepsilon-1)f}{m} = \delta_m \left(\frac{m(\varepsilon-1)}{\varepsilon} \right)^{-\varepsilon} W_r^{-\varepsilon} \sum_{s=1}^R I_s T_{sr}^{-\varepsilon} P_s^{\varepsilon-1} \tag{16.A8}$$

—which can easily be solved for the wage rate W_s in region r:

$$W_r = \left[\frac{(\varepsilon-1)}{\varepsilon} m^{(1-\varepsilon)/\varepsilon} \left(\frac{\delta_m}{(\varepsilon-1)f} \right)^{1/\varepsilon} \right] \left(\sum_{s=1}^R I_s T_{sr}^{-\varepsilon} P_s^{\varepsilon-1} \right)^{1/\varepsilon} \tag{16.A9}$$

As in Technical Note 16.1, the awkward constant in square brackets on the right-hand side disappears if we impose the normalization $m = (\varepsilon-1)/\varepsilon$ and $f = \delta m/\varepsilon$. Doing that implies that equation 16.5 is a special case for two regions ($R = 2$), applied to the first region ($r = 1$).

Technical Note 16.3 Structural gravity

Structural gravity equations depend on (i) spatial allocation of expenditure for the importer and (ii) market-clearing for the exporter. Regarding expenditure allocation, let i be the origin, n the destination, and $\pi_{ni} \geq 0$ the share of importer n's expenditure allocated to country i. Equation (16.A10) holds as an accounting identity. Obviously, the sum of all expenditure shares is 1: $\sum_i \pi_{ni} = 1$. The expenditure shares must be expressed in the multiplicative form of equation (16.A11), with the B_n as the accessibility-weighted sum of exporter capabilities, to ensure that the shares sum to 1.

$$X_{ni} = \pi_{ni} X_n \tag{16.A10}$$

$$\pi_{ni} = \frac{S_i \theta_{ni}}{B_n}; \; B_n = \sum_i S_i \theta_{ni} \tag{16.A11}$$

One can view B_n as a measure of the degree of competition in the market. As discussed in the main text, a range of micro-economic foundations give rise to equation (16.A11).

Regarding market-clearing for the exporters, the sum of country i's exports to all destinations (including its own markets) is equal to the total value of production Y_i: see equation (16.A12). Solving for S_i gives equation (16.A13). The term A_i is referred to as market potential in economic geography; relative access is measured by θ_{li}/B_l, so A_i is an expenditure-weighted average of relative access.

$$Y_i = \sum_n X_{ni} = S_i \sum_n \frac{\theta_{ni} X_n}{B_n} \qquad (16.A12)$$

$$S_i = \frac{Y_i}{A_i}; \quad A_i = \sum_l \frac{\theta_{li} X_l}{B_l} \qquad (16.A13)$$

Substituting equation (16.A13) in (16.A11) gives equation (16.A14). Substituting this in equation (16.A10) gives equation (16.A15). Equations (16.A13)–(16.A15) are summarized as equation 16.9 in the main text.

$$B_n = \sum_l \frac{\theta_{nl} Y_l}{A_l} \qquad (16.A14)$$

$$X_{ni} = \frac{Y_i}{A_i} \frac{X_n}{B_n} \theta_{ni} \qquad (16.A15)$$

 ## Notes

1 We prefer the term 'geographical economics', partly in order not to offend the older and respected economic geography literature.

2 We take the natural log of (rank-0.5) rather than simply the rank for technical reasons as it leads to an unbiased estimate of the slope coefficient, see Gabaix and Ibragimov (2011). The reported high significance is based on an estimated standard error using their methodology.

3 The discussion in the text is based on city limits. Similar results hold when we analyse agglomerations, in which case there are 55 agglomerations with more than one million people, Mumbai is the largest agglomeration with 21.9 million people, the slope of the line is −1.23 and 97 per cent of the variance is explained. Data are then from http://www.populationdata.net.

4 Strictly speaking, 'Zipf's Law' applies if the estimated coefficient in equation 16.1 is equal to minus one, otherwise the 'Rank-size rule' holds. This phenomenon also holds for comparative advantage as measured by the Balassa index, see Hinloopen and van Marrewijk (2012).

5 Luxembourg is combined with Belgium in trade flows, hence there are only eight neighbours from a trade perspective.

6 The regression is based on 184 German trade partners for which relevant data is available.

7 We assume that the fraction of the workers in the manufacturing sector is equal to the fraction of income spent on manufactures and normalize the workforce to one. This eases notation without substantially affecting the (dynamic) equilibrium, as discussed in Brakman, Garretsen, and van Marrewijk (2001).

8 The box information is based on Radelet and Sachs (1998), Davis (1998), and Hummels (1999a, b).

9 Why did we choose this set of base-scenario parameters? To some degree, the choice is arbitrary. The share of income spent on manufactures and the elasticity of substitution have been chosen based on reasonable empirical estimates. Given these choices, the value of the transport costs is chosen to show an important aspect of the geographical economics model as illustrated in Figure 16.8 and discussed below.

10 The simulation exercises in the study guide are based on a more user-friendly Excel program.

11 If there is complete agglomeration, the relative real wage cannot actually be calculated since there are no manufacturing workers in one of the regions. Points A and E in the figure are therefore limit values.

12 Provided the share of income spent on manufactures is less than 50 per cent. If this share is more than 50 per cent not all manufactures can be produced at one location and the 'periphery' also produces some manufactures, requiring a slight adjustment of the tomahawk diagram.

13 The apparently peculiar choice of T results from a different parameterization used by Stelder, which we have respecified here using our parameterization.

Questions

Question 16.1

a. What is 'hysteresis' or 'path-dependency', and what is its importance for geographical economics?

b. What does this imply for empirical research?

The two-region geographical economics model predicts that manufacturing activity will spread over the two regions or agglomerate in one region depending on the size of three economic parameters:

- The (iceberg) transport cost (T)
- The elasticity of substitution (ε)
- The share of income spent on manufactures (δ_m)

c. Do high transport costs lead to spreading or agglomeration of manufacturing activity? Explain.

d. Does a high elasticity of substitution lead to spreading or agglomeration of manufacturing activity? Explain.

e. Does a high share of income spent on manufactures lead to spreading or agglomeration of manufacturing activity? Explain.

Question 16.2

Figure 16.18 displays part of a diagram from the Geographical Economics model.

a. What is the name of this diagram?

b. Complete the diagram: What is on the axes? What is the meaning of points B and S?

c. What is the meaning of the arrows and why are some lines dashed?

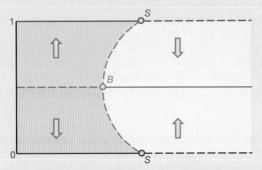

Figure 16.18 A diagram from the Geographical Economics model.

Question 16.3

Occasionally, the Chinese government contemplates building a tunnel underneath the Bohai Sea, more or less from Dalian to Yantai (see Figure 16.19).

Discuss the economic benefits to building a tunnel from Dalian to Yantai based on the Geographical Economics model. In particular:

a. Which city / cities benefit most in relative terms? Why?

b. Do you think Beijing–Tianjin benefits? Why?

c. Do you think Shanghai benefits? Why?

Figure 16.19 Proposed Dalian–Yantai tunnel.

*See the **online resources** for a Study Guide and questions:*
www.oup.com/uk/vanmarrewijk_it/

17 Growth and competitiveness

Objectives

- To be familiar with the large differences in income per capita levels between countries.
- To know the most important stylized facts of economic growth.
- To understand the importance of capital accumulation in the economic growth process.
- To understand the importance of human capital in the economic growth process.
- To have an idea how economic agents make decisions based on forward-looking behaviour.
- To know what total factor productivity is and how it is measured.
- To understand the meaning of the terms accumulability, rivalness, and excludability.
- To understand the role of knowledge spillovers and accumulation for the growth process.
- To know what a Dupuit triangle is and what it measures.
- To have a feeling for the dynamic costs of trade restrictions.
- To have an understanding of the components determining a nation's global competitiveness.

17.1 Introduction

In the long run a country's development level is determined by dynamic processes interacting with other countries in the global economy. This chapter discusses the main aspects of this interaction. First, we provide an overview of stylized facts of economic growth (Section 17.2). Second, we discuss the role of physical and human capital in the economic growth process (Sections 17.3 and 17.4) and how economic agents make forward-looking decisions (Section 17.5). Third, we explain what total factor productivity is and how it is measured (Section 17.6). Fourth, we discuss the meaning of the terms accumulability, rivalness, and excludability and how these are useful for explaining the role of knowledge spillovers in the economic growth process (Sections 17.7 and 17.8). Paul Romer is the most important contributor to this discussion (see Box 17.1). Fifth, we discuss Dupuit triangles and the dynamic costs of trade restrictions (Section 17.9). We provide an indication of the size of these costs for China (Section 17.10). We conclude with an overview of the components that determine a nation's global competitiveness (Section 17.11).

BOX 17.1 Paul Romer

Figure 17.1
Paul Romer (1955–).

After studying mathematics, physics, and economics at the University of Chicago, where he received his PhD in economics, Romer (Figure 17.1) worked at Rochester, Chicago, and Berkeley, before settling at Stanford University. He was the instigator and most important developer of 'endogenous growth theory', which seeks to better understand the economic forces leading to innovation and improvements in standards of living. It all started with Romer's article 'Increasing returns and long run growth', published in the *Journal of Political Economy* in 1986. His research in this area culminated in 'Endogenous technological change', published in the same journal in 1990. We should also mention his 1994 work 'New goods, old theory, and the welfare costs of trade restrictions', published in the *Journal of Development Economics*, on the difficulty of comprehending, appreciating, and measuring the effects of not introducing new goods and services in an economy.

17.2 Stylized facts

We observed in Section 1.5 that there are big differences between countries in terms of income per capita. Using information from the Penn World Tables, Figure 17.2 provides an indication of how big those differences really are using a logarithmic scale for 167 countries, together accounting for about 96 per cent of the world population. The population-weighted average income level is $10,673. This ranges from a low of $291 for the Democratic Republic of Congo to a high of $124,720 for Qatar. The average income level in Qatar is thus an enormous 429 times higher than in Congo. Note that Qatar has a small population (about 2 million people) and is rich in oil. Similar observations hold, however, for countries with large populations that do not depend on a single commodity for generating their income. The USA is the richest sizeable country in terms of population (about 315 million people). It has a per capita income level of $42,646, which is 147 times as much as Congo (67 million people), 54 times as much as Ethiopia (85 million people), 18 times as much as Nigeria (163 million people), 12 times as much as India (1,242 million people), and more than 5 times as much as China (1,324 million people). The research topic of this chapter is to explain to some extent the main causes of these big differences.

In trying to confront the performance of theoretical models with the empirical evidence some economists have constructed lists of *stylized facts*. We mention five 'facts' from two lists.

The Kaldor list of stylized facts is (Kaldor, 1961):[1]

1. The continued growth in the aggregate volume of production and in the productivity of labour at a steady trend rate.

2. A continued increase in the amount of capital per worker.

3. A steady rate of profit on capital.

4. Steady capital–output ratios over long periods.

5. A steady investment coefficient and a steady share of profits and wages.

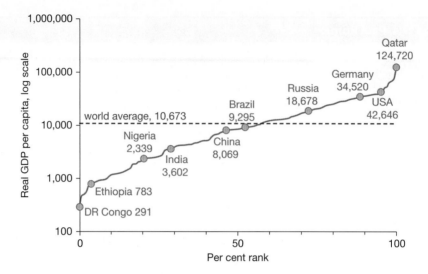

Figure 17.2 Ordering of real income per capita.

Source: author's calculations based on PWT8.0, data for 2011; income in constant 2005 USD PPP; world average is population-weighted; 167 countries included.

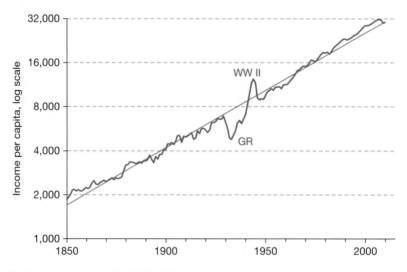

Figure 17.3 Income per capita: USA, 1850–2010.

Source: based on Maddison Project Database (www.ggdc.net); income in 1990 international GK $ (PPP corrected); the thin line is a regression line; GR = Great Recession; WW II = World War II.

We illustrate Kaldor's stylized fact 1 for the USA in Figure 17.3 using data for the period 1850–2010. Over a period of 160 years the income per capita increased 16.5 times (from 1,849 to 30,491 dollars).[2] That is a formidable increase indeed, within about five generations. Figure 17.3 uses a logarithmic scale and also shows a thin regression line to illustrate how stable the development of income per capita has been, except for a dip during the

Great Recession and a peak during World War II. According to the regression line, per capita income growth is a little over 1.8 per cent per year, which is a doubling of the income level within 40 years. We must note, however, that this stability does *not* hold for many other countries, and as such is questionable. Kaldor's stylized facts 2–4 hold reasonably well empirically, but stylized fact 5 is also questionable (see Box 17.4 later in the chapter).

The foundations of the endogenous growth theory were laid by Paul Romer, who in response to Kaldor's list produced a list of his own (Romer, 1994). The Romer list of stylized facts is:

1. There are many firms in a market economy.
2. Discoveries differ from other inputs in that many people can use them at the same time (non-rival goods).
3. It is possible to replicate physical activities.
4. Technological advance comes from things that people do.
5. Many individuals and firms have market power and earn monopoly rents on discoveries.

The empirical validity of Romer's stylized facts is hardly disputed. They turn out to be useful for constructing a proper theoretical model (see Section 17.8).

17.3 Capital accumulation

If you look at a construction site in a developing country, such as the Philippines, you observe an impressive number of workers labouring in the heat using relatively simple tools. If you look at a construction site in Australia, on the other hand, you see a fairly small number of workers operating impressive-looking cranes and other machinery, in many cases from air-conditioned cabins. One important explanation for differences in per capita income is therefore related to differences in the amount and quality of tools available for the average worker, which we refer to as capital per worker. The neoclassical growth model focuses on capital accumulation over time as the main driving force of economic growth (Solow, 1956). As we discuss below, the neoclassical model is based on strong restrictions regarding technology and type of competition. See Box 5.2 for a discussion of the importance of capital per worker and the differences between countries. See Box 17.2 for information regarding income per capita and the average number of hours worked in a country.

Output Y is a function $F(K, L)$ of the inputs capital K and labour L. Since the neoclassical production function has constant returns to scale, we can write the variables in *intensive* form, which is per worker units. We use lower case letters to denote these variables, so $y = Y/L$ is output per worker, $k = K/L$ is capital per worker, and so on. The production function is then $y = f(k) \equiv F(k, 1)$. We denote its first derivative by $'$ and its second derivative by $''$. A neoclassical production function has a positive marginal product of capital which diminishes as the capital stock increases, so $f' > 0$ and $f'' < 0$. We also impose the Inada conditions: $f(0) = 0$, $\lim_{k \downarrow 0} f'(k) = \infty$, and $\lim_{k \to \infty} f'(k) = 0$.[4]

We are interested in changes of the variables over time. We denote these changes by a dot over the variable; $\dot{k} = dk/dt$ is thus the change of capital per worker over time, and so on. The gross capital stock K increases if we invest I in new capital and decreases as a result of the depreciation rate δ times the capital stock K, such that $\dot{K} = I - \delta K$. We will assume that the working population grows at a constant rate n, such that $\dot{L}/L = n$. Differentiation

BOX 17.2 Do people in rich countries work longer hours?

Economics is about choosing optimally given the restrictions that you face. One such choice is, given that you want to work, to determine how many hours you want to work. Occasionally, you may enter conversations where somebody argues that the income level in country X is low because the people in country X do not like to work long hours.[3] We have to keep in mind, however, that people in different countries face different circumstances, and for that reason alone may make different choices.

The Penn World Table provides reliable information on the average annual number of hours worked per person engaged for only 52 countries, which excludes most developing countries. Figure 17.4 ranks these countries from low to high. The simple average is 1,809 hours worked per year. This is close to the Irish average of 1,802 hours. People in Hong Kong, a rich country, work the longest: 2,344 hours per year. People in the Netherlands, another rich country, work the shortest: 1,382 hours per year. This is about 40 per cent less than people in Hong Kong. One reason for the low number of hours worked in the Netherlands is that people can choose to work part-time, an option not always available or widely accepted in other countries. Focusing on the minimum and maximum suggests only that there is no connection between the number of hours worked and income per capita. Figure 17.4 also provides some examples that suggest otherwise: the UK and USA are both below the world average, while Turkey and Poland are above the world average.

Figure 17.5 provides a more clear picture on the relationship between the number of hours worked and income per capita. In general, people in high-income countries work *less*, not more. This suggests that spare time is a luxury good of which you start to consume more if income rises. The Netherlands, which works the shortest hours, confirms this rule, while Hong Kong, which works the longest hours, is an exception to this rule. In any case, this information shows that we can clearly rule out the hypothesis that people in lower-income countries are poor because they work shorter hours. Instead, the opposite holds in general: people in advanced countries have high income levels despite the fact that they work shorter hours.

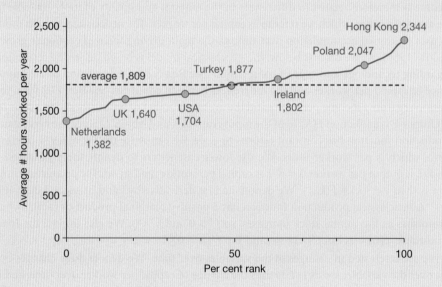

Figure 17.4 Ordering of hours worked per year.

Source: author's calculations based on PWT8.0, data for 2011; simple average; 52 countries.   (*continued...*)

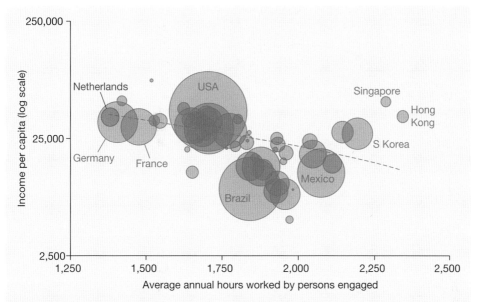

Figure 17.5 Income per capita and number of hours worked per year.

Source: author's calculations based on PWT8.0; 52 countries; bubbles proportional to population size.

of the definition $k = K/L$ over time gives the first part of equation 17.1.[5] It says that capital per worker increases if investment per worker i is higher than $(\delta + n)k$, which is what is needed to keep the amount of capital per worker constant.[6] The second part of equation 17.1 follows by assuming that a constant fraction s of income is saved and invested in the capital stock ($I = sY$ or $i = sy = sf(k)$).

$$\dot{k} = i - (\delta + n)k = sf(k) - (\delta + n)k \qquad 17.1$$

The implied dynamics of the amount of capital per worker given in equation 17.1 is illustrated in Figure 17.6. Since capital is essential for production ($f(0) = 0$), the curve starts at zero. It then becomes positive (since the marginal product of capital is arbitrarily large if the capital stock is arbitrarily small), reaches a peak, and becomes negative (since the marginal product of capital becomes arbitrarily small if the capital stock becomes arbitrarily large). If we start out with a given stock of capital per worker k_0 then this stock first increases rapidly (as indicated by point a in Figure 17.6) and then gradually slower and slower until long-run equilibrium point E is reached. At that point the amount of capital per worker is constant, denoted by k^*.

Note that the steady-state capital per worker k^* depends on the parameters in equation 17.1. In particular, it rises if the savings rate s increases, the depreciation rate δ falls, or the population growth rate n falls. Countries with a high savings rate thus converge to a high capital stock per worker and countries with a high population growth rate to a low capital stock per worker. Also note that output per worker y^* of course increases if k^* increases, since $y^* = f(k^*)$. The same does not hold, however, for consumption per worker c^*, since $c^* = y^* - i^* = f(k^*) - sf(k^*)$. In fact, it is easy to determine the 'optimal' savings rate that

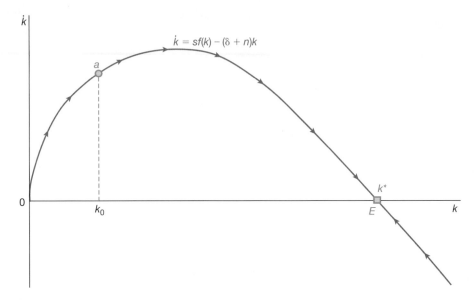

Figure 17.6 Capital accumulation in the neoclassical model.

maximizes consumption per worker in the steady state. This so-called *golden rule of accumulation* must ensure that $f'(k^*) = (\delta + n)$, so the marginal product of capital must be equal in the steady state to the population growth rate plus the depreciation rate.[7]

One problem of the neoclassical model discussed so far is that in the steady state the amount of capital per worker and the output per worker do not actually increase, which is in contrast to facts 1 and 2 on the Kaldor list (Section 17.2). To remedy this shortcoming we can impose *exogenous labour-augmenting technical change* (at a constant growth rate g). The term exogenous indicates that this technical change will increase production but is not explained within the model. The term labour-augmenting indicates that this technical change makes the input labour more productive (as will be discussed). Let A denote our measure of the level of technology. We assume it grows at a constant rate $g = \dot{A}/A$. Gross output Y is now given by the production function $Y = F(K, AL)$, which has all the neoclassical properties. We can again write the model in intensive form, but this time all variables are in *effective* worker units. We thus have $y = Y/AL$, $k = K/AL$, and so on. All results above still hold, provided we change equation 17.1 to $\dot{k} = sf(k) - (g + \delta + n)k$. The economy thus moves over time to a constant level of capital per *effective* worker. In *worker* units this means that the capital stock is ultimately growing at the exogenous rate g (and so is output per worker), which allows us to explain all five stylized facts on Kaldor's list. The *golden rule of accumulation* must now be adjusted to ensure that $f'(k^*) = (g + \delta + n)$.

17.4 Human capital

Section 17.3 has argued that the accumulation of capital over time is crucial for understanding differences in per capita income levels. The discussion so far has focused attention implicitly on *physical* capital. Box 6.6 discussed the large differences between countries in terms of the availability of human capital. This section shows how we can incorporate both types of capital in the neoclassical growth model.

How can we most easily accommodate human capital in the neoclassical growth model? By treating it essentially the same as physical capital (Barro, 1991).[8] Suppose, therefore, that there are two types of capital: physical capital K and human capital H. We ignore technical change, so output Y is a function of physical capital, human capital, and (unskilled) labour L, with the standard neoclassical properties (and Inada conditions for both types of capital): $Y = F(H,K,L)$. We can write this in per-worker terms as $y = f(h,k)$. As before, physical capital rises because we save and invest a constant fraction of income s_k and falls as a result of depreciation and the increasing work force. Equation 17.1 is thus replaced by equation 17.2. Similarly, human capital rises because we save and invest a constant fraction of income s_h and falls as a result of depreciation and the increasing work force.[9] This gives us equation 17.3. Both equations together determine how capital accumulates over time.

$$\dot{k} = s_k f(h,k) - (\delta + n)k \tag{17.2}$$

$$\dot{h} = s_h f(h,k) - (\delta + n)h \tag{17.3}$$

Figure 17.7 illustrates the dynamics in physical capital–human capital (k,h)-space.[10] The curve $\dot{k} = 0$ depicts combinations of (k,h) for which the physical capital per worker is not

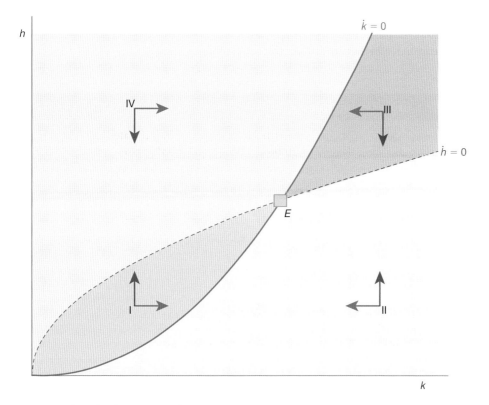

Figure 17.7 Physical and human capital accumulation.

changing. Physical capital rises to the left of this curve and falls to the right of it, as indicated by the horizontal arrows. The curve $\dot{h}=0$ depicts combinations of (k,h) for which the human capital per worker is not changing. Human capital rises below this curve and falls above it, as indicated by the vertical arrows. Taken together, the two curves divide the (k,h)-space into four different areas, labelled I, II, II, IV. Starting from any point on the plane, we will evolve over time to the stationary point E. During this process, self-reinforcing dynamics are important: as physical capital accumulates the marginal product of human capital rises, as human capital accumulates the marginal product of physical capital rises, and so on. In the end, this approach implies that a larger share of total output is accounted for by accumulable inputs (capital).[11] The distinction between these types of input is not really important.

17.5 Forward-looking behaviour

The discussion in Sections 17.3 and 17.4 assume that a constant fraction of income is saved and invested. This is, of course, not true in reality: there are large differences across time for most countries, see Box 17.3. Economic agents (consumers and entrepreneurs) make a *choice* at each point in time of how much to save and invest, depending on the expected future returns to savings and investments. Proper economic modelling of this forward-looking behaviour by economic agents thus implies dynamic optimization over time (Ramsey, 1928) in a framework of uncertainty and expectations formations (Muth, 1961). This requires technical analysis beyond the scope of this book, but we can nonetheless illustrate the main issues that are at stake in a simple framework.

BOX 17.3 Gross savings rates

In order for an economy to grow fast it has to invest intensively in order to accumulate physical capital (Section 17.3), accumulate human capital (Section 17.4), or improve technology (Sections 17.6 to 17.8). All these investments require access to savings in order to make them possible. The International Monetary Fund (2015) provides statistical information on the gross savings rate as a percentage of income for all years in the period 1980–2014 for 136 different countries.[12] The average savings rate for these countries is about 20 per cent of income. There is, however, considerable variation across countries and over time (in contrast to Kaldor's stylized fact in Section 17.2); see Figure 17.8.

The three countries with the highest average savings rates (around 40 per cent of income) are Singapore, China, and Qatar (see panel a.). This has been consistently high for rapidly developing Singapore and China. It is much more volatile for Qatar, which depends on the fluctuating oil price for its main source of revenue. The three countries with the lowest average savings rates (around 5 per cent of income or less) are Guyana, Central African Republic, and Sierra Leone (panel b.). All three are developing countries. The three countries with the most volatile gross savings rates (measured by the standard deviation) are Kuwait, Cape Verde, and Equatorial Guinea (panel c.). Note that the vertical scale of this panel differs from that of the other three panels in order to accommodate the enormous fluctuations, in particular associated with the Kuwait war after the Iraq invasion in 1990. The three countries with the most stable gross savings (around 21 per cent of income) are the European countries Italy, Spain, and France.

(continued...)

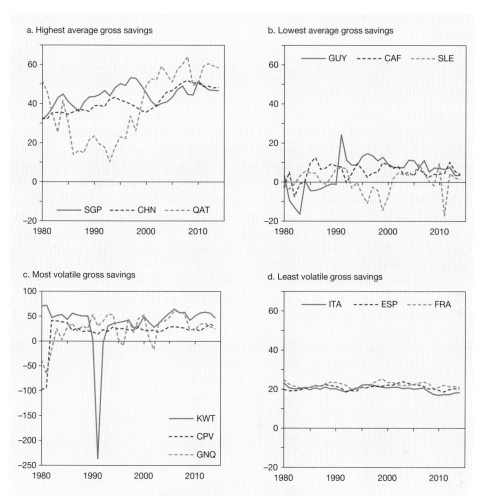

Figure 17.8 Gross savings rates: high, low, and volatility, per cent of income.

Notes: volatility measured by standard deviation; SGP = Singapore; CHN = China; QAT = Qatar; GUY = Guyana; CAF = Central African Republic; SLE = Sierra Leone; KWT = Kuwait; CPV = Cape Verde; GNQ = Equatorial Guinea; ITA = Italy; ESP = Spain; FRA = France; note that the vertical scale is different for panel c.

Source: data from IMF (2015).

Our framework is the same as in Section 17.3, without exogenous technological change. In a dynamic setting, consumers try to choose their consumption level c optimally at any point in time from now until the indefinite future, to maximize the discounted value of (instantaneous) utility $u(c)$, which depends on their consumption level c at that point in time. Discounting the future at some exogenous rate of time preference $\rho > 0$ reflects the fact that consumers prefer to consume now rather than tomorrow, or it reflects the inherent uncertainty associated with future outcomes. Let $\sigma(c) > 0$ be the intertemporal elasticity of substitution, indicating how difficult it is to substitute consumption now for consumption tomorrow.[13] The crucial equations for the optimization problem are given by

$$\dot{k} = f(k) - c - (\delta + n)k \qquad\qquad 17.4$$

$$\dot{c}/c = \sigma(c)\left[f'(k) - (\rho + \delta + n)\right] \qquad\qquad 17.5$$

Equation 17.4 is essentially the same as equation 17.1; the only difference is that we have replaced i with $f(k) - c$ to highlight the fact that we can choose the consumption level c optimally. Equation 17.5 dictates the dynamic behaviour of consumption over time. The most important thing to note is that $\dot{c}/c$ can only be equal to zero if $[f'(k) - (\rho + \delta + n)]$ is equal to zero (since $\sigma(c) > 0$). This holds for a particular level of the capital stock per worker. We denote this by k^{**} as determined by $f'(k^{**}) = (\rho + \delta + n)$. In other words, the consumption level is constant if, and only if, the marginal product of capital is equal to the sum of the rate of time preference, the depreciation rate, and the population growth rate. This so-called *modified golden rule of accumulation* simply adds the rate of time preference to the earlier condition, such that $k^{**} > k^*$.

The equilibrium dynamics for the economy are illustrated in Figure 17.9. It is constructed by looking at combinations of (k,c) for which $\dot{k} = 0$ and $\dot{c} = 0$. Capital per worker is rising below the $\dot{k} = 0$ curve and falling above it, as indicated by the horizontal arrows.

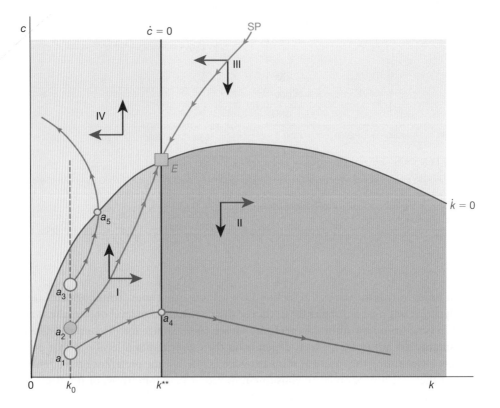

Figure 17.9 Economic growth and forward-looking behaviour.

Consumption per worker is rising to the left of the $\dot{c} = 0$ curve and falling to the right of it, as indicated by the vertical arrows. As in Figure 17.7 this divides the plane into four areas, I, II, III, IV. This time, however, some arrows point towards the long-run equilibrium at point E (where (k,c) is stationary) and some arrows point away from it. At first, this may seem to be a problem as it seems unclear how the economy would move over time towards the stationary point. It turns out, however, that forward-looking agents *ensure* that the stationary point is reached over time, as it is part of the necessary conditions for solving the optimization problem.

Suppose that we are initially *not* at the equilibrium point E, but rather have an initial level of capital per worker k_0 below this equilibrium level: $k_0 < k^*$. We know that the capital stock can be only gradually adjusted over time through investments and depreciation, while we can choose optimal consumption at any point in time. This implies that at time 0 the capital stock–consumption level combination must be somewhere along the vertical line given by k_0 in Figure 17.9. We now discuss where on this line the consumption point should be. Figure 17.9 illustrates three possible trajectories out of an infinite number of possibilities to assist us in determining this equilibrium.

- First, suppose that the initial capital stock–consumption level combination is given by point a_1 in the figure. As this point is in area I, we know that the capital stock is increasing, as is the consumption level. The speed at which this occurs is determined by equations 17.4 and 17.5. As we follow the trajectory from point a_1 in Figure 17.9, we note that at some time in the future we reach point a_4 and cross over from area I to area II, such that henceforth the capital stock is increasing and the consumption level is falling. This trajectory moves away from the long-run equilibrium at point E. Instead, we start to consume less as we need to invest more and more resources to increase the capital stock. Asymptotically, we are no longer consuming anything, so this trajectory cannot possibly solve our optimization problem.

- Second, suppose that the initial capital stock–consumption level combination is given by point a_3 in the figure. Again, this point is in area I such that the capital stock and consumption level are both increasing. As we follow the trajectory from point a_3 in Figure 17.9, we note that at some time in the future we reach point a_5 and cross over from area I to area IV, where the consumption level is rising and the capital stock is falling. Again, this trajectory will not lead us to the long-run equilibrium at point E. Instead, it ensures that the capital stock is completely depleted at some time in the future, at which time production becomes zero and consumption must jump to zero too. Such a trajectory also cannot possibly solve our optimum problem.

- Third, suppose that the initial capital stock–consumption level combination is given by point a_2 in the figure, a well-chosen point in between the points a_1 and a_3. It is determined such that all points below a_2 will eventually cross over from area I to area II, while all points above a_2 will eventually cross over from area I to area IV. Point a_2 is therefore very special, as the trajectory determined by equations 17.4 and 17.5 does not cross over from area I to area II or from area I to area IV. Instead, the trajectory will lead us on a delicate path to the long-run equilibrium at point E. It is 'delicate' because if the initial consumption level is just a little bit higher or a little bit lower, the trajectory will lead us in a completely different direction. Such a path is called a saddle path (SP).

The economic agents with forward-looking behaviour thus *choose* the right consumption level given by point a_2 in Figure 17.9 to ensure that the long-run equilibrium point is reached. They know that the saddle path leading to this point is the only viable solution. Note that the fact that the saddle path is 'delicate' (there is only one solution leading to point E) is actually not a problem but helps the economic agents to determine the equilibrium. If there were several solutions leading to point E, the agents would have to somehow determine the optimal path or they would have to coordinate their actions in determining which one to pick. This principle of selecting the saddle path which leads to some balanced growth or stationary equilibrium underlies all dynamic optimization models.

17.6 Total factor productivity (TFP)

Section 17.3 emphasizes the importance of physical capital accumulation K to explain rising output Y, while Section 17.4 emphasizes the importance of human capital accumulation H. We also emphasized the importance of the accumulation of knowledge A to explain rising output per capita. One simple way to summarize the discussion so far is thus to define output Y as a function of these different inputs: $Y = AF(K,H,L)$. If we have data available on all of these variables, we can also estimate the contribution of the individual components to explain actual economic growth, an exercise known as 'growth accounting'. If we define the *growth rate* of a variable by a tilde above it (such that $\tilde{Y} = \dot{Y}/Y$, $\tilde{K} = \dot{K}/K$, and so on), we can differentiate the production function above to determine the growth accounting exercise in terms of growth rates:

$$\tilde{Y} = \alpha_K \tilde{K} + \alpha_H \tilde{H} + \alpha_L \tilde{L} + \tilde{A} \qquad\qquad 17.6$$

In equation 17.6 the variable α_K is the elasticity of output with respect to capital, defined as the marginal product of physical capital times the amount of capital used, divided by total output.[14] Similar definitions hold for α_H and α_L. The term $\alpha_K \tilde{K}$ in equation 17.6 reflects the contribution of the change in physical capital to rising output. In a neoclassical framework of perfect competition the return to capital is equal to its marginal product, in which case α_K is simply the share of output paid for using the input physical capital, and so on. In that case the shares sum to 1 ($\alpha_K + \alpha_H + \alpha_L = 1$) and the growth of output is the weighted average of the growth of inputs plus technical change.

In practice, we have reasonably reliable information on the growth of output Y, the contribution of the inputs K, H, and L, and ways to estimate the elasticities. We lack, however, reliable information for measuring the level of knowledge A. The growth accounting exercise now turns equation 17.6 around: rather than using it to explain rising output levels, we use it instead to estimate changes in the level of knowledge A, referred to as *total factor productivity* (TFP): $\tilde{A} = \tilde{Y} - (\alpha_K \tilde{K} + \alpha_H \tilde{H} + \alpha_L \tilde{L})$.

Table 17.1 provides information on the contribution of different components for explaining economic growth for 120 countries over the period 1990–2014 using data from the Conference Board, a business membership and research association. The data provides estimates of the contribution from the quantity and the quality of labour (similar to our variables L and H) and two types of capital goods (a subdivision into two parts of our variable K), namely ICT capital and non-ICT capital.

Table 17.1 Income, inputs, and total factor productivity (per cent growth): averages, 1990–2014

	average	median	min	max	count
a. Period-average growth rates					
GDP	3.75	3.63	0.68	10.17	120
Labour quality	0.34	0.30	−0.06	1.37	111
Labour quantity	1.64	1.70	−1.97	7.77	120
ICT capital services	14.35	13.84	1.46	27.90	69
Non-ICT capital services	3.67	3.41	−1.85	13.10	120
b. Contribution to GDP growth					
Labour quality	0.19	0.16	0.01	0.69	111
Labour quantity	0.71	0.75	−1.45	3.88	120
ICT capital services	0.67	0.58	0.00	2.31	69
Non-ICT capital services	1.68	1.44	−1.18	7.07	120
c. Total factor productivity (TFP) growth: part of GDP growth not explained by input growth					
TFP	0.75	0.49	−2.88	5.43	120

Notes: reported values are country level averages for the period 1990–2014; min = minimum; max = maximum; count = number of countries; the 'average' column for GDP thus reports the average GDP growth rate for 120 countries in the period 1990–2014 (equal to 3.75 per cent), and so on for other rows and columns.

Source: The Conference Board Total Economy Database, May 2015.

In Table 17.1*a* we see that the median growth rate of output over the period 1990–2014 is 3.6 per cent per year, ranging from a low of 0.7 per cent to a high of 10.2 per cent. The median growth rate of labour quality is 0.3 per cent, of labour quantity is 1.7 per cent, of ICT capital is 13.8 per cent, and of non-ICT capital is 3.4 per cent per year.[15] On the basis of this information alone, the contribution from labour quality to economic growth would appear to be lowest and of ICT capital would appear to be highest. This would ignore, however, the importance of the elasticity terms in equation 17.6. ICT capital grows the fastest, but its importance as an input into the production process is still smaller than that of non-ICT capital. Table 17.1*b* gives estimates of the contribution of the four types of input taking the elasticity terms into consideration. From low to high, the median values are 0.2 per cent for labour quality, 0.6 per cent for ICT capital, 0.8 per cent for labour quantity, and 1.4 per cent for non-ICT capital. This implies that non-ICT capital explains the largest part of actual economic growth, followed by increases in the quantity of labour.

The part of economic growth that is left unexplained by rising quality or quantity of inputs is used to estimate changes in total factor productivity in panel *c* of Table 17.1. The median value is about half of a per cent and the average value about three-quarters of a per cent of economic growth. The lowest TFP estimate is −2.9 per cent (for Senegal) and the highest is 5.4 per cent (for Armenia). The average and median contribution of the different components to explain economic growth is illustrated in Figure 17.10 for the 69 countries for which all relevant information is available, including ICT capital information. As explained in Box 17.4, total factor productivity estimates tend to fall if more detailed information on the quantity and quality of inputs becomes available. For the countries in Figure 17.10 the median growth rate is 2.9 per cent. The contribution of labour quality to economic growth remains the lowest (0.2 per cent) and the contribution of non-ICT capital remains the highest (1.2 per cent). The contribution of labour quantity and ICT

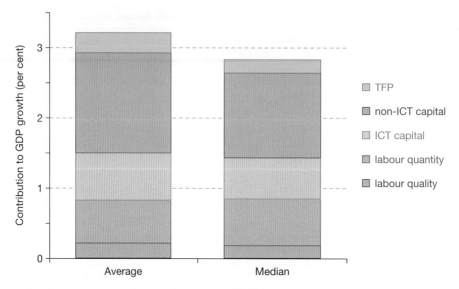

Figure 17.10 Decomposition of economic growth, 1990–2014.

Source: see Table 17.1; only 69 countries with complete information are included.

capital is now about equally important (around 0.6 per cent). The contribution of TFP to economic growth is about 0.2 per cent. The average values are a little bit higher, but the picture remains the same.

BOX 17.4 Available information and TFP estimates

Table 17.1 provides total factor productivity (TFP) summary statistics for 120 countries, while Figure 17.10 provides a decomposition of the contribution to economic growth for the four different types of input and TFP for 69 rather than 120 countries. The reason for doing this for a smaller group of countries only is that we have to be careful in drawing conclusions regarding TFP if we have limited information available. By construction, TFP is measured as a residual: it is the part of output growth we cannot explain from a rise in input quantity or quality.[16] If we have limited information available regarding these inputs, we thus automatically allocate the missing information to TFP changes, thereby tending to overestimate the contribution of TFP.

This tendency to overestimate TFP if limited information is available is illustrated in Table 17.2. The table identifies three groups of countries. The first group consists of 69 countries for which information is available on all four inputs (labour quality, labour quantity, ICT capital, and non-ICT capital). For this group of countries the average share of economic growth that is 'explained' by TFP is a modest 8.9 per cent and the median is 6.4 per cent. The second group consists of 42 countries for which no ICT capital information is available. For this group of countries the share of economic growth that is attributed to TFP is a substantial one-third of total output growth. The rather small third group consists of nine countries for which no information on ICT capital and no information on labour quality is available. For this group of countries the share of economic growth that is attributed to TFP is about one-fourth or one-fifth. Compared to the group of countries with complete information on all inputs available, the TFP estimates are substantially higher for both the second and the third group.

(*continued...*)

Table 17.2 Available information, TFP estimates, and contribution to growth, 1990–2014

Country group	TFP estimate per cent per year		TFP contribution to growth, per cent total	
	average	median	average	median
69 all input information	0.29	0.19	8.9	6.4
42 no ICT capital info	1.44	1.29	34.5	30.7
9 no labour quality or ICT capital info	0.99	1.36	17.4	25.9

Source: as Table 17.1.

17.7 Accumulability, rivalness, and excludability

Section 17.6 shows that non-ICT *capital accumulation* is the most important component for rising output, since it explains about 42 per cent of output growth (see Figure 17.10). As such the neoclassical focus on capital accumulation is understandable. We can, however, also look at this from a different perspective: the sum of the *other* components is even more important! Recall that these components are labour quantity, labour quality, ICT capital, and TFP. We could argue that this is the *human* component of the contribution to output growth, which as a whole is thus more important than capital accumulation.[17] Since both components must be compensated for their contribution somehow, a crude indication of their relative importance for a specific country is to analyse the share of labour compensation in total income: see Figure 17.11.

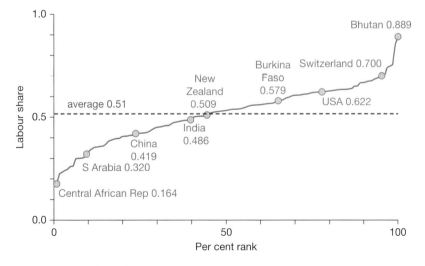

Figure 17.11 Ordering of share of labour compensation in income.

Source: authors' calculations based on PWT8.0; data for 2011; simple average; 127 countries.

The average share of labour compensation in income is about 51 per cent, close to the level of New Zealand. There is substantial variation between the countries, ranging from a low of 16 per cent in the Central African Republic to a high of 89 per cent in Bhutan. In Figure 17.11 large emerging markets, such as China and India, are below the average, while some advanced countries, such as the USA and Switzerland, are above the average. There is, however, considerable variation across per capita income levels, as illustrated for developing countries by Central African Republic, Burkina Faso, and Bhutan in Figure 17.11. In fact, a figure with the logarithm of income per capita on one axis and the share of labour compensation on the other axis shows that there is virtually *no* relationship between these two variables. To understand why this is the case, it is useful to distinguish between the three main types of sectors that together comprise the economy, namely agriculture, services, and manufacturing. It turns out that (see Section 4.10):

- The share of agriculture in total output *falls* if per capita income rises.
- The share of services in total output *rises* if per capita income rises.

If we view manufacturing activity as the residual of these two main trends, its share tends to be small at low levels of income per capita (because most people work in agriculture) and at high levels of income per capita (because most people work in services). This suggests that there is a tendency for manufacturing activity to peak at intermediate income levels. As Figure 17.11 illustrates, this is true to some extent. For example, the share of manufacturing activity in total output is rather low for Ethiopia (12 per cent; income per capita $1,380), substantially larger for India (31 per cent; income per capita is $5,418), and even larger for China (44 per cent; income per capita $11,907), but then declines and is much lower for the USA (21 per cent; income per capita $53,042). As Figure 17.12 shows, the effect is not so strong if we consider all countries in the world and the variation is substantial. Since manufacturing activity tends to be relatively capital-intensive, such that the share of labour compensation is low if the share of manufacturing activity is high,[18] this explains why there is no overall relationship between income per capita and the share of labour compensation in income.

Before we analyse the importance of the human component in continued economic growth through knowledge creation in the next section, we need to discuss three important characteristics of inputs, namely *accumulability, rivalness,* and *excludability* (Romer, 1990).

An input is *accumulable* if its value can potentially increase without bound. This holds, for example, for the (economic) value of the capital stock.[19] The labour force, interpreted as the number of people at work, has been increasing for thousands of years. Nonetheless, given the finite space available on earth (and ignoring extra-terrestrial possibilities) the labour force cannot continue to rise forever. It is therefore ultimately non-accumulable. If we analyse in per capita terms, the labour force is already fixed at 1. The production value of a worker may, of course, rise indefinitely if she is working with ever-rising amounts of capital or ever more available knowledge. In Section 17.4 we discussed the importance of human capital, focusing on the level of schooling for workers that enables them to work with new knowledge and more complex capital goods. In that section human capital was essentially treated the same as physical capital and could accumulate indefinitely. Paul Romer, however, convincingly points out that human capital is incorporated in a person and that this person cannot pass on that human capital to someone else when she dies. Ultimately, therefore, human capital is *not* accumulable.

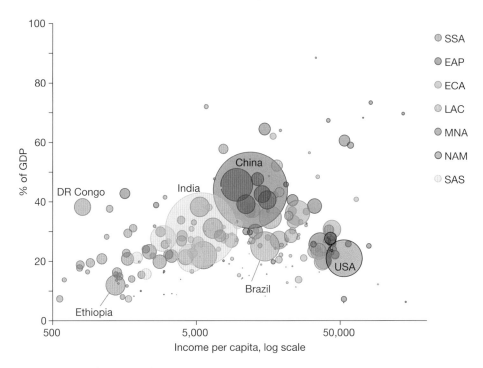

Figure 17.12 Manufacturing and income per capita.

Notes: income in current GDP PPP; see Chapter 4 for the World Bank region abbreviations; bubbles proportional to population size; 195 countries.

Source: based on the most recently available information in the World Development Indicators online for the period 2010–2014 and CIA World Fact book for missing data.

An input is a *rival* good if only one person can use it at a point in time. I can work on a computer, and so can you. But we cannot work on the same computer at the same time. A computer is therefore a rival good, as is a desk, a chair, a copy machine, and so on. In principle, labour and capital are rival inputs. Knowledge, however, is special as it is in general a non-rival good. I can apply the principles of addition, subtraction, or double entry book keeping at the same time as you can. And we can do this in different sectors.

An input is *excludable* if the owner can prevent others from using it. Most rival goods are excludable. Most knowledge, such as a newly invented intermediate good, is partially excludable. You may try to keep your design a secret, or the patent office may grant you exclusive rights to your new invention for a number of years. Eventually, however, others may benefit from the new knowledge you created because the secret is leaked or the patent runs out. The creation of knowledge thus usually leads to knowledge spillovers that are valuable to other people.

On the basis of the rivalness and accumulability characteristics we can identify three major types of input for our analysis in the next section (van Marrewijk, 1999):[20]

- rival, not accumulable inputs, such as *labour L* (or human capital);
- rival, accumulable inputs, such as *capital K*;
- non-rival, accumulable inputs, such as *knowledge A*.

17.8 **Knowledge and endogenous growth**

To explain rising levels of output and capital per worker we introduced *exogenous* technical change at the end of Section 17.3. As a result, the growth rate of output per worker is g because we assumed it to be g. This is, of course, not satisfactory because technical change, the development of new goods and services, and the creation of new knowledge are the outcomes of costly and risky investment decisions by firms, governments, and individuals. All these investment decisions taken together must somehow determine the growth rate of knowledge (and the economy). The objective of the endogenous growth literature is to explain this growth rate within the framework of the model itself, rather than imposing it exogenously. There are important contributions regarding the invention of new varieties of goods (Romer, 1990), the introduction of quality improvements (Aghion and Howitt, 1992), and an integration of both approaches (Grossman and Helpman, 1991). For simplicity we focus on the variety approach.

Paul Romer starts by pointing out that on the basis of two of his stylized facts (see Section 17.2), namely non-rivalness of knowledge (fact 2) and a replication argument (fact 3), there *must* be increasing returns to scale in the aggregate. This gives rise to imperfect competition (fact 5), although to a limited extent because there are many firms in a market economy (fact 1). Since accumulating knowledge, testing and developing new products, and achieving scientific breakthroughs is costly and takes a lot of effort from talented individuals (fact 4), he argues that a proper model of economic growth should allow these efforts to be determined and remunerated within the model.

Romer identifies three sectors: (i) a perfectly competitive final goods sector, (ii) an intermediate goods sector with monopolistic competition, and (iii) a research and development (R&D) sector for inventing new varieties of intermediate goods. There is free entry in the R&D sector to ensure that the expected return is equal to the expected revenue. The development of a new variety is equivalent to the creation of new knowledge A. Entrepreneurs can recover the costly development of a new variety by using their market power in the intermediate goods market to earn positive operating profits. A slightly simplified version of the model can be summarized in equations 17.7 and 17.8, where the intermediate goods sector is represented by the capital stock K.

$$Y = F(L_Y)A^{\alpha}K_Y^{1-\alpha} = C + \dot{K} \qquad\qquad 17.7$$

$$\dot{A} = R(L_A)A \qquad\qquad 17.8$$

There are three inputs: a rival and non-accumulable input labour L (which is taken as constant), a rival and accumulable input capital K, and a non-rival and accumulable input knowledge A. There are two production functions: one for output Y and one for new knowledge $\dot{A}$. For the rival inputs L and K there is a sub-index Y or A to indicate in which sector this input is used. There is no sub-index for the non-rival input A since the same knowledge can be used *simultaneously* in both sectors. If I use certain knowledge in the output sector I can still use the same knowledge in the R&D sector. It is, after all, a non-rival input.

The production function for output uses labour, capital, and knowledge as inputs. Output can be consumed or added to the capital stock. The production function in the R&D sector is special in two ways. First, it does not use capital as an input, only labour and knowledge. We thus have $K_Y = K$. Second, the non-excludable part of new knowledge leads to knowledge spillovers in the R&D sector. Entrepreneurs pay only for the use of labour in R&D, and this labour becomes more productive as A rises. As a result of these assumptions, only the allocation of labour across the two sectors is relevant (since capital is only used in the final goods sector and knowledge is non-rival): $L_Y + L_A = L$. This allocation depends, of course, on the return to labour in the two sectors. Note that for a given level of labour the growth rate of knowledge is constant ($\tilde{Y} = R(L_A)$), because of the imposed knowledge spillovers and constant returns to scale for the accumulable factor A). If we impose $\tilde{Y} = \tilde{K}$ (Kaldor's stylized fact 4) it follows easily from equation 17.7 that the growth rate of output is equal to the growth rate of knowledge ($\tilde{Y} = \tilde{A}$ because of constant returns to scale to the accumulable factors A and K). The growth rate is thus determined endogenously within the model based on the investment decisions of entrepreneurs who use their monopoly power in the intermediate goods market to cover the R&D costs. The process is self-sustaining as a result of constant returns to scale for knowledge spillovers in the R&D sector. The decentralized economy is not socially optimal since the entrepreneurs do not take these spillovers into consideration when making their investment decisions (the economy grows too slowly and the government should stimulate innovation).

Some of the restrictions on the production functions imposed in the Romer model are not necessary. We can allow for a framework where the rival inputs labour and capital are used in all sectors: to produce output, intermediate goods, and R&D (van Marrewijk, 1999). Such a setting allows for a non-trivial role for both (neoclassical) capital accumulation and (endogenous growth) knowledge spillovers. In this framework, capital accumulation and innovation are complementary processes, neither of which would take place in the long run without the other. The restrictions needed to make this work are intuitive. There must be constant returns to scale to accumulable factors (A and K) for both output and R&D and there must be labour-augmenting knowledge spillovers in the intermediate goods sector and the R&D sector.

17.9 Dupuit triangles and the costs of trade restrictions

As far as we know, the first analysis of the value of a new good to society—that is, the first attempt to try to measure the value of something that does not yet exist—was provided by the French engineer Jules Dupuit in 1844. As head of an engineering district, he was responsible for building roads, bridges, and canals. He was therefore interested in developing practical rules for determining if a specific project should be built, for which he described a demand curve and a revenue curve, which allowed him to identify an important problem associated with the introduction of new goods.

The main issue is illustrated in Figure 17.13, depicting a downward-sloping demand curve for a good (say a bridge) that has not yet been introduced. The vertical axis represents the price to be paid each time the bridge is crossed. If the price is too high (above p_{max}), nobody will use the bridge. If the price is zero, the bridge will be used most intensively at q_{max}. As we know from standard microeconomic theory, the area under the demand curve measures the value of the bridge to the consumers at any given quantity. At a price of 0, for example, the total value of the bridge to consumers is equal to the triangle area $0q_{max}p_{max}$.

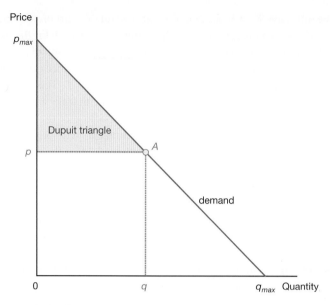

Figure 17.13 The Dupuit triangle.

Suppose that a private company is interested in building this bridge, and evaluates whether or not it is worthwhile to go ahead with the project. In Figure 17.13 we assume that the firm charges price p, resulting in q crossings of the bridge and total revenue pq, equal to the area $0pAq$. How the firm determines the price p it charges for one crossing of the bridge is immaterial for our argument. What is important is the fact that the total area under the demand curve at q, that is the area $0P_{max}Aq$, is strictly larger than the revenue generated by the firm from the crossings of the bridge, the area $0pAq$. The difference between the value to consumers and the revenue for the firm, that is the triangle $p_{max}Ap$, represents a welfare gain for which the firm building the bridge is not compensated in terms of revenue. If the firm decides that the total revenue generated by the bridge is not enough to compensate it for the costs of building and maintaining the bridge, it will decide not to build the bridge. Romer calls the area $p_{max}Ap$ the Dupuit triangle and argues that it is equal to the welfare loss to society of not building the bridge (Romer, 1994).

In general, the above reasoning shows that there are costs involved, in terms of a welfare loss to society as a whole, of *not* introducing a good on the market. The Dupuit triangle can be interpreted as a measure for this welfare loss.[21] Moreover, it is evident that we cannot rely on market forces to ensure that all new goods that are valuable to society will actually be introduced, because the firm introducing a new good can only appropriate part of the surplus it generates.[22] Romer continues by pointing out that one of the most important consequences of imposing trade restrictions is the fact that they might lead to new goods and services not being available on the market. He illustrates his argument for a small developing economy, say Developia, which does not invent its own capital goods. Instead, those intermediate capital goods and services are invented abroad. After a successful innovation, the foreign inventors face the decision whether or not to introduce the intermediate good on Developia's market, which gives them an operating profit as the price they

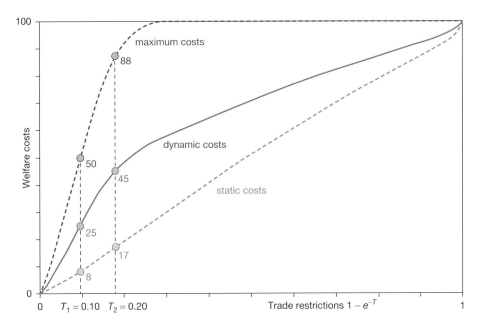

Figure 17.14 Dynamic costs of trade restrictions.

Source: van Marrewijk and Berden (2007).

charge will be higher than the marginal costs of production and transport. They will only introduce the new intermediate good on Developia's market if the operating profits are higher than the fixed costs of introduction, say for setting up a local consulting office. This criterion determines the number of varieties introduced on the market. Romer discusses the impact of 'expected' versus 'unexpected' tariffs for Developia's market. This approach has been extended to a dynamic setting (van Marrewijk and Berden, 2007).

Suppose the government of Developia imposes an ad valorem tariff T on the purchases of all foreign goods. We discuss the consequences of the welfare loss (measured as the percentage reduction in output relative to the output level without tariffs) for a specific numerical example, see Figure 17.14. The *static costs* of this policy assume that all capital goods continue to be introduced on the market; this leads to a welfare loss of 8 per cent if the tariff level is 10 per cent. The *maximum costs* of this policy assume that all inventors at any point in time already know that this policy will be imposed (also into the indefinite past) and thus maximizes the number of goods not introduced on the market; this leads to a welfare loss of 50 per cent if the tariff level is 10 per cent. The *dynamic costs* of this policy assume that inventors are completely taken by surprise at the time the policy is introduced, and hence only a certain range of newly developed goods will not be introduced on the market; this leads to a welfare loss of 25 per cent if the tariff level is 10 per cent. The important thing to remember is that the true costs of trade restrictions should include the dynamic costs of trade restrictions (goods not introduced on the market), which are much larger than the static costs of trade restrictions. Moreover, these costs rise rapidly if trade restrictions increase. If the tariff level is 20 per cent, the dynamic costs already amount to a welfare loss of 45 per cent (rather than the static costs of 17 per cent). We now turn to a case study of these costs.

17.10 **China: a case study**

The main difficulty of calculating the dynamic costs of trade restrictions as explained in Section 17.9 is the fact that even if you think that these costs are important, it is almost impossible to estimate their size. How do you estimate the size of the welfare loss as a result of goods and services that are not introduced using a generally accepted method-ology? It is virtually impossible. We can, however, provide circumstantial evidence that the dynamic costs are important. An example is the difference in economic development between North Korea and South Korea after the Korean ceasefire in 1953. North Korea isolated itself economically from virtually all outside influences, thus not benefiting from the knowledge increases and inventions of new goods and services in the rest of the world. The result was a stagnant, or slowly deteriorating, North Korean economy for more than five decades, eventually resulting in large famines. The developments in North Korea con-trast sharply with those in South Korea, which focused aggressively on expansion on the world market, using knowledge and capital goods from all over the world. Unfortunately, lack of reliable data on the North Korean economy prevents me from going into further detail here.[23] Instead, we will briefly focus attention on the developments in mainland China.

China is a large country with an impressive cultural, economic, and military history, dat-ing back thousands of years. According to recent estimates, there are more than 1.3 billion Chinese inhabitants. Since we want to get a feel for the importance of international trade and capital flows, and of openness to the outside world, even for such a large country as China, we will measure economic development in China relative to the outside world. To this end, Figure 17.15 depicts China's income per capita as a percentage of world average income per capita in any given year.

In 1949 Mao Zedong proclaimed the founding of the People's Republic of China and installed a new political and economic order modelled on the Soviet example. In 1958, Mao broke with the Soviet model and started a new economic programme called the Great Leap Forward. Its aim was to raise industrial and agricultural production by forming large cooperatives and building 'backyard factories'. The results of the market disruption and poor planning, leading to the production of unsaleable goods, were disastrous. Within a year, starvation appeared even in fertile agricultural areas, resulting in famine from 1960 to 1961. The relationship with the Soviet Union deteriorated sharply, leading to the restric-tion of the flow of scientific and technological information to China and the withdrawal of all Soviet personnel in 1960. When compared to the world average, the impact of the Great Leap Forward shows up in Figure 17.15 as a deterioration of China's living standards from an already low 4.97 per cent in 1960 to an even lower 2.56 per cent in 1962 (a relative decline of 36 per cent!).

In the early 1960s Liu Shaoqi and his protégé Deng Xiaoping took over direction of the party and adopted pragmatic economic policies at odds with Mao's revolutionary vision. In 1966, when the Chinese economy had almost recuperated from the consequences of the Great Leap Forward and Chinese per capita GNP had bounced back to 3.39 per cent of the world average, Mao started the Cultural Revolution, a political attack on the prag-matists who were dragging China back towards capitalism. The Red Guards, radical youth organizations, attacked party and state organizations at all levels. Again, Mao's insightful

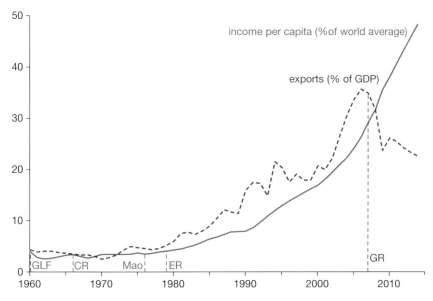

Figure 17.15 Economic development in China, 1960–2015.

Notes: income per capita is GDP in constant 2005 USD (relative to world average of that year in per cent); exports of goods and services as per cent of GDP; GLF = Great Leap Forward; CR = Cultural Revolution; Mao = Mao's death; ER = Economic Reform; GR = Great Recession.

Source: World Development Indicators online.

ideas were disastrous to the Chinese standard of living, which dropped to 2.73 per cent of the world average in 1968 (this time a relative decline of 'only' 19 per cent). The Chinese political situation stabilized after some years along complex factional lines, resulting in living standards of around 3.5 per cent of the world average. Deng Xiaoping was reinstated in 1975 but then stripped of all official positions one year later by the Gang of Four (Mao's wife and three associates).

Mao's death in September 1976 set off a scramble for succession, leading to the arrest of the Gang of Four and the reinstatement of Deng Xiaoping in August of 1977. In a pivotal meeting in December 1978 the new leadership adopted economic reform policies to expand rural incentives, encourage enterprise autonomy, reduce central planning, open up to international trade flows with the outside world, establish foreign direct investment in China, and pass new legal codes in June of 1979. The positive consequences of the economic reforms, which were continued with some interruptions by successive governments, for the Chinese standard of living were enormous, dramatically illustrating the dynamic costs of trade restrictions. In relative terms, income per capita in China increased twelve-fold in 34 years, from 4 per cent of the world average in 1979 to 48 per cent in 2014. A monumental achievement indeed, with enormous consequences for more than one billion people.

The policy of openness is illustrated in Figure 17.15 by exports relative to income, which rose from 5 per cent in 1979 to more than 35 per cent in 2006. Remember that this is a sharply increasing share of a rapidly rising income level. These trade flows have been vital for Chinese development. Relative exports declined once the Great Recession started in

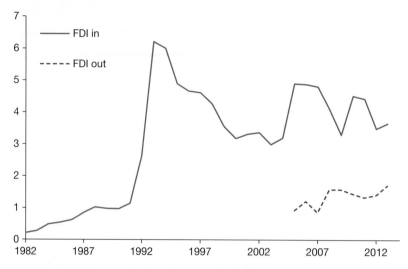

Figure 17.16 China: FDI inflows and outflows (per cent of GDP), 1982–2014.

Source: World Development Indicators online; FDI = foreign direct investment.

2007 (to about 23 per cent in 2014), but this has not slowed down Chinese development. Apparently, China was rather successful in its transition process to the next stages of economic development (see Section 17.11), such that it can also rely on domestic factors for continued economic growth. Another indicator of the policy of openness is provided by the foreign direct investment (FDI) flows relative to income in Figure 17.16. There are no data available before 1982, but we can be sure that FDI flows were virtually absent before that time. After the economic reforms, FDI into China rose rapidly from a meagre 0.2 per cent of income in 1982 to an average level above 4 per cent from 1992 to 2013. Associated with these investments is an enormous transfer of knowledge by multinational firms. Since around 2005 China has also been increasingly active as an investor in the rest of the world. FDI outflows increased from about 0.9 per cent of income in 2005 to more than 1.7 per cent in 2013. The more decentralized and outward-oriented economic policies that started around 1980 have been enormously important for China's economic development.

17.11 Global competitiveness: an overview

Many aspects that are also important for economic growth and development are not discussed in this chapter. We should mention the role of institutions in laying a solid foundation for the economic growth process, and the role of finance for development. In addition, workers need to be healthy, well-trained, and educated in order to function properly in our increasingly complex society, and so on. This section concentrates on providing a rough overview of the main issues that are at stake in order for an economy to be globally competitive, also at different stages of development. Such an overview is provided, for example, by the *Global Competitiveness Report* (World Economic Forum, 2015), which uses a specific methodology discussed below.

The 2015 Global Competitiveness Index (GCI) framework distinguishes between 12 different so-called pillars of competitiveness for three main types of economies, at different stages of economic development: factor-driven economies, efficiency-driven economies, and innovation-driven economies. Associated with each type of economy is a sub-index contributing to overall competitiveness, namely a basic requirements sub-index (consisting of four pillars), an efficiency enhancer sub-index (consisting of six pillars), and an innovation and sophistication sub-index (consisting of two pillars), as follows:

A. *Factor-driven* economies: *basic requirements* sub-index

   1.   Institutions

   2.   Infrastructure

   3.   Macroeconomic environment

   4.   Health and primary education

B. *Efficiency-driven* economies: *efficiency enhancers* sub-index

   5.   Higher education and training

   6.   Goods market efficiency

   7.   Labour market efficiency

   8.   Financial market development

   9.   Technological readiness

  10. Market size

C. *Innovation-driven* economies: *innovation and sophistication* sub-index

  11. Business sophistication

  12. Innovation

This approach thus acknowledges that many different aspects are important for determining a country's competitiveness and economic growth. The relative importance of individual components for total competitiveness is, of course, up for discussion. The GCI, however, uses detailed information to estimate how well a country is scoring on each of the individual components. The institutions pillar, for example, is estimated using 21 different indicators, including property rights, diversion of public funds, judicial independence, organized crime, ethical behaviour of firms, and so on. To take another example, the business sophistication pillar is estimated using 11 different indicators, including local supplier quantity, local supplier quality, value chain breadth, extent of marketing, and so on. Similarly for the other ten pillars.

The GCI also takes into consideration the relative importance of different pillars for countries in different stages of economic development, as measured by income per capita (see Figure 17.17). For factor-driven economies (income per capita up to 2,000), the weight for the basic requirements index is 60 per cent, for the efficiency enhancers is 35 per cent, and for innovation and sophistication is 5 per cent. There is then a transition (income per capita in between 2,000 and 3,000) to the next stage for efficiency-driven economies (income per capita between 3,000 and 9,000), where the weight for the basic requirements index is 40 per cent, for the efficiency enhancers is 50 per cent, and for innovation and

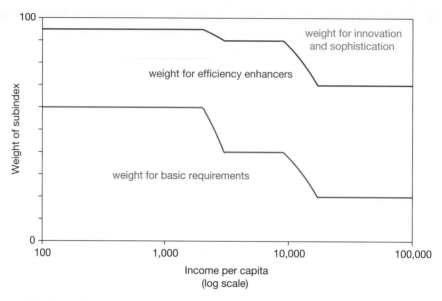

Figure 17.17 Stages of development and sub-index weights in global competitiveness.

Source: based on data from World Economic Forum (2015).

sophistication is 10 per cent. Finally, there is a transition (income per capita in between 9,000 and 17,000) to the next stage for innovation-driven economies (income per capita above 17,000), where the weight for the basic requirements index is 20 per cent, for the efficiency enhancers is 50 per cent, and for innovation and sophistication is 30 per cent.

Figure 17.18 provides an indication for the score on each of the 12 pillars for four sample countries in four panels using a radar diagram. For each pillar the score ranges from 0 to 7, where a higher score indicates better performance. A low score for a particular pillar is reflected in an observation close to the radar centre for that particular pillar, and a good score far away from that centre. Each panel in Figure 17.18 also shows the average score for all countries (in grey) for all pillars for ease of reference.

Panel a. depicts the score for Switzerland, the country with the highest GCI. Switzerland scores above the world average for all pillars, and thus essentially has no weak spots. Switzerland's weakest point in relative terms (that is compared to the world average score for that pillar) is for health, followed by market size. Switzerland's relatively strong points are innovation, followed by infrastructure. Panel b. depicts the score for the USA, number 3 in the ranking. With the exception of the macroeconomic environment (which is therefore its relatively weakest point) the USA scores above the world average for all pillars. The USA's relatively strongest point is market size, followed by innovation. Panel c. depicts the score for China, number 28 in the ranking. With the exception of technological readiness (which is therefore its relatively weakest point) China also scores above the world average for all pillars, although only marginally so in six cases. China's relatively strongest point is market size, followed by the macroeconomic environment. Panel d., finally, depicts the score for Nigeria, number 124 in the ranking. With the exception of market size and labour efficiency (which are therefore its relatively strongest points) Nigeria scores below

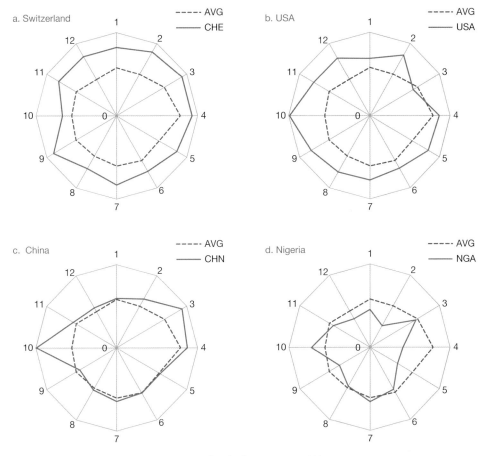

Figure 17.18 Global competitiveness in 12 pillars for four countries, 2015.

Notes: the pillars 1, ..., 12 are listed in the main text; the score for each pillar ranges from 0 (lowest) to 7 (highest); AVG = world average score, for reference.

Source: based on data from World Economic Forum (2015).

the world average for all pillars. Nigeria's lowest scores in relative terms are for health and infrastructure. As this discussion shows, one of the advantages of the GCI approach is that it helps countries to identify which pillars of economic growth and competitiveness need improvement, particularly in their specific stage of development.

17.12 **Conclusions**

Many issues play a role in determining a country's level of economic development. We summarize the main issues at stake on the basis of the Global Competitiveness Report. Many of these issues are discussed in more detail in other chapters. The remainder of this chapter focuses on the main theories of economic growth. First, we emphasize the importance of investing in (physical and human) capital accumulation for maintaining economic growth and we explain how economic agents make forward-looking decisions. A disadvantage of this approach is that we have to impose *exogenous* technical change in order to keep the economy growing on a per capita basis. Second, we emphasize the important role of innovation and firms with market power which invest in R&D as well as the role of knowledge spillovers for explaining total factor productivity and per capita economic growth *endogenously*. To do so, we discuss the terms accumulability, rivalness, and excludability, which are important for modelling the structure of the economy and firm behaviour. In the end we concluded that capital accumulation and innovation are complementary processes, neither of which would take place in the long run without the other. Third, we discuss the role of openness by evaluating the dynamic costs of trade restrictions using Dupuit triangles, as illustrated with a case study for China.

 ## Notes

1 Kaldor also noted that countries have very different long-run growth rates.

2 Measured in so-called 1990 international Geary–Khamis dollars, which corrects for purchasing power parity.

3 The terms 'lazy' or 'lying on the beach' may be heard.

4 Named after Ken-Ichi Inada (Uzawa, 1963). In words: capital is indispensable for positive production, the marginal product of capital becomes arbitrarily large if the capital stock becomes arbitrarily small, and the marginal product of capital becomes arbitrarily small if the capital stock becomes arbitrarily large.

5 Note that $\dot{k} = \frac{\dot{K}}{L} - k\frac{\dot{L}}{L} = \frac{I - \delta K}{L} - nk = i - (\delta + n)k$.

6 Since you have to replace depreciated capital δk and provide new workers with capital nk just to keep k constant, the term $(\delta + n)k$ is the minimum investment level required to keep k constant.

7 Note that $c^* = f(k^*) - sf(k^*) = f(k^*) - (\delta + n)k^*$ in the steady state from equation 17.1.

8 See Section 17.6 for a critical evaluation of this approach.

9 For simplicity the depreciation rate of human and physical capital is the same, but this is not essential.

10 It is based on a simple production function: $y = h^{0.30}k^{0.35}$, with depreciation 10 per cent, population growth rate 2 per cent, savings for physical capital 30 per cent, and savings for human capital 25 per cent.

11 In the example of Figure 17.7 we note that 35 per cent of output is attributed to physical capital and 30 per cent to human capital, so in total 65 per cent to accumulable inputs.

12 There is additional information for 37 other countries for part of this period.

13 It is defined as $\sigma(c) = -u'(c)/cu''(c)$.

14 That is: $\alpha_K = (\partial F/\partial K)(K/F)$.

15 Note that the growth rate of output is roughly the same as the growth rate of non-ICT capital, which is in line with Kaldor's stylized facts (Section 17.2).

16 Indeed, before the term TFP became popular, this estimate used to be called the 'Solow residual'.

17 ICT capital is included as it largely consists of software written by humans. There may also be a human component in capital accumulation arising from poorly measured improvements in quality.

18 The correlation of the labour share in income and the manufacturing share in GDP was −0.45 in 2011.

19 The physical amount of the capital stock may be finite. Its value in the production process is not.

20 The fourth possibility (non-rival and not accumulable) can be trivially included.

21 Actually, the Dupuit triangle probably overestimates this loss. If the bridge is not built, an alternative means of crossing the river, such as a ferry, will be viable. The ferry will have a similar Dupuit triangle which mitigates the welfare loss of not building the bridge.

22 Price discrimination cannot solve this problem (Romer, 1994).

23 Similar examples of neighbours with different openness of economic systems, and corresponding differences in economic development, are East versus West Germany (before German reunification), and Thailand versus Myanmar.

 Questions

Question 17.1

Briefly answer the following questions.

a. What is the main driving force for economic growth in the neoclassical (Solow) model?

b. Briefly describe the role played by human capital in the growth model of Section 17.4.

c. How is the Ramsey model (Section 17.5) different from the Solow model (Section 17.3)?

d. What is the main contribution of endogenous growth models?

Question 17.2

a. What is / measures the Dupuit triangle?

b. Explain how the Dupuit triangle can be useful to understand the differences in economic development observed for North Korea and South Korea (see Figure 17.19) in relationship to trade costs.

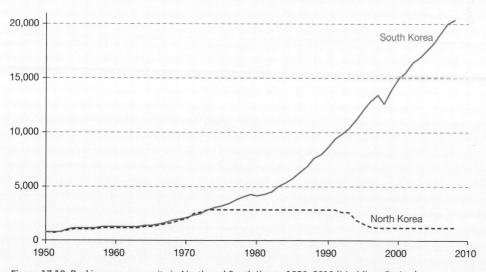

Figure 17.19 Real income per capita in North and South Korea; 1950–2010 (Maddison Project).

Question 17.3

Briefly answer the following questions:

a. What is total factor productivity?

b. How important are the four inputs below for explaining income growth relative to TFP growth? (based on observations for about 70 countries in the period 1990–2014)

- Labour quantity

- Labour quality

- ICT capital services

- Non-ICT capital services

c. Which three main drivers of economic growth does the Global Competitiveness Index (GCI) identify? How are these related to a country's development level?

d. What is the relationship between GCI and international trade- and investment flows?

 See the **online resources** *for a Study Guide and questions:*
www.oup.com/uk/vanmarrewijk_it/

References

Aggarwal, V.K., and S.J. Evenett (2015), 'A fragmenting global economy: A weakened WTO, mega FTAs, and murky protectionism', CEPR Discussion Paper No. 9781, CEPR: London.

Aghion, P., and P. Howitt (1992), 'A model of growth through creative destruction', *Econometrica* 60: 323–51.

Albert, M. (1993), *Capitalism Against Capitalism*, Vintage, London.

Allen, W.R. (ed.) (1965), *International Trade Theory: Hume to Ohlin*, Random House, New York.

Amanpour, C. (2016), 'Brexit: truths, myths, and media "neutrality"', CNN online, 29 June 2016.

Anderson, J.E., and E. van Wincoop (2003), 'Gravity with gravitas: A solution to the border puzzle', *American Economic Review* 93(1): 170–92.

Antràs, P., and S.R. Yeaple (2014), 'Multinational firms and the structure of international trade', in: G. Gopinath, E. Helpman, and K. Rogoff (eds), *Handbook of International Economics*, Vol. 4, Chapter 2, pp. 55–130.

Armington, P.S. (1969), 'A theory of demand for products distinguished by place of production', *International Monetary Fund Staff Papers* 16: 159–78.

Arrow, K.J. (1962), 'The economic implications of learning by doing', *Review of Economic Studies* 29: 155–73.

Aw, B.-Y., and A.R. Hwang (1995), 'Productivity and the export market: A firm-level analysis', *Journal of Development Economics* 47: 313–32.

Baier, S.L., J.H. Bergstrand, and M. Feng (2014), 'Economic integration agreements and the margins of international trade', *Journal of International Economics* 93(2): 339–50.

Bajona, C., and T. Chu (2010), 'Reforming state owned enterprises in China: Effects of WTO accession', *Review of Economic Dynamics* 13(4): 800–23.

Balassa, B. (1965), 'Trade liberalization and "revealed" comparative advantage', *Manchester School of Economic and Social Studies* 33: 92–123.

Balassa, B. (1966), 'Tariff reductions and trade in manufactures', *American Economic Review* 56: 466–73.

Balassa, B. (1989), '"Revealed" comparative advantage revisited', in: B. Balassa (ed.), *Comparative Advantage, Trade Policy and Economic Development*, New York University Press, New York, pp. 63–79.

Baldwin, R.E. (2014), 'Multilateralising 21st century regionalism', OECD Global Forum on Trade, February 2014.

Baldwin, R.E., and P. Martin (1999), 'Two waves of globalisation: Superficial similarities, fundamental differences', NBER Working Paper 6904, National Bureau of Economic Research, Cambridge, MA.

Barkin, J.S. (2006), *International Organizations: Theories and Institutions*, Palgrave McMillan, New York.

Barrell, R., and N. Pain (1999), 'Domestic institutions, agglomeration and foreign direct investment in Europe', *European Economic Review* 43: 925–34.

Barro, R.J. (1991), 'Economic growth in a cross-section of countries', *Quarterly Journal of Economics* 106(2): 407–43.

Bartelsman, E.J., and R.M.W.J. Beetsma (2003), 'Why pay more? Corporate tax avoidance through transfer pricing in OECD countries', *Journal of Public Economics* 87: 2225–52.

Berden, K. (2011), 'The effect of Somali piracy on trade flows and welfare – a partial equilibrium analysis', research paper, Ecorys Nederland BV.

Berden, K., J. Francois, S. Tamminen, M. Thelle, and P. Wymenga (2009), *Non-tariff Measures to EU–US Trade and Investment: An Economic Analysis*, Ecorys Nederland BV, Rotterdam, December.

Bernard, A.B., and J.B. Jensen (1995), 'Exporters, jobs, and wages in US manufacturing: 1976–1987', *Brookings Papers on Economic Activity, Microeconomics*: 67–112.

Bernard, A.B., and J.B. Jensen (1999), 'Exceptional exporter performance: Cause, effect or both', *Journal of International Economics* 47. 1–25.

Bernard, A.B., and J. Wagner (1997), 'Exports and success in German manufacturing', *Review of World Economics* 133(1): 134–57.

Bernard, A.B., J.B. Jensen, S.J. Redding, and P.K. Schott (2015), 'Global firms', mimeo.

Bernard, A.B., S.J. Redding, and P.K Schott (2007), 'Comparative advantage and heterogeneous firms', *Review of Economic Studies* 74: 31–66.

Beugelsdijk, S., S. Brakman, H. Garretsen, and C. van Marrewijk (2013), *International Economics and Business: Nations and Firms in the Global Economy*, Cambridge University Press, Cambridge, UK.

Bhagwati, J. (1965), 'On the equivalence of tariffs and quotas', in: R.E. Baldwin (ed.), *Trade, Growth and the Balance of Payments*, North-Holland, Amsterdam.

Blaug, M. (1985), *Great Economists before Keynes*, Wheatsheaf Books Ltd, Brighton, Sussex.

Bowen, H.P., A. Hollander, and J.-M. Viaene (1998), *Applied International Trade Analysis*, University of Michigan Press, Ann Arbor.

Bowen, H.P., E.E. Leamer, and L. Sveikauskas (1987), 'Multicountry, multifactor tests of the factor abundance theory', *American Economic Review* 77: 791–809.

Bown, C.P., and K.M. Reynolds (2015), 'Trade flows and trade disputes', *Review of International Organization* 10: 145–77.

Brainard, S.L. (1997), 'An empirical assessment of the proximity–concentration trade-off between multinational sales and trade', *American Economic Review* 87(4): 520–44.

Brakman, S., and C. van Marrewijk (1998), *The Economics of International Transfers*, Cambridge University Press, Cambridge, UK.

Brakman, S., and C. van Marrewijk (2007), 'Transfers, non-traded goods, and unemployment: An analysis of the Keynes–Ohlin debate', *History of Political Economy* 39(1): 121–43.

Brakman, S., H. Garretsen, and C. van Marrewijk (2001), *An Introduction to Geographical Economics*, Cambridge University Press, Cambridge, UK.

Brakman, S., H. Garretsen, and C. van Marrewijk (2009), *The New Introduction to Geographical Economics*, Cambridge University Press, Cambridge, UK.

Brakman, S., T. Kohl, and C. van Marrewijk (2015), 'The impact of the Transatlantic Trade and Investment Partnership (TTIP) on low income countries', Report for the Dutch Ministery of Foreign Affairs, The Hague.

Brakman, S., C. van Marrewijk, and M. Partridge (2015), 'Local consequences of global production processes', *Journal of Regional Science* 55(1): 1–9.

Brander, J.A. (1981), 'Intra-industry trade in identical commodities', *Journal of International Economics* 11: 1–14.

Brander, J.A., and P.R. Krugman (1983), 'A "reciprocal dumping" model of international trade', *Journal of International Economics* 15: 313–21.

Brander, J.A., and B.J. Spencer (1983), 'International R&D rivalry and industrial strategy', *Review of Economic Studies* 50: 707–22.

Brander, J.A., and B.J. Spencer (1985), 'Export subsidies and international market share rivalry', *Journal of International Economics* 18: 83–100.

Brülhart, M. (2008), 'An account of global intra-industry trade', University of Nottingham Research Paper Series, *Globalisation, Productivity and Technology*, Research paper 2008/08.

Bulow, J.I., J.D. Geanakoplos, and P.D. Klemperer (1985), 'Multimarket oligopoly: Strategic substitutes and complements', *Journal of Political Economy* 93(3): 488–511.

Caves, D.W., L.R. Christensen, and W.E. Diewert (1982), 'The economic theory of index numbers and the measurement of input, output, and productivity', *Econometrica* 50(6): 1393–1414, <http://www.jstor.org/action/showPublication?journalCode=econometrica>.

Chamberlin, E.H. (1933), *The Theory of Monopolistic Competition: A Re-orientation of the Theory of Value*, Harvard University Press, Cambridge, MA.

Chang, H.-H., and C. van Marrewijk (2011), 'Firm heterogeneity and development: Evidence from Latin American countries', Tjalling C. Koopmans Research Institute Working Paper No. 11-14.

Chipman, J.S. (1965), 'A survey of the theory of international trade: Part 1, the Classical theory', *Econometrica* 33: 477–519.

Coase, R.H. (1937), 'The nature of the firm', *Economica* 4(16): 386–405.

Collier, I. (1999), 'Laudatio for Paul Krugman', in Ehrenpromotion Paul Krugman, 4. Dezember 1998, Reden und Festvorträge. Fachbereich Wirtschaftswissenschaft der Freien Universität Berlin. Published in German, translation as the Nachwort to Paul Krugman's Die Große Rezession, Campus Verlag, Frankfurt/New York., 1999.

Costinot, A., and D. Donaldson (2012), 'Ricardo's theory of comparative advantage: Old idea, new evidence', *American Economic Review* 102(3): 453–8.

Cournot, A. (1838), *Recherches sur les principes mathématiques de la théorie des riches*, translated by N. Bacon (1897), Macmillan, New York.

Davis, D.R. (1998), 'The home market, trade, and industrial structure', *American Economic Review* 88: 1264–77.

Debreu, G. (1959), *Theory of Value*, Wiley, New York.

De Melo, J., and A. Panagariya (1993), *New Dimensions in Regional Integration*, Cambridge University Press, Cambridge, UK.

De Volkskrant (2015), 'Een op drie "Syrische" asielzoekers Duitsland komt niet uit Syrië', 25 September.

Diewert, W.E. (1981), 'The economic theory of index numbers: A survey', in: A. Deaton (ed.), *Essays in the Theory and Measurement of Consumer Behaviour*, Cambridge University Press, Cambridge, UK, pp. 163–208.

Dixit, A., and G. Grossman (1986), 'Targeted export promotion with several oligopolistic industries', *Journal of International Economics* 21: 233–50.

Dixit, A., and A.S. Kyle (1985), 'The use of protection or subsidies for entry promotion and deterrence', *American Economic Review* 75: 139–52.

Dixit, A., and V. Norman (1980), *Theory of International Trade*, Cambridge University Press, Cambridge, UK.

Dixit, A.V., and R.S. Pindyck (1994), *Investment Under Uncertainty*, Princeton University Press, Princeton, NJ.

Dixit, A., and J. Stiglitz (1977), 'Monopolistic competition and optimal product diversity', *American Economic Review* 67: 297–308.

Dornbusch, R., S. Fischer, and P. Samuelson (1977), 'Comparative advantage, trade and payments in a Ricardian model with a continuum of goods', *American Economic Review* 67: 823–39.

Dunning, J.H. (1977), 'Trade location of economic activity and MNE: A search for an eclectic approach', in: B. Ohlin, P.O. Hesselborn, and P.M. Wijkman (eds), *The International Allocation of Economic Activity*, Macmillan, London.

Dunning, J.H. (1981), *International Production and the Multinational Enterprise*, Allen and Unwin, London.

Eaton, J., and G.M. Grossman (1986), 'Optimal trade and industrial policy under oligopoly', *Quarterly Journal of Economics* 2: 383–406.

Egger, P., and M. Larch (2011), 'An assessment of the Europe Trade Agreements' bilateral trade, GDP, and welfare', *European Economic Review* 55(2): 263–79.

Ethier, W.E. (1982), 'National and international returns to scale in the modern theory of international trade', *American Economic Review* 72: 950–9.

Feenstra, R.C., and G.H. Hanson (1996), 'Foreign investment, outsourcing, and relative wages', in: R.C. Feenstra, G.M. Grossman, and D.A. Irwin (eds), *The Political Economy of Trade Policy: Papers in Honor of Jagdisch Bhagwati*, MIT Press, Cambridge, MA.

Feenstra, R.C., R. Inklaar, and M. Timmer (2015), 'The next generation of the Penn World Table', *American Economic Review* 105(10): 3150–82.

Felbermayr, G., W. Kohler, R. Aichele, G. Klee, and E. Yalcin (2015), 'Mögliche Auswirkungen der Transatlantischen Handels- und Investitionspartnerschaft (TTIP) auf Entwicklungs-und Schwellenländer, Studie des Ifo Instituts gemeinsam mit dem IAW Tübingen im Auftrag des Bundesministeriums für Wirtschaftliche Zusammenarbeit und Entwikkelung (BMZ) Endbericht', Ifo Institute, Munich.

Feldstein, M., and C. Horioka (1980), 'Domestic savings and international capital flows', *Economic Journal* 90 (June): 314–29.

Findlay, R., and J.G. O'Rourke (2001), 'Commodity market integration, 1500–2000', NBER Working Paper No 8579, National Bureau of Economic Research, Cambridge, MA.

Fletcher, M. (2016), 'Who is to blame for Brexit's appeal? British newspapers', *The New York Times*, 21 June.

Forslid, R., and G. Ottaviano (2003), 'An analytically solvable core–periphery model', *Journal of Economic Geography* 3: 229–40.

Francois, J.F., and H.K. Hall (1997), 'Partial equilibrium modeling', in: J.F. Francois and K.A. Reinert (eds), *Applied Methods for Trade Policy Analysis: A Handbook*, Cambridge University Press, Cambridge, UK, pp. 122–55.

Francois, J., M. Manchin, H. Norberg, O. Pindyuk, and P. Tomberger (2013), 'Reducing transatlantic barriers to trade and investment: An economic assessment', Report Trade 10/A2/A16 for the European Commission: http://trade.ec.europa.eu/doclib/html/150737.htm.

Fujita, M., P. Kungman, and A. Venables (1999), *The Spatial Economy: Cities, Regions, and International Trade*, MIT Press, Cambridge, MA.

Gabaix, X., and R. Ibragimov (2011), 'Rank-1/2: A simple way to improve the OLS estimation of tail exponents', *Journal of Business and Economic Statistics* 29(1): 24–39.

Gandal, N., G.H. Hanson, and M.J. Slaughter (2000), 'Techonology, trade, and adjustment to immigration in Israel', NBER Working Paper 7962.

Gourevitch, P., R. Bohn, and D. McKendrick (2000), 'Globalization of production: Insights from the hard disk drive industry', *World Development* 28(2): 301–17.

Grossman, G.M., and E. Helpman (1991), *Innovation and Growth in the Global Economy*, MIT Press, Cambridge, MA.

Grossman, G.M., and E. Rossi-Hansberg (2008), 'Trading tasks: A simple theory of offshoring', *American Economic Review* 98(5): 1978–97.

Grossman, S.J., and O.D. Hart (1986), 'The costs and benefits of ownership: A theory of vertical and lateral integration', *Journal of Political Economy* 94(4): 691–719.

Grubel, H.G., and P.J. Lloyd (1975), *Intra-Industry Trade: The Theory and Measurement of International Trade in Differentiated Products*, John Wiley, New York.

Grubert, H., and J. Mutti (1991), 'Taxes, tariffs, and transfer pricing in multinational corporate decision making', *Review of Economics and Statistics* 79: 285–93.

Harberger, A.C. (1954), 'Monopoly and resource allocation', *American Economic Review* 44: 77–87.

Harberger, A.C. (1959), 'Using the resources at hand more effectively', *American Economic Review* 49: 134–46.

Head, K., and T. Mayer (2014), 'Gravity equations: Workhorse, toolkit, and cookbook', in: G. Gopinath, E. Helpman, and K. Rogoff (eds), *Handbook of International Economics*, Vol. 4, Chapter 3, pp. 131–95.

Helpman, E. (1984), 'A simple theory of international trade with multinational corporations', *Journal of Political Economy* 92 (3): 451–71.

Helpman, E. (1985), 'Multinational corporations and trade structure', *Review of Economic Studies* 52: 443–58.

Helpman, E., and P.R. Krugman (1985), *Market Structure and Foreign Trade*, MIT press, Cambridge, MA.

Helpman, E., M.J. Melitz, and S.R. Yeaple (2004), 'Export versus FDI with heterogeneous firms', *American Economic Review* 94: 300–16.

Hertz, N. (2001), *The Silent Take-over*, William Heinemann, London.

Heston, A., R. Summers, and B. Aten (2011), Penn World Table version 7.0, Center for International Comparisons of Production, Income and Prices at the University of Pennsylvania.

Hinloopen, J., and C. van Marrewijk (2001), 'On the empirical distribution of the Balassa Index', *Weltwirtschaftliches Archiv* 137: 1–35.

Hinloopen, J., and C. van Marrewijk (2012), 'Power laws and comparative advantage', *Applied Economics* 44(12): 1483–1507.

Hopenhayn, H. (1992a), 'Entry, exit, and firm dynamics in long run equilibrium', *Econometrica* 60: 1127–50.

Hopenhayn, H. (1992b), 'Exit, selection, and the value of firms', *Journal of Economic Dynamics and Control* 16: 621–53.

Horn, H., Mavroidis, P.C., and A. Sapir (2010), 'Beyond the WTO? An anatomy of EU and US preferential trade agreements', *World Economy* 33: 1565–88.

Horst, T. (1971), 'The theory of the multinational firm: Optimal behavior under different tariff and tax rates', *Journal of Political Economy* 79: 1059–72.

Horstman, I.J., and J.R. Markusen (1986), 'Up the average cost curve: Inefficient entry and the new protectionism', *Journal of International Economics* 20: 225–48.

Hummels, D. (1999a), 'Towards a geography of trade costs', research paper, Purdue University, http://www.krannert.purdue.edu/faculty/hummelsd/research/toward/tgtc.pdf.

Hummels, D. (1999b), 'Have international transport costs declined?', mimeo, Purdue University.

Hymer, S.H. (1960), *The International Operations of National Firms: A Study of Direct Foreign Investment*, PhD dissertation, Massachusetts Institute of Technology, Department of Economics; published posthumously (1976), MIT Press, Cambridge, MA.

IMF (1996), *Balance of Payments Textbook*, Washington, DC.

Irwin, D. (1996), *Against the Tide: An Intellectual History of Free Trade*, Princeton University Press, Princeton, NJ.

Jones, R.W. (1965), 'The structure of simple general equilibrium models', *Journal of Political Economy* 73: 557–72.

Kaldor, N. (1961), 'Capital accumulation and economic growth', in: F.A. Lutz and D.C. Hague (eds), *The Theory of Capital*, Macmillan, London, pp. 177–222.

Karns, M.P., and K.A. Mingst (2009), *International Organizations: The Politics and Processes of Global Governance*, Lynne Rienner Publishers, Boulder, CO.

Kemp, M.C., and H.Y. Wan, Jr (1976), 'An elementary proposition concerning the formation of customs unions', *Journal of International Economics* 6(1): 95–7.

Kenen, P.B. (2000), *The International Economy*, 4th edn, Cambridge University Press, Cambridge, UK.

Kennedy, P. (1995), 'The threat of modernization', *New Perspectives Quarterly* 12: 31–3.

Keynes, J.M. (1919), *The Economic Consequences of the Peace*, Macmillan, London.

Keynes, J.M. (1939), 'Professor Tinbergen's method', *Economic Journal* 49: 558–68.

Klein, N. (2001), *No Logo*, Flamingo, London.

Kohl, T., S. Brakman, and J.H. Garretsen (2015), 'Do trade agreements stimulate international trade differently?' *World Economy* 39(1): 97–131.

Koopman, R., W. Powers, Z. Wang, and S.-J. Wei (2010), 'Give credit where credit is due: Tracing value added in global production chains', National Bureau of Economic Research Working Paper 16426.

Krugman, P.R. (1979), 'Increasing returns, monopolistic competition and international trade', *Journal of International Economics* 9: 469–79.

Krugman, P.R. (1980), 'Scale economics, product differentiation, and the pattern of trade', *American Economic Review* 70: 950–9.

Krugman, P.R. (1990), *Rethinking International Trade*, MIT Press, Cambridge, MA.

Krugman, P.R. (1991), 'Is bilateralism bad?', in: E. Helpman and A. Razin (eds), *International Trade and Trade Policy*, MIT Press, Cambridge, MA.

Krugman, P.R. (1993), 'Regionalism versus multilateralism: Analytical notes', in: J. De Melo and A. Panagariya (eds), *New Dimensions in Regional Integration*, Cambridge University Press, Cambridge, UK.

Krugman, P.R., and A.J. Venables (1995), 'Globalization and the inequality of nations', *Quarterly Journal of Economics* 110: 857–80.

Lancaster, K.J. (1979), *Variety, Equity and Efficiency*, Columbia University Press, New York.

Lanjouw, G.J. (1995), *International Trade Institutions*, Longman and Open University, London, New York, and Heerlen.

Leamer, E.E. (1980), 'The Leontief paradox reconsidered', *Journal of Political Economy* 88: 495–503.

Leontief, W.W. (1956), 'Factor proportions and the structure of American trade: Further theoretical and empirical analysis', *Review of Economics and Statistics* 38.

Lerner, A.P. (1952), 'Factors, prices and international trade', *Economica* new series 19(73): 1–15.

Liesner, H.H. (1958), 'The European common market and British industry', *Economic Journal* 68: 302–16.

Linden, G., K.L. Kraemer, and J. Dedrick (2009), 'Who captures value in a global innovation network? The case of Apple's iPod', *Communications of the ACM* 52(3): 140–4.

Linden, G., K.L. Kraemer, and J. Dedrick (2011), 'Innovation and job creation in a global economy: The case of Apple's iPod', *Journal of International Commerce and Economics* 3(1): 223–39.

Los, B., M.P. Timmer, and G. de Vries (2015), 'How global are global value chains? A new approach to measure global fragmentation', *Journal of Regional Science* 55(1): 66–92.

Maddison, A. (2001), *The World Economy: A Millennial Perspective*, OECD, Paris and Washington, DC.

Maddison, A. (2011), 'Statistics on world population, GDP and per capita GDP, 1–2008 AD', available at: http://www.ggdc.net/MADDISON/oriindex.htm.

Maggi, G. (2014), 'International trade agreements', in: G. Gopinath, E. Helpman, and K. Rogoff (eds), *Handbook of International Economics*, Vol. 4, Chapter 6, pp. 317–90.

Markusen, J.R. (1981), 'Trade and the gains from trade with imperfect competition', *Journal of International Economics* 11: 531–51.

Markusen, J.R., and A.J. Venables (1998), 'Multinational firms and the new trade theory', *Journal of International Economics* 46: 183–203.

Markusen, J., and A. Venables (2000), 'The theory of endowment, intra-industy, and multinational trade', *Journal of International Economics* 52: 209–34.

Marrewijk, C. van (1999), 'Capital accumulation, learning, and endogenous growth', *Oxford Economic Papers* 51: 453–75.

Marrewijk, C. van (2002), *International Trade and the World Economy*, Oxford University Press, Oxford.

Marrewijk, C. van (2009), 'Collapsing Trade Flows', inaugural lecture, Utrecht University.

Marrewijk, C. van (2012), *International Economics: Theory, Application, and Policy*, 2nd edn, Oxford University Press, Oxford.

Marrewijk, C. van, and K. Berden (2007), 'On the static and dynamic costs of trade restrictions for small developing countries', *Journal of Development Economics* 84: 46–60.

Mayer, T., and G.I.P. Ottaviano (2007), *The Happy Few: The Internationalisation of European Firms*, Bruegel Blueprint Series, Volume 3, Bruegel, Brussels.

Mayer, T., and G.I.P. Ottaviano (2008), 'The happy few: The internationalisation of European firms', *Intereconomics* 43(3): 135–48.

McDonald, F., and F. Burton (2002), *International Business*, Thomson, London.

Melitz, J. Marc (2003), 'The impact of trade on intra-industry reallocations and aggregate industry productivity', *Econometrica* 71(6): 1695–725.

Melitz, M.J., and S.J. Redding (2014), 'Heterogeneous firms and trade', in: G. Gopinath, E. Helpman, and K. Rogoff (eds), *Handbook of International Economics*, Vol. 4, Chapter 1, pp. 1–54.

Muth, J.F. (1961), 'Rational expectations and the theory of price movements', *Econometrica* 29: 315–35.

Neary, J.P. (1978), 'Short-run capital specificity and the pure theory of international trade', *Economic Journal* 88: 477–510.

Neary, J.P. (2001), 'Of hypes and hyperbolas: Introducing the new economic geography', *Journal of Economic Literature* 39(2): 536–61.

Neary, J.P. (2003), 'Globalisation and market structure', Presidential address to the European Economic Association, *Journal of the European Economic Association* 1: 245–71.

Neary, P. (2004), 'Europe on the road to Doha: Towards a new global trade round?', *CESifo Economic Studies* 50(2): 319–32.

NRC Handelsblad (2001), 'Minder EU-hulp suiker', 23 May (in Dutch).

NRC Handelsblad (2003), 'Hoe Amsterdam de VS verdubbelde', 20 December, p. 27 (in Dutch).

O'Rourke, K.H., and J.G. Williamson (1999), *Globalization and History: The Evolution of a Nineteenth-Century Atlantic Economy*, MIT Press, Cambridge, MA.

O'Rourke, K.H., and J.G. Williamson (2000), 'When did globalization begin?', NBER Working Paper 7632, National Bureau of Economic Research, Cambridge, MA.

O'Rourke, K.H., and J.G. Williamson (2002), 'When did globalization begin?', *European Review of Economic History* 6: 23–50.

Obstfeld, M., and A.M. Taylor (2003), 'Globalization and capital markets', in: M.D. Bordo, A.M. Taylor, and J.G. Williamson (eds), *Globalization in Historical Perspective*, National Bureau of Economic Research and University of Chicago Press, Chicago.

Ohlin, B. (1933), *Interregional and International Trade*, Harvard University Press, Cambridge, MA.

Orefice, G., and N. Rocha (2014), 'Deep integration and production networks: An empirical analysis', *World Economy* 37(1): 106–36.

Ostrup, F. (2002), 'International integration and economic policy', research paper, University of Copenhagen.

Putterman, L., and D. Weil (2010), 'Post-1500 population flows and the long-run determinants of economic growth and inequality', *Quarterly Journal of Economics* 125(4): 1627–82.

Radelet, S., and J. Sachs (1998), 'Shipping costs, manufactured exports, and economic growth', research paper, AEA meetings, Harvard University, http://earthinstitute.columbia.edu/sitefiles/file/about/director/pubs/shipcost.pdf.

Ramsey, F.P. (1928), 'A mathematical theory of saving', *Economic Journal* 38: 543–59.

Rauhut, D. (2010), 'Adam Smith on migration', *Migration Letters* 7(1): 105–13.

Roberts, M.J., and J.R. Tybout (1977), 'The decision to export in Colombia: An empirical model of entry with sunk costs', *American Economic Review* 87: 545–64.

Romer, P.M. (1990), 'Endogenous technological change', *Journal of Political Economy* 98(5): S71–S102.

Romer, P.M. (1994), 'New goods, old theory, and the welfare costs of trade restrictions', *Journal of Development Economics* 43: 5–38.

Rougoor, W., and C. van Marrewijk (2015), 'Demography, growth, and global income inequality', *World Development* 74: 220–32.

Rybczynski, T.M. (1955), 'Factor endowments and relative commodity prices', *Economica* 22: 336–41.

Samuelson, P.A. (1948), 'International trade and the equalisation of factor prices', *Economic Journal* 58: 163–84.

Samuelson, P.A. (1949), 'International factor price equalisation once again', *Economic Journal* 59: 181–96.

Samuelson, P.A. (1952), 'The transfer problem and transport costs: The terms when impediments are absent', *Economic Journal* 62: 278–304.

Samuelson, P.A. (1971), 'Ohlin was right', *Swedish Jounal of Economics* 73: 365–84.

Scitovsky, T. (1954), 'Two concepts of external economies', *Journal of Political Economy* 62: 143–51.

Solow, R.M. (1956), 'A contribution to the theory of economic growth', *Quarterly Journal of Economics* 70: 65–94.

Sorge, A.M., and A. van Witteloostuijn (2004), 'The (non)sense of organizational change: An essay about universal management hypes, sick consultancy metaphors and healthy organization theories', *Organization Studies* 25: 1205–31.

Spence, A.M. (1976), 'Product selection, fixed costs and monopolistic competition', *Review of Economic Studies* 43: 217–35.

Stelder, D. (2000), 'Geographical grids in new economic geography models', paper presented at the International Conference on the Occasion of the 150th Anniversary of Johann Heinrich von Thünen's death, Rostock, 21–24 September.

Stiglitz, J. (2002), *Globalization and its Discontents*, W.W. Norton, New York.

Stolper, W., and P. Samuelson (1941), 'Protection and real wages', *Review of Economic Studies* 9: 58–73.

The Economist (1997), 'Peace in our time', 26 July (*The Economist* website).

The Economist (2000a), 'So that's all agreed, then', 14 December (*The Economist* website).

The Economist (2000b), 'Thank you, Singapore', 30 September (*The Economist* website).

The Economist (2001), 'A fruity peace', 19 April (*The Economist* website).

The Economist (2005), 'Beet a retreat', 23 June (*The Economist* website).

The Economist (2015), 'Take-off delayed: A Chinese planemaker will find it hard to break the Airbus–Boeing duopoly', 7 November (*The Economist* website).

The Economist (2016a), 'Brexit: Taking stock', daily chart, 28 June.

The Economist (2016b), 'Debunking years of tabloid claims about Europe', daily chart, 22 June.

The Economist (2016c), 'International banking in a London outside the European Union', 24 June.

The Economist (2016d), 'David Cameron quits Downing Street with a ruined legacy', 24 June.

The Economist (2016e), 'A tragic split: How to minimise the damage of Britain's senseless, self-inflicted blow', 24 June.

Thweatt, W.O. (1976), 'James Mill and the early development of comparative advantage', *History of Political Economy* 8: 207–34.

Tinbergen, J. (1939), *Statistical Testing of Business Cycle Theories*, League of Nations, New York.

Tinbergen, J. (1956), *Economic Policy: Principles and Design*, North Holland, Amsterdam.

Tinbergen, J. (1962), *Shaping the World Economy*, Twentieth Century Fund, New York.

Tinbergen, J. (1976), *Reshaping the International Order*, Dutton, New York.

Tirole, J. (1988), *The Theory of Industrial Organization*, MIT Press, Cambridge, MA.

Trefler, D. (1995), 'The case of the missing trade and other mysteries', *American Economic Review* 85: 1029–46.

UNCTAD (2000), *World Investment Report 2000*, United Nations, New York.

UNCTAD (2015), *World Investment Report 2015: Reforming International Investment Governance*, United Nations, New York and Geneva.

Uzawa, H. (1963), 'On a two-sector model of economic growth II', *Review of Economic Studies* 30(2): 105–18.

Vanek, J. (1959), 'The natural resource content of foreign trade, 1870–1955, and the relative abundance of natural resources in the United States', *Review of Economics and Statistics* 41(2): 146–53.

Verdoorn, P.J. (1960), 'The intra-block trade of Benelux', in: E.A.G. Robinson (ed.), *Economic Consequences of the Size of Nations*, Macmillan, London.

Viner, J. (1950), *The Customs Union Issue*, Carnegie Endowment for International Peace, New York.

Weibull, J. W. (1995), *Evolutionary Game Theory*, MIT Press, Cambridge, MA.

Whalley, J. (1998), 'Why do countries seek regional trade agreements?' in: J. Frankel (ed.), *The Regionalization of the World Economy*, University of Chicago Press, Chicago.

Williamson, O.E. (1985), *The Economic Institutions of Capitalism*, Free Press, New York.

Wood, A. (1994), *North-South Trade, Employment and Inequality: Changing Fortunes in a Skill-Driven World*, Clarendon Press, Oxford.

World Economic Forum (2015), *The Global Competitiveness Report: 2015–2016*, World Economic Forum, Geneva.

World Trade Organization (2010), *World Trade Report 2010*, WTO, Geneva.

Zipf, G.K. (1949), *Human Behavior and the Principle of Least Effort*, Addison Wesley, New York.

Index

Tables, figures, and boxes are indicated by an italic t, f, and b following the page number.